Microsoft® Windows® XP Networking and Security Inside Out: Also Covers Windows 2000

Ed Bott

Carl Siechert

PUBLISHED BY
Microsoft Press
A Division of Microsoft Corporation
One Microsoft Way
Redmond, Washington 98052-6399

Library of Congress Control Number 2005920808

Printed and bound in the United States of America.

1 2 3 4 5 6 7 8 9   QWT   8 7 6 5

Distributed in Canada by H.B. Fenn and Company Ltd. A CIP catalogue record for this book is available from the British Library.

Microsoft Press books are available through booksellers and distributors worldwide. For further information about international editions, contact your local Microsoft Corporation office or contact Microsoft Press International directly at fax (425) 936-7329. Visit our Web site at www.microsoft.com/mspress. Send comments to mspinput@microsoft.com.

Microsoft, Active Directory, ActiveX, Authenticode, Excel, FrontPage, Hotmail, InfoPath, JScript, Microsoft Press, MSDN, MSN, NetMeeting, Outlook, PowerPoint, SharePoint, Visio, Visual Basic, Visual Studio, Win32, Windows, Windows Media, Windows NT, and Windows Server are either registered trademarks or trademarks of Microsoft Corporation in the United States and/or other countries. Other product and company names mentioned herein may be the trademarks of their respective owners.

The example companies, organizations, products, domain names, e-mail addresses, logos, people, places, and events depicted herein are fictitious. No association with any real company, organization, product, domain name, e-mail address, logo, person, place, or event is intended or should be inferred.

This book expresses the author's views and opinions. The information contained in this book is provided without any express, statutory, or implied warranties. Neither the authors, Microsoft Corporation, nor its resellers, or distributors will be held liable for any damages caused or alleged to be caused either directly or indirectly by this book.

Acquisitions Editor: Juliana Aldous
Project Editor: Sandra Haynes

Body Part No. X11-11225

Contents At A Glance

Contents At A Glance

Table of Contents

Chapter 4
Managing User Accounts and Passwords   81

Chapter 5
Securing a Shared Computer   135

Chapter 6
Preventing Data Loss   179

Chapter 7
Keeping Your System Secure   213

Part 2
Smart, Secure Networking

Chapter 8
Setting Up a Secure Home or Small Business Network 239

Chapter 9
Sharing an Internet Connection 301

Chapter 10
Wireless Networking 329

Chapter 11
Working with a Corporate Network 347

Part 3
Protecting Your Personal Computer

Chapter 12
Making Internet Explorer More Secure   385

Chapter 13
Blocking Spyware, Adware, and Other Unwanted Software   431

Chapter 14
Stopping Viruses, Worms, and Trojan Horses   457

Chapter 15
Securing E-Mail and Instant Messages   493

Chapter 16
Blocking Spam   527

Chapter 17
Securing Your Computer by Using a Firewall   561

Chapter 18
Protecting Your Privacy   585

Part 4
Extreme Security

Chapter 19
Securing Ports and Protocols   627

Chapter 20
Installing and Using Digital Certificates   671

Chapter 21
Encrypting Files and Folders 699

Chapter 22
Managing Security Through Group Policy 729
and Security Templates

Acknowledgments

Every book is a collaborative effort, and on this one we had the very able assistance of many friends and colleagues, for which we're grateful.

The production schedule for this book turned out to be a rollercoaster ride, with some really fast parts, some excruciatingly slow sections (while we waited as plans for Microsoft security products changed repeatedly), and lots of unexpected twists and turns. Throughout it all, Joan Preppernau and her crew at Online Training Solutions, Inc. did an incredible job of keeping everything on track. It takes a lot of skill to perform copy editing, technical editing, illustration, page layout, proofreading, and indexing even on a normal schedule, but Joan, Susie Bayers, Jan Bednarczuk, R.J. Cadranell, Liz Clark, Jaime Odell, and Lisa Van Every did an outstanding job in difficult circumstances.

Our friends at Microsoft Press, Juliana Aldous and Sandra Haynes, made sure that we had everything we needed and provided the ideas and support that we've come to expect—and greatly appreciate. It was also through their efforts that this entire book was reviewed for accuracy and consistency by the folks at Microsoft who know the products inside out, members of the Security Content Review Board. Rich Benack, Kimmo Bergius, Heiko Böhm, Barbara Chung, Coleman Craig, Duane Crider, Fidelis Ekezue, Eric Fitzgerald, Doug Neal, Steve Patrick, Shawn Rabourn, David Ross, George Spanakis, and Brad Warrender each reviewed one or more chapters in their area of expertise. Kai Axford reviewed the entire book and, like the others, provided many useful suggestions for improvement. Their input was invaluable, but we made the final decisions on every word that went into this book—if you see a mistake, blame us, not them!

Others at Microsoft who generously answered questions and provided much-needed information include Brendan Foley, Rob Franco, Jason Joyce, Sterling Roeser, and Aaron Margosis.

Our agent, Claudette Moore of Moore Literary Agency, helped to conceive the book, asked for the moon, and managed to keep everyone happy, as she so ably does.

Lori Paxton of DigitalPersona, Inc. provided a fingerprint reader for evaluation and, more important, provided answers to our questions about biometric logon devices.

This book incorporates some material that was originally written by Craig Stinson and Dave Methvin for *Microsoft Windows Security Inside Out for Windows XP and Windows 2000*.

Our sincere thanks to all.
—Ed Bott and Carl Siechert

We'd Like to Hear from You!

Our goal at Microsoft Press is to create books that help you find the information you need to get the most out of your software.

The Inside Out series was created with you in mind. As part of an effort to ensure that we're creating the best, most useful books we can, we talked to our customers and asked them to tell us what they need from a Microsoft Press series. Help us continue to help you. Let us know what you like about this book and what we can do to make it better. When you write, please include the title and author of this book in your e-mail, as well as your name and contact information. We look forward to hearing from you.

How to Reach Us

E-mail: nsideout@microsoft.com

Mail: Inside Out Series Editor
Microsoft Press
One Microsoft Way
Redmond, WA 98052

Unfortunately, we can't provide support for any software problems you might experience. Please visit Microsoft Help and Support at *http://support.microsoft.com* for help with any software issues.

About the CD

The companion CD that ships with this book contains many tools and resources to help you get the most out of your *Microsoft Windows XP Networking and Security Inside Out* book.

What's on the CD

Your Inside Out CD includes the following:

***Microsoft Windows XP Networking and Security Inside Out* eBook.**

- This section contains the electronic version of the book.

Reference eBooks.

- In this section, you'll find the following eBooks in PDF format: *Microsoft Computer Dictionary, Fifth Edition*; *Microsoft Encyclopedia of Networking, Second Edition*; and *Microsoft Encyclopedia of Security*.

Insider Extras.

- This section includes sample batch and script files referenced in the book as well as a set of sample security templates for you to use. These templates include e-mail messages and presentation materials that you can use to educate others about security-related issues.

Windows XP Downloads.

- In this section, you'll find a listing of Windows XP downloadable resources, including information about security.

Expert Zone Columns.

- This section provides a downloadable compilation of Web articles written by Windows expert Ed Bott.

Windows XP Tips Sites.

- In this section, you'll find links to third-party sites maintained by Ed Bott and by a number of Windows MVPs, such as Bob Cerelli, Chris Pirillo, Doug Knox, Jerry Honeycutt, Jim Boyce, Kelly Theriot, and John "PapaJohn" Buechler.

The companion CD provides detailed information about the files on this CD, and links to Microsoft and third-party sites on the Internet.

> **Note** Please note that links to third-party sites are not under the control of Microsoft Corporation and Microsoft is therefore not responsible for their content, nor should their inclusion on this CD be construed as an endorsement of the product or the site. Please check third-party Web sites for the latest version of their software.

Software provided on this CD is in English language only and might be incompatible with non-English language operating systems and software.

Using the CD

To use this companion CD, insert it into your CD drive; a license agreement should appear. If AutoRun is not enabled on your computer, run StartCD.exe in the root of the CD to display the license agreement.

System Requirements

Following are the minimum system requirements necessary to run the CD:

- Microsoft Windows 2000 or Windows XP Service Pack 2
- 266-MHz or higher Pentium-compatible CPU
- 64 megabytes (MB) RAM
- 8X CD-ROM drive or faster
- 80 MB of free hard disk space (to install the eBook files)
- Microsoft Windows-compatible sound card and speakers
- Microsoft Internet Explorer 5.01 or higher
- Microsoft Mouse or compatible pointing device

Note System requirements might be higher for the add-ins available on the CD. Individual add-in system requirements are specified on the CD. An Internet connection is necessary to access the hyperlinks in the "Windows XP Tips Sites" section. Connection time charges might apply.

Support Information

Every effort has been made to ensure the accuracy of the book and the contents of this companion CD. For feedback on the book content or this companion CD, please contact us by using any of the addresses listed in the "We'd Like to Hear from You" section.

Microsoft Press provides corrections for books through the World Wide Web at *http://www.microsoft.com/mspress/support/search.asp*.

For support information regarding Windows XP, you can connect to the Microsoft Windows XP Help and Support page at *http://support.microsoft.com/windowsxp/*. A similar page for Windows 2000 is available at *http://support.microsoft.com/ph/1131/*.

Conventions and Features Used in This Book

This book uses special text and design conventions to make it easier for you to find the information you need.

Text Conventions

Convention	Meaning
Abbreviated menu commands	For your convenience, this book uses abbreviated menu commands. For example, "Choose Tools, Track Changes, Highlight Changes" means that you should click the Tools menu, point to Track Changes, and select the Highlight Changes command.
Boldface type	**Boldface** type is used to indicate text that you enter or type.
Initial Capital Letters	The first letters of the names of menus, dialog boxes, dialog box elements, and commands are capitalized. Example: the Save As dialog box.
Italicized type	*Italicized* type is used to indicate new terms.
Plus sign (+) in text	Keyboard shortcuts are indicated by a plus sign (+) separating two key names. For example, Ctrl+Alt+Delete means that you press the Ctrl, Alt, and Delete keys at the same time.

Design Conventions

 Inside Out

These are the book's signature tips. In these tips, you'll get the straight scoop on what's going on with the software—inside information on why a feature works the way it does. You'll also find handy workarounds to deal with some of these software problems.

Tip　Tips provide helpful hints, timesaving tricks, or alternative procedures related to the task being discussed.

Troubleshooting sidebars

Look for these sidebars to find solutions to common problems you might encounter. Troubleshooting sidebars appear next to related information in the chapters. You can also use the Troubleshooting Topics index at the back of the book to look up problems by topic.

Cross-References

Cross-references point you to other locations in the book that offer additional information on the topic being discussed.

 This icon indicates sample files or text found on the companion CD.

Caution   Cautions identify potential problems that you should look out for when you're completing a task or problems that you must address before you can complete a task.

Note   Notes offer additional information related to the task being discussed.

Sidebars

The sidebars sprinkled throughout these chapters provide ancillary information on the topic being discussed. Go to sidebars to learn more about the technology or a feature.

Part 1

Windows Networking and Security 101

Setting up a computer network is easy, even for an amateur. Building a secure, reliable, fast network takes a little more time and skill. Keeping that network running smoothly and securely is a constant challenge.

Our goal in this book is to arm you with the information you need to handle most networking or security issues on home or small business networks made up of computers running Microsoft Windows XP or Windows 2000. (Although we touch on the unique security issues of large corporate networks at several points in this book, our primary emphasis is on small networks that do not include a Windows domain controller.) In this chapter, we cover essential Windows networking concepts. In Chapter 2, "Computer Security: Are You at Risk?" we identify the security threats you need to consider when you use either of these operating systems; in Chapter 3, "Windows Security Tools and Techniques," we introduce the set of tools and technologies you can use to protect yourself from these perils. In later chapters, we examine each of these issues in depth, with detailed technical information, hands-on advice, and step-by-step instructions for setting up and securing your Windows-based network.

It's practically impossible to discuss networking without at least touching on security issues. Physical locks and passwords can effectively protect a stand-alone computer, but connecting computers in a network creates new opportunities for unauthorized access to information and resources. The security risks increase dramatically and the stakes get noticeably higher when you connect the network to the Internet. Setting up a secure network requires that you strike a delicate balance between providing legitimate users with easy access to shared resources and locking out those who have no business poking around in files or exploiting shared resources.

Building a Network with Security in Mind

Even for Windows experts, network security is a challenging and demanding area of technology. Oh, sure, it's easy to get started. Thanks to cheap and ubiquitous hardware and fill-in-the-blanks wizards, just about anyone can combine two or three computers running Windows into a reasonably secure local area network in a matter of minutes. Ensuring that your network *stays* secure, however, requires constant attention. Although you don't necessarily need to earn your credentials as a Microsoft Certified Systems Engineer to manage a network, your chances of success improve greatly if you have a solid understanding of network hardware, communications protocols, TCP/IP addressing, and access controls.

> **Note** In this chapter, we assume that you've correctly installed and configured a baseline configuration for all of the Windows computers on your network, including the most recent service pack and all current critical updates and security updates. We also assume that all users on your network have received basic training on security, and that every computer on the network has antivirus software that is configured for regular automatic updates. We cover each of these tasks in more detail later in this book, beginning in Chapter 8, "Setting Up a Secure Home or Small Business Network."

In general, you should ask the following questions when setting up a local area network:

Is the network physically secure? Just as with a stand-alone computer, physical security should be your first priority. On a wired home network, this might not be a pressing concern, but in a small business or department, you should guard against the possibility of an attacker using an unattended workstation or plugging into the network. On any home or business network with a wireless access point, you should guard against the possibility of an unauthorized user connecting to the network; in a worst-case scenario, an intruder could use "sniffer" software to eavesdrop electronically on your network communications.

Are shared network resources adequately protected? Your goal is to restrict access to shared resources (files, folders, and peripheral devices) so that only authorized users can connect to those resources across the network. To do so, you need to ensure that you have set up the proper mix of user accounts on each computer that contains shared resources, with administrative accounts limited to only trusted users. You can then assign appropriate permissions for the shared resources, using a combination of share permissions and NTFS file permissions. Because the sharing and security model varies in different versions of Windows, this task might be more complicated than it appears.

Do you have consistent procedures for auditing shared resources? Security breaches on corporate networks can often be traced to user accounts that were originally assigned to employees who have resigned or have been fired. It's crucial to pay close attention to user accounts (especially on servers), file and share permissions, and access that is granted to guests and temporary users.

Do you need to administer your network from a central location? Trying to manage a business network that consists of more than 10 computers can run anyone ragged, especially if the computers are in separate locations. If your network has outgrown the "workgroup" label, you'll need to create a Windows domain with at least one computer running Microsoft Windows Server 2003 or Windows 2000 Server. A Windows domain supplies some powerful security features, including the ability to enforce security policies through Active Directory directory service, a database of user and group accounts that is available to all computers on the network. Peer-to-peer networks—consisting of computers running any combination of Windows XP Professional, Windows XP Home Edition, Windows 2000 Professional, Windows Millennium Edition (Windows Me), Windows 98, or

Windows 95—can be configured to be reasonably secure, although administration is more difficult.

Is your private network secured from unauthorized access via the Internet? Firewalls, routers, and access control policies can safeguard your network from outside intruders, but only if they're properly installed and configured. Likewise, remote access software can provide an open door through which outsiders can connect to individual computers on your network, and from there to any network resource.

> For information on how you can prevent unauthorized access to your local network, see Chapter 9, "Sharing an Internet Connection."

Is your network protected from viruses, worms, Trojan horses, and other types of unauthorized software? Malware—the generic name for hostile software of all kinds—can spread over network connections, which is why it's so important to have a comprehensive program to identify and block potential threats. A single networked computer, if infiltrated by a Trojan horse program or with keystroke-logging software, can allow an outsider to view confidential data, steal passwords, and masquerade as a trusted user. Appropriate security precautions on servers and access points can minimize this risk. It's also essential that you remain alert to warning signs of intrusion.

Which Windows? A Comparison of Networking Features

Throughout this book, we assume you're using either Windows XP or Windows 2000, with the most recent service pack, security updates, and critical updates installed. Later in this book, we discuss the details of configuring a network using either of these operating systems. For this brief discussion, it's important to know the fundamental differences between these versions of Windows.

Windows XP was built on the same code base as Windows 2000, so it shouldn't be surprising to find many common features. Regardless of which operating system you use, you'll find networking features installed as part of the core operating system. Both operating systems use TCP/IP as the default network protocol; both support a wide variety of network devices, including different types of Ethernet networks; and both enable a set of network services that allow file and printer sharing and other common network activities.

Windows XP has several significant networking improvements, including a built-in firewall that is available to all network connections. The most noteworthy change is built-in support for wireless networking hardware. On computers running Windows 2000, you must use drivers and management software supplied by a third party to configure wireless connections; Windows XP supports wireless networks, including drivers for popular hardware and options for configuring wireless encryption.

Windows XP also fundamentally changes the way in which network users share files and folders. In Windows 2000, share permissions are based on user names and passwords of individual users; Windows XP replaces this system with a scheme known as Simple File Sharing, which provides access to shared resources by using the built-in

Guest account. To make matters even more confusing, older versions of Windows used a resource sharing scheme based on passwords assigned to shared folders. We explain these confusing concepts in this chapter; you'll find more specific details on how to share files and folders in Chapter 3, "Windows Security Tools and Techniques."

Installing service packs and security updates is an essential part of a normal maintenance program for any version of Windows. Historically, service packs have "rolled up" previously released updates into a single package for the sake of convenience. In the case of Windows XP Service Pack 2 (SP2), however, the changes are far more profound. In addition to bundling previously issued bug fixes and security updates, SP2 introduced a sweeping collection of new features, most of them aimed at improving security. We discuss these security-related changes in more detail in Chapter 2, "Computer Security: Are You at Risk?" From an administrator's or user's perspective, the two most significant new networking features in SP2 are the following:

- **Windows Firewall.** The original release of Windows XP included rudimentary intruder-blocking capabilities in its Internet Connection Firewall. SP2 introduced a significant upgrade and a new name, Windows Firewall. The updated firewall component is enabled by default (a change from the original release of Windows XP) and is designed to permit file and printer sharing on local networks. We explain how to configure and troubleshoot Windows Firewall in "Using Windows Firewall in Windows XP," page 277, and "Configuring a Host Firewall," page 564.

- **Wireless networking support.** Secure high-speed networks based on wireless technology were expensive and relatively rare when Windows XP was first introduced. Today, wireless networks are inexpensive and extraordinarily popular. SP2 includes a new Wireless Network Setup Wizard that makes it much easier to secure networks from intruders using advanced encryption techniques.

For information about installing and configuring wireless networks, see Chapter 10, "Wireless Networking."

Using a Hardware Firewall Appliance

If you have more than one computer connected to the Internet, you should consider using a hardware firewall appliance—also known as a router, residential gateway, or network address translation (NAT) device. A *firewall* is a program or a device that filters network packets based on rules intended to discriminate between legitimate and unwanted traffic. Firewall appliances provide good protection from external attacks and can be a terrific complement to a personal firewall program. (As we note a bit later in this chapter, some personal firewall programs filter outgoing traffic as well as incoming traffic; most hardware firewalls for home and small business use are unable to perform these tasks in any meaningful way.) In fact, even if you have only a single computer connected to a high-speed Internet connection, you can benefit from the protection provided by a router, which can effectively deflect unauthorized connection attempts without requiring any effort on your part, even if your personal firewall software is temporarily disabled.

> **Note**   If your network includes a server running Windows 2000 Server or Windows Server 2003, you might consider using Microsoft Internet Security and Acceleration (ISA) Server as an alternative to—or, better yet, a supplement to—a hardware firewall appliance. ISA Server provides a secure perimeter firewall with capabilities far exceeding those of a personal firewall such as Windows Firewall. For more details, see *http://www.microsoft.com/isaserver/*.

One of the most effective tricks that a firewall appliance adds to your defensive measures is network address translation (NAT). In short, a NAT device uses a single IP address to communicate with the Internet, and it assigns an IP address within a range of private addresses to each computer on your network. The NAT device translates each private IP address into its public address, never exposing your computers' addresses to the network.

> For more information about NAT, see "How Network Address Translation Works," page 303. For information about selecting and configuring a firewall appliance, see "Sharing an Internet Connection Through Hardware," page 310.

> **Tip**   Two good sources of information about firewall appliances, including up-to-date reviews and analysis, are *http://www.practicallynetworked.com* and *http://www.firewallguide.com/hardware.htm*.

Configuring Network Hardware

These days, most small networks are built around the Ethernet and Fast Ethernet standards (which run at 10 and 100 megabits per second, respectively).The Gigabit Ethernet standard, which transfers data at a theoretical maximum of 1000 megabits per second, is becoming popular for owners of business and home networks who want fast transfers of large files such as video clips. In the past few years, wireless networking technologies have become increasingly popular; these can be used in lieu of or in addition to conventional wired network adapters. (As of this writing, the two most common wireless standards are IEEE 802.11b, also known as *Wi-Fi*, and IEEE 802.11g, which uses similar technologies but operates at higher speeds.) A much smaller number of home networks use alternative networking technologies, such as HomePNA and HomePlug, which communicate over phone or power lines. Regardless of the specific technology used, however, the basic networking concepts work in much the same way.

> For information about the security issues that are unique to wireless networks, see Chapter 10, "Wireless Networking."

For starters, every computer needs a network adapter (also called a *network interface card*, or NIC) to communicate with the other computers on the network. These adapters can be internal (usually installed in a PCI slot or, on a portable computer, in a PC Card slot) or external (typically connected to a USB port). To connect multiple computers in an Ethernet network, you need a hub or switch (which is sometimes integrated into a router or residential gateway).

Routers and firewall devices are essential components of a secure network, and the differences between competing hardware designs are profound. (We discuss hardware-based network security options in more detail in Chapter 9, "Sharing an Internet Connection.") By contrast, most network adapters and hubs are interchangeable from a security standpoint, with one noteworthy exception: If you use Internet Protocol Security (IPSec) to encrypt traffic on a local area network (LAN), you might benefit from products such as Intel's PRO/100 S and 3Com's 10/100 Secure NIC, both of which incorporate separate coprocessors designed to perform IPSec encryption on the network card without overtaxing the computer's CPU. For extremely bandwidth-intensive applications, such as those involving high-resolution video, you might benefit from Gigabit Ethernet adapters. For all other network needs, any Windows-compatible Ethernet or Fast Ethernet card should be sufficient.

For more information about using and configuring IPSec, see "Restricting Ports by Using IP Security," page 640.

One attribute of every standard Ethernet card has the potential to affect your network's security and your personal privacy. The Media Access Control (MAC) address is a 48-bit code that uniquely identifies a particular Ethernet device. The MAC address consists of 12 hexadecimal digits (using the numbers 0–9 and the capital letters A–F), broken into six 2-digit groups. In Windows 2000 and Windows XP, you can view the MAC address for a specific Ethernet adapter by entering **ipconfig /all** in a Command Prompt window. The MAC address appears on the line labeled Physical Address. In Windows XP, you can view this information from the status dialog box for the network connection in question by following these steps:

1 From Control Panel or the Start menu, open the Network Connections folder.

2 Double-click the connection icon (or right-click and choose Status from the shortcut menu).

3 On the Support tab, click the Details button. The MAC address appears on the first line, in the field labeled Physical Address.

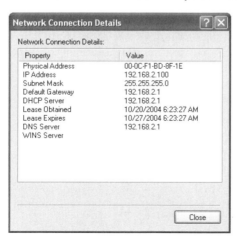

> **Tip** Decode a MAC address
>
> MAC addresses are not randomly assigned. The first half of the address (6 hexadecimal digits, or 24 bits) consists of an Organizational Unique Identifier (OUI) that is specific to the manufacturer of your Ethernet card. These vendor codes are assigned by the Institute of Electrical and Electronics Engineers (IEEE), which maintains a searchable database of OUIs at *http://standards.ieee.org/regauth/oui/index.shtml*. For more information and some excellent links to detailed technical information on MAC addresses, see Charles Spurgeon's "Ethernet Numbers" article at *http://www.ethermanage.com/ethernet/descript-troubleshoot.html*.

In Windows XP, you can also use the Getmac command-line utility to return the MAC addresses for one or more network adapters on a system. This command has one big advantage—you can run it remotely to gather this information from a group of network computers without leaving your desk. Unfortunately, if you have more than one Ethernet adapter in a given system, the results are inscrutable, because the output of the command associates each MAC with an Ethernet GUID rather than a name. To see the full syntax for this command, open a Command Prompt window and type **getmac /?**.

Because each MAC address is (in theory, at least) unique to a specific hardware device and is transmitted with every TCP/IP packet, network managers can use this information for two purposes:

- Using software, an administrator can configure a network to allow or deny access based on MAC addresses. Many cable companies restrict users in this fashion by configuring the broadband connection to work with only a specific MAC address. If you replace your network adapter or install a router, you are required to call the cable company and register the new MAC address. Similarly, some routers and wireless access points allow you to designate which MAC addresses are allowed to send and receive data through that device, rejecting packets from other addresses.

  The former restriction is annoying; the latter seems like a promising addition to your security arsenal. Unfortunately, both solutions fall apart quickly because of the ease with which MAC addresses can be "spoofed." Changing the MAC address of the router so that it matches the address of the Ethernet card in your computer leaves your broadband configuration unchanged, even though you've actually added an entire network behind the router. Most Ethernet routers enable you to change their unique address through a menu. Figure 1-1 on the next page, for instance, shows an advanced setup screen from an SMC Barricade router; clicking the Clone MAC Address button copies the address from the Ethernet adapter in the computer.

- By examining the logs of a router or a Web server, a network administrator might be able to monitor your actions on the Internet. In this scenario, the MAC address functions much like a browser cookie, except that it remains identical as you surf from site to site. Fortunately, MAC addresses are routinely stripped from packets at the first router they encounter; as a result, most Web sites will never see your MAC address. This information will, of course, always be available to your Internet service provider.

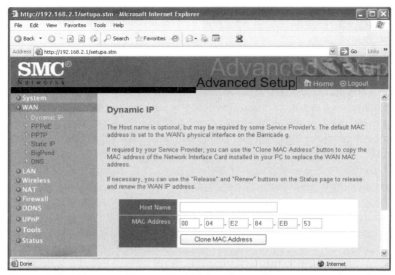

Figure 1-1. You can change the MAC address of most routers by using a menu.

Blocking Attacks by Using a Firewall

Many of the dire events we discuss in this book can be prevented by using a properly configured firewall. (Properly configured personal firewall software can protect a computer from any outside attack, whether it originates from the Internet or from another computer on the same network. Network-based firewall devices are usually designed to protect computers inside the firewall—those on the same network segment—from threats that originate from the Internet. The combination can provide a level of security that is extremely effective.) As shown in Figure 1-2, a firewall prevents entry of packets that don't meet the criteria you specify, while allowing transparent passage to authorized connections.

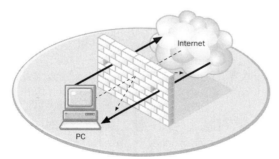

Figure 1-2. A firewall blocks unauthorized intrusion attempts and unsafe content while allowing legitimate communications and safe content to pass through.

Packet Filtering

Most firewalls work (at least in part) by packet filtering; that is, they block or allow transmissions depending on the content of each packet that reaches the firewall.

Packet filter rules can be configured in a firewall to block or allow transmissions from or to certain IP addresses or ports. A packet filter examines several attributes of each packet and either routes it (that is, forward it to the intended destination computer) or blocks it, based on any of these attributes:

- **Source address.** The IP address of the computer that generated the packet.
- **Destination address.** The IP address of the packet's intended target computer.
- **Network protocol.** The type of traffic, such as Internet Protocol (IP).
- **Transport protocol.** The higher level protocol, such as Transmission Control Protocol (TCP) or User Datagram Protocol (UDP).
- **Source and destination ports.** The number that communicating computers use to identify both ends of a communications channel.

> For more information about TCP/IP ports, see Chapter 19, "Securing Ports and Protocols."

Stateful-Inspection Packet Filtering

Blocking based on addresses, ports, and protocols is very fast, but it's an inadequate solution by itself. When a TCP connection is made to a destination port (usually on one of the well-known low-numbered ports with numbers less than 1024), an arbitrarily numbered source port (somewhere in the range between 1024 and 65535) is opened on the client computer. You certainly wouldn't want to leave all ports in this range open to incoming connections, which would present a huge target for attackers. This is where *stateful-inspection* packet filtering comes in. Here's how it works, using a Web browser as an example:

1. You type a URL in your browser's address bar and press Enter.
2. The browser sends one or more packets of data, addressed to the Web server. The request itself contains HTTP instructions. The destination port is 80, the standard port for HTTP Web servers. The source port is an arbitrary number between 1024 and 65535 that is used to define the current connection request. The outgoing request has only the SYN flag turned on. (For more information about the SYN flag, see the following sidebar.)
3. The firewall saves information about the connection in its state table, which it will use to validate returning inbound traffic.
4. After the Web server and your computer complete the handshaking needed to open a TCP connection, the Web server sends a reply (the contents of the Web page you requested) addressed to your computer's IP address and source port.
5. The firewall receives the incoming traffic and compares its source and destination addresses and ports with the information in its state table. If the information

matches (and if the incoming packet has only the ACK and SYN flags turned on), the firewall permits the reply to pass through to the browser. If the data doesn't match in all respects, the firewall discards the packet.

6 Your browser displays the received information.

TCP, SYN, ACK, and Other TLAs

TCP is a "connection-oriented" protocol, which means that it goes through an elaborate process to establish and confirm reliable communications before it can transmit data. TCP uses flags in the TCP header to perform this process, as follows:

1 One computer sends a packet with the SYN (short for *synchronize*) flag turned on. This says, in effect, "Hey, I'd like to open a connection."

2 The receiving computer responds with a packet that has both the SYN and ACK (acknowledge) flags turned on. In other words, "Okay, let's chat."

3 The first computer then sends a packet with only the ACK flag turned on.

This sequence—which is actually much more complex than this simplified explanation might suggest—is sometimes called the TCP three-way handshake, which is described in detail in Knowledge Base article 172983. Oh, and TLA? That's geek speak for *three-letter abbreviation*.

Application Filtering

More-sophisticated personal firewalls can filter based on the content of traffic directed at the firewall, scanning for viruses, malicious code, ActiveX controls, Java applets, cookies, and so on. In addition, and perhaps more importantly, these firewalls can limit outbound connections to approved applications only. A rule for each application that attempts to connect to another computer (on your LAN or on the Internet) determines whether the connection is allowed or blocked. Some personal firewalls come with pre-configured rules for common applications.

Most personal firewalls offer some sort of rule assistant that makes it easy for you to create new rules to accommodate other applications. For example, ZoneAlarm Pro displays a message similar to the one shown in Figure 1-3 when you use an application for which you haven't previously allowed access to the network. Click Allow or Deny to specify how you want the firewall to handle this packet; by selecting the Remember This Setting check box, you can specify that you want your choice to apply to all future traffic emanating from the specified application.

Because a firewall controls *all* TCP/IP communications through a particular network connection, it can block communications with other computers on your network if the same connection joins your computer to the LAN and the Internet. To give you unfettered access to your LAN while still enjoying protection from the Internet, many personal firewall programs allow you to segregate computers into security zones, typically by defining a range of "trusted" IP addresses. Although these zones are conceptually similar to the security zones used by Internet Explorer, Outlook Express, and other applications, they are not the same. Each firewall program implements zones in a slightly different way. For example, ZoneAlarm has three zones: a trusted zone (for computers you explicitly trust, such as those on your LAN), a blocked zone (for computers you explicitly distrust), and an Internet zone (for all other computers). ZoneAlarm makes it easy to configure your zones. For example, when ZoneAlarm Pro detects the presence of a network, it starts a wizard like the one shown in Figure 1-4 on the next page, which allows you to define security settings for your LAN.

Figure 1-3. When an application attempts to connect to an external computer and you haven't previously authorized it, a personal firewall might display a message like this.

> **Note** Windows Firewall, included with Windows XP SP2, does not explicitly use security zones; it does, however, allow you to define the scope of a particular rule so that it applies to all incoming connections, to those on your network, or to a range of IP addresses. If you use Windows Firewall on the network connection that connects your computer to the LAN, you might need to make some manual adjustments to allow certain applications to work on your network. For details, see "Configuring a Host Firewall," page 564.

One type of exploit that outbound filtering is likely to prevent is your computer's participation in a distributed denial-of-service (DDoS) attack, in which your computer becomes part of a network of computers taken over by an outsider to attack an external site. Most firewalls are configured to block the ports used by known DDoS tools. In addition, if you inadvertently install such a tool in the guise of a Trojan horse (by opening a malicious e-mail attachment, for example), a firewall with outbound application filtering might block the outbound packets from joining the attack.

In addition to stopping Trojan horse programs, application-based outbound filtering can be used to notify you when a program attempts to make a connection to an external host on its own. If you know how to interpret the data, you can use this type of alert to identify spyware programs and prevent them from "phoning home." In the hands of an inexperienced or unsophisticated user, however, these alerts can be more confusing than helpful, because legitimate programs from reputable publishers routinely connect to external servers—to download updates, gather news headlines, and transmit status reports, for example.

Figure 1-4. Upon detecting a new network—usually your LAN—ZoneAlarm Pro launches a wizard in which you can define security settings for the network.

Caution   Some personal firewalls come with a large number of predefined rules or automatically generated rules that allow certain applications to access the Internet without ever asking your permission. The danger of this convenience is that the developer who defines the rules might not share your standards for determining which programs should be given access. If you place a high value on controlling outbound connections, be very wary of a firewall program's "automatic rule generation" feature. Instead, configure the program so that it asks for confirmation the first time a program attempts access. (This confirmation prompt is sometimes referred to in a program's documentation as a "rule wizard," "rule assistant," or "learning mode.") This one-time task, which usually involves only a single click per program, ensures that *you* control which applications have access.

Note   Windows Firewall does not provide outbound traffic filtering. Don't be fooled by the dialog boxes that ask your permission to make an external connection; those settings control inbound connections only. Whether this limitation is significant is subject to heated debate. For information about some of the problems with outbound traffic filtering, see the sidebar "Firewalls Are Vulnerable, Too—Especially When Controlling Outbound Traffic," page 15.

Firewalls Are Vulnerable, Too—
Especially When Controlling Outbound Traffic

Want to start a raging argument in a room full of computer security experts? Just ask whether the definition of a firewall has to include filtering of outbound packets. By long-standing definition, a firewall's primary purpose is to prevent outside intruders from gaining access to a protected network or host. Windows Firewall sticks to this traditional role and makes no attempt whatsoever to monitor outbound traffic. In 2001 and 2002, several vocal privacy advocates published tests that demonstrated how some firewall programs failed to detect programs that make unexpected connections to external host systems. As a result, they succeeded in expanding the criteria that are widely used to evaluate personal firewall software, and today it's virtually impossible to purchase a third-party personal firewall package that doesn't monitor and control incoming *and* outgoing traffic.

Outbound traffic detection is a key differentiator between third-party firewall programs. Current versions of all the firewalls listed in "Choosing a Third-Party Personal Firewall," page 280, provide application-level protection. Most allow you to define programs that are authorized to make outbound connections, and then store a cryptographic signature—sometimes called an *MD5 hash*—of each trusted program along with the program's name. This prevents a rogue program from appropriating the name of a trusted program (such as Iexplore.exe, the executable file for Internet Explorer); packets sent by a program whose name matches an entry in the list of trusted programs are blocked if the program's signature doesn't match the stored value.

It's important to recognize that hackers will continue to pound on firewalls, and at least some will find ways to sneak past outbound filtering features. (Like Windows itself, firewall programs are usually updated by their publisher soon after any vulnerability is discovered. You'll want to periodically visit your firewall vendor's Web site to check for updates and patches.)

Security researcher Bob Sundling has argued that "the added protection provided by outbound filtering is entirely illusory," adding, "if a firewall is going to allow some program to transmit and receive data over the Internet, and that program allows other programs to control its actions, then there's no point in blocking anything at all." While we don't fully share his bleak outlook, we do agree with the general conclusion that a firewall offers no protection if you allow an intruder to bypass your defenses. The first requirement for a would-be attacker to exploit an outbound firewall is to convince you to install a program, especially if you do so from an account that has full administrative privileges. You can prevent such attacks by not executing untrusted programs, by normally using an account that does not have administrative privileges, and by promptly patching security holes. This bears repeating: An attacker must place a program on your computer—by exploiting a security hole, or by attaching an executable file to an e-mail message or offering an attractive-sounding program on a Web site and then persuading you to run the program. Don't succumb! Use up-to-date antivirus and antispyware programs to detect malware in real time, keep your e-mail program in the Restricted Sites zone, and never open unexpected executable attachments.

For information about installing, configuring, and using antivirus software, see Chapter 14, "Stopping Viruses, Worms, and Trojan Horses."

No firewall is impervious to attack. A good firewall, however, provides yet another barrier, another defensive layer. Although a dedicated attacker might ultimately be able to penetrate a firewall, either because of its inherent vulnerabilities or improper configuration, upon encountering yours the attacker is more likely to move on to easier prey.

Who Needs a Firewall?

In reality, any computer that's connected to the Internet needs firewall protection. Always-on broadband connections (such as cable, DSL, and satellite) are perhaps more vulnerable to attack than dial-up connections. Because of shorter connection times and assignment of a different IP address with each connection, dial-up connections provide something of a moving target. In addition, because of their slower speed, dial-up connections are less attractive to some attackers (depending on the attacker's goal).

Nonetheless, you should seriously consider firewall protection for any of the following:

- A computer connected to the Internet through a dial-up connection
- A computer connected to a cable modem or DSL modem
- A computer that serves as an Internet gateway for other computers on a network (for example, by using Internet Connection Sharing)
- A computer that is connected to the Internet through a wireless connection, either at home or through a wireless "hot spot" in a public place
- Computers that are connected to a hub that is also connected to a cable modem or a DSL modem

In short, any computer that is connected directly to the Internet must use a firewall. Computers that connect to the Internet indirectly, either through a router or through another computer on the network, are less vulnerable but should have a firewall installed as well. In this case, the firewall software should be configured to allow the use of shared resources by other addresses on the local network but not from outside the network. Third-party firewall solutions can offer additional intrusion protection and additional security features (such as content filtering, cookie management, and privacy protection).

For more information about firewall protection in a networked environment, see Chapter 9, "Sharing an Internet Connection."

Caution   A sensible defensive strategy has multiple layers, including password protection, NTFS permissions, antivirus protection, and a firewall. And it can make sense to have a personal firewall on a workstation in addition to a hardware firewall device or network protection such as a router or a proxy server. But you should not install more than one software firewall on a single computer.

Restricting Network Access to Files and Folders

Sharing files over a network is usually a fairly simple process, at least in mechanical terms: Open the properties dialog box for a folder, select a check box, give the shared resource a name to identify it over the network, and wait for other network users to connect to the shared resource.

Sharing files *securely* over a network is a different story. Different versions of Windows offer different mechanisms for sharing files, and the task becomes even more complicated when computers on a network use differing versions of Windows. If you're concerned about restricting access to shared folders on a Windows network, read this section carefully.

Windows Sharing and Security Models

How do you control access to shared files and folders? The answer depends on which version of Windows you're running. One or more of the following sharing models is found in every version of Windows:

Simple File Sharing.   Simple File Sharing is the default configuration on all installations of Windows XP other than on computers running Windows XP Professional that are joined to a domain. In this configuration, you share folders and printers by selecting a single check box; Windows XP sets the appropriate shared resource permissions and (on volumes formatted with NTFS) file permissions. With Simple File Sharing, Windows uses the Guest account to authenticate all network logons. As a result, shared resources are accessible to all network users; you cannot selectively set permissions so that some users have access and others are locked out.

Classic sharing.   The classic sharing model is used on computers running Windows 2000 Professional and on those running Windows XP Professional with Simple File Sharing disabled. (In Windows XP Home Edition, Simple File Sharing cannot be disabled.) When you share a folder, you have the option to set access permissions on a per-account basis; by combining these permissions with NTFS file permissions, you can tightly control access to a shared folder. You can set varying permissions for individual users or groups (allowing full control to some, read-only access to some, and locking out others altogether, for example). You can also limit the number of simultaneous connections. This additional flexibility comes at the cost of complexity, however. You not only need to understand the sometimes confusing mix of permissions and how to set them, but also need to set up local accounts on each computer for users who should be allowed network access.

Share-level access control.   If any of the computers on your network are running Windows 95/98/Me (or if you recently upgraded from one of these older versions of Windows), you might be familiar with this third sharing model. In a workgroup setting, these operating systems control access to shared resources by using passwords (one for read-only access and one for full access). When a network user tries to connect to a shared resource, Windows requests a password. Which password the user enters—the full control password, the read-only password, or an incorrect password—determines the user's level of access to the share. Windows makes no attempt to determine who the user is; therefore, any user on the network who obtains (or guesses) the password has access to the share.

Anyone who upgrades from Windows 95/98/Me to Windows 2000 Professional or Windows XP is practically certain to be confused by the sudden shift in sharing models. Instead of using a single password to allow full access to a particular shared folder or printer, Windows 2000 and Windows XP employ *user-level access control*, which means that each shared resource can be accessed only by specified user accounts. To gain access to a shared resource over the network, a user must be authenticated using the credentials of an account that has access to the share. If Simple File Sharing is enabled, the only account used is the Guest account, which requires no password.

> For more details about Simple File Sharing, including instructions on how to disable it, see "Viewing and Changing NTFS Permissions," page 143.

Understanding how Windows controls access to shared folders can be tricky. Often, the most difficult challenge is understanding fully what permissions have been applied to a folder and which credentials are in use by each network user. Start by recognizing this fundamental principle: *All network access is controlled by the computer with the shared resources.* Regardless of what operating system is in use on the computer attempting to connect to a network share, it must meet the security requirements of the computer on which the resource is shared.

Simple File Sharing in Windows XP

Windows XP Home Edition uses Simple File Sharing exclusively. Windows XP Professional can use either Simple File Sharing or classic sharing. When Simple File Sharing is enabled and SP2 is installed, the following settings are in effect for any folder you designate as shared:

- **Share permissions.**   The built-in Everyone group has Change or Read access, depending on the Sharing tab setting.
- **NTFS permissions.**   The Everyone group (which includes the Guest account) has Modify or Read & Execute access, depending on the Sharing tab setting.
- **How to connect.**   All network users are authenticated as Guest and therefore can open any shared folder simply by double-clicking its shortcut in Windows Explorer.

When Simple File Sharing is in use, you cannot selectively protect shared resources over a network. All users connecting over the network have identical permissions because Windows XP ignores their credentials and uses the Guest account for authentication. Clearly, this configuration is not appropriate for all networks. It is probably sufficient on most home networks, where users can be trusted and the most common use of sharing is to expand access to digital music and other media files. In business networks, however, the limitations of Simple File Sharing are sufficient to disqualify Windows XP

Windows Networking and Security 101

Home Edition for use on any computer on which selective access to shared resources is necessary.

Classic File Sharing in Windows XP Professional and Windows 2000

Compared with Simple File Sharing, the classic sharing model is far more powerful—and more complex. With classic sharing, which is available only in Windows XP Professional and Windows 2000 Professional, you can specify different levels of access to resources on your computer based on user and group accounts. You also can specify which users can access each resource (instead of allowing access to everyone on the network) and what permissions they have (instead of allowing the same access—modify or read-only—to everyone who connects over the network). When classic sharing is in use on a computer with Windows XP SP2 installed, the following settings are available for shared folders:

- **Share permissions.** By default, the Everyone group has Read access. Administrators on the sharing computer can grant or deny permissions to any user or group.
- **NTFS permissions.** By default, a folder inherits the permissions of its parent folder, but administrators on the sharing computer can grant or deny permissions to any user or group.
- **How to connect.** If your local account has the same user name and nonblank password as an account on the sharing computer, you're authenticated using that account and therefore have the access privileges granted to that account. If your local account does not match one on the sharing computer, you're authenticated as Guest and therefore have only the access privileges explicitly granted to Everyone or Guest. (If the Guest account is disabled on the sharing computer, only users with an account matching a local account can connect to the share.)

Classic sharing is the only option available for Windows 2000 Professional. To enable classic sharing in Windows XP Professional, go to Control Panel and open Folder Options (in the Appearance And Themes category), click the View tab, and then clear the Use Simple File Sharing (Recommended) check box.

Classic sharing imposes three fundamental changes in the way you control network access:

- You specify shared resource permissions on a per-user basis. (Simple File Sharing sets shared resource permissions only for the Everyone group.)
- If the shared folder is on an NTFS volume, you specify access control lists (ACLs) for each object in the share. (Simple File Sharing sets NTFS permissions only for the Everyone group and hides the ability to view or modify ACLs.)
- Users who connect to your computer over the network are not automatically authenticated as Guest. If a network user's user name and nonblank password match the user name and password of an account on your computer, Windows authenticates the user as the local account. If the user name and password of the network user do not match a local account, he or she is authenticated as Guest.

19

How Shared Resource Permissions and NTFS Permissions Work Together

On the surface, shared resource permissions and NTFS permissions are confusingly similar. In fact, avoiding this confusion is the primary reason that Microsoft introduced Simple File Sharing in Windows XP. If you use Windows 2000 or if you demand the greater level of security that comes with using the classic sharing model in Windows XP Professional, you need to understand how these two separate levels of access control work together.

Shared resource permissions control *network* access to a particular resource. Shared resource permissions do not affect users who log on locally. You set shared resource permissions in the Permissions dialog box, which is opened from the Sharing tab of a folder's properties dialog box.

NTFS permissions apply to folders and files on an NTFS-formatted drive and provide extremely granular control over an object. For each user to whom you want to grant access, you can specify exactly what they're allowed to do: run programs, view folder contents, create new files, change existing files, and so on. NTFS permissions affect all users, whether they log on locally or from across the network. You set NTFS permissions on the Security tab of the properties dialog box for a folder or a file. (Note that this tab is unavailable on a computer running Windows XP with Simple File Sharing enabled.)

For more information about NTFS permissions, see "Using NTFS Permissions for Access Control," page 143.

Only accounts that successfully pass both tests are granted access. It's important to recognize that the two types of permissions are combined in the most restrictive way. If, for example, a user is granted Read permission on the network share, it doesn't matter whether the user's account has Full Control NTFS permissions on the same folder; the user can only read files and cannot modify them when connecting over the network. Conversely, a user might have Modify permissions on the network share, but that means nothing if the user attempts to open a file whose NTFS permissions restrict the user to Read access only.

An account that attempts to connect over the network must first have its shared resource credentials validated. The account is either denied access or allowed to enter with certain permissions, at which point Windows checks the NTFS permissions for the requested object. Based on the user's access token, Windows might strip away (but not add to) some or all of the permissions granted at the first doorway.

In determining the effective permissions for a particular account, you must also consider the effect of group membership. NTFS permissions are cumulative; an account that is a member of one or more groups has the permissions granted explicitly to the individual account in addition to all permissions granted to each group of which it's a member. The only exception to this rule is Deny permissions, which take precedence over any conflicting Allow permissions.

If Windows cannot authenticate a user trying to connect from the network, the user sees a logon dialog box. (Figure 1-5 shows what you'll see if you're using Windows XP Home Edition to connect to another computer on the network.) To gain access, enter the user name and password of an account that has been granted the permissions you need. If this account is a local account on the computer that contains the shared resource (as is always the case in a workgroup), enter the user name in the form *computername\username* (for example, if user Ed is logged on to a computer named Fellini, use **Fellini\Ed**). To use a domain user account when your computer is not joined to the domain, use the form *domain\username*; if your computer is joined to the domain, you can enter the user name alone. If you're using Windows XP Professional, the logon dialog box includes a check box that you can select to save the user name and password so that you are automatically authenticated whenever you connect to that resource.

Figure 1-5. To connect to a shared folder on a computer using classic sharing, you must enter the user name and password of a user with an authorized account.

If you get an "access denied" error message instead of a logon dialog box when you try to connect to a shared resource, Windows cannot match your logon credentials to an account that is authorized to access the resource in question. This problem is inevitable if you are authorized to access shared resources on another computer using a different user name/password combination than the one you use to log on to your computer.

If you're running Windows XP Professional, you can solve this problem by storing the user name and password in the Protected Storage subsystem, where it's available when you log on. If you select the Remember My Password check box, Windows does this automatically. You can also add credentials for another network computer manually. Follow these steps if your computer is not joined to a domain:

1. From Control Panel, open User Accounts.
2. Click your name in the Pick An Account To Change list.
3. Under Related Tasks, click Manage My Network Passwords.
4. Click Add, and then enter the name of the server, protected Web site, or network location for which you want to store your credentials, and a valid user name and password.

Follow these steps if your computer is joined to a domain:

1 From Control Panel, open User Accounts.

2 In User Accounts, click the Advanced tab and then click Manage Passwords.

> You might need to log off and log on before you can access the shared folder.

These options, available if you're using Windows XP Professional, allow Windows to save your credentials so that you need never enter them again to access the same resource. Unfortunately, the same is not true of Windows XP Home Edition or of Windows 2000. Both of these operating systems remember your credentials only as long as you remain logged on. If you log off or restart your computer, you need to reenter the user name and password to access a shared resource. With a little effort, you can work around these limitations and connect to a network share with an alternative user name and password. One way to accomplish this task is to create a batch file that includes the Net Use command, adding a valid user name and password at the end of the command. (The complete syntax is available by typing **net use /?** in a Command Prompt window.) Unfortunately, this option unnecessarily compromises your security by storing the password in plain text; anyone can open the batch file in a text editor and learn your password.

A much better option is to map the shared folder to a drive letter. Although this option is primarily designed to make browsing files easier by replacing a cumbersome path with a single drive letter, it also includes the option to pass a different set of credentials with which to connect to the network share. By mapping a share on a remote server and connecting to it automatically at startup, you can force Windows to save your logon credentials and reuse them for all connections to the same server. Follow these steps:

1 In Windows Explorer, choose Tools, Map Network Drive.

2 Select any available drive letter from the drop-down list in the Drive box. The exact letter doesn't matter.

3   In the Folder box, type the path to the folder you want, using UNC syntax.

4   Select the Reconnect At Logon check box; this option instructs Windows to connect to this shared folder automatically each time you log on.

5   Click the Different User Name link, enter the user name and password of an account that is authorized to access the shared resource, and then click OK.

6   Click Finish.

Shared Folders in Windows 95/98/Me

If your network includes any computers running Windows 95/98/Me, those computers rely on passwords to protect shared resources. When a user authenticates from across the network, Windows ignores the user name and checks only the password. These settings apply to the shared folders:

● **Permissions.**   When a folder is shared, it can be protected with a password for read-only access, a password for full access, both, or neither.

● **How to connect.**   Any network user can open any shared folder simply by double-clicking its icon in Windows Explorer. If the password for the current user account matches the password assigned to the folder, the folder opens immediately. If not, Windows asks you to provide the password in a dialog box similar to the one shown in Figure 1-5 (on page 21). You don't need to provide a user name; that box is disabled.

Inside Out

Understand the secrets of long share names

In Windows 2000 and Windows XP, share names can be up to 80 characters long, including spaces and punctuation. In Windows 95/98/Me, share names are limited to a total of 12 characters in length. If your network includes computers running different versions of Windows, you can take advantage of this technical difference to prevent users of older versions of Windows from accessing shared resources on computers running Windows 2000 or Windows XP. If you name a share Projects, for example, any user can see it, even from a computer running Windows 98. But if you name the share Secret Projects (a total of 15 characters, including the space), only users of computers running Windows 2000 or Windows XP can see the share. Because you can easily prevent an untrusted user from logging on to computers running Windows 2000 and Windows XP, this technique is surprisingly effective.

Workgroups vs. Domains

Computers on a Windows network can be joined together in a workgroup or in a domain.

In a *workgroup*, the security database (including, most significantly, the list of user accounts and the privileges granted to each one) for each computer resides on that computer. When you log on to a computer in a workgroup, Windows checks its local security database to see whether you've provided a user name and password that matches one in the database. Similarly, when network users attempt to connect to your computer, Windows again consults the local security database. A workgroup is sometimes called a *peer-to-peer network*.

By contrast, a *domain* consists of computers that share a security database stored on one or more domain controllers running a member of the Windows Server 2003, Windows 2000 Server, or Microsoft Windows NT Server families. When you log on using a domain account, Windows authenticates your credentials against the security database on a domain controller.

In general, our advice throughout this book is predicated on the assumption that your network does not include a domain controller. In a domain environment, security is managed at the server, and the task of configuring a domain server is significantly more complex than we can cover in this book. Nonetheless, we can point out the security-related differences you're likely to encounter if you connect your computer to a domain-based network. The following list provides a basic overview of these differences; for a more detailed discussion of this and other issues that are unique to larger business networks, see Chapter 11, "Working with a Corporate Network."

Logon and Logoff.　The Windows XP Welcome screen is unavailable in a domain environment. Instead, you use the "classic" logon, which prompts you to press Ctrl+Alt+Delete and then enter your user name (if it isn't already entered from your last session) and password. If you use Windows 2000, the logon procedures are identical except for the addition of a Domain box at the bottom of the logon dialog box.

Passwords.   A domain administrator can change the password for your domain account. Any user who is a member of the local Administrators group can change the password for any local account. In Windows XP, the option to create or use a Password Reset Disk is not available.

File Sharing and Security.   Although the Simple File Sharing option is available in the Folder Options dialog box on a computer running Windows XP Professional in a domain, selecting that option has no effect. A computer joined to a domain uses classic sharing, just as in Windows 2000. (If you use Windows XP Home Edition, you're stuck with Simple File Sharing and are unable to join a domain, although you can access a domain's resources by supplying the proper user name and password.)

Logon Scripts and Group Policy.   In a domain environment, a domain administrator can set up scripts that run automatically each time you log on to your computer. These scripts, which are usually stored and administered on the domain controller or another network server, can be used to provide software updates, new virus definitions, and other information to your computer; set up network connections; start programs; and perform other tasks. Group Policy settings are centrally managed and can be selectively applied to computers, users, groups, domains, and other divisions. On a managed network, the combined effect of these features can severely limit your ability to control your own system's configuration.

Chapter 2

Computer Security: Are You at Risk?

Every year, personal computers become more powerful, more complex, more connected... and more vulnerable.

In 1995, when the Internet was still in its infancy, a leading computer security clearing-house, the CERT Coordination Center (*http://www.cert.org*), reported the discovery of 171 vulnerabilities that thieves and vandals could exploit to attack widely used operating systems and applications. In 2000, the number of newly discovered vulnerabilities jumped to 1,090; and in 2002, the total skyrocketed to more than 4,100, with 37 of those flaws considered serious enough to warrant formal security alerts. Since hitting that dubious high-water mark, the rate of growth in reports of new vulnerabilities in computer operating systems and networks has leveled off, but the raw numbers are still depressingly high. With an average of more than 10 new vulnerabilities every day in 2003 and 2004, the problem shows no signs of abating.

Those alerts are aimed at users of many operating systems and hardware platforms, of course, not only at those of us who run Microsoft Windows. But the world's most popular operating system makes a tempting target. Destructive, fast-spreading viruses and newly discovered bugs in the Windows operating system make for juicy headlines. And for every security threat that makes the nightly news, a hundred more might be reported only on Web sites and mailing lists aimed at security professionals. Make no mistake about it: What you don't know *can* hurt you.

As personal computers weave themselves ever more tightly into the social and economic fabric of our lives, the potential for damage from viruses, malicious Web sites, cyber-vandals, and thieves increases. A successful attacker can vaporize data files and wipe out installed programs on your computer, drain funds from your online bank and brokerage accounts, ruin your credit, send forged e-mail messages using your Internet connection, and hijack your computer for use in attacks on other computers and networks. Viruses and worms can scramble data and render entire networks unusable for days.

The cost to clean up after a major outbreak of a new virus or worm can be staggering. Estimates of the economic impact of viruses, worms, and other security-related

Microsoft Windows XP Networking and Security Inside Out

outbreaks are always suspect, but there's no question that the direct costs of preventing attacks on computers and business networks add up to billions of dollars each year, and cleaning up the damage caused by successful attacks adds untold billions of dollars to the price tag. Even if you're responsible for only a single computer, the costs can be significant. Imagine how much you would lose if the computer that runs your business were rendered unusable for several days or a week and all your saved files were destroyed.

Fortunately, you don't need a degree in computer science to protect your computer. We wrote this book with the specific intent of helping ordinary Windows users break through the haze of misinformation, myth, and technobabble that defines most of the currently available information about Windows security. If you want to take control of your personal computer and protect yourself from online threats, you've come to the right place. Our focus is on vulnerabilities and threats that affect anyone running Windows XP (Home Edition or Professional) or Windows 2000 Professional. We'll explain how each vulnerability works, how it can affect you, and how you can close the security hole.

Note This book focuses on Windows XP (Home Edition and Professional) and Windows 2000 Professional. If you're using Windows 95, Windows 98, or Windows Millennium Edition (Windows Me), some of the information in this book will be relevant to you, but most of our recommendations rely on features found only in Windows XP and its predecessor, Windows 2000. Both of these operating systems were designed from the ground up with security in mind; features such as the NTFS file system, built-in encryption, and support for multiple users are essential building blocks of a comprehensive computer security program. If you're serious about protecting your personal computer and you're still running an older version of Windows, we've got one word of advice: Upgrade.

In this chapter, we examine the most common threats to your computer's security and list the basic steps you need to take as part of a comprehensive security program. In Chapter 3, "Windows Security Tools and Techniques," we describe the arsenal of security tools and technologies built into Windows 2000 and Windows XP and explain how you can put them to best use. Elsewhere in the book, we explore each type of threat in detail, providing in-depth technical information, expert tips, additional resources, and checklists you can use to stop even the most determined intruder.

Balancing Safety and Convenience

Let's start with a simple, inescapable truth: There is no such thing as a perfectly secure personal computer, just as there is no such thing as a perfectly secure house.

Keeping your personal data and your Internet connection safe from hostile software and unwelcome visitors is, by definition, a balancing act. Some of the features available in Windows that ease your online life can inadvertently expose confidential information to an untrusted stranger. For instance, a feature in Microsoft Internet Explorer called AutoComplete enables you to save logon names and passwords associated with Web sites so that you can access your data with a single click instead of having to remember your password and enter it each time. But that time-saving trick works equally well for any person who sits down at your computer. In a matter of minutes, anyone with physical access to your computer can poke around in your banking records, view sensitive information, and even transfer funds.

To protect yourself, you can disable features of the operating system and its components that pose unnecessary risks to your security. You can increase the complexity of the passwords you use to access your computer and online accounts. You can also add third-party security software and hardware devices to make life more difficult for intruders. Unfortunately, each additional layer of security also makes performing even simple computing tasks more difficult for you.

> For a much more detailed discussion of these fundamental security concepts, see the Appendix, "The Ten Immutable Laws of Security."

How do you find the right balance between security and convenience? The role of the computer and the value of the data stored there determine the level of security that's appropriate. If you're an analyst for the Central Intelligence Agency or an auditor for a multinational bank, you need world-class security, and you should be prepared to pay a steep price for that level of protection. On the other hand, if you have a home computer located in your den, accessible only to members of your family, you can tip the scales in favor of convenience.

Before you can decide how to protect yourself, however, you need to understand the different types of threats that confront every computer user, every day.

Know Your Enemy: Seven Threats to Your Computer's Security

If you pay attention only to the mainstream media, you might think that credit card thieves and occasional outbreaks of e-mail–borne viruses are the only serious threats to your computer and its data. Nothing could be further from the truth. Attacks can come from just about anywhere, including your own office. Every year, the Computer Security Institute and the San Francisco office of the FBI survey American corporations, government agencies, financial institutions, medical institutions, and universities to determine trends in computer security; their 2004 survey revealed that roughly two-thirds of the businesses and institutions surveyed experienced at least one instance of unauthorized access to their systems and data by insiders—disgruntled current or former employees. And some of the most serious attacks on the global Internet in recent years have come as a result of "Trojan horse" programs planted on Windows computers by technically unsophisticated amateur attackers.

In this section, we list seven common categories of threats you're likely to encounter.

Threat #1: Physical Attacks

The most basic breach of your computer's security doesn't require the attacker to have any technical skill at all. If you leave a notebook computer unattended for even a few seconds in a busy airport or train station, a thief can pick it up and carry it away, along with all your personal data and access to any passwords stored there. Stealing a desktop computer is logistically more challenging, but the resulting loss can be equally disastrous. And don't assume that a complex, hard-to-guess password or even well-encrypted files will protect you. If a technically savvy crook can cart away your computer, he (the overwhelming majority of malicious hackers and high-tech thieves are male) can work on it for days or weeks. Given enough time, bad guys can break into any computer, no matter how well it's protected.

As bad as that sounds, some physical attacks on your computer can be even more devastating. Consider the consequences, for instance, if you leave your office door open and your computer on and unlocked while you go to lunch or a meeting. A brief absence is long enough for an intruder to sneak into your office, sit down at the keyboard, and copy data files to a portable storage device or upload them to another computer over the Internet. A malicious intruder could sabotage your work by altering numbers in a spreadsheet or changing the wording of a contract or letter. A really determined spy could even install surveillance software that runs in the background on your computer, sending the information to a remote computer.

Figure 2-1, for instance, shows typical setup options from a "stealth monitoring" program called WinSpy (*http://www.win-spy.com*). The program installs in a few seconds and is nearly undetectable when running on the victim's computer. After the software is installed, it monitors every keystroke—including passwords, credit card numbers, confidential memos, online chat sessions, and love letters—and also captures images of the screen's contents at regular intervals. The resulting files can be sent to an e-mail address or uploaded to a Web site. With a separate remote console module, the intruder can monitor activities on your computer in real time, browsing files and folders and transferring files at will.

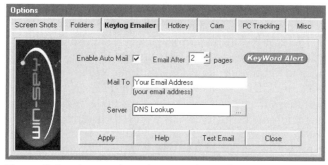

Figure 2-1. An attacker who gets physical access to your computer for even a few minutes can install surveillance software and literally take control of your computer from a remote location.

For more details about how you can detect and remove Trojan horses, keystroke loggers, and other remote control software, see "Repairing an Infected System," page 490.

Physical Security: A Checklist

As the experts at the Microsoft Security Response Center note, "If a bad guy has unrestricted physical access to your computer, it's not your computer anymore." That's why, as part of a comprehensive computer security plan, your absolute first line of defense is to make sure that your computer is physically protected. Follow these guidelines:

- Keep any computer containing sensitive information behind a locked door. Cubicles make it too easy for intruders to attempt a break-in.

- In high-traffic areas, use external locks to physically bolt a computer to a desk. This extra level of protection won't stop a determined professional thief, but it will prevent crimes of opportunity.

- Take extra precautions to protect portable computers and handheld devices, especially when they contain sensitive information. Consider using a radio-controlled alarm that sounds an alert if you and your notebook carrying case are unexpectedly separated.

- At work, make a habit of logging out or locking the computer every time you leave your desk. Casual snoops can learn a lot just by looking at the names of files and folders, without even touching your keyboard. Don't make their job easy.

- Watch out for "shoulder surfers" who try to steal passwords by watching your fingers as you log on. Arrange your work space so that your keyboard is not in plain view.

- Use a password-protected screen saver. Set your screen saver to kick in after a short period of inactivity—no more than five minutes—and choose the option to display a password prompt when resuming.

- Convert FAT32 disks to NTFS format to prevent snoops from booting with a floppy disk and accessing data files without having to log on. (For details on making this conversion, see "Use NTFS for All Drives," page 72.)

- If your computer contains ultrasensitive data, consider using the encrypting file system (for details, read Chapter 21, "Encrypting Files and Folders"), and add a hardware-based logon device such as a smart card or a biometric identification system.

Do some of these precautions sound extreme? They're not. In fact, most of this advice is common sense. You wouldn't think of leaving your front door unlocked when you go to bed at night. Why then would you want to leave your personal computer unlocked, especially when you know that would-be intruders are constantly on the prowl, rattling virtual doorknobs in search of unsecured computers?

Chapter 2

31

Caution   Encrypting data is a superb way to lock out thieves, as long as you're also diligent about setting strong passwords and logging off when you're not using your computer. Just make sure to keep a backup copy of the encryption key! If anything happens to the hard disk containing your Windows system files, you must be able to replace the encryption key. Without it, you're permanently locked out from all your encrypted files, even if you're able to restore them from a backup copy. Before you even think about using the encrypting file system built into Windows XP Professional and Windows 2000, read Chapter 21, "Encrypting Files and Folders."

Threat #2:   Pilfered Passwords

On the overwhelming majority of computers and secure Web sites, entering a password is the only way to establish that you are who you say you are. If someone else borrows, steals, or guesses your password, that person has complete access to all your files and network resources. By logging on with your password, a malicious intruder can read your e-mail, poke around in your sensitive files, access protected network resources such as corporate databases, and perform all sorts of mischief, leaving you to clean up the mess.

Surprisingly, the newest and most secure version of Windows, Windows XP, actually encourages sloppy password habits. When you install Windows XP (Home Edition or Professional) on a computer that's not connected to a Windows domain, the Setup program creates new user accounts with blank passwords and full administrative rights—hardly a secure configuration (although, in the system's defense, its default settings disable any access to shared files from across the network until you create a password). When you run the Network Setup Wizard and enable file sharing, Windows XP encourages each user to create a password and add a hint, like the one shown in Figure 2-2. The hint makes it easy to remember your password later; unfortunately, it also makes things easier for anyone trying to guess your password.

Strong, effective passwords are at least eight characters long and contain a random mix of uppercase and lowercase letters, numbers, and punctuation marks. Sad to say, most people do a lousy job of picking passwords and personal identification numbers, using easy-to-remember and easy-to-guess combinations of numbers and letters, such as birthdates or the names of children or pets. Worse still, most people reuse the same password at every opportunity, which means that an intruder who steals the password for your favorite online bookstore might also be able to access your bank account, log on to your computer, and read or send messages using your e-mail account.

Using a strong password increases your online security dramatically. Widely available password-cracking utilities can unlock a simple password by trying millions of combinations of words and numbers; this process, aptly described as brute-force cracking, can be accomplished in a few minutes. It can take thousands of times longer—days, weeks, even months—to crack a complex password that mixes random letters, numbers, and symbols.

For more details about how password-cracking utilities work, see "Recovering a Lost Password," page 115.

Computer Security: Are You at Risk?

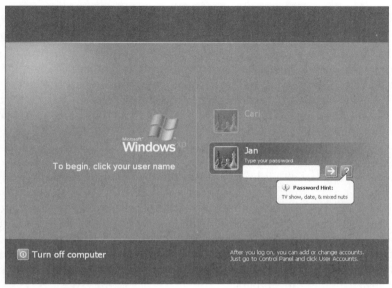

Figure 2-2. Avoid using hints like the one shown here, which weaken the security of your logon password.

Of course, even the strongest password offers scant protection if it's written on a sticky note tacked to the side of a monitor or stuffed in the top desk drawer. Enterprising thieves also use "social engineering" to trick a gullible computer user into giving up passwords to a complete stranger over the phone or through e-mail. A con artist using social-engineering techniques might pretend to be a technical support specialist diagnosing trouble with your computer. By interspersing details about your company, its network, and your applications, the would-be thief tries to lull the victim into a false sense of security. ("Mr. Bott? Yes, this is Carl in the network operations center. We've been trying to track down a problem on the 16th floor Ethernet run and wonder whether you can help us. We think there are some problems in the fiber runs between your wing and the server room. Do you have a minute to help me do some testing so I can figure out what's going on?") Although the technique fails more often than it succeeds, it's still surprisingly effective. Even seasoned computer support professionals sometimes fall for social-engineering scams, in which an outside caller pretends to be a user experiencing password problems. ("Can you reset my password, please? I've forgotten it.") On corporate networks, where individual users have access to a broad range of resources, the results can be devastating.

> For technical details on how Windows saves passwords and how you can increase the security of password-protected resources, see "Using Passwords Effectively," page 108.

Threat #3:   Nosy Network Neighbors

Do you trust the person in the next cubicle? Misplaced trust and misconfigured systems can lead to security headaches on computer networks of any size. Networks promote collaboration by enabling users to share files, folders, and other resources in real time. Used effectively, networks can have a dramatic positive effect on productivity. Used carelessly, however, networks can contribute to security problems. The most common weaknesses occur when users don't pay sufficiently close attention while sharing resources and setting up user accounts.

The three most common security problems on networks are the following:

- **Sharing files that should remain confidential.**   Users can inadvertently create this problem by sharing a folder filled with several subfolders, some of which contain data files that should remain confidential. Simple carelessness can also cause data to be compromised, as when a user copies sensitive files to a removable disk or to a local workstation or a portable computer that isn't properly secured. Creating policies that define what types of local files can be shared or copied and training users in proper techniques for managing confidential data are essential steps in avoiding this problem.

- **Allowing unrestricted access to shared files.**   Some types of information need to be shared with a small, tightly restricted group of network users. A Microsoft Excel workbook containing your company's budget and salary details, for instance, might need to be shared among a group of senior executives. If share permissions are too broad, unauthorized users might inadvertently be able to access these files. This is a particular problem on peer-to-peer networks running Windows XP, in which the default Simple File Sharing configuration enables all network users to access shared resources.

> For more details about your alternatives when setting up shared access to sensitive files, see "Restricting Network Access to Files and Folders," page 17.

- **Allowing users to change files without permission.**   Many collaborative environments depend on a team of workers being able to share information. Sensible management policies often dictate that only one or two team members have responsibility for making changes to files. What happens if a network share is set up incorrectly, so that everyone who has access to files in a particular folder also has the capability to edit, replace, or delete those files? In that scenario, a single distracted user can wipe out a frightful amount of work by accidentally saving a new file using the same name as an existing file or by deleting a group of files in a misguided cleanup effort. Good backups can undo some of the damage (a topic we cover in depth in Chapter 6, "Preventing Data Loss"), but configuring the shared resources correctly can prevent the problem from occurring in the first place.

Inside Out

For extra security, add a server

If the data stored on your business network is truly sensitive, we strongly recommend that you augment the basic protections afforded by access controls in Windows 2000 Professional and Windows XP Professional. In this type of environment, consider setting up at least one server running Microsoft Windows Server 2003 or Windows 2000 Server and creating a Windows domain. When all user data is stored on domain servers, a trained administrator can manage security policies and enforce them across the entire network, instead of relying on each user to maintain secure data. Using network servers also makes it easier to ensure that data is backed up regularly. Although this book doesn't cover server configuration in detail, you can learn more about how to work with domains in Chapter 11, "Working with a Corporate Network."

Threat #4: Viruses, Worms, and Other Hostile Programs

Mainstream media outlets reserve their most breathless headlines for outbreaks of viruses and worms, often prompted by press releases from companies that sell software intended to fight those hostile programs. In recent years, a handful of new viruses and worms have caused massive amounts of damage to the computers they infected and have disrupted the flow of information on the Internet. In addition, the list of unsafe or unwanted programs has expanded to include software that doesn't meet the technical definition of a virus or worm but still has unwanted consequences, such as displaying pop-up windows or taking over some functions of a Web browser. Sadly, Windows users who pay attention to the threat of viruses only when a new outbreak occurs are most likely to become victims of a new attack.

Understanding how hostile software works is essential to keeping them out of your computer and network. Let's start with some definitions:

- A *virus* is a piece of code that replicates by attaching itself to another object. A virus doesn't have to be a self-contained program; in fact, many outbreaks of seemingly new viruses actually involve rewritten and repackaged versions of older virus code. When a virus infects a computer running Windows, it can attack the registry, replace system files, and take over e-mail programs in its attempt to replicate itself. The virus *payload* is the destructive portion of the code. Depending on the malicious intent and skill of the virus writer, the virus can destroy or corrupt data files, wipe out installed programs, or damage the operating system itself.

- *Worms* are independent programs that replicate by copying themselves from one computer to another, usually over a network or through e-mail attachments. Many modern worms also contain virus code that can damage data or consume so many system resources that they render the operating system unusable.

- *Spyware* is a catch-all term commonly used to describe a class of programs that are installed on a computer through deceptive means. Originally, this term referred to keystroke loggers, browser add-ins, and other programs that gather and transmit information about you and your activities without your knowledge and informed consent. In recent years, the definition has broadened to include all sorts of potentially unwanted software.

- *Adware* refers to a class of programs that display advertisements—usually in pop-up windows, on the desktop, or in the browser window. These programs often contain spyware-like features in that they monitor your movements around the Web so that they can provide ads that are ostensibly related to your interests. The most aggressive forms of adware use a variety of tricks to hide themselves and to make uninstalling the software as difficult as possible.

Computer viruses date back to the 1980s, when they were most commonly transmitted through infected floppy disks. In recent years, though, virus outbreaks have become faster and more destructive, thanks to the ubiquitous nature of the Windows platform and popular e-mail programs such as Microsoft Outlook and Outlook Express, coupled with the soaring popularity of the Internet. Virus writers have become more sophisticated, too, adding smart setup routines, sophisticated encryption, downloadable plug-ins, and automatic Web-based updates to their dangerous wares. Polymorphic viruses can mutate as they infect new host files, making discovery and disinfection difficult because no two instances of the virus "look" the same to virus scanners. So-called stealth viruses can disguise themselves so that installed antivirus software can't detect them. If you know where to look in the virus underground, you can find point-and-click virus-authoring software, which lets even a nonprogrammer build a fully functional, destructive virus.

Many viruses and worms spread by attaching themselves to e-mail messages and then transmitting themselves to every address they can find on the victim's computer. Some bury the virus code in an executable file that masquerades as a seemingly innocuous graphic file. When the victim opens the attachment, the animated file plays in its own window, disguising the virus activity.

Some viruses hidden in e-mail attachments try to cloak their true identity by appending an additional file name extension to the infected attachment. This strategy relies on the intended victim using the default settings of Windows Explorer, which hides extensions for known file types. (Recent versions of Microsoft Outlook and Outlook Express show all extensions for file attachments, regardless of Windows Explorer settings.) Today, many Internet mail servers block executable attachments; as a result, the majority of recent viruses deliver their payload in compressed files that use the .zip format.

Although most viruses and worms arrive as e-mail attachments, that's not the only method of transmission. Malicious code can also be transmitted to unprotected machines through network shares, through ActiveX controls and scripts, and by HTML-based e-mail messages or Web pages. The infamous Code Red and Nimda worms represent particularly virulent examples of "blended threats" that replicate using multiple vectors.

> **Caution** "Underground" Web sites that host pornography, illegal software, and other questionable content are disproportionately likely to transmit viruses and worms. If novice computer users have access to your computer, make sure they understand the dangers of downloading and installing software from unknown sources. Up-to-date antivirus software is imperative on multiuser computers.

How can you stop viruses and worms before they cause damage to your computer or network? Here are four general guidelines to follow.

> For more details, including how to identify a virus or worm and how to recover from a virus infection, see Chapter 14, "Stopping Viruses, Worms, and Trojan Horses."

- **Learn how to spot the warning signs of viruses.** This is especially important in the first few hours or days after a new virus or worm appears on the scene, before antivirus software makers have developed updates that can detect the new strain. Unexpected e-mail attachments, even from familiar correspondents, should always be treated with extreme caution. (For a complete list of the telltale clues, see "Identifying Malicious Software," page 470.)

> **Tip** When in doubt, delete suspicious files
>
> When a new virus outbreak occurs, articles in the mainstream press often advise users to avoid opening attachments from strangers. That advice is dangerously incomplete. It's equally important to avoid opening attachments from friends and colleagues. Most viruses that target Windows computers distribute themselves by combing the victim's hard drive for e-mail addresses and randomly using those addresses in the To and From fields of the outgoing message. The infected attachment might be a real file, plucked from the victim's My Documents folder. If you receive an unexpected attachment from anyone, *especially* someone you know, don't open it until you can verify that it's safe. When in doubt, press the Delete key.

- **Install antivirus software and keep it up to date.** A good antivirus program monitors downloads and e-mail attachments in real time instead of relying on after-the-fact scans to identify infected files. Be sure to update the virus definitions regularly. Out-of-date antivirus software is worse than none at all because it promotes a false sense of security without offering any protection against recent virus strains.

- **Train other network users on how to avoid viruses.** Make sure that people you share a network with develop a healthy suspicion of file attachments and questionable Web pages. Impress on them how important it is to have antivirus software running at all times.

- **Build additional barriers to prevent viruses from attacking computers.** The best protection against viruses and worms is to keep them from ever reaching the user. Some third-party firewall programs offer extra layers of protection that block malicious code. Recent versions of Outlook and Outlook Express also include features that can disable potentially dangerous attachments. On a corporate network that includes an e-mail server, e-mail gateways can quarantine dangerous mail before it has a chance to reach users.

Chapter 2

Threat #5: Outside Intruders and Trojan Horse Takeovers

If you've been to the movies, you've seen Hollywood's stereotypical hacker—brilliant, antisocial, fueled by pizza and Mountain Dew, and so skilled that he can break into any bank, corporate database, or international spy headquarters with just a few taps on the keyboard.

In the real world, malicious hackers are far less glamorous and, for the most part, far less skilled than their counterparts on the silver screen. Unfortunately, even a novice hacker can do a frightful amount of damage by targeting an inadequately protected computer over the Internet.

> **Note** Some security professionals bristle at what they perceive as the misuse of the term *hacker*, especially by the mainstream news media. In the computer underground, a hacker is anyone who spends time poking into computers and operating systems, testing their limits and discovering their vulnerabilities. "White hat" hackers who find and fix vulnerabilities in operating systems, applications, and networks are widely respected for their skills. "Black hat" hackers, or crackers, are more interested in breaking into computers and networks without authorization, either for the sheer fun of it or to steal valuable information, such as credit card numbers. In this book, we use the more precise terms *attacker* and *intruder* to refer to anyone who tries to access an unauthorized computer system from outside.

Most would-be intruders don't bother aiming at a particular computer or network. Instead, they use widely available underground utilities to automate the process of breaking and entering. These tools scan hundreds or thousands of IP addresses in search of specific, known vulnerabilities; they're most effective against always-on Internet connections, such as cable modems and DSL lines, whose IP addresses remain constant for long periods of time. Here are some examples of what they're looking for:

- **Unprotected shared resources.** In theory, shared resources should be accessible only to other users on your network. In practice, poorly secured shares might be accessed from other computers on the same network segment (users connected to the same dial-up modem or cable router, for instance) and in some circumstances by any computer, anywhere on the Internet. A malicious intruder who finds an open share that isn't protected by a password can do anything with the files and folders in that location.

- **Open service ports.** An intruder who finds a server running on your computer can probe it for weak passwords or known security holes; if you haven't applied the latest software updates to fix those vulnerabilities, the intruder can exploit the weakness to access your computer. Web servers, FTP servers, remote access programs like pcAnywhere, and messaging clients such as ICQ are especially susceptible to this sort of attack. For information about identifying open service ports, see "Determining Which Ports Are Active," page 632.

- **Trojan horses.** Also known as "back door" programs, these pieces of hostile software act as stealth servers that allow intruders to take control of a remote computer without the owner's knowledge. Like the Greek myth after which they're

Chapter 2

named, Trojan horse programs typically masquerade as benign programs and rely on gullible users to install them. Computers that have been taken over by a Trojan horse program are sometimes referred to as *zombies*. As we'll see shortly, armies of these zombies can be used to launch crippling attacks against Web sites.

To prevent intruders from breaking into your computer from the Internet, follow these three general guidelines:

- **Shut down services you're not using.** If you once installed a personal Web server to experiment with Web page design but no longer use it, make sure it's not still running on your computer, inviting intruders to take a crack at it. (For details about turning off unused services, see "Shutting Down Unneeded Services," page 650.)

- **Use firewall software to block access to your computer and to monitor intrusion attempts.** Windows Firewall, which is installed when you upgrade Windows XP to Service Pack 2 (SP2), provides effective basic protection from outside intrusion attempts. As Figure 2-3 shows, you can configure the firewall to allow certain types of traffic through, while blocking all others. Third-party firewall software offers additional capabilities, including the capability to block unwanted outbound connections and to restrict Internet access on a per-application basis.

- **Use hardware barriers for an extra layer of protection on networks.** A simple router or residential gateway provides basic Network Address Translation, which shields the IP addresses of computers on the network and rebuffs many attempts at intrusion. More sophisticated (and more expensive) firewall devices add the capability to block specific ports and protocols that outside attackers might be able to exploit.

Figure 2-3. Windows Firewall, included with Windows XP Service Pack 2, provides basic but effective protection from intruders.

For more details about blocking intruders, see "Securing Network Connections," page 276.

Threat #6: Invasions of Privacy

When a hacker, cracker, or attacker connects to your computer, the threat to your security is immediate and personal. But threats to your online privacy are more subtle, and different users have different reactions to features in Windows and Internet Explorer that deliberately or unintentionally reveal personal information about you.

Every time you visit a Web page, for example, Internet Explorer reveals extensive details about your browser—which version you're using, which optional components you've installed, and which site contained the link that brought you to the current page. It also betrays a few details that might be able to help the owner of a Web site pin down your location: your IP address and time zone, for instance.

Those details are relatively minor and are primarily intended to improve communication between your Web browser and the sites you visit. But another feature that's common to all modern browsers is considerably more controversial. *Cookies* are tiny data files that contain persistent bits of information about you and your interaction with a particular Web site. They're also a source of raging controversy among people who are passionate about privacy. In Chapter 18, "Protecting Your Privacy," we explain how cookies work and how you can control them. For the purposes of this discussion, you should know these four facts:

- Cookies can contain personal information only if you provide it. Most cookies simply create a serial number that allows the Web site to recognize that you're a repeat visitor. If you enter personal details—by entering an online contest or filling in a registration form, for instance—the cookie can keep track of those details and match them with your browsing history from previous visits to the same site. Cookies are especially helpful for online shopping applications and at sites where you need to establish your identity for access.

- Internet Explorer 6 (an upgrade for Windows 2000 users, a standard part of Windows XP) includes a Privacy dialog box that lets you control cookies en masse or individually. Figure 2-4 shows an expanded version of the dialog box that appears when you configure Internet Explorer to prompt you before accepting a cookie.

- The most troubling threats to privacy come from third-party cookies, which enable advertisers and marketing companies to track your movements between different sites that include elements (such as banner ads) from that third party's site. Using Internet Explorer 6, you can handle third-party cookies using different rules than those that apply to cookies associated directly with a site. A variety of add-on utilities for Internet Explorer and other browsers let you exercise even more precise control over which sites are allowed to set cookies on your computer.

- An emerging standard called the Platform for Privacy Preferences (P3P) allows Web sites to define the privacy standards they follow and publish that policy in a compact form as part of their Web site. Internet Explorer 6 can read this compact privacy policy and compare its settings to the preferences you entered. In theory, at least, this feature should let you automatically handle cookies at some sites.

Figure 2-4. Most cookies consist of identifying numbers, not personal details.

Your browser has an impact on your privacy in one other way as well: The browser's history keeps a record of every site you visit—going back, by default, almost three weeks. Anyone who has physical access to your computer can examine the list of sites you've visited and learn a lot about you—perhaps more than you'd like them to know. Sweeping away this evidence of where you've been in cyberspace is more difficult than it appears, because traces of your movements are scattered all over your hard drive. We'll show you how to clean up all those scattered bits and pieces and also explain why even reformatting your hard disk might not be enough to eliminate all evidence of where you've been on the Web. For details, see "Covering Your Tracks," page 618.

Threat #7:   E-Mail Threats

You're exposed to a myriad of threats every time you start your e-mail software. We've already discussed e-mail as a delivery mechanism for viruses, but other security issues are equally important, if not as obvious. Incoming messages can contain misleading content intended to fool you into revealing confidential information; outgoing messages can be intercepted by unauthorized parties as they wend their way across the Internet.

By its very nature, e-mail lends itself to scam artists. Anyone who's ever used an e-mail account knows about its dark side—unsolicited commercial e-mail, more popularly known as *spam*. For most of us, spam is a nuisance rather than a serious threat to our computer's security. But spam can carry viruses and other hostile software. Unwanted ads for Web-based casinos and pornography can cause embarrassment or threaten your job security if they land in your work inbox. And some of the tactics people use to fight back against spam actually make the problem worse, as we explain in Chapter 16, "Blocking Spam."

We can't promise to eliminate the problem completely, but we can provide a series of steps designed to dramatically reduce the accumulation of e-mail in your inbox.

Spam is mostly just annoying, but another form of unsolicited e-mail is far more dangerous. Online con artists take advantage of the anonymity of e-mail to create fraudulent messages that appear to have been sent by a legitimate company. All it takes is a few lines of HTML code snipped from a Web page to create these "phishing" attacks, which are designed to fool the recipient into visiting a Web site that mirrors the look and feel of a bank, an Internet service provider (ISP), or an online auction firm. The victim, who thinks he is updating an account or confirming a transaction, enters personal financial data—credit card numbers, account user names and passwords, Social Security numbers, and so on—which the con artist can then use to make fraudulent purchases or electronic fund transfers. Although the phenomenon (and the colorful word that describes it) are as old as the Internet, these scams have become alarmingly popular in recent years. According to the Anti-Phishing Working Group (*http://www.anti-phishing.org*), more than 2,800 phishing sites were active in April 2005, using brand names from 79 well-known companies; that's a 150 percent increase from the monthly total only six months earlier.

In general, phishing attacks are aimed at American audiences and are launched from other countries, where law enforcement is lax. Most give themselves away with odd grammar, typographical errors, or other inauthentic details. But these fraudulent messages can be surprisingly realistic looking, and the most successful con artists can dupe as many as 5 percent of recipients into responding to the bogus appeal.

For details on how to avoid being hooked by a phishing attack, see "Avoiding Losses from 'Phishing' Attacks," page 591.

By comparison, outgoing messages are less likely to pose a significant problem. Still, you should be aware of the perils and pitfalls of including sensitive information in e-mail messages. If you use Internet-standard e-mail servers, every message you send travels in plain text on an unpredictable path that can pass through dozens of intermediate computers or routers before it reaches its destination. At any step along the way, your message can be intercepted and read; it can also be altered. In fact, it's easy for a moderately tech-savvy crook to forge your name and address on a message so that it appears to have come from you. Because of that fundamental insecurity, you should never send confidential information such as credit card details or your Social Security number in a normal e-mail message; likewise, you should never rely on ordinary e-mail messages for important business transactions.

However, if you're willing to endure some hassles, you can protect a message from prying eyes by using strong encryption and digital signatures so that the recipient can be certain the message was sent by you and hasn't been tampered with. Full details are available in Chapter 15, "Securing E-Mail and Instant Messages."

How Can You Protect Yourself?

Now that you have a basic overview of the security threats that can affect you, what should you do next? The most important step you can take is to put together a comprehensive security plan. It should incorporate the following elements:

- Make sure you install critical updates for Windows and the applications you use regularly. Configure Windows XP and Windows 2000 to download critical updates automatically; you can choose when to install those updates. Visit Microsoft Update at least once a month to check for other important updates that might apply to your computer. Eliminating vulnerabilities as soon as they're discovered is a crucial first step in protecting your data and your network. (See Chapter 7, "Keeping Your System Secure," for pointers to Microsoft Update and other sources of fixes and updated system files.)

- Be sure that your computer is physically secure.

- Use strong passwords that are difficult or impossible to guess. Don't use the same password for multiple accounts, and be sure to change your passwords every few months. Don't use automatic logons for your main Windows account.

> **Tip** **Get help remembering passwords**
> If your memory isn't up to the challenge of remembering dozens of randomly selected passwords, don't worry—help is available. You can download any of several Windows utilities that can help you securely store your password list in encrypted form; some of these utilities even include password generators that help you create truly random, hard-to-break passwords. For some suggestions, see "Managing Passwords," page 119.

- Install antivirus software and update it regularly.

- Use firewall software and hardware to protect yourself from outside intruders.

- Back up critical data regularly, and store the backups in a safe location, away from your computer.

Above all, don't think of security as a chore or a one-time task. Keeping your data, your computer, and your network secure is an ongoing process. The day you let your guard down is the day you're most likely to become a victim.

In Chapter 3, we'll walk you through important security-related features of Windows XP and Windows 2000.

Windows Security Tools and Techniques

Who do you trust?

That's not a rhetorical question. Trust is the fundamental underlying principle of all Microsoft Windows security features. As the administrator of a computer or the owner of data, you have the power to decide who can be trusted with access to your computer and its files and who should be locked out. The desktop operating systems Windows XP and Windows 2000 Professional provide an assortment of system components and tools that can help you reliably identify anyone trying to access protected resources. In this chapter, we introduce each of the pieces that form this security infrastructure.

We start with the most basic of building blocks, the user account. By setting up a password-protected account for each individual who needs to access your computer, you can share files, folders, printers, and other resources with coworkers and family members. More importantly, you can lock out unknown users and restrict who has access to files that are private or confidential. We also explain how Windows enables you to create security groups, which ease the administrative burden of managing shared resources on business networks. Although the concept of user accounts sounds simple enough, its implementation in Windows is complex. The more you understand about how Windows stores and manages the details of user accounts and security groups, the better prepared you are to defend your computer and network from unauthorized access.

Next we introduce a set of system components that provide logon and authentication services. Any user who sits down in front of a computer running Windows XP or Windows 2000 must prove his or her identity by providing the user name and password for a valid account. It's a rather simple test, really, but we show you how the process works and, more importantly, how you can customize it to make it as easy as possible for legitimate users to log on while still barring users who shouldn't have access.

After a user successfully logs on, Windows uses the security information in his or her account to determine which resources are available to the user and which are forbidden. You can apply permissions to files, folders, and network shares; and, for extra security, you can encrypt data files so that they are literally unreadable by anyone without the correct credentials, even if he or she is able to bypass your security settings and access the files. As we explain in this chapter, however, your options vary greatly, depending on your version of Windows, the file system used on a particular disk, and the choices you (or the computer manufacturer) made during Windows setup. We'll explain how each of these options work.

Last, but certainly not least, this chapter concludes with a checklist of security tweaks and tune-ups that every Windows user should implement immediately. It also includes a handful of advanced security tweaks that aren't for everyone but might be appropriate for you.

What Are User Accounts?

In Windows XP and Windows 2000, *access control* (the method of controlling access to specific files, folders, computers, and other resources) depends on the system's ability to uniquely identify each user. A user account provides that unique identity. Each person who uses a computer should be given a user account. (An exception to this rule is if your computer is used by many people who need identical privileges—for example, if it is a kiosk computer with public access or a business computer used by many employees with the same job function. For computers like these, you could instead create a single user account—usually with very limited privileges—that's shared by all such users.)

> For information about applying access control to protect local computer resources, see Chapter 5, "Securing a Shared Computer." We discuss access control for network resources in Chapter 1, "Windows Networking and Security 101."

Internally, Windows stores information about each user account in a protected database called the Security Accounts Manager (SAM). Although you're most likely to identify an account by its user name, Windows uses a variable-length value called a *security identifier* (SID) to track each account and its associated rights and permissions. When you create a user account, Windows assigns a unique SID to that account. In both Windows XP and Windows 2000, all SIDs begin with S-1. The remainder of the SID consists of groups of numbers that uniquely identify each account.

Most of the time, Windows represents accounts by their friendly names—Ed, Carl, or Administrator, for instance—and keeps track of the SID for each account in the background. However, if you look in the Windows registry, you can see the SIDs for all accounts on the current computer. Figure 3-1 shows the HKEY_USERS key for an installation of Windows XP Home Edition. The three short values are *well-known SIDs* that identify accounts common to all Windows installations; S-1-5-18 is the System account, for instance. The two much longer SIDs represent user accounts on this computer.

Each SID is used only once. The SID created along with a new user account remains uniquely associated with that account until the account is deleted. The SID is never used again—for that user or any other. After deleting an account, you cannot re-create that account and recover its permissions and other settings; if you create a new account with the same user name and password, Windows assigns a new SID to that account.

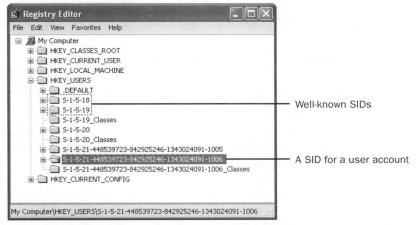

Well-known SIDs

A SID for a user account

Figure 3-1. Windows XP and Windows 2000 use security identifiers—the oddly-named keys shown under HKEY_USERS—to identify user accounts and their associated rights and permissions.

Inside Out

Find all SIDs associated with your user account

Want to see all the SIDs associated with your account? The command-line Whoami utility, included with Windows XP Professional and Home Edition, lets you examine this information in detail. To use it, you must install Windows Support Tools. Insert the Windows XP CD, browse to the Support\Tools folder, and run Setup. After installing Windows Support Tools, open a Command Prompt window (Cmd.exe) and enter the command **whoami /all /sid**. The output lists the name and SID of the currently logged-on user as well as the name and SID of each security group to which that account belongs.

Fortunately, users are never required to know their SID. Users log on to a computer running Windows by providing their user name and (if one has been assigned) the password for the account.

Tip Decode well-known SIDs
A Windows installation may include any of 59 well-known SIDs, which remain constant on different computers. For a detailed listing of these SIDs, their friendly names, and their uses, see *http://www.microsoft.com/resources/documentation/windows/xp/all/reskit/en-us /prnc_sid_cids.asp*.

User Accounts in Earlier Versions of Windows

You might be familiar with *user profiles* in Windows 95/98 and Windows Millennium Edition (Windows Me). This feature, accessed through the Users icon in Control Panel, provides a way to create a unique operating environment for each user. Each user gets to have a unique Start menu, maintain a separate My Documents folder, maintain a cache of passwords to network resources, and choose his or her desktop background, colors, and icons.

In these earlier versions of Windows, the ability to maintain separate profiles—which is also a benefit of user accounts in Windows XP and Windows 2000—is a feature of convenience, not security. Although you can set up Windows 95/98 or Windows Me so that Windows requests a password at startup, you can circumvent the request simply by clicking Cancel or pressing Esc when you see the logon dialog box. Using this option logs you on without loading the personal settings in a user profile, but still gives you full access to all information in all user profiles. The password cache files for other users remain locked, but you can easily crack these files using widely available utility programs.

By contrast, Windows XP and Windows 2000 require each user to log on with a user account. Don't confuse this crucial security feature with user profiles in earlier versions of Windows. Although the features are superficially similar, the difference in security is like night and day.

Local vs. Domain Accounts

In this chapter, our focus is on *local* accounts—user accounts and security groups that are stored in your computer's SAM. A stand-alone computer or a computer in a workgroup uses only local accounts. Each computer in the workgroup maintains its own SAM with local accounts for that computer only. With local accounts, users can log on only to the computer on which the accounts are stored and can access only resources on that computer. Other users on your network can access resources on your computer only if they authenticate themselves using a local account. (In many cases, the Guest account is used for this purpose.)

For more information about sharing resources over a network in a workgroup configuration, see "Restricting Network Access to Files and Folders," page 17.

By contrast, domain accounts are stored on a central computer called a *domain controller*. If your computer is joined to a domain—a network that has at least one computer running Microsoft Windows Server 2003 or Windows 2000 Server and serving as a domain controller—you ordinarily log on using a domain account. (Microsoft Windows NT Server can also act as a domain controller, but it does not use Active Directory or the Kerberos V5 authentication protocol, two features that define most current domains.) In the Log On To box in the Log On To Windows dialog box, you specify either your computer name (to log on using a local account) or the name of a domain (to log on using a domain account).

With a domain account, you can log on to any computer in the domain (subject to your privileges set at the domain level and on individual computers), and you can gain access to permitted resources anywhere on the network. The logon dialog box shown here displays the extra information used to log on to a domain. Notice that the user name is followed by an @ sign and the domain name.

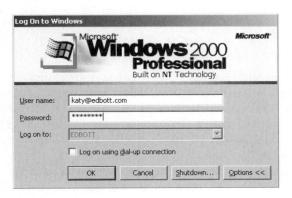

Note Users running Windows XP Home Edition can connect to shared resources on a Windows domain by entering an authorized user name and password, but they cannot join the domain, save a roaming user profile on the domain, or save the user name and password for a domain account locally. If you want to join a domain, you must upgrade to Windows XP Professional.

Domains are unnecessary for small networks, but they add security and make administration easier as networks grow. On a four-computer network, for instance, where each computer has a single user, it's not particularly difficult to create matching user accounts on each computer and coordinate file sharing. On a network with 20 or 200 or 2,000 computers, however, the task of synchronizing identical sets of user accounts on each of those computers would be overwhelming. Adding a domain controller allows a network administrator to centralize security settings.

Domain user accounts, each with its own unique SID, are stored in the domain's directory, which is managed by the domain controller. Every member of the domain can connect to this database and use its list of accounts for security purposes. Thus, an individual computer user can grant access to a shared resource by using the name of a domain security group. When the network administrator adds a new user to the network and assigns that user to the group in question, the new user automatically has access to the shared resource without requiring the local computer user to take any action.

Even in a domain environment, the local computer's SAM plays a role. Accessing resources on the local computer requires a local user account or membership in a local group. For that reason, when you join your computer to a domain, Windows adds the Domain Admins group (a domain-based security group for administrators) to the local Administrators group and adds the Domain Users group to the local Users group.

Domain-based accounts and groups are also known as *global accounts* and *global groups*.

For more details about using Windows XP and Windows 2000 as part of a domain, see Chapter 11, "Working with a Corporate Network."

Built-In User Accounts

Every installation of Windows 2000 or Windows XP has at least two built-in user accounts that are preconfigured with certain privileges and restrictions:

● **Administrator.** This account has full rights over the entire computer. As a permanent member of the Administrators group, this account has unrestricted access to all files and registry keys on the computer. The Administrator account can create other user accounts. See "Securing the Administrator Account," page 99.

Tip Bring back the Administrator account

In Windows XP, the Administrator account normally doesn't appear as a logon choice on the Welcome screen. (It appears only if no other user account exists that is a member of the Administrators, Guests, Power Users, or Users groups or when you boot into Safe Mode.) Rest assured: The account exists. If you want to log on using the Administrator account (or any other account that doesn't appear on the Welcome screen), press Ctrl+Alt+Delete two times to display the Log On To Windows dialog box, in which you can enter any user name.

● **Guest.** The Guest account is intended for occasional or one-time users, and its default privileges are quite limited. A user who logs on using this account can run programs and save documents on the local computer only. In Windows XP, the Guest account can also provide access to shared network resources when the Simple File Sharing option is enabled. See "Securing the Guest Account," page 101.

Computers running Windows XP have two or more additional built-in accounts. Unlike Administrator and Guest, these built-in accounts can be moved to a different security group or deleted by an administrator. These additional accounts include the following:

● **HelpAssistant.** The HelpAssistant account, which is used for Remote Assistance sessions, is disabled by default (and protected by a strong password). The HelpAssistant account on the computer belonging to the novice is used for logon by the remote expert.

● **SUPPORT_xxxxxxxx.** Windows XP can include one or more accounts designed for use by vendors, such as Microsoft and your computer's manufacturer, for online support and service. (*xxxxxxxx* represents a vendor-specific number.)

On some computers running Windows XP Home Edition, you might find an Owner account, which is the equivalent to the built-in Administrator account in Windows XP Professional.

Windows also includes one or more *service accounts*–special-purpose user accounts that the operating system uses to run services. (Most Windows-based programs run using the security settings of the user who started the application. Services must run in the context of a particular account, too, but because services can run before a user logs on and can continue running after all users have logged off, they need to use service accounts. The use of service accounts provides control—they have limited privileges—and accountability.) In Windows 2000, most services run using Local System privileges; others run as a particular user or have their own special-purpose user account. Windows XP adds two other service accounts with varying privileges. Services can run as LocalService only on the local computer or as NetworkService only on the network.

Security Groups

Security groups, which represent collections of user accounts, are another type of security principal. (A *security principal* is any entity that can be authenticated. In Windows XP or Windows 2000, a user, group, computer, or service can be a security principal.) Security groups provide a way to organize user accounts into groups of users with similar security needs. For example, you might want to create a security group at home for the kids in your family; in the office, you might create a group that includes all the people in the accounting department. You can then assign security permissions to the group rather than to individual users. A user account can belong to one group, more than one group, or no group at all.

Groups are a valuable tool for administering security. They simplify the job of ensuring that all user accounts with common access needs have an identical set of privileges. Although you can grant privileges to each user account individually, doing so is tedious and prone to error—and usually considered poor practice. You're better off assigning permissions and rights to groups and then adding user accounts to the group with the appropriate privileges.

Built-In Security Groups

Windows includes several built-in security groups, each with a predefined set of rights, permissions, and restrictions. Table 3-1 provides a brief description of the groups and specifies which ones are included in each version of Windows.

Table 3-1. **Built-In Security Groups in Windows**

Group	Windows XP Professional	Windows XP Home Edition	Windows 2000 Professional	Description
Administrators	Yes	Yes	Yes	The most powerful group, with full control over the system.
Power Users	Yes		Yes	Includes many, but not all, privileges of the Administrators group.
Users	Yes	Yes	Yes	Limited privileges for users who don't need to administer the system.

Chapter 3

Table 3-1. **Built-In Security Groups in Windows**

Group	Windows XP Professional	Windows XP Home Edition	Windows 2000 Professional	Description
Guests	Yes	Yes	Yes	Provides limited access for occasional users and guests.
Backup Operators	Yes		Yes	Provides the privileges needed to back up and restore folders and files, including ones that members aren't otherwise permitted to access.
Replicator	Yes		Yes	Members can manage file replication, a feature of domain-based networks.
Network Configuration Operators	Yes			Members can set up and configure network components. (For details, see Microsoft Knowledge Base article 297938.)
Remote Desktop Users	Yes			Provides access to a computer by using Remote Desktop Connection.
HelpServices Group	Yes	Yes		Allows technical support personnel to connect to your computer.

Roles of Security Group Members

Members of the Administrators group have total control of the computer. By default, administrators have full, unfettered access to all files and to all keys in the registry. And administrators can grant to themselves any right or permission they do not already have. Administrators' privileges include the ability to do the following:

- Create, change, and delete user accounts and security groups
- Install programs
- Share folders
- Set permissions
- Access all files
- Take ownership of files
- Grant rights to other user accounts and security groups as well as to themselves
- Install or remove hardware devices
- Log on in Safe Mode

By default, the Administrators group includes all local user accounts that you create during setup. If you upgrade to Windows XP from Windows NT or Windows 2000, the Administrators group retains all its members from your previous operating system. If your computer is joined to a domain, the Domain Admins group is a member of the local Administrators group.

Security Groups and Account Types

You'll encounter the term *security group* in Windows NT, Windows 2000, and Windows Server 2003, but it's less apparent in Windows XP. Although the function and use of security groups remain largely the same, in Windows XP you're more likely to see the term *account type*, particularly when you run the User Accounts tool from Control Panel. *Account type* is a simplified way of describing membership in a security group. Although you can have any number of security groups—indeed, a default installation of Windows XP Professional has nine built-in groups and you can create more—Windows XP categorizes each user account as one of only four account types:

- **Computer administrator.** Members of the Administrators group are classified as computer administrator accounts.
- **Limited.** Members of the Users group are classified as limited accounts.
- **Guest.** Members of the Guests group are shown as guest accounts.
- **Unknown.** A user account that is not a member of the Administrators, Users, or Guests group appears (somewhat alarmingly) as an Unknown account type. Because accounts you create through User Accounts in Control Panel are assigned to the Administrators group or the Users group, you'll see the Unknown account type only if you upgraded from an earlier version of Windows (for example, new users in Windows 2000 are assigned by default to the Power Users group) or if you use the Windows 2000–style User Accounts application, the Local Users And Groups console, or the Net Localgroup command to manage group membership.

There's nothing wrong with "unknown" accounts, and if you need to use other security groups to classify the user accounts on your computer, you should do so. In User Accounts, all the usual account-management tasks are available for accounts of Unknown type, but if you want to view or change group membership, you'll need to use one of the other account-management tools: Local Users And Groups, the Windows 2000–style Users Accounts, or the Net Localgroup command. We describe all three of these tools in detail in "Managing User Accounts for Security," page 82.

Members of the Power Users group hold most of the same privileges as users in the Administrators group. Power users cannot take ownership of files, back up or restore files, load or unload device drivers, or manage the security and auditing logs. Unlike ordinary users, however, power users can share folders; create, manage, delete, and share local printers; and create local users and groups.

Members of the Users group should not be able to inflict damage on the operating system or installed programs. By default, members of the Users group are not allowed to do the following:

- Modify machine-wide registry settings—those that affect all users (for example, anything in the HKEY_LOCAL_MACHINE hive).
- Modify operating system files.
- Modify files of programs installed by an administrator for all users.
- Install programs that others can use or run programs that other members of the Users group have installed. This important restriction limits the effect of a Trojan horse, which can be run only when started by the user who (inadvertently) installed it.

In addition to the groups just discussed, Windows automatically maintains a number of built-in security principals that are not shown in the Local Users And Groups list and whose membership cannot be managed by an administrator. Some of these groups exist for obvious special purposes. For instance, anyone who connects to a computer over a dial-up connection is automatically added to the Dialup group and is subject to any restrictions assigned to that group. Two built-in groups deserve special mention:

- **Everyone.** This group includes all users who access the computer, including users in the Guests group. In Windows 2000, but not in Windows XP, this group also includes members of the Anonymous Logon group.
- **Authenticated Users.** This group includes any user who logs on with an account that is authenticated locally. This group does not include guest accounts or members of the Anonymous Logon group.

With the exception of the Everyone group, built-in groups are not routinely used for assigning file access. Instead, their purpose is to control specific user rights, such as the right to access a computer over the Internet. An individual's right to access shared folders, however, will be controlled by a different set of file permissions.

Rule of Least Privilege

User accounts and groups provide the means with which you enforce the rule of least privilege. This fundamental rule of information security states that you give only enough access for a person (or a program or other entity) to do their job. The ideal implementation of this rule strikes a balance that allows a person to do everything they need to do to perform their job without obstruction, but prevents them from doing anything they're not supposed to do.

The rule of least privilege is not intended only for people you don't trust. (Hopefully you don't live or work with too many of them!) Using least privilege also reduces the risk of inadvertent damage (from acts as simple as deleting someone else's file or innocently installing a program that turns out to be malicious, for example) by limiting allowable actions. Best practices suggest that you use the least privileged account necessary as well as imposing restrictions on others who use your computer and your network.

> **Tip   Use administrator accounts sparingly**
>
> Microsoft's security experts routinely recommend that anyone responsible for a computer running Windows avoid logging on for everyday use with an account that belongs to the Administrators group. Instead, they suggest using an account with fewer system privileges for everyday activities such as running applications and browsing the Web, and logging on as an administrator only on those infrequent occasions when you need to perform administrative tasks. This is a key method for implementing the rule of least privilege.
>
> In theory, at least, this practice helps you avoid the risk that you'll damage the system configuration or allow a virus or Trojan horse to infect it. In Windows 2000, you can easily assign your everyday account to the Power Users group without encountering many inconveniences in normal use. When Windows XP was initially released, restricting yourself to a limited account in Windows XP could be a frustrating experience because its set of built-in privileges interferes with many programs that weren't specifically written for Windows XP. Fortunately, most newer programs can properly do their job without requiring you to log on as an administrator. (You will, however, need to log on as an administrator or, better yet, use the Run As command to obtain administrative privileges, when you install a program.) If you can work around the frustrations, you can significantly increase your security with this simple safeguard.

> For more information about using the rule of least privilege, see "Following Best Practices for Your Everyday Account," page 103, and "Using Least Privilege When Browsing the Internet," page 404. In his blog at *http://blogs.msdn.com/aaron_margosis*, Aaron Margosis explains in great detail how to run using a least privileged, nonadministrative account.

Controlling the Logon and Authentication Process

The purpose of logging on to Windows—providing a user name and password—is to allow Windows to *authenticate* you. In theory, the process of logon and authentication verifies that you are who you claim to be (because, presumably, only the owner of a user account knows its user name and its password). On the surface, the process is quite simple: Depending on how your computer is configured, you press Ctrl+Alt+Delete to display the Log On To Windows dialog box, or you click your user name on the Welcome screen; you enter your password (your user name is already entered) and click OK; and a few moments later your desktop appears.

Under the hood, a lot is going on to allow this seemingly simple task to be performed as securely as possible—all under the control of the Local Security Authority (LSA). This process is explained in great detail in *Microsoft Windows XP Professional Resource Kit,*

Third Edition (Microsoft Press, 2005). In this chapter, we concentrate on the type of logon used on stand-alone computers and on computers that are not joined to a Windows 2000 Server or Windows Server 2003 domain: an interactive logon using NTLM authentication.

An *interactive logon* is one of four types of logon processes handled by Windows XP and Windows 2000. It's the process of logging on to a local computer to which you have direct physical access or to which you connect with Remote Desktop Connection or Terminal Services. The other logon types are *network*, which is used for accessing another computer on your network; *service*, which is used by services to log on using the LocalSystem account or the credentials of a user account, depending on how the service is configured; and *batch*, which is for applications that run as batch jobs (such as a program that updates a corporate database server overnight) and is almost never used in small networks.

During the authentication process, the computer that's asking for permission to access a resource must exchange information with the computer that manages security for that resource. From a security standpoint, it is almost never acceptable to send a user name and password over any network in unencrypted form (referred to as *plain text* or *clear text*). In Windows XP and Windows 2000, this communication is encrypted using one of two authentication protocols: *Kerberos V5* or *NTLM*. Kerberos is the default authentication protocol on computers running Windows XP and Windows 2000; however, these computers fall back to NTLM authentication when they are not joined to a Windows 2000 Server or Windows Server 2003 domain—in other words, on stand-alone computers and on workgroups of any size that consist of a mix of computers running Windows.

The Kerberos protocol uses extremely sophisticated encryption to prevent unauthorized intruders from intercepting traffic on the network and breaking a password. By contrast, the NTLM protocol uses a challenge/response authentication mechanism: The computer managing security for the resource issues an encrypted challenge to the computer that's requesting access, which in turn must provide the correct encrypted response, using an encryption key based on the password for that user account.

NTLM authentication in Windows XP and Windows 2000 supports three NTLM variants:

- **LAN Manager (LM).**   This is the least secure authentication method in Windows XP. It's used only when you connect to shared folders on computers running Windows for Workgroups, Windows 95/98, or Windows Me.

> **Tip**   If you must maintain some systems that run older versions of Windows, configure those computers to use NTLM version 2. See Microsoft Knowledge Base article 239869 for details.

- **NTLM version 1.**   More secure than LM, this variant is needed only when you connect to servers in a Windows NT domain in which a domain controller is running Windows NT 4 Service Pack 3 or earlier.

- **NTLM version 2.** This is the most secure form of challenge/response authentication. It is the one used to connect to other computers running Windows XP or Windows 2000 or to servers in a domain where all controllers are running Windows NT 4 Service Pack 4 or later.

Inside Out

Shut down LM to tighten network security

If all the computers on your network run Windows XP or Windows 2000, you can disable the weaker authentication variants, thereby closing a couple of additional avenues that attackers might use. To disable these variants, follow these steps:

1 At a command prompt, type **secpol.msc** to start Local Security Settings.

2 Open Security Settings\Local Policies\Security Options.

3 In the details pane, double-click Network Security: LAN Manager Authentication Level (in Windows XP) or LAN Manager Authentication Level (Windows 2000).

4 In the dialog box that appears, select Send NTLMv2 Response Only\Refuse LM & NTLM.

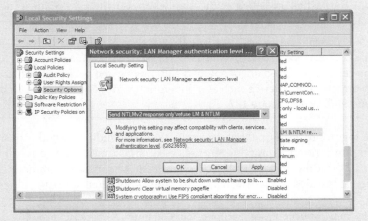

Making this setting helps to stymie password-cracking tools that capture password-bearing packets from network traffic. Note, however, that taking this step will effectively break communications between your computer and those running earlier versions of Windows.

How Interactive Logons Work

In an interactive logon, a complex sequence of events occurs:

1 As the last step of the boot process, Winlogon.exe starts.

2 Winlogon calls the Microsoft Graphical Identification and Authentication dynamic-link library (Msgina.dll), which obtains your user name and password using one of the following two techniques:

   ■ If you're using the Welcome screen in Windows XP (also known as the secure desktop), a list of available user accounts appears. Click a user name to display an input dialog box and enter your password.

   ■ On a computer running Windows 2000 (or Windows XP with the classic logon option), press Ctrl+Alt+Delete to display the Log On To Windows dialog box, and then enter your user name and password.

3 Winlogon passes the user name and password to the LSA, which then determines whether the logon is to be authenticated on the local computer or over the network. (This depends on the choice you make in the Log On To box.)

4 For local logons, the LSA consults the SAM, a protected database that manages user and group account information.

5 If the user name and password are valid, the SAM returns to the LSA the user's SID and the SIDs for all groups to which the user belongs.

6 The LSA uses this information to create an *access token*, an identifier that accompanies the user throughout the session. An access token is a sort of "badge" that the LSA flashes on behalf of the user whenever the user requests access to a protected resource.

7 Winlogon starts the Windows shell with the user's access token attached.

> **Tip**   You can avoid the tedium of entering a user name and password with each logon by using a biometric logon device such as a fingerprint reader. For details, see "Logging On with a Biometric Device," page 127.

A secure logon process—one that prevents unauthorized users with physical access to your computer from logging on—requires disabling some of the convenience features available in Windows. Specifically, you might want to consider eliminating the following convenience features, each of which represents a potential security vulnerability:

> For step-by-step instructions, see "Securing Your Computer: A Checklist," page 66.

Replace the Welcome screen with the classic logon dialog box.   Available only in Windows XP and only when the computer is not joined to a domain, the Welcome screen, shown in Figure 3-2, presents a friendly face and lets you log on with a simple click (and entry of a password, if your account requires one). The Welcome screen exposes the user names of all users to anyone who walks by. In addition, password hints for all users are available with a couple of clicks. Knowing the user name and a password hint, an attacker is well on the way to an authenticated logon.

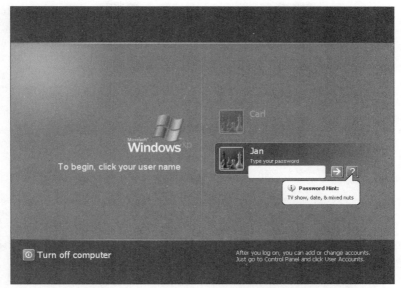

Figure 3-2. The Welcome screen in Windows XP offers too much information to passersby.

Force Windows to display a secure logon screen. The Welcome To Windows dialog box, shown in Figure 3-3, asks you to press Ctrl+Alt+Delete, known as the secure attention sequence. Although this extra key combination might seem inconvenient, it's your guarantee that Winlogon is calling Msgina.dll to request your user name and password. Only Windows 2000 or Windows XP can respond to this reserved key combination properly; the Ctrl+Alt+Delete sequence will cause a system reboot or display a Task Manager dialog box if a stealthily installed password-stealing program is displaying its own counterfeit version of the password-request screen in an effort to collect your password and send it off to an attacker.

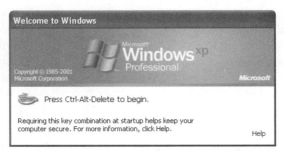

Figure 3-3. Displaying this screen ensures that Windows—not a Trojan horse—is capturing your logon information.

Disable automatic logons. Under Windows XP and Windows 2000, your computer can be configured to bypass the Log On To Windows dialog box completely. In this configuration, Windows automatically enters a default user name and password

59

whenever your computer starts up. This means that anyone who has physical access to your computer can log on by flipping the power switch—even if your computer is currently turned on and you're logged off. (Think autologon is safe on a home computer? Think again. We advise against it because of the risk that a thief might steal the computer and gain access to sensitive information just by turning it on.) As Figure 3-4 shows, you can configure this option to use any account and password.

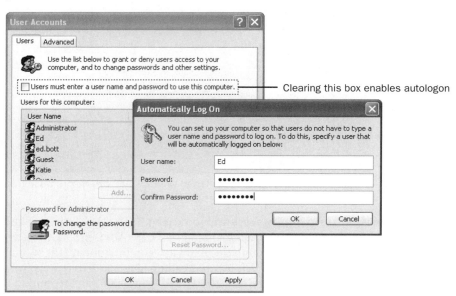

— Clearing this box enables autologon

Figure 3-4. The autologon feature automatically enters the specified user name and password at startup. For most Windows users, this is a security risk.

> **Tip Set up a safe autologon option**
>
> In general, we strongly discourage the use of autologon—especially when the default account is a member of the Administrators group. However, in one circumstance, autologon is safe and sensible. For a computer shared by several workers who log on with the same account, or for one set aside for use by the public (in the lobby of an office building, for example), it makes sense to set up a highly restricted user account and use it as the default account. In case of a power failure or accidental reset, the system will automatically start up with this default account rather than leaving users at a cryptic logon screen.

Safeguarding the Security Accounts Manager

The Security Accounts Manager stores account password information in the registry. Although this information is encrypted using a 128-bit encryption key, it presents a tempting target to attackers, as you might imagine. In Windows NT 4, in fact, a number of well-publicized vulnerabilities made it possible for attackers to break into the SAM and extract the encrypted password values (called *hashed* values), after which they

Windows Security Tools and Techniques

could work on the stored data with password-cracking utilities. Microsoft's response was to tighten security with a utility called Syskey, introduced in Service Pack 3 for Windows NT 4. Syskey, which is enabled by default in Windows XP and Windows 2000 (it was optional in Windows NT 4), protects account information stored in the SAM by using multiple levels of encryption. (That is, the password information is encrypted by a per-user-account password encryption key, which is encrypted by a master protection key, which is encrypted by the startup key. Did you follow all that?)

By default, the startup key is a machine-generated random key stored on the local computer. This ordinarily provides excellent protection for the password information in the registry. On a computer whose SAM has been protected with Syskey, it is nearly impossible for unauthorized users to extract the hashed passwords, even if they have physical access to the computer. On computers that require extra-high levels of protection, it's possible to ratchet this already high level of security another notch, by removing the Syskey code from the computer and copying it to a floppy disk.

> For details on the pros and cons of this technique, as well as step-by-step instructions, see "Adding Another Layer of Protection with Syskey," page 132.

Using Group Policy to Restrict Access

One of the most powerful features of Windows XP Professional and Windows 2000 is support for Group Policy settings. After logging on as an administrator, you can use a fairly straightforward tool called the Group Policy snap-in to define security settings for a local computer, to control more than 700 aspects of the operating system's behavior, and to automate what happens at startup and shutdown and when users log on or off. (A part of the Group Policy snap-in, called Local Security Policy, handles a subset of these settings and can be a useful tool also.) On a Windows domain, Group Policy is especially powerful, giving administrators complete control over user settings for everyone who logs on to the domain.

> **Note** The features described in this section do not work in Windows XP Home Edition. If you attempt to run the Local Security Policy snap-in, Windows displays an error message.

To open the Group Policy console, enter **gpedit.msc** at a command prompt. Figure 3-5 on the next page shows the resulting window, with the User Rights Assignment category expanded.

Because Group Policy settings can be applied to users and groups, you can use this feature to customize security settings quite effectively. Items in the Computer Configuration category include access control settings for users and groups. Using settings in the Password Policy group, for instance, you can force all limited user accounts (members of the Users group) to create complex logon passwords, require that they change the password at regular intervals, and prevent them from reusing old passwords. (Unfortunately, there's no policy that will keep users from writing passwords on sticky notes and slapping them on the side of their monitor!) Similarly, the User Rights Assignment section allows you to prevent certain users or groups from shutting down the computer or resetting the system clock.

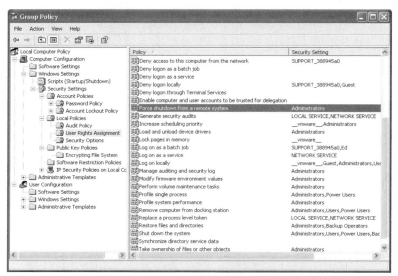

Figure 3-5. Use the Group Policy console to adjust what users and groups can do on the local computer.

Settings listed under User Configuration apply to all users of the local computer and can be overridden only by an administrator. When you make changes in Group Policy in Windows XP Professional and Windows 2000, your new settings are stored in the registry. If you're using Group Policy under Windows 2000, you can see a detailed explanation of a particular setting when you double-click any item on the list. If you use Windows XP Professional, the same help text is visible on the Extended tab so that you can scroll through the list of settings and learn how each one works, as shown here, without having to open each item individually.

Chapter 3

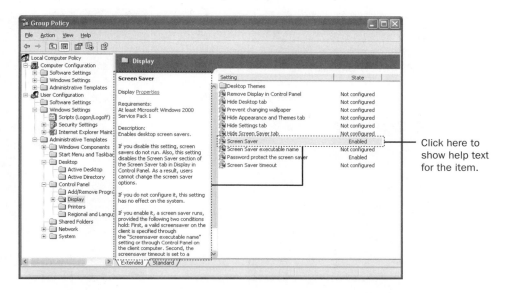

Click here to
show help text
for the item.

For more details about using Group Policy, see Chapter 22, "Managing Security Through Group Policy and Security Templates."

Ensuring the Security of Files

Among the most powerful security features of Windows XP and Windows 2000 are those that enable you to restrict access to files and folders, both on the local computer and across network shares. In this section, we look at the sometimes confusing mechanisms you need to master to take advantage of these features.

Using NTFS Permissions

For every object stored on a volume formatted with the NTFS file system, Windows maintains an *access control list* (ACL). As its name implies, this list defines which users are allowed access to that object—typically a file or folder—and which users are denied access. Individual items in the ACL are called *access control entries* (ACEs) and are made up of the following information:

- The SID for a user or group. (Remember that Windows uses SIDs, not user or group names, to keep track of access rights.)
- The list of permissions that make up the access right, drawn from a long list of basic and special permissions—Full Control, Read, and Write, for instance.
- Inheritance information, which determines whether and how Windows applies permissions from the parent folder.
- A flag that indicates whether access is being allowed or denied.

Chapter 3

Microsoft Windows XP Networking and Security Inside Out

Probably no subject in Windows XP and Windows 2000 is more confusing than NTFS permissions. Figuring out the interaction of inherited permissions and determining which take precedence in the case of conflicts between individual and group ACEs can be a daunting task. In Windows 2000, you can inspect these details by right-clicking an object, choosing Properties, and clicking the Security tab. As Figure 3-6 shows, this tab offers a concise, although hardly intuitive, display of the current ACL.

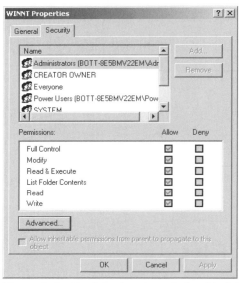

Figure 3-6. Deciphering the ACL for this folder can be a challenge.

In Windows XP Professional, the Security tab is essentially the same (although it's slightly better organized), but many Windows users never see it at all, thanks to a feature called Simple File Sharing. When this configuration option is enabled (as it is in a default installation on any computer that is not part of a Windows domain), Windows drastically reduces the number of options available to users and sets permissions only when you choose to make files in your personal profile private. On a computer running Windows XP Home Edition, Simple File Sharing is always on, and the only time you see the Security tab is when you boot into Safe Mode.

For more details about how Simple File Sharing works, see "Simple File Sharing in Windows XP," page 18. For instructions on how to disable this feature, see "Viewing and Changing NTFS Permissions," page 143.

Inside Out

See all permissions at a glance

Windows XP includes a new feature, not found in Windows 2000, that helps you sort out the interaction of permissions. This capability can be a helpful troubleshooting tool if you've assigned several sets of permissions to different users and groups and the results are not what you expect. To use this option, you must have Simple File Sharing disabled. Right-click the icon for an object, choose Properties, and then click the Security tab. Click Advanced, and then click the Effective Permissions tab to see a summary of the access controls in effect for the selected object.

By default, Windows 2000 does a fairly good job of setting permissions on default directories. If you store all your data in the My Documents folder associated with your personal profile, for instance, access is automatically restricted to your account, the System account, and the Administrators group. Windows XP does the same and goes a step further, adding an option to automatically make all files in your personal profile private, which removes the Administrators group from this list so that only you can access your personal files. Anyone else who logs on to the computer is locked out.

Default permissions in other locations are less predictable, however. Under Windows 2000, if you create a new folder in the root of drive C, the default permissions assign Full Control to the Everyone group, which means that any users who log on to that computer can add, remove, or change files in that folder, even if they've logged on using the restricted Guest account. By contrast, when you create the same sort of folder under Windows XP, the default permissions enable limited users (including the Guest account) to read existing files and create new ones but not to rename, edit, or delete existing files.

Learning the ins and outs of Simple File Sharing is essential to maintaining security with Windows XP. After you understand how this restricted menu of permissions works, you might choose to disable Simple File Sharing and return to the Windows 2000–style NTFS Security dialog box. If that's your choice, it's especially important to learn how to apply NTFS permissions properly.

Sharing Files Over a Network

In Windows XP and Windows 2000, any user who is a member of the Administrators or Power Users group can designate a folder for shared access. (Limited users cannot create a shared folder.) Sharing a folder has no effect on users who log on to the computer locally; it affects only users who want to access data over the network.

Understanding the basics of shared folders is essential to maintaining the security of shared files:

- When you share a folder, all files in that folder are available to network users with the appropriate permissions. You cannot selectively share files within a folder.

- In Windows XP and Windows 2000, you can designate a shared folder as read-only, or you can give network users permission to change files in the shared folder.

- You cannot assign a password to a shared folder (as you can in Windows 95/98 or Windows Me). You can, however, specify that some folders allow only read access, while others allow full access.

- By default, Windows 2000 grants the Everyone group full access to a shared folder. You can change these permissions so that different users and groups have different levels of access (Full Control, Change, or Read) from the network.

- If files in a shared folder are secured with NTFS permissions, those permissions apply to anyone accessing the files over the network. Thus, even when permissions on a shared folder allow the Everyone group full access over the network, you can still lock out unauthorized users and groups by selectively applying NTFS permissions to files or to the folder itself.

- When you use Simple File Sharing, Windows XP authenticates all access to shared folders using the Guest account. As a result, any shared folder is accessible to any user who can reach it over the network. This can cause an unacceptable security risk if a folder you want to share holds sensitive files. In that case, you must disable Simple File Sharing and use the Windows 2000–style sharing interface instead. The option to disable Simple File Sharing is not available with Windows XP Home Edition.

For more details about sharing folders over a network, see "Restricting Network Access to Files and Folders," page 17.

Encryption Options

On drives that use the NTFS file system, you can significantly increase the security of individual files and entire folders by encrypting those files. When you do so, Windows uses your public encryption key to encrypt the files so that they can be unlocked only by your private key, which is available only when you log on to your user account. The protection offered by the encrypting file system is extremely difficult to crack. Even if intruders can gain access to the files, they will not be able to decrypt the data without your private encryption key, which is separate from your password. To an intruder, the encrypted files look like random combinations of letters and numbers and are literally unreadable. That's good news if you're trying to protect files from prying eyes. It's very bad news, however, if you lose the encryption key. If you plan to use NTFS encryption, be sure to read "Before You Begin: Learn the Dangers of EFS," page 703.

Securing Your Computer: A Checklist

Maintaining a secure computer isn't something you do in your spare time every few weeks or months. The most effective security program is one that's built around a sensible and comprehensive security policy. To get you started, we've put together a checklist of tasks you should perform right now to eliminate any existing security holes on your computer.

1. Install and Configure a Firewall

A firewall is a device or software that controls the flow of traffic between computers and protects your computer or network from intruders. This extra layer of protection is especially important on any computer with an "always on" Internet connection, such as a DSL line or cable modem. Firewalls vary widely in their cost and features, but in general they consist of hardware, software, or a combination of the two, which prevents unauthorized users from interactively logging on to network resources from the outside. On most networks, a firewall acts as a single point of access to the outside world, making it easier to enforce security settings and to keep a log of intrusion attempts.

Consider one or more of the following additions to increase security on a single computer or a small to medium-sized network:

Configure custom ports.   The built-in Windows Firewall included with Windows XP SP2 effectively blocks all incoming traffic from the outside except on ports where you've requested data. Windows Firewall is automatically configured when you run the Network Setup Wizard. Many Windows-based programs can work seamlessly through the firewall (all traffic from the local machine is allowed out), although you might need to configure some ports manually before you can run a server or a third-party program that uses nonstandard ports. To adjust Windows Firewall settings, open its icon in Control Panel or in Security Center. Note that Windows Firewall has preconfigured exceptions for a number of common server types, as shown in Figure 3-7.

> For more details about how Windows Firewall works and how you can configure it, see "Using Windows Firewall in Windows XP," page 277, and "Configuring a Host Firewall," page 564.

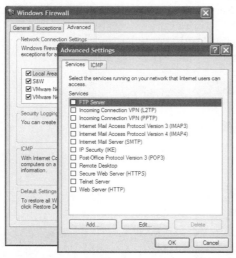

Figure 3-7.   Selecting any of these preconfigured server options in Windows Firewall allows traffic to flow through the firewall.

Upgrade the firewall software.   Third-party firewall programs are appropriate for use with Windows 2000, which includes no firewall utility of its own, and for Windows XP administrators who want more protection than Windows Firewall provides, such as the capability to block or filter outbound traffic. In addition to intrusion detection and logging, many of these programs supply tools to help you configure traffic on a per-application basis, allow virtual private network connections, and alert you when intrusion attempts are taking place.

Add hardware protection.   Hardware-based firewall products range from simple routers that offer Network Address Translation services and port filtering, to complex devices that inspect every packet entering a network to determine whether and how it should be allowed to pass. On small networks, the combination of a simple hardware device and desktop firewall software can be a very effective form of protection.

> For a more detailed discussion of hardware-based firewall products, see "Using a Hardware Firewall Appliance," page 6.

2.   Install All Windows Security Updates

Without exception, every version of Windows ever released includes bugs and defects that open the door for intruders. Over time, as these security problems are identified, Microsoft's developers release patches and updates (sometimes referred to as *hotfixes*) that repair the problems. From time to time, Microsoft releases service packs, which incorporate all fixes and security updates to that point. You can use any or all of the following options to determine which fixes are necessary for your computer:

In Windows XP, configure the Automatic Updates feature to check for critical updates at regular intervals. You can choose to receive notifications only, download the updates automatically, or (if you have Service Pack 1 or later installed) have Windows update your system files automatically. To configure this feature, open the Systems option in Control Panel (under Performance And Maintenance if you're using Category view) and click the Automatic Updates tab.

Connect to the Windows Update online service manually to download and install all service packs and critical updates that are appropriate for your version of Windows. Point your browser to *http://windowsupdate.microsoft.com*, or use the shortcut at the top of the All Programs or Start menu, on the Tools menu in Microsoft Internet Explorer, or in the Help And Support Center in Windows XP. Windows Update scans your system using an ActiveX control and presents a list of suggested updates for point-and-click download and installation. Windows Update works with Windows 2000 and Windows XP as well as Windows 95/98 and Windows Me. Users of Windows XP and Windows 2000—but not earlier versions of Windows—can instead use Microsoft Update (*http://www.update.microsoft.com*), which installs updates for other Microsoft applications (including Microsoft Office) in addition to updates for Windows.

Use the Microsoft Baseline Security Analyzer (MBSA) to analyze your local computer or your entire network for missing security updates and service packs. This free utility works by downloading an XML file that lists the updates needed for your computer and then scanning to see which ones have been installed. In addition to scanning for missing security updates, MBSA scans and reports on other system vulnerabilities in Windows, IIS, and SQL Server, including blank user account passwords, the file system type used, all available shares with their configured permissions, and more. MBSA, which works with Windows 2000, Windows XP, and Windows Server 2003, comes with a graphical user interface and command line version.

 Inside Out

Ensure timely updates

Windows Update is a terrific and useful service, but for extremely security-conscious Windows users it might fall short. Windows Update includes updates for the Windows operating system and related components (including Internet Explorer and IIS); it does not offer updates for non-Windows products like SQL Server. In addition, you'll often find a delay of days or weeks between the time a security bulletin is published and when it is available on Windows Update. If you prefer to receive notification of security updates for all Microsoft products as soon as they're released, subscribe to Microsoft's Security Notification Service. To join the list, visit *http://www.microsoft.com/security/bulletins/alerts.mspx*.

For more details about Windows Update, service packs, and Microsoft Baseline Security Analyzer, see Chapter 7, "Keeping Your System Secure."

3. Install and Configure Antivirus Software

Given the pandemic spread of viruses on the Internet in recent years, it's foolhardy to even think of connecting a computer to the Internet without robust, up-to-date antivirus software. Dozens of options are available, most at relatively modest prices. More important than installing the software, of course, is making sure that its virus signatures are current. The best antivirus programs include software agents that handle this chore automatically. After installing the software and the latest updates, scan your system to ensure that you're virus-free.

For more information about antivirus software, see Chapter 14, "Stopping Viruses, Worms, and Trojan Horses."

4. Eliminate or Disable Unused Accounts

One common avenue that intruders use to attack Windows is to look for user accounts that are poorly secured. On business networks, an all-too-common mistake is to fail to remove a user account after an employee quits or is fired. If the account remains active and the password is unchanged, a disgruntled ex-worker can break into the computer and steal data or sabotage the system. The potential for damage is even worse if the former employee has remote access privileges that haven't been promptly revoked. To view the complete list of user accounts in Windows XP Professional or Windows 2000 Professional, open the Local Users And Groups snap-in from the Computer Management console. (To open this console, right-click My Computer and choose Manage.)

Figure 3-8 shows the list of accounts on a computer running Windows XP Professional. To remove an account, right-click its entry in the Users list and choose Delete from the shortcut menu. To temporarily disable an account without removing its associated files and permissions, double-click its entry in the Users list and select the Account Is Disabled option on the General tab of the properties dialog box.

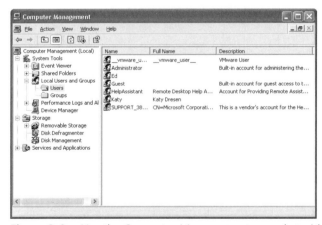

Figure 3-8. Use the Computer Management console to identify and eliminate unused accounts so that they can't be accessed by intruders.

Unfortunately, if you use Windows XP Home Edition, the Local Users And Groups option is missing from the Computer Management console, and trying to run it manually (either by adding the Local Users And Groups snap-in to an MMC console or by running the **lusrmgr.msc** command) produces only an error message. To work with the complete list of user accounts, try the **net user** command; you'll find full details in "Disabling or Deleting User Accounts," page 91.

5. Set Strong Passwords for All User Accounts

Weak passwords are the would-be intruder's best friend—a point we make repeatedly in this book. By default, all new accounts created in Windows XP have a blank password and belong to the Administrators group. If you're serious about security, assign a password to every account; your password should be at least eight characters long and composed of a random selection of letters, numbers, and symbols in a combination that can't be found in any dictionary. Longer (much longer) is better—even if your password includes a collection of ordinary words. For details, see "Creating Strong Passwords," page 111.

6. Tighten Logon Security for All Users

In Chapter 2, "Computer Security: Are You at Risk?," we discussed the tradeoffs between security and convenience. Tipping the balance too heavily in favor of convenience can be catastrophic to your security. Why make life easier for a would-be intruder? Forcing a secure logon can significantly decrease the likelihood that an unauthorized person will be able to break into your computer while you're away.

To disable the Windows XP Welcome screen, open Control Panel and run the User Accounts option. Click Change The Way Users Log On Or Off and then clear the Use The Welcome Screen box. Click Apply Options to make the change effective. Note that making this change disables the Use Fast User Switching option as shown here:

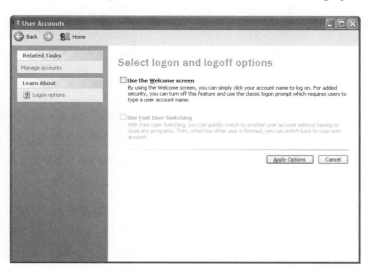

If you're using the so-called classic logon prompt (the default setting in Windows 2000 and an option in Windows XP), configure Windows so that every user is required to press Ctrl+Alt+Delete and provide his or her password to log on. The Secure Logon option is available on the Advanced tab of the User Accounts dialog box, shown in Figure 3-9 on the next page. Windows 2000 users can access these settings from the

Users And Passwords option in Control Panel; if you're using Windows XP and your computer is not joined to a domain, enter the command **control userpasswords2** at a command prompt to open this dialog box.

Figure 3-9. For additional logon security, select the check box at the bottom of this dialog box so that every user must press Ctrl+Alt+Delete to log on.

Finally, make sure that the autologon feature is not enabled. Open the Users And Passwords dialog box as described in the previous paragraph, and on the Users tab, select the Users Must Enter A User Name And Password To Use This Computer check box.

For many more details about removing vulnerabilities in the logon process, see "Configuring the Logon Process for Security," page 122.

7. Use NTFS for All Drives

If you've upgraded from Windows 98 or Windows Me to Windows XP, one or more drives on your system might still be using the FAT32 file system. Even on a clean installation of Windows 2000 or Windows XP, you have the option to choose FAT32 or NTFS. Some users do choose FAT32, either from force of habit or because they want to be able to access the data on that drive from earlier versions of Windows. The security benefits of NTFS (as well as advantages in reliability) are overwhelming in comparison to FAT32 drives, however. Continuing to use FAT32 is justifiable only on computers where data security is less important than the ability to boot into multiple operating systems.

To quickly determine the file system in use on a given drive, open the My Computer window, right-click the icon for any drive, and choose Properties. The current file system is listed on the General tab, as shown here:

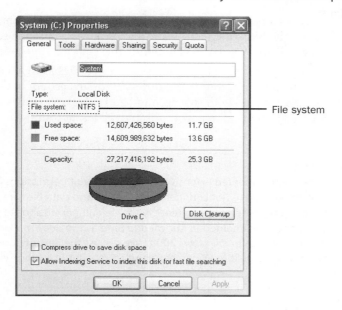

File system

To convert a FAT32 drive to NTFS, you must use the command-line Convert utility with the /FS:NTFS switch. If you attempt to run this command on a drive that contains Windows system files or the system paging file, Windows schedules the conversion to take place at startup after you reboot the computer.

> **Note** Converting a FAT32 drive to NTFS on a computer that was upgraded to Windows XP from an earlier version of Windows can have unintended negative consequences for performance. For a discussion of the best way to carry out this conversion, see the chapter titled "Managing Disks and Drives," in *Microsoft Windows XP Inside Out, Second Edition* (Microsoft Press, 2005).

8. Review NTFS Permissions on All Data Directories

Tinkering with NTFS permissions is a tricky business. Unless you fully understand how these permissions work (including how permissions are inherited from higher-level folders and how permissions are transferred when folders or files are moved or copied), you should be wary of changing any permissions. In general, follow these guidelines whenever possible:

- Use default storage locations. Install programs in subfolders under the Program Files folder and store personal data in the My Documents folder; in both cases, Windows applies a known set of permissions that you can tighten if necessary. If you have data files that are stored outside the default locations, consider moving them.

● On Windows XP installations that are not joined to a domain, use the Simple File Sharing interface and the Network Setup Wizard to establish a baseline set of file and folder permissions. Afterward, you can modify these permissions as needed.

● Test the effect of permissions by trying to access protected files from a limited account. Create a limited local account (Windows XP) or an account in the Users group (Windows 2000), log on with that account, and try to access files in the protected locations. (Be sure to eliminate or disable the test account when you're finished!)

> **Tip** Go back to square one
> If you (or someone else) have experimented extensively with the default permissions on an existing Windows installation and you're not confident that system and data files are properly protected, you can use a security template to reapply the default permissions to your computer. This procedure is fully documented in Knowledge Base article 266118, "How to Restore the Default NTFS Permissions for Windows 2000." We discuss the Security Configuration And Analysis snap-in and the built-in Windows security templates in "Using Security Templates," page 761.

9. Review All Network Shares

With Windows, you can specify that all files in a particular folder should be available for sharing with other users over the network. You can create a multitude of individual shares on your computer for use with individual projects. If you're not meticulous about cleaning up after each project is finished, however, you could end up with shared folders that are open to view by anyone on the network. Every so often, it's a good idea to review the complete list of network shares and eliminate any that are no longer needed. To see the full list of shares, right-click My Computer and choose Manage. In the Computer Management window, double-click Shared Folders and then click Shares. Figure 3-10 shows one such list.

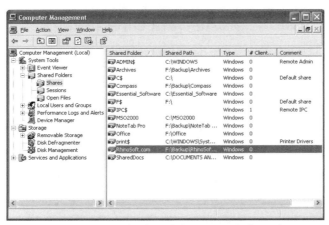

Figure 3-10.   Inspect the list of shares regularly and remove any that are no longer needed.

In Windows 2000, you can right-click any entry in the Shares list and inspect its properties or remove the share. In Windows XP Professional, these options are available only if you've disabled Simple File Sharing; in a default, non-domain installation of Windows XP Professional, this list is read-only. That's also true on a computer running Windows XP Home Edition, where Simple File Sharing cannot be disabled.

In Windows XP Home Edition and Windows XP Professional with Simple File Sharing enabled, you can use Windows Explorer to stop sharing a folder. Right-click the icon of the shared folder, choose Properties, and then click the Sharing tab. Under Network Sharing And Security, clear the Share This Folder On The Network check box.

Inside Out

Remove administrative shares

Windows XP Professional and Windows 2000 Professional include a long list of administrative shares whose names end with a dollar sign. For instance, every drive includes an administrative share that consists of the drive letter and a dollar sign (C$ for drive C, for instance); these administrative shares are accessible to anyone in the Administrators group. If you're using Windows 2000 Professional or Windows XP with Simple File Sharing disabled, you can right-click the entry for any default share and choose Stop Sharing. However, Windows will automatically create the share the next time you restart the computer.

To permanently remove an administrative share from Windows XP Professional or Windows 2000 Professional, start Registry Editor (Regedit.exe) and navigate to the registry key HKLM\SYSTEM\CurrentControlSet\Services\lanmanserver\parameters. Right-click the key name and choose New, DWORD Value. Give it the name AutoShareWks and use the default value data of 0. After making this change, the administrative shares will no longer be re-created after each restart.

Removing the default shares on drives that contain program or data files is a sensible security precaution. Don't delete the ADMIN$ or IPC$ shares, however. These are system-level shares that are invisible to network browsing and are not available for interactive use; they're essential for interprocess communications and remote administration.

10. Use Your Screen Saver as a Security Device

With modern monitors, screen savers aren't really needed to prevent images from "burning in" to a CRT or flat-panel display. But a properly configured screen saver can be a valuable security aid, especially in homes and offices where physical security is lacking and you're often away from your desk. Open the Display option in Control Panel and click the Screen Saver tab. Select any screen saver, and then adjust the following two options, as shown in Figure 3-11 on the next page.

- Select the On Resume, Password Protect check box (Windows XP) or the Password Protected check box (Windows 2000).

Chapter 3

● In the Wait box, dial the default setting down to the minimum level you can tolerate. For maximum security, make this value no more than 5 minutes. This is the period that Windows will wait following any inactivity before the screen saver kicks in.

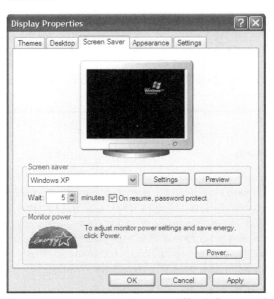

Figure 3-11. To make it more difficult for unauthorized users to access your computer when you step away from it, set screen saver options as shown here.

11. Create a Backup

Accidents happen. Even the most security-conscious Windows user can fall victim to a power failure, a hardware glitch, or an attack that slips through a newly discovered security hole. Regardless of the cause, it's crucial that you have a reliable current backup at all times so that you can quickly recover data that's been damaged or destroyed. We discuss your backup options in detail in Chapter 6, "Preventing Data Loss." Make a backup plan, and then make a backup.

Advanced Security Options

The 11 steps outlined in the previous sections apply to every Windows user. The suggestions in this section include steps that aren't essential but might be useful to advanced users or those with special configurations.

Configure Windows Explorer to show all file name extensions.   Some viruses and Trojan horse programs use a cheap trick to try to slide past a Windows user's defenses, adding a second, innocent-looking file name extension to disguise the true executable extension. In a default Windows installation, extensions are hidden. As a result, a file with the name Letter.doc.vbs will appear to a casual user as Letter.doc. Sophisticated Windows users will have no trouble seeing through this trick, but a less experienced or distracted user might be fooled long enough to launch a dangerous file. To protect yourself, open Windows Explorer and choose Tools, Folder Options. On the View tab, clear the Hide Extensions For Known File Types check box, as shown in Figure 3-12. For a discussion of how hostile software uses multiple file name extensions to attack Windows, see "Identifying Malicious Software," page 470.

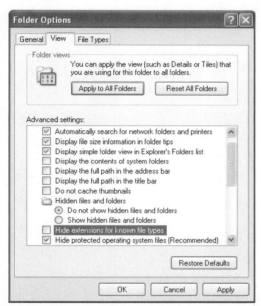

Figure 3-12.   Display all file name extensions so that you can more easily detect hostile software that tries to hide its true extension.

Tip   Selectively show extensions

If you can't stand the clutter caused by the full display of file name extensions, you can customize specific file types so that their extensions are always visible, while still keeping other, less dangerous extensions hidden. If you're concerned about files with the .vbs, .pif, and .scr extensions, for instance, you can ensure that those extensions are always visible by following the steps outlined in "Blocking Dangerous Attachments," page 485. You can also use a custom script to toggle the display of file name extensions and hidden folders as needed; the CD included with *Microsoft Windows XP Inside Out* includes one such script, called ToggleHiddenExplorerStuff.

Adjust Internet Explorer security options.   The zone-based security settings in Internet Explorer 6 and later provide excellent protection against most garden-variety attacks. With advanced security options you can significantly increase the level of security in your browser. We explain these options in full in Chapter 12, "Making Internet Explorer More Secure."

Adjust Internet Explorer privacy options.   Are you concerned that browser cookies are disclosing too much information about you? Internet Explorer uses a fairly complex system to control the information that flows between you and Web sites. You can customize these settings significantly by using the built-in privacy controls in Internet Explorer 6, shown here. If you're willing to roll up your sleeves and work with XML files, you can create and share custom privacy settings as well, as we document in "Setting Cookie Preferences in Internet Explorer," page 600.

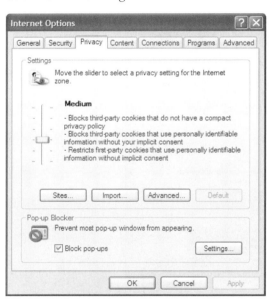

Review saved passwords and form data in Internet Explorer.   By default, all versions of Internet Explorer offer to save form data, user names, and passwords for Web sites you visit. This saved information can unintentionally reveal information about you, such as searches you've made, and can allow unauthorized users to access password-protected Web sites that contain confidential information about you. Your browser's history can also divulge sites you've visited. Read "Covering Your Tracks," page 618, to learn how to configure these features to match your preferences and how to eliminate any stored information.

Obtain a personal certificate for signing and encrypting e-mail.   Electronic mail is not secure. If you routinely send and receive sensitive mail, consider purchasing and installing a personal digital certificate from a certification authority such as VeriSign or Thawte Technologies. This option allows you to digitally sign and encrypt messages so that they can't be read or tampered with by anyone who intercepts the traffic. We provide full instructions (and a number of important cautions) in "Obtaining a Personal Certificate," page 678, and "Protecting E-Mail from Prying Eyes," page 515.

Chapter 3

Restrict executable file attachments in e-mail. The overwhelming majority of viruses that attack Windows arrive through e-mail. Recent versions of Microsoft Outlook (a component of Microsoft Office) and Outlook Express 6 restrict a user's ability to view, save, or execute file attachments whose extensions are on a restricted list. These features are controversial, and their implementation varies widely, depending on the specific e-mail client you use. In Outlook 2003, for instance, certain file types are automatically blocked, and the user cannot disable or tweak this setting. In Outlook Express, by contrast, the option to block dangerous attachments is turned off by default, as shown here. We explain your options fully in "Blocking Dangerous Attachments," page 485.

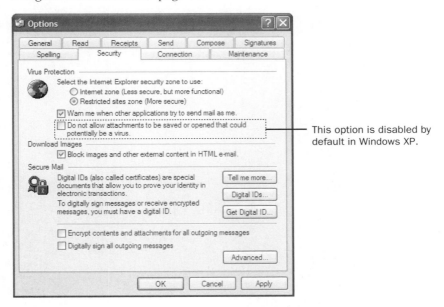

This option is disabled by default in Windows XP.

Chapter 3

Set up virtual private network connections for remote access. To allow remote access to a computer on your network, set up a VPN connection, restrict it to only those users who need access, and protect those accounts with strong passwords. VPN connections encrypt traffic over the Internet and provide dramatically better security than other remote access options. For Windows 2000, the complete set of steps is described in Knowledge Base article 257333, "How to Configure Windows 2000 Professional to Windows 2000 Professional Virtual Private Network Connections." In Windows XP, you can use the Create A New Connection Wizard in the Network Connections folder to quickly create a VPN connection. To explore VPN connections further, read "Connecting Remotely to a Corporate Network," page 373.

Set up encryption for wireless networks. Unlike conventional wired networks, wireless networks add security risks. Unless you take special precautions, anyone who roams into the range of your wireless access point can intercept network traffic and potentially break into any computer on the network. You have a number of configuration options; we explain how to tighten wireless security in Chapter 10, "Wireless Networking."

Chapter 4

Managing User Accounts and Passwords

In this chapter, we explain how to create and customize one of the basic building blocks of security in Microsoft Windows XP and Windows 2000: the user account. By carefully managing user accounts, you can increase your level of security dramatically by imposing restrictions and granting privileges to particular users or groups of users. This is a fundamental difference from how security is implemented in the Windows 9x family and in Windows Millennium Edition (Windows Me). In these operating systems based on Windows 9x code, security—such as it is—is applied by assigning a single password that controls all access to a resource (such as a shared folder). Anyone who knows or can crack the password for a shared resource can gain access to it. A Windows 9x user can assign separate passwords for read-only access and for read-write access, but he or she cannot control access on a per-user basis.

Because each user account is associated with certain rights and privileges, along with permissions to access various computer resources such as files and printers, best security practices dictate that you configure each user account with the least privileges necessary. The concept of least privilege and how you implement it for everyday accounts is the topic of this chapter's second section.

Passwords are another main topic of this chapter, and we explain how to use them effectively. By appropriately applying password policies and practices, you can minimize the chance that an attacker will figure out your password and gain access to your protected information, plant a Trojan horse on your computer, or do other damage.

With user accounts and passwords firmly established, the next step is to put them together in the logon process. Making the logon process more secure is the final topic of this chapter.

Security Checklist: User Accounts and Passwords

Here's a quick checklist of security practices you can follow to secure your user accounts, passwords, and logon process. Some items might not be appropriate for your situation; review the information in this chapter before you forge ahead.

- Create a user account for each person who uses the computer.
- Disable or delete unnecessary accounts.
- Assign each account to appropriate security groups.
- Assign a strong password to each account.
- Secure the built-in Administrator account.
- Set password policies to ensure that users create strong logon passwords and change them regularly.
- Create a Password Reset Disk.
- Use a password-management program to securely manage your collection of passwords.
- Disable the Welcome screen in favor of the classic logon screens.
- Require users to press Ctrl+Alt+Delete and enter a user name and password before logging on.
- Display a legal notice that warns users about unauthorized logon attempts.
- Set account lockout policies to lock out password guessers.
- For ultra-high-security needs, consider removing the system's startup key so that a password or floppy disk is required before the logon screen appears.

Managing User Accounts for Security

Because so much in Windows security depends on the identification of users, the first step in securing your computer and your network should be to configure your user accounts. You'll need to do the following:

- Create a user account for each person who uses the computer. (See page 89.)
- Disable or delete unnecessary accounts. (See page 91.)
- Assign each account to appropriate security groups. (See page 94.)
- Assign a strong password to each account. (See page 97.)
- Secure the built-in Administrator and Guest accounts. (See pages 99 and 101.)

In the following sections, we explain how to perform each of these security-related tasks. As you might imagine, you can configure a number of other options for local user accounts—everything from changing the picture that appears on the Welcome screen and at the top of the Start menu to specifying a profile and a logon script. Windows XP users can find information about those topics in our earlier book, *Microsoft Windows XP Inside Out, Second Edition* (Microsoft Press, 2005).

Domain user accounts, which are stored in Active Directory on a server running Microsoft Windows Server 2003 or Windows 2000 Server, offer a wealth of additional configuration options, including phone numbers, mailing addresses, and much, much more. Active Directory configuration and, indeed, security options for an Active Directory–based domain are topics beyond the scope of this volume. Microsoft Press offers a number of books on these topics.

> For an explanation of how user accounts identify each user on your computer and on your network and how they fit into the overall security infrastructure of Windows, see "What Are User Accounts?" page 46.

Finding the Account-Management Tools

With Windows 2000, you have a choice of three methods for creating and maintaining user accounts:

- **Users And Passwords.**   Located in Control Panel, Users And Passwords provides a simple dialog box for performing common tasks. Although the capabilities of this tool are few (you can add or remove local user accounts, set passwords, and place a user account in a single security group), it has a handful of unique abilities that aren't available with the other GUI (graphical user interface) tools. With this tool, you can:

    - Change an account's user name.
    - Configure automatic logon.
    - Configure the Ctrl+Alt+Delete requirement.

    > For information on these last two features, see "Configuring the Logon Process for Security," page 122.

    To start Users And Passwords, shown in Figure 4-1 on the next page, open Control Panel and double-click Users And Passwords.

- **Local Users And Groups.**   This Microsoft Management Console (MMC) snap-in, shown in Figure 4-2 on the next page, provides access to more account-management features than Users And Passwords and is friendlier than the command-line utilities (described next). You can start Local Users And Groups in any of the following ways:

    - In Computer Management (under Administrative Tools in Control Panel), open System Tools\Local Users And Groups.
    - At a command prompt, type **lusrmgr.msc**.
    - In Users And Passwords, click the Advanced tab and then click the Advanced button.

- **Net commands.**   Two command-line utilities, Net User and Net Localgroup, although not particularly intuitive, provide the most complete and direct access to various account tasks.

Chapter 4

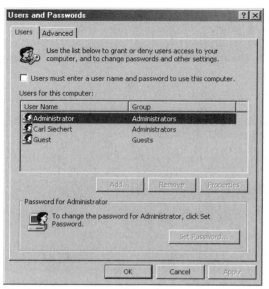

Figure 4-1. Users And Passwords in Windows 2000 has a Windows XP counterpart, called User Accounts, that is nearly identical in appearance and function. You can open User Accounts by typing **control userpasswords2** at a command prompt.

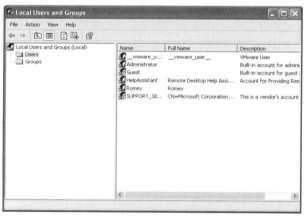

Figure 4-2. Local Users And Groups, like most MMC consoles, resembles Windows Explorer.

For detailed information on these commands, type **net help user** or **net help localgroup** at a command prompt. For a quick refresher course on the syntax and available options, type **net user /?** or **net localgroup /?**.

> **Tip** **Use a Command Prompt window for Net commands**
> Although you can issue Net commands in the Run dialog box (and they will be effective), you should always open a Command Prompt window and enter the commands there instead. That's because Net displays the command results in the same window; if you enter the command in the Run dialog box, the window closes before you have a chance to see the results. (To open a Command Prompt window, press the Windows logo key+R to open the Run dialog box, type **cmd**, and press Enter. If your keyboard doesn't have a Windows logo key, open the Start menu and choose Run.)

In addition to these three account-management tools, Windows XP offers a fourth, simpler tool for managing user accounts:

- **User Accounts.** This wizard-based account-management tool, shown in Figure 4-3, is designed for novice computer administrators. Its choices are limited, but it provides assistance every step of the way. To start User Accounts, open Control Panel and double-click User Accounts.

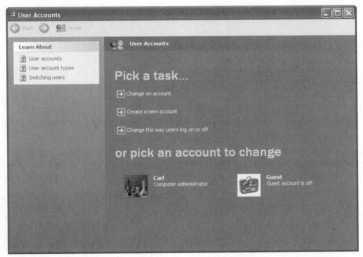

Figure 4-3. Choosing User Accounts in Control Panel on a Windows XP computer that's not joined to a domain offers this friendly face.

> **Note** If your computer is running Windows XP Professional and is joined to a domain, opening User Accounts in Control Panel produces a version of User Accounts that's nearly identical to Users And Passwords in Windows 2000, shown in Figure 4-1.

With varying degrees of ease, the three tools available in Windows 2000—Users And Passwords, Local Users And Groups, and Net commands—enable an administrator to perform the basic tasks of creating, modifying, and deleting local user accounts and security groups. Which one you choose depends in large measure on which user interface you prefer: Do you like the direct, concise method of working with a command-line interface? Or do you prefer the friendly guidance provided by a graphical interface? Are you comfortable working with MMC consoles? Do you want to automate account-management procedures with batch programs?

Selecting an account-management tool in Windows XP becomes a little more complicated (in part because of its developers' zeal to make things simpler):

- If you have Windows XP Home Edition, Local Users And Groups is not available. (You can start the program, but it won't let you do anything.)
- If your computer is in a workgroup, clicking User Accounts in Control Panel displays the new, simplified version of User Accounts. If you prefer to work with the version that resembles Users And Passwords in Windows 2000, type **control userpasswords2** at a command prompt. (To add to the confusion, the title bar identifies both versions as User Accounts.)
- As noted earlier, if your computer is joined to a domain, clicking User Accounts in Control Panel displays the Windows 2000–style User Accounts dialog box. The simple version of User Accounts is not available.

None of the tools can perform all account-related tasks, so for certain tasks your choice of user-management tool is dictated by each tool's capabilities. Table 4-1 shows which common tasks for managing local user accounts you can perform with each of the four tools.

Table 4-1. **Local User Account-Management Tasks**

Task	Users And Passwords (User Accounts in Windows XP)	Local Users And Groups	Net Commands	User Accounts*
Create user account	Yes	Yes	Yes	Yes
Delete user account	Yes	Yes	Yes	Yes
Place account in a security group	Yes, but you can add an account to only one group	Yes	Yes	Yes, but you can add an account only to the Administrators group or the Users group
Change user name	Yes	Yes	No	No
Change full name	Yes	Yes	Yes	Yes
Change description	Yes	Yes	Yes	No
Change picture	No	No	No	Yes

Table 4-1. Local User Account-Management Tasks

Task	Users And Passwords (User Accounts in Windows XP)	Local Users And Groups	Net Commands	User Accounts*
Set password	Yes, but only for a local account other than the one with which you're currently logged on	Yes	Yes	Yes
Set password hint	No	No	No	Yes
Set password restrictions	No	Yes	Yes	No
Set logon hours	No	No	Yes	No
Enable or disable account	No	Yes	Yes	Yes, but only the Guest account
Unlock account	No	Yes	Yes	No
Set account expiration date	No	No	Yes	No
Specify profile and logon script	No	Yes	Yes	No
Link account to a Microsoft .NET Passport	Yes, but only in Windows XP	No	No	Yes

* User Accounts is not available in Windows 2000 or in Windows XP Professional when the computer is joined to a domain.

For managing local security groups, you'll need to use either Local Users And Groups or the Net Localgroup command. Both of these tools enable you to:

- Create a local security group.
- Delete a group.
- Rename a group.
- Set group membership by adding or removing local user accounts and groups.
- Add a domain user account to a local security group.

Chapter 4

Inside Out

Add your domain user account to a local group

Users And Passwords (called User Accounts in Windows XP) lets you perform only one group-management task—but it's an essential one if your computer is a member of a domain. With Users And Passwords, you can add a domain user account to a local security group, giving your domain account (presumably the one with which you normally log on) privileges on your local computer. To do that, follow these steps:

1 In Control Panel, open Users And Passwords (Windows 2000) or User Accounts (Windows XP Professional).

2 Select the name of the domain user account that you want to add to a local group, and then click Properties.

Domain user accounts are identified by a different icon and the name of the domain (instead of the computer name) in the Domain column.

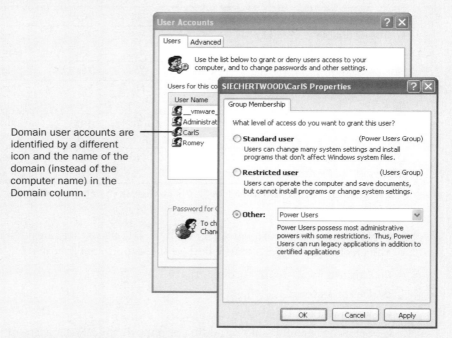

3 Select Other, and then select the name of the group to which you want to add the selected account.

You might, for example, want to add your domain account to the local Power Users group, thereby granting to it in one fell swoop all the rights, privileges, and responsibilities of a local power user.

Creating User Accounts

When you set up Windows on a new computer, you might have user accounts for yourself and others who use your computer, or you might have only an Administrator account, depending on the options you choose during setup. If you upgrade a computer that previously had user accounts, those accounts are retained. In any case, you should be sure that you have an account for each user. If you need to create an account, you can use any of the four tools, as follows:

- With Users And Passwords, click the Add button on the Users tab. The Add New User Wizard then leads you through the steps of selecting a user name, assigning a password, and adding the account to a local security group.

> **Troubleshooting**   **The Add button is unavailable**
> If the Add button on the Users tab of Users And Passwords appears dimmed, select the Users Must Enter A User Name And Password To Use This Computer check box. If the check box is already selected (or if it doesn't appear, which is the case if your computer is joined to a domain), be sure you're logged on with an account in the Administrators or Power Users group.

- In Local Users And Groups, right-click Users in the console tree and choose New User. Complete the information in the New User dialog box, shown in Figure 4-4 on the next page, and then click Create. The dialog box remains open so that you can create another user account; click Close when you've finished creating accounts.

- To create a user account with the Net User command, use the form **net user** **_username_** /**add**, where _username_ is the user name of the account you want to create. You might also want to include other command-line parameters to configure the account. Table 4-2 on the next page lists the parameters that are most useful in setting up new accounts. For example, you might enter a command and see results such as the following:

```
C:\>net user jan /add /fullname:"Jan Siechert" /random
Password for jan is: x@WY$52N

The command completed successfully.
```

- In User Accounts, you create an account by clicking its convenient Create A New Account link. You need to supply only a name for the account and decide whether you want the account to be a computer administrator account or an account with limited privileges. To configure other options—including setting a password—you must make changes after you create the account.

Chapter 4

Figure 4-4. Local Users And Groups presents a straightforward dialog box that lets you provide all the basic account information in one place.

Table 4-2. **Net User Parameters for Adding Accounts**

Parameter	Description
/Add	Creates a new user account. The user name can contain a maximum of 20 characters and can't contain any of these characters: " / \ [ ] : ; | = , + * ? < >
password or * or /Random	Sets the password. If you type an asterisk (*), Net User prompts for the password you want to assign; it does not display the password as you type it. The /Random switch generates a hard-to-crack, eight-character password.
/Fullname:"*name*"	Specifies the user's full name.
/Comment:"*text*"	Provides a descriptive comment (maximum length of 48 characters).
/Passwordchg:yes or /Passwordchg:no	Specifies whether the user is allowed to change the password. The default is yes.
/Active:no or /Active:yes	Disables or enables the account. (When an account is disabled, the user can't log on or access resources on the computer.) The default is yes.

Table 4-2. **Net User Parameters for Adding Accounts**

Parameter	Description
/Expires:*date* or /Expires:never*	Sets the expiration date for an account. For *date*, use the short date format set in Regional Options in Control Panel. The account expires at the beginning of the day on the specified date; after that time, the user can't log on or access resources on the computer until an administrator sets a new expiration date. The default is never.
/Passwordreq:yes or /Passwordreq:no*	Specifies whether the user account is required to have a nonblank password. The default is yes.
/Times:*times* or /Times:all*	Sets the times when the user is allowed to log on. For *times*, enter the days of the week you want to allow logon. Use a hyphen to specify a range of days or use a comma to list separate days. Following each day entry, specify the allowable logon times. Separate multiple entries with a semicolon. For example, use **M-F,8am-6pm;Sa,9am-1pm** to restrict logon times to those work hours. Use All to allow logon at any time; a blank value prevents the user from ever logging on. The default is all.

* These three switches enable you to make security-related settings that you can't make (or even view) using the other account-management tools. They provide powerful options that are otherwise available only with Active Directory and a server-based domain.

User Name vs. Full Name

Each of the account-management tools enable you to specify a user name and a full name. (User Accounts uses the name you provide as both the user name and the full name.) What's the difference? The *user name* is the name used internally by Windows, and it's how you refer to the account in most places. You use it when you log on without the benefit of the Welcome screen and when you specify the account name in various commands and dialog boxes for setting permissions. The *full name* is the "friendly" name that appears on the Welcome screen and at the top of the Start menu in Windows XP, as well as in a few other places. It's there for your convenience only and isn't needed by Windows.

Disabling or Deleting User Accounts

Every user account offers a potential entry point for an attacker. Therefore, it's good practice to disable or delete user accounts that are no longer needed. If an employee leaves your company, for example, you should immediately disable his or her account. (Disabling an account prevents the user from logging on or accessing the computer's resources, but it leaves the account information, its certificates, and its private files intact.

If you need to use the account later, you simply enable it again.) When you're certain that you won't need access to any of the account's private information, you should delete it.

To disable (or subsequently re-enable) an account, use either of these methods:

- In Local Users And Groups, double-click the account to display the General tab of the properties dialog box. Then select (or clear) the Account Is Disabled check box.

- In a Command Prompt window, type **net user** *username* /**active:no** (where *username* is the account's user name) to disable an account. To enable an account, enter **net user** *username* /**active:yes**.

Inside Out

Disable the Guest account with user rights

In User Accounts, you can effectively disable or enable the Guest account (but no other accounts). Click the Guest account and then click Turn Off The Guest Account or Turn On The Guest Account. In fact, enabling or disabling the Guest account in this manner does not set the account's active status, as the other methods do. When you "turn off" the Guest account, Windows adds Guest to the list of accounts with the Deny Logon Locally user right assigned. (This is actually a side effect of the way Windows XP uses the Guest account for network access when Simple File Sharing is enabled.)

If you have Windows XP Professional, you can verify this in Local Security Settings. To start Local Security Settings, open Control Panel and then open Administrative Tools, Local Security Policy, or simply type **secpol.msc** at a command prompt. Open Security Settings \Local Policies\User Rights Assignment and look at the Deny Logon Locally right. For more information about user rights and Local Security Settings, see "Exploring Security-Related Policies," page 730.

Deleting an account prevents anyone from logging on with the account. Once this change is made, it's permanent. You can't restore access to resources for which the user currently has permission by re-creating the account. These resources include the user's encrypted files, personal certificates, and stored passwords for Web sites and network resources as well as files. Access is denied because permissions are linked to the account's security identifier (SID)—not the user name. Creating a new account—even one with the same user name and password as the account you deleted—produces a new SID, which will not have the same access privileges as the original account.

Note Unless you're absolutely certain that you won't ever use Remote Assistance to obtain help from another user, you shouldn't delete the built-in HelpAssistant or SUPPORT_*xxxxxxx* accounts (Windows XP only). Instead, you should be sure that these accounts are disabled. (They'll be enabled automatically when you use features that depend on them.)

Managing User Accounts and Passwords

You can delete any account except the built-in Administrator and Guest accounts or an account that is currently logged on. To delete an account, you can use the account-management tool of your choice, as follows:

- In Users And Passwords, on the Users tab, select the name of the account you want to delete and click Remove.
- In Local Users And Groups, click Users in the console tree to display the list of users in the details pane. Right-click the name of the account you want to delete and choose Delete.
- To delete an account with the Net User command, use the form **net user** *username* **/delete**, where *username* is the account's user name.
- In User Accounts, click the name of the account you want to delete. Then click Delete The Account. User Accounts gives you the following choices, shown in Figure 4-5, about what to do with the account's files:

Figure 4-5. When you delete an account with User Accounts, Windows XP also deletes the user profile, but gives you an opportunity to save the user's files.

- **Keep Files.** If you select Keep Files, Windows copies the user's files and folders from the desktop and the My Documents folder to a folder on your desktop, where they become part of your profile and remain under your control. The rest of the user profile—such as e-mail messages and other data stored in the Application Data folder, Internet favorites, and settings stored in the registry—is deleted after you confirm your intention in the next window that appears.

- **Delete Files.** If you select Delete Files and confirm your choice in the window that follows, Windows deletes the account, its user profile, all files associated with the account (including those in its My Documents folder), and its registry settings.

Chapter 4

Microsoft Windows XP Networking and Security Inside Out

Inside Out

Delete user profiles and registry settings, too

If you use a tool other than User Accounts to delete an account, the account's profile continues to occupy space in the Documents And Settings folder and in the registry. Purging these unused items by deleting files with Windows Explorer and editing the registry directly can be risky; it's too easy to delete the wrong folders or keys. Instead, right-click My Computer and choose Properties to open the System Properties dialog box. In Windows 2000, click the User Profiles tab; in Windows XP, click the Advanced tab and then click Settings under User Profiles. Select the account named Account Unknown (the deleted account) and click Delete. (If the Delete button is not available, log off all users and then log on again.)

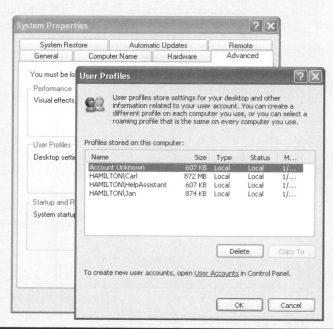

Assigning User Accounts to Security Groups

With your computer's list of users now refined to include everyone who uses the computer and no one else, you should assign each user to one or more security groups. The built-in security groups have predefined rights and permissions that are appropriate for broad classes of users, and they are usually all you need for stand-alone computers and small networks. (For details, see "Roles of Security Group Members," page 52.)

To assign a user account to only one group, you can use any of the account-management tools, as explained here. If you want to add an account to more than one group (which is likely only if you're using groups other than the built-in ones), you must use either Local Users And Groups or the Net Localgroup command.

● In Users And Passwords, click the Users tab and then double-click the user name for the account you want to change. In the properties dialog box that appears, click the Group Membership tab and then select a security group, as shown in Figure 4-6.

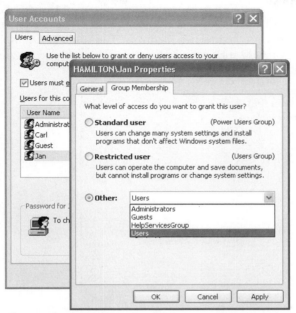

Figure 4-6. This dialog box lets you place an account in any single local security group.

Caution When you add an account to a group by using Users And Passwords, Windows removes the account from any other local groups the account was in. An account that is a member of the Remote Desktop Users group and the Administrators group, for example, loses membership in both those groups if you use this tool to move the account to the Power Users group.

Inside Out   Avoid Standard User in Windows XP Home Edition

All versions of Windows 2000 and Windows XP let you assign an account to the Power Users group by choosing Standard User in the dialog box shown in Figure 4-6. This choice produces a flurry of error messages in Windows XP Home Edition, however, because Home Edition does not have a built-in Power Users group. Although you could prevent the error messages by using the Net Localgroup command to create a Power Users group, doing so wouldn't have the intended effect. Simply creating a group with that name doesn't confer the predefined rights, restrictions, and permissions that the built-in Power Users group in Windows XP Professional enjoys. Your best bet: If your computer is running Windows XP Home Edition, avoid choosing Standard User.

- Local Users And Groups provides the best tool for managing group memberships. You can approach the task in either of two ways:

  - To manage the group memberships for a single user account, click Users in the console tree. With user accounts displayed in the details pane, double-click a user name and then click the Member Of tab in the properties dialog box that appears, as shown in Figure 4-7. Click Add and complete the ensuing dialog box to add the user account to a group, or select a group and click Remove to delete the account from the group.

Figure 4-7. From Local Users And Groups, use the Member Of tab of the properties dialog box to review and manage a user's group memberships.

  - To manage the group memberships for a single security group, click Groups in the console tree. With groups displayed in the details pane, double-click a group name to see a list of the group's members. See Figure 4-8, which shows a security group's properties dialog box. Click Add to add a user account to the group, or select an account and click Remove to delete the user from the group.

- The Net Localgroup command uses the form **net localgroup** *group* *usernames* /**add** (where *group* is the security group name and *usernames* is one or more user names, separated by spaces) to add an account to a user group. For example, to add Jan and Muir to the Power Users group, use this command:

```
net localgroup "power users" jan muir /add
```

Figure 4-8. Local Users And Groups displays a list of user accounts in a particular security group.

To delete one or more group members, use the same syntax, replacing the /Add switch with /Delete. Note that the group membership changes you make with Net Localgroup do not affect a user account's membership in other security groups.

● With User Accounts, you can assign an account only to the Administrators group or the Users group. An account's membership in either of those groups is deleted when you switch the account to the other group; however, all the account's additional group memberships remain unchanged. To make the change, click the account name in User Accounts. Then click the Change The Account Type link.

Assigning a Password to a User Account

The last step in configuring user accounts is to assign a logon password to each one. The other steps—creating user accounts, disabling unused accounts, and assigning accounts to security groups—are often performed for you automatically during setup. Windows Setup, however, does not assign passwords to most accounts; you must perform this most crucial step on your own.

In this section, we explain how to set a password by using each of the account-management tools. Before you undertake this task, however, you should think about the passwords you want to use. For information about selecting effective passwords, see "Creating Strong Passwords," page 111.

Chapter 4

Caution   You can safely set the initial password for a user account using any of the account-management tools. But if you're running Windows XP, do not remove or change another user's password unless the user has forgotten the password and has absolutely no other way to access the account. (For more information, see "Recovering a Lost Password," page 115.) If you change or remove another user's password, that user loses all personal certificates and stored passwords for Web sites and network resources. Without the personal certificates, the user loses access to all of his or her encrypted files and all e-mail messages encrypted with the user's private key. (For information about encrypted files, see Chapter 21, "Encrypting Files and Folders.") This feature, new in Windows XP, is designed to prevent an administrator from changing someone else's password to gain access to that individual's private information.

The user whose password is changed can regain access to his or her certificates and encrypted information only by changing the password back to the old password or by using the Password Reset Disk. (For details about resetting passwords, see "Using a Password Reset Disk," page 116.)

Chapter 4

- Users And Passwords lets you set the password for all local accounts except the one with which you're currently logged on. (To change your own password, press Ctrl+Alt+Delete and then click Change Password.) On the Users tab, select the user name and then click Set Password (Windows 2000) or Reset Password (Windows XP).

- With Local Users And Groups, you assign a password by clicking Users in the console tree, right-clicking a user name, and choosing Set Password.

- To set a password with the Net User command, use the form **net user *username* *password***, where *username* is the account's user name and *password* is one of these three values:

  - The password you want to assign.

  - * (Windows then prompts you to type the password you want to use.)

  - **/random** (Windows generates, assigns, and displays a strong eight-character password.)

- In User Accounts, you assign a password by clicking the account name and then clicking the Create A Password link. A window like the one shown in Figure 4-9 appears. User Accounts is the only tool that lets you specify a password hint. (The password hint is available by clicking the question mark icon that appears after you click your name on the Welcome screen.) The availability of password hints is another feature that offers added convenience at the expense of security; anyone who has access to your computer can see your hint if the Welcome screen is displayed. Therefore, if you use this feature, be *very* circumspect about the hint you provide! You're better off not using the feature at all.

Figure 4-9. User Accounts enables you to specify a password hint when you set the password.

> **Caution** Don't use the Description or Comment field to store a password hint. This field, which is displayed in all tools except User Accounts, can be read by other users on your network as well as other users on your computer.

Securing the Administrator Account

The Administrator account is a natural target for malicious attackers. First, of course, that account holds the keys to the entire kingdom; someone who can gain access as Administrator can do just about anything he or she wants with your computer. It's also attractive because nearly every computer has an account named Administrator; an intruder needs to determine only the password because the user name is already known.

The most important steps you can take to secure the Administrator account are to assign a strong password to it and to change the password frequently. For details about strong passwords, see "Creating Strong Passwords," page 111.

You can lock down your computer's Administrator account a little more by changing its user name. The name needn't be overly cryptic (like a password, for example); it should just be something other than "Administrator," the name that every hacker already knows and expects to find. Follow these steps to change the user name:

1 Open Users And Passwords. (If you are running Windows XP and your computer is not joined to a domain, type **control userpasswords2** at a command prompt.)
2 On the Users tab, double-click the Administrator account.

3 In the User Name box, type a new name for the Administrator account.

Don't use the Administrator account (or whatever you now call it) as your everyday account. And if you do need to use the Administrator account occasionally for computer maintenance, don't leave it logged on.

> **Tip** Create a phony Administrator account
>
> After you rename the Administrator account, you can create a new user account named Administrator. Put this account in the Guests security group and give it a strong password. Such an account serves two purposes: It's a decoy that'll keep attackers occupied (and won't give up anything of value if they do manage to crack it), and it helps you to determine whether someone is trying to break into your system. (Check the security log in Event Viewer to see whether someone is attempting to log on as Administrator.)

If you have an alternative administrative account (that is, another user account that is a member of the Administrators group), you can disable the built-in Administrator account to prevent anyone from using it to log on.

To disable the Administrator account in Windows XP, double-click the account in Local Users And Groups, select Account Is Disabled, and then click OK.

In Windows 2000, you can't disable built-in accounts, but you can assign a user right that prevents the account from logging on. Start Local Security Settings (type **secpol.msc** at a command prompt), and open Security Settings\Local Policies\User Rights Assignment. In the details pane, double-click the Deny Logon Locally right. Click Add, select Administrator, click Add, and then click OK.

Does Your Computer Have a Hidden Administrator Account?

Your computer might have an account named Administrator—and you might not even know it. This is a particular likelihood on computers running Windows XP and configured to use the Welcome screen for logon because by default, the Administrator account is not shown on the Welcome screen. With some manufacturer-installed versions of Windows XP, an Administrator account is created during setup without the user's knowledge, and it has no password protection. (This account is in addition to the administrative account created for the primary user during setup.) Anyone who discovers this account can log on with full administrative privileges; no password is needed. (For more information about this vulnerability, see *http://www.net-security.org/vuln.php?id=3711*.)

To see whether your computer has an unexpected account named Administrator, open Local Users And Groups and select the Users folder. If you find an Administrator account, you can right-click it and choose Set Password to lock it down with a strong password.

Securing the Guest Account

The Guest account provides convenient access for occasional users (such as a babysitter, customer, or other visitor who wants to check e-mail). Users of the Guest account (and members of the Guests group) have access to your computer's programs, to files in the Shared Documents folder, and to files in the Guest profile. Although the Guest account offers only limited access, it is another means for an intruder to get a toehold into your computer. And because ordinarily no password is required to use the account, you must be sure that the Guest account doesn't expose items that a casual user shouldn't be able to view or modify.

You can further secure the Guest account by making the following changes:

- **Turn off or disable the Guest account if you don't need it.** If you only occasionally have a visitor who needs guest access, turn on the Guest account only when necessary.

  If you are running Windows XP and your computer is not joined to a domain, log on as Administrator. In Control Panel, open User Accounts and click Guest. Click Turn On The Guest Account to enable Guest access; return to the same window and click Turn Off The Guest Account to close this entryway.

  If you are running Windows 2000 or your computer is joined to a domain, use Local Users And Groups to control Guest access. Click Users in the console tree and then double-click the Guest account in the details pane. In the Guest Properties dialog box, select the Account Is Disabled check box to disable Guest access; clear the check box to allow access.

Chapter 4

> **Tip** If you have an account lockout policy in place, a specified number of incorrect guesses of the Guest password locks out the account, even if it is disabled. In Local Users And Groups, open the Guest account and check to see whether Account Is Locked Out is selected. If so, someone has been trying (unsuccessfully) to log on as Guest. For details about account lockouts, see "Setting Account Lockout Policies," page 131.

- **Rename the Guest account.**   It's no guarantee of security, but renaming the Guest account offers a tiny bit of subterfuge, perhaps leading an attacker away to find an easier mark. If the Guest account is enabled, you can rename it with Users And Passwords, just as you can rename the Administrator account. (For details, see the preceding section, "Securing the Administrator Account.") If you want to rename the account without first enabling it, you must use Local Security Settings:

  1 At a command prompt, type **secpol.msc** to open Local Security Settings.

  2 Open Security Settings\Local Policies\Security Options.

  3 In the details pane, double-click Accounts: Rename Guest Account (Windows XP Professional) or Rename Guest Account (Windows 2000).

  4 Type the new name for the Guest account and click Apply.

- **Prevent network logon by the Guest account.**   If you do not use Simple File Sharing in Windows XP to share folders or printers with other people on your network, you can prevent anyone from using the Guest account to log on to your computer over the network. (Simple File Sharing is a Windows XP feature that requires the use of the Guest account for network access.) In Local Security Settings (Secpol.msc), open Security Settings\Local Policies\User Rights Assignment. Be sure that Guest is listed in the Deny Access To This Computer From The Network policy.

> For information about Simple File Sharing, see "Windows Sharing and Security Models," page 17.

- **Prevent a Guest user from shutting down the computer.**   If a guest can shut down the computer, he or she not only stops all running processes but also can then restart the computer—perhaps booting from a floppy disk or a CD into another operating system. To prevent someone logged on as Guest from shutting down the system, start Local Security Settings and open Security Settings\Local Policies \User Rights Assignment. Be sure that Guest is not listed in the Shut Down The System policy.

  Anyone—including guests—can shut down the system from the Welcome screen or the Log On To Windows dialog box unless you also set a policy that allows only a logged-on user to shut down the computer. In Local Security Settings, open Security Settings\Local Policies\Security Options. In the details pane, double-click Shutdown: Allow System To Be Shut Down Without Having To Log On (Windows XP) or Allow System To Be Shut Down Without Having To Log On (Windows 2000) and then select Disabled.

Of course, with physical access to the computer, a disreputable individual can simply press the power switch to circumvent this protection. These settings are effective only if your computer's system unit is securely locked away, separate from the keyboard and monitor.

● **Prevent a Guest user from viewing event logs.** Guests might be able to glean information about your computer and your habits by poring through event logs. (For more information about event logs, see "Viewing the Log of Security Events," page 781.) To prevent this, start Registry Editor and open HKLM\System \CurrentControlSet\Services\Eventlog. Visit each of the three subkeys— Application, Security, and System—and be sure that each contains a DWORD value named RestrictGuestAccess that is set to 1.

Following Best Practices for Your Everyday Account

By default, each user account you create during Windows XP setup (as well as those migrated during an upgrade from Windows 98 or Windows Me) becomes a member of the Administrators group. This account assignment is for convenience because administrative privileges are needed to run many programs (particularly older programs that were written without regard for security). But it's definitely not the most secure way to operate, and you should demote all users—yourself included—to less privileged groups if possible. Always running as a computer administrator makes your computer and your network more vulnerable to attacks from viruses and Trojan horses, simply because administrative accounts have all the requisite privileges to start such processes, albeit inadvertently. Routinely logging on and running as an administrator violates the basic security tenet of *least privilege*, a rule that states that you give only enough access for a person to perform his or her job.

Even if your programs run properly without administrative privileges, you'll almost certainly need to log on as an administrator to install most programs and occasionally to perform other administrative tasks, such as managing user accounts. (In particular, nearly all the procedures described in this chapter require administrative privileges.) Therefore, we suggest the following strategy:

● Log on as Administrator (or another administrative account you create for the purpose) and move all other accounts from the Administrators group to the Power Users or Users group. Log off and then use your normal (nonadministrative) account for everyday use.

● When you install a program, use the Administrator account. As an alternative to logging off and then logging on as Administrator, you can use the Run As command. Right-click the new application's setup program and choose Run As. (In Windows 2000, you must hold down Shift when you right-click to make the Run As command appear.) Enter the credentials for the Administrator account.

● After you install a program, if it balks when you try to run it as a nonadministrative user, you can set a compatibility mode, which attempts to convince the ill-mannered program that it's running in the earlier version of Windows for which it was designed. To set a compatibility mode, log on as Administrator (or use Run As) and follow these steps:

- In Windows XP: If you run the program from a CD or a network drive, open the Start menu and choose All Programs, Accessories, Program Compatibility Wizard. If you've installed the program on your local hard disk, right-click the program's shortcut, choose Properties, and then click the Compatibility tab.

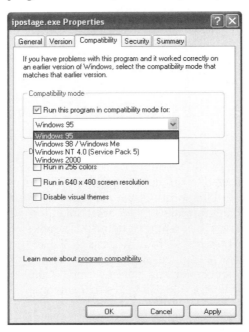

- In Windows 2000 Service Pack 2 (SP2): If you have installed SP2 or later, a Compatibility tab similar to the one shown for Windows XP is available. After installing SP2 or later, you enable the feature by typing **regsvr32 %systemroot%\apppatch\slayerui.dll** at a command prompt. (You need to do this only once.) Thereafter, the dialog box that appears when you right-click a program's shortcut and choose Properties includes a Compatibility tab on which you can select the earlier version of Windows to emulate.

- In Windows 2000 without SP2: If you haven't already installed Support Tools and the Application Compatibility tool, insert the Windows 2000 Professional CD, navigate to its \Support\Tools folder, and run Setup. To run Application Compatibility, open the Start menu and choose Programs, Windows 2000 Support Tools, Tools, Application Compatibility Tool (or simply type **apcompat** at a command prompt).

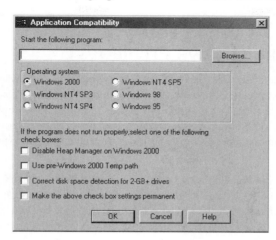

- If setting a compatibility mode doesn't solve the problem, use Run As to run your program. You can configure a program's shortcut so that it always prompts you for the credentials of the account you want to use; this lets you launch the program in the usual way instead of having to right-click and choose Run As. The user name will be filled in for you, but you'll need to provide its password each time you run the program. To configure a shortcut this way, right-click the shortcut (this works only with shortcuts to programs, not with the programs' executable files), choose Properties, and click the Shortcut tab. In Windows XP, click Advanced and then select Run With Different Credentials. In Windows 2000, the Run With Different Credentials check box is on the Shortcut tab.

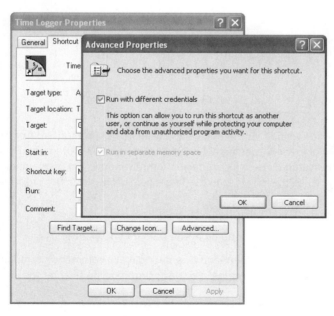

Chapter 4

Using Run As When You Need Administrative Privileges

The Run As command provides a way to run a program using the privileges granted to an account other than the one with which you're currently logged on. This lets you configure your own everyday account as a member of the Users group (a good implementation of the rule of least privilege) and use an administrative account only when necessary to run a certain program. Run As can be invoked from the Windows graphical interface or from a command prompt.

To use the graphical interface, right-click the icon for an application (.exe file name extension), Microsoft Management Console document (.msc), or shortcut (.lnk) and choose Run As. (If you're using Windows 2000, you must hold down the Shift key when you right-click. In addition, the shortcut menu for some programs and Control Panel shortcuts doesn't include a Run As command, even in Windows XP; in those cases, pressing Shift should make it appear.) In the Run As dialog box, select The Following User, select a user name from the list of Administrators group and Power Users group members, and enter the password for the account you selected.

The command-line version, Runas.exe, can be used in a Command Prompt window, in the Run dialog box, or in the Target field of a shortcut's properties dialog box. For instance, you can create a shortcut that opens a Command Prompt window (Cmd.exe) using another user's permissions by typing the following in the Target field of the shortcut's properties dialog box:

```
runas /user:username cmd
```

Replace *username* with the user name of the account you want to use.

When you invoke the Run As command by entering it at a command prompt or by opening a shortcut like the preceding example, Windows prompts you to enter the password for the specified user account.

An administrative Command Prompt window is a handy tool to have. But it's a good idea to clearly differentiate that window from Command Prompt windows that you launch in the context of your limited user account so that you can tell at a glance that you're using your "super" Command Prompt window—and be aware that its elevated powers come with elevated risks. To do that, create a shortcut as described above. Right-click the shortcut and choose Properties. On the General tab, change the name to something like "Administrative Command Prompt"; this name appears in the title bar when you run the application. On the Colors tab, select a distinctive color scheme. And on the Shortcut tab, click Change Icon and select a distinctive icon for the shortcut.

One irritation with Run As—aside from its requirement that you enter a password each time you use it—is that it doesn't work with all programs. In some cases, even when you use Run As to start a program, the program actually runs using your original logon account. (If you're not sure, you can use Task Manager [press Ctrl+Shift+Escape and click the Processes tab] or Sysinternals Process Explorer [*http://www.sysinternals.com/ntw2k/freeware/procexp.shtml*] to find out.) This usually occurs because an instance of the program is already running with your account; launching another instance reuses the already-approved security token—yours—instead of the new one you provide.

It is for this reason that by default, you can't use Run As with Windows Explorer, because as the Windows shell, Windows Explorer is *always* running. This is a significant limitation, because many of the things that you would need to do with an administrative account are most easily done from Windows Explorer. Fortunately, a simple solution exists. In Folder Options, click the View tab and then select Launch Folder Windows In A Separate Process. Note, however, that this is a per-user setting, and you must make it for the target user (that is, the account you plan to "run as"). The easiest way to do that is to log on with the administrative account, make the change in Folder Options (which you can open from Control Panel or by choosing Tools, Folder Options in Windows Explorer), log off, and then log on with your everyday (limited) account.

The graphical version of Run As has one other security-related trick that you might find handy. If you select Current User (instead of The Following User) and also select Protect My Computer And Data From Unauthorized Program Activity, the program runs using the credentials of the current user (and, therefore, that user's privileges), with some significant exceptions: It prevents the program from making any changes to the registry and prevents the program from accessing the user's profile folder. Although these severe restrictions prevent most programs from working properly, this option can be useful for trying out an untrusted program.

If these workarounds don't solve the problem—or if you tire of entering yet another password every time you need to run a frequently used program—your choices are limited: See whether a newer version of the offending program (or a reasonable alternative program) is available, or put yourself back in the Administrators group.

Aaron Margosis of Microsoft Consulting Services is a strong advocate of running with least privilege. He has written extensively about the risks of running with administrative

Chapter 4

privileges and about how to live with (and work around, when necessary) the limitations imposed by an ordinary Users account. He has also created some simple tools for temporarily changing the privilege level of your everyday account (his MakeMeAdmin program provides an alternative to logging on with a different account or using Run As when you need administrative privileges) and for providing visual feedback that lets you know the privilege level of running programs. You can find this information and download the tools from his Non-Admin blog at *http://blogs.msdn.com/aaron_margosis/*. To see a summary of the relevant blog posts, click the Non-Admin or Non-Admin For Home Users link under Post Categories.

Using Passwords Effectively

Do you need to create and use a password for Windows logon? After all, it's certainly easier to simply click your name or just press Enter when you start your computer. And if your computer is in a secure place, such as your home, you might be tempted to forgo the protection a password provides.

Before you decide, consider who has physical access to your computer. At home, your computer might be available only to you and your spouse. What about kids? House guests? Do you have any household employees such as a babysitter or cleaning service? What about repair services or other contractors? Each of these people might pose a different threat: Family members whom you trust completely might be inexperienced computer users who can inadvertently delete or otherwise destroy your data if they can too easily log in as you. Others could conceivably have more malicious intentions.

In a business, it's more likely that someone who shouldn't do so could obtain access to your computer. In addition to business associates and employees (who might at some point become "disgruntled employees"), janitorial crews (and sometimes their accompanying children), security guards, delivery persons, clients, vendors, and door-to-door framed artwork solicitors could reach your computer when you're not there to defend it. In an office environment, you should almost certainly use strong passwords for Windows logon.

You might base your decision on the presumed value of the information on your computer. In a business, of course, you're likely to have financial data, product information, proposals, customer data, and other important files. The loss of these resources, or their discovery by a competitor, might prove devastating. At home, perhaps you have your family finances on one computer that clearly needs to be protected, but you think your other computers don't have anything of "value." Think again: Do they have your photo collection, music collection, kitchen remodel plans, or correspondence with Aunt Mary? Although these types of files might not be of any use to anyone else, remember that some vandals enjoy the perverse satisfaction of destroying your data. Even if you religiously back up your data, you might be faced with restoring your system from scratch, which could take several hours or more.

It is especially important to password-protect any account that is a member of the Administrators group (which is, by default, most accounts you set up in Windows XP) because of the unrestricted power these accounts wield. If someone manages to plant a virus or a Trojan horse on your computer while logged on as an administrator (by logging on to your computer locally, by connecting over a network or the Internet, or by tricking you into running an executable e-mail attachment, for example), that malicious program can do just about anything. Two lessons here: Don't run as an administrator, and password-protect all administrator accounts.

Weak passwords trump strong security. As pointed out in "The Ten Immutable Laws of Security" (reprinted in this book's Appendix), all your other security measures are for naught if malicious attackers can get past your password defense. Don't let your password selection (or lack thereof) be your weakest link.

 Inside Out

Safely use an account with no password

Security enhancements in Windows XP mean that blank passwords aren't quite the risk that they are in earlier versions of Windows, including Windows 2000. In Windows XP, accounts with a blank password can be used only to log on interactively at the computer by using either the Welcome screen or the Log On To Windows dialog box. You can't log on to a non-password-protected account over the network or with Remote Desktop, for example. Nor can you use the Run As feature to run in the context of an account with a blank password. (And because Task Scheduler uses Run As to launch programs, you can't use a password-free account to run scheduled tasks.) These additional restrictions apply only to local accounts with no password; domain accounts are not afforded such protection. (However, sound domain policy would prevent the creation of a domain account with a blank password.)

Although these enhancements mean that if you don't use a password in Windows XP your greatest risk is from people who have physical access to your computer, you can be sure that malicious hackers are working night and day to find a way around these restrictions. Your safest bet: Don't rely on this protection. Use strong passwords—at least for your administrator accounts—even with Windows XP.

Chapter 4

Troubleshooting

Windows XP asks for a password, but you haven't set one

When you upgrade a system to Windows XP, the Setup program assigns temporary passwords for use during setup. Ordinarily, these passwords are removed when setup is completed. If they're not removed for some reason, you're effectively locked out of that account until you determine or change the password.

If you can log on using another administrative account, you can change the password for the affected user account—but be aware of the potential problems and data loss that changing someone else's password can cause. (See the caution on page 98.)

A better way to solve this problem is to determine the temporary password assigned by Setup, which you can do as follows:

1   Boot into the Recovery Console by following these steps:

   a   Insert the Windows CD and restart your computer. Follow your computer's prompts to boot from the CD. (You might need to adjust settings in the computer's BIOS to enable the option to boot from a CD.)

   b   Follow the setup prompts to load the basic Windows startup files. At the Welcome To Setup screen, press R to start the Recovery Console.

   c   Enter the number of the Windows installation you want to access from the Recovery Console.

   d   When prompted, type the Administrator password. If you're using the Recovery Console on a system running Windows XP Home Edition, this password is blank by default, so just press Enter.

2   At the command prompt, type **systemroot** to change to the %SystemRoot% folder—the folder where Windows XP files are located.

3   Type **more setupact.log** to display a file that contains the password information you need.

4   Scan the file contents for the line that begins "Random password for." Press Spacebar to display the next screen of the file. When you find the line, make a note of the user name and password. (Remember that the password is case sensitive.)

5   Reboot into Windows XP and log on using the user name and password information you found.

If Windows is installed on a FAT32 volume, you can boot from a Windows 98 or Windows Me boot floppy instead of using Recovery Console. At the command prompt, type **edit %windir%\setupact.log** to open the file. Use the Edit program's search command to locate the line beginning with "Random password for."

Creating Strong Passwords

At a security industry conference in 2004, Microsoft Chairman Bill Gates famously predicted the demise of passwords because they "just don't meet the challenge for anything you really want to secure." In the future, he said, we'll rely instead on smart cards, access tokens, and biometric devices. Smart cards and access tokens are devices that a user carries and then inserts in a smart card reader or USB port to gain access. These devices contain information that identify the user, and their use typically requires the user to also enter some unique information that only that user would know. This two-factor authentication—something you have and something you know—is difficult to bypass. For now, however, these devices are gaining a foothold only in large enterprises. Except for the recent appearance of inexpensive biometric devices (see "Logging On with a Biometric Device," page 127), users in small businesses and homes are still stuck with passwords.

It's a fact: Computer users hate passwords. Some just leave the password blank or are inclined to use an extremely simple (and obvious) password, such as *password*, *test*, or their user name. Others attempt to be a little more secure by using a special date or the name of a spouse, pet, or favorite sports team. Still others, thinking they're being more secure, use random words that occur to them. None of these approaches is any match for a sophisticated password-cracking program, which can usually correctly ascertain such passwords in a matter of minutes. (For more information about password cracking, see "Recovering a Lost Password," page 115.)

The following common practices—widely understood and exploited by attackers—must be avoided to maintain security:

- Using a word found in any dictionary, including foreign-language dictionaries
- Using the names of people, pets, places, sports teams, and so on
- Writing down your password on a note stuck to your monitor or placed in your top desk drawer

You can defend against password-cracking programs by using strong passwords. Ultimately, such passwords can also be cracked, but it can take months instead of hours. In the meantime, attackers have moved on to easier targets. And if you're following best security practices, you'll have changed to a new strong password before the current one is cracked. A strong password:

- Contains at least eight characters (longer—much longer—is better; the maximum length for logon passwords in Windows XP and Windows 2000 is 127 characters).
- Contains a mixture of uppercase and lowercase letters, numerals, and symbols.
- Changes periodically and differs significantly from previous passwords.
- Does not contain your name, user name, or any other words or names.
- Does not contain a series of consecutive letters (such as "lmnopqrs"), consecutive numbers, or adjacent keyboard keys (such as "qwerty").
- Is not shared with anyone.

Chapter 4

Unfortunately, such gobbledygook passwords can be as difficult to remember as they are to crack. You can, however, use some mnemonic tricks to create and remember them.

One effective approach is to distill an easy-to-remember phrase into a difficult-to-crack password. For example, you could use the phrase "**S**ecurity **is e**very**one's bus**iness" to come up with this password: Sie1'sbs. History buffs might use the title of the World War I marching song "It's a Long, Long Way to Tipperary" to create the seemingly random, yet memorable, password IaL,LW2T. You get the idea.

Another trick is to take a memorable phrase ("It was the best of times") and intersperse its initial letters with a memorable number (such as your anniversary). Using a date of March 18 (3-18) yields this password: I3w-t1b8ot.

Not everyone agrees that your password must be an unpronounceable collection of apparently random letters, numbers, and symbols. Some experts argue that such cryptic passwords are *less* secure than ones made up of several words interspersed with numbers and symbols, because you're almost certainly going to write down a cryptic password. One such expert is Jesper Johansson, a security program manager at Microsoft, who advocates the use of *pass phrases*. A pass phrase consists of a memorable phrase (perhaps a line from a favorite song, movie, or book) that is typically five to nine words long, with spaces between words. A pass phrase can (and indeed, should) include punctuation. A pass phrase that contains uncommon words or misspelled words will be even more difficult to crack, as is one that uses letter substitutions (such as 5 for S, the number 0 for the letter O, and so on). Johansson has written a three-part series of articles about the merits of pass phrases versus passwords; you can find the articles by going to *http://www.microsoft.com* and searching Microsoft.com for **pass phrase johansson**.

You can find another interesting discussion of password security in "Ten Windows Password Myths," an article written for SecurityFocus by Mark Burnett (*http://online.securityfocus.com/infocus/1554/*).

Tip **Generate strong passwords automatically**

You can use the Net User command to randomly generate a strong password and assign it to a user account. In a Command Prompt window, type **net user *username* /random**, where *username* is the account's user name. Similarly, a number of online services and stand-alone programs are available for randomly generating strong passwords of any length you specify. You'll find good ones at the following locations:

http://www.winguides.com/security/password.php
http://javascript.internet.com/passwords/password-generator.html
http://www.segobit.com/apg.htm
http://www.hirtlesoftware.com
http://www.mark.vcn.com/password/
http://www.roboform.com

RoboForm, the program available from the last Web site listed, does much more than generate passwords: it also serves as a password manager that keeps track of your various passwords and it fills in forms on Web sites with information such as your name and address.

Managing User Accounts and Passwords

Establishing and Enforcing Password Policies

To ensure that you and other users on your network don't leave the password door wide open, you should establish (and follow!) some effective logon password policies and guidelines. As we explain here, you can use security settings in Windows to enforce some of these policies; for others, user education is the key.

For best security, we recommend the following:

- **A password should be required for all user accounts.** At the very least, enforce this rule for members of the Administrators group.
- **Passwords must be at least eight characters long.** Shorter passwords are more easily cracked.
- **Passwords must be complex.** They should contain characters of at least three of these four types: uppercase letters, lowercase letters, numerals, and symbols. This stymies dictionary attacks, causing password crackers to rely on brute-force methods or other techniques.

> **Tip** Use spaces
> You can use any character in a Windows logon password, including spaces. With one or more spaces in a password, it's easier to come up with a long yet memorable password; you might even incorporate several words separated by spaces and other symbols. Don't use a space as the first or last character of your password, however; some applications trim spaces from these positions.

- **Passwords should not contain any form of your name or user name.** Because so many users have passwords based on this weak scheme, password-cracking programs are trained to try these variants very early in the process.
- **Passwords should be changed at least every 90 days.** The attacker's best friend is time. When dictionary attacks don't work, a determined thief can use brute-force techniques to try every combination of letters, numbers, and characters in the hope of finding one that works. This task can take months, but it will eventually pay off if you never change your password.
- **Passwords should not be written down and stored in plain view.** Not all attacks come from scurrilous characters connected to your computer only by the Internet. If your password is written on a sticky note and stuck to your monitor, anyone who walks by your computer can copy it.

Even if you convince everyone who uses your computer to use passwords, you can be sure that they won't always follow the secure practices of creating strong passwords and changing them often. To be sure that these guidelines are followed (except for the last one, which relies on user education and monitors that repel sticky notes), you can set security policies using the Local Security Settings console.

Chapter 4

113

Inside Out

Use at least 15 characters for best security

In Windows XP and Windows 2000, passwords can be up to 127 characters long. (In Microsoft Windows NT, the limit was 14 characters.) Longer passwords become exponentially more difficult to crack, but they have another seldom-documented benefit. The LAN Manager (LM) password hash, a relatively insecure method of storing passwords used in early network operating systems, is stored incorrectly in Windows XP/2000 if the password is at least 15 characters long. An identical LM hash value is used for *any* password longer than 14 characters. This little-known fact was discovered by Urity of Security Friday (*http://www.securityfriday.com*).

As a result, any password cracker that relies on LM hash extraction (as do many of those we discuss later in this chapter) will not work. Similarly, if an attacker coaxes your computer to log on using weak LM authentication, your password will not be exposed. (Windows 2000 falls back to LM authentication if Kerberos V5 or NTLM are unavailable; for details, see "Controlling the Logon and Authentication Process," page 55.)

Unfortunately, you can't use password policies (discussed next) to enforce a 15-character minimum length. You can't specify a minimum length greater than 14 characters.

To start Local Security Settings, type **secpol.msc** at a command prompt. To see the policies that set password behavior for all accounts, open Security Settings\Account Policies \Password Policy. Double-click a policy to set its value, as shown in Figure 4-10. Table 4-3 explains each policy.

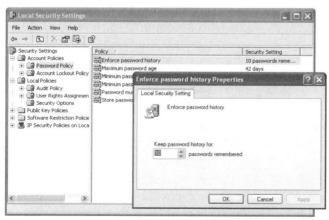

Figure 4-10. Local Security Settings lets you impose password policies on all local user accounts.

Chapter 4

Table 4-3. **Password Policies**

Policy	Description
Enforce password history	Specifying a number greater than 0 (the maximum is 24) causes Windows to remember that number of previous passwords and forces users to pick a password different from any of the remembered ones.
Maximum password age	Specifying a number greater than 0 (the maximum is 999) dictates how many days a password remains valid before it expires. (To override this setting for certain user accounts, open the account's properties dialog box in Local Users And Groups and select the Password Never Expires check box.) Selecting 0 means passwords never expire.
Minimum password age	Specifying a number greater than 0 (the maximum is 999) lets you set the number of days a password must be used before a user is allowed to change it. Selecting 0 means that users can change passwords as often as they like.
Minimum password length	Specifying a number greater than 0 (the maximum is 14) forces passwords to be longer than a certain number of characters. Specifying 0 permits users to have no password at all. *Note: Changes to the minimum password length setting do not apply to current passwords.*
Password must meet complexity requirements	Enabling this policy requires that new passwords be at least six characters long; that the passwords contain a mix of uppercase letters, lowercase letters, numbers, and symbols (at least one character from three of these four classes); and that the passwords not contain the user name or any part of the full name. *Note: Enabling password complexity does not affect current passwords.*
Store password using reversible encryption for all users in the domain	Enabling this policy effectively stores passwords as clear text instead of encrypting them, which is much more secure. You almost certainly do not want to enable this policy, which is provided only for compatibility with a few older applications.

> **Tip** If you use password history, you should also set a minimum password age. Otherwise, users can defeat the password history feature by quickly changing the password a number of times and then returning to the current password.

Recovering a Lost Password

If you can't log on to a computer because you don't know the password, you're not alone. Forgetting passwords is one of the most common problems users face, especially if they've gone to the trouble of creating strong ones. If the computer is yours, finding that password

Chapter 4

is called "recovering a lost password." If the computer is not yours, the process is called "cracking." Either way, the tools and procedures are much the same. If you find yourself in this situation, you might need to explore the murky underworld of hackers to find the tools and techniques you need.

Traditionally, the best and fastest solution is for an administrator to log on to the computer and reset your password using any of the available account-management tools. This continues to be a viable solution for Windows 2000, but it comes with a huge caveat in Windows XP: If an administrator changes or removes another user's password, that user loses all personal certificates and stored passwords for Web sites and network resources. Without the personal certificates, the user has no access to his or her encrypted files or to e-mail messages encrypted with the user's private key. Windows XP deletes the certificates and passwords to prevent the administrator who makes the password change from gaining access to them.

> **Note** If your Windows XP computer is a member of an Active Directory domain, a domain administrator can safely change the password for your domain user account without putting your certificates, stored passwords, and encrypted data out of reach. Problems arise only when the password is changed for a local user account.

Troubleshooting

You can't access your encrypted files because an administrator changed your password

When an administrator removes or changes the password for your local account on a computer running Windows XP, you no longer have access to your encrypted files and e-mail messages. That's because your master key, which unlocks your personal encryption certificate (which, in turn, unlocks your encrypted files), is encrypted with a hash of your password. When the password changes, the master key is no longer accessible. To regain access to the master key (and, by extension, your encrypted files and e-mail messages), change your password back to your old password. Alternatively, use your Password Reset Disk (see the next section) to change your password.

When you change your own password (through User Accounts or with your Password Reset Disk), Windows uses your old password to decrypt the master key and then re-encrypts it with the new password, so your encrypted files and e-mail messages remain accessible.

Microsoft Knowledge Base article 290260 provides more information about recovering from this situation.

Using a Password Reset Disk

If you use Windows XP—and if you do a little advance preparation—recovering from a forgotten password is easy (and secure). Windows XP lets each user create a Password Reset Disk, a floppy disk with which users can log on without knowing their password.

To create a Password Reset Disk, you need to know your current password; otherwise, someone could create such a disk at your computer when you've stepped away.

> **Note** You can make a Password Reset Disk only for your local user account. If your computer is joined to a domain, you can't create a Password Reset Disk as a back door to your domain logon password. However, in a domain environment a domain administrator can safely change your password, and you'll still have access to your encrypted files.

To create a Password Reset Disk, follow these steps:

1 Log on using the account for which you want to create a Password Reset Disk.

2 In Control Panel, click User Accounts.

3 If you're logged on as an administrator, click your account name.

4 Click Prevent A Forgotten Password (in the task pane under Related Tasks) to start the Forgotten Password Wizard.

Because anyone with physical access to your computer can use your Password Reset Disk to usurp your account, be sure to store the disk in a secure location away from the computer. (Not too far away, of course. You never know when you'll need it.)

When you attempt to log on and can't remember your password, Windows XP displays a message that includes a Use Your Password Reset Disk link (if your computer is configured to use the Welcome screen) or a Reset button (if you're not using the Welcome screen). Click the link or button to launch the Password Reset Wizard. The wizard prompts you to insert your Password Reset Disk and then asks you to create a new password. Log on using your new password and return your Password Reset Disk to its safe storage place.

> **Tip** Even if your computer is joined to a domain, you might want to create a Password Reset Disk for one of your computer's local user accounts. To do that, log on as the local user. Press Ctrl+Alt+Delete to open the Windows Security dialog box. Click Change Password, and then click Backup to launch the Forgotten Password Wizard.

Using Other Methods for Recovering Lost Passwords

If you don't have a Password Reset Disk and you don't know the password for an administrator account, you can resort to various hacker tricks to try to get back into your computer.

Password-cracking programs use a variety of methods to try to crack the Security Accounts Manager (SAM), the database in which password information is stored. The programs are most effective if you log on using a different user account (preferably one with administrator privileges), in which case they'll try everything: dictionary attacks; extracting password hashes from the SAM or, better yet, from memory; and brute-force attacks, where every possible combination of characters is tried. But some can work after booting from a floppy disk, after booting into another operating system (if your computer has multiple operating systems installed), or from another computer on the network.

If you need to recover a lost password (or you want to see firsthand how vulnerable your computer is to attack), try one or more of the following tools, which give an excellent perspective of how hacking tools work:

- Winternals Locksmith, a component of ERD Commander 2003 (*http: //www.winternals.com/products/repairandrecovery/erdcommander2002.asp*)
- Sunbelt Software NTAccess (*http://www.sunbelt-software.com/product.cfm?id=265*)
- ElcomSoft Proactive Windows Security Explorer, also known as PWSEX (*http: //www.elcomsoft.com/pwsex.html*)
- @stake LC 5, the latest version of L0phtCrack (*http://www.atstake.com/products/lc/*)
- Offline NT Password & Registry Editor, by Petter Nordahl-Hagen (*http: //home.eunet.no/~pnordahl/ntpasswd/*)
- Windows XP / 2000 / NT Key (*http://www.lostpassword.com /windows-xp-2000-nt.htm*)
- John the Ripper (*http://www.openwall.com/john/*)

Although some password-cracking utilities are used by and were even created by some rather unsavory characters, many such utilities (including those listed above) are from well-established software publishers and they serve a legitimate purpose: recovering a lost password.

We recommend that you try one or more of these programs, even if you haven't forgotten your password. The experience is a real eye-opener, and it might convince you that strong (very strong!) passwords are essential. (An important secondary lesson here is that physical security of your computer is paramount.) Figure 4-11 shows Proactive Windows Security Explorer in action.

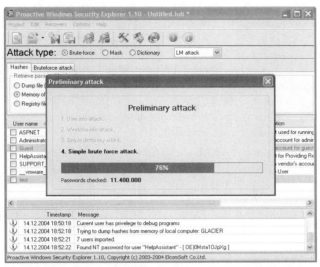

Figure 4-11. Programs like this one can use brute-force methods to try millions of combinations in short order.

You'll probably be shocked and amazed at how quickly these programs are able to successfully recover passwords. If you can get physical access to a computer and somehow log on, you can crack almost any password in less than a day. Most passwords take only a few hours, and weaker ones are revealed in minutes.

For more information about tools and techniques for recovering passwords, you'll find some excellent information at *http://www.password-crackers.com*.

Managing Passwords

Our discussion so far has focused specifically on Windows logon passwords. Indeed, a user's logon password is one of the most important to protect because with it comes access to all the user's certificates, network resources, and Internet passwords as well as access to a local computer and its resources. In other words, if your logon password is compromised, a malicious user instantly has access to virtually all the same resources that are normally yours alone.

However, passwords (sometimes in combination with a user name, sometimes not) are also used to control access to all kinds of information: network resources, Web sites, online accounts, and subscription-based data. The list goes on and on.

The cardinal rules of effective passwords—use a strong password and change it frequently—make entering and keeping track of your password for each account hard enough. But another commonly espoused rule—use a different password for each account—exponentially compounds the difficulty of managing passwords. The reason for this rule, of course, is simple: If you use the same password for all your accounts and it is compromised, the person who has your password has access to all your protected information. Rather than advocating strict adherence to this rule, however, we suggest a more manageable three-level approach:

- Use a *secure password* for your Windows logon and for any Web site or account that stores valuable financial or personal information. This would include bank and brokerage accounts, for example, as well as any e-commerce site where your credit card number or other sensitive information is stored. These passwords should follow all the rules for strong passwords detailed earlier in this chapter. Use a separate secure password for each account.

- Use a *private password* for accounts on sites where you shop or have a paid subscription but have not stored sensitive information. This password should be relatively strong, but because your personal financial well-being and privacy are not at risk if it's cracked, you don't need to go overboard. (The worst that can happen? Someone sees your shopping history or freeloads off your paid subscription.) You can reuse this password on any site that uses a secure server.

- Use a *throwaway password* for any of the numerous sites that force you to register and log on but retain no personally identifiable or valuable information. Reuse this password for all such sites.

This approach still forces you to keep track of a whole collection of passwords. Avoid the temptation to write them all down and stick them to your monitor! You should also avoid keeping the passwords in an unencrypted file of any type. If someone manages to find the file on your computer (or finds the floppy disk with the file's backup copy), you're in trouble.

A no-cost solution is to keep a master list of all your passwords in a text file or spreadsheet (or other document type if you prefer) and encrypt the file. Keep a copy of the file in a secure location away from your computer. (If you use the built-in Encrypting File System to encrypt the file, remember that the file is automatically decrypted when you—but not another user who finds the file on your hard drive—copy the file to a floppy disk. Therefore, if you use a floppy disk or other removable medium to store the backup copy, keep it under lock and key.) A better solution is to use one of the many free or low-cost password-management programs. One of our favorites is RoboForm (*http: //www.roboform.com*), a comprehensive solution that manages passwords, fills in Web forms with your stored information, and generates passwords on demand. (A solution like this makes it easy to use a different secure password for every site you visit—which is an even better solution than the strategy we outline above.) Another favorite is Password Corral, a terrific program from Cygnus Productions (*http://www.cygnusproductions.com /freeware/pc.asp*), in which you store a list of user name/password combinations along with descriptive notes; Password Corral scrambles the list contents using 128-bit encryption. You unlock the list with a master password of your choosing. (You definitely want a strong one here.) As shown in Figure 4-12 on page 122, this program optionally encrypts the on-screen display to prevent passersby from stealing your passwords.

Tip   Use Stored User Names And Passwords in Windows XP Professional

Windows XP has a feature called Stored User Names And Passwords that helps to manage logon credentials for various resources, such as a shared folder in an untrusted domain or a Web site that requires a password or certificate. When you attempt to connect to such a resource, Windows offers the logon credentials for that resource as saved in Stored User Names And Passwords. Only if that fails (either because the credentials are invalid or because you haven't previously saved credentials for the resource) does Windows prompt you to enter your user name and password. For this reason, users of computers running Windows XP face far fewer logon prompts than users of Windows 2000, which does not have a comparable credentials manager. By safely storing as part of a user profile the logon credentials for other domains, Web sites, and workgroup computers, Windows XP users approach the goal of a single sign-on experience.

Note that Stored User Names And Passwords offers logon credentials only to target computers that use an integrated authentication package, such as NTLM, Kerberos, or Secure Sockets Layer (SSL). Therefore, it works with Web sites that use SSL, but not with sites that require you to enter a credential through other means. Stored User Names And Passwords also works with .NET Passport.

You can save credentials in Stored User Names And Passwords in either of two ways: Select the Remember My Password check box in the logon dialog box, or enter credentials manually into Stored User Names And Passwords.

To manage your stored credentials, open Stored User Names And Passwords, as follows: If your computer is not joined to a domain, in Control Panel open User Accounts, select your account, and then click Manage My Network Passwords (in the task pane). If your computer is joined to a domain, in Control Panel open User Accounts, click the Advanced tab, and click Manage Passwords. Alternatively, on any computer, enter the command control keymgr.dll to open Stored User Names And Passwords. In the Stored User Names And Passwords dialog box, you can add, delete, or review credentials for various resources.

If you use Windows XP Home Edition, you can't add credentials (you can only delete or review credentials that Windows has added automatically) or store logon credentials for domain resources; the primary use of Stored User Names And Passwords in Home Edition is for .NET Passport credentials.

Chapter 4

121

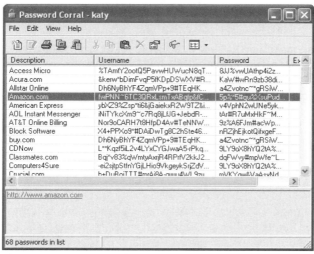

Figure 4-12. Password Corral optionally encrypts the on-screen display of user names and passwords so they can't be gleaned by passersby.

Configuring the Logon Process for Security

Logging on to a computer presents a barrier to entry for all users, authorized and unauthorized. In Chapter 3, we explained how the logon and authentication processes work. In this section, we show you how to customize the logon process to make it as easy as possible for legitimate users to log on while still barring users who shouldn't have access.

> For information about the logon process, including an introduction to the Welcome screen and the classic logon, see "Controlling the Logon and Authentication Processes," page 55.

Securing the Welcome Screen

The Welcome screen in Windows XP is wonderfully convenient; users can log on with a single click (and entry of a password, if their account requires one). But it also exposes user names and password hints to anyone who happens by. You might want to consider disabling the Welcome screen by following these steps:

1 In Control Panel, open User Accounts.
2 In User Accounts, click Change The Way Users Log On Or Off.
3 Clear the Use The Welcome Screen check box and click Apply Options.

With the Welcome screen disabled, you use the "classic" logon, which includes the Welcome To Windows and Log On To Windows dialog boxes. Note that disabling the

Welcome screen also disables Fast User Switching, the feature that lets you log on to another account without first logging off. This feature enables multiple users to be logged on simultaneously, leaving each user's programs running in the background.

If you want to retain the convenience of Fast User Switching, you can make the Welcome screen more secure in another way: by hiding certain user accounts so that they don't appear on the Welcome screen. You can use either of these two methods:

- You can modify the group membership of accounts you want to hide. Only members of the Administrators, Guests, Power Users, or Users groups appear on the Welcome screen.

- You can make a change in the registry. Use Registry Editor to open HKLM \Software\Microsoft\Windows NT\CurrentVersion\Winlogon\SpecialAccounts \UserList. Create a new DWORD value, setting its name to the user name of the account you want to hide and leaving its data set to 0.

To log on to an account that's not on the Welcome screen, press Ctrl+Alt+Delete two times to display the Log On To Windows dialog box—the same one that appears in the classic logon. Accounts that you hide in this manner aren't available with Fast User Switching, however, because the trick of pressing Ctrl+Alt+Delete twice works only when no one else is logged on.

> **Tip**   **Hide your user name from passersby**
> By default, when you set up a new user account in Windows XP, the account's user name and full name are the same. Therefore, anyone who sees the Welcome screen, which shows each account's full name, knows everyone's user name—the name they'd need to log on remotely. You can throw up a little smoke screen by changing the accounts' full names; that way, the accounts' first access credential (the user name) remains hidden from view. You can use any account-management tool to change the full name, but the easiest is probably User Accounts in Control Panel. When you change the account name in User Accounts, only the full name changes; the user name remains the same.

Securing the Classic Logon

The classic logon, which traces its roots back to Windows NT, requires you to press Ctrl+Alt+Delete to display the Log On To Windows dialog box, where you must enter your user name and password. To secure this process, follow these steps:

1   In Windows 2000, open Control Panel and double-click Users And Passwords. In Windows XP, open the Run dialog box and type **control userpasswords2**.

Chapter 4

2 To ensure that the Ctrl+Alt+Delete requirement is in place, click the Advanced tab and select the Require Users To Press Ctrl+Alt+Delete check box.

3 To disable autologon, click the Users tab and select the Users Must Enter A User Name And Password To Use This Computer check box.

Inside Out

Secure the classic logon by using registry entries

It's usually best to avoid editing the registry directly, particularly when an easier, less error-prone, and potentially less destructive method exists. But you might find it useful to change classic logon security through the use of a script, batch program, or .reg file that makes applying these settings a one-click affair. Both settings are controlled by values in the HKLM\Software\Microsoft\Windows NT\CurrentVersion\Winlogon key.

To require users to press Ctrl+Alt+Delete before logging on, set the DisableCAD DWORD value to 0, or set it to 1 to eliminate this requirement.

To disable autologon, set the AutoAdminLogon string value to 0. Delete the DefaultPassword string value if it exists.

Depending on your security needs, you might want to use some stronger measures to lock down the classic logon process even more tightly. You can make several changes through the use of local security policies. For details, see "Exploring Security Options," page 736.

Controlling Automatic Logons

The autologon feature lets you bypass the logon screens and go directly to your desktop when you start your computer. Step 3 of the procedure outlined in the preceding section disables autologon, and that's a good security practice in most cases. In some situations, however, you might want to use autologon. If your computer is in a physically secure location and you're the only one who uses it, you might enjoy the convenience of auto-logon. (Even in this situation, however, consider whether you want to allow a burglar to easily access your computer.) Paradoxically, if your computer is used in a public display area with virtually no physical security, you also might want to use autologon. Why? In such a situation, you can force users into a particular account rather than leaving them gaping at a confusing logon prompt or giving them an opportunity to guess passwords for other accounts.

The easiest way to enable autologon is to reverse the action described in step 3 of the previous procedure: On the Users tab, *clear* the Users Must Enter A User Name And Password To Use This Computer check box and click OK. Windows then asks for the user name and password of the account to be automatically logged on each time the computer starts.

Enabling autologon in this way makes several modifications to the registry's HKLM\Software\Microsoft\Windows NT\CurrentVersion\Winlogon key:

- It creates a string value named DefaultUserName and sets it to the user name you provided.
- It creates a string value named DefaultDomainName and sets it to the domain name of the specified user account (if the account is not a local account).

Chapter 4

● It adds a string value named AutoAdminLogon and sets it to 1. (A value of 0 disables autologon, but don't use this value alone to disable the feature. The DefaultPassword value should also be deleted, which happens automatically if you use Users And Passwords to disable autologon.)

> **Caution** Numerous books, articles, and Web pages—including many published by Microsoft—wrongly suggest that configuring autologon creates a string value named DefaultPassword and sets it to the password you provided. These sources go on to say that the password is stored in plain text and that anyone with registry access can read it. While it's true that you *can* use a DefaultPassword value (and indeed, if you set up autologon by manually editing the registry, you must use this value), the good news is that if you use Users And Passwords (User Accounts in Windows XP) to configure autologon, the password is stored in encrypted form in HKLM\Security\Policy\Secrets\DefaultPassword, a registry key that can't be viewed by any ordinary user accounts, including administrator accounts. Therefore, you should always use the Users Must Enter A User Name And Password To Use This Computer check box to set up autologon.

You can make other settings in the same registry key that further control the autologon process:

● Ordinarily, autologon works only for the first logon after you start the computer. After that logon, a user could log off and return to the logon screen. You can prevent that from happening by adding a string value named ForceAutoLogon. Set it to 1, and the system automatically logs on to the specified account after each logoff.

● By default, you can prevent autologon by holding down the Shift key during startup. The normal logon dialog box then appears, allowing you to log on to any account. If you want to ignore the Shift key override of autologon, add a string value named IgnoreShiftOverride and set it to 1.

● You can limit the number of times that autologon will work. This setting is normally made only by automated setup programs, but you might think of a reason to allow autologon a fixed number of times before disabling the feature. To do that, add a DWORD value named AutoLogonCount and set it to the number of times you want autologon to run. Each time the computer is restarted and autologon runs, the AutoLogonCount value is decremented by 1. When the value reaches 0, Windows changes the value of AutoAdminLogon to 0 (to disable autologon) and removes the AutoLogonCount value.

> **Caution** Be sure to leave yourself a back door. If you set up autologon and then lock it down with the additional registry settings mentioned here, you won't be able to log on using your (presumably more powerful) user account. As long as you can get to Registry Editor or Users And Passwords using the Run As capability, you're fine. But if you go to the extremes of also restricting access to Control Panel, the Run command, Command Prompt windows, and so on for the account that logs on automatically and repeatedly—you might find that your setup is *too* secure!

Tip Another way to configure autologon is with Tweak UI, a free program you can download from Microsoft. (The Windows XP version is available at *http://www.microsoft.com /windowsxp/downloads/powertoys/xppowertoys.mspx*; for the Windows 2000 version, go to *http://www.microsoft.com/ntworkstation/downloads/PowerToys/Networking /NTTweakUI.asp*.) Before you embrace this method, however, you should be aware of one security vulnerability: Although Tweak UI stores the logon password in encrypted form in an inaccessible part of the registry, the password is available in masked form in the Tweak UI dialog box. An attacker with ActMon Password Recovery XP (*http://www.actmon.com /password-recovery/*) or a similar tool for revealing masked passwords can view the password.

Logging On with a Biometric Device

For years, biometric security—retinal scans, voice identification, DNA sampling, and so on—has been the stuff of science fiction and futuristic action movies. With the recent introduction of inexpensive fingerprint readers from Microsoft, DigitalPersona, and other vendors, biometric security is now becoming mainstream.

With a fingerprint reader, instead of entering a user name and password at the logon screen, you press a finger to the fingerprint reader. It scans your fingerprint, compares it with its database of registered fingerprints (one of the first tasks with a new fingerprint reader is to register your fingerprints, as shown in Figure 4-13), and then invisibly enters the user name and password on your behalf. (Standard logon methods are also available.)

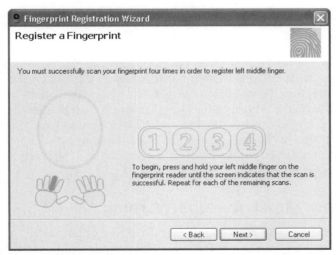

Figure 4-13. Register the fingers you'll use in lieu of entering your user name and password. Most people use just their two index fingers.

When different users have registered their fingerprints on a system, the fingerprint reader determines who is touching the reader and logs on the appropriate user account. With the Microsoft Fingerprint Reader (which is available embedded in a keyboard or as a stand-alone reader that connects to a USB port), you can use Fast User Switching in Windows XP. While one user is logged on, if another touches the reader, Windows switches to the other user—no clicks and no keystrokes required.

> **For more information about Microsoft Fingerprint Reader products, visit**
> *http://www.microsoft.com/hardware/mouseandkeyboard/productlist.aspx?fprint=yes*

You can also use fingerprint readers to enter logon credentials for programs and Web sites that require entry of a user name and password. When you visit such a site for the first time, touch the fingerprint reader and its software displays a dialog box in which you enter your user name, password, and any other required information. Thereafter, when you run the protected program or visit the protected site, press the fingerprint reader, and it enters your logon information.

Dispensing with the need to enter a user name and password at Windows logon and with Web sites and programs that require secure logon is a great convenience. Not having to remember (or look up) your password for each site and type it is a real time saver. Microsoft, in fact, bills its line of fingerprint readers as convenience devices—but specifically disclaims their use as security devices. That's because the fingerprint identification technology alone doesn't ensure security; it only ensures that a scanned fingerprint matches (or doesn't match) one in its database of registered fingerprints. But if the passwords that underlie your use of a fingerprint reader—that is, your passwords for logging onto Windows and onto secure Web sites—are not secure, then your information is still accessible to others. All they need to do is figure out your insecure password and they're in. Use strong passwords, and a fingerprint reader provides strong security. (In fact, because you never need to type your password, there's no reason not to make each one very long and very strong.)

DigitalPersona (*http://www.digitalpersona.com*) is the developer behind the Microsoft fingerprint readers, which are intended primarily for consumer use on stand-alone computers. Under the DigitalPersona and U.are.U brand names, the company also makes a line of fingerprint readers for businesses. These systems can store their databases of fingerprint and password information in a central Active Directory store as well as on stand-alone systems. Unlike Microsoft, DigitalPersona squarely positions its products as security devices. And the data backs them up: The incidence of false acceptances and false rejections is extremely minute.

Displaying a Welcome Message—or a Warning

Silly as it might sound, in some areas you might be required by law to warn people that efforts to log on by unauthorized users are illegal. Windows lets you place that warning right up front in a dialog box that appears before the Log On To Windows dialog box is displayed. (See Figure 4-14 for an example.) Whether required or not, it might be useful to display a message that warns users about the consequences of misusing company information or notifies them that their actions might be monitored. (You might also use this feature to offer a friendly welcome message!)

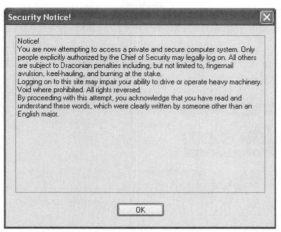

Figure 4-14. A user must click OK in this dialog box before the logon dialog box is displayed.

To create such a message, follow these steps:

1 At a command prompt, type **secpol.msc** to open Local Security Settings.

2 Open Security Settings\Local Policies\Security Options.

3 In the details pane, double-click Message Title For Users Attempting To Log On. (In Windows XP, the names of this policy and the one in step 5 are preceded by "Interactive Logon.")

4 Type the text that should appear in the title bar of the legal notice and then click OK.

5 Double-click Message Text For Users Attempting To Log On.

6 Type the text that should appear in the main part of the legal notice and then click OK.

> **Note** The legal notice dialog box appears only if you provide *both* message text and message title.

As an alternative to using Local Security Settings, you can make these changes by modifying two string values in the registry's HKLM\Software\Microsoft\Windows NT \CurrentVersion\Winlogon key. Enter the title bar text as data for the LegalNoticeCaption value. Enter the body text as data for the LegalNoticeText value.

As shown in Figure 4-15, you can also add text to the Log On To Windows dialog box through the use of two string values in HKLM\Software\Microsoft\Windows NT \CurrentVersion\Winlogon:

● The Welcome value appends text to the "Log On To Windows" message in the title bar. (For reasons unknown, the Welcome value does not add text to the logon dialog box in Windows XP.) The content of the Welcome value is also displayed

Chapter 4

in the title bar of the Windows Security dialog box—the one that appears when you press Ctrl+Alt+Delete while logged on to a system that does not have the Welcome screen enabled.

● The LogonPrompt value lets you add a message (or legalese text) above the User Name and Password boxes.

Text from the Welcome value

Text from the LogonPrompt value

Figure 4-15. Some simple registry edits let you customize the logon dialog box.

Setting Up Windows 2000 for Secure Logon

When you set up Windows 2000 on a new computer (and do not join a domain during setup), the Network Identification Wizard runs the first time you start your computer after setup is complete. Its default choice, as shown in Figure 4-16, is to configure autologon to bypass the requirements for pressing Ctrl+Alt+Delete and entering a password. It suggests the user name you entered as the registered user, for which the wizard creates a user account that is a member of the local Administrators group. It assigns the password you enter two times in this dialog box; if you don't enter a password, the account's password is blank. If you simply click Next without making any changes—a common habit when zipping through a wizard (especially when you're anxious to begin using a new machine)—Windows 2000 is configured to log on automatically at startup to an account with full administrative privileges and no password.

If your computer is already set up this way, you'll probably want to change the account's password and group membership, as well as the computer's autologon behavior, as described elsewhere in this section. When you set up your next computer, you can avoid these extra hassles by selecting Users Must Enter A User Name And Password To Use This Computer when this wizard runs. At the very least, be sure to enter a strong password, even if you plan to use autologon.

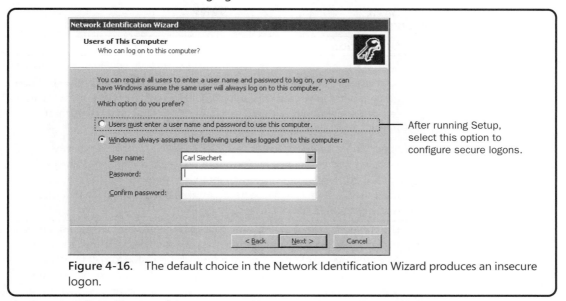

After running Setup, select this option to configure secure logons.

Figure 4-16. The default choice in the Network Identification Wizard produces an insecure logon.

Setting Account Lockout Policies

Account lockout policies enable you to lock out an account after an incorrect password has been entered too many times. Setting up this policy can be an effective defense against password-cracking attempts in which a user (or, more likely, a program) tries repeatedly to log on using different passwords.

When an account is locked out because too many wrong passwords have been entered, an administrator can unlock the account with Local Users And Groups: Double-click the user account and clear the Account Is Locked Out check box. At this point, of course, you should be on alert (unless you know that an authorized user simply forgot the password), for your system might be under attack. When you unlock the account, you should also select the User Must Change Password At Next Logon check box, thereby dealing a setback to the would-be intruder.

You set account lockout policies with the Local Security Settings console, which you can start by typing **secpol.msc** in the Run dialog box. To view or modify the account lockout policies, open Security Settings\Account Policies\Account Lockout Policy. Double-click a policy to set its value. Table 4-4 on the next page explains each policy.

Chapter 4

Table 4-4. **Account Lockout Policies**

Policy	Description
Account lockout duration	Setting a number greater than 0 (the maximum is 99,999 minutes, or about 69 days) specifies how long the user is to be locked out. After the specified time elapses, the account is unlocked. If you specify 0 (the most secure setting), the account is locked out forever—or until an administrator unlocks the account, whichever comes first.
Account lockout threshold	Specifying a number greater than 0 (the maximum is 999) prevents a user from logging on after he or she enters a specified number of incorrect passwords within a specified time interval. A setting of 10 lets an authorized user make a few inadvertent mistakes but doesn't give an intruder many chances to guess correctly.
Reset account lockout counter after	Use this policy to set the time interval (up to 99,999 minutes) during which the specified number of incorrect password entries locks out the user. After this period elapses (from the time of the first incorrect entry), the counter resets to 0 and starts counting again. A setting of 30 minutes provides good security against typical password-cracking attacks.

Adding Another Layer of Protection with Syskey

Syskey is a feature of Windows 2000 and Windows XP that uses a startup key to encrypt the Security Accounts Manager (SAM), the repository of password information. By default, the startup key is a machine-generated random key that is stored on the local computer.

For more information about Syskey protection, see "Safeguarding the Security Accounts Manager," page 60.

Because Syskey protection makes it pointless for attackers to boot into another operating system and steal a copy of the SAM or steal a backup copy (common exploits before the advent of Syskey), the default setup provides excellent protection for the password information in the registry. But attackers with physical access to your computer, high-powered password-cracking tools, and plenty of time could get your passwords. If that's a possibility in your situation, you might consider adding another layer of protection. Using Syskey, you can configure your system so that the startup key is not stored on the computer.

With this extra protection in place, an additional prompt appears before the logon sequence begins, as shown in Figure 4-17. You'll need to insert a floppy disk that contains the startup key or enter the startup key password (depending on which Syskey option you select) to unlock the password database and display the logon screens. Without the floppy disk or startup key password, no attacker has successfully retrieved user logon passwords from a computer that has been protected in this way.

Figure 4-17. Using Syskey, you can set up your computer to require a password before you can see the usual logon screen.

> **Caution** Bear in mind that this added startup requirement provides no additional protection once the computer is up and running. That is, if an attacker can reach your unattended computer while an administrator account is logged on, your passwords can be stolen. An attacker can steal the LSASS (Local Security Authority Subsystem Service) cache of hashed passwords and copy it to a floppy disk in seconds. Again, it comes down to physical security: Unless your computer is always guarded by a person or by a locked door, be sure to log off when you leave the computer and ensure that all user accounts are password protected.

To install this additional protection, follow these steps:

1 At a command prompt, type **syskey**. You'll see the following dialog box:

> **Caution** If the Encryption Disabled option does not appear dimmed, as shown here, you've got a problem. Someone has managed to disable Syskey encryption and probably has full access to your system.

2 In the dialog box, click Update. (Because Syskey protection is always enabled in Windows 2000 and Windows XP, the OK and Cancel buttons are effectively equivalent; both close the dialog box without making any changes.)

Chapter 4

3   In the Startup Key dialog box, choose one of the three options:

- **Password Startup.**   Enter a password, which you'll need to unlock the startup key each time you start the computer. For the best protection, the password should be at least 12 characters long.

- **Store Startup Key On Floppy Disk.**   Syskey generates a new startup key and stores it on a floppy disk. You must insert the floppy disk when prompted each time you start the computer.

- **Store Startup Key Locally.**   This is the default setting. By storing the startup key on the local hard disk, Windows can access it during startup without further intervention on your part.

4   Click OK. If you're changing *from* one of the first two options, provide the existing startup key password or floppy disk when prompted.

Caution   This protection is so effective that if you forget the password or lose the floppy disk with the startup key, you won't be able to start your computer. Write down the password and keep it in a safe location, away from the computer. Make several backup copies of the floppy disk and store them in different locations. If you don't have the password or floppy disk when you need it, the only solution is to use an Emergency Repair Disk (Windows 2000) or an Automated System Recovery Disk (Windows XP) to restore your registry from a backup created before you enabled startup key protection. Doing so, of course, obliterates changes that have been made in the meantime.

For more information about Syskey, see Knowledge Base article 143475.

Chapter 5

Securing a Shared Computer

Almost by definition, allowing more than one person to use a single computer creates potential security problems. If each party with access to the computer is completely trustworthy and has permissions commensurate with his or her level of experience, these security risks are relatively small. Most of the time, however, the users of a shared computer need to be protected from each other (and sometimes from themselves). As the responsible adult in charge of a computer used by the whole family, for instance, you certainly want to keep children from accessing your work files or installing untrusted software. In an office, you need to safeguard confidential information so that only authorized users can view it.

Setting up a shared computer—whether it's a stand-alone computer or a member of a workgroup—requires that someone take on the role of administrator and make the tough decisions about rights and permissions for each user. When you don your administrator's hat, your primary responsibility is to protect the privacy of each user's data and to secure the operating system so that an inexperienced user doesn't accidentally damage configuration details.

In this chapter, we focus on three distinctly different tasks:

- **Creating secure storage for each user's private files.**   Using the NTFS file system available in Microsoft Windows XP or Windows 2000, you can make certain that each user is able to save files to a location that is protected from access by any other user of the computer, including administrators.

- **Creating secure locations where users of the same computer can safely share files with one another.**   With this capability, users can collaborate easily on projects; it's also useful for securely and efficiently managing collections of data files that take up disproportionate amounts of disk space, such as music, pictures, video, and other digital media files.

- **Preventing users from changing a shared computer's configuration without authorization.**   This safeguard is equally important in small businesses and on home computers, where some users might not have the technical skills to install applications and adjust system settings, or the experience to leave crucial system files alone.

This chapter does not cover the ins and outs of sharing files with other users over a network (including the Internet). For the fine points of safely sharing information across a network, read "Restricting Network Access to Files and Folders," page 16.

Any discussion of file security in Windows begins, by necessity, with the user-based access controls that are a key part of the NTFS file system. Although the underpinnings of NTFS security are the same in Windows 2000 and Windows XP, the implementations of these controls differ greatly, thanks to a Windows XP feature called Simple File Sharing, which controls the default permissions for common data locations and provides a user interface that is dramatically different from its counterpart in Windows 2000. Before you even think about implementing user-based access controls, it's crucial that you understand how these interfaces work.

Security Checklist: Shared Computers

Follow the steps on this checklist to ensure that your file system and Windows registry are safe from unauthorized tampering:

- Convert all local drives to NTFS.
- On computers running Windows XP Professional, consider disabling Simple File Sharing to increase the range of security options you can exercise over files and folders.
- Use encryption to protect sensitive files.
- On computers running Windows XP (Professional or Home Edition), use the option to make files in your personal profile private.
- Educate users of a shared computer about safe techniques for working with the registry.

Using NTFS Permissions for Access Control

On volumes formatted with NTFS, every entry in the master file table—every file, folder, and subfolder—includes an access control list (ACL) that defines which users and/or groups have permission to access that object. Each individual item in the ACL is called an *access control entry* (ACE) and consists of the security identifier (SID) for the account it controls (a user, group, or computer, or a special account managed by the operating system) along with permissions that describe the type of access that account is permitted. Most of the time, of course, Windows hides the SID and shows you a friendlier name for the account in question—the name of a user or group, for instance.

> **Note** As we emphasize throughout this book, the NTFS file system is an integral part of the security infrastructure in Windows XP and Windows 2000. If you're still using the FAT32 file system for drives that contain sensitive data, we highly recommend that you convert those drives to NTFS. If you're not certain you should do so, we suggest that you reread "Use NTFS for All Drives," page 72.

The owner of a file or folder (typically the person who creates the item) has the right to allow or deny access to that resource. In addition, members of the Administrators group and other authorized users can grant or deny permissions by modifying ACEs (unless the owner of that resource has denied access to the Administrators group). In Windows XP, using the Simple File Sharing interface, your options for modifying permissions are severely limited. If you use Windows 2000 Professional, however, or if you disable Simple File Sharing in Windows XP Professional, you gain access to the full complement of NTFS permissions. (Users of Windows XP Home Edition must start their computer in Safe Mode to bypass Simple File Sharing.) With NTFS permissions, you can add individual users to the list of users associated with a file or folder and allow or deny specific types of file and folder actions. You can also assign permissions to built-in groups (the Administrators group, for instance) or create your own groups and assign permissions to them. As we'll explain later in this section, some permissions don't need to be explicitly defined but instead are inherited from permissions set in a parent folder.

When you first install Windows XP or Windows 2000 and choose NTFS as the file system, the Setup program applies default permissions to common locations. To view the permissions assigned to any file or folder under Windows 2000 Professional or Windows XP Professional with Simple File Sharing disabled, open Windows Explorer, right-click the icon for the object in question, choose Properties, and then click the Security tab. The resulting dialog box shows the list of users and/or groups with ACEs for that object; selecting an entry in the list reveals the permissions assigned to that user or group.

Figure 5-1 on the next page, for instance, shows the default permissions that Windows 2000 assigned to the user profile folder for the account with the user name Ed on the computer BOTT-2KPRO-VM. Because this folder was created the first time he logged on, Ed is the Creator Owner of the folder and has Full Control permissions for all files and subfolders within it. The System account and all members of the Administrators group also have Full Control permissions in this location, enabling any administrator to create, modify, and delete files and subfolders here. Any user other than Ed who is not a member of the Administrators group and tries to access files in this location will see an error message.

For commonly used storage locations where security is critical, Windows controls security by assigning different permissions to different groups of users. One such location is the %SystemRoot% folder, which contains system files, device drivers, security settings, service packs, and other essential files. Figure 5-2 on the next page shows the full permissions for this folder (in this case, C:\Winnt), with additional details about permissions that apply to subfolders; to see this dialog box, click the Advanced button on the Security tab of the properties dialog box. Figure 5-3 on page 139 shows the comparable dialog box in Windows XP.

Chapter 5

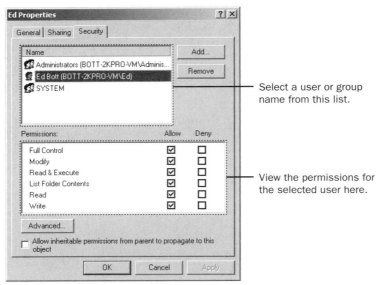

Select a user or group name from this list.

View the permissions for the selected user here.

Figure 5-1. The default NTFS permissions give each user full control over all files and folders in his or her profile; any other user who is not a member of the Administrators group is locked out.

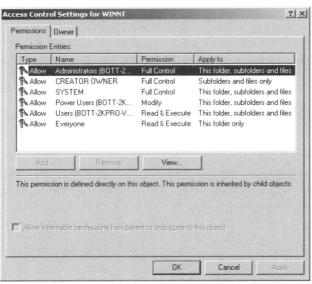

Figure 5-2. On a computer running Windows 2000, this dialog box displays the full list of access control settings for a file or folder.

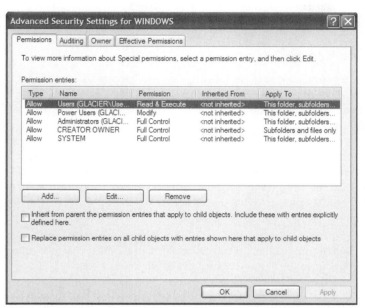

Figure 5-3. In Windows XP, the Advanced Security Settings dialog box includes a few additional tabs, but the basic functionality of the Permissions tab remains unchanged from the Windows 2000 equivalent.

In this example, the System account and the Administrators group have Full Control permissions over files in this folder and all its subfolders. Members of the Power Users group are assigned the Modify permission, which enables them to create new files and replace existing ones (when installing new software, for example) but does not allow them to delete subfolders or change permissions on existing files. Members of the Users group (also known as *limited accounts* in Windows XP) are given only Read & Execute permission for this folder and its subfolders, which effectively prevents them from installing any program or device driver that creates or replaces system files as part of its setup routine. Permissions for the Everyone group are the most limited. This group (which includes anyone logging on through the Guest account) has Read & Execute permissions for the %SystemRoot% folder only and is locked out of all subfolders. In Windows XP, the Everyone group is excluded altogether by default. Collectively, these security precautions prevent naïve or untrained users from inadvertently installing viruses and Trojan horse programs.

Chapter 5

Inside Out

Bring back default permissions

If you tinker with permissions in locations where system files are stored, you could end up with a system in which the overall security can't be trusted or easily verified. What do you do in that case? If you remember all the locations where you made changes, you can use the Security tab in the properties dialog box for each folder (or use the Cacls utility from a command prompt, as described in "Setting NTFS Permissions Using Command-Line Utilities," page 149) to restore the default permissions. If you're not certain which folders have non-standard permissions, try using the Security Configuration And Analysis tool to restore the default NTFS permissions using a Security Configuration template. (This solution also restores default registry permissions and user rights.)

> **Caution** This is a drastic measure that undoes any custom permission settings that might have been applied by applications, Windows updates, or patches. Use this technique only as a last-ditch alternative to completely reinstalling Windows.

1. After logging on as an administrator, go to any command prompt and type **mmc** to start the Microsoft Management Console.

2. Press Ctrl+M to open the Add/Remove Snap-In dialog box.

3. Click the Add button and choose Security Configuration And Analysis from the list of available snap-ins. Click Add and then click Close. Click OK to close the Add/Remove Snap-In dialog box and return to the MMC window.

4. In the console tree, right-click Security Configuration And Analysis and choose Open Database.

5. Enter a name for the file that will hold your security settings. Any descriptive name, such as Default Settings, is sufficient. Click Open to save the name you entered.

6. If the Import Template dialog box does not open, right-click Security Configuration And Analysis again and choose Import Template. In the Import Template dialog box, if necessary, change the displayed folder to %SystemRoot%\Security\Templates.

7. From the list of available templates, choose Setup Security.inf and click Open.

8. In the console tree, right-click Security Configuration And Analysis and choose Configure Computer Now.

9. In the Configure System dialog box, click OK to accept the proposed name for error log file.

Windows then applies the user rights, registry permissions, file permissions, and so on as they exist on a newly installed system with default settings.

> For more details about this procedure, see "Using Security Templates," page 761.

Basic and Advanced Permissions

Windows 2000 and Windows XP Professional let you control access to system resources by using a set of predefined basic permissions. Table 5-1 lists these basic permissions and describes the effects they have when assigned to a specific user or group.

Table 5-1. **Basic NTFS Permissions**

Permission	Effect on Users and Groups
Full Control	Gives the selected user or group full control over the file or folder. With Full Control permission, a user can do anything to an object—list the contents of a folder, read and open files, create new files, delete files and subfolders, change permissions on files and subfolders, and take ownership of files, for instance. Selecting this check box on the Security tab also selects all permissions.
Modify	Enables the selected user or group to read, change, create, and delete files but not to change permissions or take ownership of files. Selecting this check box on the Security tab also selects the permissions listed below it.
Read & Execute	Enables the selected user or group to view files and execute programs. Selecting this check box on the Security tab also selects the List Folder Contents and Read permissions.
List Folder Contents (folders only)	Available on the Security tab only for a folder, this option provides the same individual permissions as Read & Execute. The only difference is that this permission is inherited by subfolders but not by files within the folder or subfolders.
Read	Enables the selected user or group to list the contents of a folder, view file attributes, read permissions, and synchronize files. This is the most basic permission.
Write	Enables the selected user or group to create files, write data, read attributes and permissions, and synchronize files.

The final entry in the Permissions list, Special Permissions, is unlike all previous options in that you cannot select it directly to apply a set of predefined permissions. Instead, this option is shown as selected whenever the assigned permissions don't match any of the built-in basic permissions. To see details, click the Advanced button on the Security tab of the properties dialog box, select a user or group name, and then click the Edit button (Windows XP) or the View/Edit button (Windows 2000). Don't be misled by this long list of so-called special permissions. Whenever you adjust NTFS permissions, your actions ultimately result in changes to this list. Using the built-in permission options—Full Control, Modify, and so on—simplifies the process for you by setting predetermined groups of permissions from this full list. When you select the Allow check box next to the Read & Execute entry on the Security tab, for instance, Windows actually sets five individual permissions in response to the single click, as shown in Figure 5-4 on the next page.

Chapter 5

141

Figure 5-4. Assigning the Read & Execute permission to a user or group actually assigns these five individual permissions to the ACE for the selected object.

For all but the most unusual access control settings, the predefined basic permissions are perfectly adequate. In the unlikely event that you need to assign these permissions individually, your best strategy is to choose the basic permission that comes closest to the set of permissions you want to use. You can then add or remove special permissions as needed. Table 5-2 lists the full set of special permissions that are applied when you set each of the predefined basic permission options.

Table 5-2. Special Permissions Applied by Basic Permissions

Basic Permission	Special Permissions
Read	List Folder/Read Data Read Attributes Read Extended Attributes Read Permissions
Read & Execute *or* List Folder Contents	All Read permissions listed above Traverse Folder/Execute File
Write	Create Files/Write Data Create Folders/Append Data Write Attributes Write Extended Attributes

Table 5-2. **Special Permissions Applied by Basic Permissions**

Basic Permission	Special Permissions
Modify	All Read & Execute permissions listed above
	All Write permissions listed above
	Delete
Full Control	All permissions listed above
	Delete Subfolders And Files
	Change Permissions
	Take Ownership

Viewing and Changing NTFS Permissions

If you're willing to plunge into the sometimes confusing realm of NTFS permissions, you can significantly tighten control over who is allowed to access files and folders on a local computer. With Windows 2000 Professional, in fact, working directly with NTFS permissions is your only option for setting security on files and folders. With Windows XP, by contrast, direct access to NTFS permissions is blocked by default in favor of the easy-to-use but severely limited Simple File Sharing scheme; depending on the version of Windows XP you use, however, you might be able to disable Simple File Sharing and expose the Windows 2000–style NTFS permissions interface. (See "Turning Off the Simple File Sharing Interface in Windows XP," page 144, for step-by-step instructions.)

Using the full range of NTFS permissions, you can fine-tune access in the following ways:

- **Control access to files and folders on any NTFS-formatted drive.** This capability is especially useful if you use multiple volumes to store data. For instance, you might store all your digital pictures and home movies on a separate physical disk whose drive letter distinguishes it from the disk where your My Documents folder is located. Using NTFS permissions, you can restrict access to the separate disk so that you and your spouse can view and edit the files, but your kids are locked out of some subfolders and limited to read-only access in other locations. This option isn't available if you use Simple File Sharing, in which every user has unrestricted access to files and folders outside private user profiles.

- **Allow different types of access to different users or groups of users.** On a shared computer in a small office, you might set up an account for temporary workers that allows them to see only those files and folders they require to perform their tasks. You could assign a different set of permissions to your office manager, allowing access to accounting and payroll information while still restricting his or her access to sensitive legal documents.

- **Set custom permissions on any file or folder.** Using the full set of NTFS access controls, you can apply different permissions to files stored in the same folder. Permissions then depend on the account and group membership of the user trying to access those files. You might use this capability to grant access to a library of Word documents that you use as templates; by adjusting NTFS permissions for the Templates folder to limit all users except you to read-only access, you can protect your

Chapter 5

143

carefully crafted templates from being inadvertently wiped out by another user's changes.

> **Caution** Blindly experimenting with NTFS permissions when you don't understand how the various permissions interact can lead to unexpected and unwelcome results. If you're not careful, you can leave security holes that allow unauthorized users to view files, or you can inadvertently block your own access to files and folders that you use regularly. Working with the built-in permission sets—Full Control, Modify, and so on—is the safest strategy. If your security setup demands that you use special permissions, experiment first using a test folder filled with files that don't contain sensitive information. When you're certain you've worked out the correct mix of permissions, apply them to the folder containing your real working files and delete the test folder.

Turning Off the Simple File Sharing Interface in Windows XP

If you're running Windows 2000 Professional, the properties dialog box for every file and folder on an NTFS volume includes a Security tab where you can add or change access controls for individual users and groups of users. If you use Windows XP Professional in a workgroup or stand-alone configuration, this tab is normally hidden; to work with the full set of NTFS permissions, you must disable Simple File Sharing. If you use Windows XP Professional and your computer is joined to a Windows domain, the Simple File Sharing option is disabled by default and your options for setting file and folder permissions are essentially identical to those used in Windows 2000.

To disable the Simple File Sharing interface and use the full complement of Windows 2000–style file permissions, open any folder in Windows Explorer (the My Documents or My Computer folder will do) and choose Tools, Folder Options. Click the View tab, scroll to the bottom of the list, and then clear the Use Simple File Sharing (Recommended) check box.

> **Note** You must be logged on as an administrator to enable or disable the Simple File Sharing option.

If you use Windows XP Home Edition, your NTFS options are severely limited. The only way to view the Security tab for point-and-click access to the full set of NTFS permissions is to restart your computer in Safe Mode and log on as an administrator. The alternative, if you're willing to work from the command line, is to use the Cacls or Xcacls utility described in "Setting NTFS Permissions Using Command-Line Utilities," page 149.

You should disable Simple File Sharing only if you're absolutely confident that you understand the consequences your decision will have for how users can access files and folders shared over a network. You'll find a detailed explanation of the differences between Simple File Sharing and the classic sharing and security model in "Windows Sharing and Security Models," page 17.

How Simple File Sharing Sets NTFS Permissions

When you use security options in the Simple File Sharing interface, Windows XP acts on your behalf to apply a strictly defined set of permissions to selected objects while hiding the full details of what it's doing. If you know the basics of NTFS permissions, you can understand what's happening behind the scenes:

- **Default permissions (user profile).** When you create a new user account and log on for the first time, Windows XP creates an empty set of user profile folders and assigns Full Control permissions for the new user. In addition, Windows assigns Full Control permissions to the built-in Administrators group and the System account. Windows designates the logged-on user as the Creator Owner of these folders; the owner has full rights to work with the files and folders and to change the access controls on these files.

- **Default permissions (outside user profile).** When any user creates a new folder outside his or her user profile in the root of an existing volume (C:\, for instance), Windows assigns Full Control permissions to the user who created the folder, to the built-in Administrators group, and to the System account. In addition, users with limited accounts have Read & Execute permissions for the newly created folder. The permissions applied might be different in other locations for new subfolders created within existing folders, especially in system folders where special permissions are inherited. For instance, when you log on as an administrator and create a new subfolder in the Program Files folder, the Power Users group inherits Modify permissions in that subfolder, whereas Users group members have Read & Execute permissions only.

- **Private folders (within user profile).** Selecting the Make This Folder Private option removes the Administrators group from the list of permitted users, leaving only the user's account and the built-in System account on the Permissions list. (A member of the Administrators group can regain access by taking ownership of the folder.)

- **Shared folders.** As the name implies, the Shared Documents folder and its subfolders are available for use by anyone with an account on the computer. Members of the Administrators group have Full Control permissions for this folder and all its subfolders. Members of the built-in Power Users group (not available in Windows XP Home Edition) have Modify permissions, giving them all rights except the ability to change permissions or take ownership of files in this folder. Finally, those with limited accounts (members of the built-in Users group) have Full Control permissions for files they create, but Read & Execute permissions for all other files and folders. Thus, they can create new files in the Shared Documents folder and can read and open files created by other users, but they cannot modify or delete any files except those they created.

It's important to note that simply enabling or disabling the Simple File Sharing interface doesn't in itself adjust any permissions. You must move a file or make a folder private to actually change permissions. Also, Simple File Sharing options affect only those ACEs that are used for Simple File Sharing: Administrators, Users, System, and Creator Owner. Any other permissions (including those set from the command line or those carried over as part of an upgrade from Windows 2000) are unaffected.

Chapter 5

Setting NTFS Permissions Through Windows Explorer

This section assumes that you're running Windows 2000, or that you've disabled the Simple File Sharing interface in Windows XP Professional, or that you've started Windows XP Home Edition in Safe Mode. To view and edit NTFS permissions for a file or folder in any of these configurations, right-click the file or folder icon, choose Properties, and then click the Security tab. The dialog box that's displayed lists all the groups and users and the permissions set for each group or user.

If the user or group whose permissions you want to change is already listed here, you can add permissions by selecting check boxes in the Allow column or remove permissions by clearing boxes. Select check boxes in the Deny column only if you want to explicitly forbid certain users from exercising a specific permission. Deny access control entries take precedence over any other permission settings that apply to an account, such as those granted through membership in a group. If you want to completely lock out a specific user or group from access to a selected file or folder, select the Deny check box on the Full Control line.

Tip Avoid the Deny boxes

Although using the Deny options on the Security tab might sound like a great way to tighten security on confidential files and folders, we suggest that you resist the temptation to use this column. Deny permissions are typically used on large networks where many groups of users are defined, with different levels of permissions that overlap and sometimes conflict; in these circumstances, administrators use Deny permissions to exercise tight control over sensitive files in specific locations. Even for Windows experts, unraveling the interactions between Allow and Deny permissions can be a daunting task. On a computer shared by a few users in a home or a small business, you can almost always meet your security needs by selecting and clearing check boxes in the Allow column.

To set permissions for a group or user whose name isn't currently listed in the Group Or User Names box (the Names box in Windows 2000), follow these steps:

1 Open the properties dialog box for the file or folder and click the Security tab. (If you're using Windows XP Professional and the Security tab is unavailable, you need to disable Simple File Sharing, as explained in "Turning Off the Simple File Sharing Interface in Windows XP," page 144.)

2 Click the Add button.

3 In the Select Users Or Groups dialog box, enter the name of the user or group you want to assign permissions to for this file or folder. When entering multiple names, separate them with semicolons. The technique for adding names varies slightly, depending on which version of Windows you're using:

- With Windows 2000 Professional, you can select user or group names from a scrollable list at the top of the dialog box, as shown on the following page, or enter the user name (not the full name) directly.

Securing a Shared Computer

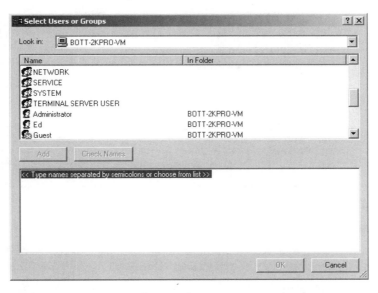

■ With Windows XP Professional, you can enter the user name (which might be different from the full name displayed on the Welcome screen) as shown here, or the group name. To choose from a list of all available users or groups (including special accounts), click the Advanced button and then click Find Now.

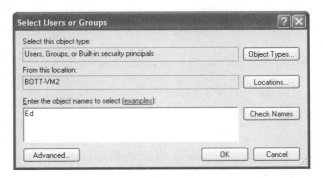

Note These instructions assume that you are adjusting permissions on a computer that is not a member of a Windows domain. In that case, Windows checks user and group names against the database for the local computer. If the computer is joined to a domain, the Select Users Or Groups dialog box automatically looks for names using the complete list in the domain directory, includes a full set of search tools, and enables you to enter full names instead of user names. If you want to assign permissions only for users with accounts on the local computer, use the Look In box in Windows 2000 to select the computer name; on a Windows XP Professional computer, click the Locations button and select the computer name instead of the domain.

Chapter 5

147

- Click the Check Names button. If the name you entered exists in the accounts database, Windows fills in missing details such as the computer name or domain name. If the name doesn't match an existing entry, you see an error message; in that case, correct the name and try again.

- Click OK to return to the Security tab and set permissions for the newly added user(s).

> For additional discussion of NTFS permissions in Windows XP, including instructions on how to work with special accounts, see the chapter titled "Securing Files and Folders," in our earlier book, *Microsoft Windows XP Inside Out, Second Edition* (Microsoft Press, 2005).

Troubleshooting

You can't change file or folder permissions

If you're unable to set permissions on a file or folder, look for the "symptom" in this list and try the following problem-solving techniques:

- **The Security tab is not visible.** If you're using Windows XP Home Edition, the Security tab is available only when you start your computer in Safe Mode. If you're using Windows XP Professional, in Windows Explorer, choose Tools, Folder Options and clear the Use Simple File Sharing (Recommended) check box on the View tab. If you see a Sharing tab only (Windows 2000 Professional or Windows XP Professional with Simple File Sharing disabled), open the My Computer window and check the properties for the drive; the most likely explanation is that the drive is formatted using the FAT32 file system, or you're looking at a CD-ROM, which uses the CDFS file system. The Security tab is visible only on NTFS drives.

- **You've made changes, but the check marks disappear.** This situation occurs in Windows XP and usually isn't a problem at all. If you set permissions and apply them to anything other than the default location—This Folder, Subfolder, And Files— Windows adds a check mark in the Special Permissions box. When you view permissions for a folder, this check box is at the bottom of the Permissions list; you have to scroll down to see it. You can view the applied permissions by clicking the Advanced button, selecting the user or group, and clicking the Edit button.

- **Permission settings are unavailable.** Check your user account rights. You must be logged on as a member of the Administrators group or be the owner of an object in order to set its permissions. These settings are also unavailable on objects stored in some protected system folders, including certain subfolders within the Program Files folder that are created during Windows Setup. If the selected object is inheriting its permissions from a parent folder you must remove the inheritance before you can set custom permissions.

Setting NTFS Permissions Using Command-Line Utilities

Cacls.exe, a command-line utility available in all versions of Windows XP and Windows 2000, provides another way to view and edit permissions. With Cacls (short for "Control ACLs"), you can view existing permissions on files and folders by typing **cacls** *filename* at a command prompt (where *filename* is the name of the file or folder whose permissions you want to inspect or change). You can also change permissions on files and folders by appending the appropriate switches and parameters to the end of the command line. To see the syntax for the command, type **cacls** in a Command Prompt window and then press Enter.

Inside Out

Use wildcards as a shortcut

The Cacls utility accepts conventional wildcard characters as arguments, including * and ?, making it easy to quickly view or change permissions on a group of files from the command line. Use *.* to apply the command to all files in the current folder, for instance. You can also narrow down the effect of the command by using wildcards with the *filename* argument; if you use the command **cacls *.doc**, for instance, followed by the correct switches, you can apply Read & Execute permissions to all Word documents currently stored in a specific folder for a specific group of users, while still allowing those users to open, edit, and save changes to other types of documents in that location. One little-known wildcard, the single period that stands for the current folder, is especially useful with the Cacls command. To see the permissions for the current folder without having to type its full name and path, add a space and a period (**cacls .**) after the command.

When you view permissions with Cacls, you see a brief list of ACEs for every file or folder that makes up the *filename* argument. Each ACE includes the user account name and a single letter for any of three standard permission settings: F for Full Control, C for Change (equivalent to the Modify option on the Security tab), R for Read (equivalent to Read & Execute permission). In addition, any permissions that are applied through inheritance from a parent folder get a separate listing in the Cacls output. Any other combination of settings from the Security tab or the Advanced Security Settings dialog box (Access Control Settings in Windows 2000) generates a list of individual special permissions that will send you scrambling to the Windows Help And Support Center for an explanation.

Cacls is useful for quickly determining the permissions for an object without having to drill down through multiple dialog boxes. If you're comfortable working in a Command Prompt window, it's never more than a few keystrokes away. If you're an administrator, especially if you're responsible for computers running Windows XP Home Edition, it's an indispensable part of your toolkit.

Chapter 5

> **Tip** Get a more powerful permission tool
>
> If you like Cacls, you'll love Xcacls. As the name suggests, it's an extended version of the basic utility included with Windows 2000 and Windows XP. With Xcacls you can set all file permissions that are accessible through Windows Explorer, including special permissions, on folders (directories) as well as on files. This utility is included in the Support Tools collection found on the Windows XP CD in \Support\Tools\Support.cab. Windows 2000 users can download it from *http://www.microsoft.com/windows2000/techinfo/reskit/tools/existing /xcacls-o.asp*. Microsoft also provides—but does not support—a version of Xcacls written in Microsoft Visual Basic Scripting Edition (VBScript); this version offers more options than Xcacls.exe. For details of its usage, along with a link to its download location, see Microsoft Knowledge Base article 825751.

In addition to viewing access control settings, you can also set permissions with Cacls and Xcacls. In fact, in Windows XP Home Edition, this utility provides the only way to adjust individual permissions without restarting in Safe Mode. Use the switches listed in Table 5-3 to modify the effects of Cacls.

Table 5-3. **Command-Line Switches for Cacls.exe**

Switch	What It Does
/T	Changes the permissions of specified files in the current folder and all subfolders
/E	Edits the ACL instead of replacing it
/C	Continues to work on additional files even if you receive one or more "Access Denied" errors; without this switch, execution stops on the first such error
/G *user:perm*	Grants the specified user access rights; if used without /E, completely replaces the existing permissions
/R *user*	Revokes the specified user's access rights (must be used with /E)
/P *user:perm*	Replaces the specified user's access rights
/D *user*	Denies access to the specified user

For the /G and /P switches, use one of the following four letters to replace the *perm* placeholder:

- F (for Full Control) is equivalent to selecting the Allow check box next to Full Control on the Security tab.
- C (for Change) is equivalent to selecting the Allow check box for Modify.
- R (for Read) is equivalent to selecting the Allow check box for Read & Execute.
- W (for Write) is equivalent to selecting the Allow check box for Write.

You can also use the letter N (for None) with the /P switch to remove access rights for the specified user.

Note that you can use wildcards to specify more than one file in a command. You can also specify more than one user in a command. For instance, if you've created a subfolder called Archives in the Shared Documents folder and you want Carl to have Full Control permission and Ed to have Read & Execute permission in that folder, open a Command Prompt window, navigate to the Shared Documents folder, and type the following command:

```
cacls archives /g carl:f ed:r
```

If you then decide to revoke Ed's access rights and give Read & Execute permission to the Administrators group, you can type this command:

```
cacls archives /e /r ed /g administrators:r
```

> **Caution** Just because you *can* set permissions with Cacls doesn't mean you *should*. It's easy to make a mistake that causes you to lose the existing permissions on a file. If you're using Windows XP Professional, there's usually no reason to use Cacls to set permissions. If you're using Windows XP Home Edition, try the Cacls command on a test folder first to ensure that your settings have the desired effect before you use this command on your actual working files.

Applying Permissions to Subfolders Through Inheritance

In addition to permissions that are set by a user or by a program (including Windows Setup), files and subfolders can *inherit* permissions from a parent folder. By default, any new permissions you assign to a folder are passed on to its subfolders as well. Thus, when you set permissions for your Accounting folder specifying that only you and your office manager have Full Control permissions for the contents of that folder, any new subfolders you create in that location inherit those permissions. You can explicitly remove inherited permissions from an object; you can also apply permissions to an object and specify that those permissions are not to be inherited by subfolders.

Under some circumstances, you might want to prevent permissions from being inherited by changing the inheritance options for a folder. In other cases, you might choose to break the link between a subfolder and the permissions it inherited from its parent folder, enabling you to explicitly define permissions for the subfolder.

To see the inheritance options for a selected folder, right-click the folder icon, choose Properties, click the Security tab, and then click the Advanced button.

With Windows 2000, an extremely subtle difference in the shading of the key icon used in each permission entry is your only clue that an entry is inherited. As you scroll through each item in the Access Control Settings dialog box, the text at the bottom discloses whether its permissions have been inherited from a parent folder or have been defined directly, as shown in the example in Figure 5-5 on the next page.

Chapter 5

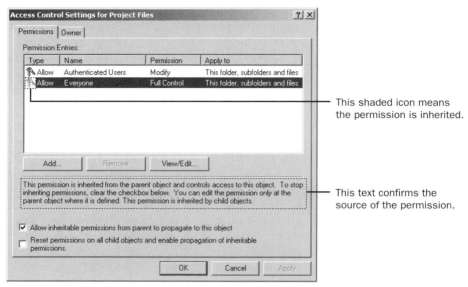

This shaded icon means
the permission is inherited.

This text confirms the
source of the permission.

Figure 5-5. On computers running Windows 2000, subtle color differences on the key icon to the left of a permission entry indicates that the permission has been inherited rather than defined directly.

By contrast, the Advanced Security Settings dialog box in Windows XP Professional makes it easy to identify inherited permissions. The Inherited From column in the Permission Entries list shows the parent folder from which a given set of permissions is inherited. In the example shown in Figure 5-6, the Users group inherits Read & Execute permissions from the ACL on the root folder of drive F, whereas the Modify permissions assigned to the Power Users group, designated as <not inherited>, have been applied directly on this folder.

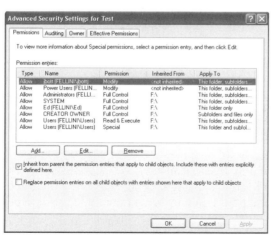

Figure 5-6. Before you can change or remove permissions inherited from a parent object, you must break the inheritance.

In this example, the inherited permissions make it possible for any user with a limited account to read the contents of the folder. If your goal is to lock out limited users and allow only members of the Power Users and Administrators groups to access the selected files, you must first remove the inherited permissions. To do so in Windows XP, clear the option labeled Inherit From Parent The Permission Entries That Apply To Child Objects. (In Windows 2000, the corresponding check box is labeled Allow Inheritable Permissions From Parent To Propagate To This Object.) As soon as you clear this check box, you see the following dialog box, which warns you to specify how you want to reset the permissions on the selected folder. (In Windows 2000, your choices are the same, although the accompanying explanatory text differs slightly.)

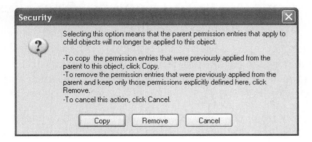

Choose one of the following three options:

- **Copy.** This option copies the permissions from the parent folder to the current file or folder and then breaks the inheritance link to the parent folder. After choosing this option, you can adjust the permissions to suit your security needs.

- **Remove.** This option completely removes the inherited permissions and keeps only the permissions that are currently assigned to the file or folder directly. In some cases, this results in an object that has no permissions and is thus inaccessible to anyone until the owner changes the permissions. If you click OK to make this change, Windows warns you with this dialog box:

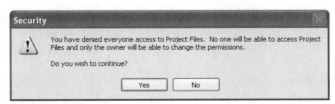

- **Cancel.** This option closes the dialog box and leaves the inheritance options intact.

When you remove inherited permissions from a folder, the folder becomes a new parent object. By default, any permissions you assign to this folder ripple down the hierarchy of subfolders and to files within those subfolders as well.

Normally, inheritance of permissions simplifies the task of administering security settings on a computer. If you designate a set of custom permissions for a folder, you can count

Chapter 5

on those permissions cascading down to subfolders and files stored in the same location and rest assured that that data is accessible only to users and groups who have permission. In some specific scenarios, however, you might want to apply two or more sets of permissions to the same folder for the same group, with each set of permissions having different inheritance settings. When you create a set of permissions for a user or group, you can specify that those permissions apply to the current folder, to files within that folder, or to subfolders. You can also choose any combination of these three options, setting one group of permissions that apply to This Folder and another set to Subfolders And Files for the same user or group.

What Happens to Permissions When You Copy or Move Files?

After you painstakingly set permissions on a group of folders to restrict access, you might be surprised to see that files you move or copy take on new permissions. Under some circumstances, in fact, double-clicking a file or folder icon can result in an "Access Denied" error message, even when the user in question has been granted Full Control permission in the current folder.

To understand why this problem occurs, you need to understand what happens when you move or copy files or folders from one location to another. During the move or copy operation, the permissions on the files or folders can change. Windows 2000 follows a strict set of rules when applying permissions during a move or copy operation. Windows XP applies the same rules when Simple File Sharing is disabled, but uses a different set of rules when Simple File Sharing is enabled.

When the Windows 2000–style rules are followed, you'll encounter the results listed here; note that the results depend on whether you're moving or copying the object and whether the destination is on the same drive (as indicated by the drive letter) or on a different drive:

When you copy a file or folder to an NTFS drive... The newly created object takes on the permissions of the destination folder, just as if you had created the object from scratch. The original object retains its permissions. This is true whether the destination is on the same NTFS drive as the original file or on a separate NTFS drive. You become the Creator Owner of the new file or folder, which means that you can change its permissions.

When you move a file or folder within a single NTFS drive... The moved object retains its original permissions and you become the Creator Owner. If you move a file from a highly restricted location on drive C to your Shared Documents folder that is on the same drive but whose ACL allows access to a wider group of users, the file remains restricted to the original, smaller group of users.

When you move a file or folder from one NTFS drive to another... The moved object picks up the permissions of the destination folder and you become the Creator Owner, as if you had copied the object to its new location and then deleted the original. If you move a file from a restricted folder on drive D to your Shared Documents folder on drive C, the file is available to everyone with access rights to the Shared Documents folder.

When you copy or move a file or folder from a FAT32 drive to an NTFS drive... The newly created object picks up the permissions of the destination folder and you become the Creator Owner.

When you copy or move a file or folder from an NTFS drive to a FAT32 drive... The moved or copied object in the new destination loses all permission settings because the FAT32 file system is incapable of storing these details.

With Simple File Sharing enabled on Windows XP, these rules change in a subtle but significant way. When you move or copy files or folders from a folder you've made private to any other location on an NTFS volume, the moved or copied objects take on the security attributes of the destination folder—in most cases, that means they're freely available to all other users. When you drag a file out of your private My Documents folder and drop it in the Shared Documents folder, for instance, that file is accessible to all other users of the local computer. Conversely, when you move a file from the Shared Documents folder into your private My Documents folder, it becomes a private file accessible only to you. It doesn't matter whether you move or copy the file; Simple File Sharing always adjusts permissions to match the destination.

In one particular set of circumstances, you might drag one or more files or folders from your My Documents folder to the Shared Documents folder, only to discover that other users are unable to access the file. This problem occurs if the following conditions apply:

- The drive that contains the Documents And Settings folder is formatted using the NTFS file system.
- You've made your entire user profile private (as you were prompted to do when you added a password to your account).
- You've disabled Simple File Sharing.

Because both locations are on the same NTFS-formatted drive, dragging any file or folder from your user profile to the Shared Documents folder moves the selected object without changing its access control list. As a result, other users can see the icon for the file or folder but are greeted with an "Access Denied" error message when they double-click it. Frustrating, isn't it? The solution to this dilemma is simple. If you've disabled Simple File Sharing, never *move* a file from your personal profile to a shared location. Instead, get in the habit of *copying* the file. The new copy inherits the permissions from the destination folder (Shared Documents) and is therefore available to every user. After copying the file or folder, you can safely delete the original from your private folder.

File permissions can behave unexpectedly in several other circumstances as well. For example, if you use the Move command from a command prompt when the source and destination folders are on the same drive but have different permissions, the moved file will retain its old permissions.

Chapter 5

How to Break into Files and Folders
When You Don't Have Access Rights

As we pointed out in Chapter 2, physical security is an absolute prerequisite for effective file and folder security. That fundamental principle means that anyone with time, a modest amount of computer smarts, and physical access to your computer can break the permissions you set on files and folders using NTFS-based access controls. In fact, any user who is a member of the Administrators group on your computer can gain access to your files and folders by taking ownership of those files. Mind you, we're not suggesting that you use these tactics to violate another person's privacy. But knowing how to forcibly take over ownership of a group of files can be useful in some perfectly legitimate circumstances—for example, if your Windows system files become corrupted and you reinstall Windows, you will be able to access the data in your user profile only by taking ownership of the file using your new security credentials.

Every file or folder on an NTFS volume has an owner, who in turn has the right to allow or deny permission for other users and groups to access the file or folder. As the owner, you can lock out every other user, including all members of the Administrators group. (That's how the Make This Folder Private option works—by removing the Administrators group from the ACL for a user's profile folder.)

One of your rights as owner is the ability to turn over responsibility for a file or folder to another user. You can accomplish that task directly by changing the owner of the object to another user, a strategy that works only if the other user is a member of the Administrators group. If the other user has a limited account, you can change the ACL for the object and allow the other user to take ownership of the object; the easiest way to accomplish this goal is to give the other user Full Control permission. In addition, any member of the Administrators group can take ownership of any file or folder, with or without your knowledge, although he or she cannot transfer ownership to another user.

Turning over the ownership of a file or folder makes sense when you want someone else to be responsible for setting permissions for that object. To ensure a smooth transition of power, use one of the following techniques:

- If you're the owner of the object, follow these steps:
    1. Right-click the file or folder icon and choose Properties.
    2. On the Security tab, click the Advanced button to open the Advanced Security Settings dialog box (Windows XP) or the Access Control Settings dialog box (Windows 2000) for the file or folder.
    3. Click the Owner tab. As the example in Figure 5-7 shows, this dialog box displays the user name of the current owner. You can transfer ownership to any user or group in the list, which typically includes the local Administrators group.

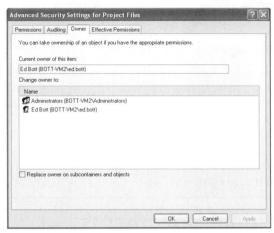

Figure 5-7. The list of names in the Change Owner To box includes all members of the local Administrators group.

4 If the selected object is a folder and you want your change to apply to all files and subfolders within that folder, select the Replace Owner On Sub-containers And Objects check box. (This option is unavailable if the selected object is a file icon.)

5 Select a name from the Change Owner To list and click OK.

● If you're an administrator, you can take ownership directly. Open the Advanced Security Settings dialog box (Windows XP) or the Access Control Settings dialog box (Windows 2000) for the selected object, click the Owner tab, and select your own name from the Change Owner To list.

● If you're not an administrator, you must first be explicitly granted the right to take ownership of a file or folder. Ask the current owner or any member of the Administrators group to add your account to the ACL for the file or folder and give you the Take Ownership permission. You can find this permission at the bottom of the list of special permissions available by clicking Edit on the Permissions tab of the Advanced Security Settings dialog box (Windows XP) or by clicking View/Edit on the Permissions tab of the Access Control Settings dialog box (Windows 2000). It's also included as part of the Full Control basic permission.

Ultimately, the ability of an administrator to take ownership of files and folders means that you cannot count on absolute privacy for any files stored on an NTFS drive unless you use additional means (such as encryption) to protect them. No matter how securely you lock up unencrypted files, an administrator can break the lock by taking ownership of the files. This is a brute-force solution, however, and it's not something that can be easily hidden. If you're concerned about security and you want to monitor changes in ownership of file-system objects, configure your system so that Take Ownership events in a particular location are audited. You'll find step-by-step instructions in "Auditing Security Events," page 773.

Chapter 5

Inside Out

Keep an eye on temporary files

Restricting access to the files and folders in your user profile is a good first step, but don't overlook other locations where copies of personal files can appear. Word processing programs, for example, often create temporary files or automatically save backups of documents as you edit. If these copies are stored in an insecure location, such as a shared folder used for storing temporary files, another user could browse through your work and uncover details that you would prefer remain hidden. Make sure you know where temporary files are being stored. For security's sake, this location should be in your user profile, where you can keep it secure and delete files as needed.

Locking Up Personal Documents

As personal computers insinuate themselves ever more deeply into the details of our daily lives, the need to protect personal data files becomes increasingly important. Even if you think your life is absolutely unexceptional, you might be surprised at the amount of confidential information stored on your computer—from medical records to credit card numbers to passwords that unlock your bank account. If you believe your personal files are no one else's business, make certain they're stored under a virtual lock and key. The exact procedures for securing their storage vary, depending on which version of Windows you're using.

Making a Folder Private with Windows XP

If you use either Windows XP Home Edition or Windows XP Professional, any files you store in your personal profile (including the entire contents of your My Documents folder) are normally accessible to any user who logs on to a computer with an account in the Administrators group. Because Windows XP assigns every new account to the Administrators group by default, the practical effect is that you cannot be certain your personal files are protected unless you specifically exercise the option to make them private.

Figure 5-8, for instance, demonstrates how Windows XP routinely makes each user's personal documents accessible to other users of the same computer. In this example, the current user has logged on using an account in the Administrators group. When she opens the My Computer folder, she sees a separate folder icon representing the My Documents folder for each user who has an account on that computer. As an administrator, she can open, delete, change, and add files in any of those folders.

By contrast, a user with a limited account sees only his or her personal documents folder in the My Computer window. Any limited user who tries to browse another user's personal files by opening Windows Explorer and navigating to that user's profile in the Documents And Settings folder will see an "Access Denied" error message. Thus, if yours is the only administrator account on a given computer and all other users have limited accounts, you can safely store your personal files in your My Documents folder, without

Chapter 5

having to worry about making them private. However, if your computer's local accounts database includes more than one account in the Administrators group, making your personal folders private is essential.

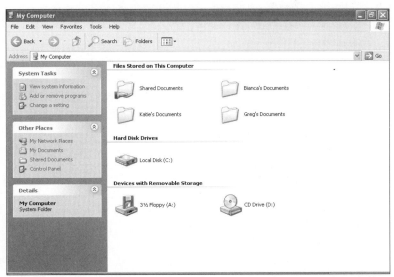

Figure 5-8.   Because Katie is logged on as a member of the Administrators group, she has full permission to work with Greg's and Bianca's files.

At first glance, protecting your personal files from unauthorized access is a simple, straightforward task that involves selecting a single check box. In practice, however, this option is deceptively complex. If you're not careful, you could end up with less protection than you bargained for. Here's what you need to know about using the Make This Folder Private option in Windows XP:

- The disk on which your personal profile is stored must be formatted using the NTFS file system. As we pointed out earlier, the Make This Folder Private feature performs its magic by adjusting NTFS permissions; it is therefore unavailable on a disk formatted using the FAT32 file system.

- The Make This Folder Private option is available only if you have Simple File Sharing enabled. On a computer running Windows XP Home Edition, Simple File Sharing cannot be disabled. On a computer running Windows XP Professional that is joined to a Windows domain, Simple File Sharing is not available at all. If your computer is running Windows XP Professional in a stand-alone or work-group configuration, Simple File Sharing is an option.

- Your user account must be protected with a password. Although you can choose the Make This Folder Private option after logging on with an account that has a blank password, the option is meaningless without a password to protect the account because any user can then log on using that account. If you attempt to make a folder private and your account is not protected with a password, Windows XP prompts you to create a password, as shown here:

- The Make This Folder Private option is available only for your user profile and its subfolders. You cannot select this check box for any other folder, including those in another user's profile.
- Making a folder private makes all files in that folder and all its subfolders inaccessible to other users. When Simple File Sharing is enabled, you cannot selectively grant or deny access on a file-by-file basis using the Windows 2000–style user interface. (You can work around this restriction in Windows XP Home Edition, however, if you're willing to boot into Safe Mode temporarily or tinker with the Cacls command-line utility; for details, see "Viewing and Changing NTFS Permissions," page 143.)
- You can reverse the decision to make a folder private by clearing the Make This Folder Private check box. Using this option resets the permissions on the selected folder, on all its subfolders, and on all files contained in that location.

Inside Out

Get easy access to profiles

To quickly view the entire contents of your personal profile in Windows Explorer, take advantage of the %UserProfile% system variable. To see the common locations that are available for all users of the current computer, use the system variable %AllUsersProfile%. Type either value (including the percent signs) in the Run dialog box or in the Address bar in Windows Explorer and press Enter to work directly with the selected profile; in a Command Prompt window, enter **cd**, followed by a space and then either variable. Alternatively, create a shortcut with either of these variables as the target and save it on the shared desktop (%AllUsersProfile%\Desktop).

In technical terms, the Make This Folder Private option performs a simple adjustment of NTFS permissions. Normally, for each user's profile on an NTFS volume, Windows XP grants Full Control access permissions to the user account that owns that profile, to the System account, and to the Administrators group. Selecting the Make This Folder Private option removes the access control entry for the Administrators group, leaving only the owner and the System account with access.

Securing a Shared Computer

The easiest way to make your entire user profile private is to let Windows XP do it. After you create a password for a user account, Windows XP presents the dialog box shown in Figure 5-9. Click the Yes, Make Private button to change the access permissions on your entire user profile.

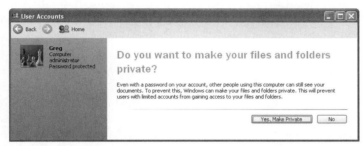

Figure 5-9. Choose the Yes, Make Private option to restrict access to all files in all subfolders in your user profile.

Don't be fooled by the text in this dialog box, however, which is at least misleading and arguably just plain wrong. The explanatory text claims that making your files private "will prevent users with limited accounts from gaining access to your files and folders." In fact, as we've pointed out, users with limited accounts are already locked out of your personal files and folders. Clicking the Yes, Make Private button will prevent *all* users, including those with accounts in the Administrators group, from accessing your files and folders.

> **Tip** **Restore the Make This Folder Private option**
> If you elected not to make your personal files private when you first assigned a password to your account, what should you do if you change your mind later? You could open Windows Explorer and browse to the Documents And Settings folder, which contains the user profile for each user who has logged on to the local computer. Right-click the icon for your user account, choose Sharing And Security, and then (if Simple File Sharing is enabled) select the Make This Folder Private check box. As an alternative, you can visit the User Accounts option in Control Panel and replace the password assigned to your account. Don't use the Change My Password option; instead, first choose Remove My Password and then create a new password. As the final step in the process, Windows XP checks the permissions on the root folder of your personal profile (typically C:\Documents And Settings*username*); if it detects that the Make This Folder Private setting is not turned on, it displays the dialog box shown in Figure 5-9.

For maximum security, you should protect your entire user profile. Because the Make This Folder Private setting applies to all subfolders, choosing this option automatically protects not only your My Documents folder but also the folders used to store personal settings and application data, including Microsoft Internet Explorer cookies and history files, Microsoft Outlook Express messages, data files on your desktop, and shortcuts to documents you've viewed or edited recently. Any of these locations can disclose personal information that you might prefer not to reveal; for instance, anyone who looks in the

Recent subfolder in your personal profile could see that you recently edited two Word documents called Employment Application.doc and Draft of Resignation Letter.doc. Even if such visitors were unable to open the files to which those shortcuts point (either because you deleted them or because they're stored in a protected folder), they could safely surmise from the document titles that you're thinking of leaving your current job. Protecting your personal profile can also prevent inadvertent damage from a nosy and careless user who accidentally deletes important files while poking around in these locations.

In one specific circumstance, you might decide to selectively protect individual subfolders within your personal profile. If your local computer's accounts database includes two or more trusted users who are members of the Administrators group and at least one limited user, you can selectively use private folders to creatively manage access. On a shared office computer, for instance, where the business owner and the office manager are each members of the Administrators group and temporary workers have limited accounts, you could set up three default locations for storing data files, each with a different level of access:

- Folders in your personal profile that you do not make private are accessible to other members of the Administrators group. If the business owner creates an Accounting subfolder in her My Documents folder and does not make it private, the office manager has ready access to that folder as well, with everyone else locked out.

- Folders in your personal profile that you make private are accessible only to you. Thus, the boss can safely store confidential correspondence with her attorney by creating a Legal subfolder in her My Documents folder and making that folder private.

- Files in the Shared Documents folder can be opened by any authorized user of your computer, even if they have a limited account. This is the appropriate place to store brochures, advertising copy, and routine correspondence for any office worker to view and edit.

If you're aware of the security risks and decide that you want to be selective about which folders you make private, follow these steps:

1 From the Run dialog box or Windows Explorer, enter the command **%userprofile%**. A window opens, displaying the files and folders in your user profile.

2 If the Application Data folder is not visible, choose Tools, Folder Options and select the Show Hidden Files And Folders option on the View tab.

3 Right-click the Application Data folder and choose Sharing And Security. Select the Make This Folder Private check box, and then click OK to change the permissions for that folder.

Securing a Shared Computer

4   Repeat step 3 for any other subfolders that you want to make private. Do not use this option on the My Documents folder, because that also makes all its subfolders private, defeating the purpose of this exercise. Instead, use subfolders within My Documents to have different privacy settings.

5   Double-click the My Documents folder and repeat step 3 for any subfolders that you want to make private.

Unfortunately, selectively applying the option to make individual folders private is cumbersome, and it has one serious drawback: There is no simple way to indicate which folders are private and which are public. If you choose this strategy, we recommend that you use a folder-naming scheme that clearly indicates which folders are private. For instance, you might add a single private subfolder in your My Documents folder, giving it a descriptive name such as My Private Files; you can then organize your private files using subfolders in that location.

Protecting Personal Files in Windows 2000

If you use Windows 2000, your personal files are stored by default in your user profile. Just as in Windows XP, the default permissions give each user full control over his or her user profile folders, with the System account and the Administrators group also getting Full Control permissions.

Unlike Windows XP, Windows 2000 does not include a one-click option that enables you to make your files private. You can accomplish the same goal manually, however, by removing the Administrators group from the ACL for your user profile folder, using the technique described in "Setting NTFS Permissions Through Windows Explorer," page 146.

Note Encrypt files for maximum protection

The ability of administrators to take ownership of files and folders makes NTFS access controls a less-than-foolproof solution for protecting truly sensitive documents. If you absolutely must store confidential information on a computer that other persons can access, make sure to encrypt it so that even if other users can gain access to the files, they can't read the contents. The Encrypting File System in Windows 2000 and Windows XP Professional offers excellent protection; third-party software utilities also allow you to scramble files so that only you can decode them. For a full discussion of this powerful capability, see Chapter 21, "Encrypting Files and Folders."

Sharing Documents Securely on a Multiuser Computer

Windows XP sets aside a group of folders that enable users to share documents with one another. The Shared Documents folder has its own icon in the My Computer window for all users who log on to the local computer. By default, the Shared Documents folder and its subfolders are located in the All Users profile (on a default setup, the path is C:\Documents And Settings\All Users). Members of the Administrators group have Full Control permissions for this folder and all its subfolders. Members of the built-in Power Users group (available only in Windows XP Professional) have all rights except the ability to change permissions or take ownership of files in this folder. Finally, those with limited accounts (members of the built-in Users group) can read and open files in the Shared Documents folder and can create new files, but they can modify or delete an existing file only if they are the file's owner.

On systems running Windows 2000, the C:\Documents And Settings\All Users folder exists, but its properties are subtly different. Under a default setup, you won't find an easy shortcut to reach this location, and its permissions are slightly more restricted, giving members of the Power Users and the Users groups the same limited rights for files created by other users.

For files and folders that you want to share with all users of a given computer, the Shared Documents folder is a suitable storage location. In other situations, however, you might want to create storage areas that are accessible to some but not all users, with differing levels of access for various users. You can accomplish this goal by managing NTFS permissions for the shared location. Carefully configured inherited permissions can be especially effective in an application of this sort.

For instance, say that several workers in your office share a computer on which they create brochures and other documents by using a desktop publishing program. All the members of the team have limited accounts, including your desktop publishing manager, Carl. You've set up a shared folder called Projects for use by everyone who has an account on the shared computer. In the main folder, you've stored a handful of templates that you want members of the team to use when creating new documents; you've also created a single subfolder for each project your team works on. Here's what you want to accomplish:

- Any user should be able to create a new document in any existing subfolder.
- Any user should be able to create a new subfolder within an existing folder, but you want to prevent users from adding new subfolders within the top-level Projects folder.
- A user should be allowed to change or delete any document he or she created.
- Users should be able to open any document in any subfolder that was originally created by another user, but they must save their changes under a new name, leaving the original file intact.
- Carl, your desktop publishing manager, should be able to modify or delete any project file created by any user. You don't want to make him a member of the Administrators group, however, because that would give him too much access to other data stored on the same computer.

To implement this scenario, start by giving the Administrators group and the System account full control over the folder, subfolders, and files. Next, give the Everyone group Read & Execute access to files within the top-level folder, with Read, Write & Execute permissions for subfolders. This allows users with limited accounts to open templates stored in the top-level folder but prevents the users from accidentally changing or deleting the templates. A limited user who tries to save a file in the top-level folder will see the error message shown here:

The more liberal set of permissions on subfolders enables users to create new files and modify previously saved documents in subfolders, but only if they created the files. Finally, you should assign Modify permissions to Carl.

Chapter 5

Creating Shared Document Shortcuts in Windows 2000

Although Windows 2000 doesn't include easy access to the Shared Documents folder through the My Computer window, as Windows XP does, you can add this feature in one of two ways. The simple solution is to create a shortcut that allows all logged-on users to access the All Users\Documents folder from the desktop or the Start menu. Begin by opening a Windows Explorer window and entering **%allusersprofile%\desktop** in the Address bar. Point to any empty space in the folder pane, right-click, and choose New, Shortcut. In the Create Shortcut Wizard, enter **%allusersprofile%\documents** as the location of the item and **Shared Documents** as the shortcut name. The resulting shortcut appears on every user's desktop. To add an identical shortcut to the Start menu, right-click the Start button, choose Open All Users, and use the New Shortcut Wizard (or copy the shortcut from the desktop to the All Users\Start Menu folder).

A much more elegant (but also more complex) solution is to customize the My Computer namespace, the section of the registry that controls which icons appear in the My Computer window. Doing so turns the All Users\Documents folder into a system folder, like other objects in My Computer. You could make the changes manually, by calling up Registry Editor and adding a half-dozen keys and accompanying values, but it's much easier to create a text file, save it with the .reg extension, and then double-click the file to import those values.

 You'll find this and other handy files on the CD that accompanies this book, in the Author Extras folder.

```
Windows Registry Editor Version 5.00

;CreateSharedDocsNameSpace-Windows2000.reg
;Creates a Shared Documents icon in the My Computer window
;for Windows 2000

[HKEY_CLASSES_ROOT\CLSID\{59031a47-3f72-44a7-89c5-5595fe123456}]
@="Shared Documents"

[HKEY_CLASSES_ROOT\CLSID\{59031a47-3f72-44a7-89c5-5595fe123456}\DefaultIcon]
@="C:\\WINNT\\system32\\SHELL32.DLL,42"

[HKEY_CLASSES_ROOT\CLSID\{59031a47-3f72-44a7-89c5-5595fe123456}
    \InProcServer32]
@=hex(2):25,00,53,00,79,00,73,00,74,00,65,00,6d,00,52,00,6f,00,\
6f,00,74,00,25,00,5c,00,73,00,79,00,73,00,74,00,65,00,6d,00,\
33,00,32,00,5c,00,53,00,48,00,45,00,4c,00,4c,00,33,00,32,00,\
2e,00,64,00,6c,00,6c,00,00,00
"ThreadingModel"="Apartment"

[HKEY_CLASSES_ROOT\CLSID\{59031a47-3f72-44a7-89c5-5595fe123456}\Shell]
```

```
[HKEY_CLASSES_ROOT\CLSID\{59031a47-3f72-44a7-89c5-5595fe123456}
    \Shell\Open Shared Documents]

[HKEY_CLASSES_ROOT\CLSID\{59031a47-3f72-44a7-89c5-5595fe123456}
    \Shell\Open Shared Documents\Command]
@="explorer /root,\"C:\\Documents And Settings\\All Users\\Documents\""

[HKEY_CLASSES_ROOT\CLSID\{59031a47-3f72-44a7-89c5-5595fe123456}\ShellEx]

[HKEY_CLASSES_ROOT\CLSID\{59031a47-3f72-44a7-89c5-5595fe123456}
    \ShellEx\PropertySheetHandlers]

[HKEY_CLASSES_ROOT\CLSID\{59031a47-3f72-44a7-89c5-5595fe123456}
    \ShellEx\PropertySheetHandlers\{59031a47-3f72-44a7-89c5-
    5595fe123456}]

[HKEY_CLASSES_ROOT\CLSID\{59031a47-3f72-44a7-89c5-5595fe123456}\ShellFolder]
"Attributes"=hex:00,00,00,00

[HKEY_LOCAL_MACHINE\SOFTWARE\Microsoft\Windows\CurrentVersion\
    Explorer\MyComputer\NameSpace\{59031a47-3f72-44a7-89c5-
    5595fe123456}]
@="Shared Documents"
```

(If you type this file yourself, note that the indented lines should be typed as part of the line above instead of starting a new line.)

This trick works by creating a globally unique identifier (GUID), which is the incredibly long string of characters that begins with 59031a47 and is used to represent the Shared Documents folder. If you choose to adapt this technique to add other items as system folders, be sure to change the GUID. (Changing the last six numbers will suffice.)

To create a Shared Documents icon on your desktop, edit the final entry in this file, replacing MyComputer with Desktop (or use the CreateSharedDocsOnDesktop-Windows2000.reg file found on the companion CD.) If you decide you want to remove the icon from your My Computer window or desktop, use the RemoveSharedDocsNameSpace.reg file, its companion registry file, which can also be found on the companion CD. This removal utility also can be helpful if you accidentally merge these registry entries into Windows XP and end up with two Shared Documents icons in your My Computer window! Don't be fooled by the status message it displays: Although it warns that you're about to add information to the registry, it does indeed remove the extra keys.

Chapter 5

167

Applying these permissions requires several steps that go beyond the basic permissions available from the Security tab. After logging on as an administrator, you need to remove any inherited permissions by clicking the Advanced button and clearing the option labeled Inherit From Parent The Permission Entries That Apply To Child Objects. (In Windows 2000, the corresponding check box is labeled Allow Inheritable Permissions From Parent To Propagate To This Object.) Next, use the tools on the Security tab to add Full Control permissions for the Administrators group and for the System account. Add the Creator Owner account (Full Control) and your desktop publishing manager, Carl (Modify), to the list. Finally, add the Everyone group to the list (Read & Execute and Write permissions).

All the permissions entered so far apply to the current folder and to all subfolders and files. To tighten permissions on the top-level folder, follow these steps:

1 On the Security tab, click the Advanced button.

2 In the Advanced Security Settings dialog box, select the permission entry for Carl and click Edit.

3 In the Permission Entry dialog box, change the Apply Onto entry from its default setting (This Folder, Subfolders And Files) to Subfolders And Files Only. Click OK to save the permission and return to the Advanced Security Settings dialog box.

4 Repeat steps 2 and 3 for the Creator Owner and Everyone entries.

5 In the Advanced Security Settings dialog box, click the Add button and enter Everyone in the Select User Or Group dialog box. Click OK.

6 The Permission Entry dialog box opens automatically. In the Apply Onto list, choose This Folder Only, and then select the following options: Traverse Folder/Execute File; List Folder/Read Data; Read Attributes; Read Extended Attributes; Read Permissions. Click OK to save the permissions. Note that a second entry for the Everyone group now appears.

7 Click OK to close the Advanced Security Settings dialog box.

Chapter 5

The resulting set of permissions should look like the one shown in Figure 5-10.

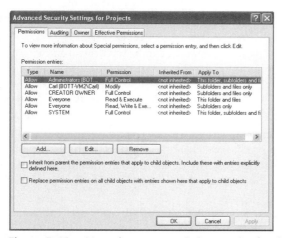

Figure 5-10. Note the two permission entries for the Everyone group; entering the second set of permissions requires that you select five individual permissions from the Advanced Security Settings dialog box.

Restricting Access to Programs

When you're wearing your administrator's hat, you might want to limit which programs users can run. Your motive might be productivity—in a small office, you might not want your employees to spend their day playing FreeCell or Pinball. Or you might decide to restrict access to programs in the interest of system stability. After all, once you have your computer running smoothly, the last thing you want is for someone else to install a poorly written program that drags down performance or causes unexplained crashes.

The good news is that you can prevent cooperative users from installing untrusted or nonsecure applications. The bad news is that an uncooperative user can almost always find a way to work around any restrictions you impose. Ultimately, your best chance for success is to educate users in the risks of installing unauthorized software.

If you're determined to protect your computer from unauthorized software, the most important step you can take is to give all users limited accounts. With this restriction in place, users can install only programs that meet Microsoft's "Designed for Windows XP" logo standards. Any application that tries to replace protected system files or tamper with registry settings outside the user's personal profile will fail to install. In general, users with limited accounts will have a difficult time installing any software.

In addition, you can try any or all of the following techniques:

- Remove program shortcuts from the %AllUsersProfile%\Desktop and %AllUsersProfile%\Start Menu folders.
- For programs that are installed in the Program Files folder (as the overwhelming majority of Windows-based applications are), change permissions on subfolders

Chapter 5

169

that contain programs you want to restrict. Remove the Everyone and Users groups from the list of available permissions, leaving only the Administrators group, the Power Users group (Windows 2000 Professional and Windows XP Professional), and any users who should have access to that program.

● Prevent users from opening a Command Prompt window, from which they can often launch a program. Look for the files Cmd.exe and Command.com, both of which are located in the %SystemRoot%\System32 folder. You can configure permissions on both of these files so that they can be executed only by administrators; or, if your users are relatively unsophisticated, you can simply rename the files.

● With Windows XP Professional only, you can use Software Restriction policies to define lists of programs that are either allowed or prohibited. This powerful but complex tool is described in more detail in Microsoft Knowledge Base article 310791, "Description of the Software Restriction Policies in Windows XP."

> **Note** For information about using Group Policy to restrict users, see "Exploring Security-Related Policies," page 730.

Restricting Access to the Registry

On a computer running Windows, every configuration detail is stored in a large, supremely organized database, the Windows registry. Most of the time, you make changes to the registry indirectly, using check boxes, drop-down lists, and other elements in the user interface, to ensure that you don't inadvertently enter the wrong data. Under some circumstances, however, editing the Windows registry directly is the only way to accomplish a particular task. To edit the registry safely, you need a basic understanding of how Registry Editor works, as well as a healthy respect for the havoc that even a simple misstep can unleash.

> If you need a refresher course on the structure of the registry and how to use Registry Editor, we recommend that you read the chapter titled "Editing the Registry," in our previous book, *Microsoft Windows XP Inside Out, Second Edition* (Microsoft Press, 2005).

You can prevent changes to individual registry keys and subkeys (but not to individual values) by editing the permissions for each such key. Registry permissions work like permissions assigned to shared resources or to files and folders on an NTFS drive; for each account or group, you can allow full control of a key, allow read access, deny access to the key, or set a bewildering array of special permissions. As we explain in this section, you can also lock out all access to the registry on a user-by-user basis.

> **Tip** **Handle registry permissions with care**
> When it comes to protecting the registry, your worst enemy is a user who knows just enough to be dangerous. Web sites and popular magazines are filled with tips that encourage would-be Windows experts to tweak the registry in search of better performance or to work around restrictions imposed by an administrator. If you're responsible for administering a computer and you find yourself doing constant battle with one such user, you might be tempted to lock him or her out of specific keys or branches using permissions. We don't recommend this strategy because of the risk that your restrictions will result in unintended consequences that add to your support woes. In a situation like this, you're much better off educating the user about the problems that registry edits can cause. If you can't reach a workable compromise, use the techniques we outline in this section to lock out the user's access to registry editing tools.

To adjust registry permissions, you must start with the correct tool. On a computer running Windows 2000, two registry editors are available. The easy-to-use Regedit.exe (also known as Registry Editor 5.0) enables you to search for keys and values and edit most data types. However, if you want to view and set registry permissions, you must run Regedt32.exe, with its distinctly old-fashioned interface. In Windows XP, this program is gone, replaced with Registry Editor 5.1, which starts up when you enter **regedit** or **regedt32** at any command prompt or in the Run dialog box.

From Windows 2000's Regedt32 program (shown in Figure 5-11), you can access the Permissions dialog box by selecting a key or subkey from the window that contains its hive and then choosing Security, Permissions.

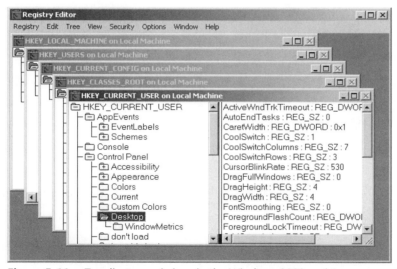

Figure 5-11. To adjust permissions in the Windows 2000 registry, you must use the Regedt32 program. Note that each main branch (or hive) of the registry appears in its own window.

On a computer running Windows XP, the new and improved Registry Editor utility lets you see the entire hierarchy in a single Explorer-style window, as shown in Figure 5-12.

Chapter 5

To view or change permissions, select a key or subkey, right-click, and choose Permissions from the shortcut menu.

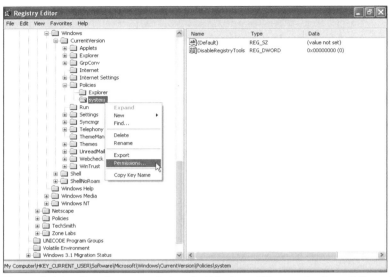

Figure 5-12. To adjust permissions in Windows XP, open Registry Editor, right-click the name of the key, and choose Permissions from the shortcut menu.

Both Windows 2000 and Windows XP display registry permissions using a dialog box that should be comfortingly familiar to anyone who has worked with permissions for a shared folder or printer.

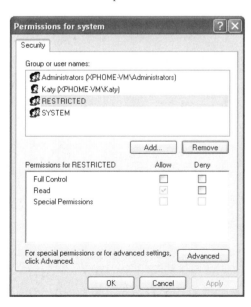

Inside Out

Protect the registry from suspicious programs

One noteworthy difference between the permissions assigned to a registry key and those assigned to files and folders is the presence of the Restricted security identifier (SID) in the Group Or User Names box for the HKEY_LOCAL_MACHINE, HKEY_CURRENT_USER, and HKEY_USERS keys. On all these keys, the Restricted SID is limited to Read permissions; by contrast, members of the Administrators group have full control over these keys, and the Creator Owner of the HKEY_CURRENT_USER key has full control over that key.

Although the Restricted SID is present on these registry keys in both Windows 2000 and Windows XP, this set of permissions has a practical effect only in Windows XP and is essentially ignored in Windows 2000. In Windows XP (Professional or Home Edition), you can launch a program by using the Run As command (right-click the icon for a program or shortcut and choose Run As from the shortcut menu). If you choose to run the program using the credentials of the current user, you can then select the Protect My Computer And Data From Unauthorized Program Activity check box. This option runs the program using your credentials but adds the Restricted token, which prevents the program from making any changes to the registry. This option is especially effective when you're trying out a new program that is untrusted; by selecting this check box, you can safely run the program and see whether it generates any error messages or displays any unusual behavior. Avoid using this option with setup programs, which are almost always designed to make changes to the registry and will surely fail given the permissions assigned to the Restricted SID.

Default permission settings in Windows XP and Windows 2000 do an excellent job of preventing limited users from damaging registry settings that affect the entire system. These users typically have Full Control permissions over portions of the registry that affect their own account (the HKEY_CURRENT_USER branch), enabling them to work with programs that install completely within their own profile. In addition, programs that use the Windows Installer for setup are able to install applications correctly, even when run from a limited user's account. Problems arise, however, when a limited user needs to install or run a program that wasn't written with Windows XP or Windows 2000 in mind. In that case, the user is likely to encounter an error message. The solution? Adjust permissions for specific keys and subkeys that affect the program, giving that user Full Control permissions over the necessary key, rather than the default Read permissions.

> **Tip** Monitor changes to the registry
>
> How can you tell which registry keys and values are being accessed by a program or process? For best results, use any of several third-party utilities that monitor the registry and report activities to you. A pair of utilities, Filemon and Regmon, developed by Mark Russinovich and Bryce Cogswell (*http://www.sysinternals.com/ntw2k/utilities.shtml#monitor*), help you identify exactly what's happening on your computer in real time, monitoring changes to files and to registry settings. SmartLine's Active Registry Monitor (*http://www.protect-me.com /arm/*), by contrast, takes before and after "snapshots" of the registry, allowing you to zero in on changes and experiment with different scenarios. Utilities such as these are essential when you're trying to keep an eye on what's really happening beneath the covers of your computer.

On a shared computer, you might decide that certain users should be denied all access to registry editing tools. To enforce the ban, you can use Group Policy, as described in "Using the Group Policy Snap-In," page 754. Unfortunately, this solution cannot be applied easily to a single user but instead locks out all users—you included. If you'd prefer to be more selective, you'll need to make a change to the registry for the user you want to lock out. Follow these steps:

> **Caution**   Be extremely careful when applying this setting. After you change this registry value, you will not be able to use Registry Editor to undo the change.

1 If the user whose access you want to disable has a limited account, change it to an administrator account. (You must have administrative rights to perform this change.) Then log on using that user's credentials.
2 Start Registry Editor by typing **regedit** at any command prompt.
3 Browse to the HKCU\SOFTWARE\Microsoft\Windows\CurrentVersion\Policies key.
4 Select the System subkey. If this key does not exist, create it.
5 Create a new DWORD value DisableRegistryTools and set it to 1 (1 = disable Registry Editor access; 0 = enable Registry Editor access).

The change is effective as soon as you exit Registry Editor and does not require you to log off or restart the computer. If you changed the account type in step 1, be sure to change it back to a limited account.

Now, whenever this user attempts to start Registry Editor, he or she will see the following error message. The same error will appear if the user attempts to merge a registry settings file (a text file with a .reg extension).

To undo this change, follow these steps:

1 Log on using the credentials of the locked-out user and create a shortcut with **regedit.exe** as the target.

2 Right-click the shortcut (hold down the Shift key when you click if you're working with Windows 2000) and choose Run As. Supply the credentials of an account in the Administrators group.

3 Browse to the HKLM\SOFTWARE\Microsoft\Windows NT\CurrentVersion \ProfileList key.

4 Select each SID under this key and look at the value ProfileImagePath. At the end of this string is the name of the user. Find the SID that matches the user whose access you're trying to restore.

5 Select the HKU*SID*\SOFTWARE\Microsoft\Windows\CurrentVersion \Policies\System key, where [*SID*] is the SID you identified in step 4.

6 Change the value for DisableRegistryTools to **0** and close Registry Editor.

Managing Removable Storage Devices and Printers

Despite an otherwise pervasive focus on security, Windows 2000 and Windows XP allow essentially unfettered access to hardware devices that are connected to a computer. If you want to prevent users from writing data to floppy disks, writable CDs, or Zip disks, for instance, you must physically lock the drive or use Group Policy, as explained in "Exploring Security Options," page 736. Unfortunately, the restrictions imposed through Group Policy are inadequate for preventing theft of files.

Restricting Access to Removable Storage Devices

The wide availability of portable storage devices such as USB flash drives (UFDs), MP3 players, and digital cameras provides a convenient method for someone who has physical access to your computer to steal your confidential files and escape undetected. If the device in question includes a signed driver, any user can plug in the device, allow Windows to install the driver automatically, and use it. (Users with limited accounts, however, cannot install unsigned device drivers.) These devices, which are small and hold gobs of data, can also hold malicious software that can be installed on your computer, either intentionally or inadvertently. Because they plug directly into your computer's USB port, firewalls and other perimeter defenses can't prevent the transmission of data to and from these portable storage devices.

Some companies have banned the use of portable storage devices to prevent the introduction of malware and the theft of corporate data. Such policies reduce the risk of inadvertent installation of Trojan horses and viruses, but are unlikely to deter someone with malicious intent. Some people have even taken the extreme measure of disabling their computers' USB ports by plugging them with epoxy—but that, of course, prevents the use of a growing number of essential peripherals.

With Service Pack 2 (SP2), Windows XP offers a partial solution: You can set a registry value that changes USB devices to read-only devices. This prevents their use for theft of files, but does nothing to prevent the introduction of malicious software. Nonetheless, it's a useful solution in some cases. To configure the USB devices as read-only, use Registry Editor to navigate to the HKLM\System\CurrentControlSet\Control\StorageDevicePolicies key. (Create this key if it doesn't already exist.) In this key, create a DWORD value named WriteProtect. Set this value to 1 to write protect your USB-based storage devices; set it to 0 (or delete the value) to restore the default full-function behavior.

An alternative registry tweak using a different registry value lets you disable USB flash devices altogether. To do that, use Registry Editor to open the HKLM\System \CurrentControlSet\Services\usbstor key. In that key, set the Start value to 4 to disable the USB Mass Storage driver. This setting doesn't stop the use of any currently connected UFDs, but prevents the driver from starting each time you insert a device thereafter. To return to normal operation, set the Start value to 3.

Using a similar tweak in different subkeys of HKLM\System\CurrentControlSet \Services, you can disable other removable storage devices. To disable the CD-ROM drive, open the Cdrom subkey; to disable the floppy drive, open the Flpydisk sub-key. In each case, set the Start value to 4 to disable the device, or set it to 3 to enable it.

By creating a custom administrative template, you can make these settings through Group Policy instead of delving into the registry. Microsoft Knowledge Base article 555324 provides the content of the template, which you save in a text file with a .adm extension. To incorporate the template into Group Policy, in Group Policy (Gpedit.msc) right-click Computer Configuration\Administrative Templates and choose Add/ Remove Templates. Add the template file you created. Then, to make its policies appear (in Computer Configuration\Administrative Templates\Custom Policy Settings \Restrict Drives, as shown on the facing page), choose View, Filtering and clear the Only Show Policy Settings That Can Be Fully Managed check box.

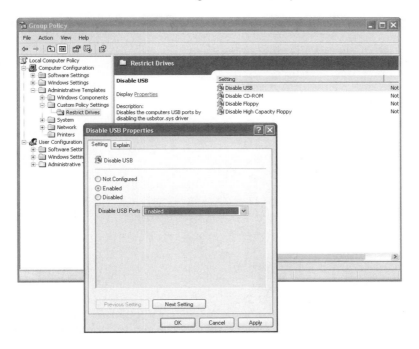

A more complete solution is provided by a utility such as DeviceLock (*http://www.devicelock.com*). This program runs as a service and lets you specify access rights for each of several device types, including floppy disk, hard disk, and CD-ROM drives; and USB, IEEE 1394 (FireWire), infrared, serial, and parallel ports. For each type of device, you can specify different access levels for different users.

Restricting Access to Printers

You can adjust permissions to restrict access to local printers in Windows 2000; in Windows XP, you might be surprised to note, this capability is available only if you disable Simple File Sharing. In Windows 2000, each printer has its own Security tab, similar to the one shown in Figure 5-13 on the next page, which enables you to specify which users can send jobs to the printer, manage jobs in the print queue, and manage printer settings. If you want only authorized users to use a particular printer—say, a color inkjet printer whose cartridges cost a small fortune—remove the Everyone group from the list of available permissions and assign Print rights on a user-by-user basis.

Chapter 5

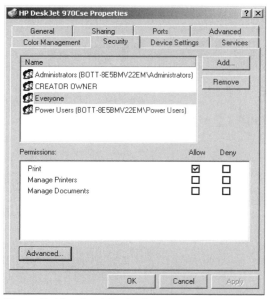

Figure 5-13. By default, the Everyone group has Print rights under Windows 2000. Adjust these permissions to prevent users from sending documents to a specific printer.

Chapter 6

Preventing Data Loss

Most of this book is concerned with keeping the bad guys at bay—viruses, Trojan horses, malicious hackers, spammers, password crackers, and other misfits who want to get into your computer. But a discussion of computer security is incomplete if it doesn't address the all-important issue of backing up your data.

Most computer experts agree that the three most important security safeguards are "backup, backup, and backup." A good backup provides a final safety net if an intruder or a virus gets past all your other defenses and destroys your data. And backups provide security against a host of other, perhaps more likely, threats to your data:

- **Hard disk crash.**   Hard disks are more reliable today than they were in years past. Some hard disk manufacturers, in fact, no longer include mean time between failures (MTBF) in their product data sheets because the number was getting ridiculously high: several *decades*, in most cases. That number no longer jibed with the manufacturer's stated component design life, which is typically five years for hard disks. The data sheets now often show an annual failure rate or annual return rate of less than 1 percent. Nonetheless, failures can occur at any time—often without warning—and can be triggered by a number of seemingly minor events, such as dropping or jarring the computer or the discharge of static electricity. If your drive happens to be that one in a hundred that dies, you'll be glad you have a backup.

- **Electrical surge and related power problems.**   While we were writing this chapter, this threat was driven home forcefully. On a calm sunny day in California (where lightning is rarely a problem), an electrical surge wiped out *all three* hard disks in a friend's computer. The surge might have been caused by a car hitting a power pole or a maintenance worker dropping a pair of pliers; we don't know. But the drives are now in hard disk heaven.

- **Fire, flood, tornado, hurricane, earthquake, and other natural disasters.** 'Nuff said.

- **Theft.**   Notebook computers are particularly vulnerable to being stolen because of their portability and because they're often out of your clutches in airports and other places with lots of strangers. Desktop computers are also high on the shopping list of burglars who prey on businesses, homes, and college dorms.

● **User error.**   It's all too easy to change or delete files inadvertently. You can make a mistake like this, for example, if you're in the habit of breezing through dialog boxes without reading them carefully: One day, without a thought, you click the wrong button, and your files disappear. Although you can restore deleted files from the Recycle Bin, some deletion methods bypass Recycle Bin protection. Deleted files that do go to the Recycle Bin don't stay there forever, either, because the oldest files are permanently deleted to make room for newly deleted files; you might not even notice that a needed file is missing until after it's gone from the Recycle Bin.

● **Faulty programs or device drivers.**   At one time or another, most longtime computer users have installed a new program or device, only to find that their computer no longer starts or operates properly. Attempts to uninstall the new item invariably leave some residual files or settings that continue to prevent the system from working. Fortunately, improvements in driver testing and qualification and in driver signing, plus the addition of the System Restore feature in Microsoft Windows XP, have largely relegated these problems to the historical dustbin. But you can still encounter trouble occasionally, and having a backup that lets you restore your system to a known working condition can be immensely helpful.

Security Checklist: Backup

Follow the steps in this checklist to be sure you have a complete and current backup of the information on your computer.

● Decide on a backup method. Back up selected folders and files, selected types of data, complete partitions, or any combination of those elements.

● Decide on appropriate media for the backup method you select.

● Delete data you no longer need.

● Using partitions, folders, or both, organize your remaining data so that files you use and modify frequently are in one area and seldom-changed files are in another.

● Devise a backup schedule and an automated way to implement it.

● Create a full system backup on a regular basis. If you use the backup program included with Windows, be sure to make an Automated System Recovery disk (Windows XP Professional) or an Emergency Repair Disk (Windows 2000).

● Create a backup of your high-use documents on a more frequent basis.

● Protect your backups with a password.

● Store crucial backups in a secure, off-site location.

● Learn how the data recovery process works, and periodically test the restore process.

Despite the experts' frequent admonitions to back up data, it's a well-known fact that most users do not have a backup plan and do not perform backups regularly (or at all). Some believe that they don't have any data worth backing up. However, nearly every computer stores something that's important to its owner. If it's not important financial, banking, or legal records, it might be a manuscript you're working on, family photos, a music collection, e-mail messages, or even the settings and top scores for your favorite game. In addition to the content of your document files, consider how much time you've invested in configuring your system and fine-tuning it to work the way you like; do you want to (or could you) go through all those steps again if your computer experiences an untimely demise?

In this chapter, we show you some backup strategies and tactics that make the chore tolerable, if not enjoyable. Without a significant investment of time or money, you can greatly improve your security and peace of mind by following these procedures.

Determining Your Backup Needs

What makes a good backup? Ideally, your backup method is one that ensures that you will never lose a file you need. In addition, if your hard disk is lost, stolen, or completely destroyed, a good backup makes it possible to get a new system up and running with minimal hassle. (That is, you won't have to locate all your original program disks, along with their patches and updates, and then meticulously rebuild your system from scratch.) If your backup system is *really* good, you'll be able to retrieve files that you deleted weeks, months, or even years earlier.

You can create good backups such as these in a number of ways. You have a wide choice of methods and media (removable disks, CD-R or CD-RW, tape cartridges, internal or external hard disks, network drives, and online storage, to name a few). What's best? The short answer: whichever system you actually *use*. It must be easy enough that it doesn't become an unbearable chore left for another time.

Because computer usage patterns, hardware capabilities, and resource constraints differ, no single method is best for everyone. In this section, we start with a list of questions that can help you determine your backup needs. We then introduce the basic building blocks of a comprehensive backup strategy so that you can put together a plan that works well for you.

Answer each of the questions in this section to identify the key factors that should be a part of your backup strategy.

How Much Data Do You Have to Back Up?

- Less than 700 MB
- Between 700 MB and 4.3 GB
- Between 4.3 GB and 20 GB
- More than 20 GB

These numbers might appear arbitrary, but they're not. Each dividing line corresponds to a common type of backup media. A single writable CD will hold up to 700 MB of data, and a writable DVD will hold approximately 4.377 GB (makers of DVD media often misleadingly label their products as having a capacity of 4.7 GB, but this is true only if you interpret a gigabyte as one billion bytes). If your backed-up data will fit on one CD

Chapter 6

181

or DVD, your choice of media is simple, and you just need to be sure that the backup software you select can write to your chosen media. Once the size of your backup set exceeds a single disc, however, your backup routine gets more complicated—if you decide to use multiple CDs or DVDs for backups, you have to be present during the backup process to manually swap media. If your data collection exceeds 20 GB—roughly five DVDs—you should consider an external hard drive as the backup medium.

What Is Your Most Important Goal?

- Being able to restore your system quickly after a hard disk crash or other system failure
- Being able to recover important working files if they're accidentally deleted or lost
- Creating a long-term archive of work-related data files
- Backing up a library of digital media files (music, pictures, video)
- Backing up saved e-mail messages, an address book, and Internet Favorites

Traditionally, backups include only data files. In the event of a hard disk crash, or if you replace your old computer with a new one, you'll have to reinstall Windows, reinstall all your software, and then restore your backed-up data files to get back to work. One option that can help you bypass this tedious process is to use drive imaging software, which takes a snapshot of an entire partition that you can restore in a single quick operation. We explain the tradeoffs involved in these approaches in "Designing a Backup Solution," page 188.

How Much Are You Willing to Spend?

- As little as possible
- A modest amount
- Whatever it takes to have an easy, reliable backup system

A reliable and effective backup routine doesn't have to be expensive. You can schedule regular backups of some or all files on any computer using only the Windows Backup program, which is included with all versions of Windows 2000 and Windows XP. If you want features not available in Windows Backup, such as data compression and the capability to save backup sets directly to CD or DVD, you'll need to pay for a third-party backup program. Online backup services typically extract monthly or annual fees as well, and of course you'll need to factor in the cost of your time, especially if you devise a complex system that requires lots of personal attention.

How Important Is Your Data?

- Nothing on your computer is that important. You're willing to reinstall all programs and start from scratch after a crash.

- You would be disappointed to lose some files, especially irreplaceable digital pictures and your e-mail address book.
- You paid 99 cents for each song in your music library and you have more than a thousand of them. Do the math.
- Your business would fail if you lost access to these files for an extended period of time.

The more valuable and irreplaceable your data, the more important the need for accurate backups. For mission-critical data files, the backup media need to be stored in a separate physical location so that they're not lost along with your hardware in a fire, flood, or other local disaster. Commercial online storage services take some of the hassle out of this process, if you're willing to pay for the convenience.

What Level of Hassle Are You Willing to Endure?

- You trust yourself to perform manual backups on a regular basis.
- You want to be reminded to perform backups, but you're willing to perform some manual tasks.
- You need a solution that is as automatic and foolproof as possible.

Using the Windows Backup program, you can schedule backups on a schedule of your choosing. You can also save settings and perform manual backups as part of your weekly or even daily routine. In either case, the most efficient strategy requires an initial investment of time and effort, after which you can kick off the process with minimal effort.

Organizing Your Data

Regardless of how much data you need to back up, you can streamline the process by judiciously deleting unneeded files and rearranging other files. Organizing your data in a logical fashion minimizes the amount of data that needs to be backed up. The more organized you are, the less time and disk space you need for each backup.

Eliminating Unnecessary Data

Begin by doing some housecleaning. Delete files that you no longer need (or archive them to CD or DVD) and uninstall programs that you no longer use. Use Disk Cleanup to empty the Recycle Bin and get rid of temporary files and other junk. (To start Disk Cleanup, right-click a drive in Windows Explorer, choose Properties, and then click Disk Cleanup. Or, more simply, type **cleanmgr** at a command prompt so that the Disk Cleanup dialog box appears.)

Chapter 6

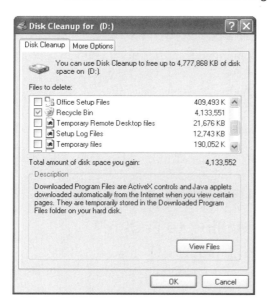

If you use Windows XP to burn CDs, clear the staging area. To do that, open the CD drive in Windows Explorer. If any files appear in the Files Ready To Be Written To The CD group, click Delete Temporary Files in the task pane.

Performing these housekeeping tasks before each backup avoids the wasted effort of backing up unnecessary data. In addition, by making a few one-time configuration changes, you can further reduce the time and space needed for your backups. Consider the following options:

- **Reduce the space allocated to the Recycle Bin.** By default, the Recycle Bin can grow to be 10 percent of the size of your hard disks' capacity. Particularly with large hard disks, this protection against accidental deletion is more than most people need—especially if they have a good daily backup routine. To reduce the maximum Recycle Bin size, right-click the Recycle Bin and choose Properties. On the Global tab (or on the tab for each drive, if you configure the drives independently), move the slider to the left.

- **Reduce the size of your Temporary Internet Files cache.** When you use Microsoft Internet Explorer, it saves files from the sites you visit so that they'll load faster when you revisit the same Web page or other pages that use the same files. By default, the cache is often ridiculously big—on a system with a large hard disk, the cache might occupy more than 1 GB of disk space. You can safely reduce the cache to 100 MB or less without any deleterious effects on performance. To set the cache size, in Internet Explorer choose Tools, Internet Options. On the General tab, under Temporary Internet Files, click Settings and then move the slider to the left.

- **Disable hibernation.**   Hibernation is a power-management feature that saves an image of your computer's RAM on your hard disk before shutting down the power; when you turn the power back on, hibernation quickly boots right to where you left off. The image is stored in a hidden file named C:\Hiberfil.sys, a file that matches your computer's RAM in size. Hibernation is a nifty power-saving feature, but if you never use it, there's no point in including that huge file in your backups, especially if you use disk-imaging software. To disable hibernation, go to Control Panel, click Performance And Maintenance if you're using Windows XP Category View, and open Power Options. On the Hibernate tab, clear the check box that enables hibernation. Doing so deletes Hiberfil.sys.

- **Move the page file to a partition that you aren't backing up.**   The page file is a large file used as virtual memory, but there's no reason to back it up. If you don't back up certain partitions (such as the one where you store backup files), consider using that partition for your page file. To make the change, right-click My Computer, choose Properties, and click the Advanced tab. Click the Settings button in the Performance box. In the Performance Options dialog box, click the Advanced tab (Windows XP only) and click Change. Select each drive and set the size of the page file for that drive.

- **Reduce the space allocated to System Restore.**   System Restore is a feature of Windows XP that saves restore points—mini-backups that let you undo configuration changes and restore your system files to a previous point in time. By default, Windows uses up to 12 percent of each hard disk's space for System Restore data. To reduce this amount, right-click My Computer, choose Properties, and click the System Restore tab. If your computer has only a single hard disk, adjust the slider in the Disk Space Usage box. If your computer has more than one hard disk, select each drive in turn and click Settings to adjust the maximum space used.

Arranging Your Data for Easy Backup

You should back up all the data that remains after you've removed or archived the files that are superfluous—but you don't need to back it all up every day. The files you actively work with day in and day out (primarily documents) have different backup needs than files that change rarely (such as program files) or documents that you no longer plan to change but need to keep for historical purposes. Your next step in developing an effective backup system, then, is to organize the data on your hard disks so that you can easily separate the files that need to be backed up frequently from those that seldom change.

You can do this by storing your frequently changed files in a separate folder or even a separate partition. To a great extent, Windows does this for you if you use subfolders of My Documents for all data files. Most recent applications store their data by default in My Documents or another subfolder of your user profile. (You can view the folders in your user profile by typing **%userprofile%** in the Run dialog box or in the Windows Explorer address bar.) Don't fight this organization; it's a good thing! For programs that don't use My Documents as a default location, move your documents to a subfolder of My Documents if the program allows it; otherwise, keep track of where the program stores data.

Chapter 6

185

> **Note** Most modern programs store data files and preferences in your personal profile. If you use any Windows-based programs that were written before 2001, they might store data or settings in a nonstandard place, such as a subfolder of the Program Files folder.

Many users prefer to store their frequently changing documents on a separate partition. Moving My Documents (and all its subfolders) is quite simple: Right-click My Documents, choose Properties, and click the Target tab. In the Target box, type a new location, or click Move to browse to a location. Remember that each user on your computer has a My Documents folder, so you must repeat this procedure for each user if you want to move all the My Documents folders to a different partition.

> **Tip** Use Tweak UI to move other folders
> To adjust the location of other folders normally created by Windows, such as My Music or My Pictures, use the Tweak UI utility. The Windows 2000 version is available at *http://www.microsoft.com/ntworkstation/downloads/PowerToys/Networking /NTTweakUI.asp*. If you use Windows XP, you'll find the correct version for your operating system at *http://www.microsoft.com/windowsxp/downloads/powertoys/xppowertoys.mspx*.

You can also redirect special folders, including the Desktop folder and My Documents, using Group Policy on a local computer or a domain. This capability is most useful when you want to redirect special folders to a shared folder on a network server, which allows you to back up data files for all users in one operation. For details, click Start, Help And Support, and search for the Help topic "Folder Redirection."

Even if you move the My Documents folder to another partition, your user profile and the profiles of other users will undoubtedly accumulate additional information that you should back up. (This data is commonly stored in the Application Data and Local Settings\Application Data subfolders of your profile.) Therefore, if you're intent on using separate partitions to isolate your changeable data, you should store the entire Documents And Settings folder on the partition to be backed up frequently. You can't just move the folder, however, because the registry is filled with references to that folder. The preferred way to set up profiles in a different location is to specify the location during Windows setup using the /Unattend switch. You can move the profiles folder after setup, but doing so is fraught with error and is not supported by Microsoft; in fact, the articles that explain how to do this specifically warn that possible consequences include "catastrophic system failure or an unstable computer." Nonetheless, you can find instructions for both options in Microsoft Knowledge Base articles 236621 (Windows 2000) and 314843 (Windows XP).

> **Tip** Archive your old documents in a different folder
> To keep the My Documents folder from becoming cluttered with files that don't need to be backed up frequently, use this location only for documents that you're actively working with. Periodically (perhaps before each full backup), move the documents you no longer use regularly to a folder that's not in My Documents—call it Archives or something similar. Your My Documents folder can then remain relatively small, and you'll need to back up the Archives folder only when you add files to it.

Choosing a Backup Location

Regardless of whether you use separate partitions for your different classes of data, you need a separate partition (or a separate physical disk) on which to save your backup images if you plan to use drive-imaging software to create comprehensive backups as described later in this chapter. Ideally, the partition should be at least as large as the rest of your partitions combined; this allows plenty of room for backups of all partitions as well as temporary files used while compressing the backup data. Through the miracle of compression, you can usually get away with a backup partition that is about one-third smaller than the largest partition you plan to back up, if need be.

Our strong recommendation is that you take the easy way out and use a separate hard disk drive as your backup location. Using inexpensive external drive enclosures and standard IDE drives, you can build your own external drive for a low cost; connect it to a USB 2.0 or IEEE 1394 (FireWire) port, and get right to work. Creating partitions is simple if you're working with a new, unpartitioned disk. The Disk Management console included with Windows has all the tools you need to create, delete, and format partitions.

If you choose not to add a new hard disk drive to your existing hardware configuration, your challenge is more daunting. Disk Management can't resize partitions on basic disks (the type most users have); the only way to divide an existing large partition into smaller partitions is to delete the existing partition (destroying all data stored there) and then carve the free space into two or more smaller partitions.

For complete details about using Disk Management, see *Microsoft Windows XP Inside Out, Second Edition* (Microsoft Press, 2005).

Third-party partition management tools can resize your existing partitions and create new partitions without destroying your data. Three popular programs of this type are Symantec's Norton PartitionMagic (*http://www.symantec.com/partitionmagic/*); Partition Manager, from Paragon Software Group (*http://www.partition-manager.com*); and BootIt Next Generation, from TeraByte Unlimited (*http://www.bootitng.com/bootitng.html*).

Ordinarily, partition-management programs safely modify your disk layout. But they do work with your data at a low level, and the publishers rightly recommend that you back up your data before you use the program. This leaves you with a Catch-22: You can't back up your hard disk until you create a backup partition, and you can't create a backup partition until you back up your hard disk. Rather than taking your chances that the partition manager will succeed, you'll need to make a backup using whatever tools are available. For example, you can use drive-imaging software to back up your existing partition directly to a CD-R. Then, after deleting the existing partition and creating new ones, you can restore the backed-up image.

Chapter 6

Designing a Backup Solution

Now that you've identified the broad outlines of your backup needs and reorganized your data, you're ready to put together a backup routine that builds on those requirements. The tools and techniques we describe in this section comprise the building blocks that you can use to satisfy your unique set of requirements. As we note at the end of this section, for most people a combination of these options represents the best backup approach.

Simple Backup Strategies

Are your most important files concentrated in relatively small "islands" of data? If all you need to back up is a relatively small collection of e-mail messages, financial files, letters, and spreadsheets, you might be able to get by with the simplest of all strategies: Copy those files to the medium of your choice. In some cases, you can find a menu option or a utility that does the work for you; or you can just open Windows Explorer and drag the files to the backup destination. If your files are well organized, the process should take just a few minutes.

You can use this technique by itself or in conjunction with more complicated backup solutions. You might decide, for instance, to back up your entire hard disk using drive-imaging software once a month, and on a daily or weekly basis you can copy your important files and settings to a safe location. In the event of a disk crash, you can restore the saved drive image and then replace the older data files with your most recent copy.

> **Tip** Use the Files And Settings Transfer Wizard
>
> Windows XP includes a Files And Settings Transfer (FAST) Wizard, which can help you transfer files and settings from your old computer to a new one running Windows XP. If you have Windows XP and if the program for which you want to back up data is supported by FAST, the wizard can be a helpful tool for an occasional impromptu backup as well as for moving files and settings to a different computer.
>
> To start the wizard, open the Start menu and choose All Programs, Accessories, System Tools, Files And Settings Transfer Wizard—or simply type **migwiz** at a command prompt. When you get to the What Do You Want To Transfer page, be sure to select the check box that lets you specify a custom list of files and settings. On the wizard page that follows, you'll need to select and then remove settings, folders, and file types that you're not interested in exporting. You'll find more details about FAST in *Microsoft Windows XP Inside Out, Second Edition* (Microsoft Press, 2005).

Backing Up Data for a Single Program

You might find it useful to back up certain data files each time you use a particular program. Because financial data is likely to be on anyone's "must back up" list, for instance, most accounting and personal finance programs offer to save your data files each time you exit the program. If you use any program whose data files are particularly important, look on the File menu for a Backup or Export command. If the program doesn't have export capabilities, you might be able to find an add-in for backing up its files and settings.

Saving E-Mail and Addresses

If you use Microsoft Outlook Express, you can back up your account settings, address book, and mail folders from within the program, although the procedures for doing so are cumbersome. Tom Koch's excellent Web resource, Inside Outlook Express (*http://www.insideoutlookexpress.com/backup/*), explains the details. (Microsoft offers similar information in Knowledge Base article 270670.) If you want to back up your newsgroup messages or program settings (such as signatures, message rules, view settings, blocked senders list, and so on), you'll need to dive into the registry, using the procedures outlined in Knowledge Base article 276511. A far simpler option is to use a third-party program such as Outlook Express Quick Backup (*http://www.oehelp.com/oebackup/*); Express Assist, from AJSystems.com, Inc. (*http://www.ajsystems.com*); or Express Archiver (*http://www.expressarchiver.com*).

Users of Microsoft Outlook can perform most backup tasks from within Outlook. Knowledge Base articles explain how: See 287070 for Outlook 2002 (part of Microsoft Office XP) or Outlook 2003, 196492 for Outlook 2000, 184817 for Outlook 98, or 168644 for Outlook 97. Here, too, using a special-purpose program makes the process easier. Microsoft offers the free Personal Folders Backup add-in for Outlook 2000 and later (*http://www.microsoft.com/downloads/details.aspx?FamilyID=8b081f3a-b7d0-4b16-b8af-5a6322f4fd01&displaylang=en*); for older Outlook versions or for more comprehensive backups, we recommend OutBack Plus, from AJSystems.com (*http://www.ajsystems.com/obp4.html*).

The Thunderbird e-mail program is a companion to Web browsers built on the Mozilla code base, including Firefox, and is also available separately. To back up messages and contacts stored in a Thunderbird e-mail profile, use the MozBackup utility (*http://mozbackup.jasnapaka.com*).

If Eudora is your e-mail program of choice, check out Eazy Backup – Eudora, a shareware program from AJSystems.com that backs up all or selected messages into a compressed file. (Eudora saves e-mail messages as individual plain-text files, which can chew up large amounts of disk space if left uncompressed.) This utility also backs up Eudora's system files and file attachments. Details are at *http://www.ajsystems.com/ezb.html*.

Saving Microsoft Office Settings

As you use Microsoft Office, it creates a profile—a collection of settings that includes your Office program preferences and options, custom dictionaries, custom templates, AutoCorrect lists, and AutoFormat lists. These settings are scattered across various files and registry entries; finding them and backing them up manually is a real chore. Microsoft has a solution: the Save My Settings Wizard. This wizard is included with Office 2003 and Office XP; users of Office 2000 can use the Microsoft Office 2000 Profile Wizard, which is described in Knowledge Base article 816003.

Chapter 6

To run the wizard, open the Start menu and choose Programs, Microsoft Office Tools, Save My Settings Wizard. The wizard backs up your Office profile to a file. You use the same wizard to restore your settings, either to the same computer or to another. (This makes it easy to configure Office on multiple computers.)

For information about backing up a Microsoft FrontPage Web to CD-R, see Knowledge Base article 825447 (FrontPage 2003), 310511 (FrontPage 2002), or 315508 (FrontPage 2000).

Backing Up Selected Folders and Files

The traditional method for backing up a system is to specify certain folders and files to be backed up and then copy them to a backup location. You apply this basic concept whether you use Windows Backup (the backup program included with Windows), command-line utilities such as Xcopy, or third-party backup solutions. Depending on the program you choose for backups, you can use a variety of criteria to specify the files to be backed up, including the following:

- File name
- Location in the folder hierarchy
- File modification date
- Whether a file has been backed up before
- Other file attributes, including whether the file is a hidden file or a system file
- Whether a file already exists in the backup location

The general strategy for doing file backups is to periodically perform a full backup of everything on your computer's hard disks. If you use your computer all day, every day, you'll probably want to schedule full backups to occur weekly; casual computer users might choose to perform a full backup only once a month or so. Then, on a more frequent basis (typically every day if you use your computer constantly), you perform a selective backup of files that have changed since the last full backup. Later in this chapter, we explain how to perform these tasks using Windows Backup.

Tip   Establish and follow a schedule

A key component of a successful backup strategy is to establish and observe a regular schedule. The frequency of your schedule depends on the type of work you do with your computer. As noted, some users will want to perform full backups weekly with daily interim backups, whereas those who use their computers infrequently or change only a few files might be adequately protected with a monthly/weekly schedule. To ensure that the schedule is followed, use the scheduling feature in your backup program or create a Scheduled Task in Windows.

Chapter 6

Preventing Data Loss

You can find a program for backing up selected files that works with just about any type of media, including the following:

- **Floppy disks.**   With a capacity of only 1.44 MB, floppy disks are practically useless for serious backups of a computer running Windows XP or Windows 2000. (The operating system files alone would occupy several hundred floppy disks, and a full backup would take days.) But in a pinch, if you have no alternative, they can be useful for backing up a handful of key files.

- **USB flash drives ("memory keys").**   These portable devices are typically the size of a house key; remove the protective cap, plug the connector into an available USB port, and Windows recognizes the flash RAM on the device as a new drive. As we write this chapter, 1-GB flash drives have just begun to appear on the market at reasonable prices; lower-capacity devices (256 MB and 512 MB) are relatively inexpensive. Their best use is as a way to transfer files between computers. For instance, you might copy files from an office computer onto a flash drive so you can transfer them onto a computer at home.

- **High-capacity floppy disks.**   Zip disks (available in 100 MB, 250 MB, and 750 MB capacities) and Jaz disks (available in 1 GB and 2 GB capacities), both from Iomega Corporation (*http://www.iomega.com*), as well as other high-capacity removable magnetic disks are well suited for interim backups, but they are generally too costly (and too slow) for full backups. These types of media have fallen out of favor in recent years as the cost of hard disks has plummeted and as writable CD and DVD technology has become more widespread.

- **Magneto-optic (MO) discs.**   MO discs are available with capacities ranging from about 128 MB to roughly 20 GB.

- **Tape.**   Magnetic tape cartridges for data backup come in a variety of formats and capacities. In the 1990s, tape was the backup medium of choice for corporate networks and for conscientious home users. In recent years, however, hard disk capacity has grown quickly, outpacing that of tape cartridges and drives. Nowadays, most tape drives that cost less than the computer in which they're installed use tapes that hold only a fraction of the computer's hard disk data. Performing a full backup is a slow process and can't be performed unattended because you must keep feeding in new tape cartridges.

- **Hard disk.**   Backing up to another hard disk with adequate free space is often the most convenient method because your backups can run unattended; you don't have to stand by to swap media as each tape or disk fills up. (As you'll see later in this chapter, backing up to a hard disk is, in fact, the method that we recommend—preferably as an intermediate stop on the way to writable CD or DVD media.) An internal hard disk (if it's a separate disk and not a separate partition on the same disk) can provide protection against data loss as the result of hard disk crashes, viruses, and accidental deletion, but it's useless against the many other threats to your data (power problems, theft, natural disaster, and so on). External hard disks that connect to your PC using USB 2.0 or IEEE 1394 (FireWire) ports are relatively inexpensive and versatile. The biggest disadvantage of hard disks is that they are rather fragile devices; throwing them in the trunk of your car or packing them in checked baggage increases the risk that a shock will damage the drive's innards and render its contents unreadable.

- **CD-R, CD-RW, and DVD+/-R/RW.**   Because the price of drives and media is so low, writable CDs and DVDs have become the backup media of choice for many users. In general, this type of media provides the least expensive backups overall. And they offer another benefit: they can be used for long-term archival storage. If you back up to reusable media (such as tape), you'll be able to go back, at most, a few months to retrieve old files (unless you buy additional expensive tape cartridges or other media for archiving). The biggest drawback to CD media is their capacity (only about 700 MB); it can take a stack of CDs to perform a full backup of a large hard disk. Writable DVD media, which can hold 4.377 GB of data per disk, are a much better choice if your goal is to back up a collection of digital media files. New DVD writable formats and media will provide capacities of 8.5 GB and 9.4 GB.

> **Note**   Not all backup programs support all media types. Windows Backup, for example, cannot back up directly to CD or DVD media. (We explain a workaround later in the chapter: Back up to a hard disk, ensure that your backup files are no larger than the CD or DVD capacity, and burn the backups in a separate operation.) If you're committed to a particular backup medium, be sure that the backup program you choose supports that medium.

- **Web-based storage.**   A number of companies allow you to back up your files over the Internet. Some companies provide a backup program that interfaces with the Internet storage location (for example, SwapDrive Backup, at *http://www.swapdrive.com*); others (such as Xdrive, at *http://www.xdrive.com*) use your Web browser. Regardless of the interface, using the Internet for backups is impossibly slow unless you have a broadband connection. Even with a fast, reliable connection, regularly backing up many gigabytes of data is impractical. The two best reasons to choose a Web-based backup are to safeguard irreplaceable work files, such as accounting data and customer records, and to provide easy access to working files from multiple locations.

> **Tip**   You can find a good list of companies offering Web-based storage by going to *http://dir.yahoo.com* and clicking links to follow this tortuous path through the Yahoo! directory: Business and Economy, Shopping and Services, Communication and Information Management, Internet and World Wide Web, Personal Information Management, File Hosting.

Using Imaging Software to Back Up Complete Partitions

One problem with file backups is that they don't copy every bit of information on your hard disk. Files that are in use—including some critical system files—are difficult, if not impossible, to back up with a program such as Windows Backup. (Windows XP adds a *volume shadow copying* feature, which creates a copy of all files in use at the time a backup job begins and then backs up the copies. This feature is designed to produce an exact duplicate of a disk volume—including any files in use—while avoiding errors caused by files that are locked by the operating system.)

Several software publishers have come up with an alternative solution: disk imaging programs. Disk imaging programs can make an exact duplicate of an entire hard disk partition. The three leading programs in this field are Symantec's Norton Ghost, a successor to the once-popular Drive Image program (*http://www.symantec.com/sabu/ghost/*); Acronis True Image (*http://www.acronis.com*); and TeraByte Unlimited's Image for Windows and Image for DOS (*http://www.terabyteunlimited.com*). Older versions of these programs required that you restart your computer into MS-DOS or a similar dedicated operating system; newer versions of all three programs enable you to create a backup image without exiting Windows and can also create a differential image or images that exclude some files.

Disk imaging programs clone an entire partition by copying it (and, optionally, compressing its data) to another hard disk partition, to a separate internal or external physical disk), to a shared network volume, or to writable CD or DVD media. Figure 6-1 shows the main interface for Norton Ghost 9.0. Because disk imaging programs can compress the data, the backup partition need not be as big as the partition you're backing up. As hard disk prices continue to drop and disk capacities increase, a relatively small investment can give you a backup system that you'll actually use.

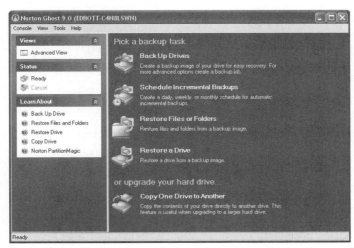

Figure 6-1. Norton Ghost allows you to save an image of an entire disk partition and then back up changes to that image later.

Although disk imaging programs were originally designed to back up only entire partitions, most modern versions include the capability to create incremental backups as well. In addition, you can typically explore the contents of an image file and restore individual folders or files as needed. Figure 6-2 on the next page shows Symantec Backup Image Browser, the component of Norton Ghost that you use for various image-file management tasks and, more important, for restoring files from a backup image.

Chapter 6

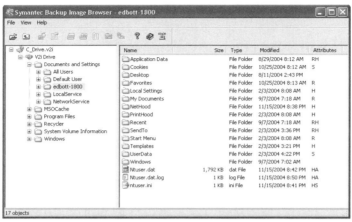

Figure 6-2. Disk imaging programs let you restore individual folders or files from a disk image.

Like file backup programs, disk imaging programs let you store backups on a wide variety of media. In fact, because a partition backup is stored as an ordinary file, you can save it on just about any type of media. (The programs include an option to split the backup file across multiple files, each sized to the maximum capacity of the target media.) If you've divided your system into multiple partitions—one for your operating system and programs, the other for data files—you can restore the complete disk image for your data partition from within Windows. To restore your system partition in the event of a hard disk failure or other catastrophe, you'll need to boot into a special recovery environment, typically by starting your computer with the disk imaging program CD. You'll need to verify that the recovery environment includes drivers for the devices on which you choose to save backup images.

Combining Methods for a Comprehensive Backup Strategy

A partition backup provides the best full backup; it includes all the bits on the disk and, if you back up to a different hard disk partition, it can be run unattended in a relatively short time. But using a partition backup for your frequent interim backups makes little sense; with a file backup, you can save only the files that have changed in a fraction of the time, and disk or media space that a full partition backup requires. Hence, our recommended solution for most small businesses and home users is a hybrid one:

● Periodically use a disk imaging program to perform a full backup of all your computer's partitions (except the one you use as a backup location). Schedule the program to run when you won't be using your computer (for most people, in the middle of the night), and save the backup files to a hard disk partition or separate physical disk reserved for the purpose. To make room for later backups, copy the image files to writable CD, DVD, or other removable media that can be accessed using the recovery CD created by your disk imaging program.

● On a more frequent basis, use Windows Backup or a similar program to back up the data files (documents, e-mail, and so on) that you use day in and day out. Schedule the program to run when your computer is idle, and save the backup files to the same drive that you use for full backups. Compress the backup file and copy it to CD, DVD, or other removable media.

That's all there is to it. You'll probably want to schedule the full backups to occur somewhere between once a week and once a month, with interim backups performed daily. Increase the frequency of your full backups when the interim backups no longer fit on one CD (or whatever medium you choose).

To obtain the safety of off-site storage and the convenience of having your backups on-site, take the CD, DVD, or other removable media to an off-site location and leave the original backup files on the hard disk partition reserved for backups. For off-site storage, you could take your office backups home and take your home backups to work, for example. You could even mail them to a friend across town or in another state. The off-site backup, on removable media, is available in case of total disaster; and the hard disk copy is available on a moment's notice if you discover that you've inadvertently deleted a file you need. Be sure to secure the off-site copy with a strong password.

The following sections explain how to use the Windows Backup program and offers additional details about how to implement and automate this two-tiered backup strategy.

Using the Windows Backup Program

Windows Backup, shown in Figure 6-3, is a full-featured backup program that lets you select folders and files to back up based on any combination of criteria. You can save a collection of backup settings as a backup job, and you can schedule the backup job to run automatically at predefined times. Windows Backup can back up data to a file (combining all the files you back up into a single file with a .bkf extension) or to tape.

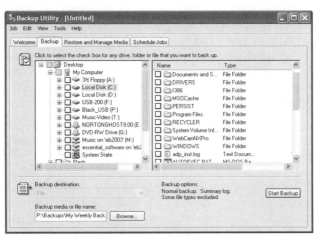

Figure 6-3. Although Windows Backup allows you to back up to tape, you're most likely to save your backup to a disk file.

Chapter 6

Note The backup program included with Windows goes by a variety of similar names, depending on which version of Windows you're using. In Windows 2000 (and in this book), it's called Windows Backup. In Windows XP, it's called Backup Utility. In both operating systems, you can start Windows Backup by opening the Start menu and choosing Programs, Accessories, System Tools, Backup. Alternatively, you can start Windows Backup by typing **ntbackup** at a command prompt.

Inside Out

Windows Backup in Windows XP Home Edition

In Windows 2000 and Windows XP Professional, Windows Backup is installed by default. In Windows XP Home Edition, however, you won't find it on the Start menu or even in Add Or Remove Programs. It *is* included, though—you just need to know where to look.

To install Windows Backup, you need your Windows XP Home Edition CD. Use Windows Explorer to open the \Valueadd\Msft\Ntbackup folder and then double-click Ntbackup.msi.

If your computer came with only a "system recovery" CD instead of a full Windows CD, finding Ntbackup.msi is not so easy. Look on the CD that was furnished and on any additional hard disk partitions set up on your computer. Some manufacturers provide the Windows files more or less intact, whereas others embed them in compressed disk image files. (Compaq systems with Windows XP Home Edition preinstalled, for example, have Windows files stored within Drive Image files on drive D.) If you happen to have the disk imaging program that was used to create the disk image files, you can extract the Windows files you need. If all else fails, borrow a Windows XP CD from a friend or co-worker, or download Ntbackup.msi from *http://www.onecomputerguy.com/windowsxp_tips.htm#backup_home*.

Once installed, Windows Backup works the same in Windows XP Home Edition as in Windows XP Professional, with one key exception: You can't restore your system using Automated System Recovery (ASR). Although Windows Backup lets you create an ASR disk, the Home Edition CD does not include the requisite files to *use* the ASR disk—so there's no point in making one. To perform a full system restore from a backup created with Windows Backup, you first need to reinstall Windows and reinstall Windows Backup. Only then will you be able to access your backup files and begin restoring. For more information about ASR, see "Restoring a System by Using an Automated System Recovery Disk," page 211.

This limitation provides another reason to use a disk imaging program for your full backups. See "Using Imaging Software to Back Up Complete Partitions," page 192, for details.

Windows Backup has plenty of competition from third-party commercial applications and shareware. Advantages offered by some third-party backup programs include the ability to back up network drives, to back up to writable CD or DVD media, to span multiple disks, and to compress backup files. (Windows Backup uses compression only on tape drives that support hardware compression, and performs no compression if you back up to a file). In this chapter, we show how to implement a backup system using Windows Backup—but other programs, perhaps with additional features that you'll find useful, work in a similar manner.

> **Tip**   **Create rescue disks with your full backup**
> Whatever tool you use for backing up your system, you should use its facility for creating a rescue disk. Typically, a rescue disk is a bootable floppy disk (or set of disks) that lets you access your backup media and fully restore your data; you'll need this disk to get going on a new system if your hard disk goes missing or belly up.
>
> In Windows XP Professional, Windows Backup can create an Automated System Recovery (ASR) disk. To create one using the Backup Or Restore Wizard, select All Information On This Computer on the What To Back Up page. In Advanced Mode, click the Welcome tab and then click Automated System Recovery Wizard. For more information, see "Restoring a System by Using an Automated System Recovery Disk," page 211.
>
> Windows Backup in Windows 2000 can create an Emergency Repair Disk (ERD). For details, see "Keeping an Up-to-Date Emergency Repair Disk," page 205.

Choosing a Backup Type

In Windows Backup, a full backup is called a *normal* backup. Windows Backup backs up all selected files, regardless of the current setting for the archive bit on each file. It then clears each file's archive attribute so that subsequent differential or incremental backups copy only files that have changed since the normal backup.

> **Note**   Virtually all backup programs, including Windows Backup, use each file's archive attribute to determine whether to include the file in a backup. The *archive attribute* is a single bit in the file's directory entry. When a file is created or modified, its archive attribute is turned on. When a file is backed up using a normal or an incremental backup, the archive attribute is cleared. You can view (and set, if you like) the archive attribute for a file by right-clicking the file in Windows Explorer and choosing Properties. On the General tab, click the Advanced button; the first check box in the Advanced Attributes dialog box represents the archive attribute.

For your frequent interim backups, Windows Backup supports two types of backups that automatically exclude files that haven't changed since the last backup:

- An *incremental* backup copies files that have changed (or have been created) since the most recent normal or incremental backup and clears the archive attributes for these files.
- A *differential* backup copies files that have changed (or have been created) since the most recent normal or incremental backup but does not clear the files' archive attributes. Subsequent differential backups continue to copy all files that have changed since the most recent normal or incremental backup.

Chapter 6

You can use either type for your frequent backups; which you choose is a matter of convenience. An incremental backup includes fewer files in each operation (because it includes only the files that have changed since the last backup), so the backup files are smaller and the backup process takes less time. A differential backup, however, makes it much easier to restore files from your backup media when necessary. With this type of backup, you can locate any file (or restore your entire system) by checking, at most, only two backup files: the most recent full backup and the most recent differential backup. With incremental backups, on the other hand, you might need to fish through the full backup and *all* the incremental backup files before you find the item you need to restore.

Therefore, unless you change a lot of data every day—so much that you can't perform an unattended backup—you're better off using the differential type for your interim backups. (An *unattended backup* is one that runs automatically and doesn't require any manual intervention such as responding to dialog boxes or changing media.)

In addition to normal, incremental, and differential backup types, Windows Backup supports two others:

- A *copy* backup copies all selected files but does not clear their archive attributes. A copy backup is useful as a way of archiving particular files without affecting your overall backup routine.

- A *daily* backup copies all selected files that have changed on the current day, without clearing the files' archive attributes. It's a way of backing up a particular day's work without affecting the overall backup routine.

Inside Out

Avoid the daily backup type

The daily backup type sounds like it might be an appropriate part of a regular backup routine. It's not. Although the daily type can be useful for occasional backups, it has two shortcomings that make it unsuitable for regular once-a-day backups.

- A daily backup includes only files created or changed on the day of the backup, up until the time of the backup. Any files that are changed after the backup is run are missed, and they won't be picked up in the next day's backup because they weren't changed that day.

- If you miss a day for any reason (the scheduled task didn't run, the drive didn't contain media, you had to rush home before starting the backup), that day's files won't be backed up.

To avoid these problems, use either an incremental or a differential backup for everyday backups.

Performing Interim Backups with Windows Backup

Windows Backup is a fine tool for frequent interim backups, for it can be scheduled to run without intervention. To set up a daily backup job, follow these steps:

1 Type **ntbackup** at a command prompt to start Windows Backup.

If you use Windows XP with the default settings, the Backup Or Restore Wizard starts. We recommend you use the wizard, which offers two preconfigured backup jobs that are ideal for interim backups: My Documents And Settings and Everyone's Documents And Settings. (See Figure 6-4.) These jobs include the important files from your profile (or profiles) and specifically exclude a number of files that should not be backed up, such as the hibernation file and the page file. When you reach the wizard's final page, click Advanced to set up a schedule for your backup job. That's it; you're done.

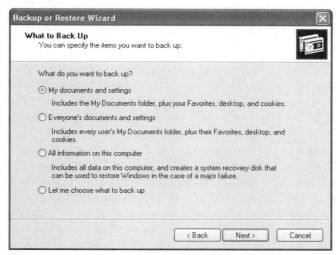

Figure 6-4. The wizard in Windows XP makes it easy to set up an interim backup of your document files and other settings.

2 To specify your own backup parameters, click the Advanced Mode link.

If you use Windows 2000, no wizard appears. Although you can summon one, the wizard in Windows 2000 doesn't have the compelling options offered by the Windows XP version. Therefore, you should continue with this procedure.

3 Click the Backup tab.

4 Select the folders that contain data you want to back up. In most cases, that would be only <d:>\Documents And Settings, where <d:> is the drive letter of your main partition.

5 In the Backup Media Or File Name box, type the name of the file on your backup partition that will contain your backup data (for example, U:\Daily.bkf).

6 Choose Job, Save Selections to save your backup job definition.

Chapter 6

7 Click Start Backup.

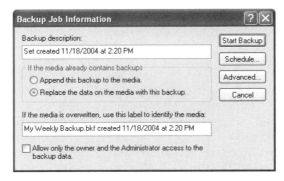

8 In the Backup Job Information dialog box, make the following settings:

- Type a description of the backup job if you like.

- Select the Replace option so that your backup job creates a new file with the same name each time you run it.

- Select the Allow check box. This allows any member of the Administrators group to restore files from your backup file, but prevents someone who does not have an account on your computer from using the file. (Later in the process, you can store the backup in a password-protected .zip file for additional protection.)

9 Click Schedule and enter your password (or the user name and password of an account with sufficient permissions; see the sidebar "Windows Backup and Permissions" for details). Click OK and then set up a schedule in the Scheduled Job Options dialog box. You can schedule the backup to run at any time because Windows Backup runs without interrupting your other work. However, if you use Windows 2000, which lacks the volume shadow copy feature, files that are open while the backup is running might not be backed up. Therefore, it's best to schedule the job at a time when you know your computer will be idle and you have shut down all running programs.

After the scheduled backup job runs, copy the single backup file from your backup partition to a CD-R. Although you can copy the .bkf file as is, we suggest that you first take an additional step: Compress the file as a .zip file. This compression offers several advantages:

- The backup file is smaller, so that your backup can contain more files and still fit on a single CD.

- Because the file is smaller, it takes less time to copy it.

- The backup file can be password-protected. Although cracking the password on a password-protected .zip file is no challenge for a determined hacker, this protection will deter most people.

- If the backup file is too large to fit on a single CD, you can split the .zip file to span multiple CDs.

Windows Backup and Permissions

Windows won't let just anybody log on to a computer, back up files, and subsequently restore them somewhere else. You must have certain permissions or user rights to back up files, whether you use Windows Backup or another file backup program designed for Windows XP or Windows 2000. Here are the provisions:

- A member of the local Administrators group or Backup Operators group can back up all files on the local computer—even files that NTFS permissions otherwise prevent the user from accessing.

- A member of the Domain Admins group or the domain Backup Operators group can back up all files on any computer in the domain.

- Users who are not members of any of these groups can back up only folders and files that they own and files for which they have one or more of the following permissions: Read, Read & Execute, Modify, or Full Control.

Tip **Back up (almost) directly to CD-R**
If you choose not to compress your backup file as a .zip file and if you use Windows XP, set up Windows Backup to store the .bkf file in the staging area for writing CDs. Creating the file in that folder doesn't write it directly to a CD-R disc, but it allows you to write the file to CD-R with only a single click. To use this trick, replace step 4 on page 199 with the following:

4 Click the Browse button. In the File Name box of the Save As dialog box, type **%userprofile%\local settings\application data\microsoft\cd burning\backup.bkf** and then click Save.

After you run the backup job, open My Computer, right-click your CD-R drive, and choose Write These Files To CD.

The backup file created by your scheduled backup job always has the same name. You'll find it easier to keep track of your frequent backups if you give them a more meaningful name; we suggest using the file date as the file name.

Changing a file name and creating a .zip file is a perfect application for a batch program. Here's one that can do the job:

```
:: Batch program to compress daily backup for storage on CD-R
@echo off
cls

:: Create environment variables with today's date values.
setlocal
for /f "tokens=1-4 delims=/ " %%i in ('date /t') do (
set Day=%%i
set MM=%%j
set DD=%%k
set YYYY=%%l
)
```

```
:: This batch program assumes that your scheduled backup file is saved
:: as D:\Backup\Backup.bkf. If you use a different folder or file
:: name, replace the values in the following lines.
cd /d d:\backup

:: Error handling: check for existence of source and target files.
if not exist backup.bkf goto nofile
if exist %YYYY%-%MM%-%DD%.bkf goto targetexists

:: Use today's date as the file name for the backup file.
ren backup.bkf %YYYY%-%MM%-%DD%.bkf

:: Use WinZip and the WinZip Command Line Support Add-On to compress
:: the backup file. Replace PASSWORD with the password you want to
:: use for protecting the compressed backup file.
"%programfiles%\winzip\wzzip" -m -ex -s"PASSWORD" %YYYY%-%MM%-%DD%.zip %YYYY%-
    %MM%-%DD%.bkf
cls
echo The backup has been compressed and saved as %YYYY%-%MM%-%DD%.zip
echo.
dir %YYYY%-%MM%-%DD%.zip | find /i "zip"
echo.
echo If the file size shown above is greater than 650,000,000, you'll
echo need to open the file in WinZip and use its Split function.
pause
goto end

:nofile
echo The expected backup file, D:\Backup\Backup.bkf, doesn't exist.
pause
goto end

:targetexists
echo A file named %YYYY%-%MM%-%DD%.zip already exists.
pause

:end
endlocal
```

 You can find this file, which we call CompressBackup.bat, on this book's companion CD. Save it on your hard disk and modify it as necessary. (In particular, you'll need to change the references to D:\Backup and Backup.bkf if you store your backup file elsewhere, and you'll need to pick a better password than PASSWORD for the .zip archive.)

> **Note** To use CompressBackup, you need WinZip and the WinZip Command Line Support Add-On. You can download them from *http://www.winzip.com*; the add-on is located at *http://www.winzip.com/wzcline.htm*. If you prefer to use a different .zip management program, you'll need to modify CompressBackup.

Open the Start menu and choose Programs, Accessories, System Tools, Scheduled Tasks and set up CompressBackup to run as a scheduled task after your daily backup runs.

When you return to your computer after both the backup and CompressBackup have run, copy the .zip file (which has the backup date as its file name) to a CD.

If the file is too big to fit on one CD, open the file in WinZip. Open the Actions menu and choose Split. In the Part Size box, select CD-ROM to create files that will fit on a CD.

Troubleshooting

The backup file won't compress

The daily backup scheme we've described has one significant limitation: It won't work if your backup file is larger than 4 GB and you're using WinZip 8.0 or earlier or another compression utility. In that case, you won't be able to compress the file because the standard .zip format doesn't support files that large. And because you can't compress it, you can't split it across multiple CD-size files. The CompressBackup batch file will fail with an error; it doesn't handle this situation with aplomb.

The simplest solution in this case is to modify your backup job so that it creates two or more smaller backup files. You should also consider increasing the frequency of your full backup, moving files that don't change out of your My Documents folder, or using differential backups, as described in the accompanying Inside Out tip.

If you don't mind spending a few dollars and tweaking the batch file accordingly, use a more modern compression algorithm. WinZip 9.0 supports 64-bit extensions to the .zip file format, which enable you to create compressed files of any size. You can also use the WinRAR archive manager instead of WinZip; it's available at *http://www.rarlab.com*. The RAR format, developed by Eugene Roshal, excels at splitting very large files into chunks sized to fit on CD and other media and doesn't suffer from the size limitations of the .zip format.

Inside Out

Use differential backups

Because our recommended strategy uses a disk image as the periodic full backup instead of using a file backup, the archive attribute isn't cleared when you perform a full (that is, disk image) backup. Therefore, you can't rely on a backup program's differential backup type to copy only the files that have changed since your last full backup—unless, that is, you clear the archive attributes for all files when you perform the full disk image backup.

You can clear the archive attribute for every file on a disk with a single use of the command-line utility Attrib. For example, to clear the archive attribute for all files on drive C, use this command:

```
attrib -a c:\*.* /s
```

By saving this single line to a batch program that is scheduled to run immediately after the full backup job runs, you're in effect doing exactly what Windows Backup does when it performs a normal (that is, full) backup. For your frequent interim backups, you can then select all the files on a system (instead of selecting particular folders) and use a differential backup type. This method ensures that every file that has changed is backed up; it doesn't rely on your ability to figure out where each program stores its files that have changed.

Note that this command doesn't change the archive attribute on hidden files or files for which your account doesn't have at least read permission. Therefore, such files that have the archive attribute turned on will be included in your differential backup unless they're specifically excluded. Many hidden files are excluded by default in Windows Backup.

Using Other Data Loss Prevention Tools Included with Windows

Windows includes some other utilities that can help to keep your data secure. Depending on which backup regimen you choose, you might want to use one or more of these tools on a regular basis to reduce the risk of data loss.

Checking for Hard Disk Errors with Chkdsk

Chkdsk is a command-line utility that checks a disk for file-system and media errors. Windows includes a graphical interface for Chkdsk (shown here), which you can display by right-clicking the disk icon in Windows Explorer, choosing Properties from the shortcut menu, clicking the Tools tab, and clicking Check Now.

Selecting Automatically Fix File System Errors in this dialog box is equivalent to running Chkdsk with the /F switch. Choosing Scan For And Attempt Recovery Of Bad Sectors is equivalent to running Chkdsk with /R. Choosing this second option implicitly chooses the first as well; that is, if you check for media errors (bad sectors), the command also fixes the file system.

Both of these options require that the system be granted exclusive control of the disk you want to check. If you have any open files or processes that require access to the disk, you are notified that the requested checkup cannot be carried out. You then have the option of having the system check your disk the next time you start your computer. If you accept, Windows performs the desired check at your next startup, before the logon screen appears.

The easiest way to perform automatic file-system and media checks at regular intervals is to create a batch program that executes Chkdsk.exe and then create a scheduled task to execute the batch program. Chkdsk has some additional options not provided by the graphical interface; to see an explanation of these options, open a command prompt window and type **chkdsk /?**.

Keeping an Up-to-Date Emergency Repair Disk

If you use Windows 2000, you should create an Emergency Repair Disk (ERD). An ERD is a floppy disk containing data that might allow Windows 2000 to get your system running again if it fails to start in the normal way. You should update your ERD regularly, as one of your routine maintenance procedures. That way, if the need ever arises, you'll have a reasonably current recovery disk at your disposal.

To create an ERD, run Windows Backup. On the Welcome tab, click Emergency Repair Disk.

The process of creating an ERD optionally creates a registry backup in %SystemRoot%\Repair\Regback. (The files are too large to fit on the floppy disk.) If your registry is damaged, the ERD recovery process can make use of this backup. However, these registry backup files, which include the Security Accounts Manager (SAM), make an attractive target for malicious hackers. Anyone who gains access to the Regback folder (which is open to all users) can view or make a copy of these files. Because of Syskey protection, the SAM is still a tough nut to crack. (For information about Syskey, see "Safeguarding the Security Accounts Manager," page 60.) Nonetheless, some security experts suggest *not* using the option of creating a registry backup. Instead, use other tools (such as a disk image backup) to protect registry data. Alternatively, move the registry data from Regback to removable media that you keep in a secure location.

For information about using the ERD, see "Restoring a System by Using an Emergency Repair Disk," page 210.

Creating System Restore Points

System Restore is a Windows XP service that runs in the background, keeping track of changes to your system. The first time you start a computer running Windows XP, System Restore creates a snapshot of system files and registry data. Then, once a day, System Restore automatically creates a new, updated snapshot of system files and registry data, storing it in hidden archives for safekeeping. In addition to the periodic snapshots (called

Chapter 6

system checkpoints), System Restore creates a restore point when you take any of the following actions:

- **Install an unsigned device driver.**   When you attempt to install an unsigned hardware driver, Windows displays a warning message. If you choose to continue, System Restore creates a restore point before the installation proceeds.
- **Install an application that uses a System Restore–compatible installer.** Applications that use Windows Installer (such as Microsoft Office XP or later) or InstallShield Professional version 7 or later trigger creation of a restore point.
- **Install a Windows update or patch.**   System Restore creates a restore point whenever you install an update using Windows Update or Automatic Updates.
- **Restore an earlier configuration using System Restore.**   When you revert to an earlier configuration, System Restore saves your current configuration so that you can undo the restore if necessary.
- **Use Windows Backup to restore data.**   When you restore files with Windows Backup, System Restore creates a restore point. If restoring the files causes problems with Windows system files, you can revert to a working configuration.

You can also create your own restore points. To do that, open System Restore by clicking the Start button and choosing All Programs, Accessories, System Tools, System Restore. In the window that appears (see Figure 6-5), select Create A Restore Point and click Next.

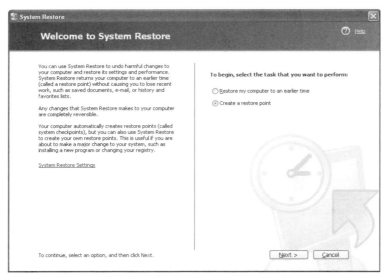

Figure 6-5.   In addition to the automatically created restore points, you can create your own.

System Restore does not back up any document files, e-mail files, or files in the My Documents, Favorites, Cookies, Recycle Bin, Temporary Internet Files, History, or Temp folders. Therefore, you can restore an earlier configuration without affecting any of the files that you have created or modified since the restore point was created. (For this same reason, of course, System Restore is useless as a backup system for your documents; that's not its purpose.)

To restore your system to a previous configuration, you must be logged on as a member of the Administrators group. Shut down all running programs, and make sure that no other users are logged on to the machine (either in inactive local sessions or across the network). Then start System Restore, select Restore My Computer To An Earlier Time, and click Next. In the window shown in Figure 6-6, you can select a date and a specific restore point on the selected date.

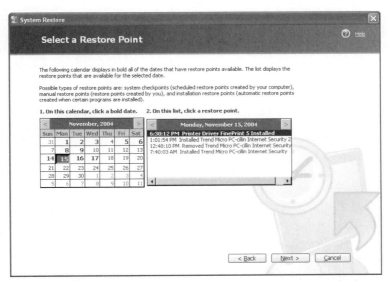

Figure 6-6. Bold numbers in the calendar indicate dates on which one or more restore points were saved.

> **Our other book, _Microsoft Windows XP Inside Out, Second Edition_ (Microsoft Press, 2005), contains more details about System Restore.**

Backing Up the Registry

When you use Windows Backup, you can include the entire registry in a backup set by including System State in your backup selections. (System State also includes the COM+ Class Registration Database and boot files, such as Ntldr and Ntdetect.com.) System State is useful if you need to rebuild your system from scratch using your Windows Backup files. But it's an all-or-nothing proposition; you can't selectively back up or restore parts of the registry.

A better tool for backing up certain registry keys—which is a good idea if you're making changes to the registry—is Registry Editor (Regedit.exe). Use its File, Export command to back up a selected key, including all its values and subkeys.

Chapter 6

You can find detailed procedures for both techniques in Microsoft Knowledge Base articles 322755 (Windows 2000) and 322756 (Windows XP).

Protecting Backups

Creating a good backup is half the battle; the rest is ensuring that the backup is in usable condition when you need it! Your backup media share some of the same risks as your primary data storage: the chance of theft, for example, or damage from fire, flood, tornado, hurricane, earthquake, and other natural disasters.

> **Tip** Safeguard valuable data
>
> A thief who steals your backup copy can restore the data and harvest any secrets contained within the backup set, including saved passwords, financial information, corporate secrets, and personal medical information. To protect yourself from this eventuality, use a strong password and encryption, if available, when you create your backup set. Be sure to store the password in a safe place—not in the same location as the backup media!

In addition, outside your computer's protective case, your media are subject to some environmental risks, such as exposure to sunlight, temperature and humidity variations, and magnetic fields. By observing a handful of simple guidelines, however, you can protect your backups from damage.

Bear in mind that magnetic media—tapes in all formats, removable disks such as Zip and Jaz disks, floppy disks, and so on—are sensitive to damage from magnetic fields. While that might seem rather obvious, it's not always obvious where those magnetic fields lie. Most speakers and CRT-type monitors have the capability to generate data-destroying magnetic fields. Be sure to store your magnetic media away from such devices.

If you're going to keep your backups on-site, you should store all backup media—magnetic or optical—in a fireproof safe. Be aware, however, that most fireproof safes, which are designed for protecting business papers and the like from fire damage, are inadequate for protecting computer media. A safe is considered "fireproof" if its internal temperature remains below 350 degrees Fahrenheit for a specified amount of time—usually 20 to 30 minutes—while exposed to fire. Although that's well below the flash point of paper (remember Ray Bradbury's *Fahrenheit 451*?), magnetic media can be damaged at temperatures as low as 125 degrees and can become unusable if exposed to temperatures of about 280 degrees or higher. Some manufacturers of fireproof safes make "media safes," which are specifically designed for protecting magnetic media (as well as film media, such as negatives, transparencies, microfilm, and the like) by keeping the internal temperature below 125 degrees during a fire. Manufacturers of media safes include the following:

- FKI Security Group (*http://www.fkisecuritygroup.com*)
- Schwab Corp. (*http://www.schwabcorp.com*)
- Sentry Group (*http://www.sentrysafe.com*)

A media safe provides protection from theft as well as fire. Not all are waterproof, however, so flooding remains a threat, as does structural damage from earthquake and storms. Your best protection against such threats is to store your backup media off-site—somewhere away from your computer. The farther you can go, the better, as you'll gain greater protection against regional disasters such as earthquakes or wildfires. By putting some distance between your original data and the backups, you're unlikely to lose both. Such an arrangement isn't feasible for everyone, of course. (It's particularly difficult if you work out of your home so that your "office" and your "home" are only a few feet apart.) Even so, you might be able store periodic full backups with a friend or relative or in a bank's safe deposit box.

Tip   **Use Web-based backup**

Another way to set up an off-site backup is to use a Web-based backup service. For reasons outlined earlier in this chapter (see "Backing Up Selected Folders and Files," page 190), such services are generally impractical for full backups, but they can be useful for off-site backup of your most important files. A number of companies offer limited amounts of storage at little or no cost, including MSN Groups (*http://groups.msn.com*), and Yahoo! Briefcase (*http://briefcase.yahoo.com*). In addition, if you have a Web-accessible e-mail account in which you can store messages with large attachments, such as those offered by Hotmail (*http://www.hotmail.com*) or Google (*http://www.gmail.com*), you can save your backed-up files in an encrypted archive and send it to yourself.

For the most effective use of off-site storage, follow these guidelines:

- Rotate media between off-site and on-site storage locations.
- Set up a schedule so that at no time are all recent backups on-site. The exchange of off-site and on-site media should occur at the off-site location (because the primary data—your hard drive—is at the on-site location) so that at least one set of recent backups is off-site at all times.
- Maintain a log of backup media—and keep a copy at an off-site location. (If you keep the log in one or more text files, you could keep the log in a folder of a Web-based e-mail account.)

Recovering Data

As its title suggests, this chapter is about *protecting* your data from loss. In this final section, we take a high-level look at some of the options available for recovering damaged or missing data.

Recovering Individual Files from Backups

Your most common data recovery task is likely to be restoring individual files. This need arises after the "Doh!" moment when you realize you've deleted or modified a file that you meant to keep. If you have a backup available, the task is simple: You can restore individual files by using the same program (or suite of programs) you use for backing up files.

Windows Backup, for example, restores files from the backup media it creates. You can use its Backup Or Restore Wizard or the "advanced" interface, just as you can when you back up. Either way, you start by choosing a backup set and then selecting individual folders and files to restore. You have the option to restore files to their original location or to an alternative folder you specify. (If you use the wizard, click Advanced on the last wizard page to set these options; see Figure 6-7.) You can also specify what should happen if the files you're restoring already exist on your computer.

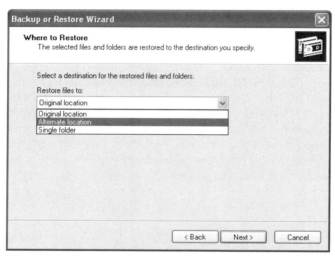

Figure 6-7. You can choose to restore your files to the original locations or to another location.

You can also use tools that back up entire partitions to selectively restore files. If you back up a partition with Norton Ghost, for example, use the Symantec Backup Image Browser (a program included with Norton Ghost) to select and restore folders and files in a partition image file. Most modern drive-imaging programs offer a utility that performs a similar function.

Restoring a System by Using an Emergency Repair Disk

In Windows 2000, the emergency repair process (the recovery measure that uses your ERD) can help you do the following:

- Repair problems with system files
- Repair problems with your startup environment, if you have a dual-boot or multi-boot system
- Repair the partition boot sector on your boot volume

To use the emergency repair process:

1 Start your computer from the Windows 2000 CD (if you can boot from a CD) or from the Windows 2000 Setup disks.

2   You'll be asked whether you want to continue installing Windows 2000. Answer yes.

3   You'll be asked whether you want to do a full install or repair an existing installation. Choose the latter by pressing R.

4   Indicate whether you want to perform a "fast repair" or a "manual repair."

5   Insert the ERD when prompted.

A fast repair requires no further decisions from you. The repair process attempts to fix your system files, the boot sector, and your startup environment. If your registry appears to be damaged, the fast repair process restores the copy of your registry that the Setup program created when you first installed Windows 2000. (If your registry does not appear to be damaged, the fast repair process does not change it.) The repair process does not restore your own profile settings—the portion of the registry stored in the file Ntuser.dat. If that part of your registry is in good shape, your personal settings will still be intact. The rest of the registry, however, will revert to the condition it was in the day you installed Windows 2000. If you had the foresight to create a backup of your registry (through the System State option in Windows Backup or the equivalent in another backup program), you'll be able to use that backup to restore the registry to a more current condition.

A manual repair lets you choose whether you want to repair the system files, the boot sector, or the startup environment (or any combination of those), but it doesn't let you do anything with the registry.

For more details about the differences between the fast repair and manual repair options, see Knowledge Base article 238359.

Restoring a System by Using an Automated System Recovery Disk

Automated System Recovery (ASR) is a feature of Windows XP Professional that's intended to restore your system in the event of catastrophic failure, such as severe physical damage to a hard drive or the loss of a computer in a fire. But it isn't fully automated, and it can recover your system only if the ASR disk is accompanied by its full system backup, which is created by Windows Backup. An ASR backup set includes the complete contents of your system volume, plus information about the current arrangement of disk partitions, system files, and detected hardware.

Caution   If you create the ASR set using Advanced Mode in Windows Backup, only the system volume is backed up. If you want to include other drives in the backup, use the Backup And Restore Wizard and select All Information On This Computer to back up all your drives.

In the event of a catastrophic failure of your system volume, you can boot from the Windows XP CD, press F2 to run Automated System Recovery when prompted by Windows Setup, and then follow the prompts to restore your system.

Chapter 6

Inside Out

Boot from floppy disks

If you can't boot into Windows—or if you need to perform certain file operations that can't be done while Windows is running—you can boot from your Windows CD. Follow the prompts, choose the option to repair your installation, and then choose Recovery Console. After you enter the password for the Administrator account, you'll see a simple command prompt. This command-line interface supports a limited number of commands, but they're plenty powerful.

> For more information about Recovery Console, see *Microsoft Windows XP Inside Out, Second Edition* (Microsoft Press, 2005).

But what if your computer doesn't support booting from CD, or what if your computer didn't come with a Windows CD? If you have Windows XP, you can download a file from Microsoft that creates a set of bootable setup floppy disks. For details, see Knowledge Base article 310994.

Recovering Data from a Damaged Hard Disk

If, despite our admonitions, you don't have a backup copy of your data when your hard disk crashes, all is not lost. Using sophisticated tools, data recovery services can often recover some or all of your data, even if your disk has been damaged by fire, flood, or other catastrophe. This service often comes at a steep price, however; it can cost thousands of dollars for recovery services. In addition, they aren't always successful; sometimes the hard disk is too severely damaged.

There's no shortage of companies offering such services (proving our statement that most users don't back up their data). An Internet search for "data recovery disk crash" turns up a large number of vendors for you to evaluate.

Chapter 7

Keeping Your System Secure

So you've set up user accounts with secure passwords, installed virus protection, configured a firewall, and implemented the other security measures described in this book. You're done, right? Unfortunately, no.

Maintaining a secure system is an ongoing process. No sooner is one vulnerability eliminated than hackers discover another—and another. In this chapter, we examine a number of resources that you can use to help keep your computer system secure. In addition, we show you some ways in which you can confirm that your system's defenses are in good shape.

Security Checklist: Staying Secure

- Use Windows Update to check for security updates.
- Consider using Automatic Updates for automatic notification and (optionally) installation of updates.
- Subscribe to a security alert service to keep apprised of new security problems.
- Periodically check for changes to your security settings. For example, check the list of trusted sites in Microsoft Internet Explorer to be sure that an installation program hasn't surreptitiously added a site. (For details, see "Using Security Zones," page 405.) Check to see whether new startup programs have been added. (See Table 13-1, page 453.)
- Test your security settings periodically using Microsoft Baseline Security Analyzer or a similar tool.

Monitoring Security in Windows XP

Microsoft Windows XP Service Pack 2 (SP2) includes Security Center, a feature that monitors your computer's basic security conditions. Security Center is not available in earlier versions of Windows. When Security Center is enabled (the default setting on computers that are not joined to a domain), it monitors three security essentials—firewall, automatic updates, and virus protection—and alerts you to any problems. In addition, Security Center provides a control panel for monitoring and managing security-related settings, as shown in Figure 7-1 on the next page.

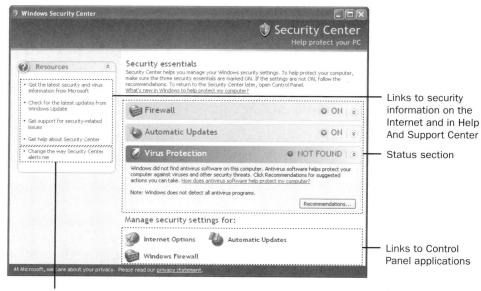

Links to security information on the Internet and in Help And Support Center

Status section

Links to Control Panel applications

Link to Security Center alert settings

Figure 7-1. Security Center consolidates monitoring and management of firewall, automatic updates, and virus protection into a single window.

> **Note** If your computer is joined to a domain, Security Center is turned off by default (unless the setting is overridden by a domain policy, which is available only with Windows Server 2003). You can open Security Center, but it does not monitor your computer's security status. The only function of Security Center when it's turned off is to provide an attractive container for links to security-related Control Panel applications and online security information. To fully enable Security Center on a domain-based computer, you must make a Group Policy setting. For details, see "Enabling Security Center," page 362.

To open Security Center, double-click its icon in Control Panel or type **wscui.cpl** at a command prompt. Alternatively, you can click the Windows Security Alerts icon when it appears in the notification area. With Security Center on the job, you might see an occasional message sprouting from the notification area icon, such as the one shown in Figure 7-2; clicking the message opens Security Center.

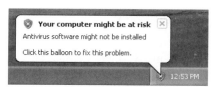

Figure 7-2. When Security Center detects a problem, it displays a message by the notification area.

> **Note** One significant security threat is overlooked by Security Center, which provides no protection against spyware. Security Center does not detect whether you have installed an anti-spyware program, nor does it monitor its status. For that one, you're on your own.

The status section in Security Center provides a quick glimpse into your computer's security settings. For each item, if everything is okay, you'll see a blue bar with the word *ON*. Clicking the blue bar expands it to display descriptive information.

Items that need your attention have an orange or red bar, and the status is indicated by phrases such as Off, Check Settings, Out of Date, Not Found, or Not Monitored. Below the bar appears explanatory text and buttons that let you correct the problem (or configure Security Center so that it won't bother you).

Security Center is designed to work with third-party firewall programs as well as with Windows Firewall, but some firewall programs written before the release of SP2 in mid-2004 are not properly recognized by Security Center. It checks for the presence of other software firewalls using Windows Management Instrumentation (WMI); some firewalls don't respond in an expected way. If you've turned off Windows Firewall in favor of an unrecognized third-party firewall, Security Center suggests with a red bar that your computer has no firewall protection. Click the Recommendations button to display the dialog box shown in Figure 7-3. In that dialog box, you can click Enable Now to turn on Windows Firewall for each of your network connections, without so much as a visit to Windows Firewall or Network Connections. But if you don't want to use Windows Firewall and you don't want to be bothered with alerts from Security Center, select the check box near the bottom of the window: I Have A Firewall Solution That I'll Monitor Myself. You won't receive any further alerts, and thereafter Security Center passively indicates the status as Not Monitored.

Figure 7-3. Selecting the check box tells Security Center to stop monitoring firewall status and to stop sending alerts about its status.

> **Note** Security Center does not detect any type of hardware firewall device. If you have one, you can select the check box in the Recommendation dialog box to avoid the warnings—or you can enable Windows Firewall. Although it's not a good idea to run more than one software firewall on a computer, there's usually no reason not to run a software firewall as an extra layer of protection behind your hardware firewall.

Similarly, Security Center is designed to work with third-party antivirus programs. Using WMI queries, it checks for the presence of antivirus software, and also checks to see if the software (including its virus definitions) is up to date and whether real-time scanning is enabled. Unfortunately, many antivirus programs that predate SP2 go unrecognized. To avoid incessant warnings from Security Center, use a workaround similar to the one for unrecognized firewalls: click Recommendations and then select I Have An Antivirus Program That I'll Monitor Myself. Better still, check with your antivirus vendor to see if an updated version is available; current versions of all the most popular antivirus programs are Security Center–aware.

> **Tip** Disable Security Center alerts
>
> Selecting the I Have... check box in the Recommendation dialog box, as described in the preceding paragraphs, causes Security Center to stop monitoring a particular security component and, therefore, to stop displaying security alert messages like the one shown in Figure 7-2. If you prefer, you can disable the alert but *not* disable Security Center monitoring. This ensures that alerts don't pop up at inopportune times. To disable alerts, in Security Center click Change The Way Security Center Alerts Me, the last link in the Resources pane on the left side. In the dialog box that appears, shown below, you can selectively disable Security Center alerts by clearing one or more check boxes.
>
>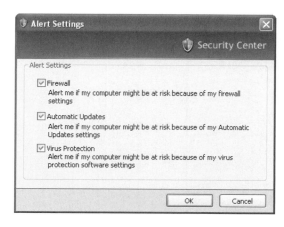

You can use the links at the bottom of the Security Center window to open Control Panel applications in which you can refine your security settings. As shown in Figure 7-1 on page 214, by default Security Center includes icons for Internet Options, Automatic Updates, and Windows Firewall. At the time of this book's publication, we're not aware of any third-party firewall or antivirus programs that add their own icons to the mix. But Security

Center is designed to easily accommodate them, so that with a complement of properly designed programs, it serves as the heart of your basic security operations.

Keeping Current with Windows Update

Windows Update is a service that provides online updates for Microsoft Windows. The intent is to offer a single location where you can obtain service packs, updated device drivers, and security updates. Certain updates are designated as "critical updates"; these patches (also known as *hotfixes*) repair bugs that can hamper your system's performance as well as compromise its security.

> **Note** Windows Update provides updates only to the Windows operating system and the various programs included with it. For updates to Microsoft Office, you can visit *http://office.microsoft.com/officeupdate*. These independent update services are still available, but in mid-2005 Microsoft introduced a one-stop update service called Microsoft Update. Microsoft Update provides updates for Windows 2000 and later, Office XP and later, and recent versions of several server applications, such as Microsoft SQL Server; support for other Microsoft applications will be added over time. To install Microsoft Update, go to *http://update.microsoft.com/microsoftupdate/*. After you install Microsoft Update, each of the startup methods listed below takes you to the Microsoft Update site—not Windows Update. Except for the addition of lists of changes to other programs you have installed, Microsoft Update is nearly identical in appearance and operation to Windows Update, which is described on the following pages.
>
> Security updates to other Microsoft products, including those that are not covered by Microsoft Update, are announced through other security newsletters and alerts from Microsoft; for details, see "Receiving E-Mail Alerts and RSS Notification," page 226.

To run Windows Update manually, do any of the following:

- In the Help And Support Center, under Pick A Task, click Keep Your Computer Up-To-Date With Windows Update (Windows XP only).
- Open the Start menu and choose All Programs, Windows Update. (In Windows 2000, simply open the Start menu and choose Windows Update.)
- At a command prompt, type **wupdmgr**.
- In Internet Explorer, open the Tools menu and choose Windows Update.
- In Internet Explorer, browse to *http://windowsupdate.microsoft.com*.

The first method displays Windows Update within the constraints of the Help And Support Center window, as shown in Figure 7-4 on the next page. If you use any of the other methods, Windows Update appears in an ordinary (full-featured) Internet Explorer window.

To begin the update process, click either Express Install or Custom Install.

Express Install queries the Windows Update server only for critical updates, security updates, service packs, and update rollups—known collectively as *high priority* updates.

After a moment's time, Windows displays a list of these updates, along with their number, total size, and estimated download time. You can click any of the listed updates to view more information, but the most expedient action is to simply click the Install button. These high priority updates should be installed as soon as they become available.

Custom Install provides access to miscellaneous noncritical software and hardware enhancements and updates in addition to the high priority updates provided by the Express Install option. Click each of the three links on the left side—Review High Priority Updates, Select Optional Software Updates, and Select Optional Hardware Updates—to view information about available updates in those categories. Read the description for each item, and then select the check box for each update that you want to install. (Because you'll almost certainly want to install all high priority updates, they're selected by default.) After you finish selecting items, click Go To Install Updates for a final review, and then click Install.

Figure 7-4. You can run Windows Update within the friendly confines of the Help And Support Center.

Note If you use Windows 2000 and you haven't updated to Microsoft Update or the most recent version of Windows Update, the procedure is slightly different from that just described. In Windows Update, click Scan For Updates. Then click each of the three links on the left side—Critical Updates, Windows 2000, and Driver Updates—to view information about and select available updates in those categories. (All critical updates are selected by default.) After you've made your selections, click Review And Install Updates. Finally, click Install Now.

Troubleshooting

Windows Update doesn't work

When you start Windows Update, it might display a "Software Update Incomplete" message. (This message appears before you have an opportunity to scan or select updates to install.)

Windows Update requires the use of an ActiveX control, which is installed the first time you access the Windows Update site. Because ActiveX controls can be used for ill as well as good, Internet Explorer erects several barriers to their installation. If your computer is running Windows XP SP2, the Information Bar in Internet Explorer drops down with a warning: "To help protect your security, Internet Explorer stopped this site from installing an ActiveX control on your computer." Click the Information Bar and choose Install ActiveX Control. A security warning box then pops up to inform you that Microsoft Corporation is the publisher of the Windows Update control. Click Install. Windows XP without SP2 and Windows 2000 provide similar warnings, which provide a way to ensure that the control is from the indicated publisher (Microsoft Corporation) and that it has not been modified. (As with any ActiveX control or other program, you must determine whether the publisher is one you trust to provide safe software.) To successfully install the ActiveX control, you must:

- Be logged on as a member of the Administrators group.
- Enable (with prompting) the download and running of signed ActiveX controls. (Use settings on the Security tab of the Internet Options dialog box; for more information, see "Using Security Zones," page 405.)
- Click Yes in the Security Warning dialog box that asks whether you want to install the Windows Update control.

You must also be logged on as an administrator to use Windows Update. Once the ActiveX control is installed, an explanatory message appears if a nonadministrative user tries to run Windows Update.

Tip   Hide updates that you don't ever want to install

Eagerly, you check Windows Update and discover that an update is available! The letdown comes on closer examination, when you discover that it's the same old update to Microsoft Movie Maker, which you never use. Windows Update will almost certainly offer some updates that you probably have no need for, including updates designed to provide compatibility with hardware you don't own, updates to components you don't use, and regional updates that don't apply to you. You can, however, customize it to eliminate the display of individual items or entire sections of updates.

In the list of updates for Windows XP presented by Custom Install, select Hide This Update for each item you don't want to see again. (The option is unavailable for high priority updates.) If you later change your mind—or if you just want to see a list of the updates you've chosen to hide—click Restore Hidden Updates (under Other Options in the left pane of Windows Update).

To customize Windows Update in Windows 2000, open Windows Update and scan for updates. Then click Personalize Windows Update (under Other Options in the left pane).

Troubleshooting

Windows Update displays an error message

When Windows Update fails to install an update, it displays a cryptic error code. You can find the decoder, lifted from a lengthy Microsoft Software Update Services Deployment Guide, at *http://faqshop.com/sus/suserrs/automatic%20update%20err%20codes.htm*. That page lists the error code and a brief description. Although it doesn't provide solutions, the description often has enough information to steer you in the right direction.

Automating Your Updates

Windows Updates are not distributed on a regular basis. Instead, they're published when the need arises, such as when a fix is developed for a newly discovered security vulnerability. You can make a habit of regularly checking Windows Update to see what's new, but there's an easier way: You can use the Automatic Updates feature.

Note Automatic Updates is not included on the Windows 2000 CD. Instead, it's available as an update from—you guessed it—Windows Update. Automatic Updates replaces an earlier updating tool called Critical Update Notification, which is no longer supported. To install Automatic Updates, you must first install Windows 2000 SP2 or later.

With Automatic Updates enabled, you don't need to remember to visit the Windows Update site periodically. Instead, Automatic Updates checks for you and (depending on your settings) downloads updates in a way that throttles its use of your Internet connection bandwidth to avoid interfering with your normal use of the connection.

Note Automatic Updates retrieves only critical updates. To view, download, and install other Windows updates and driver updates, you'll need to visit the Windows Update or Microsoft Update site.

Each Windows XP service pack has included a major overhaul of the Automatic Updates feature. In the original release of Windows XP, you could choose to be alerted when new updates were available, and Windows would download them for you to install, but the operating system wouldn't actually perform the updates. Windows 2000 still operates in this fashion by default. With Windows XP SP2 installed, the Automatic Updates dialog box includes new options, including the ability to install high priority updates on a specified schedule.

You can adjust Automatic Updates options at any time by opening Automatic Updates in Control Panel or by entering **wuaucpl.cpl** at a command prompt. (Users of computers running Windows XP SP2 can also open Automatic Updates from Security Center or by opening System in Control Panel and clicking the Automatic Updates tab.) Figure 7-5 shows Automatic Updates in Windows XP SP2, and Figure 7-6 shows the version for earlier versions of Windows.

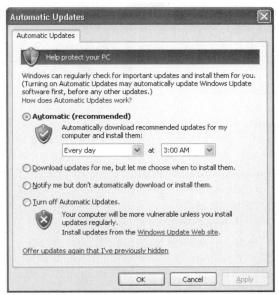

Figure 7-5. To have Windows XP SP2 automatically check for and install critical updates, select the first option.

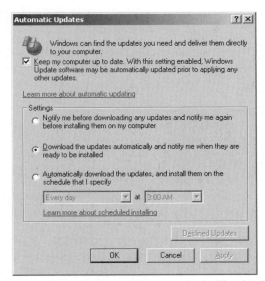

Figure 7-6. Automatic Updates looks like this in Windows 2000 and in Windows XP SP1.

To enable Automatic Updates in Windows XP SP2, select one of the first three options:

● **Automatically Download Recommended Updates For My Computer And Install Them**   Choose this option if you want the Automatic Updates process to live up to its name completely. In this "set it and forget it" configuration, Windows

Update checks for high priority updates on the schedule you specify (by default at 3:00 A.M. every day, although you can change the schedule to weekly and change the time as well), downloads each one as soon as it appears, and installs the update for you. Beware, however: If an update requires restarting your computer, Windows will do so without regard to whether any applications are open. This option is most appropriate if you leave your computer turned on.

- **Download Updates For Me, But Let Me Choose When To Install Them**   This option is most appropriate for users with high-speed, always-on Internet connections—cable modems and DSL, for instance. An icon in the notification area alerts you when a download has arrived. You can accept or reject any download.

- **Notify Me But Don't Automatically Download Or Install Them**   If you don't want to tie up your dial-up Internet connection downloading updates, choose this option. An icon in the notification area alerts you when a download is available; you decide whether and when to download and install it.

Selecting Turn Off Automatic Updates disables Automatic Updates. Doing so is appropriate if you want to manage updates from a network location instead of having each computer download and install updates individually. (For details, see the following section.)

In Windows 2000 and Windows XP SP1, you enable automatic updates by selecting Keep My Computer Up To Date. Then select one of the three options. Their descriptions and functions are similar to those listed above for Windows XP SP2, but note that the order is reversed.

If you select one of the options that does not automatically install updates when they're available, when one or more updates are ready to be downloaded or installed, Automatic Updates displays a pop-up message similar to the one shown in Figure 7-7.

Figure 7-7.   After the pop-up message disappears, you can open Automatic Updates by double-clicking its icon.

Clicking the pop-up message (or, if you're not quick enough on the draw, clicking the icon from which the message emanates) opens an Automatic Updates dialog box, as shown in Figure 7-8. To learn about the updates that are ready to be downloaded or installed, select Custom Install and click Next. In a dialog box similar to the one shown in Figure 7-9, you can select the updates you want to install. Selecting Express Install and clicking Install immediately begins the installation process for all updates.

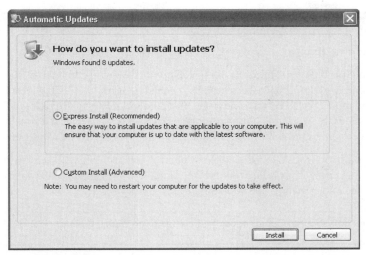

Figure 7-8. Click Cancel if you don't want to be bothered with an update installation right now.

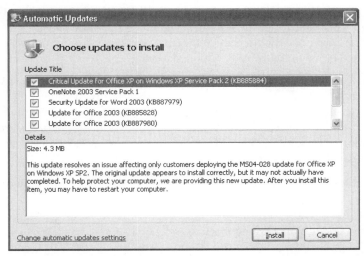

Figure 7-9. Automatic Updates displays a list of available updates when you select Custom Install in the first dialog box. This screen shows several Office updates downloaded by Microsoft Updates.

Tip Install updates on your own schedule

If you decide not to download or install a particular update and you clear its check box, you can install it at another time. To install an update that you previously rejected, open Automatic Updates. Then click the Offer Updates Again That I've Previously Hidden link (Windows XP SP2) or the Declined Updates button (Windows 2000). This option will be unavailable until at least one update has been declined.

Inside Out

Monitor Windows Update

If you encounter problems downloading or installing updates, you can enable "stepping mode." In this mode, Windows Update stops at each step along the way and displays a dialog box; you must click a button to proceed. Stepping mode is also useful for identifying download locations and viewing command-line switches, and it provides entertainment for those people who are interminably curious about the inner workings of Windows.

To enable stepping mode, use Registry Editor to open the HKLM\Software\Microsoft\Active Setup key. Create a new string value named SteppingMode and set its value data to Y. (To disable stepping mode, change the value data to N.)

For more information about stepping mode, see Microsoft Knowledge Base article 248439.

Downloading the Update Files for Multiple Computers

Some of the available updates are quite large, often exceeding 5 MB of data. And sometimes the file size shown in Windows Update is misleading; it indicates only the size of the installer for the update, not the update itself, which might be considerably larger. Particularly if you have a slow Internet connection, you'll want to minimize the bandwidth consumed by downloads from Windows Update.

Although it's not very well advertised (compared to the myriad ways to start Windows Update—only a portion of which are enumerated earlier in this chapter), Microsoft maintains a Web site where you can download stand-alone installable versions of the security fixes and other updates for Windows. Windows Update Catalog offers updates for all currently supported versions of Windows. You can search for updates based on operating system, language, date posted, content, and type of update.

To access Windows Update Catalog, visit *http://v4.windowsupdate.microsoft.com/catalog /en/default.asp.*

Tip Download updates on a fast connection
If you have a T-1 or other fast Internet connection at work and a slow dial-up connection at home, use the Windows Update Catalog to download the updates using your fast connection. Burn the files to a CD-R, take it home, and run the setup files.

Need a service pack for any Microsoft product? Visit *http://support.microsoft.com/gp/sp/*, where you'll find links to information about all released service packs, including information about how to obtain each one.

In 2005, Microsoft released Windows Server Update Services, which enables administrators of domain-based networks (running Microsoft Windows Server 2003 or Windows 2000 Server) to deliver and install updates throughout their network. For detailed information about Windows Server Update Services, visit *http://www.microsoft.com/windowsserversystem/wus/*.

Security Alert Services

In this book, we offer plenty of specific information about steps you can take to secure your computer. But we don't provide the level of detail that would, for example, suggest that you install the Internet Explorer patch described in Microsoft Security Bulletin MS04-005. Such information would be obsolete even before this book is printed. Finding out about—and responding to—newly discovered security vulnerabilities is an ongoing task.

Fortunately, you can rely on several services to keep you informed. The Automatic Updates feature advises you of Windows updates available from Microsoft. A number of other tools and services can alert you to additional security issues.

Receiving Alerts Through Instant Messaging

With Windows Messenger or MSN Messenger, you can receive an alert through your instant messaging program when new security information is available from Microsoft or when there's a virus outbreak.

> **Note** To get the latest version of Windows Messenger, use Windows Update or visit the .NET Messenger Service site at *http://www.microsoft.com/windows/messenger*. MSN Messenger is available at *http://messenger.msn.com*.

Microsoft issues an alert whenever it posts new information on its security Web site for nontechnical users. A different set of alerts is available for those who want more detailed information about breaking security issues. To sign up for either or both of these alerts, visit *http://www.microsoft.com/security/bulletins/alerts.mspx*. These alerts can also be sent to a mobile device such as a phone or PDA.

If you want to be the first on your block to know about a newly discovered virus outbreak, you can set up notification from McAfee.com through Microsoft Alerts. You can choose to receive an e-mail message, an instant message, a text message on your mobile device, or even a pager message the moment McAfee.com issues a virus alert. To sign up for McAfee.com alerts, visit *http://us.mcafee.com/alerts/*.

> **For information about other services available through Microsoft Alerts, visit**
> *http://www.microsoft.com/net/services/alerts/signup.asp*.

Although the McAfee.com instant messaging alerts are an interesting application of Microsoft Alerts, you might find the not-so-subtle reminders of the dangers of viruses and the availability of McAfee solutions a bit overbearing. The vendors of antivirus programs usually have the best and fastest information about new viruses, but remember that their goal is to sell antivirus programs and services. You can expect some exaggeration of the dangers and the pervasiveness of virus outbreaks.

Receiving E-Mail Alerts and RSS Notification

Several reliable sources offer subscriptions (usually free) to security alerts sent by e-mail or by RSS feeds. Some send a message only when a security issue is discovered (or when a patch is available, or both), whereas others publish on a regular weekly or monthly schedule, collecting that period's advisories into a single message. Popular and trustworthy security alert e-letters include the following:

- **Microsoft Security Newsletters.**   Microsoft publishes two monthly security newsletters: one for home users and one for computer professionals. The newsletter for home users provides information to help you keep your home computers safe. Along with practical tips and how-to information, the newsletter includes links to security bulletins, critical updates, and more detailed information. To sign up, visit *http://www.microsoft.com/athome/security/secnews/*. The newsletter for computer professionals includes more information about protecting corporate networks, and is generally more technical in nature. However, it's a good read even for nonprofessionals who have the responsibility for maintaining computer security in a small business. Its signup page can be found at *http://www.microsoft.com /technet/security/secnews/*.

- **Microsoft Security Updates RSS feed.**   This RSS feed delivers notification of major security updates, which are normally released on the second Tuesday of each month, along with a link to more detailed information. You can learn more about this service at *http://www.microsoft.com/security/rss.mspx*. To subscribe, point your RSS reader to *http://www.microsoft.com/security/bulletins/updates.xml*.

- **Microsoft Security Notification Service.**   Every system administrator should subscribe to this one, which delivers each Microsoft Security Bulletin as it's released. The security bulletins from Microsoft are often the most authoritative because each bulletin provides confirmation of a security vulnerability and, more important, Microsoft's update or workaround to address the vulnerability. Although the bulletins generally describe security issues honestly and accurately, they're narrowly focused on a single problem and a solution; you might find alternative solutions (as well as sometimes inflammatory discussions) from other sources. The security bulletins cover only Microsoft products. To subscribe, visit *http://www.microsoft.com /technet/security/bulletin/notify.mspx.*

Except for extraordinary events, Microsoft security bulletins are released on the second Tuesday of each month. The release of the bulletins is sometimes accompanied by a Webcast that features a brief overview of the current month's bulletins along with a question-and-answer session. Why monthly, instead of the moment a vulnerability is discovered? Most attacks are made using known vulnerabilities that have been discovered by someone else. Attacks using a newly announced vulnerability start spreading in the wild days or even hours after details of the vulnerability are made known. By releasing security bulletins (and security updates) on a known, fixed schedule, administrators can inoculate their computers at the same time that attackers are busily trying to figure out how to exploit the vulnerability. By the time that's done, computers managed by a savvy administrator are already safe.

● **CERT Advisories.** The CERT Coordination Center (CERT/CC) issues advisories that explain an Internet security problem, including information that helps you determine whether you're vulnerable and describes fixes or workarounds. To subscribe, visit *http://www.cert.org/nav/alerts.html*. (The CERT/CC also publishes a quarterly summary if you don't want to be bothered with individual advisories.)

● **Security Alert.** InfoWorld offers brief alerts of significant security issues along with links to the full story in InfoWorld magazine. To subscribe, visit *http://subscribe.infoworld.com/cgi-win/ifwd.cgi?m=newsletter*. (At the same site, you can sign up for Security Adviser, a weekly security newsletter.)

● **Secunia.** Secunia prepares a large number of security advisories and virus alerts that are available with an e-mail subscription or RSS feed. For details, visit *http://secunia.com/mailing_lists/*.

● **Security UPDATE.** This weekly security bulletin (along with occasional special alerts) from the publisher of Windows IT Pro Magazine offers security tips and capsule descriptions of newly discovered vulnerabilities. It also includes links to sites with more information and fixes. To subscribe, visit *http://www.windowsitpro.com/email/*.

● **Crypto-Gram.** This monthly newsletter by security expert Bruce Schneier covers broader security issues and cryptography instead of providing alerts about particular vulnerabilities, putting security issues in context. To subscribe, visit *http://www.counterpane.com/crypto-gram.html*.

● **BugTraq.** BugTraq is a moderated mailing list that offers announcements and detailed discussions of computer security vulnerabilities; the descriptions of vulnerabilities often explain how to exploit them as well as how to fix them. To subscribe, visit *http://www.securityfocus.com/archive/*.

● **Blogs.** Several fine Web logs (blogs), many written by leading experts in the field, are devoted to security topics. You can find pointers to some authoritative blogs at Microsoft's IT Pro Security Community page, *http://www.microsoft.com /technet/community/en-us/security/default.mspx*. Third-party blogs are quite ephemeral, even by Web standards, so we're not including a list of URLs in this book. Instead, we suggest that you search for security-related blogs. You can use a general-purpose search engine, such as Google, to search for terms like "security blog" and "security rss feed." Searches on news aggregating sites, such as Feedster and Daypop, can also lead you to terrific blogs that you'll want to read regularly.

The alerts published by these and similar services often overlap, and you probably won't want to subscribe to all of them. But you should try each one to see which best meets your needs. You'll discover that some security mailing lists merely publish raw reports without validation or control; as a result, they can be sources of wild claims that might not stand the test of time or careful investigation. You'll soon develop your own sense of which ones provide accurate information and which ones spread panic and sensationalism.

Be suspicious of security alerts you receive. Particularly if an alert directs you to a Web site to install a patch or an update, be absolutely certain that you know who it's actually coming from. It's all too easy to spoof an e-mail address; a malicious person could send a "security update" to you and make it appear that it's from Microsoft, for example. How can you tell if an alert is legitimate?

- If the message includes a "security patch" as an attachment, it's definitely not from Microsoft. Microsoft (and most other reputable companies) never distributes patches or updates by e-mail. Microsoft distributes patches only by posting them to a Web site, and they're always digitally signed.

- Be extremely suspicious of a security update that comes from an unexpected source. (For example, if you receive a security message from "Microsoft" but you don't subscribe to the Microsoft Security Notification Service, your radar should start beeping.)

- Be suspicious of a message with grammatical and spelling errors—a common trait of mail from script kiddies.

- Use the usual tools and methods for determining the true provenance of a message. For details, see "How to Decode an E-Mail Header," page 531.

- Confirm the sender's identity by examining the message's digital signature. For details, see "Ensuring the Authenticity and Integrity of Your Messages," page 520.

- Visit the Web site of the purported sender to confirm information received in an e-mail message. For example, to view an unaltered version of a legitimate Microsoft Security Bulletin, visit *http://www.microsoft.com/security/bulletins/default.mspx* or, for more technical details, *http://www.microsoft.com/technet/security/current.asp*.

Other Sources for Security Alerts

Many Web sites are devoted to issues of computer security. The roster keeps getting longer, and the following list is far from comprehensive. It's a good idea to visit one or more of these sites periodically to read about the latest security vulnerabilities:

- **Microsoft Security.** You can find links to security bulletins and virus alerts here (*http://www.microsoft.com/security*), along with numerous security checklists, white papers, and other security information.

- **Microsoft TechNet IT Pro Security Community.** TechNet is a collection of products and services geared toward computer professionals. The IT Pro Security Community home page at *http://www.microsoft.com/technet/community/en-us /security/default.mspx* provides links to newsgroups, chats, blogs, and other resources where you can learn more about security from people who have to think about it for a living.

- **CERT Coordination Center.** The CERT/CC is a federally funded research center operated by Carnegie Mellon University that studies Internet security issues, puts out advisories and incident notes, and provides a host of other security information at its site, *http://www.cert.org*.

- **SANS Institute.** The SANS (SysAdmin, Audit, Network, Security) Institute is a research and education organization of computer security professionals. Its site offers security news, research publications, and much more. Go to *http://www.sans.org.*

- **SecuriTeam.** Beyond Security (*http://www.beyondsecurity.com*), a company that performs vulnerability scans and security assessments, assembles a compendium of security news, alerts, and product reviews at *http://www.securiteam.com.*

- **eEye Digital Security.** eEye offers security products and consulting services—and has been instrumental in uncovering vulnerabilities in a number of computer programs. You can read about their discoveries at *http://www.eeye.com/html /research/advisories.*

- **Secunia.** As an alternative to Secunia's e-mail and RSS subscriptions, their site (*http://secunia.com*) provides an archive of all the security advisories and virus alerts, which can be searched, listed, and viewed in a variety of ways.

- **Security Administrator.** As part of Windows IT Pro Magazine Network, this site supplies security-related news and information from the magazine. Visit *http://www.windowsitpro.com/WindowsSecurity.*

- **SecurityFocus.** SecurityFocus offers a searchable vulnerability database and security news updates at its home page, http://www.securityfocus.com.

- **TechSpot.** Unlike the other sites in this list, TechSpot is not focused exclusively on security. It's a site for computer enthusiasts (particularly gaming enthusiasts) who are often at the bleeding edge of security issues for home users. Its OS Updates page (*http://www.techspot.com/tweaks/updates*) is created with this audience in mind, and it does a reasonable job of providing current information about security updates.

One other way to keep your ear to the ground on security issues is through the mainstream press. General circulation newspapers, television, and other broadcast media are paying more attention to computer security issues. The information they present is often sensational, only marginally accurate, and sometimes flat-out wrong. Nevertheless, it can provide a good "first alert" mechanism while you learn about the other news of the world. (After all, you don't want to spend *all* your time focused on computer security!)

Testing and Verifying Your Secure Status

Despite your best efforts, it's often difficult to know for sure whether you've succeeded in securing your computer. How do you know that you've patched all your programs, set up secure passwords for all accounts, and secured your system against intrusion by outsiders? After all, the fact that no one has broken in yet doesn't mean they can't!

Many security consultants provide various testing methods. Some will set their best attackers to work in an attempt to break into your network. Others use time-honored techniques such as creating a "honeypot"—a sacrificial system that attracts attackers. These services are typically beyond the reach of home users and small businesses.

A number of free security scanners and security assessment tools are available, however. The following Web sites check for open ports that can be used in an attack, the existence of viruses or Trojan horses on your system, and certain security-related settings. None is absolutely reliable and some have something to sell or an axe to grind—but they can be useful tools for periodically assessing your security:

- Microsoft Baseline Security Analyzer (*http://www.microsoft.com/technet/security/tools/mbsahome.mspx*)
- PC Flank (*http://www.pcflank.com*)
- Secure-Me tests in the DSLR Tools section of DSLReports.com (*http://www.dslreports.com/secureme*)
- Symantec Security Check (*http://security.norton.com*)

Checking Your Update Status with Microsoft Baseline Security Analyzer

Even with the assistance of Windows Update, it's tough to keep up with all the security updates for Windows. Fortunately, a tool is available that quickly checks the status of security updates. Microsoft Baseline Security Analyzer (MBSA) checks the very latest list of updates and compares it with the ones that have been installed on one or more computers. In addition, MBSA checks the computers for common security vulnerabilities (such as weak passwords and improper or insecure configuration) in Windows, Internet Information Services (IIS), Internet Explorer, Microsoft Office, Microsoft SQL Server, and other Microsoft server products.

> **Note** Microsoft Baseline Security Analyzer replaces two earlier tools that provided similar, but less comprehensive, security checks: Microsoft Personal Security Advisor and Microsoft Network Security Hotfix Checker (more commonly identified by the name of its executable file, Hfnetchk).

You can use MBSA to check your own computer or other computers on your network. It looks for security updates applied to the following operating systems:

- Windows 2000
- Windows XP
- Windows Server 2003

To obtain the latest version of MBSA, use your browser to display the Microsoft TechNet article at *http://www.microsoft.com/mbsa/*. This article includes a link to the download site for MBSA, along with instructions for downloading, installing, and using this tool. After you download the MBSA setup file (Mbsasetup.msi), double-click it to run Microsoft Baseline Security Analyzer Setup, a straightforward setup wizard. To run MBSA, you must be logged on as an administrator. MBSA initially displays a screen such as the one shown in Figure 7-10.

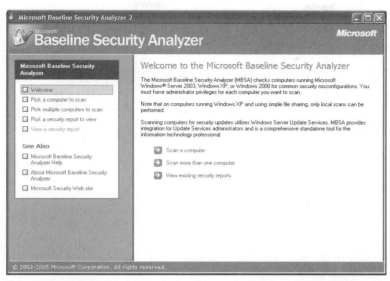

Figure 7-10. MBSA uses an interface that's similar to Windows Update.

After you click one of the links shown in Figure 7-10, MBSA asks which computer (or computers) you want to check. As Figure 7-11 on the next page shows, you can specify computers by name or by IP address. In this same window, you select which tests you want to perform from the following choices:

- **Check for Windows administrative vulnerabilities.**   Selecting this option causes MBSA to check for a variety of insecure settings. For example, it checks to see whether all hard disks are formatted as NTFS volumes, checks the status of the Guest account, and examines permissions on shared folders.

- **Check for weak passwords.**   MBSA checks the logon password for each user account and warns you if it finds blank or weak passwords.

- **Check for IIS administrative vulnerabilities.**   With this option, MBSA examines your Internet Information Services configuration for insecure settings and to see whether the IIS Lockdown Tool has been run. For information about this tool and other IIS security issues, see "Tightening Security on Internet Information Services," page 662. If you select this option and you don't have IIS installed, MBSA reports only that IIS is not running.

- **Check for SQL administrative vulnerabilities.**   This option checks for insecure settings in SQL Server. If you select this option and you don't have SQL Server installed, MBSA reports only that SQL Server is not installed.

- **Check for security updates.**   Selecting this option causes MBSA to download the latest information and scan the specified computers for installed security updates. For this scan, MBSA uses a frequently updated XML database to check for updates to each of the Microsoft products monitored by MBSA.

For each applicable update, MBSA checks the registry to see whether a particular key exists. It then checks the file version and checksum for each file installed by the update to ensure that it's the correct version and that it hasn't been modified.

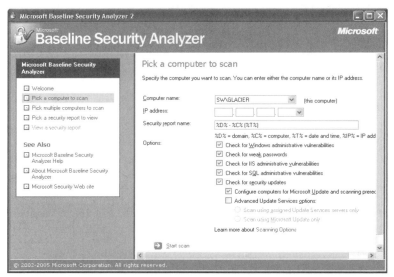

Figure 7-11. If you choose to scan multiple computers, you can specify the name of your workgroup or domain, or you can specify a range of IP addresses in a window that's only slightly different from this one.

Tip Scan your entire network
You can scan all the computers on your local network at one time. You'll need to be logged on using an account that has administrative permission on each computer. Simply click the link to scan multiple computers, and then enter the name of your workgroup or domain in the Domain Name box.

After MBSA completes its scan of the selected computers, it displays a report similar to the one shown in Figure 7-12.

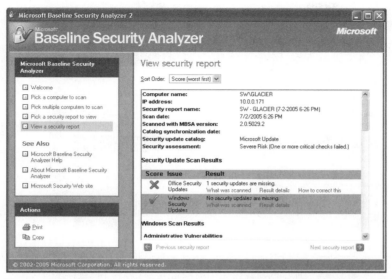

Figure 7-12. You can print the results of an MBSA scan by clicking the Print link in the left pane.

Troubleshooting

MBSA reports "no computers were found"

After you select a computer and instruct MBSA to scan it, the program cogitates for a few moments and then displays "Unable to scan all computers. No computers were found." This rather misleading message merely means that your account is not an administrator account on the computer you're attempting to scan. To scan your own computer, your account must be a member of the local Administrators group. To scan another computer on your network, you must use an account that's a member of that computer's local Administrators group.

An icon by each test shows at a glance the status of the computer's security settings. A red *X* indicates a critical vulnerability exists; a yellow *X* indicates that a computer failed a noncritical test. A green check mark, of course, is a good thing. The links beneath each test result lead to more information about the test. Figure 7-13 on the next page shows the window displayed by clicking Result Details under the first test shown in Figure 7-12.

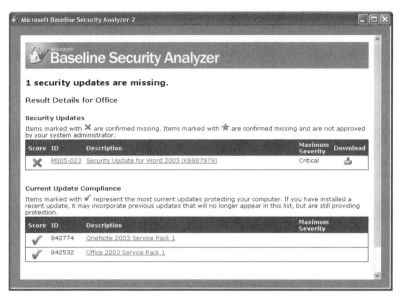

Figure 7-13. Clicking Result Details for the Office Updates Test shows which updates are missing.

Similarly, clicking Result Details for the Windows Security Updates test displays a list of updates that have not been installed, with each missing update identified by a Microsoft Security Bulletin number. (A Microsoft Security Bulletin identifier begins with *MS* followed by a two-digit number representing the year. The number following the hyphen is a sequential number.) To learn more about the missing updates, you can click the link to display the bulletin. Each security bulletin includes a link to the update, which you can download and install.

Tip Finding specific security bulletins

You can navigate to a security bulletin by starting at *http://www.microsoft.com/security /bulletins*. Alternatively, you can go directly to a security bulletin. To display bulletin MS04-44, for example, use this URL:

http://www.microsoft.com/technet/security/bulletin/MS04-044.mspx

To display another bulletin, simply replace the bulletin number near the end of the URL.

Using links in the left pane, you can print your report or copy it (in HTML format) to the Clipboard for inclusion in another document.

MBSA stores each of your test results as well. Each report is saved as an XML document in %UserProfile%\Securityscans. To view the results of a previous scan, in MBSA's left pane click Pick A Security Report To View. You can then click any report to review its results.

Using MBSA Command-Line Options

As an alternative to opening MBSA from its Start menu icon, you might find it more convenient to use a command prompt. At a command prompt, MBSA supports a rich collection of command-line parameters. By using these parameters, the most useful of which are described in Table 7-1, you can create scheduled tasks or batch programs that enable you to automate the scanning process. MBSA displays its findings in a Command Prompt window (or in a text file if you use the /F parameter), but it also creates an XML report, just as the graphical version of MBSA does.

To run MBSA from a command prompt, be sure the folder containing MBSA files (by default, %ProgramFiles%\Microsoft Baseline Security Analyzer) is the current folder and then type **mbsacli** followed by the appropriate parameters. For more information about MBSA command-line parameters, type **mbsacli /?** at a command prompt.

Table 7-1. MBSA Command-Line Parameters

Parameter	Description
Specifying Computers to Scan	
/Target *domain\computer*	Identifies the computer to scan by specifying the name of the domain (or workgroup) and the name of the computer. If you don't include the /Target, /R, or /D parameter, MBSA scans the local computer.
/Target *xxx.xxx.xxx.xxx*	Identifies the computer to scan by specifying its IP address.
/R *xxx.xxx.xxx.xxx-xxx.xxx.xxx.xxx*	Identifies the computers to scan by specifying a range of IP addresses.
/D *domainname*	Specifies scanning of all computers in the named domain or workgroup.
Specifying Scan Options	
/N	Specifies options to skip. You can follow /N with any of the following options: Updates (skips update checks); IIS (skips Internet Information Services checks); OS (skips Windows operating system checks); Password (skips password checks); SQL (skips SQL Server checks). To skip multiple options, separate the option names with a plus sign (for example, /Niis+sql).
Specifying Output	
/O *template*	Specifies the name of the report file. The default template is *%d% - %c% (%t%)*; these replaceable parameters represent the domain name, computer name, and date/time.
/L	Lists all saved report files.
/Ls	Lists reports from the latest scan.

Table 7-1. **MBSA Command-Line Parameters**

Parameter	Description
/Lr *reportname*	Displays the overview report from the saved *reportname* file. Enclose *reportname* in quotation marks.
/Ld *reportname*	Displays the detailed report from the saved *reportname* file. Enclose *reportname* in quotation marks.
/Qp	Hides display of scan progress.
/Qe	Hides display of the error list.
/Qr	Hides display of the report list.
/Q	Hides display of scan progress, error list, and report list.

Learning More About MBSA

Two convenient resources supply additional information about MBSA:

- Knowledge Base article 895660 provides detailed information about MBSA.
- The newsgroup microsoft.public.security.baseline_analyzer offers a discussion forum.

Going Beyond MBSA

The company that developed Hfnetchk and MBSA for Microsoft, Shavlik Technologies, offers HFNetChkPRO and other products for monitoring and verifying security settings. These enhanced versions are designed for administrators of large networks and they provide a complete patch management solution. For details, visit *http://www. shavlik.com*.

Part 2

Smart, Secure Networking

Setting Up a Secure Home or Small Business Network

Because we emphasize security in this book, you might be under the impression that the only secure computer is one that is not connected to the Internet or to any other computer. Fortunately that's not the case.

Microsoft Windows XP and Windows 2000 Professional were both designed with networking *and* security in mind. And unlike the early days of networking, setting up a trouble-free, secure Windows-based network is generally a straightforward process. This is particularly true with Windows XP, which includes a Network Setup Wizard to assist in configuring each computer on the network—even those running other versions of Windows.

> **Note** In this chapter, we focus on peer-to-peer networks for small workgroups (typically comprising 10 or fewer computers). Although much of the hardware setup and network configuration information is common to all networks, you'll find information specifically about domain-based networks—client/server networks that include a domain controller running Microsoft Windows Server 2003 or Windows 2000 Server—in Chapter 11, "Working with a Corporate Network."
>
> One other note about this chapter: Here we concentrate on setting up and securing a local area network (emphasis on *local*), or LAN. Although we lay the groundwork for connecting the LAN to the Internet—an integral part of most modern networks—you'll find the details of connecting your network to the Internet and managing that connection in Chapter 9, "Sharing an Internet Connection."

Security Checklist: Network Setup

Don't let your network fall prey to outside attackers. Follow these steps to secure your borders:

- On a computer running Windows XP, use the Network Setup Wizard to configure your network properly. This wizard sets permissions, enables file sharing, configures the Guest account, and turns on Windows Firewall, if needed.
- If you share an Internet connection through a hub or switch (not a recommended configuration), configure Windows Firewall (or a third-party alternative) so that file sharing over TCP/IP is allowed only on the local subnet.
- Disable file sharing on your Internet connection.
- On a computer running Windows XP Professional, consider disabling Simple File Sharing for extra security.
- Don't share the root folder of any drive unless that drive contains only non-sensitive data files.

Connecting two or more computers to form a workgroup provides several benefits:

- **Shared storage.**   By sharing folders across a network, you can transport files from one computer to another without relying on removable media or e-mail. And you don't need to maintain duplicate copies of files, because everyone on the network can access shared files, such as a collection of digital photos or a music library, stored in a single location.
- **Shared hardware resources.**   A shared printer attached to a computer can be accessed by all users on the network. Without this capability, each computer would need its own printer. Similarly, shared CD-ROM and DVD-ROM drives can be accessed by other network users.
- **Shared Internet connection.**   By using Internet Connection Sharing (ICS), you can set up Internet access on one computer and allow every computer on the network to share that connection. For a dial-up connection to the Internet, ICS lets all computers share a single modem and phone line. Furthermore, users on each computer needn't worry about whether the line is already in use before making a connection. Users of high-speed Internet connections such as DSL and broadband cable can also use ICS to great benefit. However, as we discuss in Chapter 9, in this situation using a hardware router offers significant security and performance advantages over ICS.

Although Windows XP uses a different sharing model by default, a mixed network of Windows XP and Windows 2000 workstations generally poses no problems. (For details about the sharing models, see "Windows Sharing and Security Models," page 17.) The Network Setup Wizard included with Windows XP, in fact, can be used to properly configure Windows 2000 computers to share the same network.

Chapter 8

Choosing a Network Type

When you set up a network for use in a home or small office, you must first decide which of several network types is best suited for your use. Ethernet and wireless—each of which has several variants—are by far the most popular types, but several other options exist, and all are supported by Windows XP and Windows 2000.

Ethernet Networking

Ethernet is a time-tested networking standard that was developed in the 1970s, and it remains the most popular standard for networks of all sizes. Networking hardware devices for Ethernet, such as network adapters, hubs, and routers, are widely available.

The physical layout of an Ethernet network is called a *star-bus topology*, because all computers connect (via cable) to a central hub. As shown in Figure 8-1, this layout bears some resemblance to rays of light from a star—at least on paper. (The tangle of cables in real-life hubs is often a different picture altogether!)

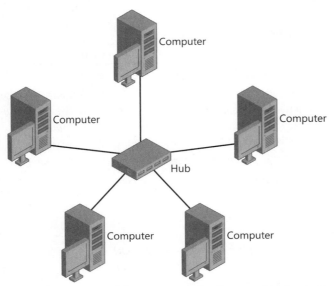

Figure 8-1. On an Ethernet network, all computers (and other network devices) connect to a central hub.

On an Ethernet network, you can connect a hub to another hub. This enables you to connect more devices than the number of ports on a single hub. For example, one of the computers shown in Figure 8-1 could be replaced with a hub and it, in turn, could have a number of computers connected to it. So much for our nice, neat star.

Connections between Ethernet devices use cables with RJ-45 modular connectors. (An RJ-45 connector is similar to, but slightly wider than, the RJ-11 connector used with a standard telephone jack.)

The Ethernet standard includes definitions of several data transfer speeds:

- The original Ethernet standard, known as 10Base-T, has a maximum speed of 10 megabits per second (Mbps). (The name *10Base-T* means 10 Mbps baseband over twisted-pair wiring. *Baseband* carries a single message at a time, as opposed to *broadband*, which can carry multiple messages simultaneously.)

- Fast Ethernet, also known as 100Base-T, can transfer data at 100 Mbps. Most currently available hubs and adapters offer auto-switching (10/100) capability that you can use to combine Ethernet and Fast Ethernet devices on the same network. Without this capability, traffic on a mixed network is reduced to the speed of the slowest link.

- Gigabit Ethernet (1000Base-T) is a recent standard that transfers data at up to 1 gigabit per second (Gbps), or 1000 Mbps.

- The 10 Gigabit Ethernet system (10GBASE) operates at speeds up to 10 Gbps. Because it requires fiber optic media instead of more common copper wire, 10GBASE hasn't yet been widely adopted.

Table 8-1 summarizes the advantages and disadvantages of an Ethernet network.

Table 8-1. **Ethernet Network Evaluation**

Pros	Cons
Network adapters, hubs, and cables are widely available and relatively inexpensive.	Requires a hub.
Many other types of network devices, such as routers, residential gateways, print servers, storage devices, and printers, are available with a built-in Ethernet adapter.	Requires an Ethernet jack in the proximity of each computer.
Installation and configuration of network adapters is easy.	Cabling can be difficult, particularly if you want to install concealed wiring in an existing structure.
At speeds up to 10 Gbps (and even at the current norm of 100 Mbps), Ethernet is the fastest network type for homes and small offices.	
Extremely reliable.	
Secure. (Unless an intruder can physically connect to your network—through an unguarded jack that's connected to the hub, for example—eavesdropping is impractical.)	

Wireless Networking

The popularity of wireless networking has soared in recent years due to improvements in ease of use (in particular, Windows XP provides much better support than previous versions of Windows, including Windows 2000) and decreasing hardware prices. Although wireless networks were originally developed for use with portable computers, they're becoming increasingly popular for desktop users, particularly in homes and offices where wiring is impossible, impractical, or—at best—unsightly.

Like Ethernet networks, wireless networks use a star-bus topology, in which each device connects to a central hub, known as a wireless access point (WAP). A key difference, of course, is that the devices connect via radio waves instead of copper wire. The WAP is often incorporated into a router or residential gateway, which lets you bridge the wireless network to an Ethernet network.

The most popular wireless networks use one of two variants of the IEEE (Institute of Electrical and Electronics Engineers) 802.11 standard, also known as Wi-Fi. Wi-Fi networks using the 802.11b standard transfer data at a maximum frequency of 11 Mbps (comparable to Ethernet speeds). The newer 802.11g standard works at approximately five times the speed (54 Mbps). Most 802.11g hardware works with 802.11b networks as well. A third variant, 802.11a, is less common, but because it offers better reliability at speeds up to 54 Mbps, it's sometimes used for streaming media (for example, in some computers that use Windows XP Media Center Edition). Because it broadcasts on a different frequency, 802.11a equipment is incompatible with 802.11b and 802.11g networks.

For more information about these and other wireless networking standards, see "802-Dot-Whatever: Decoding Wireless Standards," page 333.

Table 8-2 summarizes the advantages and disadvantages of a wireless network.

Table 8-2. **Wireless Network Evaluation**

Pros	Cons
● Network adapters and hubs are widely available.	● Although prices have dropped dramatically in recent years, wireless devices are usually more expensive than comparable Ethernet devices.
● Installation and configuration of network adapters is easy.	● Requires a hub.
● No wiring is needed between devices.	● Connections are not always reliable, particularly when walls or floors separate devices.
	● Speed (and reliability) drops as distance between devices increases.
	● Because the signal is broadcast into open space, it's more vulnerable to intrusion.

For details about installing, configuring, and securing a wireless network, see Chapter 10, "Wireless Networking."

HomePNA Networking

Networks that comply with the Home Phoneline Networking Alliance (HomePNA) standard connect computers through ordinary telephone wire. This enables you to use the existing phone wiring in your home or office instead of running new wire for an Ethernet network. HomePNA transmits data on the same wires that carry telephone and fax signals, without interfering with those communications. You connect the network

Chapter 8

adapter in each computer to a telephone wall jack using an ordinary modular phone cord with RJ-11 connectors.

HomePNA networks, which operate at speeds of approximately 10 Mbps, don't require a central connection point such as a hub; instead, they use a daisy-chain topology in which all network adapters communicate directly.

A once promising technology, HomePNA has been largely displaced by inexpensive wireless networks. Although the HomePNA 3.0 specification, released in 2003, promises speeds of 128 Mbps and higher, no products that meet the specification are currently available. For more information about HomePNA, visit the Home Phoneline Networking Alliance Web site at *http://www.homepna.org*.

Table 8-3 summarizes the advantages and disadvantages of a HomePNA network.

Table 8-3. HomePNA Network Evaluation

Pros	Cons
● Installation and configuration of network adapters is easy.	● Few new products are being developed.
● Uses existing telephone wiring.	● Requires a telephone jack in the proximity of each computer.
● No hub required.	● At 10 Mbps, it's slower than current Ethernet networks.
● Excellent reliability.	● Because it doesn't use modern encryption, it's vulnerable to intrusion, particularly to an attacker who has access to an unguarded telephone jack or telephone wires outside the building.

HomePlug Powerline Networking

The HomePlug Powerline Alliance (*http://www.homeplug.org*) has developed a standard that uses electric power wiring to connect network devices. A network adapter in each device plugs into an ordinary power outlet; data is transferred at speeds up to 14 Mbps without interfering with power transmission. (Furthermore, according to manufacturers, powerline devices do not interfere with X-10 and similar products that also communicate over powerlines.)

Emerging powerline networking standards enable its use for connecting devices other than computers. HomePlug AV is designed to support delivery of digital audio and video to entertainment devices, and Broadband Powerline (BPL) promises to offer high-speed Internet access from your electric power utility as an alternative to cable and DSL. Because HomePlug 1.0, HomePlug AV, and HomePlug BPL are designed to work together seamlessly, this could develop into an exciting system that integrates computing and home entertainment. The specifications are still in development and, aside from a handful of HomePlug 1.0 networking devices, few products exist—so much remains to be seen. The whole effort could be short-circuited if the technology doesn't develop as promised or if consumers don't buy it.

Table 8-4 summarizes the advantages and disadvantages of a powerline network.

Table 8-4. HomePlug Powerline Network Evaluation

Pros	Cons
● Installation and configuration of network adapters is easy.	● Relatively few networking products are available.
● Uses existing power wiring.	● At speeds of up to 14 Mbps, it's slower than current Ethernet networks.
● No extra cables are required, as network devices plug directly into a power outlet.	
● No hub required.	
● Reasonably secure, as it uses 56-bit encryption.	

Other Network Types

Several other types of networks are available for use with Windows-based computers. Because of their expense and complexity, the following types are seldom used in networking homes and small offices. They are more likely to be found in large corporate networks.

- **Token Ring.** Token Ring is a networking technology originally developed by IBM. In a Token Ring network, all network devices are connected in a loop, or ring.
- **Fiber Distributed Data Interface (FDDI).** FDDI uses fiber-optic cable to transfer data around a ring topology.
- **TCP/IP over Asynchronous Transfer Mode (ATM).** ATM is a packet-switching networking technology that provides transmission speeds of up to 1 Gbps; it's often used for wide area network (WAN) connections.
- **ATM LAN emulation (LANE).** An emulated LAN client uses an ATM network adapter, letting it connect to an ATM switch that provides LAN emulation services.

Working with Mixed Networks

Each of the network types described on the preceding pages is, to some degree, incompatible with all the others. Yet you might not be able to settle on a single network type. For example, you might want to have a wired Ethernet network setup for all your desktop computers, because it offers the best price, speed, and reliability. But because you want to be able to use your laptop computer throughout the house, using a wireless network is more practical than dragging a network cable around. In another scenario, you might use powerline networking to connect the computers on your internal LAN, but you need to use an Ethernet connection to a cable modem to connect the LAN to the Internet.

Seamlessly passing data between networks is done with a bridge. A bridge can take the form of a hardware device. Most wireless residential gateways, for example, include several Ethernet ports; the gateway bridges the wireless and Ethernet networks. Alternatively, a computer that has an adapter for each network can act as a bridge. For details, see "Bridging Connections," page 274.

Setting Up Your Network Hardware

Before you can configure network software and begin sharing resources, you must install and configure the proper hardware. To set up a home or small office network, you'll need a network adapter for each computer, a central connection point, and cable to tie it all together. The following sections provide additional details for these steps in setting up a network:

1 Install a network adapter in each computer.

2 Set up the central connection point—typically a hub, switch, router, or residential gateway.

3 Connect the cables.

When those steps are complete, you can configure the network connections.

> **Note** The descriptions in the following sections pertain specifically to Ethernet networks. The process of setting up other types of networks is nearly identical, but you should check the documentation provided with the network hardware for further details.

Installing and Configuring a Network Adapter

Regardless which type of network you choose, the first step in setting up a network is to install a network adapter in each computer. A network adapter (also known as a network interface card, or NIC) might take the form of an internal expansion card, a PC Card, or an external device that plugs into a USB or IEEE 1394 (Firewire) port. Some systems have a built-in network adapter; in that case, your work is already done.

Follow these general guidelines and the manufacturer's instructions for installing the adapter:

● If you're installing an internal adapter, for your own safety and to avoid damage to the adapter or the computer, turn off and disconnect the computer's power before you open the case.

● If you plan to use an external adapter, check the instructions to see whether you need to install a driver *before* you connect the adapter.

On most systems, you don't need to take any special configuration steps to install a network adapter. The Plug and Play functionality in Windows XP and Windows 2000 detects the newly installed device and then installs the necessary drivers. If Windows includes a driver, it installs automatically when the adapter is detected; if it can't find a built-in driver, Windows prompts you to supply the location of the driver files.

Connecting with Hubs, Switches, and Routers

Throughout our description of network types in this chapter, we've used the term *hub* in its generic sense to refer to a central connection point for networks that use a star-bus topology, such as Ethernet. However, a *hub* (using its more precise definition) is just one of several types of connection points commonly used in home and small office networks:

- **Hub.**   A hub, like the other devices described in this list, is a hardware device that has several jacks into which you can plug cables attached to computers and other network devices. Each of these jacks is called a *port*. In a hub (which is sometimes called a *repeater*), data that is received on one port is broadcast to all its other ports, even if the data is destined for only one other connected device. This simplistic method ensures that data reaches its intended destination, but it produces a lot of unnecessary network traffic and therefore can lead to slow network response times. Further reducing throughput is the fact that, with a hub, the maximum available bandwidth (10 Mbps on an Ethernet hub, for example) is divided among all the active ports.

- **Switch.**   A switch keeps track of the MAC address for each connected device. When a switch receives data, it sends it only to the port to which the destination computer is attached. This provides several performance and security benefits compared to a hub. Extraneous network traffic is reduced manifold, of course. Unlike a hub, a switch dedicates full bandwidth to each port, so that two computers on the same switch communicate at full speed without having to share bandwidth with other computers. From a security standpoint, directing network traffic solely to the intended destination reduces the possibility that an eavesdropper can intercept network traffic. In short, a switch is faster and more secure than a hub.

- **Router.**   Unlike hubs and switches, which are used to connect computers on a single network, a router is typically used to connect two or more networks. However, routers are commonly used in even the simplest of home networks when you need to connect that network to the Internet. In effect, what a router does in that situation is connect the home LAN (which might consist of only one computer) to the network at an Internet service provider (ISP), such as MSN.

  A router uses the logical addressing information that characterizes packets at the network layer to route information between networks. (By contrast, hubs and switches work at the data-link layer to handle the data type known as frames, which incorporate physical addressing information into packets received from network layer services.) That is, a router (on a TCP/IP network) uses the IP address to direct traffic, whereas switches use the MAC address.

> **Note**   "Network layer" and "data-link layer" refer to two of the seven layers in the Open Systems Interconnection (OSI) reference model, a networking standard introduced in 1978 by the International Organization for Standardization (ISO). The OSI model describes communication within a computer (data is passed from one layer to another) and between computers (data is passed from a layer on one computer to the same layer on another computer). Details of the OSI model are beyond the scope of this book; the Windows 2000 Server Resource Kit provides a good description, and it's available online at *http://www.microsoft.com/resources/documentation/windows/2000/server/reskit/en-us/cnet/cnfh_osi_OWSV.asp*.

Chapter 8

Despite the physical resemblance between these devices—each is a small box with a row of jacks (ports) that accept RJ-45 connectors—hubs and switches work quite differently from, and serve a different purpose than, routers. So why have we conflated them in this discussion? Because they're often integrated into a single device, sometimes called a broadband router or residential gateway. Most broadband routers—the type of router typically sold for use in homes and small offices—incorporate a 4-port or 8-port Ethernet switch (or hub) and a router that connects to an external DSL or cable modem. (Some even have that modem—which is a misnomer, as it's actually a router—built in.) Many include a bridged wireless access point, which provides access to a wireless network, and between all three networks: Internet, Ethernet, and wireless. In addition, broadband routers typically include network address translation (NAT), Dynamic Host Configuration Protocol (DHCP) server, proxy server, and firewall capabilities, providing Internet connection, networking, and security products in a single box.

So, which do you use? For a small network that's not connected to the Internet, use a hub or switch. To connect a small network to the Internet, use a router. In addition, use hubs and switches within your local area network to expand it to include more devices than you can connect to a single router, switch, or hub. Figure 8-2 shows a typical configuration that uses a broadband router to connect a network to the Internet, and a separate switch to connect additional computers to the network.

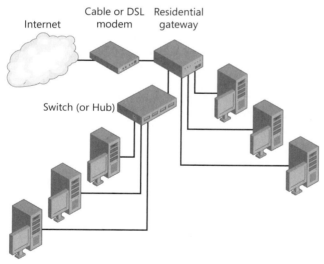

Figure 8-2. Connect the WAN port on the residential gateway to the cable or DSL modem.

When you set up your hubs, switches, and routers, keep in mind one limitation of Ethernet networks: Each cable segment can be no longer than 100 meters (328 feet). Although this is seldom a problem in most homes and small offices, centrally locating the hub gives you greater range of computer placement.

It doesn't matter which ports you use on a hub, unless one is identified as *uplink*. Uplink ports are used to expand a network's capacity by connecting a hub to another hub or router. On most hubs, you can't use the uplink port—which is an ordinary port with its two pairs of wires crossed—to connect to a computer (unless you use a crossover cable). Note also that some hubs with an uplink port share that port with the first (or last) port; that is, you can plug a cable into the uplink port or port 1, but not both. More-capable hubs can detect whether a port is connected to a computer or another hub (in which case it switches the port to act as an uplink port).

Tip   Set up Ethernet without a hub

If you're connecting only two computers, you can simply connect their network adapters with a crossover cable; if you do that, you don't need a hub. You can even use this setup to connect the two computers to the Internet: One of the computers must connect to the Internet by using a network adapter that is separate from the one used to connect to the other computer. (This could be a dial-up connection or a second Ethernet adapter that connects to a cable or DSL modem.) On the computer with the two adapters, configure ICS; for details, see "Sharing an Internet Connection Through Software," page 316.

Selecting Cable for an Ethernet Network

Cable suitable for use in modern Ethernet networks is readily available, but you should be sure to get the right type for your network:

- **Category 5 Unshielded Twisted Pair (UTP).**   More commonly known as *Cat 5*, this cable contains four sets of twisted-pair conductors. (Because Ethernet uses only two pairs, some cables contain only two pairs—and that's okay for ordinary networks.) Twisting the pairs helps to prevent unwanted interference. The design specifications of Cat 5 cable make it suitable for Ethernet or Fast Ethernet—that is, speeds up to 100 Mbps.

- **Category 5E.**   The *E* is for "enhanced," as Cat 5E cable is made to a more stringent standard than Cat 5. That improved standard makes Cat 5E suitable for speeds up to 1 Gbps (Gigabit Ethernet).

- **Category 6.**   Category 6 is made to even more stringent standards and, like Cat 5E, it's designed for transmission speeds up to 1 Gbps.

Understanding the different cable types is essential if you're installing network wiring into the walls of a home or office, as you'll want to be sure that the cable you install works for your current network and, hopefully, your *future* network. Similarly, if your building has existing cable, you'll want to be sure it's adequate for the type of network you plan to use. The cable type is usually printed on the cable's outside insulation.

Ethernet *patch cables* (a patch cable is a length of cable that has a male RJ-45 connector attached to each end) are generally available in two forms:

- A standard cable is wired straight through. That is, pin 1 at one end of the cable connects to pin 1 at the other end, pin 2 connects to pin 2, and so on. Use a standard cable for most Ethernet connections: a computer to a hub, computer to a wall jack (which, in turn, is connected to a hub or patch panel), printer to a hub, hub to hub (as long as you use the uplink port on one of the hubs), and so on.

● In a crossover cable, two pairs of wires are crossed. The pair connecting to pins 1 and 2 at one end of the cable is connected to pins 3 and 6 at the other end, and vice versa. Use a crossover cable to connect two hubs (without using an uplink port). A crossover cable is useful in certain other special situations; for example, you can connect two computers without a hub by using a crossover cable.

Configuring Your Network

After you've installed your networking hardware and configured its drivers, Windows creates a local connection that includes the following networking components:

● **Client For Microsoft Networks.** A *network client* provides access to computers and resources on a network; with this client, you can connect to computers running any 32-bit or 64-bit version of Windows.

● **File And Printer Sharing For Microsoft Networks.** This service allows other computers on your Windows-based network to access shared resources on your computer.

● **QOS Packet Scheduler.** This component (which is not installed on systems running Windows XP Home Edition or Windows 2000) enables Quality Of Service features provided on corporate networks and by ISPs. For the most part, these advanced features will not be widely used until Internet Protocol version 6 (IPv6) is also widely used.

● **Internet Protocol (TCP/IP).** TCP/IP is the default protocol in Windows XP and Windows 2000. It provides easy connectivity across a wide variety of networks, including the Internet. Although TCP/IP has plenty of options you can configure, most users can safely accept the default settings without having to make any configuration changes.

> For information about TCP/IP configuration, see "Setting IP Addresses," page 268. For details about TCP/IP networking services in Windows (as well as general information about TCP/IP, how it relates to the OSI model, and so on), visit *http://www.microsoft.com/technet/prodtechnol /windowsserver2003/library/ServerHelp/d1e53415-9a93-4407-87d2-3967d62182dc.mspx.*

This default collection of clients, services, and protocols is generally all you need to work with a Microsoft network (that is, one where all the computers are running a 32-bit or 64-bit version of Windows). For a full discussion of other protocols and networking components, see "Managing Network Connections," page 259.

Using the Network Setup Wizard in Windows XP

Windows XP (but not Windows 2000) includes a Network Setup Wizard that sets the proper permissions on shared folders, adds required keys to the registry, configures protocols and binds them to network cards, and enables or disables Windows Firewall. Windows XP Service Pack 2 (SP2) adds an extra step to the wizard, with which you can enable or disable file and printer sharing and, if necessary, adjust system policies so that file sharing works properly over the network.

After you've successfully installed all the required hardware for your network, run the Network Setup Wizard. Even if your network seems to be working just fine, you should run the Network Setup Wizard anyway. If your network contains a mix of workstations running Windows XP and Windows 2000 or other versions of Windows, run the wizard on one of the Windows XP workstations. In its last step, the wizard creates a Network Setup Disk that you can use to configure network settings on the other computers.

Inside Out

Even if you hate wizards, use the Network Setup Wizard

Are you a Windows expert? Do you have a disdain for all wizards? You're not alone. But even if you speak fluent TCP/IP and have multiple certifications in advanced networking, you should make an exception in this case and run the Windows XP Network Setup Wizard on every system that's connected to your network. Doing so is the only reliable way to ensure that your network has the proper baseline configuration. Afterward, you can manually adjust settings and enable or disable features as required.

If your network includes one computer that you want to use as an ICS host, be sure to configure the Internet connection on that computer first (for details, see "Sharing an Internet Connection Through Software," page 316), and then run the Network Setup Wizard on that computer. If all your networked computers have separate Internet connections, or if you use a router or residential gateway to share an Internet connection, you can start with any computer. To start the Network Setup Wizard, open Control Panel, double-click Network Connections (in the Network And Internet Connections group, if you use Category view), and then click the Set Up A Home Or Small Office Network link under Network Tasks in the left pane. This choice is also available in the My Network Places folder. If you've turned on the Folders bar so that the task pane isn't visible in Windows Explorer, you can access the wizard from the All Programs menu—choose Accessories, Communications, Network Setup Wizard.

Tip   Determine which connection is which
If you have two or more network connections defined, the Network Setup Wizard asks you to specify which one you plan to use for your Internet connection. It can be difficult to tell which one is the Internet connection to be shared and which one belongs to your local network. The easiest way to determine which is which is to open the Network Connections window and then temporarily unplug the connection between your external DSL or cable modem and your computer. Within a few seconds, a red *X* should appear on one of the connections—note the name of that connection and select it when prompted by the Network Setup Wizard. (And don't forget to reconnect that cable before resuming the wizard!)

Even better: In the Network Connections window, rename the connections to give each one a more meaningful name. For details, see "Managing Network Connections," page 259.

After starting the Network Setup Wizard, follow these steps:

1   Click Next twice to skip past the two introductory screens. If the wizard detects that your computer is connected to a router or residential gateway, or if you are running the wizard on other computers after setting up ICS, it offers the choice of using the shared connection or choosing an alternate connection method. Select the first option: Yes, Use The Existing Shared Connection For This Computer's Internet Access. Click Next and skip to step 4.

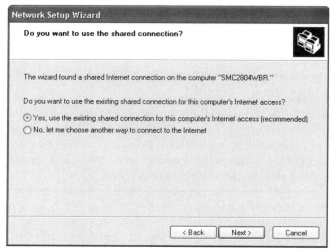

2   If your network doesn't include a router, or if you selected the second option on the previous page, the Select A Connection Method page appears. Select one of these three options:

- **This Computer Connects Directly To The Internet. The Other Computers On My Network Connect To The Internet Through This Computer.** Select this option if you have multiple network connections on the computer and you plan to use one to share Internet access with other computers on the network. Click Next to continue.

- **This Computer Connects To The Internet Through A Residential Gateway Or Through Another Computer On My Network.** If you use a router or residential gateway to manage shared Internet access and it was not detected by Windows XP, select this option and click Next to continue. If you use ICS and you see this screen, stop and check your Internet connection. If ICS is properly set up, the wizard should display a different page of the wizard, as described at the end of this section.

- **Other.** Select this option if your computer is connected to the Internet directly or through a hub, or if your network has no Internet access. If you select this option and click Next, you will see the Other Internet Connection Methods page, shown below.

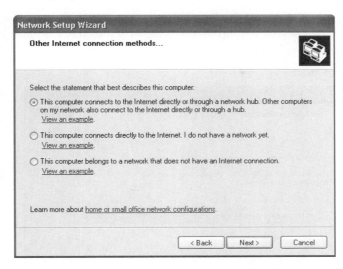

3   If you selected Other on the previous page, select one of the following options. Otherwise, skip to step 4.

■ **This Computer Connects To The Internet Directly Or Through A Network Hub. Other Computers On My Network Also Connect To The Internet Directly Or Through A Hub.**   If your external DSL or cable modem is connected directly to the hub along with all networked computers, select this option. Click Next to continue.

Caution   This configuration, in which all computers have individual Internet connections and direct access to other networked computers, potentially exposes your system to serious security risks. On computers running Windows XP Service Pack 1 (SP1) or earlier, the Network Setup Wizard displays a stern warning about the risks of this configuration immediately after you select it; the resulting configuration turns on the old Internet Connection Firewall (ICF) and blocks all access to shared resources on the local network. By contrast, with Windows XP SP2 installed, you'll see a smaller warning dialog box if you enable file and printer sharing over your network. If you override this choice and enable file and printer sharing anyway, Windows Firewall allows computers on your local subnet to access shared resources. You should verify that your local subnet doesn't include any untrusted computers, such as those belonging to other customers of your cable company sharing the same IP address range.

■ **This Computer Connects Directly To The Internet. I Do Not Have A Network Yet.**   Select this option if you have only one computer and it is directly connected to the Internet. Click Next to continue.

■ **This Computer Belongs To A Network That Does Not Have An Internet Connection.**   Select this option if no computer on your network has an Internet connection you want to share. Click Next to continue.

4 If your computer has more than one network connection, one of which is directly connected to the Internet, the Select Your Internet Connection page appears. Confirm that the wizard has selected the correct connection, and click Next to continue.

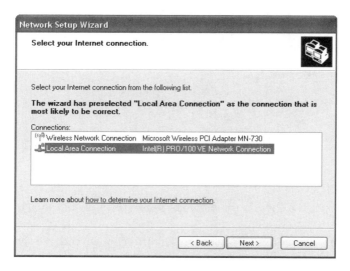

The Give This Computer A Description And Name page appears.

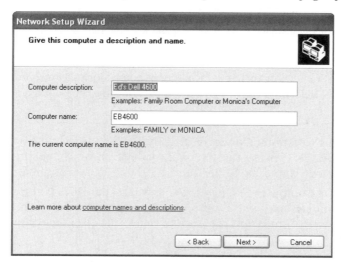

5 Check the name of the computer listed in the Computer Name box. Adjust the name and description if necessary, and click Next to continue.

> **Caution** Under normal circumstances, you establish the computer name during Setup. There's rarely a good reason to rename a computer. In fact, doing so can cause problems with some ISPs, which insist that your computer have a specific name. It can also cause inconvenience to other users who have created shortcuts to shared resources on your system. One circumstance in which it is desirable to rename a computer is if your preferred logon name is the same as your computer name. With Windows XP, you cannot create a user account whose name is the same as the computer name. In that case, it might be preferable to change the computer name so that you don't have to adopt a different user name.

6 On the Name Your Network page, enter the name of your workgroup. Note that this page is not like the previous page, in which the wizard correctly remembers your computer name. If you don't want to use the default workgroup name of MSHOME, you must manually change it here. Click Next.

> For more details about assigning workgroup names, see "Configuring Workgroup Settings," page 258.

With this File And Printer Sharing page, which was introduced to the wizard as part of Service Pack 2, you can enable or disable file and printer sharing. If you enable this option, the wizard creates an exception in Windows Firewall so that traffic from your local network can use TCP ports 139 and 445 and UDP ports 138 and 139. In addition, selecting Turn On File And Printer Sharing sets up share permissions on the Shared Documents folder so that it can be accessed by other network users.

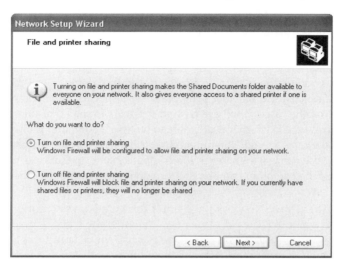

7 Select an option and click Next.

The Ready To Apply Network Settings page appears.

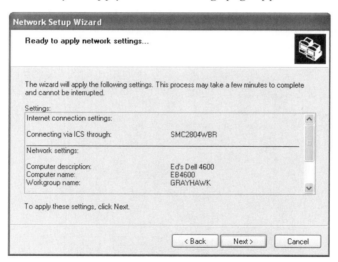

8 Scroll through the summary of changes the wizard is about to make to your network configuration. To make any changes to the settings you chose on the previous pages, use the Back button. If you're satisfied with the results, click Next to apply the changes immediately. The wizard displays an animated graphic while it works.

> **Caution** When you change your network configuration, the Network Setup Wizard temporarily shuts down your Internet connection and breaks off communication with the rest of your network. Do not run the wizard if you're currently in the middle of downloading files from the Internet or if other people are using shared resources on your computer.

9 After the wizard applies your changes, it offers to create a network setup disk for use on systems running previous versions of Windows that are connected to the same network. If your network consists of Windows XP systems only, choose Just Finish The Wizard and click Next to close the wizard.

If your network includes computers running Windows 2000 or other versions of Windows, select Create A Network Setup Disk and click Next. With the wizard pages that follow, you can select the drive where the disk will be created (you need a removable disk drive, such as a floppy drive or USB flash drive) and explain how to use the resulting disk on other networked computers.

Configuring a Connection in Windows 2000

After you set up your network hardware in Windows 2000, you should have basic networking functionality on your LAN. You should be able to see all the computers on your network by launching My Network Places and double-clicking Computers Near Me. (Computers Near Me appears in My Network Places only if your computer is joined to a domain.)

> **Note** If your network includes computers running Windows XP in addition to computers running Windows 2000, first use the Network Setup Wizard in Windows XP to configure the connection on the Windows XP computer and create a network setup disk. (For details, see "Using the Network Setup Wizard in Windows XP," page 250.) Then use the network setup disk to configure your Windows 2000 computers by running the Netsetup program that's on the disk.

Without the benefit of the Network Setup Wizard, you might (depending on whether your network uses default settings throughout) need to configure the connection manually by completing some or all of these tasks:

- Set the name of the workgroup, as described in the following section, "Configuring Workgroup Settings."
- Set up your Internet connection by running the Internet Connection Wizard. (It should run automatically the first time you run Internet Explorer; alternatively, you can start it manually from its shortcut in Start, Programs, Accessories, Communications.)
- Set up shared folders. (For details, see "Setting Up Shared Folders," page 285.)
- Install and configure a personal firewall by following the manufacturer's instructions.
- Configure the IP address, additional protocols, and other settings, as described in "Managing Network Connections," page 259.

If your network doesn't use default settings throughout, you might need to supply additional information for each network connection, as described in "Managing Network Connections," page 259.

Configuring Workgroup Settings

To communicate properly with one another, all computers on your peer-to-peer network must be members of the same workgroup. When you install a network adapter, Windows makes the computer a member of a workgroup called WORKGROUP; by default, the Network Setup Wizard in Windows XP changes the workgroup name to MSHOME. As the workgroup administrator, you might want to change the workgroup name to something that better describes your organization or family.

Tip   **Don't let the wizard change your workgroup**
Every time you run the Network Setup Wizard, it displays a page where you enter the name of your workgroup. One usability glitch in this wizard has the potential to isolate you in your own workgroup if you blast through the wizard without paying enough attention. The wizard automatically defaults to MSHOME as the workgroup name, even if you've specified a different name during Windows Setup, manually, or when running the wizard on previous occasions. Don't just idly click the Next button. Be sure to enter the correct name for your workgroup.

If you're using Windows XP, the easiest way to change the workgroup to which your computer belongs is by using the Network Setup Wizard. If you're using Windows 2000 or you want to adjust this setting manually, use the following steps:

1   Open System Properties (right-click My Computer and choose Properties or, in Control Panel, double-click System). Then click the Computer Name tab (Windows XP) or Network Identification tab (Windows 2000).

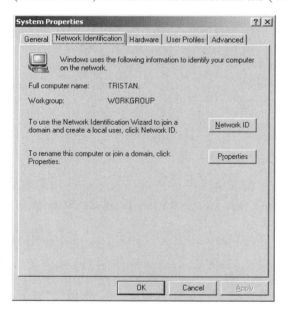

2 Click the Change button (Windows XP) or Properties button (Windows 2000). (Don't be confused by the explanatory text for this button, which mentions domains but doesn't use the word *workgroup* at all.)

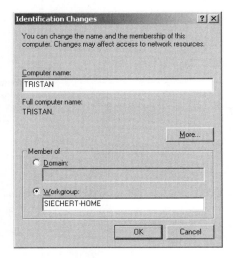

3 Select Workgroup and then replace the name of the current workgroup with the name of the workgroup you want to join or create.

4 Click OK to make the change. Two successive message boxes welcome you to the workgroup and remind you that you have to restart your computer to make the change effective.

> **Note** A workgroup name can contain up to 15 characters. It cannot be the same as the name of any computer in the workgroup, and it cannot contain any of the following characters: ; : " < > * + = \ | / ? ,

Managing Network Connections

To see information about currently defined network connections, open Control Panel, Network Connections. (In Windows 2000, the comparable Control Panel item is called Network And Dial-Up Connections, which is also accessible from Start, Settings.) Figure 8-3 on the next page shows the information and configuration options available from this window.

You can view information about each network connection, including the type of connection, whether it's enabled, the brand of the network adapter, and so on. The easiest way to see these various details in Windows XP is to select Tiles view; in Windows 2000, use Details view or select an individual icon, which causes its details to appear in the left pane.

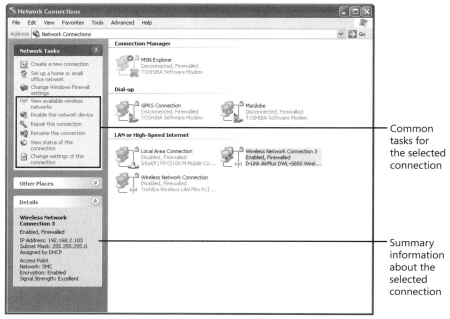

Common
tasks for
the selected
connection

Summary
information
about the
selected
connection

Figure 8-3. Windows 2000 doesn't offer all the capabilities of Windows XP (shown here), but for either operating system the Network Connections (or Network And Dial-Up Connections) window is the starting point for configuring your network.

Among other tasks in the Network Connections (or Network And Dial-Up Connections) folder, you can:

- Create a new connection. In Windows XP, click Create A New Connection under Network Tasks; in Windows 2000, double-click the Make New Connection icon.
- Open (that is, connect by using) a dial-up connection. Double-click its icon.
- Create a desktop shortcut for a connection. Right-click its icon and choose Create Shortcut.
- Copy a connection so you can make changes to the copy. (You can't copy connections associated with a network adapter; this capability is for dial-up connections and the like.)

Tip Sometimes it's easier to copy and modify an existing connection than to start from scratch with the New Connection Wizard.

- View or modify a connection's properties. Right-click the icon and choose Properties or, in Windows XP, select the icon and click Change Settings Of This Connection.
- Rename a connection. Right-click the connection icon and choose Rename from the shortcut menu; then type the descriptive name.

Tip Rename if you have multiple network adapters

Windows tags your main network connection with the Local Area Connection label. When you add connections, they get equally generic titles, like Local Area Connection 2, and it's difficult to know which one is which. On a computer that's serving as an ICS host, you might give your two network adapters distinctive names such as "Comcast Cable Modem" and "Home Network Connection."

Inside Out

Display network connections on the Start menu

You can configure the Start menu to include a cascading menu of network connections. This lets you see the status of a network connection or make a dial-up connection with a single click.

To set this up in Windows XP, right-click the Start button and choose Properties. On the Start Menu tab of the Taskbar And Start Menu Properties dialog box, click Customize. From this point, several options are available:

- If you're using the default Start menu, clicking the Advanced tab and selecting Display As Connect To Menu under Network Connections (in the Start Menu Items box) adds to the Start menu a Connect To menu that includes a link to each ephemeral connection, such as dial-up and wireless connections, and a link to the Network Connections folder.

- Another option for the default Start menu: click the Advanced tab and select Display As A Menu under Control Panel. This places on the Start menu a cascading Control Panel menu, which includes a Network Connections submenu that has links to all network connections.

- If you use the classic Start menu, select Expand Network Connections. You'll then have a Network Connections submenu on the Start, Settings menu.

To set up a cascading connections menu in Windows 2000, choose Start, Settings, Taskbar & Start Menu. Click the Advanced tab, and then select Expand Network And Dial-up Connections in the Start Menu Settings box.

Checking Connection Status

To see more detailed information about a network connection, double-click its icon in the Network Connections window. Figure 8-4 on the next page, for instance, shows the status dialog box for a wireless connection.

Chapter 8

Figure 8-4. The status dialog box provides basic statistics, including uptime, throughput, and the current connection speed.

By clicking the buttons in this dialog box you can open the connection's properties dialog box (an alternative way to open the properties dialog box is to right-click the connection and choose Properties), instantly disable the connection, or open the Wireless Connection Window to access all available wireless networks.

> **Tip**   You can also view a connection's status by pointing to its icon in the taskbar's notification area. To display the notification area icon, open the connection's properties dialog box and select Show Icon In Notification Area When Connected.

The Support tab, shown in Figure 8-5, shows the IP address and other TCP/IP details. (For information about these settings, see "Setting IP Addresses," page 268.) In Windows 2000, a connection's status dialog box does not include a Support tab. You can get comparable information by opening a command prompt window and typing **ipconfig /all**. (This command also works in Windows XP.)

The Repair button on the Support tab often fixes a nonworking connection. Clicking Repair causes Windows to:

- Request a new DHCP address lease.
- Flush Address Resolution Protocol (ARP) entries.
- Flush NetBIOS and DNS caches.
- Re-register WINS and DNS names.

Command-line aficionados and Windows 2000 users can replicate the repair function by entering these commands at a command prompt:

- **ipconfig /renew**
- **ipconfig /flushdns**
- **ipconfig /registerdns**

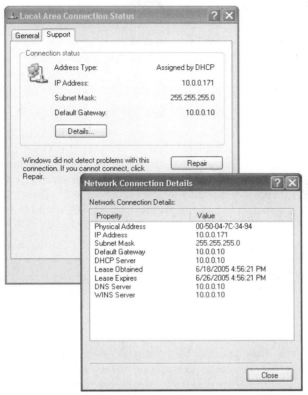

Figure 8-5. Clicking the Details button on the Support tab opens a Network Connection Details dialog box with additional information.

Installing Protocols, Services, and Clients

Network *protocols* are the common languages used to transfer data from point to point on a network. A few years ago, it was not uncommon for a computer running Windows to require multiple protocols, and earlier versions of Windows included a plethora of protocols developed for use on different types of networks—most of them completely irrelevant to home and small business users.

Because of the overwhelming popularity of the Internet, however, only one protocol is truly essential anymore. TCP/IP (Transmission Control Protocol/Internet Protocol) is the default network protocol in Windows 2000 and Windows XP. It provides easy connectivity across a wide variety of networks, including the Internet. Although TCP/IP has plenty of options you can configure, most users will accept the default settings without making any configuration changes. If you choose to use TCP/IP, you can take advantage of the full complement of security tools we describe elsewhere in this book, including IPSec and Windows Firewall in Windows XP.

If you're like most people, TCP/IP is the only protocol you'll ever need. It works exceptionally well on networks of all sizes, it's fast, and you can tighten its security with an impressive array of tools from Microsoft and third parties. We think your network is perfectly safe and secure if you configure it to use TCP/IP, add a personal firewall, and install security updates as needed.

Two protocols that were once widely used in Windows networks are still available in Windows XP and can be configured for special purposes:

- **IPX/SPX.** The Internetwork Packet Exchange/Sequenced Packet Exchange (IPX/SPX) protocol was originally developed for use on networks running Novell NetWare. It's available in Windows XP as an installable option. In the past, using IPX/SPX in addition to TCP/IP provided a workaround for security issues resulting when all network computers share an Internet connection through a hub. Because of the security improvements in Windows XP SP2, we no longer recommend this configuration. Some older games rely on IPX/SPX.

- **NetBEUI.** This protocol (short for NetBIOS Extended User Interface) is available as an unsupported option in Windows XP. It was originally developed for use on small networks running Windows 3.x. Because it works by indiscriminately broadcasting packets over the network, NetBEUI can cause performance problems and should only be used when an existing network configuration requires it.

Tip If you must, use IPX/SPX—not NetBEUI

In general, the only reason to install a protocol other than TCP/IP is to be able to communicate with other computers that use another protocol exclusively. But if you're considering adding a protocol to enhance security (an idea we don't support, by the way; see "Is TCP/IP Unsafe?" on page 267), which should you choose?

Microsoft no longer provides technical support for computers running NetBEUI, and all development has ceased on this protocol. IPX/SPX, on the other hand, is still actively supported and developed. Because installing either protocol accomplishes the same goals on a small network, we recommend choosing the one that offers the fewest configuration and support headaches: IPX/SPX.

In addition, a relatively new protocol called TCP/IP version 6 (IPv6) is included with Windows XP SP2. This protocol is still in its infancy but will someday be widely used; it is included for use in advanced and experimental applications. If you use an application that requires TCP/IP version 6, the software developer should instruct you to install this protocol.

For more information about IPv6, visit *http://www.microsoft.com/ipv6/* or *http://www.ipv6.org*.

To install an additional protocol, follow these steps:

1 If you're not planning to install NetBEUI or you're using Windows 2000 (which already has the necessary NetBEUI installation files in place), skip to step 2. If you

want NetBEUI and you're using Windows XP, insert your Windows CD. Use Windows Explorer to copy the following files from the CD's \Valueadd\Msft \Net\Netbeui folder:

- Copy Nbf.sys to the %SystemRoot%\System32\Drivers folder.
- Copy Netnbf.inf to the %SystemRoot%\Inf folder. (This is a hidden folder. You can navigate directly to it by typing its name in the Address bar.)

2 From Control Panel, open the Network Connections folder.

3 Right-click the icon for the connection you want to edit, and choose Properties from the shortcut menu. (In Windows XP, you can instead select the icon and then click the Change Settings Of This Connection link under Network Tasks.)

4 On the General tab of the properties dialog box, click the Install button. The Select Network Component Type dialog box opens.

Chapter 8

5 Select Protocol and click Add. The Select Network Protocol dialog box appears.

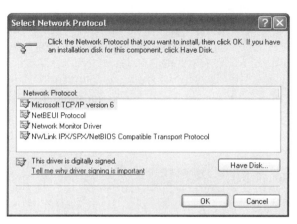

6 Select the protocol you want to add:

- To install IPX/SPX, select NWLink IPX/SPX/NetBIOS Compatible Transport Protocol and click OK.
- To install NetBEUI, select NetBEUI Protocol and click OK.
- To install TCP/IP version 6, select Microsoft TCP/IP version 6 and click OK.

You can use the new protocol immediately. In some configurations, you might be required to restart the computer before the new configuration is fully usable.

To temporarily enable or disable the use of a protocol with a specific connection, open the properties dialog box for that connection and select or clear the check box to the left of the protocol.

To permanently delete a protocol, select it in the properties dialog box and click Uninstall. Doing so removes it from *all* connections; if your intent is to remove it from a single connection, disable the protocol instead.

The procedures for installing, removing, enabling, and disabling network services and network clients are identical to those for working with protocols. For an ordinary network in a home or small office, however, you won't need any additional protocols, services, or clients.

Is TCP/IP Unsafe?

A few security specialists argue that TCP/IP is inherently unsafe. They claim that the greatest strength of TCP/IP—its ubiquitous presence on the Internet—is also its greatest weakness, because TCP/IP packets intended for use on your local network can be forwarded out to the Internet. Adherents of this approach argue that you should reserve TCP/IP strictly for your Internet connection and install a second protocol, such as IPX/SPX, for use on your LAN. By unbinding File And Printer Sharing from the TCP/IP protocol, they contend, you make it less likely that a hacker can break into your network and access shared files and printers.

Although this argument seems logical, it doesn't stand up to a close examination. Specifically:

- This security routine was originally recommended for Windows 95 and its successors, during the era when most people used dial-up connections and hardware routers were exotic, expensive devices. These days, routers are dirt-cheap and offer effective protection from unsolicited outside connections. In addition, Windows XP incorporates security features that block outside access to shared resources by default, and the Network Setup Wizard enables the Windows Firewall on network configurations that are potentially unsafe.

- Windows XP has been in widespread use for more than four years. During that time we have not found a single documented instance where this configuration would have prevented an attack. The justification is completely theoretical.

- Unbinding File And Printer Sharing does nothing to protect you from attacks on other ports through your TCP/IP-based connection to the Internet. If you neglect the basics of Internet security—installing critical updates and configuring Windows Firewall or a third-party alternative—a would-be attacker could exploit a security hole and install a Trojan horse program that gives him complete control over your computer and your network.

- Adding multiple protocols creates needless complexity and increases the chance that some applications will fail to work properly.

With all that said, we must point out one network configuration that does expose your computer to access from the Internet, and should be avoided. This can occur if your network configuration does not include a dedicated router but instead uses a simple hub or switch that connects all the network's computers to each other and to the Internet. In this configuration, your entire network is public, and every computer is open to outside attacks. If you absolutely insist on setting up your network this way, you need to protect yourself by unbinding file and printer sharing from the TCP/IP protocol and by sharing only on the NetBEUI or IPX/SPX protocol. Then install a personal firewall on each computer to block outside TCP/IP traffic. Many better solutions exist for connecting your computers to the Internet; see Chapter 9, "Sharing an Internet Connection," for details.

The bottom line? A properly networked computer running Windows XP or Windows 2000 works best and is most secure when it uses only TCP/IP, configured with appropriate security precautions. We strongly advise against installing additional protocols unless you specifically need them to communicate with other computers and servers on your network—and even then, these protocols should be used in addition to, not in place of, TCP/IP.

Setting IP Addresses

Networks that use the TCP/IP protocol rely on *IP addresses* to route packets of data from point to point. On a TCP/IP network, every computer has a unique IP address, which consists of four 8-bit numbers (each one represented in decimal format by a number from 0 through 255) separated by periods. In addition to the IP address, each computer's TCP/IP configuration has the following settings:

- A *subnet mask*, which tells the network how to distinguish between IP addresses that are part of the same network and those that belong to other networks.

- A *default gateway*, which is a computer that routes packets intended for addresses outside the local network.

- One or more *Domain Name System (DNS) servers*, which are computers that translate domain names, such as *www.microsoft.com*, into IP addresses.

Windows XP and Windows 2000 provide several methods for assigning IP addresses to networked computers:

- **Dynamic Host Configuration Protocol (DHCP).**   This is the default configuration for Windows XP Professional and Home Edition. Most ISPs start with a pool of IP addresses that are available for use by their customers. ISPs use DHCP servers to assign IP addresses from this pool and to set subnet masks and other configuration details as each customer makes a new connection. When the customer disconnects, the address is held for a period of time and eventually released back to the pool so it can be reused. Many corporate networks use DHCP to avoid the hassle of managing fixed addresses for constantly changing resources; Windows 2000 Server and Windows Server 2003 both include this capability. The Internet Connection Sharing feature in Windows XP includes a full-fledged DHCP server that automatically configures all TCP/IP settings for other computers on the network. Most routers and residential gateways also incorporate DHCP servers that automatically configure computers connected to those devices.

- **Automatic Private IP Addressing (APIPA).**   When no DHCP server is available, Windows automatically assigns an IP address in a specific private IP range. (For an explanation of how private IP addresses work, see "Public and Private IP Addresses," page 272.) If all computers on a subnet are using APIPA addresses, they can communicate with one another without requiring any additional configuration. APIPA was first introduced in Windows 98 and works the same in all versions of Windows released since that time.

> **Note**   For detailed technical information about APIPA, including instructions for disabling it, read Knowledge Base article 220874, "How to Use Automatic TCP/IP Addressing Without a DHCP Server."

- **Static IP Addressing.** By entering an IP address, subnet mask, and other TCP/IP details in a dialog box, you can manually configure a Windows workstation so that its address is always the same. This method takes more time and can cause some configuration headaches, but it allows a high degree of control over network addresses.

  Static IP addresses are essential if you plan to set up a Web server, a mail server, a virtual private network (VPN) gateway, or any other computer that needs to be accessible from across the Internet. Even inside a local network, behind a router or firewall, static IP addresses can be useful. For instance, you might want to configure the router so that packets entering your network on a specific port get forwarded to a specific computer. If you use DHCP to assign addresses within the local network, you can't predict what the address of that computer will be on any given day. But by assigning that computer a static IP address that is within the range of addresses assigned by the DHCP server, you can ensure that the computer always has the same address and is thus always reachable.

- **Alternate IP Configuration.** This feature, which is new in Windows XP, enables you to specify multiple IP addresses for a single network connection (although only one address can be used at a time). This feature is most useful with portable computers that regularly connect to different networks. You can configure the connection to automatically acquire an IP address from an available DHCP server, and then assign a static backup address for use if the first configuration isn't successful. Note that this configuration affects only IP addresses; it doesn't resolve logon issues caused by mismatched account names or switching between workgroup-based and domain-based networks.

To set a static IP address, follow these steps:

1. From Control Panel, open the Network Connections folder and select the connection whose settings you want to change.

2. Use any of the following techniques to open the properties dialog box for the selected connection:

   - Select the connection and click the Change Settings Of This Connection link under Network Tasks (Windows XP only).

   - Right-click the connection icon and choose Properties from the shortcut menu.

   - Double-click the connection icon to open the Status dialog box and then click the Properties button on the General tab.

3. From the list of installed network components, select Internet Protocol (TCP/IP) and then click the Properties button.

4. In the Internet Protocol (TCP/IP) Properties dialog box, select Use The Following IP Address and fill in the blanks. You must supply an IP address, a subnet mask, and a default gateway.

5. Select Use The Following DNS Server Addresses and fill in the numeric IP addresses for one or more DNS servers.

Chapter 8

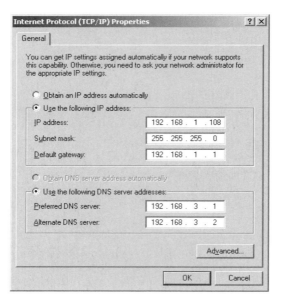

6 Click OK to save your changes. You do not need to restart the computer after changing your IP configuration.

To set up an alternate IP configuration in Windows XP (this feature is not available in Windows 2000), follow these steps:

1 From Control Panel, open the Network Connections folder and select the connection whose settings you want to change.

2 Click the Change Settings Of This Connection link under Network Tasks, or right-click the connection icon and choose Properties from the shortcut menu.

3 From the list of installed network components, select Internet Protocol (TCP/IP) and then click the Properties button.

4 On the General tab of the Internet Protocol (TCP/IP) Properties dialog box, select Obtain An IP Address Automatically.

5 Click the Alternate Configuration tab and then select the User Configured option.

6 Enter the IP address, subnet mask, default gateway, and DNS servers for the alternate connection, as shown here.

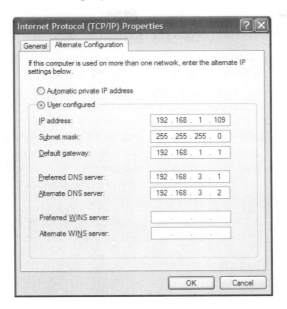

Note You can safely ignore the fields that ask you to enter a preferred and alternate WINS server. WINS stands for Windows Internet Name Service, a name resolution system that maps a computer's NetBIOS name to an IP address. WINS servers are used on large corporate networks to allow domain servers to communicate with computers running older Microsoft operating systems, including Microsoft Windows NT, Windows 95, Windows 98, and Windows Millennium Edition. For virtually all home and small business networks, the WINS server details are unnecessary and irrelevant.

7 Click OK to save your changes. You do not need to restart the computer after setting up an alternate configuration.

When you've configured an alternate IP configuration for a network connection, Windows XP looks first for a DHCP server to assign an IP address automatically. If no DHCP server is available, the system falls back to the static IP address defined on the Alternate IP Configuration tab.

Chapter 8

Public and Private IP Addresses

Any computer that is directly connected to the Internet needs a public IP address—one that can be reached by other computers on the Internet, so that information you request (Web pages and e-mail, for instance) can be routed back to your computer properly. On a home or small office network, each computer needs to have an IP address, but it's not necessary to have a *public* IP address. In fact, configuring a network with all public addresses increases security risks and usually requires an extra fee from your ISP. To communicate with the Internet, the computer or router on the edge of the network uses a technology called network address translation (NAT) to pass packets back and forth between the single public IP address and the multiple private IP addresses on the network. (For details, see "How Network Address Translation Works," page 303.)

The Internet Assigned Numbers Authority (IANA) has reserved the following three blocks of the IP address space for use on private networks that are not directly connected to the Internet:

- 10.0.0.0 – 10.255.255.255
- 172.16.0.0 – 172.31.255.255
- 192.168.0.0 – 192.168.255.255

In addition, the Automatic Private IP Addressing feature in all post-1998 Windows versions uses private IP addresses in the range from 169.254.0.0 to 169.254.255.255.

If you're setting up a small business or home network that will not be connected to the Internet, or that will be connected through a single proxy server, you can freely use these addresses without concern for conflicts. Just make sure that all the addresses on the network are in the same subnet.

Configuring Network Bindings and Provider Order

Each network adapter has one or more protocols, services, and clients with which it is configured to work. These protocols, services, and clients are said to be *bound to* the network adapter, and the association is called a *binding*. To manage your bindings, you use the Advanced Settings dialog box, shown in Figure 8-6.

To display the Advanced Settings dialog box, in the Network Connections (or Network And Dial-Up Connections) folder, click the Advanced menu and choose Advanced Settings. When you select a connection in the Connections area, Advanced Settings shows the bindings for that connection in the lower part of the dialog box.

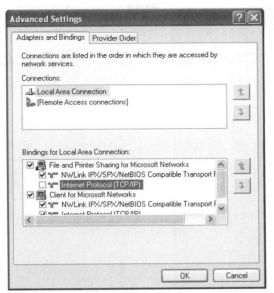

Figure 8-6. Clear the check box for a protocol you don't want to use on the selected connection.

The purpose of the Adapters And Bindings tab in the Advanced Settings dialog box is twofold:

- You can specify the order in which connections are used and, for each service and each client on each connection, the order in which protocols are used. When Windows communicates over a network, the connections and bindings are attempted in the order shown. For example, if you have three connections, Windows attempts to communicate by using the first one and, failing that, tries the second one, and so on. For best performance, you should adjust the order of the connections and protocols to place the ones you use most often at the top of the list. To change the order, select a connection or protocol and click the arrow buttons.

- You can unbind protocols you don't want to use on a particular connection. You might do this for security reasons; for example, if you use only IPX/SPX for file and print sharing on your LAN, you could unbind TCP/IP from the LAN connection. Or you might unbind an unused protocol to improve performance, as each bound protocol adds some unnecessary network traffic. To unbind a protocol, clear its check box.

The other tab in the Advanced Settings dialog box, Provider Order (shown in Figure 8-7 on the next page), works in a similar fashion. It displays a list of network providers and the services they provide. To improve performance, move the services you use most often to the top of the list.

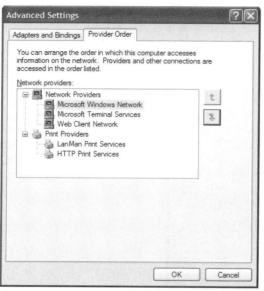

Figure 8-7. To change the order of services, select one and then click either arrow button.

Bridging Connections

A network *bridge* is a specialized type of switch that connects two or more network segments. Like a switch, a bridge directs data based on its intended MAC address. The key difference is that a bridge can work across different types of networks or across different subnets. For example:

- If the computers in your home communicate on a HomePNA network and you have an Ethernet broadband Internet connection, you need a bridge. (See the following caution, however.)
- If you want to add another workgroup to your network (perhaps another small network in your office), you need a bridge.

The traditional solution to these situations is a dedicated hardware bridge. Windows XP (but not Windows 2000) can act as a software bridge to let disparate networks communicate seamlessly. Once you've set it up, data intended for a device on the other side of the bridge flows transparently across the bridge. In each of the preceding examples, you can bridge the two networks by installing two network adapters in a computer—one for each network—and then bridging the connections, as explained below.

> **Note** With the software bridge in Windows XP, you can bridge only LAN or high-speed Internet connections. You can't bridge dial-up connections, VPN connections, or direct cable connections.

Not all types of mixed networks require setting up a separate bridge, either in Windows or with a dedicated hardware bridge. Most notably, wireless and Ethernet networks are usually bridged through the wireless access point, which connects to both networks.

> **Caution** To prevent opening your network to attack from outside, never bridge a LAN connection with an Internet connection that has a public IP address. All connections to be bridged should be inside a router or firewall. If you're trying to provide Internet access to the rest of your network, use Internet Connection Sharing instead; for details, see Chapter 9.

To create a network bridge in Windows XP, follow these steps:

1 Open the Network Connections folder.

2 Be sure that the connections you want to bridge are not configured for Internet Connection Sharing. (You can tell at a glance: An ICS connection has an outstretched hand at the bottom of its icon. To disable ICS on a connection, open its properties dialog box, click the Advanced tab, and clear the check box under Internet Connection Sharing.)

3 Hold down the Ctrl key and click each of the connections you want to bridge.

4 Right-click one of the selected connections and choose Bridge Connections.

Windows creates the bridge, and the bridge appears in the Network Connections folder, as shown in Figure 8-8.

Figure 8-8.   This bridge links two different Ethernet networks.

Chapter 8

> **Note** You'll need to keep the bridge computer turned on and running Windows for the bridge to work.

You can add or remove bridge connections at any time. Simply right-click the connection you want to change and select Add To Bridge or Remove From Bridge. Alternatively, you can open the properties dialog box for the bridge; then select the check boxes for the connections you want to bridge, and clear the others. Although you can have only one network bridge in Windows XP, you can use it to bridge up to 64 network connections.

To temporarily stop bridging, right-click the network bridge and choose Disable. If you no longer need the bridge, you can remove it by right-clicking it and choosing Delete.

Securing Network Connections

When your computer is connected to the Internet, it becomes a node on a huge global network. A *firewall* provides a barrier between your computer and the network to which it's connected by preventing the entry of unwanted traffic while allowing transparent passage to authorized connections.

Using a firewall is simple, essential, and often overlooked. You'll want to be sure that all network connections are protected by a firewall. Even if your portable computer is protected by a corporate firewall when you're at work and its home connection uses a firewalled broadband connection, consider the dial-up connection you use when you travel or the wireless connection you use at a cafe.

It makes sense to run a firewall on your computer (sometimes called a *personal firewall*) even when you're behind a corporate firewall or broadband router. Other people on your network might not be as vigilant as you about defending against viruses, so if someone brings in a Sasser-infected portable computer and connects it to the network, you're toast—unless your network connection has its own firewall protection.

> **Note** This bears repeating. In today's environment, you should run firewall software on each networked computer; don't rely on corporate gateway firewalls and gateway antivirus solutions to protect your computer from another infected computer inside the perimeter. It was this kind of vulnerability that led to the Blaster worm's quick and wide proliferation throughout supposedly protected networks in 2003.

For more information about how firewalls work, see "Blocking Attacks by Using a Firewall," page 10.

Using Windows Firewall in Windows XP

Windows Firewall, which is part of Windows XP SP2, replaces the Internet Connection Firewall (ICF) that was included in earlier versions of Windows XP. Like ICF, Windows Firewall is a stateful filtering firewall that drops all inbound traffic except traffic sent in response to a request sent by your computer and unsolicited traffic that has been explicitly allowed by creating an exception.

ICF was widely (and justifiably) criticized because it was not enabled by default, not very configurable, and rather inadequate. Windows Firewall offers a number of significant improvements over ICF, including the following:

Chapter 8

- **Windows Firewall protects internal and external connections.** Internet Connection Firewall was intended to protect your computer's Internet connection, but it wasn't easy to properly configure for connections to your LAN. Because many security threats can come from your own network, Windows Firewall works well with LAN connections.

- **Windows Firewall is enabled by default for all connections.** By default, Windows Firewall is enabled for all network connections: wired LAN connections, wireless connections, dial-up connections, and VPN connections. Any new connections you create have Windows Firewall enabled by default.

- **Global configuration options apply to all connections.** With ICF, you had to make firewall settings, such as exceptions to allow incoming traffic, separately for each connection. With Windows Firewall, you can make settings globally. Windows Firewall also lets you make settings for individual connections; any per-connection settings override the global settings.

- **You're protected during startup.** If Windows Firewall is enabled, Windows provides stateful filtering while connecting to your network. During this phase of startup, firewall protection allows basic network startup tasks such as obtaining an IP address from a DHCP server and Group Policy updates from a domain controller, registering with the local DNS server, and so on. Full protection according to your Windows Firewall configuration become effective when the Windows Firewall service starts.

- **You can specify a scope for each exception.** Windows Firewall enables you to restrict the scope for exceptions by limiting it to traffic from an IP address that is part of your local subnet or from a list of IP addresses that you specify.

- **You can create exceptions for programs.** With Windows Firewall, you can create an exception by specifying the name of the program or service for which you want to allow unsolicited incoming traffic; you don't need to know which port(s) and protocol(s) are used by a program to create an exception.

- **Windows Firewall supports two profiles on domain-based computers.** Windows Firewall switches automatically between a profile it uses when the computer is connected to the domain and a different profile it uses when the computer is not connected or is connected to a different network. Each profile has a separate list of exceptions and settings.

- **Internet Protocol version 6 (IPv6) is supported.** IPv6, sometimes called "the next generation Internet," is a protocol that will someday supplant the current Internet Protocol, which is more accurately called IPv4. When that day arrives, Windows Firewall is ready.

- **Configuration can be done with command lines or Group Policy.** The user interface for configuring Windows Firewall is convenient for ad hoc management of the firewall on a single computer. But if you perform certain tasks repeatedly, or if you have to configure multiple computers, it's much easier to set up a batch program or script that contains the commands needed to perform the task. Likewise, Group Policy (particularly in a domain environment) eases the burden of repetitive tasks.

> For details about working with firewall exceptions and other advanced configuration options, see "Configuring a Host Firewall," page 564.

Enabling or Disabling Windows Firewall

You manage Windows Firewall through its Control Panel application, which is new with Service Pack 2. (In previous versions of Windows XP, ICF was managed through a tab in the properties dialog box for each network connection.) You can, of course, open Windows Firewall directly from Control Panel. Category view users will find the Windows Firewall icon in Network And Internet Connections as well as in Security Center. Other ways to open Windows Firewall include:

- In Security Center, click the Windows Firewall link.
- In the Network Connections folder, click Change Windows Firewall Settings (in the task pane under Network Tasks).
- In the properties dialog box for a network connection, click the Advanced tab and then click Settings in the Windows Firewall area.
- At a command prompt, type **firewall.cpl**.

> **Note** Security Center and Network Connections make ideal launch pads for Windows Firewall because both show at a glance whether Windows Firewall is enabled. Security Center dedicates the top part of its status section to firewall status. In Network Connections, when you use Thumbnails, Tiles, or Icon view, each connection for which Windows Firewall is enabled has a small padlock in its icon.

Regardless of how you open Windows Firewall, you'll see a dialog box like the one shown in Figure 8-9. To enable Windows Firewall for all network connections, select On. To disable Windows Firewall, of course, select Off. In general, the only reason to turn off Windows Firewall is if you have installed a third-party firewall that you plan to use instead of Windows Firewall.

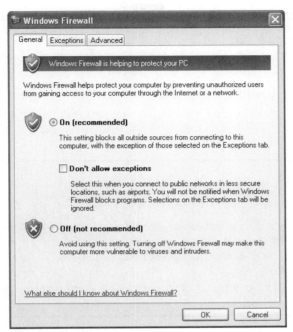

Figure 8-9. The General tab contains the main on/off switch for Windows Firewall.

 This book's companion CD includes a script called Firewall Quick Switch, which displays the current status of Windows Firewall and lets you change it without venturing into the more cumbersome Windows Firewall dialog box.

Preventing All Incoming Traffic

The Don't Allow Exceptions check box on the General tab provides additional safety. When it's selected, Windows Firewall rejects *all* unsolicited incoming traffic—even traffic that would ordinarily be permitted by an exception. (For information about exceptions, see "Allowing Connections Through Windows Firewall," page 565.) Invoke this mode when extra security against outside attack is needed. For example, you might disable exceptions when you're using a public wireless hotspot or when you know that your computer is actively under attack by others.

> **Note** Selecting Don't Allow Exceptions does not disconnect your computer from the Internet. Windows Firewall does not block outbound traffic, so even in "no exceptions" mode, you can still use your browser to connect to the Internet. Similarly, other outbound connections—whether they're legitimate services or some sort of spyware—continue unabated.

Disabling Windows Firewall for Individual Connections

Windows Firewall ordinarily monitors all network connections for unwanted traffic. In some situations, you might want to disable its protection for one or more connections while leaving it on for others. That's easily done, as follows:

1 In Windows Firewall, click the Advanced tab.

2 Clear the check box for each connection on which you want to disable Windows Firewall.

 Troubleshooting

You need more information to solve a Windows Firewall problem

Microsoft offers several online resources with troubleshooting information for Windows Firewall. If you encounter problems, start with KB article 875357. If that doesn't address a problem you're encountering, check out the document titled "Troubleshooting Windows Firewall in Microsoft Windows XP Service Pack 2." To retrieve it, visit the Microsoft Download Center (*http://www.microsoft.com/downloads/*) and search for keywords **windows firewall troubleshooting**.

Choosing a Third-Party Personal Firewall

If some computers on your network are running versions of Windows that don't include an integrated firewall, or if you're looking for features that aren't included in Windows Firewall, you need to consider other software publishers. You'll find no shortage of firewalls, intrusion detection systems, port monitors, and other programs that purportedly fill this need. Some are good, some are mediocre, and some are downright dangerous. To identify legitimate security software, ask yourself the following questions:

- **Is the developer reputable?**   In recent years, scam artists have perfected the art of selling programs that closely resemble legitimate products but are actually either counterfeit or, worse, act as vehicles for delivering viruses and Trojan horse software. Before purchasing a program, especially one offered through tiny ads or potentially deceptive e-mail offerings, check out the company. Be especially suspicious of Web sites that are loaded with testimonials from anonymous customers and claims of "awards" that don't include a link to the original source. Developing security software is a complex business; if you can't find detailed information about the company, its founders, and its products, look elsewhere.

- **Does the program use application-based outbound filtering?**   Properly configured, such programs can prevent Trojan horses, spyware, and other untrusted programs on your computer from accessing the Internet. Give a program extra points if it also prevents programs from disabling or modifying firewall protection without your approval.

Chapter 8

- **How difficult is it to configure rules?** Some programs with application-based filtering have preconfigured rules—but these rules might not be configured the way you would like. Better programs provide a combination of preconfigured rules and an easy way to add or modify rules.

- **Does the program use security zones?** A program that lets you specify trusted IP addresses provides easy LAN connectivity as well as secure Internet connections.

- **Does the program use stealth mode?** Stealth mode drops unwanted packets silently rather than sending back a "connection denied" message. The result is to make your computer essentially invisible, because an attacker has no way of discerning whether your computer is connected to the Internet.

- **Is the program compatible with the hardware that manages your Internet connection?** A properly secured network typically uses a hardware router at the point where the network connects to the Internet. As an alternative, you can use ICS, a feature in Windows that allows you to designate a single computer on your network as a gateway to the Internet and distribute its connection to all computers on the network. Be sure that the firewall software supports your router or ICS. If your network includes a server that manages Internet access, e-mail, virtual private network (VPN) connections, and other advanced features, consider installing a software firewall on that computer and select compatible personal firewall software for workstations on your network.

- **Does the program offer other, nonfirewall features?** Many programs in this category are more than simple firewalls; some publishers strive to offer a one-stop Internet protection package. You'll need to decide whether you view that as a convenience or a "feature bloat." Among the available features: some programs perform content filtering (for example, to block pornography), advertisement blocking, e-mail filtering (to isolate messages with active content or potentially dangerous attachments), and cookie management. Several security suites include antivirus software as part of the bundle.

- **How much does the program cost?** Evaluating the cost is not as simple as it might seem. Some publishers set different prices depending on who is using the software and where. (For example, some publishers charge only business users, allowing home users to use their product for free.) You'll also need to determine which computers on your network need firewall protection and whether you'll need to purchase a separate license for each computer. (Some publishers offer a network license that lets you protect all computers on your LAN.) And some personal firewall publishers have embraced the trend toward subscription-based licensing; be sure to include this in your cost calculations. Subscriptions for some products entitle you to updated data files (for example, predefined rules or lists of sites for content filtering or ad blocking) as well as program updates.

- **Is a trial version available?** The best way to evaluate a program is to try it yourself. Many personal firewall programs are available for download and limited-time trial.

Chapter 8

The following pages provide information about 12 leading makers of personal firewall software. The list is presented alphabetically and is not comprehensive. All of the products listed here, however, are generally held in high regard by security experts. Each company listed offers personal firewall software that is compatible with Windows 2000 Professional and all versions of Windows XP. Where appropriate, we have also listed higher-end firewall software that can be used on small to medium-size business networks.

> **Tip** Find current comparative information online
> You can find additional lists of personal firewalls, along with reviews of current versions, at *http://www.firewallguide.com/software.htm.*

Agnitum, Ltd.

- **Products:**   Outpost Firewall Free, Outpost Firewall Pro
- **At a glance:**   Outpost Firewall Pro is a full-featured firewall that can be extended through the use of plug-ins, including those developed by independent programmers. A limited free version of the software is available for home users.
- **Web site:**   *http://www.agnitum.com*

Computer Associates International, Inc.

- **Products:**   eTrust EZ Firewall, eTrust EZ Armor Security Suite
- **At a glance:**   Default settings for eTrust EZ Firewall provide automatic program control, which reduces the number of pop-ups asking permission to allow a program to access the Internet. The program also includes support for VPNs. The suite version bundles integrated antivirus protection with the personal firewall component.
- **Web site:**   *http://www.my-etrust.com*

Deerfield.com

- **Products:**   VisNetic Firewall, Kerio WinRoute Firewall, Kerio Server Firewall
- **At a glance:**   Although it's more expensive than many products listed in this chapter, VisNetic Firewall includes many security and logging features that are usually found only on expensive corporate firewall products. It can be used on servers or workstations. WinRoute Firewall and Kerio Server Firewall are intended for use on server-based networks.
- **Web site:**   *http://www.deerfield.com*

Chapter 8

F-Secure Corporation

- **Products:** F-Secure Internet Security, F-Secure Anti-Virus Client Security
- **At a glance:** F-Secure Internet Security is designed for use by home users and small offices without a dedicated computer support staff. It includes antivirus protection as well as a personal firewall. F-Secure Anti-Virus Client Security includes firewall protection and is designed for use on managed corporate networks.
- **Web site:** *http://www.f-secure.com*

Internet Security Systems, Inc.

- **Products:** BlackICE PC Protection, Proventia Desktop
- **At a glance:** BlackICE Defender (the product's original name) was an early leader in the personal firewall business. Early versions of this software focused on intrusion detection, but recent versions also include outbound filtering and application monitoring. Proventia Desktop provides a similar list of features for corporate networks that require central management.
- **Web site:** *http://www.iss.net*

Kerio Technologies Inc.

- **Products:** Kerio Personal Firewall, Kerio WinRoute Firewall
- **At a glance:** The developers who created the first version of Tiny Personal Firewall went on to produce Kerio Personal Firewall. It monitors outbound traffic and its stealth mode hides your computer from outsiders. The full version provides some content filtering features and will run on a server or ICS host. Kerio WinRoute Firewall is intended for installation on a dedicated computer used as an Internet gateway on corporate networks; it integrates with e-mail servers and provides secure VPN connections.
- **Web site:** *http://www.kerio.com*

McAfee, Inc.

- **Products:** McAfee Personal Firewall Plus, McAfee Desktop Firewall, McAfee Internet Security Suite
- **At a glance:** McAfee's firewall products are offered as an online subscription service. In addition to firewall protection, these products provide protection over personal data. The two suite versions add related security features, including virus protection and spam blocking. McAfee Desktop Firewall is designed for use on centrally managed corporate networks.
- **Web site:** *http://www.mcafee.com*

Chapter 8

Sygate Technologies, Inc.

- **Products:** Sygate Personal Firewall, Sygate Personal Firewall Pro
- **At a glance:** Sygate pioneered the use of stealth mode, and its firewalls continue to be technology leaders. Sygate Personal Firewall Standard is free for personal use. The Pro version provides advanced configuration options for small and medium businesses and supports VPN connections.
- **Web site:** *http://smb.sygate.com*

Symantec Corporation

- **Products:** Norton Internet Security, Norton Personal Firewall, Symantec Client Security
- **At a glance:** Norton Internet Security provides a collection of security software, with Norton Personal Firewall included as its firewall component. In terms of disk space, it's one of the largest you can find—but it's packed with features that control every aspect of your Internet connections. Symantec Client Security provides a similar feature set for centrally managed corporate networks.
- **Web site:** *http://www.symantec.com*

Tiny Software, Inc.

- **Products:** Tiny Firewall
- **At a glance:** True to its name, this software requires a minuscule amount of disk space. But it works well and includes innovative features such as the ability to prevent untrusted programs from modifying sensitive registry keys. It can be used on workstations and servers.
- **Web site:** *http://www.tinysoftware.com*

Trend Micro Incorporated

- **Products:** Trend Micro PC-cillin Internet Security
- **At a glance:** PC-cillin is a suite of security products that includes antivirus software and spam-filtering capabilities. With the personal firewall component, you can choose from predefined profiles appropriate for use in different network configurations or to create a custom profile. Beginning with the 2005 version, it also includes features to control and monitor wireless network connections.
- **Web site:** *http://www.trendmicro.com*

Zone Labs LLC

- **Products:**   ZoneAlarm, ZoneAlarm Pro, ZoneAlarm Security Suite
- **At a glance:**   Almost since the inception of the personal firewall category, ZoneAlarm has been a leader in capabilities, effectiveness, and market share. (In 2004, Zone Labs was acquired by Check Point Software, a leading enterprise security firm.) In addition to its long-established use of security zones and application-based outbound filtering, newer versions provide content filtering and protection for popular instant messaging products. The Suite version incorporates antivirus protection.
- **Web site:**   *http://www.zonelabs.com*

Sharing Information Across Your Network

With your network hardware installed, the connections configured, and firewalls in place, what's next? This section explains how to actually *use* your network to share information.

Setting Up Shared Folders

To create a shared folder, you must be logged on as a member of the Administrators, Power Users, or Server Operators group. (After a folder has been shared, however, the share is available to network users no matter who is logged on to your computer—or even when nobody is logged on.) On a computer running Windows 2000, you can create a shared folder at any time. If you're using Windows XP, however, you must first jump through one preliminary hoop.

Enabling File Sharing in Windows XP

On a clean installation of Windows XP in a workgroup setup (where your computer is not joined to a domain), sharing is disabled. That's because sharing in this configuration relies on the Guest account, which is disabled by default.

The easiest way to configure your computer for sharing folders, files, and printers is to run the Network Setup Wizard. If you haven't already done so, Windows prompts you to run the Network Setup Wizard the first time you try to share a folder. When you right-click a folder icon and choose Sharing And Security, you might see the warning shown in Figure 8-10, which indicates that sharing is currently disabled. (If the Sharing tab instead displays a pair of check boxes and a text input box, sharing is already enabled.)

As described earlier in this chapter, running the Network Setup Wizard leads you through a series of actions designed to install and configure TCP/IP, set your workgroup and computer names, and enable Windows Firewall, if appropriate for your network configuration. As far as sharing is concerned, it performs two specific actions:

- It enables the Guest account. If you prefer, you can do this manually by typing **net user guest /active:yes** at a command prompt. (Note that enabling the Guest account does not add it to the Welcome screen. To do that, you must open User Accounts in Control Panel, click the Guest account icon, and choose Turn On The

Guest Account. This extra step enables Guest—if it's not already enabled—*and* removes the Deny Logon Locally user right for the Guest account.)

Click to run the Network Setup Wizard

Click to bypass the wizard

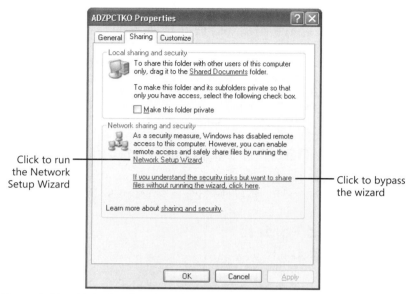

Figure 8-10. If sharing hasn't yet been enabled, you'll see a dialog box like this when you try to share a folder.

● It removes the Guest account from the list of accounts with the Deny Access To This Computer From The Network user right. To perform this task manually in Windows XP Professional, you need to open Local Security Settings (Secpol.msc) and navigate to Local Policies\User Rights Assignment. This option is not available in Windows XP Home Edition.

You might be curious about the link just below the warning text: If You Understand The Security Risks But Want To Share Files Without Running The Wizard, Click Here. If you take Windows up on this offer, you see the dialog box shown here:

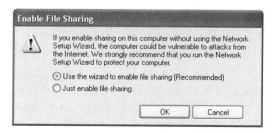

The top choice offers you one last chance to run the Network Setup Wizard. If you've already configured your network and don't want to tamper with any other aspects of your connection, you can safely choose the bottom option, Just Enable File Sharing.

Chapter 8

Doing so enables the Guest account and removes it from the list of accounts with the Deny Access To This Computer From The Network user right.

If you use Windows XP Professional and you don't plan to use Simple File Sharing, you don't need to enable sharing in the manner described in this section. In fact, by *not* enabling the Guest account, you can create a more secure environment in which only users you designate can access your computer's shared resources. For full details, skip ahead to "Sharing a Folder by Using Classic Security," page 291.

Inside Out

Use a nonadministrative account for managing shared folders

By default, setting up and managing shared folders (and printers) requires an account with administrative privileges. As we point out in this book, using an administrative account as your everyday logon account is not recommended because such an account also has many other system-level privileges, which can endanger your computer if the account is compromised. Aaron Margosis (*http://blogs.msdn.com/aaron_margosis/*), a leading proponent at Microsoft of implementing the rule of least privilege, has developed a procedure for granting to other user accounts you specify the ability to manage shared resources—enabling you to manage shares without using an administrative account. To complete this process, you need to be running Windows XP, and you need to have installed Tweak UI, an unsupported Power Toy you can download from *http://www.microsoft.com/windowsxp/downloads/powertoys /xppowertoys.mspx*. Run Tweak UI using an administrative account (only an administrative account has the ability to grant these privileges) and follow these steps:

1 In the left pane of Tweak UI, select Access Control.

2 In the right pane, select Manage File/Print Server Connections under Access Control, and then click Change.

3 Click the Add button, type the name of the account to which you'd like to grant share management privileges, and click OK. If you want to grant the privilege to anyone who logs on locally, type **interactive**.

4 With the new user's name selected in the Group Or User Names box, select the Allow check box for Enumerate Connections; all other check boxes should be cleared. Then click OK.

5 Repeat steps 3 and 4 for these privileges, which are also in the Access Control list of Tweak UI:

   ■ For Manage File Shares, grant Full Control.

   ■ For Manage Print Shares, grant Full Control.

6 Click OK in the Tweak UI window, and then restart the computer.

Thereafter, a person using the account you specified (or anyone who logs on locally, if you specified the Interactive account) can perform all the tasks outlined in this "Sharing Information Across Your Network" section—regardless of whether that account is in the Administrators, Power Users, or Server Operators group.

Configuring a Shared Folder with Simple File Sharing

When you use Windows XP with Simple File Sharing enabled, running the Network Setup Wizard automatically shares your computer's Shared Documents folder on the network. It appears on other computers as SharedDocs, and all network users can view, modify, and add files in this folder. After you enable sharing, you can share any drive or any folder, with the following exceptions and limitations:

- You cannot share the Program Files folder, although you can share subfolders within the Program Files folder.
- You cannot share the Windows folder or any of its subfolders.
- If you attempt to share the root folder of a drive, Windows first displays the warning shown here. If you are certain that you want to do so anyway, click the link to bypass the warning.

To share a folder or a drive, follow these steps:

1 In Windows Explorer, right-click the folder or drive you want to share and choose Sharing And Security from the shortcut menu.

2 In the Network Sharing And Security box, select the Share This Folder On The Network check box.

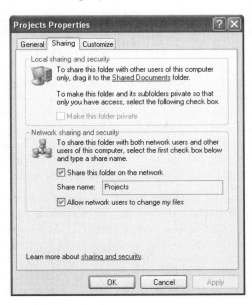

3 Specify a name for the shared resource in the Share Name box. (This is the name that network users see when they browse to your shared folder.) Windows proposes the name of the folder or, for a drive, the drive letter. Making a change here affects only the name visible on the network; it doesn't change the name of the folder on your computer.

4 By default, Windows selects the Allow Network Users To Change My Files check box, which means network users can create and modify files in your shared folder (subject to the limitations imposed on the Guest account). If you want to allow network users to view files in your shared folder and its subfolders but not allow them to create or modify files, clear this check box.

When you complete these steps, all network users will be able to find your shared folder in their My Network Places folder (or in the Network Neighborhood folder, if they're using older versions of Windows). They can also connect to your shared folder by entering its name in UNC format: *computername**sharename*. After making the connection, they can view the folder's contents and change any files or subfolders located there, unless you configured the shared folder for read-only access. With Simple File Sharing enabled, Windows ignores the logon name and password of network users and instead authenticates them as if they were using the Guest account. Thus, for folders you share over the network, network users have the same privileges as those granted to someone using the Guest account to log on locally.

Inside Out

Don't share your system's root folder!

The warning against sharing the root of a drive is well-founded, especially on a computer running Windows XP, where anyone who can connect to the computer can potentially gain access to sensitive locations. Remember that sharing a drive shares all its subfolders as well; if you share the root of a drive, everything on the drive is available. And because Simple File Sharing enables any network user to access your shared resources, the full content of your shared drive is open to anyone on your network. (If the drive is formatted as an NTFS volume, NTFS permissions might be configured to restrict Guest access to some folders, however.)

What's the risk? An attacker can gain a significant amount of control over a computer by placing an executable file in the root folder of the drive that contains system or boot files (typically C:\) or in a system folder such as Windows or System32. The risk is especially serious if the attacker can then convince the owner of the compromised system to visit a Web page or open an e-mail message that exploits an unpatched vulnerability in the operating system. Using a buffer overflow or other exploit, the attacker can cause the planted file to run by using the permissions associated with the logged-on user—or, in a worst-case scenario, as the System account.

It's always safe to share a read-only volume, such as a CD drive—provided that the data in that location is not sensitive. However, the only time you should share the root of a hard drive is when you have dedicated a volume exclusively to storage of data and you want other network users to be able to tap that data. For instance, if you install a second hard disk on your computer, format it as drive F, and use it to store your digital music files, you can safely share the root of that drive.

Behind the scenes, here's what Windows XP does when you share a folder with Simple File Sharing enabled:

- It creates a share and grants shared resource permission to the built-in Everyone group. (The Guest account is a member of the Everyone group.) Depending on whether you select the Allow Network Users To Change My Files option, Windows grants Read permission (if the option is not selected) or Full Control permission to Everyone.

- If the shared folder is on an NTFS-formatted drive, Windows adds an entry for Everyone to the folder's access control list (ACL). If Allow Network Users To Change My Files is not selected, the ACL allows Read & Execute permission; otherwise, the ACL allows Modify permission. Be aware that, by default, NTFS permissions are inherited by child objects (that is, files and folders in the folder, as well as the files and folders they contain).

> For details about the interaction of shared resource permissions and NTFS permissions, see "How Shared Resource Permissions and NTFS Permissions Work Together," page 291. For information about inheritance, see "Applying Permissions to Subfolders Through Inheritance," page 151.

Sharing a Folder by Using Classic Security

On a computer configured to use the classic security model, you define access permissions for shared folders by granting permissions to user and group accounts. In a workgroup, these accounts are maintained in a security database on your computer; each account must have a nonblank password. In a Windows domain, information about user accounts is stored in a global security database on a domain controller. All computers in the domain refer to the domain controller when they need account information.

> **Note**   Accounts that you intend to use for network access to shared folders must have a password. Except for the Guest account, Windows security prohibits network access by accounts with a blank password.

Provided you are logged on as a member of the Administrators, Power Users, or Server Operators group, you can share folders on your own computer with other users on your network.

> **Tip**   **Set permissions before sharing**
> If you're sharing a folder on an NTFS drive, you should set the NTFS permissions as you want them before you share the folder. That way, security restrictions are in place before you make the folder available on the network.

To share a folder or a drive, follow these steps:

1   In Windows Explorer, right-click the folder or drive you want to share and then choose Sharing And Security from the shortcut menu.

2   On the Sharing tab of the folder's properties dialog box, select the Share This Folder option.

3   Accept or change the proposed share name.

> **Note**   If the folder is already shared, click New Share and then type the share name. Local drives always have a default administrative share whose share name consists of the drive letter and a dollar sign (for example, C$). This share name is not visible to others, and you can't set permissions for the default share—so you'll want to create a new share.

The share name is the name that other users will see in their My Network Places folders. Windows initially proposes to use the folder's name as its share name. That's usually a good choice, but you're not obligated to accept it. If you already have a shared folder with that name, pick a different name instead.

Chapter 8

> **Tip**   **Don't let share names give away information**
>
> A little curiosity is a dangerous thing. When sharing folders that contain especially sensitive data, don't use share names that encourage a casual observer to try to break in. Instead, choose codes that describe the contents in terms you can understand but that won't unnecessarily tempt others. For instance, if you need to share payroll data with an accountant on your small business network, use a share name such as Pr-2005 instead of Payroll Data. A casual observer who sees the former share name is likely to skip right over it, whereas anyone who sees the latter name is sure to mention it around the water cooler.

4   Type a description of the folder's contents in the Comment box. Although this step is optional, a descriptive comment is helpful to other users, who will see this information when they inspect the folder's properties dialog box in their My Network Places folders (or use Details view).

5   To limit the number of users who can connect to the shared folder concurrently, select Allow This Number Of Users and then specify a number. On a small network, this option is rarely needed. The default choice, Maximum Allowed, permits up to 10 concurrent users. (If you need to share a folder with more than 10 users at once, you must use a server version of Windows.)

Hiding a Shared Folder

Whether you're using Simple File Sharing or classic sharing, you can hide any share name so that it's invisible to anyone browsing over the network (using the My Network Places folder or Windows Explorer). The secret is to append a dollar sign to the share name—for example, Projects$. Users who know the exact name of the shared folder can still connect to it by typing its name—including the dollar sign—into any place network paths are accepted, such as the Address bar, the Add Network Place Wizard, the Map Network Drive dialog box, and so on. They can also create shortcuts that open the hidden folder directly.

Like many Windows security features, hiding share names is not foolproof and doesn't guarantee that your shared folders will remain untouched. The convention that a share with its name ending with a dollar sign should be hidden is a function of the client computer, not the computer serving up the shared folder. All versions of Windows hide such shares, but if your network includes Apple Macintosh computers or computers running Linux, users of those computers can view the "hidden" shares. In addition, a would-be intruder who knows how to program in a scripting language such as Perl can easily enumerate all the shares on an entire network, hidden or not. To completely secure your sensitive shared data, you must also set permissions appropriately.

Stopping Access to a Shared Folder

To stop sharing a folder on a computer running Windows XP with Simple File Sharing, open the folder's properties dialog box, click the Sharing tab, and clear the Share This Folder On The Network check box. If you're using the classic sharing option, select Do Not Share This Folder.

Assigning Permissions to a Shared Folder

In Windows 2000 and Windows XP, the default shared resource permission associated with a new share is Full Control to Everyone. (By contrast, in Windows Server 2003, new shares allow Read Only access to Everyone by default.) That means that anyone on your network can do whatever they want to files stored in that location, including deleting or changing them. (If the shared folder resides on an NTFS volume, individual subfolders and files can have their own access restrictions, however.) If you use classic sharing, you can place limits on what particular users or groups of users can do with your shared files by clicking the Permissions button on the Sharing tab. This action displays the Permissions dialog box shown in Figure 8-11.

Chapter 8

Figure 8-11. To set share permissions, right-click the shared folder in Windows Explorer and open its properties dialog box. Then click Permissions on the Sharing tab.

Follow these steps to view or set permissions:

1   In the Group Or User Names list in the Permissions dialog box, select the user or the group you want to manage. The shared resource permissions for the selected user or group appear at the bottom of the dialog box.

2   Select Allow, Deny, or neither for each access control entry:

   ■ **Full Control.**   Controls whether users can create, read, write, rename, and delete files in the folder and its subfolders. If Allow is selected, users can change permissions on and take ownership of files on NTFS volumes. Selecting this option automatically selects the corresponding check boxes for the Change and Read permissions.

- **Change.** Allows or denies permission to read, write, rename, and delete files in the folder and its subfolders, but not to create new files.
- **Read.** Allows or denies permission to read files but not write to, rename, or delete them.

If you select neither Allow nor Deny, the user or group is implicitly denied permission to the resource. However, any user or group can still inherit the permission through membership in another group that has the permission.

To remove a name from the Group Or User Names list, select it and click Remove. To add a name, click Add to open the Select Users Or Groups dialog box, where you can enter the names of the users and groups you want to add. For more information about this dialog box, see "Using NTFS Permissions for Access Control," page 136.

Tip   Disable Guest access to shared folders

Setting up a share grants permission to the built-in Everyone group by default. In Windows XP, the Guest account is included in Everyone, and because Windows authenticates network users who don't have an account on the local computer as Guest, anyone on your network has access to a share. If you want to exclude anyone who does not have a user account on your computer, in the Permissions dialog box, select Everyone and click Remove. Then click Add, type **Authenticated Users**, and click OK. (The built-in Authenticated Users group does not include the Guest account.) Select Authenticated Users in the Group Or User Names box, and then select the Allow check box for Full Control.

Caution   In Windows XP, files and folders that are created in a shared folder on an NTFS drive while Simple File Sharing is enabled are owned by the local Guest account. Ownership of files doesn't change when you disable or enable Simple File Sharing. Be aware that, even if you change to classic sharing and impose tighter security on your shared folders, users who log on as Guest (locally or remotely) continue to have full control over files that were created by *any* remote user while Simple File Sharing was enabled (assuming they still have access to the shared folder). To remedy this situation, take ownership of the folder and its contents, and remove Everyone from the ACLs of the folder and its contents.

Managing Shared Folders

Although you can create, remove, and change permissions for individual shared folders from Windows Explorer, this technique has one significant disadvantage: It offers no way for you to quickly and effectively review the settings for all shared folders on a computer. You have to browse through the entire hierarchy of folders to see which ones are shared. If you forget that you've temporarily shared a folder, you could end up sharing important data. For a more centralized approach, use the Shared Folders snap-in for Microsoft Management Console (MMC).

To start the Shared Folders snap-in, open Computer Management (right-click My Computer, and choose Manage) and then navigate to System Tools\Shared Folders. You can open Shared Folders in its own console window—without all the clutter of Computer Management—by typing **fsmgmt.msc** at a command prompt. Figure 8-12 shows the Shared Folders snap-in, which works essentially the same under Windows 2000 and Windows XP.

Figure 8-12. Use the Shared Folders MMC snap-in to view and manage all shared folders from one central location.

To use the Shared Folders snap-in, you must be a member of the Administrators or Power Users group. And to use it for anything other than merely viewing shares, sessions, and open files, you must have Simple File Sharing disabled (which means that Shared Folders is of limited use to anyone running Windows XP Home Edition).

When you open Shared Folders, all the shared folders on your computer are visible in the Shares folder. If you use Windows XP Home Edition, you can view shares, sessions, and open files—period. If you're using Windows 2000 or Windows XP Professional with Simple File Sharing disabled, on the other hand, you can modify the properties of any folder by right-clicking it and choosing Properties. The folder's properties dialog box appears, as shown in Figure 8-13 on the next page. Notice that using the Share Permissions tab shown here achieves the same result as opening the properties dialog box from a folder in Windows Explorer and clicking the Permissions button on the Sharing tab.

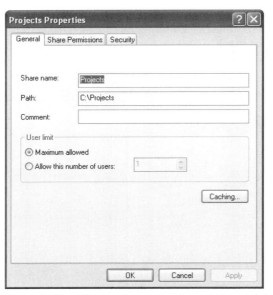

Figure 8-13. Choose Properties in the Shared Folders snap-in to open a dialog box like this.

Managing Administrative Shares

A handful of the shares you see in the Shared Folders list are created by the operating system. Most of these share names end with a dollar sign ($), which makes them "invisible" when another Windows user browses through the list of shares on your computer. They are not inaccessible, however. Any user who knows the name of an administrative share can attempt to connect to it simply by typing the share name at a command prompt rather than selecting it from the browse list. (Use UNC format to make such a connection: \\*computername*\\*sharename*.) If the computer that contains the administrative shares is running Windows 2000 or Windows XP Professional with Simple File Sharing disabled, the connection will be successful if the remote user supplies a user name and password that match the credentials of a local administrator. With Simple File Sharing enabled, however, all interactive logons to administrative shares are blocked. In fact, because Simple File Sharing cannot be disabled in Windows XP Home Edition, this version of Windows creates only the IPC$ share by default.

In general, you cannot view or set permissions on administrative shares, as you can for shares you create; the operating system hardwires access controls so that only members of the local Administrators group and select built-in accounts can connect to administrative shares.

You can stop sharing administrative shares only temporarily. The share reappears the next time the Server service starts or you restart your computer. With a registry edit, it's possible to disable this feature so that when you delete an administrative share it is not automatically re-created the next time you restart your computer. For details, see the Inside Out tip on page 31.

Chapter 8

Table 8-5 describes the administrative shares you are most likely to see on a computer running Windows 2000 Professional or Windows XP.

Table 8-5. **Administrative Shares**

Share Name	Description
C$, D$, E$, and so on	With each of these shares, members of the Administrators and Backup Operators groups can connect to the root folder of a volume. Windows creates a share for the root folder of every partition and volume on a local hard drive, using the drive letter of the volume (followed by a dollar sign to hide the share) as the share name. These shares are often used by backup programs and by centralized network administration tools such as Microsoft Systems Management Server.
ADMIN$	This share maps to the %SystemRoot% folder (C:\Windows on a typical clean installation of Windows XP; C:\Winnt on a typical clean installation of Windows 2000). This share is most often used by remote administration programs.
IPC$	This share enables interprocess communications (IPC) using named pipes. IPC allows data transfer between programs and processes over a network—during remote administration and when viewing a computer's resources, for instance.
PRINT$	This share is used for remote administration of printers.
FAX$	This share exists only if you have fax server software installed and is rarely used on desktop versions of Windows; it is used by clients to send faxes and access cover pages stored on the server.

Newcomers to Windows 2000 and Windows XP are sometimes unnerved to learn that the operating system sets up administrative shares and makes them accessible from the network. In normal use, these shares are perfectly safe from attack. For high-security environments, however, expert users might choose to disable these shares.

Creating a New Share

Although the easiest way to share a folder is to start from Windows Explorer, you can also create a new share by using the Shared Folders snap-in. The Create Shared Folder Wizard is available in the Shared Folders snap-in only if you are using Windows 2000 or Windows XP Professional with Simple File Sharing disabled. To start the wizard, right-click Shares in the console tree and choose New File Share and then follow the prompts to select the folder you want to share and set up basic security options, as shown in Figure 8-14 on the next page. Unlike the default share permissions applied when you create a share in Windows Explorer (whether Simple File Sharing is enabled or not), the wizard enables you to set different permissions for administrators (members of the Administrators group) and other users (Everyone).

Figure 8-14. The Create Shared Folder Wizard provides an alternative to sharing a folder from Windows Explorer.

You don't need to open the Shared Folders console to get to the Create Shared Folder Wizard; you can run it by typing **shrpubw** at a command prompt. Surprisingly, this shortcut works in Windows XP (including Home Edition) when Simple File Sharing is enabled. Unfortunately, using the wizard to create a share with custom permissions is of no use in this configuration because when Simple File Sharing is enabled (as it is all the time in Windows XP Home Edition), all network users are authenticated as Guest. Even if you set up different permissions for different network users, Windows XP ignores these permissions and uses the permissions assigned to the Guest account instead.

Managing Sessions and Open Files

Each user who connects to your computer creates a session. Using the Shared Folders snap-in, you can see a list of all active sessions, revealing who is currently connected to the computer as well as what files they have open. Click Sessions in the console tree to have the current sessions appear in the details pane, as shown in Figure 8-15.

> **Tip** See who is authenticated
>
> If you're trying to determine why some users have access to certain folders and others don't, it's helpful to know whether they're being authenticated using their unique logon credentials or using the Guest account. That's easy to do with Shared Folders. In the Sessions folder, the rightmost column is titled Guest; its value is either Yes (authenticated as Guest) or No (authenticated as named user).

Click Open Files in the Shared Folders console tree to see a list of shared files that are currently open for other users. This viewing tool is especially useful if you're receiving an error message when you try to open a file that's in use by someone else.

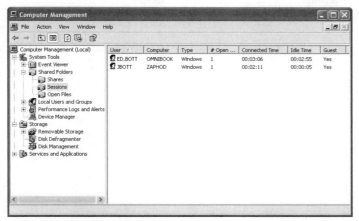

Figure 8-15. The Sessions folder shows which network users are connected to your computer.

Besides seeing who is connected, you can disconnect any or all sessions and close any open files. That's an effective way of kicking out unauthorized users when you find them connected to shared resources on your computer. Right-click a session and choose Close Session to close a single session. Right-click Sessions in the console tree and choose Disconnect All Sessions to close all the open sessions. You can close an individual file by right-clicking it and choosing Close Open File. You can close all the open files at once by right-clicking Open Files in the console tree and choosing Disconnect All Open Files. Taking any of these measures is a drastic step that can cause other users to lose data, so you should avoid disconnecting users or closing open files unless the situation is a genuine emergency.

Chapter 8

Chapter 9

Sharing an Internet Connection

Protecting a local area network in a home or small office is relatively easy. You can sit down in front of each computer to check its security settings, and you can stroll down the hallway and see exactly who's using each computer on the network. But all that changes as soon as you connect your network to the Internet.

Unless you carefully consider security when configuring your Internet connection, you could end up inadvertently extending the borders of your local area network far beyond those you intended. In a worst-case scenario, where your Internet connection is inadequately protected and you haven't installed the latest security updates for Microsoft Windows, a stranger from halfway around the world could join your network, which would then no longer seem nearly so local. Given enough time and motivation, an attacker from the outside could poke around in confidential data, sabotage files, or hijack your connection and use it as a conduit for spam or a launching pad for attacks on other vulnerable computers.

As we explain in this chapter, you can choose from a wide range of options for connecting your local network to the Internet. Cost and complexity are the two considerations that most people focus on first, but we believe security should be at the top of your list.

Security Checklist: Internet Connections

Here's a list of steps you should be sure to take in securing your network's Internet connection:

- Add a router or residential gateway to your network, or use Internet Connection Sharing. Either solution uses Network Address Translation (NAT) to hide your local computers from the outside world and thereby increases your network's security.

- Disable file and printer sharing and the Microsoft network client on your Internet connection.

- Add a personal firewall to protect your Internet connection from outside attacks. Windows XP Service Pack 2 (SP2) automatically turns on Windows Firewall; you can replace it with a third-party option if you prefer.

- If you have a router that doesn't support the UPnP home-networking standard, look for a UPnP-compatible firmware upgrade or consider replacing the hardware.

- Set a strong password on your router.

- Disable access to Web-based administrative tools from the Internet.

Connecting Your Network to the Internet

When bringing the Internet into your network, you can choose any of the following configurations:

- **Each computer has its own physical connection to the Internet.** If you're limited to dial-up speeds and each computer has its own modem and access to a telephone line, this option is simple, direct, and quite inexpensive. With broadband connections such as a cable modem or a digital subscriber line (DSL), the cost of multiple physical connections (including hardware for each computer) can be prohibitive, and the task of installing multiple connections can be daunting. In either case, you need to take extra steps to ensure that outsiders are blocked from accessing your network, as we explain in "Using Direct Internet Connections on a LAN," page 305.

- **Each computer has a direct connection to the Internet through a network hub or switch.** In this configuration, your external DSL or cable modem is plugged into a hub or switch, as are all computers on the network. Microsoft strongly recommends against using this setup, and so do we. For starters, it will work only if your Internet service provider (ISP) is willing and able to supply separate IP addresses to each computer. (Some ISPs limit customers to a single IP address or charge extra for each additional address.) Because each computer is communicating with the Internet and the local network using the same TCP/IP connection, this configuration has the potential to leave your network wide open to outside attackers. If you understand the risks and choose this configuration anyway, be sure to tighten security by using the techniques we outline in "Why You Shouldn't Use One Connection for Both Internet and LAN Access," page 310.

● **All computers on the network are connected to a router or residential gateway.** This configuration is probably the most secure you can choose for a small business or home network and is the one we strongly recommend. The hardware router serves as your gateway to the Internet, using Network Address Translation (NAT) to supply private IP addresses to computers on the local network. The router distributes all TCP/IP traffic from the network to the outside world and then routes the returning packets to their correct destination. To the outside world, your entire network appears as a single computer with its own IP address. We explain the best strategies for securing this network configuration in "Sharing an Internet Connection Through Hardware," page 310.

● **All computers on the network are connected to a single computer running Internet Connection Sharing (ICS).** ICS, which has been a part of every version of Windows since Windows 98 Second Edition, transforms the computer that is running ICS into the functional equivalent of a hardware router. Like a router, ICS uses NAT to assign private IP addresses to every computer on the network and then manages the flow of TCP/IP traffic to and from the Internet. Using ICS requires that you accept a few compromises, most notably that you leave the ICS host machine turned on at all times. In Windows XP, ICS is tightly integrated with Windows Firewall; we explain the configuration do's and don'ts in "Sharing an Internet Connection Through Software," page 316.

How Network Address Translation Works

When you connect to the Internet directly, using a dial-up modem or broadband connection, your ISP typically assigns you an IP address from a pool of addresses that it owns. These addresses are public; their location is listed in routing tables that are a crucial part of the Internet's standard procedure to guide packets of data as they move from point to point. When you click a link to a Web page or check for new messages on your e-mail server, the outgoing packet includes your IP address; the server on the other end of the connection returns the requested data to your IP address, and the Internet sees to it that those packets are routed to your computer properly.

On a home or small office network, having a unique public IP address for every computer is unnecessary and possibly dangerous. By sharing an Internet connection instead, you can get by with a single public IP address assigned to a single hardware device (a router, typically, or a computer running ICS). Each of the computers on the local network has a private IP address that is not reachable from the outside world but is known to other computers on the local network. To communicate with Web sites, external e-mail servers, and other Internet hosts, computers on the network funnel their requests through the computer or router on the edge of the network—the one with a public IP address. As each packet goes out onto the Internet, the gateway device makes a note of where it came from. When the return packets arrive, the gateway machine uses NAT to pass those packets back to the correct private IP address on the network.

The Internet Assigned Numbers Authority (IANA) has reserved three blocks of the IP address space for use on private networks that are not directly connected to the Internet:

- 10.0.0.0 – 10.255.255.255
- 172.16.0.0 – 172.31.255.255
- 192.168.0.0 – 192.168.255.255

Routers, switches, and residential gateways that use NAT almost always assign addresses from these private ranges. The Internet Connection Sharing feature in Windows XP (as in previous versions of Windows), for instance, assigns private IP addresses in the 192.168.0.*x* range (where *x* is a randomly assigned number between 1 and 255). On our test network, an older RG-1000 residential gateway from Agere Systems assigns addresses in the 10.0.0.*x* range; Linksys routers we've used typically assign addresses starting with 192.168.1.*x*; the SMC router currently in use on our production network uses addresses beginning with 192.168.2.*x*. Unlike public IP addresses, which must be unique across the entire Internet, private IP addresses need be unique only on your local network. Although it is technically possible to use IP addresses from publicly available ranges on a private network, doing so is not recommended; use only addresses from the three reserved blocks of private IP addresses.

Using private IP addresses offers a significant security advantage because the computer or router that is managing the connection through NAT can inspect each incoming packet and decide whether to forward it or drop it. If a computer on the local network requested the connection, the NAT gateway will forward it; on the other hand, if a computer outside the network is trying to make an unsolicited connection, the gateway assumes that the traffic is hostile (or at least unwanted) and discards it.

Troubleshooting

When you check your IP address, it appears in the 169.254.*x.y* range and you can't access the Internet

This range of addresses is assigned by your computer using a feature called Automatic Private IP Addressing (APIPA). APIPA kicks in only when no DHCP server is available. If you're using ICS or a router or residential gateway that automatically assigns IP addresses and your computer is unable to acquire an IP address from the DHCP server, APIPA assigns a default address. This problem is often caused by a faulty network connection or by a firewall that is configured incorrectly. Disable any third-party security software, confirm that all physical connections are set up properly, and run through the Network Setup Wizard to see if you can repair the problem.

If you use Windows 2000, you must set all security and sharing options for your network manually; in Windows XP, the Network Setup Wizard does the grunt work of configuring TCP/IP settings, installing and configuring Internet connections, setting up ICS (if your network doesn't include a router or residential gateway), and enabling Windows Firewall. In most cases, the wizard's default settings are correct and you should avoid tampering with them. In a few unusual configurations, however, you might need to tweak connection settings to achieve the result you want.

Using Direct Internet Connections on a LAN

Is the local network connection to your computer physically separate from your Internet connection? Is the Internet connection (dial-up or broadband) yours and yours alone? If the answer to both of these questions is yes, your security challenge is simple: Make sure that data packets from outside can't reach your computer (and your network) unless you specifically request them and that shared resources on your computer are accessible only from addresses on your local network. To be sure your two connections remain separate, you can and should disable file and printer sharing on the Internet connection. In addition, you should install and configure a personal firewall program that isolates the Internet connection from the LAN. Windows Firewall (included as part of Windows XP Service Pack 2) passes this test in its default configuration; with Windows 2000, you need to ensure that a third-party firewall is configured properly.

Configuring a Dial-Up Connection

By default, both Windows 2000 and Windows XP disable the File And Printer Sharing service when you create a new dial-up connection. To confirm that your existing dial-up connection is secure, follow these steps:

1 Open the folder that contains your dial-up connections. In Windows 2000, click Start, Settings, Network And Dial-Up Connections. In Windows XP, double-click the Network Connections icon in Control Panel (if you use Category View, look under Network And Internet Connections).

2 Right-click the icon for your dial-up connection and choose Properties.

3 On the Networking tab, ensure that the File And Printer Sharing For Microsoft Networks and Client For Microsoft Networks boxes are not selected. Figure 9-1 on the next page shows this dialog box as it appears in Windows XP; the Windows 2000 version is nearly identical.

Figure 9-1. Make certain that file and printer sharing is disabled on any dial-up connections.

Configuring a Broadband Connection

With broadband connections, the task of preventing anonymous intruders from browsing shared folders and other resources on your LAN is trickier. In this configuration, you have two Ethernet adapters—one providing connectivity to your LAN, the other connecting you to the Internet. If you use the Network Setup Wizard in Windows XP to install and enable file and printer sharing, this setting applies to all network connections. Thus, your first priority should be to shut down this service on the Internet connection, while leaving it in place on the LAN connection. To do so, follow these steps:

1 Open the Network Connections folder (Windows XP) or the Network And Dial-Up Connections folder (Windows 2000). You should see at least two Local Area Connection icons.

2 Right-click the icon for your Internet connection and choose Properties from the shortcut menu.

3 On the General tab, clear the check boxes to the left of File And Printer Sharing For Microsoft Networks and Client For Microsoft Networks.

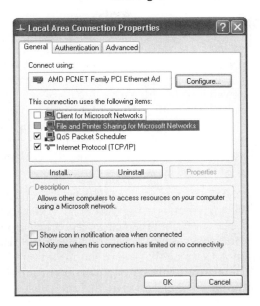

4 Click OK to save your changes.

 Inside Out

Differentiate between your connections

When you have two or more network connections, how can you tell which is which? Windows isn't much help—it applies the generic label Local Area Connection for each one, tacking a number onto the end of the name for the second and subsequent connections. If the network adapter and the IP address don't give you enough information, use each connection's IP address to figure out which is which. From the Network Connections window, double-click each connection icon to open its status dialog box. On the Support tab, look at the IP address. The connection with the IP address in a private range is your LAN connection; the one with a public IP address is the Internet connection.

If you can't decipher the IP addresses, try either of these easy shortcuts: Unplug the Ethernet cable from your Internet connection, and note which icon changes to disconnected status. Alternatively, right-click one icon and choose Disable from the shortcut menu. Leaving the other icon enabled, try to connect to a Web page. If you see an error message in your browser window, you know that the disabled icon belongs to your Internet connection and the other one goes with your local network. If the page appears, the roles are reversed. Armed with this information, right-click each icon in turn and choose Rename; then enter a descriptive label for each one so that you won't have to go through this rigmarole the next time you want to know which network connection is which!

Adding Firewall Protection

After disabling file and printer sharing services, your next responsibility is to install a personal firewall to block unsolicited inbound traffic on the Internet connection. In Windows 2000, you must use a third-party product for this task because the operating system doesn't include any firewall features. In Windows XP, you can use a third-party product, but you remain perfectly secure with the help of the built-in Windows Firewall. We explain the ins and outs of firewalls in "Blocking Attacks by Using a Firewall," page 10, so we won't repeat those details here. In this section, we focus instead on how to work around some of the occasionally confusing choices that the Windows XP Network Setup Wizard offers when you add an Internet connection to your LAN.

To start the wizard, open the Network Connections folder from Control Panel and choose File, Network Setup Wizard (if you're using the Category view of Control Panel, click Network And Internet Connections and then click Network Setup Wizard). After you click through its two introductory screens, the wizard displays the dialog box shown in Figure 9-2. The first two options assume that you're sharing an Internet connection over your network using either a hardware router or a computer running ICS software. As we emphasize repeatedly in this chapter, this is indeed the safest and simplest way to add Internet access to a LAN.

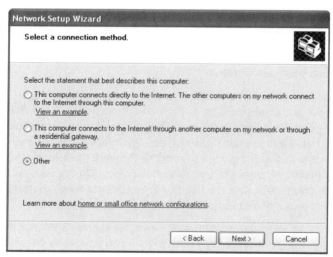

Figure 9-2. If your computer is connected directly to the Internet and a LAN, select the Other option.

Select the Other option and click Next. In the Other Internet Connection Methods dialog box, shown in Figure 9-3, select the top choice, This Computer Connects To The Internet Directly Or Through An Internet Hub, and click Next to continue.

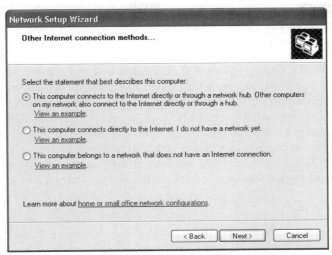

Figure 9-3. If other network users are not accessing the Internet through your computer, choose the top option from this list.

In a step that is new with Service Pack 2 (SP2), the wizard next offers you the option to enable or disable file and printer sharing. If you choose to enable sharing, the wizard displays the dire warning shown in Figure 9-4.

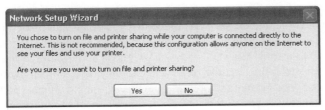

Figure 9-4. If your Internet connection is firewalled and you're confident that no other network computers have Internet access, you can proceed despite this warning.

Although the warning is generally accurate, you may safely disregard it and continue if you are certain that no other computer on your network has an active Internet connection or that all other Internet connections are protected by a firewall.

If there is any chance that another computer on your network can connect to the Internet without the protection of a firewall, you run the risk that an intruder can break in to that computer and then access resources on your computer using your TCP/IP–based LAN connection. If you're confident this can't happen, click Next and finish the wizard. After prompting you for the computer and workgroup names, the wizard turns on Windows Firewall on both connections, with file and printer sharing restricted to computers on your local network. Because you've already disabled the File And Printer Sharing service on the Internet connection, you can be confident that your network is secure from unauthorized access.

Why You Shouldn't Use One Connection for Both Internet and LAN Access

Safely sharing an Internet connection requires at least a slight investment in extra hardware. Routers and residential gateways cost more than simple network hubs or switches. The less expensive Internet Connection Sharing option requires that you install a second Ethernet adapter on the computer that will serve as the ICS host. Windows users with a broadband connection and a very tight budget might be tempted to cut corners by plugging a cable or DSL modem directly into the network hub or switch alongside two or more networked computers. In this configuration, every computer acquires an IP address directly from the ISP and uses the same Ethernet adapter to communicate over the Internet and across the local network.

Without additional precautions, this configuration is horrendously insecure. An intruder who breaks in to any computer on the network has access to the entire network. In Windows XP, the Network Setup Wizard first delivers a warning message (shown in Figure 9-4) and turns on Windows Firewall. In the original release of Windows XP, this solution protected the network by disabling all communication with other computers on your LAN. Beginning with SP2, Windows XP handles the situation more gracefully by configuring Windows Firewall to allow file and printer sharing only on the local subnet. However, this precaution is effective only if your ISP segments your block of addresses properly. It's possible, in this configuration, that other users with addresses in the same range may be able to access shared resources on your network.

If you insist on using this configuration, we recommend that you install a third-party personal firewall program in place of Windows Firewall. (You'll find a list of firewall programs in "Choosing a Third-Party Personal Firewall," page 280.) Choose a full-featured firewall product that enables you to define security zones and explicitly define which IP addresses are part of your local network. Configured properly, the firewall should enable you to freely exchange data among network computers while blocking all unsolicited inbound traffic on the Internet connection.

Sharing an Internet Connection Through Hardware

The single most effective way to protect your local network from outside intruders is to place a barrier between the Internet and your LAN. Although businesses can justify sinking thousands of dollars into sophisticated hardware firewalls, you can protect your home or small business network for a fraction of that amount by installing a simple hardware router (sometimes referred to as a residential gateway). This piece of hardware sits between your network and your Internet connection (usually an external DSL or cable modem, although you can also use a conventional modem in this configuration). To the outside world, this gateway device looks like just another computer, although it's considerably more secure because it does not have any running programs or disk storage that can be attacked. Because it's always on, any computer can access the Internet at any time through the gateway device.

> **Note** What's the difference between a router and a residential gateway? Very little, at least today. A router is designed primarily for computer networks; its role is to sit at the edge of the network and serve as the secure interface between a local network and the rest of the world. Most products currently sold as residential gateways are nothing more than routers aimed at home users. Someday, residential gateways might take on more ambitious assignments and live up to their high-falutin' name by integrating video, telephony, and home control systems with PC-based home networks. For now, though, you can consider the terms essentially interchangeable.

Routers and residential gateways typically use NAT to assign private IP addresses to computers on your network, although you can also assign static IP addresses that are within the IANA-approved private IP address ranges.

Inside Out

Mix and match IP addresses

By default, most routers have DHCP enabled, allowing the router to dynamically assign IP addresses to computers on your network. This removes some of the hassles of administering a network, but it also creates problems if you want to allow certain ports to pass through the router and be sent directly to a specific local computer. If you power down the local computer for a few days, it might acquire a new address the next time it's turned on. To work around this problem, you can assign static IP addresses to one or more computers on your network. Be sure the addresses are in the same range and on the same subnet as those assigned dynamically by your router, and be sure to exclude the fixed addresses from the list used by the router's DHCP server.

Despite what you might read in some advertising literature, a router is *not* the same as a firewall. A basic router is designed to do exactly what its name implies: route packets between networks. An increasing number of routers sold for use in home and small business networks incorporate features typically found in firewalls, such as packet filtering, port blocking, and NAT. By making the individual computers on your network essentially invisible to the outside world, the router accomplishes one of the key tasks of a firewall; but your network will be much more secure if you combine this hardware solution with a software firewall. (See "Blocking Attacks by Using a Firewall," page 10, for more details on the additional layers of protection you can expect.)

Why Your Router Should Be UPnP-Compatible

When you go shopping for a router or residential gateway, you'll encounter a wide variety of options, from simple one-port routers to pricey devices that incorporate software firewalls and virtual private network (VPN) technology. For any router that you intend to use with computers running Windows XP, we recommend that you study the specifications carefully and make certain it supports the UPnP home-networking standard. UPnP-compatible routers (including firmware upgrades to add UPnP support to older routers) have been available for several years, and most hardware makers now support this capability. A well-publicized security flaw in the initial release of Windows XP in late 2001 led to a blizzard of negative publicity about this feature. However, subsequent security updates have fixed this flaw and there is no good reason to avoid UPnP on a properly configured Windows network.

A router that supports UPnP can offer a variety of features designed to streamline administrative tasks. With UPnP, for instance, other computers on the network can automatically sense that the router is available and configure their Internet connections without any effort on your part. Administrators can also use UPnP features to configure and manage the router without having to remember specific IP addresses or load custom software.

The most important benefit of UPnP, however, is its support for *NAT traversal*. With a router or residential gateway that doesn't support UPnP, the use of private addresses makes it impossible for communications programs like Remote Assistance to establish a connection. Likewise, the use of NAT makes it impossible for Windows Messenger users to communicate using audio or video features. With UPnP, the router understands how to work seamlessly with private network addresses and can maintain these connections properly.

If you have an older router that doesn't work properly with these types of applications, you might want to replace it with a newer, UPnP-compatible device. Before you go to that trouble, though, be sure to check with the hardware manufacturer. You might be pleasantly surprised to find that UPnP features are available with a simple firmware upgrade.

Configuring a Router or Residential Gateway

Connecting a router to your network isn't a particularly difficult task. First plug your cable or DSL modem into the WAN port on the router; then plug the hub or switch that connects computers on your local network into the LAN port on the router. (If your router includes an integrated hub or switch, you can plug computers on your network directly into the LAN ports on the router.)

Most routers include a configuration utility, typically accessed through a Web-based interface. With the popular Linksys BEFSR41 and BEFSR81 routers, for instance, you load the configuration page shown in Figure 9-5 by typing the URL *http://192.168.1.1* and entering the default password, **admin**.

Chapter 9

Sharing an Internet Connection

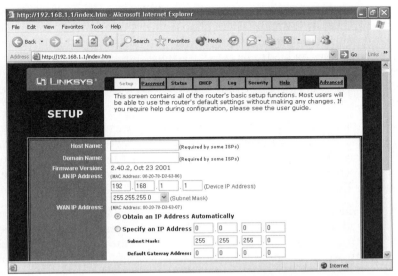

Figure 9-5. Most routers, like this Linksys model, use a Web-based configuration utility.

 ## Troubleshooting

You can't connect to the configuration page for your router

When setting up a router, you need to supply its IP address, typically by typing it into the Address bar in Internet Explorer. If your computer and the router have IP addresses on different subnets, you'll be unable to connect. Your computer should acquire an IP address automatically from the DHCP server on the router. This option will fail if the router's DHCP capabilities have been previously disabled, or if another DHCP server is running elsewhere on the network. Try any of these strategies to solve the problem:

● Check your router's documentation to see whether it requires software to be installed on your computer in order to locate the router.

● Disconnect all other computers from the network, leaving only the LAN connection for your computer and the WAN connection enabled. Make sure your computer is set to acquire an IP address automatically and try again.

● Press the router's reset switch to apply the default settings. This should enable the DHCP capabilities again.

● If all else fails, assign a temporary static IP address to your computer. Make sure this address is on the same subnet as the router, and specify the router's IP address as the gateway. For instance, if the router's address is 192.168.1.1, assign your computer the address 192.168.1.2, with a subnet mask of 255.255.255.0 and a gateway of 192.168.1.1.

The first step is to establish your Internet connection. If you normally acquire an IP address automatically through DHCP, choose this option for your router. Depending on your ISP, you might need to supply a fixed IP address, enter the addresses of DNS servers, or both. You might also have to perform additional steps, such as setting up a Point-to-Point Protocol over Ethernet (PPPoE) logon for the router or changing the Media Access Control (MAC) address of your router so that it matches the MAC address of your primary computer.

Next, set up the router's internal DHCP server. When this feature is enabled, the router responds to requests for an IP address from computers on your local network. You can typically specify a range of private IP addresses. Depending on the router, you might be able to map specific IP addresses to specific MAC addresses so that each computer on your network always receives the same IP address when connecting to the network.

Finally, close the configuration utility and configure each computer on the network to acquire an IP address automatically. (For computers running Windows XP, you should use the Network Setup Wizard for this task.) After confirming that the router is doing its job, you can set up advanced features, such as packet filtering and port forwarding.

Inside Out

Bypass ISP restrictions on servers

Some routers enable you to create virtual servers inside your network, passing specific ports through the router to a designated IP address. This capability can be a useful (but potentially dangerous) way to get around the blocks that many ISPs place on Web and FTP servers. You might want to run a personal Web server on which you can share photos with other family members, but access from the outside will fail if your ISP blocks port 80, the standard port used by Web servers. One solution is to configure the Web server to use a port that isn't blocked, such as 8080, and then use the router's port-forwarding features to pass all outside traffic on port 8080 directly to the IP address of the computer running the Web server. Anyone making a connection to the server will need to specify the public IP address of the router, followed by a colon and the port number. If you choose this option, be certain that you update the Web server software regularly with the latest security updates. And don't try to use this "under the radar" capability for a high-volume Web site unless you're prepared for a confrontation with your ISP.

Tightening Security on a Router

Adding a router to your network isn't a panacea. Simple NAT and packet-filtering capabilities provide a baseline level of security for your network, but don't underestimate the resourcefulness and tenacity of outside attackers. A determined intruder who figures out that you're using a specific type of router can craft an attack against the router and might succeed if you aren't thorough in your preparation. To increase the security of the network, follow these tips:

- **Set a strong password for the router.** Out of the box, every router uses a simple default password, and you can bet that every one of those default passwords is on a list that would-be attackers try right away.

- **Disable remote administration capabilities.** Many routers enable you to connect to the router's configuration utility from inside your local network or from the outside. To block a major avenue of attack, disable the capability to manage the router from the Internet.

- **Configure how the router responds to unsolicited outside traffic.** If you're running a server inside your network, forwarding specific ports to the IP address of the computer running the server software, you need to allow outside access to the computer. But you should disable all other unsolicited outside traffic. In particular, if you can configure the router to discard Internet Control Message Protocol (ICMP) packets from the Internet, you should do so. This step prevents outsiders from "pinging" your network and determining that the IP address exists. It also prevents an entire class of attacks that use malformed ICMP packets to cause havoc to the network.

- **Enable firewall or antivirus features, if available.** Some routers integrate with specific antivirus and personal firewall programs. Using this capability, you can enforce a security policy that allows Internet access through the router only to computers that are running up-to-date versions of supported security programs. Routers designed for business use might also offer firewall features that go beyond basic address translation and packet filtering, such as VPN support.

- **Carefully configure advanced firewall options.** Every router is different. Depending on the specific capabilities of your router, you might be able to block specific incoming ports or block access to particular ports by time of day. The latter capability can be especially useful if you want to prevent kids from browsing the Web after 10:00 PM, for instance.

> **Caution** Many routers include an option to place one or more computers on the local network in a perimeter network (also known as DMZ, demilitarized zone, and screened subnet). Putting a computer in this zone bypasses the router, giving it direct access to the Internet. Using this option might be the only way to make some types of connections, such as those used in multiplayer games. Just be aware that bypassing the router also gives outsiders unfiltered access to the computer in the perimeter network. If you must use this option, we recommend enabling it only when you need it and removing the local computer from the perimeter network when direct access to the Internet is no longer required.

Chapter 9

Sharing an Internet Connection Through Software

You don't have to invest in a dedicated router or residential gateway to share a single Internet connection and simultaneously protect your network. Using Internet Connection Sharing, you can turn a single computer with an active Internet connection into the functional equivalent of a router. The connected computer acts as the ICS host and shares its Internet connection. All other computers on the network route their Internet traffic through the ICS host computer.

ICS is most effective with high-speed (cable or DSL) connections, although it works acceptably with dial-up Internet connections. To share a broadband connection, the ICS host computer must have separate network adapters for the Internet connection and the LAN connection. The single biggest drawback of ICS, of course, is that the shared connection is available only if the ICS host computer is turned on.

Although ICS is included as a feature in Windows 98 Second Edition, Windows Me, and Windows 2000, we strongly recommend that you use a computer running Windows XP (Home Edition or Professional) as your ICS host. The security and usability features of this version of ICS are head and shoulders above those found in earlier versions of Windows. Most notably, Windows Firewall, found only in Windows XP SP2, is tightly integrated with ICS and adds a measure of security that is unmatched in earlier versions.

Note The Network Setup Wizard, which runs from CD or floppy disk to set up ICS on client computers, does not work with Windows 95 or Windows 3.1. If computers running either of these operating systems are present on your network, you must either upgrade those computers or configure the networking components manually to take advantage of an ICS host.

Do not use ICS on any network that includes a domain controller running Microsoft Windows Server 2003 or Windows 2000 Server or any other computers or devices running a DNS server, DHCP server, or Internet gateway. In addition, if any computers on the network are configured with static IP addresses, you might need to reconfigure them to be in the private address range that is automatically assigned by ICS.

Using ICS does not expose your computer to any security risks different from those that you should be concerned about on a computer that is directly connected to the Internet. Be sure to install SP2 and all post-SP2 security updates on the ICS host and all client computers on the network.

Setting Up Internet Connection Sharing in Windows XP

To configure ICS, use the Network Setup Wizard. (The procedure is identical for Windows XP Home Edition and Professional, and you must be logged on as an administrator to perform this task.) Run the wizard on the ICS host first, and then on each network computer where you plan to use the shared connection. If any computers on the LAN are running different versions of Windows, you can use the Windows XP CD to set up the client computers. If you're unable to run the CD on a networked computer, take advantage of the option in the wizard's final step, which creates a setup disk you can use with any 32-bit version of Windows.

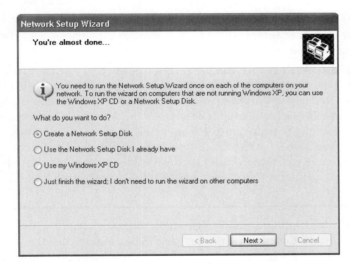

Chapter 9

Setting up ICS in Windows XP makes the following changes to your network configuration:

- The shared connection on the ICS host acquires an IP address from the Internet service provider.
- The wizard turns on Windows Firewall on the shared connection.
- The connection to the local network from the ICS host uses the static IP address 192.168.0.1, configured with a subnet mask of 255.255.255.0.
- The Internet Connection Sharing service runs automatically on the ICS host.
- A DHCP allocator on the ICS host automatically assigns IP addresses to other computers on the network. The default range is from 192.168.0.2 to 192.168.0.254, with a subnet mask of 255.255.255.0. A DNS proxy on the ICS host eliminates the need to specify DNS servers on other computers on the network.
- The wizard enables autodial on the ICS host.

Troubleshooting

Your shared Internet connection isn't working

Any of the following circumstances can prevent ICS from working properly:

- **The Internet Connection Sharing service is not running.**   From Control Panel, open the Administrative Tools folder (available from the Performance And Maintenance category if you're using Category view), double-click the Services icon, and then check to see that the Status column alongside the Windows Firewall/Internet Connection Sharing (ICS) service reads Started. If necessary, right-click the service entry and choose Start or Restart from the shortcut menu.

- **The wrong network adapter is shared.**   Run through the Network Setup Wizard again and confirm that you've selected the correct adapters.

- **The settings on other network computers are incorrect.**   Computers running Windows 98, Windows Me, Windows 2000, or Windows XP should be able to connect to the Internet through an ICS host, when configured to obtain an IP address automatically and obtain DNS servers automatically. Leave the default gateway field blank. If necessary, rerun the Network Setup Wizard on the other computers. (The wizard will not run on Windows 95 or Windows 3.1 or on computers running other operating systems. In this case, you must manually specify that the computer is to acquire its IP address through DHCP, set the gateway to 192.168.0.1, and leave the DNS server settings blank.)

After completing the initial, automated configuration, you can manage the shared connection from the Network Connections folder on the ICS host. Right-click the icon for the shared connection, choose Properties, and then click the Advanced tab. Use the resulting dialog box, shown in Figure 9-6, to enable or disable the connection and to control whether users at other computers on the network can enable or disable the connection. (The Establish A Dial-Up Connection option is available only if your shared connection is through a modem.)

Giving other network users the capability to turn Internet access on or off is most useful when you have a dial-up connection where you pay for each minute you're connected. However, you can also use this capability as a rudimentary security function or to regulate Internet access (on a home network, for instance). Clear the Allow Other Network Users To Control Or Disable The Shared Internet Connection check box if you want to maintain complete control over Internet access; with this option selected, you can shut down the Internet connection whenever you want. Other users will need to log on to your computer (the ICS host) locally, using an account with administrative rights, or ask your permission to restart the Internet connection.

Figure 9-6. Clear the last check box in this dialog box to prevent other network users from disabling Internet access.

> **Tip   Get easy access to network connections**
>
> If you frequently access the properties dialog box for a network connection, shared or otherwise, you'll quickly tire of drilling through dialog boxes to get to it. Instead, create a shortcut on the Start menu, the Quick Launch bar, or the desktop. From the Network Connections folder, right-click the network icon and choose Create Shortcut. A dialog box warns you that you can't create a shortcut in this folder and asks if you want to create it on the desktop instead. Click Yes to create the shortcut, and then move it to your preferred location.

When you open the Network Connections folder on a computer that gets its Internet access from an ICS host, you see an Internet Gateway icon in the Network Connections folder. Double-clicking this icon displays the status dialog box shown in Figure 9-7 on the next page.

Click the Disable button to shut down Internet access immediately. (You must be an administrator to perform this action.) When the connection is shut down, the label for this button switches to Enable; click the button to restart the connection. Use the Properties button to manage Windows Firewall settings on the ICS host. This dialog box is the same one you see if you open the properties dialog box for the connection and click the Settings button on the Advanced tab.

Figure 9-7. Use the two buttons at the bottom of this dialog box to manage a shared Internet connection remotely.

Setting Up Internet Connection Sharing in Windows 2000 Professional

If at least one computer on your network runs Windows 2000 Professional and you don't have any Windows XP installations to choose from, you can set up ICS on that computer instead. The basic operation of ICS in Windows 2000 is the same as in Windows XP, with the following exceptions:

- No wizard is available to help you set up the connection. All configuration options are set manually on the ICS host and on local computers.

- Windows 2000 does not include a firewall, so all computers that share this Internet connection are vulnerable to outside intruders. For this reason, you should install and configure a third-party firewall program before setting up ICS.

- Network users cannot control access to the shared connection.

To enable ICS, you must have two separate network connections, one for the Internet, and the other for LAN access. Open the Network And Dial-Up Connections folder, right-click the icon for the Internet connection, and then choose Properties. On the Sharing tab, select the Enable Internet Connection Sharing For This Connection check box. Click OK to close the dialog box. The Internet connection acquires an IP address using the current settings; your LAN connection is reset to a static IP address of 192.168.0.1 and subnet mask of 255.255.255.0; and the DHCP allocator assigns addresses in the 192.168.0.2 to 192.168.0.254 range.

If you gain Internet access through a dial-up modem, you'll find the Sharing tab in the properties dialog box for the dial-up connection, as shown here. Note the extra check box that allows you to enable on-demand dialing.

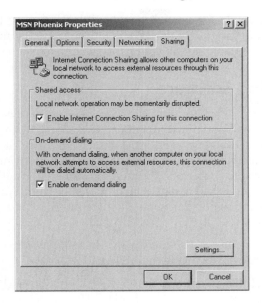

On a network with a Windows 2000 ICS host, you must configure client computers manually. Specify that the computer is to acquire its IP address automatically through DHCP, set the gateway to 192.168.0.1, and leave the DNS server settings blank.

Controlling Inbound Access to Your LAN

If you follow the advice we outline in this chapter, all the computers on your network are well secured from unauthorized access by anyone who isn't directly connected to your network. So, what do you do when you actually want to allow people to share resources on your network from the Internet? You open up connections very selectively, and you pay a great deal of attention to security. And, if possible, you find an alternative that accomplishes the same goal without requiring you to compromise the security of your network or your computer.

In general, any solution that allows outside access to your network involves two potentially dangerous actions: running a server program that listens for incoming connections, and then opening one or more ports to accept those connections. In this section, we discuss the pros and cons of the three most common scenarios in which you might be tempted to use this risky configuration, as well as some alternatives:

- **Sharing files using peer-to-peer (P2P) software.** Using a P2P program allows other users of compatible software to download files stored in a shared location on your computer.

- **Making Web pages or files available over HTTP or FTP connections.** As we noted earlier in this chapter, you can use a computer running Windows XP Professional or Windows 2000 Professional as a light-duty Web server.

Chapter 9

● **Remote access to one or more desktop computers.** Using the Remote Desktop capability of Windows XP Professional or third-party software, you (or another authorized user) can control a computer on your network from a remote location.

Using Peer-to-Peer File-Sharing Software

Are you thinking about connecting to an underground file-sharing system to trade movies, music, or other files? Our advice can be summed up in one word: Don't. By their very nature, file-sharing systems exist in a shadowy world that attracts unsavory characters, making it difficult to identify and fix security issues. Some of the most popular programs in this genre have been fingered as the source of unwanted software that installs itself along with the main executable module and can be difficult to remove. On a computer that contains sensitive personal or business information, installing any kind of file-sharing software is asking for trouble.

If you (or another user of your computer) absolutely insist on installing file-sharing software, minimize the security risks by following this advice:

● **Choose your software carefully.** Research alternatives thoroughly and find a program that you can be reasonably confident is free of hostile or deceptive software (spyware and adware) and is well supported. If you choose the free version of any such program, read the license agreement from start to finish to see what you're authorizing. You might not want to install the program when you see the terms.

● **Make sure you know what you're sharing.** Most file-sharing programs enable you to designate a location for sharing files. Check to be sure you haven't inadvertently included any extra files in that location, and make sure you haven't accidentally designated any other locations for sharing.

● **Be suspicious of incoming files.** Trojan horses, viruses, and other forms of hostile software can sneak in disguised as otherwise innocuous programs.

● **Disable sharing when you're not actively using the program.** Maintaining an unlimited 24/7 incoming connection is like hanging out a sign on your network saying "Hack me."

● **Watch for the warning signs of intrusion.** Monitor the activity log for your firewall and be especially sensitive to any signs that might indicate your computer has been compromised.

Running a Web Server on Your Network

Both Windows 2000 Professional and Windows XP Professional include Internet Information Services (IIS), the same Web server software found in Windows 2000 Server and Windows Server 2003, respectively. (The only difference is that the Professional versions limit the number of simultaneous connections to 10, whereas the server versions allow unlimited connections.) In addition, a thriving third-party development community offers numerous choices of free or inexpensive Web-server software that runs on desktop versions of Windows.

Having a Web server on a local network can be extremely useful. If you manage a Web site that's hosted elsewhere, you can use the local server as a staging area for files that are under development, and you can create your own intranet for sharing information with other members of your family or organization.

But everything changes when you allow outsiders to connect to that Web server. For starters, as we noted earlier in this chapter, many ISPs explicitly forbid their users from running Web or FTP services, and many go so far as to block incoming connections to the well-known public ports (21 for FTP, 80 for HTTP). Web server software is also an attractive target for intruders, and as a result, managing a Web server requires that you be vigilant about applying security updates. If you miss an update, you could expose your entire network to a security flaw.

If you're considering running a Web server on your local network, we recommend that you avoid opening it up to the outside world. Instead, choose one of the many free or inexpensive Web hosting services that are available. Many broadband ISPs include basic Web hosting as part of their standard package, and you can find high-quality, full-featured third-party hosting packages for a few dollars a month. (Type "cheap web hosting" into your favorite search engine's input box and be prepared to sift through thousands of options!) When you use an independent hosting company, you don't have to worry about backups or downtime, and you don't have to expose your network to an increased risk of attack.

If your business has reached a size where you really do need your own Web server, then give that server the support it needs. Don't run it on a desktop operating system; instead, use a server operating system such as Windows Server 2003, which was designed with the appropriate level of security for this role. In addition, locate the server outside your network's firewall; with this precaution, an intruder who is able to compromise that server will still be unable to do any damage to the rest of your network.

Connecting to Your Desktop from a Remote Location

Keeping two computers in perfect sync is an impossible task. If you have a computer at the office and another at home, you know how difficult it is to be equally productive in both locations. With a crucial deadline looming, you decide to put in a late night, only to discover that the files you need are back at the office. Or worse, you remember to bring home those important data files, but the program you need to finish the job isn't installed on your home computer. You could hop in the car and drive back to the office, but there's a much better choice: log on to your office computer remotely and work with the data files and installed software directly, just as if you were sitting in front of the remote computer.

To take advantage of remote-access solutions, you need to do some initial setup work. You can use third-party software or the Remote Desktop feature in Windows XP Professional to accomplish your goal. (If you are trying to connect to a computer behind a corporate firewall, you might have to use a virtual private network, or VPN connection.

See "Connecting to a VPN," page 375, for more details on how to make these two features work together.)

> **Tip** Be safe, not sorry
>
> If you allow remote access to your computer, we recommend that you observe basic security principles. Use strong passwords, change those passwords regularly, and activate remote-access capabilities only when you need them. In addition, if your network includes a hardware or software firewall (or both), you'll need to create exceptions to allow incoming traffic on the appropriate ports.

Third-Party Remote Access Software

To allow remote access to a single desktop computer, you can install a program like Symantec's pcAnywhere (*http://www.symantec.com/pcanywhere/*) or Laplink Software's Laplink Gold (*http://www.laplink.com/products/llgold/*). Both of these programs are mature, full-featured packages that offer remote access to computers running nearly any version of Windows. If your budget is tight or you just want a simple, no-frills solution, consider the free open-source VNC (short for Virtual Network Computing). The VNC server provides password-protected, encrypted access to just about any operating system, including every 32-bit version of Windows; use the matching client program to make connections over the Internet.

An interesting third-party alternative is the Web-based GoToMyPC service (*http://www.gotomypc.com*), which provides secure remote access through a Web browser. A small server program runs on the computer to which you want to allow remote access, and a lightweight browser plug-in enables remote clients to connect from computers running nearly any operating system. The underlying technology is provided by Citrix, which has a well-deserved reputation for providing secure remote access solutions to demanding corporate clients.

Windows XP Remote Desktop

If you use Windows XP Professional, you can use the built-in Remote Desktop feature to allow remote access. Enabling this feature starts Terminal Services, a stripped-down version of the remote access software used in Windows 2000 Server and Windows Server 2003. (The major difference is that Remote Desktop allows only a single client to log on at any time. If you log on using Remote Desktop, you kick off any user who is currently logged on locally. Likewise, if you log on locally, you disconnect any remote users.) This service is not available on a computer running Windows XP Home Edition; however, you can use the client portion of the software on a computer running any 32-bit version of Windows to connect to a computer running Remote Desktop. Thus, the Remote Desktop feature will work just fine if you want to connect to your office computer running Windows XP Professional, even if your computer at home is running Windows XP Home Edition or Windows 98.

Note Don't confuse Remote Desktop with the Remote Assistance capability of the Windows XP Help And Support Center. Remote Assistance enables a remote user—a friend or Help Desk professional, typically—to take over a remote computer temporarily to diagnose or repair a problem. Remote Assistance is available in all versions of Windows XP. We don't recommend that you try to use the Remote Assistance feature as a substitute for Remote Desktop, to connect remotely to a computer running Windows XP Home Edition. The security features and interface were expressly designed for situations where someone is sitting in front of the remote computer to grant you access.

To use Remote Desktop, you need two computers that are connected through a local area network, the Internet, or a dial-up connection. The remote computer must be running Windows XP Professional and must be connected to a LAN or to the Internet. If you plan to connect over the Internet, the computer must have a known, public IP address, or be connected to a router with a public IP address that can be configured to pass the remote connection on port 3389 to the correct computer. (For more details, see the documentation for your router.) To set up your computer to accept Remote Desktop connections, follow these steps:

1 Log on as a member of the Administrators group.
2 Open the System Properties dialog box (press the Windows logo key+Break or, in Control Panel, open Performance And Maintenance, System) and then click the Remote tab.

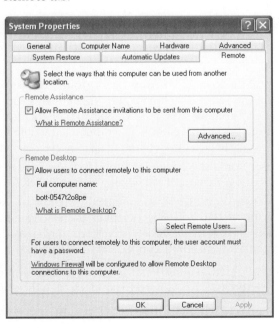

3 On the Remote tab, select Allow Users To Connect Remotely To This Computer. At this point, any of the following user accounts (as long as the account has a logon password) can be used to connect remotely to the computer:

- The account currently logged on
- All members of the local Administrators group
- All members of the local Remote Desktop Users group

> **Note** Remote access is allowed only for user accounts that require a password to log on. An account without a password cannot be used to make a remote connection.

4 If you want to change which users can connect remotely, click Select Remote Users. The Remote Desktop Users dialog box appears.

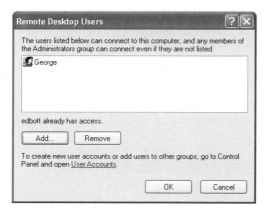

- To add a user to the Remote Desktop Users group, click Add. Then type the user's name in the Select Users dialog box that appears (or click Advanced, Find Now to select names from a list). You can type the name of any local user account or, if your computer is in a domain, any domain user account. You can add multiple users by separating each user name with a semicolon.
- To delete a user from the Remote Desktop Users group, select the user's name in the Remote Desktop Users dialog box and click Remove.

As part of this setup process, Windows XP automatically creates an exception for Remote Desktop in Windows Firewall. This exception is created automatically when Remote Desktop is enabled; if you use a hardware firewall or a third-party firewall program, you'll need to configure it to allow incoming connections on TCP port number 3389.

Your computer is now configured to allow incoming Remote Desktop requests. If you want to restrict which IP addresses are allowed to connect, take these additional steps:

1 With Remote Desktop selected on the Exceptions tab in Windows Firewall, click Edit.

2 In the Edit A Service dialog box, click Change Scope.

Chapter 9

3 In the Change Scope dialog box, select Custom List and specify the IP address of the computers you want to allow.

> **Note** You can use a different port for Remote Desktop connections. Although there's seldom reason to do so, changing to a different port can provide increased security because you don't expose a listening port where a would-be intruder expects to find Remote Desktop. For details about changing the port, see Microsoft Knowledge Base article 306759.

To set up the client computer, use the Remote Desktop Connection software included with all versions of Windows XP. If the computer you're using is running Windows XP, click Start, and then choose All Programs, Accessories, Communications, Remote Desktop Connection. If you use any other version of Windows, you'll need to install Remote Desktop Connection, which is included on the Windows XP CD. The easiest way to do so is to insert the CD and, on the menu that appears, click Perform Additional Tasks, Set Up Remote Desktop Connection. (If the menu doesn't appear, start the Remote Desktop Connection setup program directly by double-clicking Msrdpcli.exe in the \Support\Tools folder on the CD.)

> **Note** Msrdpcli.exe has been updated since Windows XP was first released. If you have an original Windows XP CD instead of one that has SP1 or SP2 integrated (or if you're not sure), download the latest version of the client installation program from Microsoft, at *http://www.microsoft.com/windowsxp/pro/downloads/rdclientdl.asp*. For the sake of convenience, consider copying this file to a USB flash drive and carrying it with you when you travel; that way, you can be assured of quick access to your Remote Desktop without having to hassle with CDs.

In the Remote Desktop Connection dialog box, enter the name or IP address of the remote computer and click Connect. You'll be prompted for a user name and password; after your credentials are verified, you can work with the remote computer as if you were sitting in front of it.

The experience of using a Remote Desktop connection can be less than ideal, especially over slow dial-up connections. For more details about how to fine-tune your connection for better performance and how to use shortcuts to navigate, see our earlier book, *Microsoft Windows XP Inside Out, Second Edition* (Microsoft Press, 2005).

Chapter 9

Chapter 10

Wireless Networking

Just a few years ago, wireless networks were an expensive, esoteric choice, used only in specialized business applications where their benefits outweighed their tremendous cost and complexity. In recent years, however, the price of wireless networking hardware has plummeted. In most portable computers and in a growing number of desktop computers and home entertainment devices, wireless technology is built in as a matter of course. Setting up a wireless network no longer takes an advanced engineering degree, either—if you use Microsoft Windows XP, wireless adapters literally configure themselves, and the task of setting up an untethered network usually takes only a few minutes.

The benefits of wireless networking are practically irresistible. Using a lightweight notebook computer equipped with an inexpensive wireless LAN adapter, you can browse the Web and access shared files and printers from anywhere within radio range of a wireless access point. At home, you can use your computer on the couch, on the back porch, or while lying in bed. On the road, you can connect to a wireless network in a coffee shop or airport lounge and check your e-mail or change your flight schedule. In the office, you can bring your computer to a conference room and still have access to information on your company's intranet or on the Web, and you can e-mail the minutes of the meeting as soon as it's over.

Unfortunately, all that convenience comes at the expense of serious security trade-offs. If you can connect to your network from a distance, so can anyone with a computer, a wireless adapter, and enough knowledge and persistence to take advantage of any gaps in your security configuration. Likewise, when you connect your portable computer to someone else's access point, you have to assume that every keystroke you transmit is being read by someone else.

In this chapter, we explain how to set up and secure your wireless connection and your wireless access point. Enabling encryption is a crucial part of this process, and we explain the difference between the two most widely used wireless security standards. We also offer suggestions on advanced security techniques if you use wireless networking in a business network.

Security Checklist: Wireless Networks

If you have a wireless network, follow these steps to safeguard your shared resources:

- Change the network name (also known as the service set identifier, or SSID) of your wireless access point to one that doesn't match the hardware defaults and doesn't give away any information about you or your business.

- Configure your wireless access point with a strong password.

- Consider disabling remote administration of the access point; if you need to change settings, you can do so directly by using a wired Ethernet connection.

- Upgrade the firmware of your wireless hardware to the most recent version, which might incorporate security fixes.

- If the pool of computers connected to your wireless network is small and fixed, restrict access to your wireless network based on the unique media access control (MAC) address of each authorized computer's wireless adapter.

- Enable the strongest form of encryption that is compatible with your hardware and set strong encryption keys.

- Change your encryption keys at regular intervals.

- Scan your wireless network to determine whether you are vulnerable to attack from widely used hacking tools.

- Consider using VPNs for wireless connections.

The Risks and Rewards of Wireless Networking

To understand the security problems inherent in wireless networking, you first need to understand the basic architecture of a wireless network. Wireless networking adapters use the same protocols as wired networks—the only difference is in setting up the hardware to transmit and receive packets of data. Today, most popular wireless networks use the IEEE 802.11 standard, adopted in 1997. Variations of this standard include the widely used IEEE 802.11b (also known as Wireless Ethernet, or Wi-Fi), which transmits data at a maximum speed of 11 megabits per second (Mbps), roughly the same speed as a conventional wired Ethernet connection. A newer standard called 802.11g uses the same underlying technology as Wi-Fi to transfer data at speeds of up to 54 Mbps. (For an explanation of the differences between the various components of the 802.11 standard, see the sidebar "802-Dot-Whatever: Decoding Wireless Standards," page 333.)

Collectively, the 802.11 standards define mechanisms by which network data literally floats through the air, using radio frequencies in the 2.4 gigahertz (GHz) or 5 GHz range. Network adapters with small antennas—built into newer portable computers, installed in a PC Card slot on older notebooks, or attached to a USB port on a desktop computer—transmit and receive data to communicate with the rest of the network. The most common wireless network configurations include a hardware device called a wireless access point (sometimes referred to as a WAP), which incorporates its own transmitter/receiver and connects directly to the Internet or to a network hub or switch, often acting as a bridge between wireless and wired networks. Strictly speaking, an access point isn't required; small networks can get by using "ad hoc mode," in which network adapters communicate directly with one another in a peer-to-peer setup.

Because wireless networking uses radio frequencies, anyone who has a computer equipped with a wireless adapter and is within the effective range of the access point or an individual wireless adapter can attempt to connect to the network. With a modest investment in hardware and little or no technical skills, an outsider can compromise the security of your network in any of the following ways:

- **Theft of service.** Even if an intruder can't break into individual computers on your network, he might be able to access the Internet using your connection. The result could degrade the quality of your Internet service. This risk is especially noticeable in high-density areas such as apartment buildings, where any of your neighbors with a wireless network adapter might be within the effective range of your access point.

- **Denial of service.** An intruder who is unable to connect to your network can still cause some degree of havoc by flooding the network with connection requests. With enough persistence, an attacker could completely deny legitimate users access to the network.

- **Theft or destruction of data.** Outsiders who successfully connect to your network can browse shared folders and printers. Depending on the permissions assigned to these resources, they can steal sensitive information contained in files stored here; change, rename, or delete existing files, or add new ones.

- **Network takeover.** An intruder who manages to log on to the network and exploit an unpatched vulnerability can install a Trojan horse program or tamper with permissions, potentially exposing computers on the LAN to attacks from over the Internet.

Out of the box, most wireless networks are designed to be easy, not secure. Properly protecting a wireless network requires some extra effort. If you work in a large organization, with access to a Windows domain, multiple firewalls, VPNs, and a server that can authenticate computers against a central database, you can lock down a wireless network impressively. In a home or small network, your options are more limited but still effective for all but the most demanding security needs.

Chapter 10

Inside Out

Take extra precautions in public places

Do you use your portable PC's wireless connection in public "hotspots"? If so, you need to take extra precautions. Before you connect to a network that can expose you to connections from other, untrusted users, ratchet up the security level on your personal firewall software to its most restrictive settings. If you use the Windows Firewall installed as part of Windows XP Service Pack 2, open the Windows Firewall dialog box from Control Panel and select the No Exceptions check box.

In addition, be vigilant about the types of data you allow to pass over an untrusted network. An attacker who has access to an insecure wireless access point can monitor packets as they pass through the wireless network. If you check your e-mail or access a password-protected account at a Web site that doesn't provide an encrypted (SSL) connection, you risk allowing a stranger to steal your logon credentials. You can have greater confidence if the hotspot provides an end-to-end encrypted connection. Connections to T-Mobile's public wireless network using its Connection Manager software use Wi-Fi Protected Access (WPA) encryption for all communications between your computer and the access point.

For maximum security, use a virtual private network (VPN). If you're dialing in to a corporate network, this option may be available through your network's infrastructure. No corporate network? Consider using a third-party VPN provider, such as HotSpotVPN (*http://www.hotspotvpn.com*), or PersonalVPN (*http://www.witopia.net*). This type of service requires a monthly financial commitment but offers effective security for travelers who use public hotspots extensively.

You can add a wireless workstation to an existing network or set up a new network based exclusively on wireless hardware. In either case, getting your wireless network up and running is a three-step process:

1. Install your wireless access point and configure it to accept requests for connections. If your access point also includes a router, you can connect it to your cable or DSL modem; if you're adding the access point to an existing network, plug it directly into the router.

2. Enable data encryption on the access point. You typically need to choose the type of encryption and enter or create the key that will be used to encrypt information.

3. Finally, configure the wireless connection on each computer that you plan to use with that access point.

On computers running Windows XP, many of the setup tasks are completely automated; you'll need third-party drivers and configuration software to set up a wireless connection on a computer running Windows 2000 or any older Windows version. After setting up a wireless network connection in Windows XP, you can set up additional connections and add them to the list of preferred networks.

802-Dot-Whatever: Decoding Wireless Standards

Working Group 802.11 of the Institute of Electrical and Electronics Engineers is responsible for all wireless network specifications. That's a big job, it turns out—so big that the group has split into a number of smaller groups to tackle individual parts of the job. The result is a host of standards, all in varying degrees of completion and with confusing names that sound almost alike. Here are explanations of those that are most likely to impact your security planning for a wireless network:

- **802.11b**, also known as Wi-Fi, is the original standard in wireless networking technology. It uses the 2.4 GHz frequency to send and receive data at a maximum rate of 11 Mbps. Most wireless networking equipment sold today still supports this standard for backward compatibility. Many 802.11b products, especially older models, support only the flawed Wired Equivalent Privacy (WEP) standard and cannot be upgraded to more secure encryption standards.

- **802.11a** uses hardware that looks similar to its 802.11b cousins; however, it broadcasts in a different frequency range, 5 GHz, and can reach maximum speeds of 54 Mbps, roughly five times faster than Wi-Fi. It is not widely used in home and small business networking equipment. It may survive as a niche technology in consumer electronic devices designed for streaming digital media to TVs and audio systems; the advantage of using 802.11a equipment is its reduced susceptibility to interference from computers that use 802.11g-based gear.

- **802.11g** is an alternative to the 802.11a standard that can also blast data across the network at 54 Mbps. Because this hardware uses the same 2.4 GHz frequency range as Wi-Fi adapters, manufacturers are more likely to make devices that support both standards, easing the transition for people who have a mix of Wi-Fi hardware and don't want to throw away that investment.

- **802.11h** is an addition to the 802.11a standard that reduces the likelihood of interference with other wireless devices and complies with regulations in a number of European countries.

- **802.11n** is an emerging high-throughput standard that is expected to offer speeds of at least four times the data rate of any currently available 802.11-based product. The final standard is not expected to be ratified before November 2006.

- **802.1X** provides a mechanism for authenticating computers that connect to a wireless access point, typically through a Remote Authentication Dial-In User Service (RADIUS) server. This emerging standard is impractical for small networks but is ideal for large organizations that already have one or more authentication servers. (And no, the name is not a typographical error—because this standard applies to conventional wired networks as well as wireless, it contains only a single 1 in its name.)

- **802.11i** officially replaces the WEP standard and associated security technologies that were part of 802.11b. Many hardware products, especially those built from 2003 through early 2005, incorporate an interim version of this standard under the name Wi-Fi Protected Access (WPA). The final 802.11i standard, which uses a stronger encryption technique than the interim, was approved in June 2004; products that incorporate the final standard are certified under the Wi-Fi Protected Access 2 (WPA2) label.

Other task groups are working on aspects of wireless technology that affect quality of service (802.11e) and communications between access points (802.11f). In addition, a proposed standard called WiMAX (802.16) promises to deliver broadband Internet access over wireless connections.

A techie humorist once wrote, "The best thing about standards is that there's so many of them." That's certainly true with wireless networking. Products based on wireless technology have become enormously popular during the past few years—a period during which different portions of the 802.11 standards were in different stages of development; as a result, you might find products that are missing some technologies found in newer devices, and you might find other hardware makers that have incorporated technologies based on draft standards rather than the final version. For the latest technical details, you can read the sometimes dense and dry commentary at the official site of the 802.11 working group, *http://www.ieee802.org/11/*. For a more readable summary, try the Web site run by the Wi-Fi Alliance, at *http://www.wi-fi.org*.

Controlling Connections to a Wireless Access Point

Most wireless access points intended for use in homes or small businesses include a simple setup wizard designed to help you quickly configure your access point. That quick configuration is not guaranteed to be secure, however. Your first line of defense in securing a wireless network is to make it more difficult for outsiders to connect to the network. That's not an easy task. The antenna in a wireless access point can broadcast its signal hundreds of feet in any direction. That's bad news if you live in a densely populated apartment complex, but even if you have no neighbors within range of the access point, you could still be vulnerable. An enthusiastic community of "drive-by" hackers has turned wireless breaking and entering into a hobby, devising booster antennas and software utilities (with colorful names like AirSnort and NetStumbler) that enable them to sniff out the details of unprotected networks as they drive through neighborhoods or sit in public areas of an office complex.

> **Tip** Don't let bad guys reconfigure your network
>
> When you set up your wireless access point for the first time, be sure to change the default password that unlocks the configuration utility. This crucial precaution protects the access point (and the rest of your network) from being reconfigured by an outsider. A would-be intruder who finds your access point is certainly going to try the default password first; change the password to one that's easy for you to remember but difficult for a stranger to crack. (If you need some ideas on how to create an effective password, see "Creating Strong Passwords," page 111.) If your hardware supports disabling wireless administration completely, consider doing without that feature and using a direct connection—through Ethernet, USB, or a serial port—instead.

The network name configured in the access point is called the *service set identifier*, or SSID. Many manufacturers use default names for the SSID, and any potential intruder who has spent more than a few minutes researching the subject already knows the most common defaults (one of the most popular default SSIDs, amusingly, is *default*). If you've secured your access point properly, a would-be intruder will see this default name in the list of available networks but won't be able to connect to it. If you haven't used any security precautions, however, the intruder could join your network just by clicking on the SSID. In fact, if you live in an apartment building with thin walls and your next-door neighbor uses the same hardware as you, it's conceivable that one or both of you could inadvertently connect to the wrong network!

You can take any or all of the following three measures to make your wireless network harder to discover. None of these steps will stop a determined attacker with the right tools and expertise, but they should prevent a casual snooper or nosy neighbor from discovering the SSID of your network and trying to connect to it:

- **Choose a new network name.** This precaution isn't required, but it is a sensible step if your hardware automatically assigns a default name that is identical to those used by other people with the same hardware. Whatever you do, don't use a name that identifies yourself or your business. That bit of information can encourage drive-by hackers to probe more deeply than if you just use a random alphanumeric string.

- **Don't broadcast your network name.** If your hardware includes an option to set up the network as a "closed" system, consider enabling this option. Anyone who wants to connect to the network will need to supply the network name manually rather than having it filled in automatically by the wireless hardware and Windows XP; after the initial setup, your wireless workstations will make future connections automatically. This configuration also frustrates casual users of scanning utilities like NetStumbler.

- **Use MAC addresses to limit access.** As we noted in Chapter 1, every network adapter includes a unique MAC address. On access points that include this option, you can specify that the only wireless adapters allowed to connect to your access point are those with MAC addresses on a list you enter. If your network is small, you can easily manage the list manually. On networks that have more than five wireless computers or that guests regularly visit, the administrative burden is unacceptable. Of course, a skilled attacker can spoof a MAC address and bypass this setting, but it can still be a useful barrier to casual snoops.

If you have access to an enterprise-strength authentication server, you can configure your network so that all connection requests are forced to authenticate through that server. This option uses the 802.1X standard and Extensible Authentication Protocol (EAP). In the enterprise market, you can choose from a variety of EAP types, most of which use either a certificate or a password to authenticate the wireless client at the access point. Used with a RADIUS server and a physical device such as a smart card, this option can be extremely secure.

Chapter 10

Support for 802.1X authentication is built into Windows XP. To access these settings, open the properties dialog box for the wireless connection, click the Wireless Networks tab, select a network name (SSID) from the Preferred Networks list, click Properties, and click the Authentication tab. Figure 10-1 shows the settings with 802.1X authentication enabled.

Figure 10-1. If your network includes an authentication server, you can greatly increase the security of a wireless network.

If your network serves a home or small business, you should not tamper with the default settings. On computers running Windows XP Service Pack 2 (SP2), 802.1X authentication is disabled by default—enabling this setting on a network without a suitable authentication server won't disable an existing connection, but it won't provide any additional security either, and it might slow down performance.

Caution   You don't need an access point to set up a wireless network. By using ad hoc mode instead of the default infrastructure mode, you can directly connect two or more computers that are equipped with compatible wireless adapters. If you think of a wireless access point as a server, then a Wi-Fi network running in ad hoc mode is the equivalent of a peer-to-peer network. We strongly recommend against this practice except for temporary use when you absolutely need a network connection and a wireless access point is unavailable. In ad hoc mode, you are unable to specify encryption, and anyone can connect to your network without restrictions. This mode is especially dangerous in public places.

Encrypting Wireless Transmissions

After getting the basic configuration steps out of the way, you're ready to tackle the most important security feature on a wireless network—turning on encryption. This step protects authorized users of a wireless network from eavesdroppers by encrypting the data flow between the networked computer and the access point. Setting up encryption should be a straightforward process: enable the option on your access point, create an encryption key, and enter that key in the configuration dialog box for each wireless adapter on your network. Depending on your hardware, you should have a choice of one or more of the following options:

- **Wired Equivalent Privacy (WEP)** is the original encryption standard defined in the 802.11b standard. Typically, WEP encryption uses a secret key that is either 64 bits or 128 bits in strength. (Confusingly, you might also see references to 40-bit and 104-bit keys, which refer to the unique portion of each WEP key that is separate from the common 24-bit initialization vector. The combination produces either a 64-bit or 128-bit key, respectively.) To enter a WEP key, you supply a string of ASCII or hexadecimal characters (5 ASCII or 10 hexadecimal characters for a 64-bit key; 13 ASCII or 26 hexadecimal characters for a 128-bit key). All devices on the network must use the same encryption strength—either 64 or 128 bits. Using WEP is better than using no encryption at all—but just barely. This standard suffers from some known security flaws that make it relatively easy for an attacker to "crack" the key using off-the-shelf hardware. It also lacks any mechanism to automate deployment or allow revocation of keys that have been compromised. As a result, we strongly recommend against using WEP; if you own WEP-compatible wireless networking equipment that cannot be upgraded, just replace it.

- **Wi-Fi Protected Access (WPA)** is an interim version of the 802.11i standard that was adopted by the Wi-Fi Alliance in early 2003. It uses a stronger encryption scheme that was specifically designed to overcome weaknesses of WEP. WPA comes in two distinct flavors: WPA Enterprise supports authentication through 802.1X; WPA Personal uses a shared network password on clients and access points (called a pre-shared key, or PSK) that consists of a 256-bit number or a passphrase that is between 8 and 63 bytes long (a longer passphrase produces a stronger key). With a sufficiently strong key based on a truly random sequence, the likelihood of an outside attack is very, very slim.

- **Wi-Fi Protected Access 2 (WPA2)** is a certification provided by the Wi-Fi Alliance, indicating that a product is fully compatible with the IEEE 802.11i standard as finally adopted. Like the interim standard, WPA2 provides Enterprise and Personal support. The primary difference is that WPA2 encrypts traffic using the stronger Advanced Encryption Standard (AES) in place of the Temporal Key Integrity Protocol (TKIP) used in WPA. To use WPA2, you must upgrade all three pieces of the wireless infrastructure: access points, network cards, and device drivers (an update for Windows XP that adds support for WPA2 is available through Knowledge Base article 893357). Some older network hardware that supports the 802.11g standard can be made compatible with WPA2 through a firmware

Chapter 10

337

upgrade. Hardware that was designed before mid-2003 typically lacks the horse-power to handle AES; in these cases, you might be able to add WPA compatibility through a firmware upgrade.

> **Caution** Choosing no encryption creates an "open" network. If you own a coffee shop or bookstore and your goal is to provide free Internet access for your customers, this option is acceptable as long as you protect other computers on your network from unauthorized access. For most home or business networks, however, enabling encryption is easy, and the risks of running an open network are unacceptable.

Typically, configuring an access point to support WEP or WPA requires that you use a Web-based configuration utility. Figure 10-2, for instance, shows the configuration settings for an SMC 2804WBR Barricade, which combines a wired router and a wireless access point.

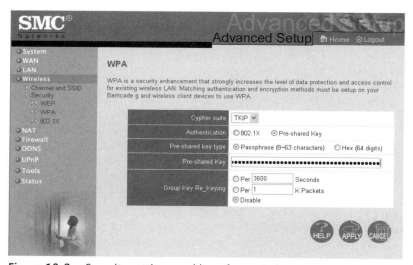

Figure 10-2. Security settings and keys for a wireless access point must match those for your wireless adapter. The Pre-Shared Key setting here works with the WPA-PSK setting in Windows XP.

Which encryption standard should you choose? WEP is completely unacceptable. WPA and WPA2, by contrast, provide robust encryption and effective security, when properly configured. If you're in the market for new wireless hardware, insist on WPA2 compatibility, and upgrade the firmware in existing equipment from WPA to WPA2 if possible. Don't worry if you have a mix of hardware on your network; you can use WPA and WPA2 encryption on a single network without untoward consequences.

In Windows XP SP2, Microsoft introduced a new standard called Windows Connect Now that enables automatic configuration of WPA or WEP encryption by using a USB flash drive. If your wireless access point supports this standard, skip to the following section and use the Windows XP Wireless Network Setup Wizard to configure your

Chapter 10

access point and each computer in a single operation. If your hardware doesn't support this standard, you must use the hardware configuration utility to enable encryption on your access point. Write down the shared key and carefully note other settings on your access point.

Note When SP2 was released in August of 2004, the Windows Connect Now architecture was widely referred to as the Network Smart Key feature. As of the writing of this chapter (mid 2005), Belkin (*http://www.belkin.com*), D-Link (*http://www.dlink.com*), and other companies had announced plans to release a wireless access point that supports the Windows Connect Now architecture.

Tip   Don't type, paste!
Manually typing a 64-digit WPA key into your computer's configuration dialog box is a recipe for frustration, especially if you have more than one or two computers to set up. You can streamline the process by using the Windows Clipboard to automate this process. When you create a WPA key on your wireless access point, copy the key to the Clipboard and paste it into a text file using Notepad or another text editor. If you can't use your access point to copy the WPA key easily, set up the workstation first. Use the Wireless Network Setup Wizard in Windows XP SP2 to generate an encryption key for you automatically. The wizard saves the key in a text file named \Smrtntky\Wsetting.txt on a USB flash drive. Open that text file on the computer you're using to configure the router or access point, copy the key to the Clipboard, and then paste it into the text box to enter or change the encryption key on the access point. This method saves typing and avoids frustrating typos that can cause connections to fail.

Because of the documented weaknesses in WEP encryption, security experts recommend that you change the WEP keys at regular intervals, at least once a month. Although this process is tedious, it's a necessary precaution on any wireless network that is not compatible with the 802.11i authentication standard.

Tip   Try this low-tech security solution
The power switch on your wireless access point is an amazingly effective security device. If most of your network consists of wired computers, and you use wireless features only occasionally, you can reduce the risk of outside intrusions by turning off the access point when you don't need to use it. On a business network that operates only during the day, consider putting the access point on a timer that automatically shuts down shortly after closing time and starts again in the morning. This low-tech solution is excellent insurance against would-be intruders who might be tempted to try to break in at night, when you're not likely to notice the unwanted traffic.

Chapter 10

Configuring a Windows Computer for Wireless Networking

Windows 2000 does not include any support for wireless networking. To configure wireless network access on a computer running Windows 2000, you must first install device drivers to enable the adapter and then use the client software supplied by the hardware manufacturer to configure the device. At a minimum, you'll need to specify the network name (SSID), specify the type of encryption used on your access point, and enter the shared encryption key.

What About Bluetooth?

Wi-Fi and other variants of the 802.11 standard are not the only wireless networking options. Beginning with Service Pack 2, Windows XP supports a wireless connectivity protocol called Bluetooth. This standard is primarily designed for short-range connections between devices, one of which might be a personal computer. Bluetooth has become especially popular in mobile phones, where it enables connections between hands-free handsets and the phone itself. Some luxury cars now include Bluetooth connections to enable hands-free operation of mobile phones.

To use a Bluetooth device with Windows XP, you need to first install a Bluetooth adapter and configure it to discover external devices. You then need to create a password-protected "partnership" between the external device and your PC's Bluetooth adapter. For more details, see Microsoft Knowledge Base article 883259.

In sharp contrast, Windows XP handles most of the details of connecting to a wireless LAN without requiring a lot of manual tweaking. A feature called Wireless Auto Configuration, which was introduced in the original release of Windows XP, adds the following interface elements to a computer that is equipped with a Wi-Fi adapter:

- A Wireless Networks tab in the properties dialog box for the wireless adapter.
- Messages in the notification area that indicate the availability of wireless networks and the status of the current connection.
- A Wireless Network Connection dialog box that lists networks available for connection.
- An entry in the Services console that enables management of the new Wireless Zero Configuration service. This service is enabled by default on all computers running Windows XP.

After the original release of Windows XP, Microsoft issued several updates that provided additional security and wireless configuration features, including support for WPA. Windows XP SP2 adds a new Wireless Network Setup Wizard that automatically configures compatible wireless computers, peripherals, and access points and sets security keys using either WEP or WPA. The SP2 version of the Wireless Network

Connection dialog box is also different, designed with the goal of making it much easier to create a secure wireless network.

When you first add a wireless network adapter to a computer and install the appropriate drivers, Windows XP scans for available wireless access points. If it finds at least one, it displays a status message in the notification area. (You must be logged in as an administrator to connect to a wireless network for the first time. After this initial setup, any user can connect to the wireless network.)

Click the status message to display the Wireless Network Connection dialog box, shown in Figure 10-3. (If the message disappears before you get around to clicking it, right-click the Wireless Network Connection icon in the notification area and choose View Available Wireless Networks; or open Network Connections from Control Panel, right-click the icon for your wireless connection, and choose the same option from the shortcut menu.) Click the network to which you want to connect, and then click the Connect button to join the network.

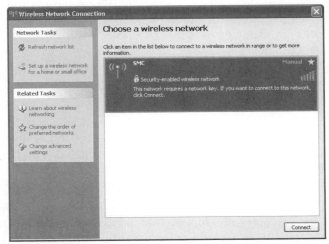

Figure 10-3. Any nearby networks that are broadcasting their network names (SSIDs) are visible here, with secure networks clearly noted.

If encryption is enabled on the network you select, as indicated by the padlock icon in its description, you'll be prompted to enter your encryption key, as shown in Figure 10-4 on the next page. After you successfully enter the key (twice), you'll be connected to the network and can begin using its resources.

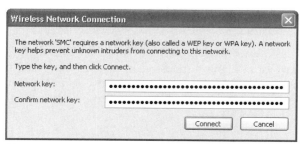

Figure 10-4. When you attempt to connect to a secure wireless network, Windows XP prompts you to enter the appropriate WEP or WPA key.

Managing Wireless Network Connections

The first time you connect to a wireless network, Windows XP adds that network to the top of the list of preferred networks. If you take your computer to a different location and successfully connect to a new network, that location is added to the list of preferred networks. Each time you turn on your computer or enable your wireless adapter, Windows XP attempts to make a connection, using the following rules:

- Wireless Auto Configuration tries to connect to each of the preferred networks in the list of available networks (those that have broadcast their SSIDs), in the order that those networks appear.

- If this does not result in a successful connection, Wireless Auto Configuration tries to connect to each preferred network that does not appear in the list of available networks. This strategy should be successful if you are trying to connect to a network that does not broadcast its network name.

- Wireless Auto Configuration next looks in the list of available networks for any ad hoc networks—that is, those that are based on direct connections to another wireless adapter rather than an access point—and attempts to connect to any that are also in the list of preferred networks.

- If all these attempts fail to make a successful connection, Wireless Auto Configuration looks in the list of preferred networks for the name of any ad hoc network that is not currently available and configures the wireless adapter as the first node in this ad hoc network, making it available for connections by other computers.

You can alter the order of networks in the preferred list, add networks manually, remove entries from the list, and configure any entry for Manual rather than Automatic connections. This type of maintenance is useful when you want to delete an entry from the list, such as the wireless network at a hotel that you don't plan to visit again. In addition, you might want to change an entry from Automatic to Manual, or vice versa, so that you can exercise control over each network connection.

To manage the settings of entries on the list of preferred networks, click Change The Order Of Preferred Networks in the list of tasks along the left side of the View Available Networks dialog box. (Or, alternatively, open the Network Connections folder, right-click the entry for your wireless connection, choose Properties, and then click the Wireless Networks tab.) This action opens the Wireless Network Connection Properties dialog box, where you can manipulate the Preferred Networks list, as shown in Figure 10-5.

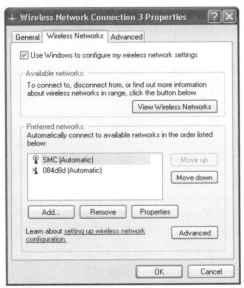

Figure 10-5. The icon to the left of each entry in the Preferred Networks list indicates whether it is currently available.

To change the order of entries in the Preferred Networks list, select the entry you want to move and then click Move Up or Move Down. Click Remove to delete an unwanted entry from the list. To change a network from Automatic to Manual, or vice-versa, select the list entry and then click Properties. Click the Connection tab and select or clear the Connect When This Network Is In Range check box.

> **Tip** Normally, Windows XP allows your wireless adapter to connect to other computers in ad hoc mode when an access point is unavailable. As we noted earlier, this represents a potential security risk. To disable this option and eliminate the possibility that you might inadvertently connect to another computer in a public place, click the Advanced button on the Wireless Networks tab of the connection properties dialog box and select the Access Point (Infrastructure) Networks Only check box. To ensure that you are notified before being automatically connected to an access point that is not on your list of preferred networks, clear the Automatically Connect To Non-Preferred Networks check box at the bottom of the Advanced dialog box.

After making a successful connection, Wireless Auto Configuration continues to scan for available networks. If a new network becomes available and it is higher on the list than the current connection, Windows drops the existing network and connects to the preferred network.

Configuring a New Wireless Network

The Wireless Network Setup Wizard, a new addition in Windows XP SP2, tries to take some of the tedium out of creating and configuring a secure network. This wizard is built around a feature called Windows Connect Now, which uses inexpensive USB flash drives to automatically configure routers and workstations on a wireless network.

Even if your router or access point lacks support for the Windows Connect Now architecture, however, you can use the Wireless Network Setup Wizard to simplify the process of setting up and securing a network. The wizard runs only on a computer equipped with a wireless adapter and running Windows XP SP2. To start the wizard, double-click its Control Panel icon or its Start menu shortcut (All Programs, Accessories, Communications), or open the Network Connections folder or the list of available wireless networks and click the Set Up A Wireless Network link under the Network Tasks heading in the task pane.

The wizard's operation is self-explanatory, so we won't walk through each step here. In broad outlines, with the wizard, you can create or specify the network name (SSID), choose authentication and encryption options for security, and automatically generate a security key of the appropriate length and complexity. Figure 10-6 shows the portion of the wizard where you specify encryption options.

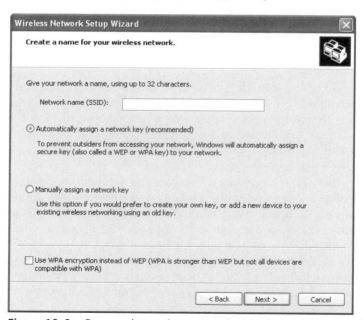

Figure 10-6. Be sure the settings you select in the wizard match those defined at the access point.

Chapter 10

In the Network Name (SSID) box, enter the name of the network as defined at the access point. This is also the place to select the following security options:

- Click Automatically Assign A Network Key to specify that you want the wizard to generate a random key at the maximum security level.

- Click Manually Assign A Network Key if your access point and/or other devices are currently configured to use a specific key and you're using the wizard to duplicate that setup.

By default, the Use WPA Encryption Instead Of WEP box is cleared, meaning your new connection will use WEP security. This default setting ensures backward compatibility with the large installed base of old Wi-Fi equipment that supports WEP but not WPA. If you know your equipment supports WPA, make sure you select this check box to take advantage of the greater security.

On the How Do You Want To Set Up Your Network page, the wizard gives you a choice of two options:

- The Use A USB Flash Drive option copies necessary configuration files to a USB-based portable storage device, along with an AutoRun file and a script that allows the wizard to operate automatically on other computers running Windows XP SP2. This is the easier of the two options.

- Use the Set Up A Network Manually option if the devices you're configuring do not support USB flash drives, or if you don't have a USB flash drive available.

If you choose this option, the final step of the wizard suggests that you need to print out the resulting settings and retype them at the destination computer. Not so: Clicking the Print Network Settings button on the final page opens Notepad, with the newly created settings file displayed as editable text. For the sake of convenience, save that text file to a common location (a floppy disk or a USB flash drive, for instance) and then open it on the computer where you're performing the next configuration step. This makes it easy to copy and paste the encryption key instead of having to type it from a printed page.

Tip **Start from scratch**
When the Wireless Network Setup Wizard finishes its work, it writes your network settings to a hidden file named LastFlashConfig.wfc, which it saves in %Appdata%\Microsoft. The data in this file is encrypted as a security measure. If you want to eliminate all traces of a previous configuration and start fresh with your wireless network, delete this file before running the wizard.

Chapter 10

Extra Security for Wireless Networks

On small networks, the measures we outline in this chapter should be sufficient to protect you from the most common forms of outside attacks aimed at your wireless network. Of course, that assumes that you've protected the rest of your network using the precautions we outline elsewhere in this book: implementing a sensible security policy, using strong passwords, limiting the use of administrator accounts, and carefully setting access to shared resources.

In businesses where the value of information stored on the network is high, you might need to implement additional precautions to safeguard a wireless network. Most of these steps involve investments in software and hardware that significantly increase the cost and complexity of your network. If your business routinely handles data that is extremely sensitive and is subject to legal restrictions on its storage (such as patient records in a medical office, or client correspondence in a law office), you should thoroughly investigate the security of wireless network equipment before purchasing and implementing it. The investment required to safeguard the data might be prohibitive.

A detailed discussion of these options is outside the scope of this book; we list the following options to give you an idea of what you should consider when setting up a wireless network in a sensitive environment:

- **Avoid connecting the wireless LAN to the wired LAN.** The wireless access point should connect to a router on a separate network or a firewalled interface.
- **Use virtual private networks for all wireless connections.** In this configuration, the access point connects to the rest of the network through the server acting as the VPN gateway. Outside intruders might be able to reach the access point, but they won't be able to transmit or receive data without authenticating against the VPN server. (For step-by-step instructions on how to set up your own VPN server on a computer running Windows XP or Windows 2000 Professional, see "Setting Up a Virtual Private Network," page 377.)
- **Use a scanning tool to test your wireless LAN for vulnerability.** The same tools that hackers use to break into wireless networks are freely available for download on the Internet. If you administer a wireless network, download a copy of AirSnort from *http://airsnort.shmoo.com*. You'll find NetStumbler at *http://www.netstumbler.com*. Both programs are well documented and easy to use—if you can figure them out, so can a world full of unsavory characters.
- **Check audit logs regularly.** Set up the Security log to monitor connections to your network, and review it regularly. Be on the lookout for account logon events (connections made over the network) that don't match the normal behavior of users on your network. You'll find details on how to set up this sort of monitoring in "Auditing Security Events," page 773.

Chapter 11

Working with a Corporate Network

Our focus in this book is on networking and security techniques for users of computers in the home and in small businesses. The network in most such cases is configured as a workgroup, or peer-to-peer network. In a workgroup, there is no central management. Each computer has its own user accounts, security settings, and group policies. Although computers in a workgroup can be managed remotely (giving the illusion of central management), there is no integration of the account, security, and group policy information on each computer. An administrator must repeat all the setup work on each computer.

That's why most larger networks rely on a domain-based model. In a domain-based network, a central repository of account, security, and group policy information resides on one or more servers. Each computer on the network refers to the server to retrieve this information. An administrator can manage user accounts, security settings, and group policies for all users and computers as a group.

This chapter does not cover the purchasing decisions, setup, configuration, deployment, or management of an Active Directory network (that is, a domain based on Microsoft Windows Server 2003 or Windows 2000 Server)—not even for a small domain used in a networked home or small business. That huge range of subjects is enough for a book in itself, and indeed, many have been written. Rather, the subject of this chapter is the use in a domain environment of workstations running either Windows XP Professional or Windows 2000 Professional.

Wondering about Windows XP Home Edition? Its use in a domain environment is severely limited. See "Accessing Domain Resources from a Computer Running Windows XP Home Edition," page 361.

Choosing Between a Workgroup and a Domain

A workgroup is good for a small collection of computers in situations where you don't need the capacity of a dedicated server. A workgroup doesn't require a network administrator, because each user decides what information on his or her computer should be shared on the network.

The lack of central administration—which is a clear benefit in small networks—becomes problematical as the number of workstations grows. If you use Windows 2000 or you use Windows XP Professional with Simple File Sharing disabled, you must maintain identical user accounts (that is, same user name and password) on all machines for each user who needs access to network resources. This configuration gives you granular control over network access—but for more than a few users and a few computers it becomes unmanageable. Alternatively, if you use Windows XP with Simple File Sharing enabled (the default setup in a workgroup), you don't have much control over who has access to which resources. For details about how to use the different sharing models in a workgroup, see "Restricting Network Access to Files and Folders," page 17.

If your network has too many computers, too many users, or too many shared resources to easily manage as a workgroup, consider Microsoft Windows Small Business Server 2003 (SBS). For small businesses, SBS provides an ideal bundle for the first domain server. The package comprises Windows Server 2003 and several server applications, including Microsoft Exchange Server 2003 (an e-mail server). SBS also includes several features that are not part of the component server products when they're sold separately—most notably, a simplified server management console and a number of wizards that make it feasible for businesses to operate a domain-based network without the need for a full-time network administrator. In short, SBS offers all the benefits of a centrally managed domain-based network, but with a lower purchase price and easier administration than the full-blown server implementations offered by Microsoft. SBS is limited to 75 users and a single domain, so it's not for everybody. For information about Small Business Server, visit *http://www.microsoft.com/sbs/*.

Introducing Windows-Based Domains

A domain-based system is centered around one or more servers called *domain controllers*. Among other functions, a domain controller stores the database of user accounts. When you log on to a computer that's joined to a domain, instead of checking your entry against the computer's local database of user accounts, Windows sends your logon information over the network to a domain controller for authentication. Part of the logon process creates an access token, which is then checked against the access control list (ACL) for each object you try to use—whether it's on your local computer or elsewhere on the network.

This is true not only in Active Directory networks, but in other types of domains, such as domains that use Microsoft Windows NT Server, a prominent domain operating system of the 1990s.

Active Directory

A key advance of Windows 2000 Server over earlier network operating systems such as Windows NT Server is the directory service called *Active Directory*. A directory provides a database of information about network resources, including computers, users, shared folders, and printers. The "service" component of the Active Directory directory service makes this information available to users and applications.

The information about each object that Active Directory stores is much more extensive than the simple user account database of earlier systems, and the information schema is extensible, which allows network administrators to customize it as needed. (An *object* is the basic element of Active Directory; an object represents a user, computer, printer, file, or other network resource. The *schema* defines which objects can be stored in the directory and which properties each type of object can have. For example, a user object has properties such as first name, last name, address, telephone number, and so on; a printer object includes properties such as location, model, and speed.)

The Active Directory database is stored on a domain controller. In a domain that has multiple domain controllers, the Active Directory database is automatically replicated on a frequent schedule so that all domain controllers have an up-to-date copy. All domain controllers in an Active Directory network are functionally peers, unlike the primary domain controller/backup domain controller distinction in Windows NT domains. In a large enterprise, with hundreds or thousands of computers querying Active Directory for information, this allows the traffic to be split among multiple directory servers. In addition, it provides redundancy in case a domain controller fails.

Domain administrators use several tools for day-to-day management of Active Directory, including the Active Directory Domains And Trusts, Active Directory Sites And Services, and Active Directory Users And Computers snap-ins for Microsoft Management Console. The latter, which is the Active Directory counterpart to Local Users And Groups, manages much more information, as you can see in Figure 11-1 on the next page.

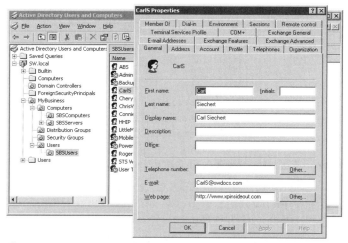

Figure 11-1. Compare the tabs in this dialog box for a user with the non–Active Directory user properties dialog box shown in Figure 4-7 on page 96.

Domain Servers

In addition to a domain controller, a domain-based network typically includes other servers that provide network services and resources, such as data storage. Other server roles can be performed on the same machine as a domain controller, or they can run on separate computers running Windows 2000 Server or Windows Server 2003, each of which comes in several versions with varying capabilities and limitations. Common server roles in an Active Directory domain include:

- **Domain controller.** Each domain must have at least one domain controller, which manages user authentication. The Active Directory database resides on the domain controller.

- **Member server.** Servers that are not domain controllers are called *member servers*, and are typically used as file servers, application servers, or print servers.

- **Dynamic Host Configuration Protocol (DHCP) server.** A DHCP server assigns a unique IP address to each network client. (For information about how a network connection uses a DHCP server, see "Setting IP Addresses," page 268.)

- **Domain Name System (DNS) server.** DNS is the naming system used on the Internet and in Active Directory networks for uniquely identifying network computers. A DNS server manages the relationships between DNS names (such as www.microsoft.com or everglades.sw.local) and IP addresses.

- **Routing and Remote Access server.** Routing and Remote Access supports several methods for providing secure remote access to a private network. It can be used to configure a virtual private network (VPN) gateway, a dial-up remote access server, network address translation (NAT) services, and more. (For information about connecting to a VPN gateway, see "Connecting to a VPN," page 375.)

- **Internet Information Services (IIS) server.** IIS provides a Web server for hosting a public Web site, an internal Web site (intranet), a Microsoft SharePoint site, and similar sites. It can also serve other Internet protocols, such as File Transfer Protocol (FTP) for sharing files over the Internet.

- **Terminal server.** Terminal server is similar to the Remote Desktop Connection feature in Windows XP, which enables clients to remotely log on to another computer (the terminal server) and operate it just as if they were sitting at that remote computer.

- **Certificate server.** A certificate server acts as a certification authority (CA) and issues digital certificates for use in digital signatures, encryption, and similar purposes. (For information about certificate services, see "Obtaining a Personal Certificate," page 678.)

Windows Server 2003 and Windows 2000 Server include the components necessary for performing any or all of the preceding server roles, as well as several others that are less common. In addition, many server applications are available. Like the server roles listed above, server applications run as a service on a computer running a server version of Windows. They can run on a domain controller or another server computer. Widely used server applications include Microsoft Exchange Server (an e-mail server), Microsoft Internet Security and Acceleration (ISA) Server (a proxy server and corporate firewall), Microsoft SQL Server (a database management system), and Microsoft SharePoint Portal Server (Web-based collaboration software). This is just a small sampling of the types of application servers designed for an Active Directory network. Naturally, other companies provide many additional options.

Domain Structure

An Active Directory domain is defined on three levels:

- Domain
- Organizational unit (OU)
- Site

A *domain* forms the basic security and organizational structure in Active Directory. A domain is a logical grouping of users, computers, and other objects for organizational and security purposes. Every object in Active Directory must belong to a domain. A domain is based on *logical* groupings, not physical location. A domain, therefore, can encompass all the computers in one physical location (such as one building or one floor) or it might span several locations (such as a corporate campus or even different cities, linked by a wide area network).

The security and organizational needs of some large networks are more easily met with multiple domains. A company might find it beneficial to create separate domains based on physical locations (for example, offices in different cities) or along organizational lines (for example, accounting versus manufacturing). Managing multiple domains can be complex, however, which is why Active Directory provides an alternative: the *organizational unit*, or OU. An OU is an object that can contain other objects, such as users, computers, or even other OUs. Like other object types, OUs are created within a domain, and they provide a method for administrators to segregate users, computers, or shared resources into different groups, each with its own administrator, but all sharing the same domain controllers. OUs provide a flexible way to divide administrative duties. For example, instead of dividing users into different OUs, a domain could have an OU that contains all the users, another OU that contains all the shared printers, another that contains all the shared folders, and so on. Prior to the advent of OUs in Windows 2000 Server, administrators of large-scale Windows NT domains faced the complexities of managing multiple domains or managing a monolithic directory that was difficult to administer because of its sheer size and lack of flexibility.

Even with the advantages provided by OUs, large organizations often require multiple domains, which provides more of a security boundary within different parts of the organization. Using trust relationships, domains can be joined into structures called *trees*, and trees can be grouped into *forests*.

Unlike the other components of Active Directory domain structure, the *site* provides organization based primarily on physical location. Sites within a domain might be connected with a slow link (compared with speeds on a local area network). With site definitions, administrators can minimize traffic over slow (or expensive) links.

Group Policy

One of the most powerful features of Active Directory networks is Group Policy. Chapter 22, "Managing Security Through Group Policy and Security Templates," provides an overview of security-related settings that can be made with Group Policy. That large number of policies is just a fraction of the available policies that enable an administrator to control all manner of computer appearance and operation details. But Group Policy (specifically, Local Group Policy) as described in that chapter applies to a single computer, and it affects all users on a computer in the same way.

With domain-based Group Policy, policies are centrally administered. An administrator can configure policies that are applied to all computers, to standardize settings throughout an organization.

But there's another huge difference in domain-based Group Policy: policies can be selectively applied to users, computers, and other objects. An administrator can configure policies so that different users on a single computer are subject to different policies. Similarly, policies can be configured so that different policies are applied to a user depending on where he or she logs on.

Domain-based policies can be applied at site, domain, and OU levels. When a user logs on, settings from the local Group Policy object are applied first, followed by site policies, domain policies, and OU policies—in that order. Policy settings applied later overwrite previously applied policies, meaning that in case of conflicting policies the highest-level policy takes precedence.

Joining a Domain

To join a domain, your computer must have a computer account set up on the domain controller. You can do this before, during, or after you install Windows XP Professional or Windows 2000 on your computer:

- Before you set up Windows, an administrator can create the computer account on the domain controller. In Windows 2000 Server or Windows Server 2003, you use the Active Directory Users And Computers console to add a computer account. With Small Business Server (SBS), a wizard handles these duties so an administrator doesn't have to work directly in Active Directory Users And Computers.

- During installation, the Setup program asks whether you want to join a workgroup or domain. If you elect to join a domain, you can create a computer account (if you haven't already set one up), provided that you can furnish the name and password of a domain administrative account that has authority to add domain computer accounts (typically, an account that's a member of the Domain Admins group). You can provide this information whether you run Setup in an interactive or unattended fashion.

- After installation, you can join a domain from the Computer Name tab of the System Properties dialog box. Details of this method are provided next. Again, if you haven't already set up a computer account on the domain controller, you can set one up from here—as long as you provide the name and password of a domain administrator account. To join a domain after you've set up Windows, follow these steps:

    1 Log on as a member of the local Administrators group.

    2 In Control Panel, open System (in the Performance And Maintenance category). Alternatively, right-click My Computer and choose Properties.

Chapter 11

3 In the System Properties dialog box, click the Computer Name (Windows XP) or Network Identification (Windows 2000) tab.

> **Tip** **Skip the Network Identification Wizard**
>
> The Computer Name tab has two buttons that perform essentially the same task. Clicking the Network ID button starts the Network Identification Wizard, which, over the course of a half dozen pages or more, helps you to join a domain. The Change button gets there with a single dialog box, as described in this section.
>
> The Network Identification Wizard does offer one advantage: It helps you add a single domain user account to a local user group. For more information about this task, see "Adding Domain Accounts to Your Local Account Database," page 357.

4 Click Change (Windows XP) or Properties (Windows 2000) to open the dialog box shown here.

5 Select Domain, type the name of your domain, and then click OK. Another dialog box appears.

6 Type the user name and password of an account that has permission to join your computer to the domain. By default, members of the global Domain Admins group have this permission.

7 Restart your computer when prompted.

Tip **Use resources in another domain**

Your computer can be joined to only one domain. But if you routinely use resources from another domain and you use Windows XP Professional, you can add credentials for other domains that allow access to those domains' resources. In Control Panel, open User Accounts. Click the Advanced tab and then click Manage Passwords. Click Add and then specify the name of the other domain's computer that has the shared resources (in the form *domainname\computername*), along with your user name and password for the other domain. (With Windows 2000, you can access other domains, but unlike Windows XP, it has no provision for saving logon credentials for other domains.)

Chapter 11

Is Your Computer Joined to a Domain?

Unless you're aware of some of the subtle visual and operational differences described later in this chapter, your computer's domain membership status might not be immediately obvious. The most reliable way to tell at a glance is to open System Properties and click the Computer Name or Network Identification tab. Below Full Computer Name appears either the word *Workgroup* or *Domain*, along with the name of the workgroup or domain.

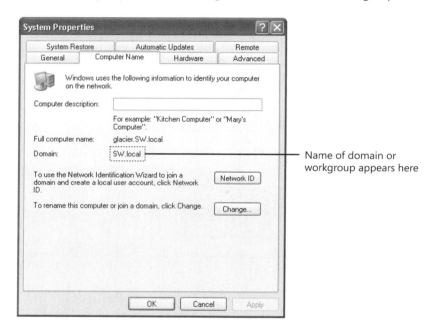

Name of domain or workgroup appears here

You can glean some other interesting information about your domain status by using the Whoami command-line utility, which you can find on the Windows XP CD in the \Support \Tools\Support.cab file. (You can install all the support tools utilities by running \Support \Tools\Setup.exe.) Open a command prompt window and type **whoami** to find out the user name of the currently logged-on user; the user name is preceded by the domain name if you're logged on using a domain account or by the computer name if you're using a local account. Type **whoami /groups** to see a list of all the local and global security groups to which your account belongs.

Inside Out

Use a command-line tool to join a domain

If you need to join several computers to a domain, as might be the case when you initially set up a new server-based network, you might find it easier to create a batch program that you can run on each computer with a simple click rather than digging into System Properties as described in the preceding steps. Netdom.exe, a command-line tool that's part of the Windows Support Tools included with Windows XP Service Pack 2 (SP2), can be used for that purpose.

To use Netdom, you need to install Windows Support Tools. If you have a Windows XP SP2 CD, you install the tools by running \Support\Tools\Setup.exe from the CD. If your copy of the Windows XP CD was created before SP2, or if you don't have a Windows XP CD, you can download the latest support tools from *http://www.microsoft.com/downloads/*; search by typing **windows xp support tools** in the Keywords box.

After you've installed Windows Support Tools, you can run Netdom to join a domain. To join a domain, at a command prompt or in a batch program, type **netdom join *computername* /domain:*domainname* /userd:*username* /passwordd:*password* /reboot**, replacing the italic text with the name of the computer and domain and the username and password for a domain administrator account. Other parameters make it possible to join a remote computer to a domain, as well as perform other domain-related tasks. For details, at a command prompt type **netdom help**.

Configuring Network Settings

In most cases, a domain server uses DHCP to provide an IP address to each computer in the network. Therefore, your network connection should be configured to obtain its IP address automatically. To confirm this setting:

1 In Control Panel, open Network Connections (in Windows 2000, Network And Dial-Up Connections).
2 Right-click your local network connection, and choose Properties.
3 Select Internet Protocol (TCP/IP), and click Properties.
4 On the General tab, be sure that Obtain An IP Address Automatically is selected.

Adding Domain Accounts to Your Local Account Database

When you join a domain by using the procedure described in the previous section, Windows adds two global security groups to your local account database:

● The domain's Domain Admins group is added to your local Administrators group.
● The domain's Domain Users group is added to your local Users group.

Chapter 11

You can confirm these additions by opening Local Users And Groups (type **lusrmgr.msc** at a command prompt) and examining the properties of the Administrators group and Users group, as shown in Figure 11-2.

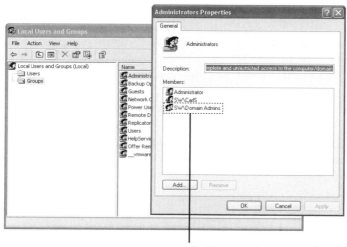

The Domain Admins group in the SW domain
is a member of the local Administrators group.

Figure 11-2. Adding domain accounts gives domain users access to local resources.

Placing these groups in your local account database gives their members the same privileges on your computer as local members of the group. For example, any member of the Domain Admins group can log on to your computer locally and have all the rights and permissions accorded to local administrative accounts.

> **Note** Don't worry: Membership in a local group doesn't automatically allow access to your files over a network connection. Only folders that you choose to share are available on the network. And permissions that you apply to the shared folder restrict who can access the folder and what they can do with its contents. For more information about sharing on a network, see "Sharing Information Across Your Network," page 285.

By default, your domain account is a member of the Domain Users group. Therefore, when you log on to your computer using your domain account, you'll have all the privileges of a member of the local Users group. (In other words, you won't have very many privileges; you'll be a limited user.) Therefore, you might want to add your domain account to a more high-powered group. You can do this in either of two ways:

● At the domain controller, add your account to a global group that has the privileges you need. For example, adding your account to the Domain Admins group gives you instant membership in the local Administrators group—not only of your computer, but of all computers in the domain. Depending on the size of your domain and your role in the organization, this might be entirely inappropriate, of course. But a domain administrator might choose to add your account to another group that has privileges that fall somewhere in between those of Domain Users and Domain Admins.

● At your computer, you can add your domain account (or another global group of which you're a member) to your local account database.

To exercise the second option—adding a domain account to your local account database—you can use either User Accounts or Local Users And Groups. User Accounts is the better tool for adding individual user accounts; Local Users And Groups lets you add groups more easily.

To add a user account, follow these steps:

1 In Control Panel, open User Accounts.

2 On the Users tab, click Add.

3 In the Add New User dialog box, type the user name and domain name of the account you want to add (or click Browse, Advanced, Find Now to select from a list of domain user accounts), and then click Next.

4 In the next dialog box, select the local group that you'd like to add the account to (see the graphic on the next page), and then click Finish.

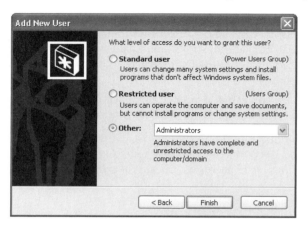

To add a global user account or global group to your local account database, follow these steps:

1 At a command prompt, type **lusrmgr.msc** to open Local Users And Groups.

2 Open the Groups folder, and then double-click the name of the group to which you want to add a user or group.

3 Click Add. If you're using Windows 2000, select the domain name in the Look In box; then skip to step 6. In Windows XP, click Advanced. The Select Users dialog box appears.

4 Be sure the domain name appears in From This Location. If it does not, click Locations and select the domain name.

5 Click Find Now to display a list of users and groups.

Chapter 11

6   Select the users or groups you want to add (hold down the Ctrl key as you click to select multiple names). In Windows 2000, click Add and then click OK in each dialog box. In Windows XP, click OK in each dialog box.

> For more information about using Local Users And Groups, see "Managing User Accounts for Security," page 82.

Leaving a Domain

The procedure for leaving a domain and joining a workgroup is similar to the procedure for joining a domain, described earlier in this chapter. To join a workgroup, follow these steps:

1   Log on as a member of the local Administrators group.

2   Open System Properties, and click Computer Name, Change. (In Windows XP, click Network Identification, Properties.)

3   Select Workgroup, and then type the workgroup name. A workgroup name can contain up to 15 characters. It cannot be the same as the name of any computer in the workgroup, and it cannot contain any of the following characters:

; : " < > * + = \ | / ? ,

4   If you're leaving an Active Directory domain, in the dialog box that appears, enter the user name and password of a domain account that has permission to remove the computer from the domain.

Accessing Domain Resources from a Computer Running Windows XP Home Edition

A computer running Windows XP Home Edition cannot be joined to a domain. Moreover, using Home Edition you can't manually add entries to the list in the Stored User Names And Passwords dialog box. However, users of Windows XP Home Edition who have a domain user account can access shared folders and printers in a domain. If your Home Edition computer is connected to the domain, either through a local area connection or a virtual private network (VPN) connection, you can use either of the following techniques to access domain resources:

- In the Windows Explorer Address bar, type the network path to the resource you want to use, in the form *servername**sharename*. For example, to open a share named Document on a server named Everglades, type **everglades****document**. A dialog box appears, in which you must enter your user name and password. Enter the credentials for your domain account, not the local account you use to log on to your own computer. The folders in the share then appear in Windows Explorer.

- Open My Network Places, and click View Workgroup Computers. If your workgroup name is the same as the domain name, other computers in the domain become visible. (If your workgroup name is not the same as the domain name, click Microsoft Windows Network under Other Places. Then double-click the domain name to see its computers.) Double-click a computer icon, and the request for user name and password appears. Enter your domain credentials, and the computer's shared resources appear.

Credentials you enter using these methods persist throughout your session, but are discarded when you log off. Therefore, typing an address or browsing to a network resource works fine for occasional connections. But if you regularly connect to the same resources, there's a better way, which lets you avoid the (sometimes lengthy) wait for the password request dialog box and the requirement to enter your network credentials repeatedly: Set up a batch program that makes your network connections, and run the batch program each time you log on (or each time you connect to the network). To set up such a batch program, follow these steps:

1 Start Notepad.

2 For each network resource you want to connect with, type a Net Use command on a separate line. Use the format **net use ***servername******sharename password* **/user:***username*, where *servername* is the name of the computer, *sharename* is the name of a shared folder, *password* is the password for your domain account, and *username* is the user name for your domain account. For example, to connect to the share named Document on the computer named Everglades using Carl's domain account, you'd enter

```
net use \\everglades\document WdYw2Gt /user:carls
```

> **Caution** Your network password is stored as plain text in this file. If you don't want to expose your password in this way, replace it with an asterisk (*). Then Windows prompts you to enter the password when you run the batch program.

3 Save the file, giving it a name with either a .cmd or a .bat extension. You might place it on the desktop or in your Startup folder.

Enabling Security Center

Security Center, a feature that was introduced with Windows XP SP2, is turned off by default on computers that are joined to a domain. With Security Center turned off, no icon appears in the notification area and, more importantly, Security Center doesn't monitor your computer's essential security settings (firewall, automatic updates, and antivirus) as it does on a workgroup computer. Opening Security Center while it's turned off produces only an assemblage of links to other Control Panel programs and related information. The status section—which monitors and advises you of the current state of Automatic Updates, your firewall, and your antivirus program—is absent.

You can enable Security Center for a computer that's joined to a domain, making it work just like a computer that is not joined to a domain. To do that, follow these steps:

1 At a command prompt, type **gpedit.msc** to open Group Policy.

2 In Group Policy, open Computer Configuration\Administrative Templates \Windows Components\Security Center.

3 Double-click the Turn On Security Center (Domain PCs Only) policy.

4 Select Enabled, and click OK.

5 Restart your computer.

> **Note** These steps explain how to use the local Group Policy object to enable Security Center for all users on a computer. This policy is also available in Windows Server 2003. Therefore, if your domain controller runs Windows Server 2003 (not Windows 2000 Server), you can use domain-based policy to make this setting. For more information, see "Local Group Policy vs. Active Directory–Based Group Policy," page 760.

> For more information about Security Center, see "Monitoring Security in Windows XP," page 213.

Working on a Domain-Based Computer

For the most part, using a computer that is joined to a domain is just like using a stand-alone computer or one that's part of a workgroup. Some important differences exist, however, and we explain those differences in the following pages.

Logging On to a Domain

When your computer is joined to a domain, you'll ordinarily log on using your domain account. Doing so loads the portions of your profile stored on network servers, applies domain-based Group Policy objects, and lets you use any domain resources for which your account has the requisite permissions.

If you have a desktop computer that's permanently attached to the network, there's seldom any reason to log on using a local account. Even most local administrative tasks are just as easily handled—either locally or remotely—by a domain account that's a member of the local Administrators group. If you have a portable computer, you might want to use a local account when your computer is not connected to the network. It's not necessary to do that, however, because Windows uses a locally cached version of your profile if the domain controller is unavailable. Using separate accounts for local and network logons can make it more complicated to manage permissions for your locally stored documents. In this situation, you might be better off not joining the domain and instead always using a local account.

> For more information on the differences between local accounts and domain accounts, see "Local vs. Domain Accounts," page 48.

To log on, wait for the Welcome To Windows dialog box to appear, and press Ctrl+Alt+Delete. Doing so displays the Log On To Windows dialog box, shown in Figure 11-3. Type the user name and password for your domain account, and be sure that

Chapter 11

363

your domain name is selected in the Log On To box. (To log on using a local user account, type its user name and password, and select the computer name in the Log On To box.)

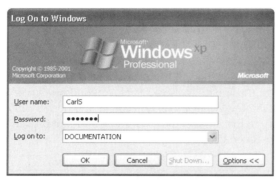

Figure 11-3. If the Log On To box isn't visible, click Options.

Entering Domain Credentials

When you enter your user name, Windows needs to know which security database to look in to find the name. In some dialog boxes (such as the Log On To Windows dialog box), you enter your user name in one box and select the name of the domain or computer in another box. Other dialog boxes, however, provide only a User Name box. Windows assumes that you're entering the name of an account on the resource you're trying to access, so in most cases you don't need to enter the name of a domain or computer. In some cases, however, you must provide the name of the computer or domain as well as your user name; you provide both pieces of information in the User Name box. If the security database is on a computer running Windows NT, use the form ***domainname\username*** (for example, **documentation\carls** or, for a local account on a computer named Sequoia, **sequoia\carls**). If the security database is on a computer running Windows 2000, Windows XP, or Windows Server 2003, you can use that form or the newer *username@domainname* form (for example, **carls@documentation.swdocs.local** or **carls@sequoia**).

Note that you can use the DNS format—the e-mail–like format used in Windows 2000 and later—even in dialog boxes that include a separate box for entering the name of the domain or computer. When you append "@*domainname*" to your name in the user name box, the domain box becomes unavailable.

Displaying My Network Places

My Network Places provides a starting point for many network operations—yet it's not always easy to find.

In Windows 2000, a shortcut to My Network Places appears on the desktop, and it can't be removed without making registry changes. A link to My Network Places also appears in the left pane of each Windows Explorer window, unless you've chosen to use Windows classic folders (an option on the General tab of the Folder Options dialog box). If you use classic folders, you can still get to My Network Places without digging down to the desktop: in any Windows Explorer window, click the Address box arrow.

In Windows XP, you can create a desktop shortcut for My Network Places if one doesn't already exist. Right-click the desktop, and choose Properties. Click the Desktop tab, and then click Customize Desktop. Select My Network Places under Desktop Icons.

You can also add My Network Places to the Start menu in Windows XP. Right-click the Start button and choose Properties. On the Start Menu tab, click Customize. In the Customize Start Menu dialog box, click the Advanced tab and then, in the Start Menu Items box, select the My Network Places check box.

Specifying Network Resources by UNC Path

Each shared folder and shared printer can be directly addressed by its Universal Naming Convention (UNC) path. A UNC path takes the form *servername**sharename*. For example, a shared folder named Accounting on a server named Everglades can be addressed as \\Everglades\Accounting. You can type a UNC path in the Address bar of Windows Explorer or in the Run dialog box to open a network folder.

Finding Files, Printers, and Users

In general, you can browse a domain to find its shared resources in much the same way as you browse a workgroup. Start by opening My Network Places:

- In Windows 2000, double-click Entire Network. In the left pane, click the Entire Contents link to display objects in the right pane. Then double-click icons to browse to the item of interest: double-click Microsoft Windows Network, the domain name, the computer name, and the share name.

- In Windows XP, you can browse the computers in your domain by clicking Entire Network (in the task pane under Other Places) and then double-clicking Microsoft Windows Network. This displays an icon for each domain and workgroup in your network; double-click a domain name to see its computers. Figure 11-4 on the next page shows a small network. (Three domains in a network this size is unusual, but we use this approach to separate test systems from our production network.)

If your domain controller uses Active Directory, a service included with Windows 2000 Server and Windows Server 2003, there's a better way. Instead of browsing for network objects (such as printers and users), you can search Active Directory. Particularly on large networks, the ability to search instead of browsing makes it much easier to find the network resources you need. Predefined searches help you locate users, contacts, and groups; computers; printers; shared folders; and organizational units. Active Directory searching is available for users of Windows XP and (to a limited degree) Windows 2000, but the process is a bit different for each.

Chapter 11

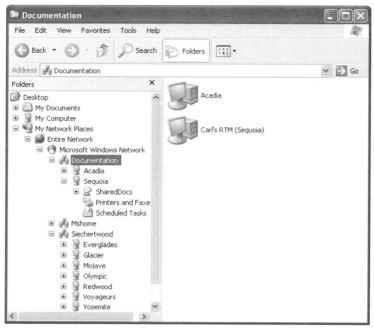

Figure 11-4. The Folders Explorer bar illustrates the network hierarchy.

Searching Active Directory in Windows XP

To start a search, click the Search Active Directory link under Network Tasks in My Network Places. Select the type of object you're searching for and then enter your criteria. The search application window, shown in Figure 11-5, is well organized and easy to figure out.

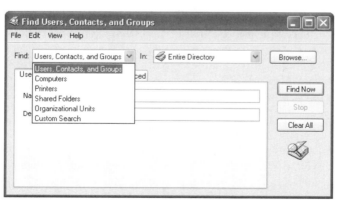

Figure 11-5. To begin an Active Directory search, select the type of object you're seeking. The window then displays search criteria for that object type.

After you enter your criteria, click Find Now. The window then enlarges, and the results of your search appear in a list at the bottom of the window, as shown in Figure 11-6.

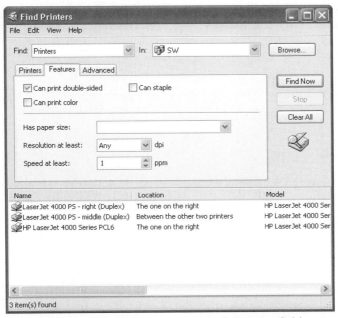

Figure 11-6. The search results include descriptive fields entered by the person who shared the resource, such as the location descriptions shown here.

Searching Active Directory in Windows 2000

Unlike the unified searching tool available for Windows XP, Windows 2000 users are faced with slightly different tools for finding shared printers, users, and computers. Unfortunately, Windows 2000 does not include a method for searching for shared folders. (You can search for folders and files within a shared folder, but you must first browse to the shared folder.)

- To search for a shared printer, in My Network Places double-click Entire Network and then click Search For Printers, which displays a dialog box similar to the one shown in Figure 11-6. Alternatively, from the Start menu choose Search, For Printers.

- To search for a user, open Entire Network and click Search For People, or click Start, Search, For People. Select Active Directory in the Look In box, and then specify your search criteria.

- To search for a computer by name, open Entire Network and click Search For Computers.

Chapter 11

Connecting to Shared Network Folders

The process of connecting to a network resource, such as a shared folder or shared printer, is much the same in a domain environment as in a workgroup setup. A domain is likely to have more available resources simply because domains are used primarily on networks with more computers, however, so the typical casual methods of browsing and connecting in a workgroup might not be the most efficient.

Two methods make it easy to return to an oft-used network folder: creating a network place, or mapping a network drive. The first method places a shortcut in My Network Places; the second assigns a drive letter to a shared folder so that it appears in Windows Explorer like a local hard drive.

Creating a Network Place

A network place can be a shortcut to a shared network folder, a Web folder, or an FTP folder. To create a network place, follow these steps:

1 Open My Network Places. If you're using Windows 2000, double-click Add Network Place, and skip to step 3. In Windows XP, click Add A Network Place, in the task pane under Network Tasks.

2 Click Next on the first page of the Add Network Place Wizard. On the second page, select Choose Another Network Location, and click Next.

3 Type the UNC network path to the shared folder you want to use. If you want a shortcut that links directly to a subfolder of the shared folder, append its path (for example, **\\everglades\doc\carl\2005**). As an alternative to typing the path, you can browse to it; click Browse, navigate to the folder you want, and click OK. Then click Next.

4 Type a name for the shortcut if you don't like the one that Windows proposes. Click Next (Windows XP only), and then click Finish.

Your network place now appears in My Network Places. Naturally, you can double-click it to open the network folder. But you can also copy the network place to another location that's more convenient for you; simply drag it to the desktop, another folder, or the Start menu.

Mapping a Network Drive

Mapping a network drive simply associates a network path with an available drive letter on your computer. You can then use the share's content like that of any drive. To map a network drive, in Windows Explorer choose Tools, Map Network Drive. A dialog box like the one shown in Figure 11-7 appears.

In the Drive box, select the drive letter you want to use. In the Folder box, type the UNC path to the shared folder. If you want to automatically remap the drive every time you use your computer, select Reconnect At Logon; if you clear this check box, the mapping is discarded when you log off.

Figure 11-7. After closing this dialog box, X:\ becomes an alternative path to the \\Everglades\Programs share.

> **Tip** Navigate to the target folder first
>
> If you browse to the shared folder you want to map to a drive letter (for example, by navigating to it in Windows Explorer), you can right-click the folder and choose Map Network Drive. Doing so displays the same dialog box as shown in Figure 11-7, but the Folder box is already filled in.

Windows XP Differences in a Domain Environment

Windows 2000 Professional, which was designed as a corporate desktop operating system at the turn of the century, works nearly identically whether it's in a workgroup or domain environment. By contrast, because Windows XP was designed to supplant all its predecessors, including those used primarily in stand-alone home systems (such as Windows Millennium Edition) and those used in corporate networks (such as Windows NT Workstation), it works differently depending on whether the system is joined to a domain. Its designers made this decision to create minimal disruption for those of all stripes who upgrade to Windows XP.

Many of these changes—some subtle and rather insignificant—are designed to make Windows XP work the same way that Windows 2000 Professional works in a domain environment, which eases the training and support burden on administrators. The following sections document the most significant differences in a domain-based computer running Windows XP Professional compared to a workgroup-based computer.

Chapter 11

369

Logon and Logoff

- **Logon screen.** The Welcome screen is unavailable in a domain environment. Instead, you use the "classic" logon, which prompts you to press Ctrl+Alt+Delete and then enter your user name (if it isn't already entered from your last session) and password.

- **Logon and logoff scripts.** A domain administrator can set up scripts that run automatically each time you log on to your computer or log off. These scripts, which are typically stored and administered on the domain controller, can be used to provide software updates, new virus definitions, and other information to your computer; set up network connections; start programs; and perform other tasks. A computer that's not joined to a domain can't run domain logon scripts. Although you can create local logon and logoff scripts for workgroup computers, they're generally less powerful and, of course, they're not centrally managed for all computers on the network.

- **Forgotten passwords.** With the classic logon that's used in a domain environment, password hints aren't available. Nor can you create or use a Password Reset Disk, with which you can set a new password if you can't remember your current one. A domain administrator can change the password for your domain account. Any user who is a member of the local Administrators group can change the password for any local account. For details about using these features in a workgroup, see "Recovering a Lost Password," page 115.

- **Fast User Switching.** Fast User Switching, which enables a user to log on without requiring the current user to first log off, is not available on domain-based computers.

- **Workstation locking.** On a computer that's joined to a domain, pressing the Windows logo key+L locks a workstation so that only the currently logged on user or an administrator can unlock it. (In a workgroup, Windows logo key+L invokes Fast User Switching.)

- **Logoff and Shutdown screens.** Instead of the big, colorful (some say cartoonish) buttons that appear when you choose to log off or shut down a workgroup computer, a computer joined to a domain displays dialog boxes similar to those in Windows 2000, as shown in Figures 11-8 and 11-9. They serve the same function and they're no harder or easier to use; they are simply intended to ease the transition to Windows XP for corporate users.

Figure 11-8. Domain users see this utilitarian Log Off Windows dialog box.

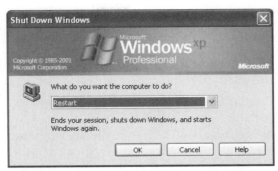

Figure 11-9. To shut down a domain-based computer, you select from a list and click OK. Windows displays your previous selection as the default option.

File Sharing and Security

- **Simple File Sharing.** Although the option to enable Simple File Sharing remains in the Folder Options dialog box (and indeed, it's selected by default), Simple File Sharing is not available in a domain environment.

    Without Simple File Sharing, the Security tab appears in the properties dialog box for all printers and for all folders and files on NTFS drives. When you're logged on as a member of the local Administrators or Power Users group, the Sharing tab, with which you set network access permissions, appears in the properties dialog box for all folders.

    Most important, without Simple File Sharing, network users are authenticated as themselves. To access local resources, their account must be granted appropriate permissions, either directly or through their membership in a group.

- **Shared Documents.** On computers in a workgroup environment, the local Shared Documents folder, %AllUsersProfile%\Documents, occupies a prominent place in My Computer. Particularly when Simple File Sharing is enabled, it is the default and easiest location for storing folders and files that you want to share with other users on your computer or on your network.

    When your computer is joined to a domain, however, you're likely to forget that Shared Documents exists. My Computer no longer includes a Files Stored On This Computer group. If your computer was in a workgroup and you ran the Network Setup Wizard before you joined a domain, the folder continues to be shared as Shared Documents. If you have not run the Network Setup Wizard, the folder is not set up as a network share by default. Either way, by default only local users and groups have permissions to access the folders and files within Shared Documents. If you want to grant permissions to domain users, you should add the appropriate domain groups to the folder's access control list (ACL). For information about modifying the ACL, see "Using NTFS Permissions for Access Control," page 136.

Chapter 11

371

Networking

- **Network Setup Wizard.** The Network Setup Wizard, which is designed to help you set up a home or small office network, does not run on a computer that's joined to a domain. For information about the Network Setup Wizard, see "Using the Network Setup Wizard in Windows XP," page 250.

- **Network Tasks.** When you open My Network Places, the task pane on a workgroup computer includes a link to View Workgroup Computers; on a domain computer, this link is replaced with a functionally similar Entire Network link, which appears under Other Places. A domain computer also includes a Search Active Directory link, which provides options for searching the network. For details, see "Finding Files, Printers, and Users," page 365.

Computer and User Management

- **User Accounts.** When you open User Accounts in Control Panel, you get a different version depending on whether your computer is joined to a domain or not. The two versions have similar capabilities; the difference is more style than substance. The workgroup version follows the newer style of Windows XP, complete with graphics and links to wizard-like dialog boxes. The domain version uses a traditional dialog box that's nearly identical to its Windows 2000 predecessor. For information about the two versions of User Accounts, see "Managing User Accounts for Security," page 82.

- **Group Policy.** A computer in a workgroup or in a non–Active Directory domain can use the local Group Policy Object to make a large number of settings and impose a number of restrictions—but these settings and restrictions apply to only a single computer, and they apply to all users on that computer. In a domain with Active Directory, many more Group Policy settings are available. More important, they're centrally managed and they can be selectively applied to computers, users, groups, domains, and other divisions. This is a huge topic that's covered in great depth in the resource kits for the Windows 2000 Server and Windows Server 2003 families. You can learn about local Group Policy—and get a hint of the power available in domain-based policy—by reviewing Chapter 22, "Managing Security Through Group Policy and Security Templates."

- **Time synchronization.** The appearance of an Internet Time tab in Control Panel's Date And Time Properties dialog box depends on domain membership. In a workgroup environment (or in a Windows NT–based domain), you use this tab to set up synchronization of your computer's clock with an Internet time server. This feature is unavailable on computers joined to a domain using Windows 2000 Server or Windows Server 2003.

In fact, this is not merely a user interface change, nor is it a feature that's missing from domain-based computers. It's actually related to the authentication method used by domain controllers. Windows 2000 Server and Windows Server 2003 use Kerberos V5 authentication, which relies on close synchronization between times on the client workstations and on the server; if transmitted data between them is tagged with a time that's not nearly identical, it's deemed to be invalid. For this reason, a computer that's joined to a domain that uses Windows 2000 Server or Windows Server 2003 as its domain controller always synchronizes its internal clock to the domain controller—not to an external time source. The domain controller should be configured to get its time from an accurate time source.

Connecting Remotely to a Corporate Network

More and more corporations allow their employees and key customers and suppliers to connect to the corporation's internal network from locations outside the network. Although it's possible to configure a small network or even a single home computer for similar access, it's often more feasible on corporate networks because of their fast Internet connections, static IP addresses, and dedicated administrative staff that can set up and maintain secure connections to the outside world.

For details on accepting an incoming connection on a small network, see "Setting Up a Virtual Private Network," page 379.

The best way for a corporation to offer remote access is through a *virtual private network* (VPN), which is a secure means of connecting to a private network (such as a corporate network) via a public network (typically the Internet). Using a VPN, you can access all your network resources just as if you were connected directly to the network, and you can do so from any location where you can make an Internet connection.

VPNs work by *tunneling* between two computers (or two networks) that are each connected to the Internet. Tunneling protocols travel across the public network using standard protocols, but each IP packet or frame (depending on the protocol) is encrypted and then wrapped inside another packet or frame with header information that allows it to travel from point to point. When the new packet or frame reaches its destination, the VPN software strips off the header, decrypts the original data, and routes it to its ultimate destination. If you were to send the original data "in the clear" over the Internet, anyone who intercepted the packets could read the content. In a VPN, however, the data is encrypted before it enters the public network and decrypted only after it's safely behind the firewall at its destination; thus, anyone who intercepts the packets sees only encrypted data that looks like gibberish.

Chapter 11

Tunneling protocols form the basis of VPNs. Although Windows supports a variety of protocols used by legacy hardware devices, three tunneling protocols are in wide use today:

- **Point-to-Point Tunneling Protocol (PPTP).** PPTP allows IP, IPX, or NetBEUI frames to be encrypted and then wrapped in an IP header to be sent across an intervening network.

- **Layer 2 Tunneling Protocol (L2TP).** L2TP allows IP, IPX, or NetBEUI frames to be encrypted and then sent over any IP, X.25, Frame Relay, or ATM intervening network.

- **IP Security (IPSec) Tunnel Mode.** IPSec Tunnel Mode allows IP packets to be encrypted and then encapsulated in an IP header to be sent across an intervening network. IPSec is often coupled with L2TP for purposes of encryption (because L2TP doesn't support data encryption).

A VPN server on a system running Windows 2000 Server or Windows Server 2003 can use any of these protocols, but the greatest security is realized when the server requires a combination of L2TP and IPSec; PPTP has been shown to be vulnerable to brute-force attacks when a weak encryption key is used. Client computers running Windows XP or Windows 2000 Professional can connect to a VPN server using any of these protocols.

Tip Outsource your VPN

Not every corporation has the budget and the ability to set up and maintain a VPN server, of course. But there is an alternative: outsourcing can sometimes offer VPN services that are faster, more reliable, and more secure than a poorly managed internal VPN server. In addition to the large telecom providers, you might want to investigate the offerings of smaller firms such as HotSpotVPN (*http://www.hotspotvpn.com*) or WiTopia (*http://www.witopia.net*).

Setting Up a VPN Connection

If your corporate network (or third-party VPN service provider) has set up a VPN server, you should be able to connect to it from any computer running Windows XP or Windows 2000. To set up a connection in Windows XP:

1 In Control Panel, open Network Connections.

2 Click Create A New Connection (in the task pane under Network Tasks). On the first page of the New Connection Wizard, click Next.

3 On the Network Connection Type page, select Connect To The Network At My Workplace, and click Next.

4 Select Virtual Private Network Connection, and click Next.

5 On the Connection Name page, enter a descriptive name; this text will be used to identify the connection in the Network Connections folder. Despite the suggestion that you supply a company name, you can enter any text you want here. Click Next.

6 On the Public Network page, select one of the following two options, and then click Next:

■ **Do Not Dial The Initial Connection.** Select this option if the computer on which you're creating the connection has a permanent high-speed Internet connection, or if you always want to connect to the Internet manually before connecting to the VPN.

■ **Automatically Dial This Initial Connection.** This option is most appropriate on a computer that normally connects to the Internet by using the same dial-up connection each time. When you select this option, you must also select the connection you want to use.

Note that a VPN connection works over an existing Internet connection. Therefore, to use a VPN connection you must first connect to the Internet.

7 On the VPN Server Selection page, enter the fully qualified domain name or IP address of the computer that is accepting incoming connections. (For most home and small business networks, you should enter an IP address here.) Click Next.

8 On the Connection Availability page, specify whether you want the connection to be available to anyone who logs on to your computer, or only to yourself. Click Next.

9 Click Finish to save your connection. (Note the convenient option to create a shortcut to the connection on your desktop. If you plan to use this VPN connection often and want to avoid having to burrow into the Network Connections folder every time, select this check box before clicking Finish.)

In Windows 2000, the procedure is similar. On the Network Connection Type page, choose Connect To A Private Network Through The Internet, and then follow the same steps outlined for Windows XP.

Tip Get the L2TP and IPSec update
Early in 2005, Microsoft issued an update to its Internet Protocol Security (IPSec) and Layer 2 Tunneling Protocol (L2TP) components that better supports VPN clients that are behind a network address translation (NAT) device. This update is included in Windows XP SP2, but if you use Windows 2000 or (shudder) Windows XP without SP2, check out Microsoft Knowledge Base article 818043 for details about the update and a pointer to the download site.

Connecting to a VPN

VPN connections work much like a dial-up connection. When you double-click the icon for the VPN connection, a connection dialog box appears, as shown in Figure 11-10 on the next page. Windows contacts the computer name or IP address (establishing a connection first, if necessary) and sends the credentials you enter. If the credentials are accepted, you can browse shared resources from the My Network Places folder or by entering addresses in UNC format.

Chapter 11

375

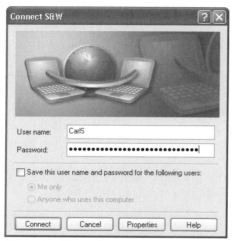

Figure 11-10. After you've established a connection to the Internet, open the VPN connection, enter your credentials, and then click Connect.

Troubleshooting

Other Internet services stop working when you make a VPN connection

When you make a VPN connection, you might find that you can no longer browse the Internet by using Internet Explorer, hold conversations by using Windows Messenger, or use other applications that access the Internet. This occurs when the VPN connection is configured to use the default gateway on the remote network for Internet access. When you make a VPN connection, Windows adds to the IP routing table a new default route that uses the connection to the VPN server. That new route is assigned the lowest metric, which means that it's used in place of your original default route—and therefore prevents access to some locations. Although this is a useful feature when you connect to some corporate networks, it's generally of little use when you're connecting to a single computer or a small workgroup.

To fix the problem, follow these steps:

1 In Control Panel open Network Connections, right-click the VPN connection, and choose Properties.

2 Click the Networking tab, select Internet Protocol (TCP/IP), and click Properties.

3 In the Internet Protocol (TCP/IP) Properties dialog box, click Advanced.

4 On the General tab of the Advanced TCP/IP Settings dialog box, clear the Use Default Gateway On Remote Network check box.

You should then be able to use other Internet applications while your VPN connection is active.

Troubleshooting

You can't find computers by name

If you connect to the Internet through a router that performs network address translation (thereby providing a private IP address to your computer), you might not be able to browse by name the computers at the other end of the VPN tunnel. To reach a computer on your corporate network, for example, you might have to specify its IP address instead of its computer name—which is not very convenient. The problem arises because network names do not route across subnets, and with the two intervening routers (one at each end of the VPN) your computer and the corporate network computers are on different subnets. The ideal solution is for an administrator who manages the VPN server to set up a DNS server (or a WINS server) to resolve names. If that's not feasible, you can solve the problem yourself with a low-tech workaround. Edit your computer's Hosts file, which is stored in the %System-Root%\System32\Drivers\Etc folder. Create an entry for each computer that you want to access by name, specifying its IP address and computer name.

Working with VPN Connection Properties

The VPN connection created by the New Connection Wizard should work fine if the VPN server was configured with default properties. Yours might not be configured that way, however, and an examination of the connection properties is in order. The properties for your VPN connection must match those of the server, so your server administrator should provide details of any settings you must make.

> **Note** It's important that the networking and security settings you make match the VPN server's configuration, or you will be unable to connect.

You can open the properties dialog box for a VPN connection in either of two ways:

- From the connection dialog box shown in Figure 11-10, click Properties.
- In Network Connections, right-click the connection, and choose Properties.

You'll first want to check the Networking tab. In the Type Of VPN box, select one of these options:

- Automatic
- PPTP VPN
- L2TP IPSec VPN

Selecting Automatic enables your computer to negotiate with the VPN server to determine which protocol it uses. If you know how your server is configured, make the corresponding selection here to save a few seconds each time you connect.

Chapter 11

The other settings you might need to change are on the Security tab.

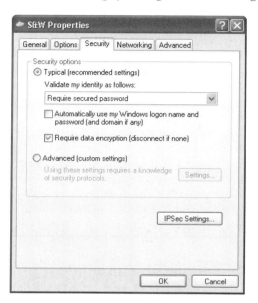

Selecting Advanced and clicking Settings displays the Advanced Security Settings dialog box, in which you can configure authentication by smart card or by certificate if your organization employs those methods. The other protocols provide methods for sending your password (or a hash of your password) to the server.

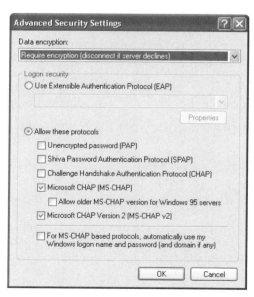

Setting Up a Virtual Private Network

Although this chapter is primarily about working with and connecting to corporate networks, after reading the preceding section you might decide that a VPN is right for your small network too. For home and small business networks, where you need only a single incoming connection at any time, Windows XP and Windows 2000 have everything built in that you need.

The procedure for setting up an incoming VPN connection is nearly identical in Windows XP and Windows 2000:

1 Open the Network Connections folder. (In Windows 2000, this folder is called Network And Dial-Up Connections.)

2 Choose File, New Connection. The New Connection Wizard appears. (In Windows 2000, it's called the Network Connection Wizard.)

3 Click Next to bypass the opening page of the wizard.

4 On the Network Connection Type page, select Set Up An Advanced Connection. (In Windows 2000, select Accept Incoming Connections.) Click Next.

5 On the Advanced Connection Options page, select Accept Incoming Connections, and click Next. (This step is not necessary for Windows 2000.)

6 If a Devices For Incoming Connections page appears, simply click Next. (These options are for setting up an incoming dial-up connection, direct cable connection, or infrared connection.) This page appears only if your computer has an installed modem, serial port, parallel port, or IrDA port.

7 On the Incoming Virtual Private Network (VPN) Connection page, select Allow Virtual Private Connections, and click Next. (In Windows 2000, this page is called Incoming Virtual Private Connection.)

8 On the User Permissions page (called Allowed Users in Windows 2000), select the check box next to the name of each user you want to allow to make an incoming connection. Windows lists all of the local user accounts on your computer. Use the Add button to create a new local account on the fly; click Properties to create or change a password.

Chapter 11

When you're finished assigning user permissions, click Next.

9 On the Networking Software page (called Networking Components in Windows 2000), select the check box next to the name of each network component you want to use for an incoming connection. For most users, the default settings, using TCP/IP, are correct. Click Next to continue.

10 Windows 2000 offers you the opportunity to give the connection a descriptive name; Windows XP does not. Click Finish to save your new connection.

After creating the incoming connection, you can adjust its settings (including adding or removing users from the list of those permitted to make a VPN connection) at any time. Open the Network Connections folder (Network And Dial-Up Connections in Windows 2000), right-click the connection icon, and choose Properties.

One change that we strongly recommend is to require that all users of your incoming VPN connection encrypt all transmitted data and passwords. (By default, this option is turned off on VPN connections.) In the connection's properties dialog box, click the Users tab and select the Require All Users To Secure Their Passwords And Data check box. Before a user can connect to a VPN with this option enabled, he or she must open the properties dialog box for the outgoing VPN connection, click the Security tab, and select Require Data Encryption (Disconnect If None).

Troubleshooting

You can't connect to the VPN from another computer

After you set up a VPN connection on another computer, you might not be able to connect. This can occur if a firewall at either end of the connection blocks VPN traffic.

When you use the New Connection Wizard in Windows XP to create an incoming VPN connection, the wizard automatically configures the built-in Windows Firewall appropriately. You can confirm that by opening Windows Firewall from Control Panel, clicking the Advanced tab, and clicking Settings under Network Connection Settings. You should see entries for Incoming Connection VPN (L2TP) and Incoming Connection VPN (PPTP), and IP Security (IKE); they should all be selected.

If you use a different firewall—software or hardware—you'll need to configure it similarly. For PPTP connections (the type most commonly used with a Windows XP–based VPN), you must open port 1723 for TCP communication. (L2TP connections, which use port 1701, require a machine certificate for authentication and are available only when the VPN server is on a network with Windows Server 2003 or Windows 2000 Server. L2TP, therefore, is a topic that is beyond the scope of this book.) IPSec uses a UDP connection on port 500.

If the firewall on your client computer filters outbound traffic as well as incoming connections, you'll need to open port 1723 on that computer as well.

If you're certain that firewalls at each end are not blocking traffic, yet you still can't connect, the problem might be in-between. Some ISPs block VPN traffic or allow it only with certain types of accounts. Check with your ISP for information about its policies.

Chapter 11

Part 3

Protecting Your Personal Computer

Making Internet Explorer More Secure

If you subscribe to one or more security notification services (a practice we strongly encourage; see "Receiving E-Mail Alerts and RSS Notification," page 226), you will almost certainly be alarmed by the steady stream of messages announcing newly discovered security holes in Microsoft Internet Explorer. If you're a casual Microsoft Windows user who reads these bulletins carefully, you might decide, quite logically, that most of the vulnerabilities described occur only under improbable circumstances and will not affect you if you observe reasonably safe browsing practices. That sort of devil-may-care attitude could easily result in catastrophe.

> **Tip** Another good way to keep abreast of Internet Explorer security issues is by joining the discussion at the microsoft.public.internetexplorer.security newsgroup.

In this chapter we describe how some of those catastrophes can occur. More importantly, we explain how to avoid them. Internet Explorer uses security zones to segregate the bad sites, the good sites, and those you're unsure of. Applying appropriate security settings to each zone ensures that the good guys can deliver a rich experience to your computer while the bad guys are severely restricted and can do no harm. We conclude the chapter with information about managing ActiveX controls, Java applets, and other add-ons—ordinarily useful Web page components that can be the vehicles for malicious attackers to do their dirty deeds.

Security Checklist: Internet Explorer

To keep unwanted code and content from hitching a ride on your Web connection, be sure to follow these sensible security rules:

- If you use Windows XP, install Service Pack 2 (SP2). If you use Windows 2000, install Internet Explorer 6 with the latest service pack.

- Make sure that your computer is protected from viruses and spyware with appropriate defensive measures.

- Use Automatic Updates to install critical updates for Windows and for your browser. Install critical updates for Microsoft Office and other network-aware applications.

- Subscribe to the Microsoft Security Notification Service to learn about new security vulnerabilities as they're discovered and as updates are released.

- Block pop-up windows.

- Check the digital signature of programs you download and, most importantly, download or install only software that you're confident is from a trustworthy source.

- Review your security zone settings, particularly for the Internet zone, which encompasses all Web sites by default. (The default settings in Internet Explorer 6 are reasonably secure, but you might want to further restrict Web sites. For better protection, set the Internet zone to High, and up the Trusted Sites zone security to Medium.)

- Do not make settings for any security zone that are lower than the default settings.

- Add to your Trusted Sites zone sites that you know to be trustworthy and that need capabilities unavailable to sites in the Internet zone.

- Add to your Restricted Sites zone sites that you visit but that you would rather visit only while wearing surgical gloves.

Number 1 Security Tip: Update!

Some of the most important features in Windows XP SP2 are specifically designed to increase your security as you move around on the Internet, making SP2 an essential update for Windows XP users. Microsoft calculates that Internet Explorer in Windows XP SP2 has 65 percent fewer vulnerabilities than Internet Explorer 6 SP1. In addition, changes such as Local Machine Lockdown preemptively eliminate entire classes of vulnerabilities. The security-related improvements include the following features:

- **Restrictions on automatic downloads in Internet Explorer.** Download prompts appear only in the Information Bar, and Web page designers can no longer repeatedly prompt you to download a file or install a program.

- **Improved handling of downloaded files, including e-mail attachments.** Windows now checks for publisher information in all executable files. When you download a file, Windows displays a dialog box that offers a clearer explanation about the file and possible risks associated with it.

- **An effective pop-up blocker.**   This option eliminates a major annoyance and lessens the likelihood that an unsophisticated user will be tricked into clicking an unsafe link. (For information about this feature, see "Blocking Pop-Ups," page 392.)

- **Tighter ActiveX security.**   ActiveX controls are executable programs that enable or enhance features in other programs, such as Internet Explorer. This powerful feature can be abused, however; ActiveX controls can deliver spyware, adware, or other hostile code. With SP2 installed,an improved notification dialog box helps you decide whether to install an ActiveX control, and you can block all downloads from publishers you don't trust.

- **An interface to control browser add-ons.**   The open architecture of Internet Explorer makes it easy to add toolbars, search panes, and utility programs that expand the capabilities of the browser. Used properly, this feature can make Web browsing more productive. Unfortunately, poorly written add-ons can cause frequent browser crashes, and some add-ons contain code that produces undesired effects, such as spawning pop-up windows or redirecting the browser to unwanted sites. With the new tool, you can see which add-ons are installed and disable or remove those you don't want as well as those that have been shown to cause crashes.

- **An Information Bar to alert you to security risks.**   The Information Bar, a narrow band just below the Internet Explorer toolbar, appears in response to events such as a blocked pop-up window or an attempt to download a program or install an ActiveX control. Clicking the Information Bar opens a menu that includes commands for accepting the blocked action and getting more information about the potential risks.

- **New advanced security settings.**   SP2 improves several important security options that are generally invisible or are buried several layers deep in dialog boxes. The most important of these settings tighten the existing Security Zone features and add new choices on the Advanced tab of the Internet Options dialog box.

Unfortunately, the Internet Explorer 6 security changes that are part of Windows XP SP2 are not available for Windows 2000. If you're using Internet Explorer 5 with Windows 2000, upgrade to Internet Explorer 6; even without the SP2 enhancements, version 6 is a significant improvement over Internet Explorer 5. You can get the newer browser version from Windows Update or by visiting *http://www.microsoft.com/downloads/*. We do not recommend the use of Internet Explorer 5, nor do we cover its features in this book.

Installing Windows XP SP2 (or Internet Explorer 6 on computers running Windows 2000) is a good first step, but it's also important to stay up to date. Because Internet Explorer is your computer's primary interface with the outside world, it's often the target of choice for attackers who are continually looking for new vulnerabilities.

In addition to periodic security updates, Windows XP users can look forward to Internet Explorer 7, which has a heavy emphasis on security improvements as well as feature enhancements. Again, Windows 2000 users are left behind; Microsoft has announced that Internet Explorer 7 will not run on that operating system.

Chapter 12

When Web Pages Go Bad

Even if you restrict your Web browsing to a carefully selected list of "safe" sites, you could fall victim to an outside attack that takes advantage of a previously undiscovered security vulnerability in Internet Explorer. (The security experts at Microsoft fix each new vulnerability as it's discovered, but you can be certain that hackers are working overtime to find new exploits.) If you mistype a Web address, for instance, you could end up at a site that contains malicious or hostile code; pranksters and miscreants are notorious for registering domain names that are similar to those of known, trusted sites, in hopes of snagging unwitting visitors. In fact, you don't even have to open a browser window to fall victim to one of these exploits. The components that make up Internet Explorer are tightly integrated into Windows and into other programs, including Microsoft Outlook Express and other e-mail programs that render HTML-based messages. Although Microsoft and other browser vendors have made huge strides in securing browsers and preventing new exploits, detecting and patching these security holes is an ongoing problem that will never be completely solved.

Some Internet security holes involve the deliberate misuse of basic features in the architecture of Internet Explorer, such as extra-long URLs that are specifically crafted to overwhelm internal buffers that hold data. These "buffer overflow" exploits can interrupt the normal execution of code, leaving the operating system in a state in which ordinary security precautions literally stop working. An attacker who sends a specific string of characters to a computer that is in this perilous state can install a virus or a Trojan horse, steal data, or alter the system configuration. Usually, the only certain defense against this sort of attack is to fix the underlying software so that it checks data buffers properly and discards URLs that are potentially harmful.

Another class of security holes in Internet Explorer involves the use—or misuse—of some form of *active content*. In Windows parlance, active content refers to scripts or executable items—in the form of ActiveX controls and Java applets—embedded in or called from the HTML code that makes up the pages you download from the Web. The powerful capabilities of these components bring the Internet to life, allowing Web pages to do more interesting things than simply display text and hyperlinks. Without these extensions, much of the Web would be about as interesting and lively as a C-SPAN marathon. Allowing scripts, ActiveX controls, and Java applets to run on your computer, however, increases the risk that a poorly written or intentionally hostile bit of code will make unauthorized use of your computer's resources.

With Microsoft and other vendors making ever more secure browsers, attackers now direct more of their attacks on users (by using various social engineering tricks to encourage you to run a malicious program) instead of on vulnerabilities in the browser. In other words, the biggest problem today is malware that users (unknowingly) choose to install, rather than malware that comes in through a browser vulnerability.

By configuring Internet Explorer properly and browsing wisely, you can manage risk so that you enjoy an acceptable level of Web functionality without endangering your computer or network.

Just Around the Corner: Internet Explorer 7

At the time of this book's publication, Microsoft engineers were hard at work putting final touches on the first beta release of Internet Explorer 7. The new version promises plenty of nifty features, from tabbed browsing to extensive support for RSS discovery and viewing. While those features are nice to have, for many the main appeal of Internet Explorer 7 is security, a primary focus of its developers. Promised security improvements include:

- "Low Rights IE," in which Internet Explorer will be run in a low-privilege context by default. Because administrative privileges are necessary for malicious software to inflict the most damage, and because ordinary Web browsing has little need for such elevated privileges, this feature should have a huge impact. (The bad news? Because Low Rights IE requires some features that are available only in Windows Vista, it won't affect Windows XP.)

- Prevention of cross-domain scripting. A comprehensive redesign of the way cross-domain boundaries and scripting interact should eliminate this source of many Internet Explorer 6 vulnerabilities.

- A more apparent and more intuitive interface for working with secure Web sites. It should be clear who owns an SSL site.

- Protection against phishing exploits. Better URL parsing, checking against a list of valid URLs and known phishing URLs, improvements to the Address bar so that a site's true URL is apparent, and warnings of possible threats should make phishing expeditions less profitable.

- Increased protection against download vulnerabilities.

- Tools and an interface to promote safe browsing practices.

We can hardly wait. Internet Explorer 7 is expected to be available for Windows XP SP2 and Microsoft Windows Server 2003 SP1 in late 2005.

Following Safe Browsing Practices

Based on one recent survey of crashes submitted via the Online Crash Analysis tool in Windows XP, Microsoft concluded that roughly half of reported failures in the Windows operating system are directly traceable to what it calls "deceptive software."

How does deceptive software end up on a computer? The simplest route is the most direct: you click a link on a Web page or in an e-mail message that leads directly to an executable file. An advertisement might make extravagant claims about a free program (often written as an ActiveX control). When an unsophisticated computer user clicks that ad, the program offers to install itself via a Microsoft Authenticode dialog box, which can easily be mistaken for an official Windows stamp of approval. In some cases, the setup routine for one program surreptitiously installs additional programs in the background. When we installed one widely used song-swapping program on a pre-SP2 version of Windows XP, for instance, we found that it installed four well-hidden add-ins along with the main application, resulting in an increase in pop-up advertisements and changes to the way the browser handles search requests and mistyped URLs. The most vicious types of deceptive software typically attempt to exploit security holes to install themselves automatically, without your approval or even your knowledge.

The makers of this sort of software employ all sorts of tricks to mislead, deceive, and cajole you into installing their wares, by extolling the program's benefits and glossing over or omitting any mention of its undesirable behavior. For someone with a basic understanding of computer security issues, the principal security concern when browsing is to ensure (insofar as it is possible) that anything you download is safe and that any potentially undesirable behavior is fully disclosed. If you share a computer or network with unsophisticated computer users who cannot reasonably be expected to consistently reject unsafe software, your goal should be to prevent them from having to make potentially confusing choices in the first place.

> **Caution**   Be especially wary of windows that pop up and indicate that you have a security problem. If you have any doubts about why a window or dialog box appeared, close it. But do not close it by clicking a "Yes," "Agree," or "OK" button, which often leads to a deceptive software purveyor's site. And don't click the "No" or "Cancel" buttons either; some crooks program those buttons to lead to the same devious sites. Instead, safely close the window by pressing Alt+F4 or clicking the Close button (the red X in the window's upper-right corner).

It is possible to browse in relative safety. Be sure to follow these safe browsing practices:

- Avoid questionable Web sites, such as sites dealing in pornography or pirated music, video, or software. For some reason, many of these shady characters also deal in undesirable software and browser-based exploits.

- Ensure that all security updates have been installed and that your virus definitions are up to date. Install an anti-spyware program with real-time scanning capability, such as Microsoft Windows AntiSpyware.

- When the Information Bar or an Internet Explorer dialog box appears, read it carefully. Be sure you understand exactly what happens if you tell Internet Explorer to proceed with a blocked action. If it's downloading or installing software, ensure that the software is safe and its publisher is trustworthy.

- Be sure that the site being displayed actually belongs to the company you think it does. "Phishing" attacks use bogus links in an e-mail message or Web site to take you to a phony Web site, where the perpetrators try to entice you to hand over personal information. Examining the Address bar isn't enough; past vulnerabilities in Internet Explorer, Firefox, and other browsers have allowed phishers to disguise it. If you have any reason to suspect a link, instead of clicking it type the URL in your browser's Address bar or use a Favorites shortcut that you created. For more information about phishing, see "Avoiding Losses from 'Phishing' Attacks," page 591.

- Send confidential information (such as credit card numbers) only to secure Web sites—that is, sites protected by Secure Sockets Layer (SSL) encryption. The URL for these sites always begins with *https:*, and Internet Explorer shows a lock icon in the status bar when you're connected to a secure site. Double-clicking the lock icon displays the site's security certificate. For details, see "Protecting Your Identity," page 587.

For more details about deceptive software and its avoidance, see "Blocking Unwanted Software" page 436.

Safe Browsing and Cookies

Proper management of cookies—the bits of information about you that a browser stores on your computer at the request of a Web site—is part of a safe browsing strategy too. But "proper" management does not mean you should block all cookies. As we explain in "Managing Cookies," page 595, most cookies are not harmful in any way. In that section, we offer a simple strategy to help you block cookies that might violate your privacy.

Using the Information Bar

Beginning with the version included with Windows XP SP2, Internet Explorer contains a new element called the Information Bar. As Figure 12-1 shows, this thin band appears above the contents of the current Web page, just below any visible toolbars.

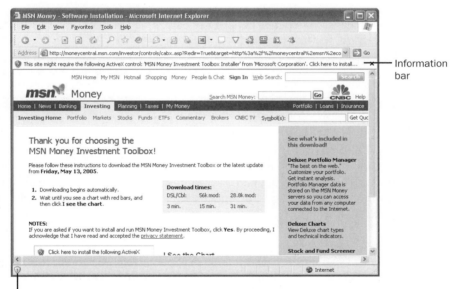

Information bar

Windows Security icon

Figure 12-1. Whenever the Information Bar appears, the Windows Security icon indicates that Windows took a security precaution on your behalf.

The Information Bar appears in response to events that previously might have triggered a warning dialog box, such as a blocked pop-up window or an attempt to download a program or install an ActiveX control. Instead of having to deal with an intrusive dialog box, this relatively subtle notification alerts you to the event; if you want to act on it, you need to click the Information Bar and choose the appropriate action from the context menu.

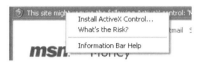

> **Tip** Use the keyboard to get to the Information Bar
>
> As with virtually every part of the Windows interface, you can navigate to the Information Bar without using a mouse. Press Tab or Shift+Tab to move the focus around the browser window. The Information Bar follows the last browser toolbar in tab sequence. When the Information Bar changes color to indicate that it has been selected, press the Application key or Shift+F10—two standard keyboard shortcuts for displaying a shortcut menu—to display its menu.

Settings for the Information Bar are enabled on the basis of security zones. If you want to disable the Information Bar for a particular type of behavior, you can do so on a zone-by-zone basis. When you disable an SP2 security feature in this fashion, Internet Explorer uses the less restrictive behavior of earlier versions of Windows XP. (For more information, see "Using Security Zones," page 405.)

> For more details about the Information Bar, the specific types of actions that trigger it, and the messages and menu options it offers, see Microsoft Knowledge Base (KB) article 843017.

Blocking Pop-Ups

Beginning with the version shipped with Windows XP Service Pack 2, Internet Explorer includes a tool called Pop-up Blocker that can eliminate most pop-up windows. With this feature turned on, you'll be spared the annoyance of advertising that appears unbidden in windows lying either over or under the Web sites you visit. Indirectly, at least, pop-ups are also a security risk, because many of them are enticements for deceptive software.

> **Note** Internet Explorer 6 in Windows 2000 does not include Pop-up Blocker. Programs with comparable capability are widely available, however. MSN Search Toolbar (*http: //toolbar.msn.com*) and Google Toolbar (*http://toolbar.google.com*), for example, include pop-up blockers. Pop-up blockers that are not part of a comprehensive toolbar package are also available; Pop-Up Stopper (*http://www.panicware.com/product_psfree.html*) and Popup Manager (*http://www.endpopups.com*) both work well.

Pop-up Blocker is turned on by default. To determine or change its status, in Internet Explorer choose Tools, Pop-Up Blocker. If the feature is on, the Pop-Up Blocker submenu displays a command to turn it off—and vice versa. You can also enable or disable

Pop-up Blocker by choosing Tools, Internet Options. On the Privacy tab, select or clear Block Pop-Ups.

In its default configuration, Pop-up Blocker suppresses most new windows that are spawned directly by Web sites you visit. (Pop-up Blocker calls these "automatic pop-ups.") If you click a link that opens a new window, Pop-up Blocker assumes you want the new window to open and does not interfere. You can configure Pop-up Blocker to be more or less permissive; see the next section, "Setting the Filter Level."

By default, Pop-up Blocker affects only sites in the Internet and Restricted Sites security zones; it does not block pop-ups spawned by sites in the Local Intranet and Trusted Sites zones. For information about changing these settings, see "Blocking Pop-Ups in the Local Intranet or Trusted Sites Security Zone," page 394.

Pop-up Blocker also maintains a list of sites that you want it to ignore. If you regularly visit a site that displays nonbothersome pop-ups, you can add it to your list of exceptions. For details, see "Allowing Pop-Ups from Specific Sites," page 394.

Tip   **Bypass Pop-up Blocker Temporarily**
You might occasionally find it convenient to allow a pop-up window from a particular site, without changing the pop-up blocker so that it always permits pop-ups from that site. To squelch the pop-up blocker temporarily, simply hold down the Ctrl key while clicking the link or command that opens the blocked window. You can also give a temporary pass to a particular site by clicking the Information Bar that appears when a pop-up is suppressed. In the menu that appears, choose Temporarily Allow Pop-Ups to display the just-blocked window.

Setting the Filter Level

Pop-up Blocker offers three levels of blocking:

- **High.**   Pop-up Blocker tries to block all new windows, including those initiated by the user. Some Web sites and ActiveX controls will not work properly with this setting.

- **Medium.**   Pop-up Blocker allows new windows that result from links you click. This is the default blocking level.

- **Low.**   Pop-up Blocker tries to permit all new windows except those that open automatically when you visit a Web site. Pop-up Blocker also allows all new windows that open from a secure (SSL) Web site.

To set the blocking level, choose Tools, Pop-Up Blocker, Pop-Up Blocker Settings. (Alternatively, you can choose Tools, Internet Options; on the Privacy tab, click Settings.) In the Pop-Up Blocker Settings dialog box, shown in Figure 12-2 on the next page, select one of the Filter Level options.

Chapter 12

Figure 12-2. In addition to setting the Filter Level, you can use the Pop-Up Blocker Settings dialog box to modify the list of exempted Web sites and configure notification options.

Allowing Pop-Ups from Specific Sites

Because some Web sites might not function properly if they aren't allowed to generate pop-ups, and because you might actually welcome pop-up advertising from particular sites, Pop-up Blocker maintains an exception list of exempted URLs. These URLs are user-specific and are stored as values in the registry key HKCU\Software\Microsoft\Internet Explorer\New Windows\Allow.

If the pop-up blocker suppresses a pop-up from a site that you want to be on the exception list, click the Information Bar, and choose Allow Pop-Ups From This Site. If you know in advance that you want to exempt a site, choose Tools, Pop-Up Blocker, Pop-Up Blocker Settings. In the Pop-Up Blocker Settings dialog box, shown in Figure 12-2, type the address of the Web site you want to exempt, and click Add. An asterisk (*) in a site address acts as a wildcard; Pop-up Blocker allows pop-ups from a site regardless of the text in the wildcard part of the address. For example, creating an exception for *.microsoft.com allows pop-ups from *www.microsoft.com*, *support.microsoft.com*, *downloads.microsoft.com*, and so on.

Blocking Pop-Ups in the Local Intranet or Trusted Sites Security Zone

By default, Pop-up Blocker pays no attention to pop-ups from sites in the Local Intranet and Trusted Sites security zones, which are presumed to be friendly. If you want to enable blocking in either or both of these security zones, follow these steps:

1 Choose Tools, Internet Options, and click the Security tab.

2 Select the zone you want to adjust and click Custom Level.

3 Near the bottom of the list in the Settings box, under the heading Use Pop-Up Blocker, select Enable.

Downloading Executable Files

Software of all types is now routinely distributed over the Internet. Many legitimate programs, particularly from smaller publishers, are available only by downloading an executable installation file; an installation CD simply isn't offered. Paying careful attention to the download process is a vital part of safe browsing.

In Windows 2000 (and in Windows XP without SP2), a single dialog box typically stands between your computer and a piece of hostile code. This dialog box, shown in Figure 12-3, appears when you click a link to download an executable file, but it displays only basic information about the file, such as its name. If you click Open, Internet Explorer begins downloading and then immediately running the file, with no further warning. If you click Save, after Internet Explorer downloads the file, it offers to run the file—again with no additional information or warnings. The burden is on you to be certain that it's a file you want and trust.

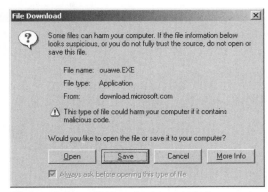

Figure 12-3.   Clicking the More Info button doesn't display more information about a particular file; it merely opens a window with general information about downloading files.

In Windows XP SP2, you have additional layers of protection. When you click a link that points directly to an executable program file, Windows displays a Security Warning dialog box like the one shown in Figure 12-4 on the next page.

Figure 12-4. When you click a download link, Windows XP SP2 provides similar information to earlier versions, but you must subsequently approve another, more detailed warning before you can install.

If you click Save, Internet Explorer downloads the file to your hard disk. After the download is complete, you can run the program by clicking Run in the Download Complete dialog box or by double-clicking the icon for the program in the folder where you saved it. In either case, you see a second Security Warning dialog box, as shown in Figure 12-5. The color of the Windows security icon in the lower left corner of the dialog box indicates whether the program is digitally signed; a red icon indicates an unsigned program, and a yellow icon identifies a signed program. (A blue icon appears for downloads that are not executable, such as Word documents.) If you're certain that the program is safe, click Run.

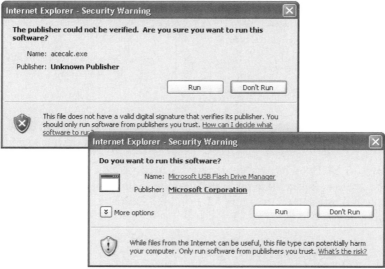

Figure 12-5. After the download is complete, Internet Explorer displays a Security Warning dialog box. The dialog box for an unsigned executable file (top) includes a sterner warning, whereas the box for a digitally signed file (bottom) includes links to its certificates.

> **Tip** How do you know a program is safe?
> When an executable file isn't digitally signed, it's impossible to make a definitive determination of who created the file and whether it's safe. In those circumstances, you can't be too cautious. In our experience, you can tip the odds in your favor by using common sense. Make sure the download is from a verifiable source. Use your favorite search engine to look for complaints about the program or its publisher—be sure to search the Web and Usenet newsgroups via Google Groups (*http://groups.google.com*)—and don't install anything until you're comfortable that you can resolve any documented problems if they crop up on your computer. Be sure to scan any downloaded files for viruses and spyware before installing. Finally, set a System Restore point before installing any software, so that you can undo the configuration changes if you're unhappy with the installation.

Dealing with Automatic Downloads

Some Web pages are designed to initiate downloads automatically when you navigate to the page in your browser. In some cases, the page designer's intent is to be helpful by supplying download or installation instructions on the page and by asking the user to approve the download. However, this tactic can be abused by unscrupulous Web site owners who display a download dialog box and use the text on the underlying page to convince the user that a potentially harmful program is actually benign. If the user tries to cancel the dialog box, it may pop back up repeatedly—a "social engineering" trick designed to confuse the visitor into clicking OK to get rid of the annoying prompts.

Automatic downloads are blocked by new security features in SP2. When you encounter a page in the Internet zone that tries to force a download that the user does not initiate by clicking on a page element, the following message appears in the Information Bar: "To help protect your security, Internet Explorer blocked this site from downloading files to your computer. Click here for options..."

> **Note** This prompt might appear even when you click a page element, if that click runs a script that opens another page that is coded to prompt for a download. Automatic downloads from Web sites that are in the Trusted Sites zone are not blocked.

If you didn't intend to download a file, you can safely ignore the prompt, and it won't be repeated—SP2 limits download prompts to once per page access. If you want to download the file, click the Information Bar and choose Download Software. This action eliminates the block; you can proceed with the download as described in the previous section.

Chapter 12

Troubleshooting

An automatic download fails

You visit a Web page that attempts to automatically download a file, but after you click the Information Bar the download doesn't begin. What happened? The most likely explanation is that the Web designer has used a script on the page that is supposed to cause the browser to begin the download and then jump to a new page. If the script doesn't check to see whether downloading blocking is in place, the download doesn't have a chance to begin—and you're left looking at a new page. Click the Back button to reenter the page. If it still fails, look for a direct link to the download; most page designers provide this alternative for use by visitors who have scripting disabled. If that fails, and you are certain the site is trustworthy, consider adding the site to the Trusted Sites zone and then reloading the page; be sure to remove the site from the Trusted Sites zone after the download is complete.

Controlling ActiveX Downloads

ActiveX controls are small programs that enhance the functionality of a Web site, using a technology developed by Microsoft. They're used for such things as enabling the capability for you to play games with other Internet users, displaying stock tickers, and displaying animation. Windows Update and Microsoft Update use an ActiveX control to compare installed updates on your system with those available on servers at Microsoft. ActiveX controls can be written in any programming language that supports the Microsoft Component Object Model (COM), and these controls are implemented as .ocx or .dll files. Like programs that you run from the Start menu or a command line, they have essentially full access to your computer's resources, although they are subject to some security restrictions.

Unlike Java applets (discussed later in this chapter), ActiveX controls are native Windows programs capable of doing nearly anything that other Windows programs can do, limited only by the permissions available to your user account. Unless you are using a severely restricted account, you should assume that any ActiveX control you download has full access to your file system, registry, and hardware. Once downloaded from the Internet and registered on your system, ActiveX controls can run automatically or be activated by external code, such as script embedded in a malevolent Web page.

Note You cannot download an ActiveX control, scan it for viruses, and install it separately. By design, ActiveX controls must be installed on the fly. Although the inability to scan for viruses might sound like a security risk, you're safe if you've configured your antivirus software to perform real-time scanning for hostile code. If the ActiveX control contains the signature of a known virus or worm, the antivirus software will intercept it and refuse to allow the installation to proceed. As with any program you download and install, of course, you must exercise caution and good judgment and ensure that the download is safe before allowing it on your computer.

The default settings for controlling the download and installation of ActiveX controls are normally sufficient, but they're not easy to check. (For details, see "ActiveX Security Settings," page 416.) We've developed a simple script that displays the current setting and provides a fast and easy way to change it. You can find the script, called ActiveX_toggle.vbs, on this book's companion CD. For a full discussion of the ActiveX_toggle.vbs script, see "Add extra security to ActiveX," page 440.

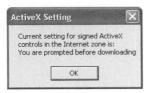

The following sections explain how to control the download and installation of ActiveX controls while you browse the Internet. For information about working with ActiveX controls after they've been installed, see "Managing ActiveX Controls," page 425. For details about security settings that control their installation and use, see "ActiveX Security Settings," page 416.

Controlling ActiveX Downloads in Windows 2000

To help you decide whether downloading an ActiveX control is an acceptable risk, Microsoft employs a digital signing technology it calls Authenticode. Internet Explorer checks the validity of the certificate and decides how to handle the control.

In the default security settings for the Internet zone (the broad category of Web sites that you have not elevated to higher-trust status or demoted to lower-trust status), Internet Explorer prompts you for permission to download a signed control and blocks any controls without a valid signature. The security warning for a signed control in Windows 2000 (and in Windows XP without SP2), shown in Figure 12-6, can be a bit difficult to comprehend.

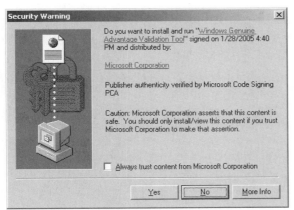

Figure 12-6. Click the company name to see the publisher's certificate.

> **Caution** It's easy for a software developer to fill the fields for the name of the software with a lengthy description practically guaranteed to fool an unsophisticated user. If you see an offer such as "Essential Windows update – Install immediately!!!" from a publisher you've never heard of, click No. (And you might consider moving a site that offers such a control to the Restricted Sites zone.)

As you can see, the Security Warning dialog box doesn't tell you much about the component you're considering downloading. You can't even tell whether the component is an ActiveX control or a Java applet. It does provide the name of the component's publisher, however, and by clicking the publisher's name, you can see the certificate that was used to sign the component, as shown in Figure 12-7.

Figure 12-7. Clicking the publisher's name lets you see the certificate that was used to sign the control.

Unless you have explicitly given the browser permission to download unsigned controls (by changing one of the default security settings), you can be assured that the signature and certificate are valid. If for some reason you want to look at the certificate, however, the time to do so is before you accept the control. Internet Explorer does not download the certificate. (You can import it, however. After clicking the publisher's name to display the certificate, click Install Certificate. Internet Explorer then installs the certificate and makes it visible on the Other People tab of the Certificates dialog box. For more information about the Certificates dialog box, see "Using the Certificates Dialog Box," page 683.)

Tip The Authenticode dialog box shown in Figure 12-6 includes a check box that, when selected, causes Internet Explorer to accept without further prompting all controls this publisher offers in the future. We recommend declining this offer. Even the most trustworthy companies that produce only the finest, fully vetted, bug-free software produce some software that you simply don't need. It's worth taking a few seconds to consider the need for new software each time it's offered.

Controlling ActiveX Downloads in Windows XP SP2

Microsoft drastically reworked the ActiveX download interface in Windows XP SP2. When code on a Web page tries to install an ActiveX control on a computer running Windows XP SP2, you see one of two warning messages in the Information Bar:

- If the control is unsigned, the message reads "To help protect your security, Internet Explorer stopped this site from installing software on your computer. Click here for options..." If you decide to overrule this decision by clicking the Information Bar and then choosing Install ActiveX Control from the menu, you see a dialog box with a red Windows security icon and the stern message shown here. Click OK to return to the page. The ActiveX control is not installed.

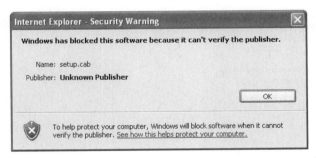

- If the control is digitally signed, the message reads "This site might require the following ActiveX control: '*control_name*' from '*publisher_name*'. Click here to install..." In this case, you can allow the download to continue by clicking the Information Bar and then choosing Install ActiveX Control from the menu. The Security Warning dialog box displays a yellow icon, along with the name of the program and its publisher. Click More Options to see the full dialog box, as shown in Figure 12-8 on the next page. If you're certain the program is safe, click Install to continue; click Don't Install if you're not confident about the program's safety.

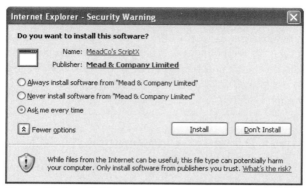

Figure 12-8. Clicking More Options gives you the choice of always allowing or always refusing future software downloads that are signed by the same publisher.

In the Security Warning dialog box, note that the publisher's name is a hyperlink. Click this link to see details about the certificate used to sign the program. This information does not guarantee that the program is safe to install or use, but it can give you a high degree of confidence about the developer of the software—information you can use to make an informed decision about whether to install the program.

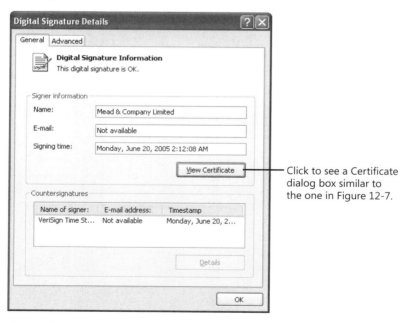

Click to see a Certificate dialog box similar to the one in Figure 12-7.

If this form of acceptance is too liberal for your tastes, you can tighten ActiveX-related security settings; for details, see "ActiveX Security Settings," page 416. If you do that and then visit a page that uses an ActiveX control, you might see this message in the Information Bar: "Your security settings do not allow ActiveX controls to run on this page.

This page may not display correctly. Click here for options..." To work around this error, you need to change the appropriate security setting for the Internet zone or add the site you're visiting to the Trusted Sites zone.

Deciding Whom to Trust

Authenticode digital signing technology attests only to its authenticity and integrity. It guarantees that the control you're about to download (or not download, as you choose) comes from the party it says it comes from and that it has not been changed in any way since the time it was signed. The digital signature verifies each bit of the signed file by comparing it to a hash value; if even a single bit of the file has changed, the comparison fails and the signature is deemed invalid. Windows XP SP2 blocks installation of any code that has an invalid signature—by definition, this indicates that the program file is corrupt or has been tampered with. The signature does *not* attest to the benevolence of the control or the competence of its creator.

For a file with a valid signature, use the information in the signature to make an additional determination: whether you trust the person or organization that signed the file. The computer can't make this determination for you; only you can decide if you trust the publisher to deliver software that is not harmful.

Windows includes a check box in the dialog box for signed downloads that allows you to specify that you always trust the publisher using that certificate. (See Figure 12-6 on page 399.) By selecting this check box, you can automatically install future downloads from your favorite publishers without having to see the Security Warning dialog box.

As shown in Figure 12-8, Windows XP SP2 adds the counterpart to that feature—a check box that lets you identify a publisher as untrusted. If you determine that a particular company's ActiveX controls and programs don't belong on your computer, you can designate that publisher as untrusted, and no user of your computer will be able to install software that uses that publisher's digital certificate.

To block programs from a given publisher if you're using Windows XP SP2, follow these steps:

1 Visit a Web page that attempts to install an ActiveX control.
2 Click the Information Bar and choose Install ActiveX Control. The Authenticode dialog box opens.
3 Choose the Never Install Software From *Publisher* option.
4 Click Don't Install.

After you make this choice, Internet Explorer notifies you any time you visit a site that tries to install or use software from the untrusted publisher. A Manage Add-Ons icon appears in the status bar, along with a balloon tip to alert you that an add-on or program has been disabled or blocked, as shown on the next page.

To remove a publisher from the Untrusted Publishers list, in Internet Explorer choose Tools, Internet Options. On the Content tab, click Publishers. In the Certificates dialog box, click the Untrusted Publishers tab, select the publisher name, and click Remove.

Caution   Do not remove the two Microsoft Corporation entries from the Untrusted Publishers list. As the text in the Friendly Name column alludes, these two entries represent certificates that VeriSign mistakenly issued several years ago to an untrusted source claiming to represent Microsoft Corporation. The revocation means that a ne'er-do-well can't exploit these phony certificates to install a virus or Trojan horse program that appears to have been published by Microsoft.

Using Least Privilege When Browsing the Internet

Programs that you run while logged on to your computer generally enjoy all the privileges that are granted to your user account. If your account has sufficient user rights and has been granted permission to access certain files, change certain registry keys, and perform other tasks—tasks that can be essential to completing your job if done properly, but potentially disastrous if done maliciously—then programs you run can perform those same tasks, with the same risks. It's for this reason that computer security professionals recommend using a "least privilege" account—one that provides only enough access for a person to perform his or her job. Aaron Margosis of Microsoft is a strong proponent of this approach; his blog (*http://blogs.msdn.com/aaron_margosis/*) offers detailed advice and tools for its implementation.

For more information, see "Following Best Practices for Your Everyday Account," page 103.

Unfortunately, that's not always feasible and most people end up routinely using an account with administrator (or near-administrator) privileges. However, even if you log on using an administrator account, you can limit your exposure to malicious programs while browsing the Web, the source of most attacks. You do that by running Internet Explorer (or whatever browser you use) with a restricted, or "low-rights" token—one that has severely limited privileges. In a low-rights context, for example, a program cannot make changes to the registry or to files in the %SystemRoot%\System32 folder.

Tip   Using a low-rights context is a smart way to run your e-mail and instant messaging programs too, as they provide other common ways for attackers to try to take over your computer.

If, while running as an administrator, you let your guard down and are enticed to download and install a program that turns out to be a worm or other type of malware, you'll suddenly have a greater appreciation for browsing the Web and e-mail using least privilege. As an example, several variants of the Bagle worm that circulated widely throughout much of 2005 rely on administrator-only tasks such as disabling Windows Firewall, writing files to system folders, and deleting registry values. Without administrative privileges, the worm is effectively neutered—even if you do make the mistake of running it.

The Run As command provides one way to run a program with low privileges, but it's somewhat inconvenient. (For information about Run As, see "Using Run As When You Need Administrative Privileges," page 106.) Michael Howard, a Senior Security Program Manager with the Microsoft Secure Engineering group, has written a program called DropMyRights that makes it easy to run your browser, e-mail, instant messaging, and other programs with low privileges. You can read all about the program and download it by visiting *http://msdn.microsoft.com/security/securecode/columns/default.aspx?pull= /library/en-us/dncode/html/secure11152004.asp.*

Note DropMyRights uses a feature called Software Restriction Policy, which is available only with Windows XP and Windows Server 2003. Therefore, you can't use DropMyRights to protect a computer running Windows 2000.

Note Running a browser with the most limited privileges enabled by DropMyRights, "constrained" or "untrusted," can cause some legitimate sites not to work properly. In particular, you cannot browse secure (SSL) sites.

The future of Web browsing involves low rights; it's just too dangerous out there to run as an administrator. Using low rights now is a bit of a chore, but Microsoft has announced that this capability will be built in to Internet Explorer 7 running on Windows Vista, the successor to Windows XP, which is due in 2006. Although Internet Explorer 7 promises many other security improvements and feature enhancements for Windows XP users (Internet Explorer 7 will not be available for Windows 2000), the so-called "Low Rights IE" feature relies on security features available only in Windows Vista.

Using Security Zones

The principal tool that all versions of Internet Explorer since 4.0 have provided is a set of security "zones." With these zones, you can segregate the Web sites you visit into categories, depending on the degree of trust you accord them. To each zone, you can apply a constellation of security settings so that the sites you trust are given greater latitude than the ones you do not trust.

Chapter 12

Caution Changes to Internet Explorer's security settings also affect other applications that use the Windows HTML rendering engine, including (among others) Outlook Express, Microsoft Outlook, and other e-mail clients; Microsoft Windows Media Player; Help and Support; Microsoft Money; and Quicken. This shared functionality has its benefits, of course: by securing Internet Explorer you also secure the HTML component of other applications that rely on Internet Explorer for HTML rendering. But shared functionality can also mean shared vulnerabilities. For example, the Klez worm—a piece of malware that spread widely in 2002—exploits a vulnerability that allows it to execute itself when you open or merely preview an infected message in Outlook Express or Outlook. Because Microsoft fixed this particular vulnerability early in 2001, users of Windows XP or Windows 2000 who applied the update or a subsequent service pack have not been affected. (Such users can, however, still contract the virus by manually running the file attached to an infected message.) The Klez episode offers two important lessons: vulnerabilities in Internet Explorer can have impacts on other applications, and you must keep current on security updates.

Security zones provide a primary line of defense against Internet exploits. By default, all Web sites you visit are assigned to the Internet zone, and Internet Explorer severely restricts the types of actions that can be taken by sites in the Internet zone. As we explain in this section, you can lock down the Internet zone and other security zones even more tightly if you like.

Internet Explorer gives you four configurable security zones by default:

- The Local Intranet zone is for sites within your organization or behind your firewall. These sites are typically accorded a high level of trust.

- The Trusted Sites zone is for sites where you want to allow certain actions, such as running ActiveX controls or scripts, that you might not permit on other sites in which you have a lower degree of trust. This zone is empty on a clean installation of Windows.

- The Restricted Sites zone is for sites where you want to prevent actions that might otherwise be permitted. This zone, which is also empty on a clean installation of Windows, is the default zone for HTML-formatted e-mail messages you read with Outlook or Outlook Express.

- The Internet zone is for all sites that don't fall into any of the other categories.

Note The right end of the status bar in Internet Explorer displays the icon and the name of the zone for the currently displayed Web page. A page identified as Unknown (Mixed) zone contains one or more frames from different zones.

Inside Out

Lock down the Local Machine zone

A fifth zone, called Local Machine (often referred to as My Computer), is not normally configurable and its settings are not displayed on the Security tab of the Internet Options dialog box. This zone is for content that is stored on the local computer. In Windows 2000 (and in Windows XP without SP2), content opened from a local file system is considered secure, which, it turns out, is not always true. Items such as ActiveX controls that were installed on your computer by Windows itself (as opposed to being downloaded from the Internet) run under the security settings of the Local Machine zone. File URLs that reference local documents also run in the Local Machine zone. Although this design seems logical, it also allows security vulnerabilities that outside attackers have successfully exploited. By convincing Internet Explorer that a Web page or a chunk of hostile code is running in the Local Machine zone, an attacker could read files and install programs, actions that aren't permitted in the Internet zone.

That all changes with SP2, which introduced a new set of restrictions called Local Machine Zone Lockdown that block scripts, objects (such as ActiveX controls), and actions that are potentially dangerous in the Local Machine zone. Web pages that you save to the desktop or a local folder run under tighter security settings than in pre-SP2 configurations.

With a bit of registry surgery, users of Internet Explorer on Windows 2000 can obtain the same protections afforded by Local Machine Zone Lockdown in SP2. For detailed instructions, see Microsoft KB article 833633. An alternative solution for locking down the Local Machine zone is to first make it visible in the Internet Options dialog box, which you can do with a simple registry change, as explained in KB article 315933. You can then apply settings to it in the same manner as other zones; to lock it down, you'll want to make its settings like those of the Internet zone.

When you open a Web page in Internet Explorer, Windows applies restrictions on what that page can do, based on the security zone for that page. Initially, any sites you connect to internally (that is, your own company's sites, which you access by means of an intranet connection) are automatically assigned to the Local Intranet zone, and the Local Intranet zone is accorded a "medium-low" level of security settings. All the rest of the Internet is lumped into the Internet zone, which is given a "medium" level of security settings. As you roam the Internet, if you come upon a site that you trust implicitly, you can move that site into the Trusted Sites zone. Internet Explorer, by default, applies a "low" level of security settings to the Trusted Sites zone. When you discover a site that warrants a high degree of wariness, you can move that site into the Restricted Sites zone. The security settings that apply there, by default, are described as "high."

Using security zones effectively requires awareness of the types of hazards that exist, an understanding of the various security settings that can be applied to each zone, and some discernment about which Web sites to put in which zones.

To assign sites to zones or configure zones' security settings, start by choosing Tools, Internet Options, and clicking the Security tab. The available zones appear at the top of the tab, as shown in Figure 12-9.

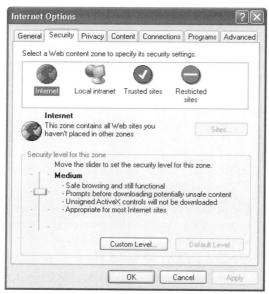

Figure 12-9. The Security tab in the Internet Options dialog box is your starting point for all security-zone operations.

Note   Use the Restricted Sites zone for your e-mail program
Outlook Express, Outlook, and other programs that use Internet Explorer for HTML rendering also use its zones. You can configure such programs to use a particular security zone, and thereafter any HTML that is displayed is subject to the restrictions of that zone. For e-mail, which can harbor more nasties than a tuberculosis ward, you should use the Restricted Sites zone.

To make the setting in either Outlook Express or Outlook, choose Tools, Options, click the Security tab, and then select Restricted Sites Zone. This is the default setting in recent versions of both programs, but it's worth diving into the Options dialog box to confirm that it's set properly.

For more information about securing your e-mail program, see Chapter 15, "Securing E-Mail and Instant Messages."

Configuring the Local Intranet Zone

By default, the Local Intranet zone is set up to include the following site categories:

- All local sites, excepting any that you have added to a different zone
- All sites that you have set up to bypass your proxy server, if your network has one
- All network servers accessed by UNC paths or via My Network Places

Internet Explorer regards any URL without dots, such as *http://localhost*, as a local site. Although this interpretation of URLs led to a vulnerability several years ago when hackers realized that a full 32-bit IP address has no dots, the vulnerability does not affect any version of Internet Explorer 6.

To remove one or more of these default categories from the Local Intranet zone, select Local Intranet on the Security tab of the Internet Options dialog box and click Sites. Then clear the appropriate check box or check boxes on the Local Intranet dialog box, shown in Figure 12-10.

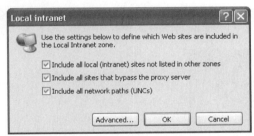

Figure 12-10.   By default, all check boxes are selected in the Local Intranet dialog box.

Adding Sites to a Zone

To add a Web site to a zone, select the zone's icon on the Security tab of the Internet Options dialog box, and then click Sites. (To add a site to the Local Intranet zone, click Sites, and then click Advanced.) A dialog box appears, comparable to the one shown in Figure 12-11 on the next page.

Type or paste the site's URL into the Add This Web Site To The Zone box, and then click OK. To remove a site, select it, and click Remove. Note the following:

- Internet Explorer assumes the HTTP protocol. Entering *www.microsoft.com* is equivalent to entering *http://www.microsoft.com*.
- The Require Server Verification (HTTPS:) For All Sites In This Zone option, included in the dialog boxes for the Local Intranet and Trusted Sites zones (and selected by default), ensures only that the zone you're currently entering is secured with SSL. You can mix and match secure and nonsecure sites in either zone. Simply clear the check box when you want to enter a site that doesn't use the HTTPS protocol.

Chapter 12

- Entering the full path to any page at a Web site adds the entire site to the selected zone. For example, entering *http://www.msnbc.msn.com/id/8487520/* is equivalent to entering *http://www.msnbc.msn.com*. On the other hand, *http://www.msn.com* is not equivalent to *http://www.msnbc.msn.com* or even *http://msn.com*; Internet Explorer treats each of these variants as distinct sites. To cover all these variants with a single entry, use an asterisk wildcard, like this: http://*.msn.com

- If you are accustomed to accessing a Web site by either its DNS name or its IP address, you'll need to create separate security-zone entries for each. For example, suppose you add *http://www.microsoft.com* to your Restricted Sites zone. If you subsequently visit the Microsoft site by navigating to *http://207.46.250.119*, you'll find that the site remains in the Internet zone because you didn't create a separate Restricted Sites entry for the IP address.

- To move a site from one zone to another, first delete it from its current site. Internet Explorer rejects duplicate entries. Note, however, that Internet Explorer will let you put functionally equivalent but differently expressed URLs (IP address and DNS name, for example, or DNS without protocol and DNS with protocol) in different security zones.

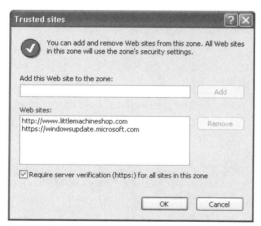

Figure 12-11. You can add or remove sites from any zone except the Internet zone.

Tip Check the list of trusted sites periodically

Programs that run on your computer can add sites to a security zone, thereby giving those sites powers (or restrictions) that you don't intend to grant. America Online, for example, puts its site in the Trusted Sites zone without notifying you. You should periodically review the added sites (especially Trusted Sites) and remove any that you don't want included.

Inside Out

Administering Internet Explorer security settings for others

If you need to create standardized security settings for a workgroup or a domain, you'll want to download the Internet Explorer Administration Kit (IEAK) from *http://www.microsoft.com/windows/ieak/*. The IEAK lets you create and distribute a customized version of Internet Explorer.

If you need to enforce a common security policy for all user accounts at a single computer, you'll find it simpler to use Group Policy (Gpedit.msc). To ensure that all users operate under the same security settings and with the same sites assigned to each security zone, in Group Policy open Computer Configuration\Administrative Templates\Windows Components \Internet Explorer. Enable the policies Security Zones: Do Not Allow Users To Change Policies and Security Zones: Do Not Allow Users To Add/Delete Sites. Then use User Configuration\Windows Settings\Internet Explorer Maintenance\Security\Security Zones And Content Ratings to configure the site assignments and security settings you want to enforce.

You can also use Group Policy to create a machine-wide security policy. (Ordinarily, each user can establish his or her own security settings.) In Computer Configuration\Administrative Templates\Windows Components\Internet Explorer, enable Security Zones: Use Only Machine Settings. (And use User Configuration\Windows Settings\Internet Explorer Maintenance\Security\Security Zones And Content Ratings to set up the machine-wide policies.) Internet Explorer then derives its security settings from the HKLM branch of the registry, instead of from HKCU.

For more information about Group Policy, see "Using the Group Policy Snap-In," page 754.

Configuring Security Settings

Internet Explorer includes four "prepackaged" constellations of security settings and applies them by default to the four standard security zones, as follows:

Security zone	Default security settings
Local Intranet	Medium-Low
Trusted Sites	Low
Restricted Sites	High
Internet	Medium

To change from one group of settings to another, select a zone on the Security tab of the Internet Options dialog box, and then move the Security Level For This Zone slider. If the slider isn't visible, that means that some custom security settings have already been set for that zone. To make the slider reappear, click Default Level. Notice that the settings applied by default to your Trusted Sites zone are more lenient than those applied

Chapter 12

to sites within your organization (Local Intranet zone). If you stick with these defaults, don't give Trusted Sites status to any Web site that you don't trust as much as the servers in your own building. Also be aware that the default settings for the Restricted Sites zone disable essentially anything that moves.

Inside Out

Find custom settings

One problem with the Security tab is that, when one or more nondefault settings are made, the tab simply says "custom," without offering any clues as to what changes have been made. (This longstanding problem in Internet Explorer is supposed to be addressed in Internet Explorer 7.) A partial solution comes from an unexpected place: Microsoft Baseline Security Analyzer (MBSA). (For information about this program, see "Checking Your Update Status with Microsoft Baseline Security Analyzer," page 230.)

Among the many configuration settings that MBSA checks, it examines your security zone settings for possible weaknesses. Near the bottom of an MBSA security report, you should find an issue named IE Zones (under Desktop Application Scan Results, Administrative Vulnerabilities). By that issue, click Result Details and, if any of your security zone settings is lower than Microsoft recommends, it lets you know. Moreover, if a zone is not set to a predefined level at or above the recommended level, a Custom link leads to a list of nonstandard settings.

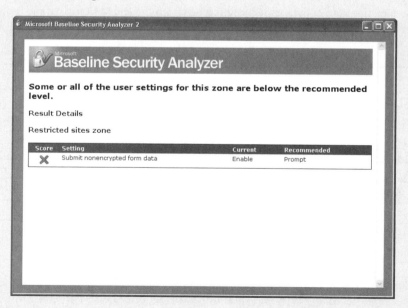

MBSA doesn't check all security tab settings, and it provides details only if your settings are weaker than Microsoft recommends. But at least you get some indication of what "custom level" means.

Making Internet Explorer More Secure

The individual settings associated with each of the security levels in Internet Explorer 6 are listed in Table 12-1. Note that these are factory defaults (as are all defaults mentioned in the following pages). If you are using a copy of Internet Explorer that has been customized by your administrator, your defaults might differ.

> **Caution** Do not make settings in any zone that are lower than the default, and don't change any zone to a lower level than the default. If you do, you can almost certainly look forward to something bad happening. Although more secure settings can mean more inconvenience while browsing, that pales in comparison to the "inconvenience" of a nasty spyware infestation. If you feel compelled to make changes to the security zone settings, make them higher! Consider moving the Internet zone to High security and Trusted Sites to the Medium level.

Table 12-1. **Default Security Settings in Internet Explorer 6**

Security Setting	Low	Medium-Low	Medium	High
.NET Framework-reliant components				
Run components not signed with Authenticode	Enable	Enable	Enable	Disable
Run components signed with Authenticode	Enable	Enable	Enable	Disable
ActiveX controls and plug-ins				
Automatic prompting for ActiveX controls*	Enable	Enable	Disable	Disable
Binary and script behaviors*	Enable	Enable	Enable	Disable
Download signed ActiveX controls	Enable	Prompt	Prompt	Disable
Download unsigned ActiveX controls	Prompt	Disable	Disable	Disable
Initialize and script ActiveX controls not marked as safe	Prompt	Disable	Disable	Disable
Run ActiveX controls and plug-ins	Enable	Enable	Enable	Disable
Script ActiveX controls marked safe for scripting	Enable	Enable	Enable	Disable

Table 12-1. **Default Security Settings in Internet Explorer 6**

Security Setting	Low	Medium-Low	Medium	High
Downloads				
Automatic prompting for file downloads*	Enable	Enable	Disable	Disable
File download	Enable	Enable	Enable	Disable
Font download	Enable	Enable	Enable	Prompt
Java VM (formerly Microsoft VM)				
Java permissions	Low safety	Medium safety	High safety	Disable Java
Miscellaneous				
Access data sources across domains	Enable	Prompt	Disable	Disable
Allow META REFRESH	Enable	Enable	Enable	Disable
Allow scripting of Internet Explorer Web-browser control*	Disable	Disable	Disable	Disable
Allow script-initiated windows without size or position constraints*	Enable	Enable	Disable	Disable
Allow Web pages to use restricted protocols for active content*	Prompt	Prompt	Prompt	Disable
Display mixed content	Prompt	Prompt	Prompt	Prompt
Don't prompt for client certificate selection when no certificates or only one certificate exists	Enable	Enable	Disable	Disable
Drag and drop or copy and paste files	Enable	Enable	Enable	Prompt
Installation of desktop items	Enable	Prompt	Prompt	Disable
Launching programs and files in an IFRAME	Enable	Prompt	Prompt	Disable
Navigate sub-frames across different domains	Enable	Enable	Enable	Disable
Open files based on content, not file extension*	Enable	Enable	Enable	Disable

Table 12-1. **Default Security Settings in Internet Explorer 6**

Security Setting	Low	Medium-Low	Medium	High
Software channel permissions	Low safety	Medium safety	Medium safety	High safety
Submit nonencrypted form data	Enable	Enable	Prompt	Prompt
Use Pop-up Blocker*	Disable	Disable	Enable	Enable
Userdata persistence	Enable	Enable	Enable	Disable
Web sites in less privileged web content zone can navigate into this zone*	Prompt	Enable	Enable	Disable
Scripting				
Active scripting	Enable	Enable	Enable	Disable
Allow paste operations via script	Enable	Enable	Enable	Disable
Scripting of Java applets	Enable	Enable	Enable	Disable
User Authentication				
Logon	Automatic	Automatic logon with current user-name and password	Automatic logon only in Intranet zone	Prompt for user name and password

* Windows XP SP2 only

> **Caution** If you use Windows 2000, you should recognize that certain default settings in Internet Explorer 6 are more restrictive than in Internet Explorer 5, the version installed with Windows 2000. However, if you upgrade Internet Explorer 5 to version 6, most of your security settings are retained. To get the tighter Internet Explorer 6 default settings, visit each zone and reset it to default levels.

Now let's look at the individual security settings. To configure any of these settings, select a zone, click Custom Level, and then fill out the dialog box shown in Figure 12-12 on the next page.

Chapter 12

415

Microsoft Windows XP Networking and Security Inside Out

Figure 12-12. You can configure individual security settings for any zone by using this dialog box.

Note **Before you switch from Enable to Disable, try Prompt**

If you're trying to tighten security but you don't understand what a particular setting does or whether it affects your browsing (which is likely because many of the setting names are inscrutable and not much explanatory information is available), try Prompt for settings where it's an option. (You can always decline the prompt to prevent anything from happening.) That way, you'll find out during the course of browsing whether you're likely to encounter problems by disabling a feature.

.NET Framework Settings

The two settings for .NET Framework-reliant components appear only if you have installed the .NET Framework, an optional component of Windows. Many modern Web-based components are based on the .NET programming platform. Because .NET confines its programs to a secure sandbox without exposing the rest of your computer's resources (in particular, a .NET program is far less capable of inflicting damage than an ActiveX control, and its sandbox is even more restrictive than that of a Java virtual machine), the default settings allow .NET components to install and run in all zones except the Restricted Sites zone, regardless of whether the component is Authenticode-signed. You might consider changing to Prompt or Disable in the Internet zone, particularly for unsigned components.

ActiveX Security Settings

ActiveX controls, because their power makes them potentially dangerous, are tightly restricted by default. Some businesses disallow the use of any ActiveX control that is not approved by an administrator. (For information about this option, see "Permitting Only Administrator-Approved ActiveX Controls to Run," page 428.) Others disallow all ActiveX controls.

The settings in the ActiveX Controls And Plug-Ins group are described below:

- **Automatic Prompting For ActiveX Controls.**   This setting determines whether Windows XP SP2 displays only the Information Bar before allowing downloads (Disable); or displays a dialog box for all ActiveX controls (Enable).

- **Binary And Script Behaviors.**   This setting tightens control over advanced components that use HTML and script to add functionality to a Web page.

- **Download Signed ActiveX Controls.**   This setting determines whether Internet Explorer is allowed to download controls that can be assumed to be authentic and unaltered. No matter how much confidence you have in your most trusted sites, we recommend that you bump this setting from Enable to Prompt in the Trusted Sites zone; the default setting provides unacceptably weak security.

- **Download Unsigned ActiveX Controls.**   By default, Internet Explorer blocks unsigned ActiveX controls without a prompt in all zones but Trusted Sites. You should never download an unsigned control unless you're absolutely certain that it's trustworthy.

- **Initialize And Script ActiveX Controls Not Marked As Safe.**   This setting determines whether Internet Explorer allows initialization and/or scripting of ActiveX controls that don't have the appropriate "safe for" signatures. Unless you're testing a control under development or have some other compelling reason to practice unsafe ActiveX, you don't want to change the defaults for this setting. For information about these signatures, see "The Safe for Initialization and Safe for Scripting Flags," page 427.

- **Run ActiveX Controls And Plug-ins.**   Internet Explorer's default security settings allow it to run downloaded ActiveX controls and plug-ins without a prompt in all zones except Restricted Sites, where controls and plug-ins are disabled. (A plug-in is an installed application used to render Internet content. Adobe Acrobat Reader, which renders the PDF file type, is a widely used plug-in.) If you have concerns about the safety of ActiveX, you might want to tighten this setting—or take advantage of a fourth option, which allows only administrator-approved controls to run. (For details, see "Permitting Only Administrator-Approved ActiveX Controls to Run," page 428.)

- **Script ActiveX Controls Marked Safe For Scripting**.   This setting determines whether ActiveX controls are allowed to interact with scripts. Note that safe-for-initialization controls loaded with <param> tags are not affected by this option.

> For information about what ActiveX controls are and how they're used in Internet Explorer, see "Controlling ActiveX Downloads," page 398.

Chapter 12

Download Settings

Like the corresponding ActiveX setting, the Automatic Prompting For File Downloads setting determines whether Windows XP SP2 displays only the Information Bar before allowing downloads (Disable) or displays a dialog box for all downloads (Enable).

File and font downloads are enabled by default for all zones except Restricted Sites. (File downloads from Restricted Sites are disabled by default; font downloads generate a confirmation prompt.) Provided you have an up-to-date virus checker installed, the defaults are reasonable.

Java Security Settings

The Java VM (Microsoft VM in Windows 2000) section of the Security Settings dialog box appears only if you have a Java virtual machine (VM) installed. (Windows 2000 and the original version of Windows XP include a Java VM, and any installed VM remains in place if you upgrade to Windows XP SP2. A clean installation of Windows XP SP2 does not include Java support by default, although you can install a Java VM separately.) This section of the Security Settings dialog box includes the following options:

- Custom
- Disable Java
- High Safety
- Low Safety
- Medium Safety.

If you choose a High, Low, or Medium Safety setting, Internet Explorer allows applets in the zone to run, provided the permissions requested by the applet do not exceed a certain level. If they do exceed that level, the browser issues a prompt and awaits your decision.

The High Safety setting corresponds to the traditional Java sandbox. For information about the permissions accorded a sandboxed applet, see "Managing Java Applets," page 430.

The Medium Safety setting allows the applet to do the following (in addition to what it can do under High Safety):

- Access scratch space—a storage area on your computer that lets the applet create temporary files without having full use of your file system.
- Perform user-directed file input and output.

Under Low Safety, the applet can also do the following:

- Perform other (not user-directed) file input and output
- Execute other applications on your computer
- Create and use dialog boxes
- Provide thread group access in the current execution context

- Open network connections with computers other than the one hosting the applet
- Load libraries on your computer
- Make calls to Windows dynamic link libraries (DLLs)
- Create a pop-up window without the customary warning that the window was created by an applet
- Exit the Microsoft VM
- Read and write to the registry
- Print
- Create a class loader

In other words, a Java applet running under low security (the default setting for the Trusted Sites zone) could, if it were signed with corresponding permissions requests, become comparable in power to an ActiveX control. If you're not comfortable with that level—and you probably shouldn't be—choose a higher one. Remember that applets that need more power than you grant can still run (unless you disable Java altogether); they just require you to answer a prompt.

If the standard Java security settings don't meet your needs, choose custom and then click the Java Custom Settings button that appears. In the ensuing dialog box, you can do a considerable amount of fine-tuning.

Miscellaneous Security Settings

Virtually every configuration process in Windows has a collection of settings that don't neatly fit anywhere else. Security Settings is no exception, and you'll find that collection under the Miscellaneous heading.

- **Access Data Sources Across Domains.** This setting determines whether a component (an ActiveX control or an applet) that needs to connect to a data source is allowed to connect to a domain other than the one from which it was downloaded. Because cross-domain access is potentially hazardous, Internet Explorer does not permit this by default in the Internet or Restricted Sites zone.
- **Allow META REFRESH.** A META REFRESH tag redirects you to a different server after a specified delay. Usually, this service is benign and welcome because it gives Web site operators a way to leave a forwarding address if they move to a different URL. Because you might not trust the site you're being redirected to, however, Internet Explorer gives you the means to turn META REFRESH off. (With the setting configured to Disable, you can still read the forwarding URL at the site from which you would otherwise be redirected, and can copy it into the Address bar if you trust the destination site.)
- **Allow Scripting Of Internet Explorer Webbrowser Control.** This setting determines whether scripts can access the Webbrowser control, the Internet Explorer component that renders Web pages. For ordinary browsing, there's no reason to enable this setting in any zone.

Chapter 12

419

- **Allow Script-Initiated Windows Without Size Or Position Constraints.** A feature in Internet Explorer allows scripts to open new windows, and to control the size, position, and appearance of those windows, even allowing a programmer to omit all the usual window accoutrements, such as borders and menus. This feature has been exploited by attackers who create windows to cover up parts of the screen with phony information, including the text of Security Warning dialog boxes, the status-bar lock icon that indicates a secure Web site, and even the Start button. Selecting Disable prevents Web sites from using that feature.

- **Allow Web Pages To Use Restricted Protocols For Active Content.** This setting determines whether a Web page that's accessed using a protocol that's restricted in the current security zone can run active content. Protocol restrictions are set through Group Policy.

- **Display Mixed Content.** By default, Internet Explorer prompts for permission in all security zones when a site wants to display both secured and unsecured content. This can occur, for example, if a Web page on a secure site draws images or framed content from an unsecured site. The risk here is that, if such a page asks you for confidential information, it's difficult to know whether your response will be transmitted over a secure, encrypted connection. There's no risk in viewing information on pages with mixed content, but you should be cautious about sending information (by completing a form, for example) from a mixed-content page. If you find the prompts annoying, you can change the setting to Enable.

Tip To determine whether a form or other part of a mixed-content page is secured, right-click the part of the page in question, choose Properties, and check the URL. If it begins with *https://*, you can proceed safely.

- **Don't Prompt For Client Certificate Selection When No Certificates Or Only One Certificate Exists.** Certain secure Web sites are configured to request a client certificate—that is, a personal certificate that identifies you and has a root trusted on the server. With this setting disabled, Internet Explorer displays a list of certificates that you can use. If you have only one personal certificate that's trusted by the site's server, you can bypass this prompt by enabling this setting.

- **Drag And Drop Or Copy And Paste Files.** With this setting enabled, the possibility exists that a control or a script could move from a site where it's restricted to a lower-security site where it could party till dawn. If you don't have 100 percent confidence in your Trusted Sites or Local Intranet sites, consider changing this setting to Prompt.

- **Installation of Desktop Items.** This setting, when set to Enable, allows a Web page to place icons or active content on your Windows desktop. However, under particular circumstances, this seldom-needed feature could allow a user to gain unauthorized privileges, so it's best set to Prompt or Disable.

- **Launching Programs And Files In An IFRAME.** IFRAMEs are in-line, or floating, frames often used for pop-up windows.

- **Navigate Sub-Frames Across Different Domains.**   This setting allows you to work with pages that use frames. In some cases, a Web site uses a frame to encapsulate a page from another site on a different domain. Disabling this setting blocks frame spoofing.

- **Open Files Based On Content, Not File Extension.**   Internet Explorer uses several methods for determining the type of each file it downloads so that it can properly—and safely—render pages; this process is called MIME sniffing. This setting's more secure option—Disable—turns on the newest forms of MIME sniffing, but if a Web server is improperly configured, this setting can cause pages not to display properly. (Typically, you'll see HTML code in plain text format, for example, instead of a fully rendered page with properly formatted text and graphics.) Because this situation is all too common, you might find it necessary to enable this setting.

- **Software Channel Permissions.**   This setting controls the permissions given to software distribution channels. Three options are available: High Safety, Low Safety, and Medium Safety. High Safety prevents you from being notified about software updates by e-mail and keeps software from being automatically downloaded and installed onto your computer. Low Safety allows you to receive e-mail notification and allows automatic downloading and installation. Under Medium Safety, you get the e-mails and downloads (provided the software is digitally signed), but no automatic installation.

- **Submit Nonencrypted Form Data.**   This setting affects the transmission of forms data over non-SSL connections. Disable prevents; Enable allows; and Prompt prompts.

- **Use Pop-Up Blocker.**   This setting specifies whether you want to use Pop-up Blocker, a feature in Windows XP SP2 that prevents Web sites from opening unwanted windows. For more information, see "Blocking Pop-Ups," page 392.

- **Userdata Persistence.**   Userdata persistence is a feature that allows a Web site to create XML files that can store a large quantity of personal information for subsequent reuse by the Web site. These files, called "supercookies" by some, don't present any particular security risk, because they can store only items that you choose to enter yourself, either directly through a form you type in or indirectly through database recordsets returned to your computer as the result of a query. The benefit of these files is avoiding the need to fill in a form again or to run a Web query again; some online merchants rely on userdata persistence to make their shopping cart feature work. Nonetheless, if you regard this innovation as an end-run around the privacy protection afforded by Internet Explorer 6's support of the Platform for Privacy Preferences (P3P), you can set Userdata Persistence to Disable.

For more information about cookies and P3P, see "Managing Cookies," page 595.

- **Web Sites In Less Privileged Web Content Zone Can Navigate Into This Zone.**   This setting determines whether a site that's in a security zone with a higher security level than the current zone can navigate into the current zone.

Chapter 12

421

Scripting Security Settings

Scripts are programs embedded within a Web page, and have the potential to engage in dangerous behavior.

- **Active Scripting.** The Active Scripting setting determines whether scripts are allowed to run on Web pages.

- **Allow Paste Operations Via Script.** In 1999, a security flaw was found in Internet Explorer 5 that allowed scripts, under certain conditions, to copy data from the user's Clipboard to the host Web site. Microsoft recommends that if you are concerned about this possibility, you should set Allow Paste Operations Via Script to either Prompt or Disable. Note that the setting is enabled by default in all zones but Restricted Sites.

- **Scripting Of Java Applets.** This setting determines whether scripts are allowed to interact with Java applets. The setting is enabled in all zones except Restricted Sites.

Should You Disable Active Scripting?

Scripts are small snippets of code, written in a scripting language such as JavaScript or Microsoft Visual Basic Scripting Edition (VBScript), that run on the client computer (that is, your computer, not the Web provider's) to enhance the functionality of a Web page. (A scripting language is a simple programming language designed to perform limited tasks.) These should be distinguished from Active Server Pages (Web pages with the extension .asp), which employ a server-side scripting technology and don't, by themselves, represent a security hazard.

Note that scripts can also be saved as stand-alone files (the extensions are .vbs for VBScript files and .js for JScript or JavaScript files) and executed outside the context of Internet Explorer by means of the Windows Scripting Host (WSH). Downloaded to users' systems by way of e-mail attachments, scripts have a disreputable history, having served as the basis for several notorious mail-borne viruses. To avoid infection by script-based e-mail viruses, it's smart to use an e-mail program that blocks dangerous attachments (as well as blocking the execution of script embedded in messages' HTML). For details, see "Protecting Yourself from Hazardous Attachments," page 494.

Malicious scripts have also been used to extract data from other domains and send that information back to their own Web sites. The potential for cross-domain privacy breaches of this kind was discovered by Microsoft and first described thoroughly in February 2000 by the CERT Coordination Center at Carnegie Mellon University's Software Engineering Institute.

However, with improvements in browser security (and with proper antivirus protection in place to handle stand-alone scripts) scripts are generally harmless and are widely used in modern Web design. Nonetheless, a would-be attacker can construct a hostile script to take advantage of security holes on a computer running Windows 2000 or Windows XP without SP2; when embedded in Web pages or in HTML-formatted e-mail messages, that script can wreak havoc on an unpatched computer. Security experts sometimes advise disabling active scripting as a security measure. If you decide to take this extreme step, be prepared for some of your favorite Web sites to stop working properly. For example, you can't search for articles in the Microsoft Knowledge Base when scripting is disabled. To work around this limitation, you can add sites—manually, one at a time—to the Trusted Sites zone.

If this option is too extreme but you're still concerned about security risks from scripts, consider choosing Prompt instead of Disable. For sites in the Internet zone that use scripting, you'll be forced to endure a blizzard of prompts, but as long as your mouse finger holds up you'll be able to successfully navigate through even the most script-heavy page.

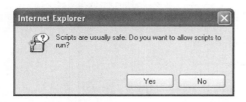

User Authentication Settings

The Logon options determine what happens if a Web site requests your logon credentials. You might think it convenient to have Internet Explorer log you on automatically—but don't allow automatic logon anywhere except (possibly) in the Local Intranet and Trusted Sites zones. The reason is that a malicious Web site operator could, without your knowledge or permission, request your logon credentials. (Internet Explorer actually responds with your user name and an encrypted hash of your password—not the actual password. But given enough time, the perpetrator could use this information to crack your password.)

Managing Browser Add-Ons

Internet Explorer is extraordinarily customizable. Developers can extend its capabilities in highly visible ways, by adding new toolbars, Explorer bars, menus, and buttons. A programmer can also hook into the browser's core features to extend its search capabilities, manage the process of filling in forms, and save bookmarks—to name just a few of the tricks that popular add-ons can perform. These add-ons take the form of browser extensions, browser helper objects (BHOs), toolbars, Java applets, ActiveX controls, and other types.

Chapter 12

Unfortunately, add-ons have a dark side as well. A poorly written add-on can interfere with the smooth operation of Internet Explorer, resulting in mysterious crashes and other glitches; a malicious add-on can cause unnecessary pop-up windows, slow system performance, and reveal details about you and your browsing habits to an untrusted third party.

Beginning with SP2, Windows XP offers a Manage Add-Ons dialog box that shows you all currently installed add-ons and allows you to disable those that are suspicious or known to cause problems. To open this dialog box, shown in Figure 12-13, choose Manage Add-Ons from the Tools menu.

Figure 12-13. This dialog box shows add-ons currently in use by Internet Explorer as well as those you've blocked.

The Manage Add-Ons dialog box displays a fair amount of detail about each add-on, including its publisher (if known), type, and the specific file with which it is associated. Use this list to enable or disable installed add-ons; select an entry in the list, and then select Enable or Disable under Settings. In the case of installed ActiveX controls, you can click the Update ActiveX button to check for a newer version than the one currently installed.

The Show list near the top of the dialog box allows you to toggle between a full list of all available add-ons and a shorter list of only those that are currently in use.

Unfortunately, the Manage Add-Ons dialog box does not include a mechanism for removing add-ons. If you want to permanently remove one of the items on this list, you need to find the program that originally installed it and then remove that program. If you can't identify which program is responsible for a specific add-on, use your favorite search engine to look for clues, using the name of the add-on and the file with which it's associated as search terms.

> **Tip** Although the Manage Add-Ons dialog box provides plenty of information about each add-on, it doesn't tell you whether a particular add-on is beneficial or harmful. For that information, we recommend the CastleCops CLSID / BHO List / Toolbar Master List, which offers judgments on hundreds of BHOs, toolbars, and other add-ons. You can find it at *http://castlecops.com/CLSID.html*.

Managing ActiveX Controls

ActiveX controls are compiled components that can be used by multiple programs or Web sites. Your system probably has dozens or hundreds of them because they're used by the operating system and by applications that have nothing to do with the Internet—as well as by many Web sites.

After you have downloaded an ActiveX control, you can learn more about it as follows:

1 Choose Tools, Internet Options.
2 On the General tab of the Internet Options dialog box, click Settings.
3 In the Settings dialog box, click View Objects.

As Figure 12-14 on the next page shows, these steps take you to the Downloaded Program Files folder (%SystemRoot%\Downloaded Program Files), where you can see a listing of installed ActiveX controls and Java applets, and view the properties of each item. (Scripts are embedded in Web pages, not downloaded as separate files, so they don't appear in the Downloaded Program Files folder.)

> **Note** This listing is by no means complete. Windows includes an enormous collection of ActiveX controls that it uses for various functions, and programs like Microsoft Office also install ActiveX controls that don't appear in the Downloaded Program Files folder. As the name suggests, this listing shows only ActiveX controls that you've downloaded and installed using your Web browser.

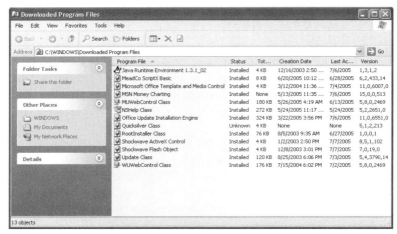

Figure 12-14. The Downloaded Program Files folder lists all ActiveX controls and Java applets downloaded to the computer.

Updating an ActiveX Control

In Details view, the Downloaded Program Files folder provides some useful information about each component. The Status column, for example, tells you whether a component has become damaged in some way, and the Creation Date column tells you the age of your components. If a component has become damaged for some reason or is starting to look a little gray around the temples, you can right-click it in the Downloaded Program Files folder and choose Update from the shortcut menu. Internet Explorer checks the original source of the component to see whether a newer version is available. If one is available, you'll see another confirmation prompt (assuming you've set Internet Explorer to prompt for download permission) and be given the chance to replace the old component with the newer version.

> **Caution** While it might be tempting to select a control marked Damaged and press the Delete key, resist this temptation. Simply deleting a control, damaged or not, gets rid of the .ocx or .dll file but leaves the registry unchanged. The next time a Web site needs the component, it will assume the component still exists somewhere on your system but will be unable to find it. To remove a control, right-click it in the Downloaded Program Files folder and choose Remove from the shortcut menu.

Reading a Control's Properties

Right-clicking a component and choosing Properties from the shortcut menu (or simply double-clicking it) reveals other useful information. (See Figure 12-15.) On the General tab, for example, the Type field tells you whether the component in question is an ActiveX control or a Java applet, and the CodeBase field tells you where the component came from. Internet Explorer uses the security zone to which the CodeBase URL is assigned to determine how to handle the control when an application or a Web page wants to use it. (Notice that the CodeBase URL might in some cases be different—and in a different security zone—from the site you were visiting when you initiated a download. In such a case, Internet Explorer applies whichever settings are more restrictive.)

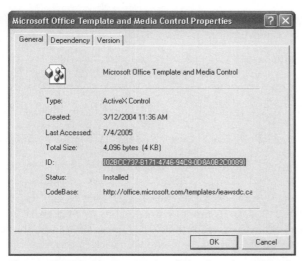

Figure 12-15. The properties dialog box for a downloaded component provides useful information about the component's source and purpose, as well as the unique ID under which the component is registered.

On the Version tab of the properties dialog box, you can often find the name of the component's publisher, as well as the version number. The Dependency tab identifies other files used by the component.

The Safe for Initialization and Safe for Scripting Flags

ActiveX controls can be initialized with either local or remote data. If this data happens to come from an untrustworthy source, it's possible that initialization of the control could cause a security breach. ActiveX controls also support a set of methods, properties, and events that are accessible to scripts. The ability of a rogue script to use an ActiveX control to do things it wasn't intended to do—such as read, write, or delete files—represents another security hazard.

As a way of dealing with these risks, publishers can mark their ActiveX controls as *safe for initialization* and/or *safe for scripting*. If a control is marked safe for initialization, the publisher asserts that the control will do no harm, regardless of how it's initialized. If a control is marked safe for scripting, the publisher asserts that the control will do no harm, regardless of how its properties, events, and methods are used.

Under the default security settings assigned to the Internet zone and Local Intranet zone, Internet Explorer blocks the initialization and scripting of controls not marked as safe for those actions, and it permits the scripting of controls marked safe for scripting. In the Trusted Sites zone, the browser prompts for permission to initialize or script controls not marked as safe, and in the Restricted Sites zone, initialization and scripting of all controls are blocked. You can customize these settings to suit your needs. For example, if you're certain that controls obtained from sites on your local intranet are safe—whether or not they are so marked—you can remove Internet Explorer's default restrictions or request a prompt for permission.

The presence of the following registry key identifies a control as safe for scripting:

```
HKCR\CLSID\GUID\Implemented Categories\{7DD95801-9882-11CF-9FA9-00AA006C42C4}
```

The presence of the following key indicates a control marked safe for initialization:

```
HKCR\CLSID\GUID\Implemented Categories\{7DD95802-9882-11CF-9FA9-00AA006C42C4}
```

In both of these registry paths, *GUID* represents the control's globally unique identifier.

> **Tip** To locate the appropriate parent key for the safe-for-scripting or safe-for-initialization subkey, select the control's GUID in its properties dialog box (see Figure 12-15) and press Ctrl+C. Open Registry Editor, navigate to HKCR\CLSID, press Ctrl+F (the shortcut for the Find command in Registry Editor), press Ctrl+V, and then click Find Next.

Deleting a Downloaded ActiveX Control

If you decide you no longer need an ActiveX control that you downloaded from the Internet, open Add Or Remove Programs in Control Panel to see whether the control can be uninstalled there. (Some can and some cannot.) If you don't find an entry for the control there, open the Downloaded Program Files folder (you can get to it from the Internet Options dialog box or by typing **%systemroot%\downloaded program files** in the Run dialog box or in the Windows Explorer Address bar), right-click the control you want to remove, and choose Remove from the shortcut menu.

Using either of these methods deletes the control and clears it from your registry. Do not simply delete the control from the Downloaded Program Files folder because this will leave your registry in a damaged state, potentially causing your browser to crash the next time a Web site comes looking for the deleted control.

Permitting Only Administrator-Approved ActiveX Controls to Run

With one of the security settings that can be assigned to security zones in Internet Explorer, you can restrict the use of ActiveX controls to an administrator-approved list. If you want to create a set of approved controls and restrict all users at your computer to that set, the best procedure is to use the Internet Explorer Administration Kit (IEAK), which you can download from *http://www.microsoft.com/windows/ieak/*. The IEAK creates a list of all controls already installed on your computer and lets you choose the ones you approve from that list.

If you don't want to use the IEAK, you can use Group Policy. At a command prompt, type **gpedit.msc**, and in Group Policy navigate to User Configuration\Administrative Templates\Windows Components\Internet Explorer\Administrator Approved Controls. You'll find a list of controls there, nearly all of which are from Microsoft. To add one of these controls to the approved list, double-click it and select Enabled. After you have made your selections from this list of controls, you can add other controls to the approved list by means of a registry edit.

Start by getting the CLSID of a control you want to add (display the properties dialog box for the control, select the CLSID, and press Ctrl+C to copy the GUID to the Clipboard). Then open Registry Editor and navigate to HKCU\Software\Policies\Microsoft \Windows\CurrentVersion\Internet Settings\AllowedControls.

Add a DWORD value for the CLSID that represents the control you want to approve, and set the data for that value to 0.

To limit Internet Explorer to the list of approved controls, configure the Run ActiveX Controls And Plug-ins security setting to Administrator Approved. (See "ActiveX Security Settings," page 416.) This is a per-security-zone setting.

Deactivating an ActiveX Control

If you remove an ActiveX control—perhaps because you no longer need it or trust it—nothing prevents Internet Explorer from downloading the control again the next time you visit a site that wants to use the control. If you want to make sure that a control never runs on your system again, you need to make a small change to the registry. Start by copying the CLSID of the control to your Clipboard. (On the General tab of the properties dialog box, select the entire ID field if it isn't already selected, and press Ctrl+C.)

Now run Registry Editor and navigate to HKLM\SOFTWARE\Microsoft\Internet Explorer\ActiveX Compatibility. With this key selected, do the following:

1 Choose Edit, New, Key.

2 Name the key by pressing Ctrl+V to paste the CLSID that you put on the Clipboard. (If the registry already has a key for the CLSID you paste, Registry Editor refuses to accept the new name and prompts you for a different one. Simply delete the unnamed new key, and navigate to the existing one.)

3 With the control's CLSID key selected, choose Edit, New, DWORD Value.

4 Name the new DWORD value Compatibility Flags.

5 Double-click the Compatibility Flags value.

6 In the Edit DWORD Value dialog box, enter the hexadecimal value 400 (or click the Decimal option button and enter 1024).

Chapter 12

429

With the Compatibility Flags value set to 0x00000400, your ActiveX control becomes inactive—permanently. Windows will not run the control, no matter who calls it and no matter whether it's updated or downloaded again. To resurrect the control, you need to remove the Compatibility Flags value that you just created.

> **Caution**   If you explore HKLM\SOFTWARE\Microsoft\Internet Explorer\ActiveX Compatibility, you might find one or more CLSID entries that have Compatibility Flags values set to 400. Don't mess with these—or, for that matter, with any of the other Compatibility Flags values. Microsoft has used this "kill bit" in the past to terminate troublesome ActiveX controls with known vulnerabilities; some of these controls still have a valid digital signature and the kill bit is the most effective way to prevent their reuse. It would be unwise to dig up a bad apple that has been successfully buried.

Managing Java Applets

A Java applet is a component written in Java, a cross-platform programming language created by Sun Microsystems. Unlike ActiveX controls, Java applets are not compiled to native Windows code. Rather, they run within a "virtual machine" (VM)—a software environment that emulates a hypothetical "native" Java computer.

Downloaded Java applets, like downloaded ActiveX controls, are listed in your %SystemRoot%Downloaded Program Files folder. You can view their properties, update them, and remove them by right-clicking entries in that folder.

Unlike ActiveX controls, Java applets normally do not have unrestricted access to your computer's resources. Java technology originally limited applets to running in a restricted area of memory called the "sandbox," where they were allowed to do only the following:

- Access threads in the current execution context
- Open network connections to the applet host so that the applet could download additional files if necessary
- Create a pop-up window with a banner warning users that the window was created from an applet
- Access reflection application programming interfaces (APIs) for classes from the same loader
- Read base system properties, such as processor type, Java version number and VM vendor, and operating system

The sandbox restrictions provided a high degree of security at the expense of capability. For more details, see "Java Security Settings," page 418.

Chapter 13

Blocking Spyware, Adware, and Other Unwanted Software

When we wrote the first edition of this book in 2002, spyware was a relatively new phenomenon. For most people, it was either a minor nuisance or a non-issue, and in that earlier edition we dismissed the topic in four paragraphs. Three years later, the rogue's gallery of potentially unwanted software—also known as spyware, adware, browser hijackers, and a host of other, often unprintable names—has grown exponentially. Today, it is arguably the single largest annoyance afflicting Microsoft Windows users worldwide. It's also a serious security issue, and in this edition we have expanded our coverage into a full-fledged chapter.

According to a 2005 survey by the Pew Internet & American Life Project (*http: //www.pewinternet.org*), 68 percent of home computer users in the United States— roughly 93 million adults—have experienced problems that are consistent with those caused by spyware, adware, or viruses. The Pew study found that about 28 million people spent an average of $100 to get their computers working again. In October 2004, America Online and the National Cyber Security Alliance conducted a research project that scanned the personal computers in 329 American homes for potentially harmful software. In an accompanying survey, 53 percent of respondents thought they were afflicted with spyware or adware; the scan revealed that in fact 80 percent of the respondents had at least one such program installed.

What kind of problems do spyware victims experience? The list includes unwanted pop-up ads, including come-ons for pornography and other offensive products; mysterious Internet shortcuts on the desktop, Start menu, and the Favorites list; slowdowns in performance; an increase in hung programs, browser errors, and operating system crashes; a change to the browser's home page that can't easily be reversed; and code that takes you to a site other than the one you expect when you click a link in your browser window. And that's just for starters—many of these programs include modules that download and install new software without any notice or permission.

Purveyors of spyware and adware go to great lengths to push their wares onto unsuspecting users, and removing the unwanted code can be a challenge for even an expert. A thriving anti-spyware industry has grown up in the past few years, with free and commercial utilities to detect, remove, and block the installation of spyware programs.

Vibrant online communities have become popular as well, offering general advice and detailed instructions on how to deal with the spyware plague.

In this chapter, we explain how this type of software does its dirty work and how you can prevent it from being installed on your computer. We also explain how to find out whether spyware or adware is installed on your computer and what your options are when you uncover unwanted software.

Security Checklist: Stopping Spyware

Follow these steps to help prevent computers on your network from being infected with spyware, adware, and other forms of harmful and deceptive software:

● Install Windows XP Service Pack 2 (SP2) on every computer running Windows XP. Changes in the way SP2 handles ActiveX and file downloads can go a long way toward protecting users from mistakenly installing spyware.

● Install all security updates for Windows and Microsoft Internet Explorer. The nastiest forms of spyware exploit security flaws in Windows to install themselves automatically, without your knowledge or consent.

● Never agree to install any software unless you are certain that it is safe and free of unwanted side-effects. When in doubt, search the Web for information that can help you make an informed decision.

● Set a System Restore point before installing any new program so that you can roll back any changes if it displays spyware-like behavior.

● Read the license agreement for every program before you install it. Be especially vigilant for any program that reserves the right to display "targeted advertisements," "personalized offers," or other euphemisms for pop-up ads.

● Restrict the ability of untrusted users to install software without your permission. This precaution is especially important if you administer a computer used by children.

● Install a reputable program that monitors your system for changes that are typical of spyware installation.

● Be alert to symptoms that can indicate possible spyware infestation, including the appearance of unwanted pop-up ads, unexplained crashes, or unsolicited changes in your browser's home page or default search engine.

What Is Spyware?

Any discussion of spyware starts with the difficult topic of defining terms. Consumer groups, security experts, and software developers often disagree on the definition of spyware and how you can protect yourself most effectively from being a victim.

The term spyware was first used to refer to computer software in 1999 by Zone Labs, makers of the popular ZoneAlarm firewall. In 2000, Steve Gibson of Gibson Research Corporation defined the term as "any software that employs a user's Internet connection in the background (the so-called 'backchannel') without their knowledge or explicit permission." A white paper written that same year by independent security consultant Richard Smith agreed with Gibson's definition and added a new term, adware, which Smith defined as "advertiser sponsored software ... that uses your Internet connection to download and store advertisements on your machine [that] are then displayed when you run the host program."

That old definition of spyware focused on identifying programs that track browsing habits through the use of cookies and then "phone home" to report the results to a third-party server. Today, the term is used in a much broader sense, as a catch-all for many types of potentially unwanted software. Some such programs display pop-up ads; others redirect Internet Explorer to a search engine or home page that's different from the one you specify; still others replace the advertisements in Web pages you visit with ads of their own. In addition to the distinction between spyware and adware, security experts and developers of anti-spyware software have a long list of labels for programs they identify.

For the purposes of this chapter, our definition of spyware is "any program that is installed without the user's full and informed consent, often through deceptive means, and that displays advertising, records personal information, or changes a computer's configuration without the user's explicit permission."

The Microsoft anti-spyware team uses the term *spyware* but prefers the broader label *potentially unwanted software*. In a white paper entitled "Windows AntiSpyware (Beta): Analysis approach and categories" (*http://www.microsoft.com/athome/security/spyware /software/isv/analysis.mspx*), Microsoft lays out the criteria it uses for defining whether a program should be considered a potential threat and, if so, how it should be classified. The categories include the following:

- **Deceptive behaviors.** Does the program give adequate notice of its behavior? Does it provide the user with sufficient opportunity to consent to the installation? After installation, does the user have control over the program's actions? Is there a readily accessible mechanism to remove the program at the user's discretion?

- **Privacy.** Does the program collect, use, or communicate personal information without the user's explicit consent?

- **Security.** Does the program have a negative impact on the security of the user's computer? Does it attempt to circumvent or disable security or conceal evidence of malicious behavior?

- **Performance impact.** Does the program have an adverse impact on performance, reliability, and quality of the user's computing experience? For example, does it slow down computer performance, cause reduced productivity, or cause corruption of the operating system?

- **Industry and consumer opinion.** Do other security experts and individual users consider the program's behavior suspicious?

The answers to the above questions aren't black and white. In fact, the Microsoft Windows AntiSpyware research team suggests that potentially unwanted programs display a wide range of behaviors, on a continuum from relatively innocuous to downright dangerous. The figure shown here, taken from the white paper, illustrates this continuum.

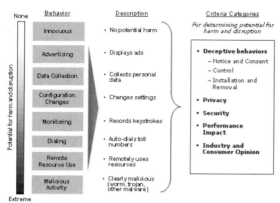

The Anti-Spyware Coalition, an industry group led by the Center for Democracy and Technology, has launched an effort to create a consensus among consumer groups and makers of anti-spyware software. The group, whose membership at the time we wrote this chapter included Microsoft, AOL, and 10 makers of security software as well as an assortment of related companies and consumer groups, is actively involved in creating a final standard that can be used to identify programs and components that a computer user might want to remove or disable. A preliminary document from the ACS defines spyware and other potentially unwanted technologies as

Technologies implemented in ways that impair users' control over:

- *Material changes that affect their user experience, privacy, or system security*
- *Use of their system resources, including what programs are installed on their computers*
- *Collection, use, and distribution of their personal or otherwise sensitive information*

Why is it so difficult to classify a program as spyware? Unlike viruses, which are clearly hostile programs created and distributed by shadowy sources, most spyware and adware programs come from known companies whose activities are questionable. Any attempt to create definitive rules is, by its very nature, subjective and controversial. Some software programs are universally considered to be spyware, but others aren't so easy to classify. If a user voluntarily agrees to accept some advertising in exchange for getting a program for free, that piece of software is adware, but it isn't unwanted. In addition, makers of security software differ on their classifications: One anti-spyware program might advise the user that a program is relatively benign and can be safely ignored; another might recommend that the same program be removed and banned. Which definition should prevail? Most anti-spyware solutions include a way of classifying possible threats on a scale and providing the user with additional information about the possible threat; armed with that information, the user can decide which alerts to heed and which to ignore.

> **Note** Most security experts agree that cookies, even so-called tracking cookies used by third-party advertisers, do not qualify as spyware. Confusingly, some popular anti-spyware programs include tracking cookies in their list of detected "threats." As the Anti-Spyware Coalition has noted, tracking cookies are incapable of having a substantial effect on computer reliability, security, or performance. These text files do raise legitimate privacy issues, which can be effectively dealt with through a combination of browser settings. For more details, see "Managing Cookies," page 595.

Of course, most people who are victimized by unwanted software don't care about labels or tests. They begin to care about spyware when it has a negative effect on their computer's performance and they can't get rid of it.

If you want to know why spyware, adware, and their unwanted cousins have become such a plague, just follow the money. Some Web sites, typically those run by online merchants, pay commissions to independent third parties (known as affiliates) who convince Web users to click links that take them to the merchant's Web site. Many of these pay-per-click affiliate arrangements are perfectly legitimate, of course, but spyware and adware publishers stretch the rules to the breaking point and beyond. On a computer where an aggressive adware program is installed, for instance, a user might click a link to purchase a book or to search for information about real estate. The adware program intercepts that legitimate click and sends the user to a different page than the one they requested—a page that, naturally, pays the adware maker or one of its affiliates a commission. Similarly, visiting sites that contain certain keywords or searching for those terms on a search engine like MSN or Google can trigger a pop-up from an installed adware program. The pop-up contains a link that leads to a page that in turn rewards the adware maker with an affiliate commission.

How does spyware, adware, or similar unwanted software get on your system in the first place? The following four mechanisms are collectively responsible for virtually all spyware and adware installations:

- **You willingly install a program with full knowledge of its actions.** This is the least common avenue by far. Most people, if confronted with a clearly written description of what a spyware or adware program does, will refuse to install it.

- **You install a program that is presented to you with a misleading or incomplete description.** Spyware developers are notorious for using misleading program names and license agreements to trick naïve users into installing a piece of software that they don't really want. This problem is especially acute with ActiveX controls. The program offered in Figure 13-1 on the next page, for instance, claims to allow you to view song lyrics. In fact, if you click the link and read the license agreement, you'll see that it actually attempts to download and install at least nine browser add-ons, none of them in any way related to lyrics.

The paragraph shown below, buried near the end of a license agreement that is several thousand words long, offers one example of how a spyware distributor technically satisfies the requirement to disclose its activities while ensuring that most of its victims will never read the disclosure. Anyone who clicks OK in the dialog box that contains the link to this epic license agreement accepts the license terms, essentially giving the software complete freedom to take over the targeted computer.

16. UPDATES. You grant Integrated Search Technologies permission to add/remove features and/or functions to the existing Software and/or Service, or to install new applications or third party software, at any time, in its sole discretion with or without your knowledge and/or interaction. By doing so, you agree to the terms of the new applications. You also grant Integrated Search Technologies permission to make any changes to the Software and/or Service provided at any time.

- **You visit a Web site that incorporates scripts designed to exploit security holes.** Not surprisingly, these sites are typically targeted at people searching for "shady" content—pornography, bootleg music files, and illegal software downloads, among others. But unscrupulous Web site authors also load spyware downloads onto Web sites aimed at kids, including those that promise song lyrics, downloadable fonts, and information about professional wrestling. Even an innocent Web surfer can be caught just by mistyping a Web site address; spyware distributors often engage in "typo-squatting," where they register a domain that is similar in spelling to a much more popular site and then attempt to foist unwanted software on accidental visitors.

- **You install a "free" program that in turn installs one or more adware programs.** Peer-to-peer file-sharing programs are among the most popular entries in this category. Ben Edelman, a highly regarded security researcher from Harvard University, performed a detailed analysis of five programs in this category and found that four of them were riddled with bundled adware.

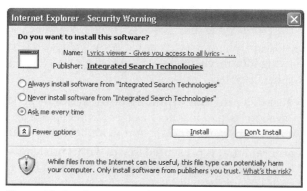

Figure 13-1. Spyware makers routinely mislabel ActiveX download prompts to deceive visitors into thinking that the program is necessary to continue.

Blocking Unwanted Software

The best offense is a good defense. That's especially true with spyware, because its developers go to great lengths to make it difficult to remove. The most insidious forms of spyware burrow into well-hidden corners of the file system and the registry and immediately begin downloading additional components. Getting rid of unwanted software can be a trying experience, and some of the most pernicious programs can stubbornly resist even an expert's attempts at removal; many are programmed to reinstall themselves if not excised with surgical precision. Even if you succeed at removing the parts that cause pop-up ads and general system slow-downs, you can't really be certain you got rid of every trace of the offending program. It's far, far better to prevent the infestation in the first place, if possible.

An in-depth defense strategy against spyware and other unwanted software combines four elements:

- Technological measures that alert you to potential threats as soon as they appear, giving you the opportunity to block installation.
- Education for all computer users, to help them learn how to recognize threats and avoid being victimized.
- Reasonable controls to prevent untrusted or naïve users from inadvertently installing harmful software.
- A regular monitoring program that scans for the presence of known threats that slip past your other layers of defense.

Inside Out

Avoid high-risk behavior

The purveyors of spyware do everything they can to mislead users into making incorrect decisions. Does that let the user completely off the hook? Not necessarily. If you regularly download files from unknown sources over peer-to-peer networks or browse adult-oriented Web sites, you are at far greater risk of getting zapped by unwanted software. The risk increases dramatically if you aren't diligent about installing security patches and critical updates. If you're going to visit dangerous neighborhoods, it makes sense to pay extra attention to your surroundings so you don't get mugged.

Healthy skepticism goes a long way toward keeping you secure. A sensible approach to spyware starts with a willingness to say no to software installations. We recommend a simple rule: If you're not sure whether to install a program, don't install it. Do some online research to investigate whether the program has known problems, unfortunate interactions with other programs, or unwanted behavior. Every Windows user has at least one horror story about installing a program that caused so many problems the only cure was a complete reinstall. Most such problems (including spyware-related issues) are well documented; you'll save yourself a lot of grief if you do your research before you click the Install button.

As anyone who has ever tackled an infested system can testify, trying to remove spyware/ adware/viruses is a difficult proposition. You're much better off if you can prevent an unwanted program from being installed in the first place. We recommend the 10 best practices on the next two pages to dramatically reduce the likelihood that an unwanted program will appear on your computer without your full knowledge and consent.

1 **Avoid questionable Web sites and untrusted downloads.**   Pushers of hostile software lurk on sites that promise "cracked" programs, pirated music and video files, or X-rated pictures. If you're a parent of a teenager who insists on using Kazaa or another unsafe file-sharing tool, you'll have to combine active prevention with education.

2 **Protect yourself from forced installations through security holes.**   The most virulent forms of spyware and adware can be installed on a system by exploiting weaknesses in the operating system, the browser, or an application. The sad part is that virtually all such attacks are preventable if you follow these simple steps:

- Install all security-related updates for Windows, Internet Explorer, and any other software that has networking features.

- Configure Automatic Updates to download and install new updates as needed.

- Use a good antivirus program and configure it to download and install new virus definitions automatically. An antivirus program will protect you from Trojan horse programs that can install other software.

3 **Block "drive-by downloads."**   Many adware and spyware programs are installed when the user clicks Yes or Install in response to an ActiveX dialog box. Unscrupulous Web site operators try to make spyware and adware programs sound essential or desirable, when the truth is exactly the opposite. You can reduce the odds that you'll be fooled into accepting a drive-by download by taking these steps:

- If you use Windows XP, install Service Pack 2 (SP2). The new Information Bar feature virtually eliminates ActiveX pop-ups.

- Configure your system to block the installation of new ActiveX controls. Using an alternative browser that doesn't support ActiveX is one measure that partially achieves this goal. Firefox and Opera ignore ActiveX prompts completely, and browser add-ons for Internet Explorer, such as Maxthon (*http://www.maxthon.com*) and Avant (*http://www.avantbrowser.com*), allow you to enable or disable ActiveX (and other) capabilities. Don't assume that using a browser other than Internet Explorer makes you immune, however. Regardless of which browser you use for everyday tasks, be sure to configure Internet Explorer properly, because other programs might launch it unexpectedly. (See the sidebar "Add extra security to ActiveX," page 440, for details on how to increase the security of Internet Explorer 6.)

- Add known good sites to the Trusted Sites zone; do so sparingly, and only for sites that you are certain can be trusted. Use the Restricted Sites zone to block sites that are known to be a source of unwanted software. Eric L. Howes's IE-SPYAD (*https://netfiles.uiuc.edu/ehowes/www/resource.htm#IESPYAD*) is an excellent starting point.

- Block pop-ups. These are a common source of come-ons for unwanted software.

- Avoid clicking links in unsolicited e-mail, which can lead to untrusted sites.

4   **Don't install any new program unless you are certain it is trustworthy.**
Most people are far too trusting of software and are willing to install a program
on a whim or a casual recommendation. You'll do best if you assume that any
new program is untrustworthy until proven otherwise. If you're not 100 percent
sure about a program's safety or reliability, don't allow it to be installed.

5   **If you have any doubts, read the license agreement and privacy policy!**
Many spyware and adware programs bury deep in a license agreement the disclosure that they display pop-up ads, clutter your browser with unwanted toolbars,
and download additional programs. If the license agreement is too long or difficult
to read, or if it incorporates agreements for other programs and requires you to
click to another site to read those agreements, that should be a warning sign that
you need to do additional research before agreeing to the installation.

6   **Do your homework.**   You can find out a lot about a program and its developer
by doing some basic research using your favorite search engine before agreeing
to install the program. (When entering the search terms, enter the program's name
and add the word *spyware* to increase the chances that you'll find pages that provide useful information about whether a program is safe.)

7   **If you do agree to install a program, set a System Restore point first.**   Give the
entry a descriptive name of your choosing, something like "Just before installing
new file-sharing utility." Save the restore point and continue with the installation.
If anything goes wrong, run System Restore again (in safe mode if necessary),
and select the manual restore point you created. That undoes all your changes and
removes any executable files and Registry entries that were added during the installation. System Restore works best if you use it as soon as possible after making
a system change.

8   **Don't install multiple programs at the same time.**   If you experience a problem
after installing several programs or utilities, you'll find troubleshooting is more
difficult than it should be. When you install a new program, use it for at least a day
or two and verify that it behaves as expected. After you're satisfied that it's safe and
reliable, you can add another program.

9   **Keep a close eye on your computer.**   Be sure you know when a program tries
to set itself up to run automatically or to hook into your browser. Take advantage
of utilities that can help you monitor common software installation locations.
("Choosing and Using Anti-Spyware Tools," page 442, includes a list of reliable
programs.) Be especially alert for symptoms of unwanted software, such as
unexplained pop-up ads and unidentified processes.

10 **Maintain good backups.**   Many adware and spyware programs can be uninstalled by using one or more removal tools. But some are so persistent that they
require manual removal, a process that can take hours even in the hands of an
expert. If you're confronted with a severe infestation, you might find it simpler to
reformat your hard disk and start over. In that case, you'll be in much better shape
if you have a current backup of your data files. (For detailed advice on how to
create and maintain useful backups, see Chapter 6, "Preventing Data Loss.")

Inside Out

Add extra security to ActiveX

Internet Explorer's capability to download and run ActiveX controls is a double-edged sword. When used properly, ActiveX controls greatly expand the power of Internet Explorer. Unfortunately, the developers of spyware, adware, and other forms of unwanted software figured out long ago that ActiveX is a great way to sneak unwanted programs onto an unsuspecting user's computer.

So how do you protect yourself? If you disable ActiveX programs completely, you cut off access to the good along with the bad. A better approach is to configure each user's account so that existing ActiveX programs run as expected in Internet Explorer, but new ActiveX controls from any site in the Internet zone are blocked. (Sites in the Restricted zone are always blocked, and sites that you specifically place in the Trusted Sites zone are unaffected by this change). This configuration change makes it impossible for a Web site to "push" spyware or adware onto your computer, by fooling you (or another logged-on user) into clicking Yes when you should click No.

To make the changes manually, follow these steps:

1   Close all instances of Internet Explorer and open Internet Options from Control Panel.

2   In the Internet Properties dialog box, click the Security tab, select Internet from the list of available zones, and click Custom Level.

3   In the ActiveX Controls And Plug-ins section, change the Download Signed ActiveX Controls setting to Disable.

4   Verify that all other settings in this section are as follows:

   - Automatic Prompting For ActiveX Controls - Disable
   - Binary And Script Behaviors - Enable
   - Download Unsigned ActiveX Controls - Disable
   - Initialize And Script ActiveX Controls Not Marked As Safe - Disable
   - Run ActiveX Controls And Plug-ins - Enable
   - Script ActiveX Controls Marked Safe For Scripting – Enable

5   Click OK to save your changes, click Yes in the Warning dialog box to confirm the changes, and then close the Internet Properties dialog box.

These settings will allow any previously installed ActiveX controls to run but won't allow you to install new ones. If you visit a page that uses an ActiveX control you need, reverse these changes temporarily to install the control.

If you'd prefer a more automated approach, we have created a simple script file that is included on the CD that accompanies this book. Copy the ActiveX_toggle.vbs file to a convenient location, such as the desktop, and double-click the file to run the script. To create the script manually, type the following code into any plain text editor and save it using the .vbs extension.

```
Option Explicit
Dim strWMI, strComputer, strStatus, strPrompt, strTitle, strKeyPath
Dim strValueName
Dim dwHKEY_CURRENT_USER, dwValue
Dim objReg

dwHKEY_CURRENT_USER = &H80000001
strWMI = "winmgmts:\\"
strComputer = "."
strStatus = "Current setting for signed ActiveX" & vbNewLine
strStatus = strStatus & "controls in the Internet zone is: " & vbNewLine
strPrompt = "Allow download of signed ActiveX controls?"
strTitle = "ActiveX Setting"
strKeyPath = "Software\Microsoft\Windows\CurrentVersion\Internet Settings"
strKeyPath = strKeyPath & "\Zones\3"
strValueName = "1001"
Set objReg = GetObject(strWMI & strComputer & "\root\default:StdRegProv")

objReg.GetDWORDValue dwHKEY_CURRENT_USER, strKeyPath, strValueName, dwValue


' Display current ActiveX setting
Select Case dwValue
    Case 0
        MsgBox strStatus & "Enabled - This setting is highly insecure", _
            vbOKOnly, strTitle
    Case 1
        MsgBox strStatus & "You are prompted before downloading", _
            vbOKOnly, strTitle
    Case 3
        MsgBox strStatus & "Disabled - signed controls are not " & _
            "downloaded", vbOKOnly, strTitle
    Case Else
        MsgBox "Download signed ActiveX components from a Web page " & _
            "(Zone 3):  The value is either Null or could not be " & _
            "found in the registry.", vbOKOnly, strTitle
End Select


' Display the message box and act on resulting button click
Select Case MsgBox(strPrompt, vbYesNoCancel, strTitle)
    Case vbYes    'Enable ActiveX
        objReg.CreateKey dwHKEY_CURRENT_USER, strKeyPath
        strValueName = "1001"
        dwValue = 1
        objReg.SetDWORDValue dwHKEY_CURRENT_USER, strKeyPath, _
            strValueName, dwValue
    Case vbNo     'Disable ActiveX
        objReg.CreateKey dwHKEY_CURRENT_USER, strKeyPath
        strValueName = "1001"
        dwValue = 3
        objReg.SetDWORDValue dwHKEY_CURRENT_USER, strKeyPath, _
            strValueName, dwValue
    Case vbCancel 'Do nothing
End Select
```

The script displays two dialog boxes. The first displays your current ActiveX security settings for the Internet zone.

After you click OK, the second dialog box allows you to change the current setting.

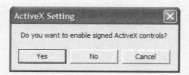

Click Yes to allow ActiveX controls to be downloaded (you will always be prompted for permission before a download takes place). Click No to disable downloads. Click Cancel to leave your current settings in place.

Note that you must be logged on as an administrator to run this script; it will fail if you are logged on as a standard user. Also, some antivirus and anti-spyware programs might display a warning (or just fail to run the script, without any notice) when you attempt to run any script written in Microsoft JScript or Microsoft Visual Basic, Scripting Edition (VBScript). In its default settings, Windows AntiSpyware attempts to block most scripts as well. If this script won't run on your computer, look at the settings for your antivirus or anti-spyware software to see what you need to do to make it work properly.

Finally, this script runs on a per-user basis. For maximum security, be sure to run the script for each user account on your computer.

Choosing and Using Anti-Spyware Tools

Relying on software alone to keep you safe from spyware is a short-sighted strategy. Unlike leading antivirus programs, which approach 100 percent effectiveness when kept up to date and used properly, many anti-spyware tools simply don't do as good a job as they promise. In late 2004, security researcher Eric L. Howes put 17 popular anti-spyware programs to the test to see how they fared at removing a series of common spyware programs. The best of the bunch detected and removed only 63 percent of the unwanted software, and the remainder were able to clean up less than half of the mess. (Brian Livingston compiled the results into a highly readable article in his Windows Secrets Newsletter, available at *http://windowssecrets.com/comp/050127/*.)

What's the problem? The biggest failure is relying on software to detect and remove unwanted software after it has already been installed. The two anti-spyware programs that originally defined the category, Spybot - Search & Destroy and Ad-Aware, were initially developed as scan-and-remove utilities. Over time, however, spyware makers learned to disguise their code so that it could evade detection, and they added modules that reinstalled the unwanted software after it was removed.

Today's best anti-spyware programs emphasize prevention over detection and removal. These programs run in the background, just as antivirus programs do, monitoring the Windows file system, the registry, and your browser's settings for behaviors that are typical of spyware installations. When the software detects an attempt to install a known threat, it alerts the user. That's the philosophy behind the Resident TeaTimer feature in Spybot 1.3 and the real-time protection features in Windows AntiSpyware, for example. Figure 13-2 shows one such warning, issued by Windows AntiSpyware, after the user clicked OK in response to a deceptive ActiveX prompt. Anti-spyware software can also detect suspicious activity, such as a change in your browser's home page or an attempt to add a program to a common start-up location, providing a warning and an opportunity to block the change.

Figure 13-2. The most effective anti-spyware strategy is to detect spyware before it is installed, as in this example from Windows AntiSpyware.

Scanning and removal tools still have a place, of course. Their primary goal is to verify that your preventive strategy is working properly. If you perform a daily or weekly scan of a well-protected computer, you should get a clean bill of health every time. When a piece of unwanted software slips past your defenses, you should remove it as quickly as possible and then determine how it got there, so that you can plug the gap.

The following list of anti-spyware programs is not exhaustive, but it includes the most popular and generally effective entries in the category. For everyday use, we recommend that you pick an anti-spyware program that does the best job possible of preventing unwanted software from getting on your system in the first place. If, despite your best efforts, you find yourself needing to remove an unwanted program, use whatever tools it takes. If your preferred tool can't get rid of the pest, go ahead and use a second or third scanner. And then, after you get rid of it, figure out how you can prevent the same thing from happening again.

Except where noted, all of the following programs run on Windows XP and Windows 2000. The list appears in alphabetical order, sorted by company name.

Aluria Software

- **Product:**   Spyware Eliminator
- **At a glance:**   This commercial product includes standard features you'd expect from a spyware scanner. Unlike most competitors, it also includes a database of ActiveX controls and hostile sites, providing protection similar to that offered by SpywareBlaster. The company offers a separate, server-based product called Paladin for use on enterprise networks.
- **Web site:**   *http://www.aluriasoftware.com/homeproducts/spyware/*

Computer Associates International

- **Product:**   eTrust PestPatrol Anti-Spyware
- **At a glance:**   Computer Associates offers its package in Home, Small and Medium Business, and Enterprise editions. An annual subscription gives you automatic downloads of updates, and the program offers the usual mix of scanning, removal, and protective features.
- **Web site:**   *http://www.ca.com/products/pestpatrol/*

ewido networks

- **Product:**   ewido security suite
- **At a glance:**   Preventing the installation of Trojan horse programs and spyware is the primary purpose of this utility. The free version scans for known threats and cleans or quarantines anything it finds. The Plus (paid) version provides real-time monitoring.
- **Web site:**   *http://www.ewido.net*

FaceTime Communications

- **Products:**   X-Cleaner Anti-Spyware Trace Eraser, Real-Time Guardian
- **At a glance:**   X-Cleaner scans for spyware and adware using a frequently updated database. It also bundles a suite of privacy-oriented tools, including a password generator, file shredder, and utilities to clean the browser's history and cached files. A trial version and an enterprise version are available. Real-Time Guardian provides spyware-blocking capabilities in enterprises, with a special emphasis on securing instant messaging applications and peer-to-peer networks.
- **Web sites:**   *http://www.xblock.com, http://www.facetime.com*

Javacool Software

- **Products:**   SpywareBlaster, SpywareGuard
- **At a glance:**   Online communities give this pair of programs (both free for personal and educational use) consistent thumbs-up ratings. Unlike all-in-one tools that scan and remove unwanted software, SpywareBlaster is strictly for prevention. Using frequently updated "block lists," it modifies the registry to prevent installation of ActiveX programs known to be hostile, and it adds entries to the Internet Explorer Restricted Sites zone that limits access to sites known to distribute hostile software. SpywareGuard runs as a background process, scanning executable files in real time to detect and prevent installation of spyware.
- **Web site:**   *http://www.javacoolsoftware.com/spywareblaster.html*

Lavasoft

- **Product:**   Ad-Aware
- **At a glance:**   Ad-Aware was among the first programs to tackle spyware head-on, and it's still a leader in the category. A free version is available for personal use; Plus and Professional editions (shareware) offer additional features, including a real-time monitor that blocks common spyware/adware installation techniques. An enterprise version is available as well. Ad-Aware uses definition files to scan files, processes, and registry settings and offers the option to remove anything it detects.
- **Web site:**   *http://www.lavasoft.com*

McAfee

- **Product:**   McAfee AntiSpyware
- **At a glance:**   Like most makers of antivirus software, McAfee has branched out with this package to block, detect, and remove spyware. It is also available in bundles with other McAfee products. Database updates require an annual subscription.
- **Web site:**   *http://us.mcafee.com/root/package.asp?pkgid=206&cid=10107*

Merijn.org

- **Product:**   Hijack This
- **At a glance:**   This unusual free tool doesn't identify or remove anything. Instead, it scans specific registry keys and system folders and then creates a log file that lists the contents of those locations. Several online communities specialize in decoding HijackThis logs and offering instructions for manual removal of spyware/adware infestations that don't respond to general-purpose removal tools. An excellent quick-start tutorial is available at the TomCoyote Forums (*http://tomcoyote.com/hjt/*), and additional help is available at SpywareInfo (*http://forums.spywareinfo.com/*) and Castle Cops (*http://castlecops.com/forums.html*).
- **Web site:**   *http://www.spywareinfo.com/~merijn/downloads.html*

Microsoft Corporation

- **Product:**   Windows AntiSpyware
- **At a glance:**   In December 2004, Microsoft purchased the whimsically named GIANT Company Software and promptly renamed its flagship product. An initial beta release of this product is essentially unchanged from its predecessor; its best feature is strong protection from spyware/adware attacks, in the form of Security Agents that monitor applications and behaviors used by unwanted software. As we prepared this chapter, Microsoft was planning a second beta release of the program. (For more details, see "A Closer Look at Windows AntiSpyware," on page 448.)
- **Web site:**   *http://www.microsoft.com/spyware/*

PC Tools Software

- **Product:**   Spyware Doctor
- At a glance: Older versions of this program got mixed reviews, but recent updates have been widely praised, especially in the crucial area of preventing spyware and adware from being installed in the first place. It can be configured to download updates automatically and perform scans on a user-defined schedule. Site Guard, an anti-phishing feature, prevents your browser from going to Web sites that might install unwanted software or impersonate a legitimate business.
- **Web site:**   *http://www.pctools.com/spyware-doctor/*

Safer Networking

- **Product:**   Spybot - Search & Destroy
- **At a glance:**   Spyware experts usually mention Spybot - S&D in the same breath as Ad-Aware. The free program, developed by Patrick M. Kolla, is widely respected and well maintained. A clever feature called the Resident TeaTimer monitors new processes, detects potentially malicious processes spawned by spyware or adware, and allows you to block or approve those processes. In addition to scanning for unwanted software, it also monitors tracking cookies and checks for home page hijackers in most major browsers.
- **Web site:**   *http://www.safer-networking.org*

Sunbelt Software

- **Product:**   CounterSpy
- **At a glance:**   If this commercial program looks familiar, that's probably because it's based on the scanning engine originally developed as GIANT AntiSpyware, which was in turn purchased by Microsoft and rebranded as Windows AntiSpyware. CounterSpy gets consistently high ratings in comparative reviews, and its ability to monitor and block changes to key system settings is noteworthy. Database updates require an annual subscription. A free 15-day trial version is available.
- **Web site:**   *http://sunbeltsoftware.com/CounterSpy.cfm*

Symantec

- **Product:**   Norton Internet Security AntiSpyware Edition
- **At a glance:**   Symantec's all-in-one package adds spyware detection, removal, and prevention capabilities to its existing feature list, which includes antivirus capabilities, a personal firewall, and parental control features. Updates are included with antivirus signatures and require an annual subscription.
- **Web site:**   *http://www.symantec.com/sabu/nis/nis_ase/index.html*

Tenebril

- **Product:**   SpyCatcher
- **At a glance:**   This commercial program includes the standard set of blocking, scanning, and removal tools. The Reinstall Shield feature claims to prevent even persistent pests from reappearing after you've removed them. Tenebril also offers an Enterprise version that allows support professionals to apply protection policies on computers from a central management console.
- **Web site:**   *http://www.tenebril.com*

Trend Micro

- **Product:**   Trend Micro Anti-Spyware
- **At a glance:**   Trend Micro added anti-spyware features to its PC-cillin antivirus suite in 2004, but the feature was roundly panned. So the company went out and bought SpySubtract Pro from Intermute, a product with a much better reputation for blocking and removing unwanted software. As part of the purchase, Trend Micro also acquired CWShredder, a unique free tool that zaps many variants of the extraordinarily hard-to-remove CoolWebSearch spyware infection.
- **Web site:**   *http://www.trendmicro.com/en/products/desktop/as/*

Webroot Software

- **Product:** Spy Sweeper
- **At a glance:** In comparative reviews, this commercial program gets consistently high marks for its ability to block, detect, and remove unwanted software. Its purchase price includes a one-year subscription. The Enterprise edition allows central management through the use of an administrative console.
- **Web site:** *http://www.webroot.com*

 Inside Out

Avoid phony anti-spyware tools

For every legitimate anti-spyware program, you'll find at least one piece of software that doesn't do what it's supposed to do. Ironically, many of these bogus tools are pitched through advertisements that appear on pages users find when they're trying to find information about how to clean up a computer that's afflicted with spyware. Some entries in this category are knock-offs of legitimate products, often using outdated detection databases. Others are inferior offerings that are sold using scare tactics—typically through online "scans" that detect nonexistent threats and try to convince the user to pay for the full version of the software. The worst offenders actually deliver spyware in a package that promises to remove it!

To avoid being stung, visit the Spyware Warrior site and check out Eric L. Howes's list of rogue/suspect anti-spyware products and Web sites at *http://www.spywarewarrior.com /rogue_anti-spyware.htm*.

A Closer Look at Windows AntiSpyware

Through the years, with only rare exceptions, Microsoft has stayed out of the business of providing security software to users of its desktop operating systems. In 2005 that policy began to change, with the release of a beta version of Windows AntiSpyware. This Microsoft-branded product was originally designed by GIANT Company Software and released as GIANT AntiSpyware. The beta release we describe here is essentially the same as that version, with a few changes in branding. As we wrote this chapter in the summer of 2005, an updated beta version was due from the Microsoft AntiSpyware team, and a final release was expected in late 2005 or early 2006.

Other programs offer similar features; Microsoft's entry in this category is noteworthy in that it incorporates an exceptional level of real-time protection, which is designed to prevent spyware from being allowed to install or run. The program also includes scan-and-remove capabilities commonly found in other anti-spyware programs as well as a smattering of diagnostic tools and privacy-protection features.

Blocking Spyware, Adware, and Other Unwanted Software

In Windows AntiSpyware, real-time protection is implemented as a collection of Security Agents that start up automatically when your computer does. Available Security Agents are broadly divided into the following three categories, each containing a number of check-points that the program monitors for suspicious behavior:

- Internet Agents keep watch over core networking functions, including dial-up and wireless connections, TCP/IP settings, and the Windows NetBIOS Messenger Service. The Winsock Layered Service Providers checkpoint is particularly useful for blocking insidious forms of spyware and adware that try to attach themselves to your TCP/IP protocol stack as a layered service provider (LSP).

- System Agents prevent unwanted changes to core components of Windows itself, including the Windows Hosts file, Windows services, Logon policies, and shell extensions.

- Application Agents monitor processes, startup files, ActiveX installations, and a wide range of settings related to Internet Explorer. Figure 13-3 shows the configuration screen for the Running Process checkpoint, which alerts you when an unknown process attempts to execute.

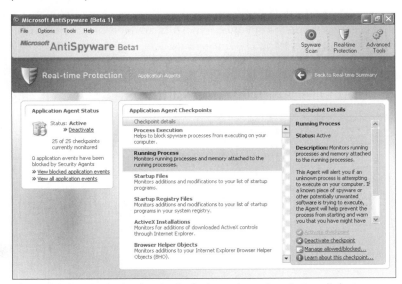

Figure 13-3. Each checkpoint includes a short description, links to a more detailed explanation, and links that allow you to manage settings for that checkpoint.

When a Security Agent detects a suspicious activity, it alerts you. The exact form of the alert varies, depending on whether the behavior is known to be benign, known to be dangerous, or unknown. You have the option to allow or block the action. The color of the warning dialog box is significant: red for known spyware, green for approved programs, blue (such as the one shown on the next page) for unknown actions.

Microsoft Windows XP Networking and Security Inside Out

Using its default settings, Windows AntiSpyware performs a daily scan. You can also scan on demand. In either case, the program inspects memory processes, files, and registry keys in search of files and settings that are either suspicious or are known to be associated with spyware and adware. When a scan turns up one or more traces of an unwanted program, the program gives you the option to remove, quarantine, or ignore the item. Figure 13-4 shows the results after Windows AntiSpyware detected a known Trojan horse program.

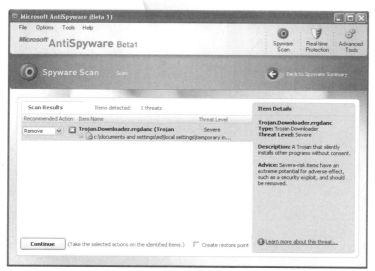

Figure 13-4. When a scan detects potentially unwanted software, you can take the recommended action or choose an alternate action. Note the option to create a restore point before making a change.

Finally, Windows AntiSpyware includes an assortment of advanced tools. Browser Restore allows you to roll back changes to various Internet Explorer settings. Tracks Eraser gives you the option to clean out cookies, saved passwords, and an assortment of history settings. The most interesting advanced feature, however, is a set of System Explorers (shown here), which allow you to view and edit lists of running applications, Internet Explorer browser helper objects and toolbars, and other useful system objects.

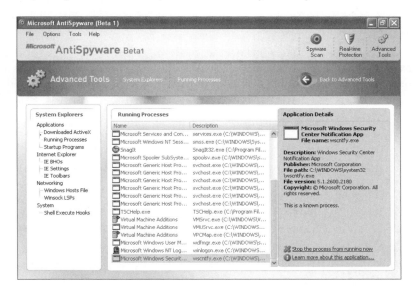

As we've emphasized throughout this chapter, the most effective strategy to defend yourself against spyware and adware is to prevent it from being installed in the first place. Using Windows AntiSpyware or a program with similar preventive features is an important component of that strategy.

Rooting Out Spyware

Cleaning a computer that's been infected with spyware can be a long, difficult, and frustrating task. If you're lucky enough to notice the unwanted software immediately, removal might be as simple as visiting Add Or Remove Programs in Control Panel and then using System Restore to roll back to a previous configuration. But the job is much more complicated if the program includes a Trojan horse component that has downloaded additional software, especially when some of the components have been specifically designed to reinstall themselves upon removal. Unless you find and remove every trace of every unwanted program, you'll probably see some of the software again.

To rid yourself of pesky programs, start by confirming the exact nature of the infestation. Then use the appropriate tools to remove the offending program. In some cases, a general-purpose anti-spyware tool will do the trick. For more persistent pests, you might need to find specialized removal tools or manually remove files and associated registry keys. In the worst cases, be prepared to back up all data, reformat the hard drive, and reinstall Windows and associated programs.

Identifying Potentially Unwanted Software

As we noted at the beginning of this chapter, there is no consensus on the definition of spyware. For obvious reasons, that greatly complicates the task of identifying programs that might represent a threat to your computer or your network. Every manufacturer of anti-spyware software has its own criteria for evaluating what constitutes adware and spyware, and few publish their lists.

If you suspect that a computer has been compromised, your first step should be to scan it using one of the tools listed in the previous section. If you're unable to download and install one of those utilities, you can use one of the following free online spyware scanning services (all use ActiveX controls):

- CounterSpy Spyware Scan, *http://www.sunbelt-software.com/dell /counterspy_scan.cfm*
- eTrust PestPatrol, *http://home.ca.com/dr/v2 /ec_main.entry25?page=PestScan2&client=ComputerAssociates&sid=35715*
- Trend Micro Anti-Spyware for the Web, *http://www.trendmicro.com/spyware-scan/*
- Webroot Spy Audit, *http://www.webroot.com/services/spyaudit_03.htm*
- XBlock X-Cleaner Micro Edition, *http://www.spywareinfo.com/xscan.php*

If a scan turns up no known spyware installations, you'll need to dig deeper. Start by looking for suspicious processes in Windows Task Manager (press Ctrl+Shift+Esc and click the Processes tab).

Inside Out

Dig deeper into processes and programs

If you're determined to hunt down an unwanted program, we highly recommend two free tools available from Sysinternals.

Process Explorer shows a wealth of detail about all running processes, including a description of the process and the name of the company that developed the associated executable file or DLL. (Author Mark Russinovich notes that processes spawned by malware typically live in the Windows folder and have no description, company name, or associated icon; they also frequently contain URLs that point to suspicious Web sites.) With Process Explorer, you can also suspend a process rather than kill it, which can help you work around spyware installations that automatically restore themselves as soon as you terminate the process.

Autoruns shows all locations where programs and services are currently set up to run when you start your computer or log on. It also shows shell extensions for Windows Explorer and browser helper objects associated with Internet Explorer. You can hide signed Microsoft entries, making it easier to zero in on third-party programs that are likely to be the source of problems. The latest versions of both programs are available at *http://www.sysinternals.com /ProcessesAndThreadsUtilities.html*.

Don't automatically assume that an unknown or obscurely named process is hostile. Some perfectly legitimate programs use cryptic filenames; randomly killing processes and deleting files can result in chaos, poor performance, and a loss of essential functions. If you spot an unknown process, see if you can find out what the process actually does. The Computer Associates Spyware Information Center (*http://www3.ca.com /securityadvisor/pest/*) includes a searchable index that identifies which piece of spyware or adware is associated with a particular file; most entries also include manual removal instructions.

If you determine that a process is unwanted, the next task is to figure out how it started. Table 13-1 contains a list of all known locations where programs can insinuate themselves on your computer to be started automatically. You can scan each location manually in search of the responsible entry, or use the Sysinternals utility Autoruns to scan all locations and present you with a convenient list. (See the previous Inside Out tip for more details on using Autoruns.) If you can't identify the source of an item on the list, check the CastleCops StartupList Index (*http://castlecops.com/StartupList.html*), which includes an alphabetical list of more than 10,000 programs known to configure themselves for automatic startup, with recommendations for handling each one and a forum for asking additional questions.

Table 13-1. Common Locations for Programs That Start Automatically

Location	Description
Startup folder (User)	The %UserProfile%\Start Menu\Programs\Startup folder contains shortcuts that run when a specific user account logs on.
Startup folder (Common)	Shortcuts in the %AllUsersProfile%\Start Menu\Programs\Startup folder run automatically whenever any user logs on.
Run key (Machine)	Programs listed in the registry's HKLM\SOFTWARE\Microsoft \Windows\CurrentVersion\Run key are available for all users.
Run key (User)	Programs listed in the HKCU\Software\Microsoft\Windows \CurrentVersion\Run registry key run when the current user logs on. A similar subkey, HKCU\Software\Microsoft\Windows NT \CurrentVersion\Windows\Run, might also be used.
Load value	Programs listed in the Load value of the registry key HKCU\Software \Microsoft\Windows NT\CurrentVersion\Windows run when any user logs on.
Scheduled Tasks folders	You can use Scheduled Tasks to specify per-user tasks that run at startup. In addition, an administrator can set up startup tasks for your user account; by default, such tasks are listed only in the administrator's Scheduled Tasks folder, not your own. Other users can also schedule tasks that run when you log on; these tasks run as background processes only.
Win.ini	Programs written for 16-bit versions of Windows can add commands to the Load= and Run= lines in the [Windows] section of this startup file (a legacy of the Windows 3.1 era), located in %SystemRoot%.

Table 13-1. **Common Locations for Programs That Start Automatically**

Location	Description
RunOnce and RunOnceEx keys	This group of registry keys identifies programs that run once and only once at startup. These keys can be assigned to a specific user account or to the machine. HKLM\SOFTWARE\Microsoft\Windows\CurrentVersion\RunOnce HKLM\SOFTWARE\Microsoft\Windows\CurrentVersion\RunOnceEx HKCU\Software\Microsoft\Windows\CurrentVersion\RunOnce HKCU\Software\Microsoft\Windows\CurrentVersion\RunOnceEx
RunServices and RunServicesOnce keys	As the names suggest, these rarely used keys can control automatic startup of services. They may be assigned to a specific user account or to a computer.
Winlogon key	The Winlogon key controls actions that occur when you log on to a computer running Windows XP. Most of these actions are under the control of the operating system, but you can also add custom actions here; if you set up automatic logon using the Windows XP version of Tweak UI, for instance, your saved settings are stored here. The HKLM\SOFTWARE\Microsoft\Windows NT\CurrentVersion\Winlogon\Userinit and HKLM\SOFTWARE\Microsoft\Windows NT\CurrentVersion\ Winlogon\Shell subkeys can automatically launch programs.
Group Policy	Group Policy has two policies (both called Run These Programs At User Logon) that contain a list of programs to be run whenever anyone logs on. In Group Policy, you'll find the policies in Computer Configuration\Administrative Templates\System\Logon and User Configuration\Administrative Templates\System\Logon.
Policies\Explorer\Run keys	Using policies to specify startup programs, as described in the previous paragraph, creates corresponding values in either of two registry keys: HKLM\SOFTWARE\Microsoft\Windows\CurrentVersion\Policies\Explorer\Run or HKCU\Software\Microsoft\Windows\CurrentVersion\Policies\Explorer\Run. It is possible for a legitimate program or rogue process to create or modify these registry values directly—that is, without using the Group Policy object. Note that disabling the Run These Programs At User Logon policies in Group Policy Editor does not prevent Windows from launching the items listed in the Policies\Explorer\Run registry keys.

Table 13-1. **Common Locations for Programs That Start Automatically**

Location	Description
BootExecute value	By default, the multi-string BootExecute value of the registry key HKLM\SYSTEM\CurrentControlSet\Control\Session Manager is set to autocheck autochk *. This value causes Windows, at startup, to check the file-system integrity of your hard disks if your system has been shut down abnormally. It is possible for other programs or processes to add themselves to this registry value. (Note: Microsoft warns against deleting the default BootExecute value. For information about what to do if your system hangs while Autocheck is running, see Knowledge Base article 151376, "How to Disable Autochk if It Stops Responding During Reboot.")
Logon scripts	Logon scripts, which run automatically at startup, can open other programs. Logon scripts are specified in Group Policy in Computer Configuration\Windows Settings\Scripts and User Configuration \Windows Settings\Scripts (Logon/Logoff).
Shell service objects	Windows loads a number of helper dynamic-link libraries (DLLs) to add capabilities to the Windows shell. The list of authorized objects includes a DLL to create the CD Burning folder, for instance, as well as another that permits Internet Explorer to check Web sites for updates. Writers of viruses and Trojan horse programs have also discovered the HKLM\SOFTWARE\Microsoft\Windows\CurrentVersion \ShellServiceObjectDelayLoad key, however, and some have used this location to surreptitiously start up unauthorized software.

After you've identified the source of the problem, you can move on to the task of removing the associated files.

Using Automated Removal Tools

Most of the programs listed earlier in this chapter (see "Choosing and Using Anti-Spyware Tools," page 442) include the option to remove any threat that is detected by a scan. Experts who specialize in spyware removal generally recommend that you perform a full scan with at least two tools to increase the chances that you remove all traces of the infection. This procedure is likely to be effective for garden-variety spyware and adware installations, especially those that are distributed by large companies that at least pay lip service to consumer rights. These all-purpose scanners are likely to be ineffective with stealthy spyware and adware programs from companies that build in code to resist automated removal techniques.

Chapter 13

Using Special-Purpose Removal Tools

If you're certain that a computer is infested with a particular pest but your anti-spyware program is unable to completely remove it, you might be able to find a tool that has been specifically designed for that purpose. The most noteworthy example is CWShredder (*http://www.trendmicro.com/cwshredder/*), which is effective at removing the persistent and constantly mutating CoolWebSearch spyware/Trojan program. Your best chance of finding similar tools for other threats is to visit a trustworthy anti-spyware community forum, such as Spyware Warrior (*http://spywarewarrior.com/index.php*) or SpywareInfo (*http://forums.spywareinfo.com*).

Removing Unwanted Software Manually

Manual removal is the most difficult route, with no guarantee of success. If all the automated tools you try are unable to clean a spyware-afflicted computer, this is your last resort. The task requires a strong working knowledge of the internal working of Windows; it might also require that you think like a devious, underhanded spyware developer.

If you're certain you've identified the source of the problem—typically one or more files that start up automatically—you need to delete the associated files and remove the registry entries or other code that allows the programs to automatically start. In many cases, you'll be unable to do so while Windows is running normally. Any attempt to delete the associated files will fail while the process is running. You can't kill the process, either. Spyware developers have learned to run multiple processes that "watch" each other; if you kill one process, the other one automatically restarts it almost immediately.

So how do you get rid of the pests? Restart the computer in safe mode and see if you're able to make the necessary changes and deletions. If that fails, you can use Sysinternals' Process Explorer to suspend each process instead of killing it. Suspending the process keeps it from performing any of its dirty work, but prevents the "watching" process from noticing that the process has been killed. After you've suspended all suspicious processes, you can kill them one by one and delete the associated files.

Avoid spending too much time trying to clean up a severely infested computer. We recommend a one-hour rule. If you're unable to completely remove a spyware/adware infection in one hour, you're in serious danger of sinking into a hole that can take all day, all night, or all week, with no guarantee of success. In the long run, you'll have better results by backing up all data files, wiping the disk clean, and reinstalling Windows and all programs from scratch.

Chapter 14

Stopping Viruses, Worms, and Trojan Horses

It's not your imagination. Computer viruses *are* becoming more prevalent, more virulent, and downright sneakier each year. Historians generally agree that the first computer virus appeared "in the wild" in 1981, many years before the release of Microsoft Windows. That first virus, disguised as a computer game, attacked the most popular computer of its day, the Apple II. It spread at a snail's pace, carried from one computer to another by infected floppy disks.

More than two decades later, the spread of computer viruses and other forms of malicious software has perversely mirrored the incredible revolution in legitimate software during the same period. Some experts estimate that *malware* (the broad term for all sorts of malicious software) grows by more than 15 percent a year. According to Sophos, a developer of antivirus software, more than 30 new viruses appear every day, and the roster of active viruses increases by more than 10,000 per year.

Most of these viruses die a natural death almost instantly, but a handful reach critical mass each year—and when that happens, look out! Thanks to the Internet, e-mail, and the incredible popularity of Windows as a host, virus outbreaks can race around the world at breathtaking speed. In May 2000, for instance, the infamous LoveLetter worm (also known as ILOVEYOU or, to antivirus specialists, VBS.LoveLetter.A) infected millions of computers and shut down e-mail servers worldwide. Researchers eventually determined that this particularly nasty bug was launched from the Philippines and spread across Asia, Europe, and the United States in a matter of hours.

In 2004, the experts at ICSA Labs published the results of their ninth annual Virus Prevalence Survey. Of the 300 qualified respondents, each represented a business or government agency with at least 500 computers and two or more Internet-connected networks. More than 30 percent of them had experienced a virus "disaster"—an infection that struck more than 25 computers in an organization—during the previous year, and 88 percent felt the virus problem was getting worse, not better. Individual users and small businesses, who don't have the luxury of full-time support staffs and dedicated firewalls, are even more vulnerable. If a piece of hostile software slips through your defenses and infects your computer or your network, you'll understand why they call it a disaster.

Cleaning up the mess can be expensive and time-consuming, and there's no guarantee you'll be able to recover all your data.

In this chapter, we discuss the complete spectrum of hostile software, often referred to as *malicious code*, or malware. We explain how viruses, worms, and Trojan horses attack your computer; how you can identify suspicious software and prevent infections; and how to clean up after an infection. We also offer practical advice on how to choose an antivirus software package that's right for you.

Security Checklist:
Viruses, Worms, and Trojan Horses

Don't let a virus or worm take over your computer or network. Use this checklist to ensure that you're protected at all times. Some items in this list might be inappropriate for your computer or network configuration; read the information in this chapter carefully before proceeding.

- Train all users of your computer and network in safe computing procedures.
- Install antivirus software on every desktop computer.
- Install and activate a personal firewall on every desktop computer.
- Ensure that you are using e-mail software that handles potentially dangerous attachments securely.
- Configure your e-mail software to block or quarantine potentially dangerous attachments.
- If you have a network server, install antivirus software at the gateway.
- Configure your antivirus software for regular, automatic updates, at least weekly and preferably daily.
- Bookmark and consult authoritative sources of information about viruses and virus hoaxes.
- Institute a regular backup program.
- Develop a recovery plan that you can implement in the event of a virus infection.

How Malicious Software Attacks Your Computer

Every year, antivirus software gets a little smarter. Unfortunately, the authors of malicious software programs are clever and persistent, too. The result is a constant struggle between legitimate software developers and the online vandals and criminals who write hostile software, with Windows users literally caught in the middle. Although viruses get a disproportionate share of the headlines, malware can actually take any of several forms. Before we explain how they work, it's important to understand the types of threats you're likely to encounter:

- A *virus* is a piece of code that replicates by attaching itself to another object, usually without the user's knowledge or permission. Viruses can infect program files, documents (in the form of macro viruses), or low-level disk and file-system structures such as the boot sector and partition table. Viruses can run when an infected program file runs; they can also reside in memory and infect files as the user opens, saves, or creates the files. When a computer virus infects a computer running Windows, it can change values in the registry, replace system files, and take over e-mail programs in its attempt to replicate itself (at which point it becomes a worm). A virus needn't be a self-contained program, nor is it necessarily destructive, although some are.

> **Note** The plural of *virus* is *viruses*. Some misguided writers, in an attempt to sound educated, insist that the correct term is *virii*. They're wrong, as a visit to a definitive reference book (such as the *Oxford English Dictionary*) or any first-term Latin primer will confirm. (And even if these writers were on the right track, *virii* would be the plural of *virius*, which isn't a word in any of our dictionaries.) If you ever need to settle a bet with someone who insists that the word *virii* exists, point them to this authoritative source, which provides a definition and pointers to several thorough and witty dissertations on the topic: *http://dictionary.reference.com/help/faq/language/v/virus.html*

- *Worms* are independent programs that replicate by copying themselves from one computer to another, usually over a network or through e-mail attachments. The most virulent outbreaks of hostile software in recent years have originated with worms. Many of these threats also contain hostile code designed to destroy data files or to launch denial-of-service attacks against other computers. The distinction between worms and viruses can be blurry, even to security experts.

- *Trojan horses* are programs that run without the victim's knowledge or consent; although they can be harmless, most Trojan horse programs in circulation today perform functions that compromise the security of the computer by exploiting the user's access rights and privileges. A Trojan horse program might arrive as an e-mail attachment or a download from a Web site, possibly disguised as a joke program or a software utility of some sort. Attackers typically rely on basic "social engineering" techniques to dupe unwitting victims into installing the software. For instance, an attacker might contact a potential victim using Internet Relay Chat (IRC) with a warning that a particularly nasty virus is going around, and then provide a link to a Trojan horse program that masquerades as a virus cleanup utility!

- *Blended threats* represent a class of sophisticated and malicious software that combines the characteristics of viruses, worms, and Trojan horses to create especially potent attacks. Unlike garden-variety viruses, which typically spread by hijacking e-mail address books on computers running Windows, blended threats often target Web servers and networks, which enable the malicious code to spread rapidly and cause extensive damage.

> This chapter focuses exclusively on viruses and other code that is unquestionably hostile. We cover the trickier forms of quasi-legitimate malware in Chapter 13, "Blocking Spyware, Adware, and Other Unwanted Software."

A Glossary of Malware

Web sites and mailing lists run by the makers of antivirus software are essential resources for tracking down details about viruses and their behavior. If you have to clean up an infected system, you can often find step-by-step instructions and downloadable utilities to assist in the process. Decoding the language of antivirus software and solutions isn't always easy, however. Here are definitions of some terms you're likely to encounter:

- **Disinfect.** To remove a virus from memory and to remove all installed components of the virus. Completely disinfecting a system that has been infected by a virus can require manual steps in addition to the automated procedures performed by an antivirus program.

- **Dropper.** The component of a virus that installs (or "drops") the virus code itself on a computer system, usually as a file.

- **File virus.** A class of virus consisting of hostile code that can attach itself to program files; also known as a *file infector*. File viruses can infect programs that have the .exe and .com file name extensions; they can also attack lesser-known types of executable files, such as those with the extensions .sys, .ovl, or .drv. File viruses often remain in the computer's memory after they run, continuing to infect any program that the user of the infected computer subsequently launches.

- **Heuristic analysis.** A technique used by some antivirus software to identify a possible virus based on its behavior rather than on a *virus signature*. In theory, this type of scan can stop a new virus even before the antivirus software developer has updated the program's signature files; however, heuristic scans can also turn up false positives when a trusted program behaves in a way that resembles virus behavior.

- **In the wild.** A phrase used to describe a virus that is actively spreading among computers and is not restricted to a laboratory environment.

- **Macro virus.** A program or fragment of code written in the internal macro programming language of an application (such as Microsoft Word or Microsoft Excel) and stored in a document file. If security settings in the program allow the macro virus to run when the document is opened, the virus can cause damage and replicate to other documents.

- **Payload.** The destructive portion of a virus. Depending on the malicious intent and skill of the virus writer, the code in the payload can destroy or corrupt data files, wipe out installed programs, or damage the operating system itself.

- **Polymorphic virus.** A virus that has the ability to change its byte pattern when it replicates; also known as a *mutating virus*. A virus writer can also incorporate encryption routines that cause the virus to look completely different on different computers or even within various infected files on the same computer. This characteristic allows the virus to avoid detection by antivirus scanners that look for specific strings of text in specific locations.

- **Proof of concept.** Example code, usually created by a security researcher, that demonstrates how a security flaw can be exploited. The gap between proof-of-concept code and an actual virus can be very short; when an example exploit appears, it's usually a signal to users and software makers that an update is critical.

- **Rootkit.** A set of tools used by an attacker to take over a computer system and simultaneously hide any trace of the intrusion. Rootkits were originally developed for systems running the Unix operating system, in which "root" is the most privileged administrative account. Rootkits that target Windows (including one ironically named Hacker Defender) have recently appeared.

- **Scanning.** The process of searching memory and saved files for viruses. Using anti-virus software, you can scan one or more files (or an entire disk) manually. Most antivirus programs also include an active, or real-time, scanning feature, which inspects files and e-mail attachments as they're accessed in order to detect and block viruses before the user can inadvertently execute the infected file.

- **Virus signatures.** The tell-tale signs that identify the content and behavior of specific viruses, worms, and Trojan horse programs; also known as *patterns* or *definitions*. All makers of antivirus software use signatures to detect viruses, and they update their virus definition files regularly in response to newly discovered strains. Without an up-to-date definition file, antivirus software is ineffective at best and potentially dangerous because of the false sense of confidence it engenders.

Some malware attempts to enter your system brazenly in the form of an executable program that disguises its true purpose. W32.Gibe@mm, for instance, is a mass-mailing worm that first appeared in 2002; it arrives as an attachment claiming to be a Microsoft security update called Q216309.exe. (Note the similarity to Microsoft Knowledge Base numbers used to identify legitimate security updates.) Other executable files might offer to install a screen saver or display an animated cartoon. An intended victim who runs the executable file might see a series of dialog boxes intended to lull the user into believing that the program ran as intended. In the background, of course, the virus code is installing itself without the victim's knowledge. The W32.Gibe@mm virus displays the dialog box shown here, which probably looks legitimate to an unsophisticated user:

Image Copyright © F-Secure Corporation

If the victim clicks the Yes button, the worm displays a progress dialog box that also looks authentic, followed by this message box:

Image Copyright © F-Secure Corporation

What's In a (Virus) Name?

When a new virus, worm, or Trojan horse appears, every maker of antivirus software rushes to identify it, determine its behavior and mode of transmission, and develop a fix that can block it. As part of the process, they have to give the virus a name. But problems can arise when different software developers call the same virus by different names. To help bring order out of this chaos, an invitation-only group called the Computer Antivirus Research Organization (CARO) has developed a naming convention for viruses. Today, many (but not all) firms that specialize in antivirus software adhere to these general guidelines; most tack on prefixes and suffixes that are unique to their products and complicate the process of comparing and collating information. Although reports in the mainstream press often refer to a virus or worm by its popular name (Mydoom, Netsky, or Bagle, for instance), technical information is typically organized using each vendor's standardized names (Email-Worm.Win32.Mydoom.ah, W32.Netsky.Q@mm, WORM_BAGLE.AZ).

A virus name consists of the following elements:

- A prefix that identifies the virus type. Most viruses that attack computers running Windows use the W32 (32-bit Windows virus), I-Worm (Internet Worm), VBS (Visual Basic Script virus), or Trojan/Troj (Trojan horse) prefix.
- A family name. This name is usually drawn from the virus code itself.
- Major variant. If this suffix is present, it's in the form of a number that identifies the file size of the virus. Most antivirus software firms omit this element.
- Minor variant. This suffix is usually a letter that distinguishes alternative versions of a single virus that are in circulation.

In addition, some names now use the suffixes @m and @mm to identify viruses that spread by e-mail or by mass mailers, respectively.

Other hostile programs attempt to disguise the fact that they are executable attachments by masquerading as innocent data files. The most common technique for virus writers who use this sort of attack is to give the attachment two file name extensions—the notorious LoveLetter worm, for instance, spread by means of an attachment named LOVE-LETTER-FOR-YOU.TXT.vbs.

The final extension is the one that actually associates files of that type with a program; in the case of the LoveLetter worm, the .vbs extension fires up the Windows Script Host and runs the payload of the virus—a destructive script that deletes a slew of data files and replaces other files with copies of the virus. Because the Windows Explorer default settings hide file name extensions for common types of files, the would-be attacker is counting on the victim to believe that the file is a harmless text document named LOVE-LETTER-FOR-YOU.TXT.

Most e-mail programs adopted effective countermeasures to this technique long ago. Today, when you receive a file attachment in Outlook Express or Microsoft Outlook, the program displays the full name, complete with all file name extensions. The only way the double-extension trick will work is if a user carelessly saves the file and then tries to view it in Windows Explorer. The tactic lives on in some viruses that spread through compressed files, however. If you receive an e-mail message with this type of infected attachment, look carefully: you might find a long line of spaces between the purported extension (typically an innocent text or image file type) and the "real" extension. The architect of this type of exploit counts on the fact that a recipient will open the archive file in a small window, where the full file name might not be visible.

Inside Out

Upgrade your e-mail program for best protection

Recent versions of Outlook and Outlook Express offer multiple layers of protection from viruses that use the "two file name extensions" trick. Regardless of the settings in Windows Explorer, attachments received by Outlook Express versions 5 and 6 always show the full name of the file, including multiple extensions. The same is true of Outlook 2000, Outlook 2002, and Outlook 2003. Even if a virus using this technique slips undetected past installed antivirus software, an alert user of any of these e-mail programs should have no problem spotting the potentially dangerous attachment before executing or saving it. To avoid being fooled by hidden file name extensions in saved files, follow the procedures outlined in "Blocking Dangerous Attachments," page 485.

The most dangerous forms of hostile software try to enter your computer system through the back door, without requiring any action by the user. Viruses in this category work by exploiting vulnerabilities in scripting engines, in ActiveX controls, in Java applets, and in the code that renders Hypertext Markup Language, or HTML (buffer overflows, for example).

For more details about how buffer overflows and other HTML exploits work, see "How Hack Attacks Work," page 562.

Attachment-Borne Viruses

By far the most common source of widespread computer virus outbreaks is the class of hostile software that replicates by sending itself to other potential victims as an attachment to an e-mail message. Although each such virus is different (some, in fact, are as complex as many commercial programs), attacks of this type have certain common features.

The accompanying message often uses "social engineering" techniques designed to lure inattentive or gullible users into opening the infected attachment. The virus writer often tries to convince recipients that the attachment is a salacious picture or that it contains details about how to gain free access to a pornographic Web site. The most widely publicized virus of 2001, VBS.SST@mm, for instance, claimed to contain a picture of tennis star Anna Kournikova. Several variants of the Mydoom virus, which spread like wildfire throughout 2004, arrived as attachments that mimicked delivery failure reports from an e-mail server administrator. The attachment, in .zip format, ostensibly included details of the failed message but actually contained the virus payload.

Tip   Beware of Zip files

These days, most mail servers reject all incoming messages with executable files attached. That simple measure completely stops most viruses written before 2003. To work around the blockade, attachment-based viruses now typically send their payloads using the standard .zip format for compressed files. If the user opens the attachment, the contents of the compressed file appear—in Windows Explorer or in the third-party utility assigned to handle .zip files. Double-clicking the executable file within the compressed archive sets the virus in motion. Virus writers use a variety of tricks with Zip files. In some cases, they include a bogus extension in the file name and then append a large number of spaces before the real file name extension, so that the actual file type doesn't appear in the window that displays archived files. Some viruses even encrypt the .zip attachment and include the password as part of the message. That allows the infected attachment to slip past some virus scanners. Most real-time scanners will detect a virus in a .zip file, either when it arrives or when the user tries to extract the file. The moral? Be wary of *all* attachments, even when they appear to be innocent.

Although most attachment-borne viruses arrive with displays written in English, a disproportionate number originate from outside the United States. Because the authors of such viruses are typically not native English speakers, the accompanying messages frequently contain grammatical errors, awkward syntax, and misspellings. These characteristics can be important clues when you're trying to decide whether a suspicious message is a virus, especially if the message was sent from an infected computer belonging to someone who normally writes in fluent English.

Early versions of mass-mailing worms and viruses took over existing e-mail client programs, such as Outlook Express and Outlook. The infamous Melissa macro virus (W97M.Melissa.A), for instance, infected a Word document with its macro virus and then hijacked Outlook 97 to send 50 copies of the infected document to addresses found in the victim's Outlook Contacts folder. More modern mass-mailing viruses often contain their own mail transport agent, allowing them to circumvent security controls on the installed e-mail client software. These hostile programs can harvest e-mail addresses from a variety of locations, including the Outlook Contacts folder and the Windows Address Book used by Outlook Express, and can even look for Mailto links in Web pages saved in the browser cache on the infected computer.

Some viruses actively try to remove or disable antivirus programs and firewall software, with varying degrees of success. Of course, for this tactic to succeed, the virus or worm must first slip undetected past the protective software, which raises the question of how effective that particular software was in the first place or whether the user missed a crucial update.

Chapter 14

> **Tip** Avoid administrator accounts
>
> In Chapter 3, "Windows Security Tools and Techniques," we explain why some security experts recommend that you log on for everyday computing tasks using an account that is not a member of the Administrators group. This precaution can pay a tremendous dividend if you inadvertently execute a piece of hostile software such as a virus or a Trojan horse. The rogue program runs using the same privileges assigned to your logged-on account. By deliberately restricting your administrative rights, you might be able to prevent the unwanted code from tampering with the Windows registry or replacing crucial system files.

Needless to say, the typical virus author doesn't usually have formal training and certainly doesn't invest in comprehensive testing and quality-control programs, as legitimate software developers do. As a result, viruses that arrive by e-mail are often riddled with bugs and programming mistakes that prevent them from carrying out all their intended functions. Ironically, those flaws can be a blessing in disguise for anyone victimized by a virus.

Attacks from the Web

Although viruses that spread through e-mail attachments have been to blame for the majority of attacks in recent years, some security experts believe that other modes of transmission represent a far greater threat and will become more prevalent in the future. By their nature, attachments require some cooperation from an unwitting or distracted user; that requirement dramatically limits their potential to spread unchecked. As a result, authors of hostile software are always on the lookout for techniques they can use to spread infections automatically.

One popular mechanism is the use of scripts, written in languages such as JavaScript, JScript, or Microsoft Visual Basic Scripting Edition (often abbreviated as VBScript or VBS), that automatically take actions on the intended victim's computer when he or she visits a Web page or views an HTML-formatted e-mail message. The Kak worm (VBS.Kak.Worm), which made its debut in December 1999, took advantage of a weakness in older versions of Outlook and Outlook Express to place the virus on a system automatically. In that example, simply viewing the infected message on a vulnerable computer was enough to trigger the virus. This particular exploit does not affect Windows 2000 or Windows XP, but it does illustrate the general problem of script-based attacks. Viruses can also spread by way of ActiveX and Java components, using the same techniques that purveyors of spyware, adware, and other deceptive software use.

For a more detailed description of these tactics and appropriate countermeasures, see "Identifying Potentially Unwanted Software," page 452.

Chapter 14

465

> **Tip** Don't click that link!
>
> Most spam is relatively harmless junk e-mail, but a small number of unsolicited messages sent through Internet e-mail contain links to sites that host viruses or Trojan horse programs. Clicking one of these links can open a browser window that invites the user to install a hostile program; if the page is able to successfully exploit an unpatched vulnerability, the damage could even occur without any action by the user. To avoid this sort of attack, try to filter out as much spam as possible before it reaches your inbox (see Chapter 16 for a full discussion of spam-blocking tactics), and emphasize to every user of every computer on your network that they should never click a Web link in a spam message, no matter how tempting.

Attackers also take advantage of unpatched vulnerabilities in the HTML-based rendering engine of all versions of Windows. Buffer overruns, for instance, can be used to overwhelm ordinary defenses and allow a hostile program to run. An unsuspecting user can encounter this sort of attack by visiting a Web page or receiving an HTML-formatted e-mail message that includes the exploit code. You have a wide variety of options for preventing Web-based attacks, including the capability to completely disable all scripts and active content such as Java applets and ActiveX controls.

> For more details about increasing the security of Internet Explorer, see Chapter 12, "Making Internet Explorer More Secure." To learn about your options for disabling HTML-based attacks that arrive by e-mail, see "Protecting Yourself from Rogue HTML," page 509.

Trojan Horse Programs

The tale of the Trojan horse is one of the most enduring in Greek mythology. A giant wooden horse was left outside the gates of Troy by the apparently defeated Greeks after a decade-long war. The Trojans hauled the "gift" inside their gates and celebrated. The horse, of course, concealed a small army of Greek soldiers; they emerged after dark, opened the gates for their waiting comrades, and led the Greek army to a decisive victory.

Trojan horse programs follow the same principles of guile, concealment, and hostile infiltration, with your computer as the target. Typically, a remote attacker lures a victim into installing the Trojan horse program by concealing the hostile code within a "wrapper" that appears to be benign. The program might masquerade as a game or a screen saver, as an update to Windows or Internet Explorer, or as a utility for downloading or viewing media files. As part of its installation routine, the Trojan horse program might actually install a harmless program, or it might pretend to fail, displaying an error message to the user. In either event, the dirty work is actually happening in the background, as the program installs its executable files, alters entries in the Windows registry, and makes other system modifications.

Trojan horse programs are not unique to Windows. Over the past two decades, security experts have discovered hundreds of these programs in the wild, infecting computers running MS-DOS, Unix, Linux, Mac OS, OS/2, Palm OS, and every version of Windows.

Once installed, a Trojan horse program can do anything that the user who installed it can do, including changing or deleting files, installing other programs, and transmitting information to a remote location. After successfully convincing a victim to install a Trojan horse program that lets them take over the remote computer, some attackers are content to use their remote connection to play pranks on the victim, but the potential for damage from a truly malevolent attacker is chilling:

- The attacker can delete files, including data files and crucial system files.

- The intruder can steal data, including credit card numbers, passwords, and sensitive business files. The mode of theft can include copying files, logging keystrokes, or capturing the contents of screens.

- Using the infected system, the attacker can try to gain access to other computers on the victim's local network or on the Internet. Using a group of infected computers as "zombies," the attacker can control them remotely and launch distributed denial-of-service attacks against Web servers, flooding the target server with massive amounts of data and effectively locking out legitimate traffic.

- By exploiting other vulnerabilities in the operating system or installed applications, an attacker might be able to launch an "escalation of privilege" attack, which can increase the level of access beyond the level normally available to the user who installed the program in the first place. Normally, running under a limited user account prevents the user from installing a Trojan horse program. A successful attack of this sort bypasses the protection of a limited user account and can give the attacker the privileges of a system service or a network administrator.

Some of the most widespread viruses and worms of recent years include a Trojan horse component in their payload. Several variations of the Bagle worm, for instance, include a backdoor component, which uses a file name such as Drvddll.exe or Sysxp.exe. It installs itself in %SystemRoot%\System32 and modifies the Windows registry so that the backdoor component automatically runs at startup.

A computer infected with a Trojan horse program often acts as a network server, accepting inbound connections on a specific port number. The Bagle backdoor, for instance, listens for connections on TCP port 1080. Attackers who run port-scanning software can detect the open port, surreptitiously connect to the Trojan horse server, and take control of the infected computer, all without the victim's knowledge.

For more details about how TCP and UDP ports work and how to block unwanted connections, see "How Ports and Protocols Allow Access to Your Computer," page 628.

Other Attacks

Viruses and other hostile software can sneak onto a computer through several avenues other than e-mail attachments and the Web. One increasingly popular mode of transmission for malware is through shared network drives. The notorious Nimda worm, for instance, searches for open network shares, attempts to copy itself to any shared drives it finds, and then executes, creating new network shares on the infected computer that allow full control by the Everyone group. The worm also creates a Guest account and adds it to the Administrators group.

Viruses and worms can also jump from one computer to another over open network connections, even in the absence of shared folders or drives. The most extreme recent example is the Sasser worm, which attacked hundreds of thousands of computers worldwide in April, 2004. The worm exploited a known security hole in the Local Security Authority Subsystem Service (Lsass.dll). An infected computer would connect with an unprotected computer on the same network over TCP port 445 and send a copy of a shell script that executed on the second computer. The newly infected computer then connected to the original infected host and downloaded the full worm, at which point it could begin seeking out more vulnerable computers on its own. Security experts who analyzed the fast-spreading Sasser worm concluded that computers that had a firewall enabled and Automatic Updates turned on were completely protected. It's no accident that those settings are the default in Windows XP Service Pack 2 (SP2).

Tip Install updates when they're released

The Kak and Sasser worms offer excellent object lessons on why it pays to install security updates and operating system patches promptly. The vulnerability that made the Kak worm possible was documented in Microsoft Security Bulletin MS99-032, which also included a patch that plugged this security hole. Likewise, the vulnerability that the Sasser worm exploited was fixed in Microsoft Security Update MS04-11. Anyone who installed these patches when they were released was protected from the worm that followed; the rapid and extensive spread of both worms is a depressing indicator of how difficult it is to convince most Windows users of the need to be alert for security updates, and why enabling Automatic Updates is so important.

Viruses that spread over a network are insidious. A single infected computer can infect dozens or hundreds of other computers, and an administrator can have a difficult and frustrating time tracking down the source of the infection. Even with effective attachment-blocking software on e-mail servers and properly configured firewalls, a network is vulnerable to this sort of attack if a user brings an infected notebook computer into the office and successfully connects to the network.

A clever virus author can also craft hostile code that spreads through instant messaging clients, such as MSN Messenger, Windows Messenger, AOL Instant Messenger, and Yahoo! Messenger. Several viruses that spread automatically through MSN Messenger and Windows Messenger have already been discovered in the wild. A worm that targeted AOL Instant Messenger has been demonstrated, although AOL patched the vulnerability that made the worm possible before attackers could take advantage of it. AOL's venerable ICQ program and variations of standard Internet Relay Chat (IRC) clients are also theoretically vulnerable to this sort of worm, although you are far more likely to be targeted by another user who is trying to plant a Trojan horse program (using social-engineering tactics to entice the victim into clicking a hostile attachment) than by a self-propagating worm.

> For detailed advice on how to lock down instant messaging programs, see "Using Instant Messaging Safely," page 524.

Finally, file-sharing programs that work over the Internet, also known as *peer-to-peer* (or *P2P*) *file-sharing software*, can also serve as vectors for viral infections. As we document in Chapter 13, "Blocking Spyware, Adware, and Other Unwanted Software," these types of programs are notorious for installing software that can have a negative impact on system performance and personal privacy. KaZaA, Grokster, and other P2P programs also offer the capability to share files of any sort, including types of files that can be infected with a virus or a Trojan horse program. Any computer that includes a P2P software installation should be considered at high risk for the installation of malware.

Don't Fall for Virus Hoaxes

The Internet is a fertile breeding ground for hoaxes, rumors, and misinformation. That's especially true when the topic is computer viruses. Well-meaning but misguided computer users routinely forward hysterical virus alerts by e-mail. Most of the time, these alerts are bogus. Some, in fact, have been around for nearly a decade.

Virus hoaxes typically have unmistakable common characteristics. Most often, the message is a forwarded copy that cannot be traced back to an authoritative source, although the message might vaguely attribute the alert to Microsoft, McAfee, IBM, or another legitimate-sounding entity. It's usually filled with breathless details of the dire fate that will surely befall anyone who is attacked by this particular virus. And, inevitably, the anonymous author urges recipients to forward the message to everyone they know. One of the earliest virus hoaxes warned recipients to beware of an incoming message with the subject "Good Times":

```
There is a virus on America Online being sent by E-Mail. If you
get anything called "Good Times", DON'T read it or download it.
It is a virus that will erase your hard drive. Forward this to
all your friends. It may help them a lot.
```

Most virus hoaxes are started by pranksters and passed on by gullible users who don't know any better. For the most part, these uninformed and erroneous messages are simply annoying, and their only deleterious side effect is the time and energy you expend deleting the message and, perhaps, responding to the sender so that he or she doesn't get sucked in by another hoax. Occasionally, though, a virus hoax includes bad advice, as was the case in the infamous Suflnbk.exe hoax of 2001 and the Jdbgmgr.exe hoax of 2002, both of which convinced an untold number of Windows users to delete perfectly legitimate system files that the hoax message misidentified as destructive viruses.

Hoaxes and hysterical warnings routinely reappear on the Internet. Occasionally, some enterprising soul revives an old warning, changing the dates and other details of a reputed virus and launching a fresh hoax into the world. If you receive a virus alert by e-mail, you

Microsoft Windows XP Networking and Security Inside Out

can quickly determine whether it's a hoax by visiting the Web site of any leading antivirus software maker; these three sites, for instance, have pages dedicated to virus hoaxes:

- Symantec Hoax Alerts: *http://www.symantec.com/avcenter/hoax.html*
- F-Secure Hoax Warnings: *http://www.f-secure.com/virus-info/hoax/*
- McAfee.com Virus Hoax Listings: *http://vil.mcafee.com/hoax.asp*

In addition, you can find excellent collections of resources for debunking all sorts of Internet hoaxes, including chain letters and phony or exaggerated virus warnings, at these sites:

- ICSA Labs Antivirus Hoaxes: *http://www.icsalabs.com/html/communities/antivirus/hoaxes.shtml*
- Rob Rosenberger's Vmyths.com: *http://www.vmyths.com*

Under rare circumstances, you can and should warn others about a virus currently making the rounds. Keep the distribution list small, and stick to the facts that your recipients need to know: the name of the virus, for instance, and a suggestion that they update the signatures for their antivirus software. Be sure to include a link to more detailed information about the specific virus, preferably from the Web site of an antivirus software vendor, so that technically minded readers can get the most recent information. And insert the current date somewhere in the body of the message (not at the top or bottom, where it can be stripped off easily during forwarding) so that recipients who get a copy of your original message will know when it was first sent.

Identifying Malicious Software

How do you know when your computer has been invaded by hostile software? The worst way to find out is to install an antivirus program, scan your computer for the first time, and discover that you've been infected for who knows how long. In the case of a Trojan horse program or a virus that disables your antivirus protection, you might not have any clear-cut warning. In those cases, you must be alert for changes in the behavior of your computer that could indicate the presence of a virus or a Trojan horse program.

Tip Don't be fooled by forged addresses
If you receive a frantic message from a friend or business associate complaining that they've just received an e-mail message with an infected attachment from your computer, don't panic. You should always take the report seriously, but don't assume that it's accurate. Most virus writers craft their code so that it forges the source of infected e-mail messages. The Klez virus, which first appeared in early 2002, introduced the strategy of searching for e-mail addresses in the Windows Address Book, the ICQ database, and local files on the infected computer and using one of those addresses in the From field on messages it sends to other potential victims. Anyone who receives a copy of a virus sent using this technique might logically (and incorrectly) assume that the apparent sender's computer is infected. If you're able to inspect the headers of the message, you might be able to find the IP address of the computer it came from, but in most cases it's easier to simply delete the message and move on.

The tendency of computers to do strange things for no apparent reason can complicate this task. Performance problems, system lockups, and odd error messages are far more likely to be caused by a buggy program or device driver than by a virus. Nevertheless, any time you observe any of the following symptoms, you should take steps to check for the presence of a rogue program:

- **Suspicious behavior from your antivirus software.** This is probably the most disturbing sign that you might have a problem. If your antivirus software shuts down for no reason, refuses to complete a scan, or is unable to update itself, one possible explanation is that a virus or worm has interfered with its normal operation. In some cases, you cannot browse to your antivirus vendor's Web page; viruses often modify the Hosts file to block access to antivirus vendor sites.

- **Unexpected disk access.** By their nature, Trojan horse programs access hard disk files when the local user is doing nothing. However, many legitimate programs, including several components of Windows, also access the hard disk in the background. In some cases—for example, when the Windows Indexing Service is building its catalog of files for a drive—this activity can take a long, long time. If you notice sudden bursts of disk activity, try to trace the responsible application.

- **Sudden system slowdowns.** A virus or a Trojan horse program can sap system resources and make other activities painfully slow. Unfortunately, so can a wide variety of system configuration problems. If you notice performance problems, try to rule out the presence of a virus as one of the first steps in your troubleshooting process.

- **Unexpected network traffic.** Many forms of hostile software attempt to hijack your network connection—to spread virus code to other computers, for instance, or to use a Trojan horse program's file-transfer and keyboard logging capabilities to steal information. Of course, a blinking red light on your network adapter is not a surefire sign of a malicious program at work; many types of programs, including antivirus packages, include features that assume you have an always-on Internet connection and check for updates at regular intervals. If you see unexplained network traffic, try to identify its source. (Many full-featured personal firewall programs offer excellent tools for identifying and, if necessary, blocking unwanted network connections; see "Identifying Intruders," page 577, for more details.)

- **Changes in the size or name of program files.** Viruses and worms spread by infecting other files. If you notice a change in the size or name of an executable file, the alteration could be a sign that the file has been infected (or that the original file has been deleted and replaced with an infected file). Although you aren't likely to notice this type of change by simply looking through file listings, some antivirus and firewall programs will alert you when they detect changes that resemble virus activity. If you're suspicious, look in Task Manager to see if strange programs are running.

Troubleshooting

Your computer is active for no apparent reason

When you're trying to figure out which application is responsible for a sudden burst of disk or CPU activity, your first stop should be the Processes list in Windows Task Manager. Press Ctrl+Shift+Esc and then click the Processes tab to display a list of all currently active processes, as shown in Figure 14-1. The CPU column shows what percentage of your CPU is in use by each process; by default, it's updated every second. To see which processes are hogging your computer, click the CPU heading twice to sort in descending order. Scroll to the top of the list and watch the display; processes that are currently active will float to the top of the list.

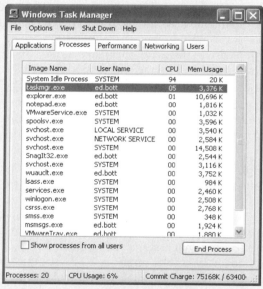

Figure 14-1. If your computer is behaving strangely and you suspect a virus, look for unexplained entries in this list.

If you can't identify an entry in the list of processes, don't assume that it's a hostile program. A much more likely explanation is that the process is a module from a program you installed. To identify the mystery process, make a note of its name as it appears in the Processes list and then use the Windows Search utility to find that executable file. Right-click the file icon, choose Properties, and look for details of the program, typically found on a Version tab. (If the process is listed as svchost.exe, the responsible program is running as a Windows service; type **tasklist /svc** at a command prompt to see the full list.)

The most reliable way to identify a virus, of course, is by scanning your system with an up-to-date antivirus program. This procedure will reliably detect any virus whose characteristics are included in the program's signature files. Virus scanning is not foolproof, however. Be aware of these two potential problems:

- **Undetected viruses.** The process of creating virus signatures is, for the most part, reactive. After a new virus appears in the wild, software developers must pick it apart, analyze its behavior, add its characteristics to the signature file for their antivirus program, and make the new signature file available. Most leading antivirus companies have "war rooms" set up to do this work at lightning speed, often resulting in updated definitions within hours of a worm's first appearance. Still, even if your antivirus program is configured to check for updates regularly, you could be unprotected from a new virus for a short period of time. This lapse in coverage can be extremely damaging in the crucial first few hours or days of a widespread virus attack.

  Because new viruses can crop up at any time, you should never rely on antivirus software alone to protect you from potential threats. To add multiple layers of protection, you should block executable e-mail attachments (see "Protecting Yourself from Hazardous Attachments," page 494, for details) and be sure to install all security updates promptly.

- **False positives.** In some relatively rare circumstances, an antivirus scan can incorrectly alert you that a program file is infected with a virus when in fact the file is perfectly safe. False positives can usually be attributed to one of two problems: a signature file that contains an erroneous definition of a specific virus; or a heuristic scan that detects the activity of a legitimate program, such as an installer or disk utility, and flags it as a possible virus.

  Whenever an antivirus program sounds an alarm, you should take it seriously, but you should also consider the possibility that it might not be the real thing. How can you tell a false positive from an actual virus? Start by looking at the alert itself. If it suggests that a heuristic scan is responsible for the alarm, you know that the suspicious behavior doesn't match any known virus in the program's signature file. If the alert includes the name of the suspected virus, head for the antivirus software maker's Web site and try to find additional identifying characteristics of that virus to confirm whether it's actually present on the system you're working with. If you can't find a definitive answer, send the suspect file to your antivirus software vendor and ask them to confirm whether it's truly infected or a false positive.

> **Caution** If you suspect that a computer on your network has been infected with a virus, avoid using it to browse the Internet or to send e-mail messages. If you are indeed infected, you risk spreading the virus far and wide by remaining connected to the Internet. In fact, because so many modern viruses can spread over network shares, a sensible precaution is to unplug the network cable temporarily until you can be certain that your computer is clean or that you've contained the infection. Find another computer, one you're certain is free of any tainted code, to research the symptoms you're experiencing; and use that clean computer to download any needed cleanup instructions or tools.

Chapter 14

The Internet is a rich source of complete and accurate information about viruses, worms, and other hostile software. Unfortunately, a random search of the Internet for information about the term "computer viruses" will also turn up a long list of links to sites that are incomplete, out-of-date, or run by scam artists. We strongly recommend that you start your search for definitive information with the vendor that supplies your antivirus software, because that company is most likely to have information and step-by-step instructions that are directly applicable to your system configuration. Virtually every major company that produces antivirus software offers a searchable Web-based list of viruses; we've included links to these invaluable information sources in the next section. In addition, we suggest bookmarking the independent CERT Coordination Center Computer Virus Resources page, which offers up-to-date, unbiased information about currently active viruses: *http://www.cert.org/other_sources/viruses.html*.

Choosing an Antivirus Program

The only computer that's absolutely safe from hostile software is one that's been unplugged and locked away. For everyone else, the risks of computer viruses are too great to ignore. Given the pandemic nature of viruses and worms, and their astonishing ability to reproduce, the conclusion is clear: No serious Windows user can afford to be without effective antivirus protection.

Even a quick survey of the marketplace turns up more than a dozen highly regarded antivirus packages. They're not all created equal. Which one is right for you? To narrow the field, ask yourself the following questions:

- **Do I need a personal or network antivirus solution?** As the name implies, personal antivirus software is designed to run on a single computer. Network-based antivirus software, by contrast, usually includes a central management console, where you can download a single copy of updated definitions and push them out to other computers on the network. Network antivirus software makes the most sense on managed networks of 25 computers or more.

- **Is the program compatible with my version of Windows?** Antivirus utilities work by hooking directly into the Windows file system, typically using file-system filter drivers. Because of the profound architectural differences between various versions of Windows, most antivirus programs and other low-level utilities will not work properly unless they were designed specifically for your version of Windows. Despite the many similarities between Windows 2000 and Windows XP, antivirus programs written for Windows 2000 might not work properly when installed on a computer running Windows XP. Insist on a guarantee of compatibility with your version of Windows.

- **Does the virus scanning engine integrate with my e-mail program?** The most effective protection against viruses that travel as e-mail attachments is to detect and quarantine them on arrival. To accomplish this task, the antivirus program needs to hook directly into the e-mail software. Several leading antivirus programs are capable of working in tandem with Outlook Express and Outlook 2000 or later. Before you pay for an antivirus program, make sure it can handle incoming e-mail properly.

- **Does it integrate with my personal or corporate firewall?** Increasingly, makers of security software are combining firewall features and virus protection in a single package. If you have a hardware router or firewall, it might be designed to work closely with a particular antivirus product. For instance, some Linksys routers can hook up with Trend Micro's PC-cillin antivirus package. If you're looking for several pieces of the security puzzle, an integrated solution could be cost-effective and easier to manage.

- **Can the software be configured to update itself automatically?** Even if you're supremely organized, this feature is crucial. As we noted earlier, for any antivirus package to be effective, it must be updated regularly. This updating works best as a background process that doesn't require any intervention on your part.

- **How much does the software cost?** Don't look only at the price tag of the software. Be sure to include subscription costs for updated virus definitions (typically renewed annually at about half the original cost of the software). If you have more than one computer to protect, budget for a separate license for each computer. (Most vendors offer discounts, sometimes substantial, for multiple copies used on the same network. But you might have to search for the best deal.) And don't ignore support. Some antivirus programs include round-the-clock support, free of any extra charges; other programs include no telephone support or provide only per-incident support, where a single incident can cost more than the original license.

> **Tip**   It's never too late to switch
>
> Many new computers arrive with a bundle of software already installed. Often, this bundle includes security software such as an antivirus program. Is this "free" antivirus software really a good deal? Only if it suits your requirements and works comfortably with your other software.
>
> We recommend that you look at the full range of antivirus options, including the bundled software that came with your computer, and make your decision based on your security needs. Don't let false economies dictate your decision—the average cost per computer to install a new antivirus program is typically between $20 and $50; after the initial grace period expires, the antivirus software vendor will probably charge you for an annual subscription to updated definition files. In addition, readily available promotional offers can reduce the cost of a new antivirus program. If you decide that the bundled software is indeed your best deal, be sure to install the latest virus definition files immediately.

Microsoft Windows XP Networking and Security Inside Out

● **Is a trial version available?**   Reviews and newsgroup postings are a helpful way to gather opinions from other people who have used a product. But they can't substitute for direct, hands-on experience. After you narrow the contenders to a few finalists, see whether you can download trial versions and use them for 30 to 60 days. Use this test period to try different options.

● **Is the software certified by ICSA Labs?**   The average computer user has no way to generate virus-infected files and e-mail messages to test an antivirus program, and the numbers that software makers include with their wares can be misleading at best. Is a program that claims to block 70,000 viruses really better than one that blocks "only" 50,000 viruses? Both programs almost certainly block every known virus likely to be found in the wild. So how do you know that a particular piece of software actually does what it's supposed to do? Look for certification by ICSA Labs, a leading independent tester of this class of software. To earn certification, a program must detect 100 percent of all known in-the-wild viruses and 90 percent of in-the-lab viruses. You can find an up-to-date list of software certified by ICSA Labs at *http://www.icsalabs.com/html/communities/antivirus /certifiedproducts.shtml*.

The following pages contain information about 13 leading makers of antivirus software. The list is not exhaustive, but it does include every company we know that makes antivirus software intended for home or small business users and compatible with Windows 2000 Professional and Windows XP Professional and Home Edition. If you visit all the Web sites, you'll detect a strong international flavor to this group; the companies listed come from Russia, Norway, Sweden, Finland, the United Kingdom, and the United States. The list is in alphabetical order.

Authentium, Inc.

● **Products:**   Command Antivirus, single-user and enterprise editions

● **At a glance:**   Command Antivirus installs as a service that runs in the background. It performs real-time scans of 70 file types (including compressed files) and on-demand scans over the Web. The antivirus module is also bundled with personal firewall, anti-spyware, and parental-control software in ESP Security Suite and Curtains for Windows. A free 30-day trial version is available.

● **Web site:**   *http://www.authentium.com*

● **Virus information:**   *http://www.authentium.com/support/threatmatrix /portal.asp*

Inside Out

Run your own virus tests

Some amateur virus-hunters maintain their own library of viruses. Support professionals in large organizations, who are regularly called on to repair infected computers, are especially tempted to hang on to viruses recovered from these infected computers. We think that keeping a virus collection is unacceptably risky behavior, about on a par with keeping scorpions or rattlesnakes in the garage. If you're evaluating a new antivirus program and you want to examine how it responds when it encounters an infected file, you don't need live viruses. Under the auspices of the European Institute for Computer Anti-Virus Research (EICAR), antivirus software makers have devised a standard test—a unique string of 68 ASCII characters—that you can embed in a file to trigger a reaction from their programs.

To create your own EICAR test file, use Notepad or another text editor to create a file that begins with the following 68 characters:

```
X5O!P%@AP[4\PZX54(P^)7CC)7}$EICAR-STANDARD-ANTIVIRUS-TEST-FILE!$H+H*
```

Note that the letters are all uppercase and that the third character is the uppercase letter *O*, not the number zero.

If your antivirus software is working and supports the EICAR test method, it will intercept the file as you attempt to save it; Trend Micro PC-cillin 2005, for instance, displays this bright red alert:

Four versions of this test file—a text file with a .com (executable) file name extension, a plain-text file with a double extension, and two .zip compressed archives—are available from EICAR's Web site. To download the files and read about their proper use, visit *http://www.eicar.org/anti_virus_test_file.htm*.

Chapter 14

Central Command

- **Products:**   Vexira Antivirus (various Home and Corporate editions)
- **At a glance:**   With this easy-to-use scanning software, you can monitor e-mail, downloads, and shared network drives. Weekly updates are available, with emergency daily updates when needed. An evaluation version of each product is available.
- **Web site:**   *http://www.centralcommand.com*
- **Virus information:**   *http://www.centralcommand.com/recent_threats.html*

Computer Associates International, Inc.

- **Products:**   eTrust EZ Armor, eTrust EZ Antivirus, eTrust EZ Firewall
- **At a glance:**   CA provides a broad range of products for home users, small businesses, and large corporations. eTrust EZ Armor combines personal firewall and virus protection for home users. All programs are available in 30-day evaluation versions.
- **Web sites:**   *http://www.ca.com, http://www2.my-etrust.com*
- **Virus information:**   *http://www3.ca.com/virus*

Eset

- **Product:**   NOD32 Antivirus System
- **At a glance:**   Provides on-demand protection and integrates with Windows Explorer and most POP3 clients. NOD32 can also scan Outlook databases. The product includes extensive update options designed for use on networks. A trial version is available.
- **Web site:**   *http://www.nod32.com*
- **Virus information:**   *http://www.nod32.com/support/pedia.htm*

F-Secure Corporation

- **Products:**   F-Secure Anti-Virus, F-Secure Internet Security
- **At a glance:**   This well-respected company offers more than a dozen versions of its flagship product, including personal and enterprise editions, as well as F-Secure Internet Security, which combines firewall and antivirus software. Evaluation copies are available.
- **Web site:**   *http://www.f-secure.com*
- **Virus information:**   *http://www.f-secure.com/virus-info/*

Grisoft, Inc.

- **Products:** AVG Anti-Virus 7.0 (Free, Professional, and Network editions)
- **At a glance:** AVG includes an on-demand scanner and e-mail protection with automatic updates. The free edition is for home users only. The network version can be used on networks with as few as two workstations. A 30-day trial of the Professional or Network edition is available for download.
- **Web site:** *http://www.grisoft.com*
- **Virus information:** *http://www.grisoft.com/us/us_vir_tt.php*

Kaspersky Lab

- **Products:** Kaspersky Anti-Virus Personal, Personal Pro, Business Optimal
- **At a glance:** Also known as AVP, this product from a respected company has an easy-to-use interface and integrates with Outlook Express and Microsoft Office applications. The Business Optimal version is designed for small to medium-sized businesses and updates itself hourly.
- **Web site:** *http://www.kaspersky.com*
- **Virus information:** *http://www.kaspersky.com/virusinfo/*

McAfee, Inc.

- **Products:** McAfee VirusScan and VirusScan Professional, McAfee Internet Security Suite, McAfee VirusScan ASaP
- **At a glance:** This huge company offers an enormous variety of security products and online services for home users, small businesses, and enterprise networks. VirusScan ASaP is an online managed support service available for as few as three users. Free trial versions are available.
- **Web site:** *http://www.mcafee.com*
- **Virus information:** *http://vil.nai.com/vil/*

Norman ASA

- **Product:** Norman Virus Control
- **At a glance:** Modular design includes an on-access scanner, an on-demand scanner, an updating engine, and a suite of utilities. Administrators can configure the software to push automatic updates to clients over the Internet, including employees with a home office. A 30-day trial version is available.
- **Web site:** *http://www.norman.com*
- **Virus information:** *http://www.norman.com/virus_info/virus_descriptions.shtml*

Microsoft Windows XP Networking and Security Inside Out

Panda Software

- **Products:**   Panda Antivirus, ActiveScan Pro
- **At a glance:**   This software offers comprehensive protection for business networks (servers and desktops). Home users can choose the Titanium or Platinum version, both of which offer daily updates. ActiveScan Pro is a browser-based solution that uses an ActiveX control to protect against viruses, spyware, and other hostile code.
- **Web site:**   *http://www.pandasoftware.com*
- **Virus information:**   *http://www.pandasoftware.com/virus_info/*

Sophos

- **Products:**   Sophos Anti-Virus, Sophos Anti-Virus Small Business Edition
- **At a glance:**   This software, which is designed specifically for use on business networks, monitors disks, programs, documents, and network drives. The Small Business Edition is appropriate for businesses with fewer than 100 employees; it offers central management tools and supports both Windows and Macintosh workstations. Free evaluation versions are available.
- **Web site:**   *http://www.sophos.com*
- **Virus information:**   *http://www.sophos.com/virusinfo/*

Symantec Corporation

- **Products:**   Norton AntiVirus, Norton Internet Security, Norton Internet Security Professional
- **At a glance:**   This large company offers versions for home users and businesses of all sizes, with firewall, anti-spam, and other capabilities included in the Internet Security bundles. The popular Norton AntiVirus integrates well with e-mail programs and corporate networks. Symantec's collection of virus removal tools is especially noteworthy.
- **Web site:**   *http://www.symantec.com*
- **Virus information:**   *http://www.sarc.com*

Trend Micro Inc.

- **Products:**   PC-cillin Internet Security, OfficeScan, HouseCall
- **At a glance:**   This well-respected company provides scanning solutions for home users, small businesses, and corporate networks. In late 2004, Microsoft chose its virus-scanning engine for use on the MSN Hotmail servers. Current versions of PC-cillin offer firewall, anti-spam, and anti-spyware capabilities. The HouseCall service offers a free Web-based scan to check for viruses.
- **Web site:**   *http://www.trendmicro.com*
- **Virus information:**   *http://www.trendmicro.com/vinfo/*

Where's Microsoft's Antivirus Software?

With Windows XP SP2, Microsoft plugged most of the security holes that existed in previous versions—with one noteworthy exception. As the Security Center notes in no uncertain terms, your computer is at risk until you install an antivirus program, and Microsoft doesn't include any antivirus features with Windows XP.

If you're a Windows trivia buff with a long memory, you might remember a program called Microsoft Anti-Virus, which was included with MS-DOS 6. It included a Windows module (licensed from Central Point Software) that offered protection for Windows 3.1 users. No subsequent version of Windows has included any real-time virus-scanning tools.

In January 2005, Microsoft released a new utility called the Malicious Software Removal Tool (MSRT). This utility, which runs on Microsoft Windows Server 2003, Windows 2000, and Windows XP, is not designed to block new viruses from entering a computer; rather, its function is to clean up systems that have been infected with known viruses. The MSRT is updated monthly and is delivered by Automatic Updates, usually along with Critical Updates that are routinely released on the second Tuesday of each month. On most computers, this tool runs silently and then deletes itself; it keeps a record of its actions, including details of any viruses it detected and removed, in a file called Mrt.log in your %SystemRoot%\Debug folder.

If you prefer to scan one or more systems manually, you can download the current executable version of the MSRT from *http://go.microsoft.com/fwlink/?LinkId=40587*. Because this utility is updated at least monthly, we do not recommend that you save this file. In addition, you can run a Web-based version of the utility by visiting *http://www.microsoft.com/security/malwareremove/default.mspx*. Because this tool uses an ActiveX control, you must run the Web-based scan using Internet Explorer and not an alternative browser.

For more details about the use of this tool, including instruction on how you can automate the task of running the MSRT on networks using batch files or Group Policy, read Knowledge Base article 890830.

Can we expect to see a full-featured antivirus program from Microsoft? The company has laid the groundwork to do so. In June 2003, Microsoft acquired the intellectual property and technology assets of GeCAD Software, a provider of antivirus software based in Romania. In December 2004, Microsoft acquired GIANT Company Software, Inc. and its GIANT AntiSpyware program. In February 2005, Microsoft announced that it had acquired Sybari Software, the maker of enterprise-level software for blocking spam and viruses on a variety of types of network servers. In July 2005, Microsoft began testing a subscription-based service called Windows OneCare, which includes antivirus and anti-spyware capabilities, a two-way firewall, backup services, and other essential consumer-focused security services. We don't know exactly when antivirus capabilities with the Microsoft brand name will be widely available for consumers and enterprise customers, but it is certainly safe to bet that those features are on the way.

Chapter 14

Protecting Your Computer from Hostile Software

Unfortunately, no one has yet designed a "silver bullet" that can protect your computer from all known threats. To effectively block the many varieties of malicious code that you're likely to encounter, you need to implement a comprehensive security program that consists of the following procedures:

- **Train every person who uses your computer or network.** At a minimum, family members and employees should know not to open unexpected attachments and not to execute software they download from the Internet until they have scanned it for viruses. In addition, they should know to be suspicious of any software that is not clearly from a trusted source. (For more details, including a checklist that you can print out for users to keep handy, see "Training Users to Avoid Viruses," page 483.)

- **Install antivirus software and keep it updated.** Installing an antivirus program is a two-part process. The initial setup enables the antivirus scanning engine—the code that checks files for possible viruses. The most important part of the package is the database of virus definitions (sometimes called the signature file). After installing an antivirus package on a new computer, update it to the latest definitions immediately. If the program has an automatic update feature, configure it to install new updates at least weekly.

- **Keep your system up to date with the latest security patches.** The most destructive viruses work by exploiting known vulnerabilities in e-mail programs and Web browsers; on an unpatched system with outdated or defective antivirus software, one of these viruses can run automatically when you view a Web page or click on an e-mail message. To prevent this nightmare scenario, use Windows Update regularly and install security updates as soon as they're available. Security patches are especially crucial for computers running Internet services, such as a Web server or an FTP server. (For details on how to download and apply patches, see "Keeping Current With Windows Update," page 217.)

- **Configure your computer to block potentially dangerous attachments that arrive by e-mail.** Many recent-vintage e-mail programs, including Outlook Express and Outlook, automatically block some or all attachments that have the potential to harm your system. You can also add this capability through third-party software; the MailSafe feature in ZoneAlarm Pro (available at *http://www.zonelabs.com*), for instance, intercepts attachments that arrive by e-mail and lets you decide how to handle them. See "Blocking Dangerous Attachments," page 485, for more details about your options.

- **Install a firewall program that can detect and block unsolicited outbound connections.** Windows 2000 doesn't include any firewall protection; the basic firewall built into Windows XP offers excellent protection against unwanted intruders, but it does nothing to detect programs that try to send data from your computer. A firewall program with two-way protection can alert you to Trojan horse programs and can also help you detect "spyware"—programs that surreptitiously connect to the Internet without your knowledge or approval. Firewalls also offer protection against network-based viruses.

● **Back up your critical data regularly.** If, despite your best efforts, a virus or other hostile program manages to slip through your defenses and cause irreparable damage to your computer, you might be forced to reformat and start over. This process is never painless, but a good recent backup can greatly ease the sting.

> **Note** Don't rely on a single layer of protection
> Protecting yourself from malware requires that you accept a few unpleasant truths: Antivirus software is not perfect. Even well-trained, experienced computer users (like you) can slip up. New vulnerabilities can result in attacks for which you're not prepared. A healthy respect for your enemy is important. If you think you can do without antivirus software because you're smarter than the cyber-hoodlums who write viruses and worms, you're practically daring them to take over your computer, and they have a better chance than you think of succeeding. To keep your computer safe from hostile software, it's important that you use more than one layer of protection and that you maintain constant vigilance against new threats.

Training Users to Avoid Viruses

Your first line of defense against any hostile software doesn't require any special hardware or software. The single most important precaution you can take is to train every user on your network (including yourself) to spot the warning signs of suspicious software. Make sure that every user understands the essential principles of safe computing. Print out a copy of these precepts (you can copy them from the electronic edition of this book, found on the companion CD) and post them near your computer:

● **Do not open any file attached to any e-mail message unless you know the sender *and* you are expecting the attachment.** If you receive an attachment from an unknown sender, delete it immediately. Be suspicious of any attachment, even if it was apparently sent by a friend, relative, or business associate, and do not open the attachment unless you are absolutely certain that it is safe to do so.

● **Never attach a file to an e-mail message without including an explanation.** At a minimum, you should explain what the attachment is and why you're sending it. Don't use generic text ("Hi, here's the attachment I promised!") that could just as easily have been generated by a mass-mailing virus. A personal note of a single sentence ("George, the attached Word document is the list of vacation rentals I promised to send you when we spoke yesterday") can reassure a recipient that the attachment is legitimate.

> **Tip** Zip attachments for safety's sake
>
> When you attach files to e-mail messages, you run the risk that the other person will be unable to open the file, especially if you're sending an executable file to someone who's using Outlook 2000 or later. To ensure that the files make it to your recipient safely, use a Zip-compatible compression program to compress them into an archive file. This precaution has a second benefit as well: "Zipping" the file reduces its size and thus lessens the time it takes to send and receive as well as the possibility that you'll run afoul of size restrictions imposed by the recipient's ISP.

- **When in doubt, check it out.** If you receive a suspicious or unexpected attachment, contact the sender and ask for an explanation. Pick up the phone, use instant messaging software, or use the Reply button to send an e-mail message. Be especially suspicious if the message that accompanies the attachment includes a generic exhortation to open the attached file ("You've got to see these pictures from my party!"). A quick visit to a reputable virus alerts Web site could help you determine whether the message and attachment are characteristic of a known virus. (For direct links to virus alerts, see the alphabetical listing of software companies in "Choosing an Antivirus Program," page 474.)

- **If it doesn't check out, delete it.** If you can't reach the sender and you aren't comfortable opening the attachment, hit the Delete key. The potential damage and the hassle of cleaning up after a virus infection greatly outweigh any possible benefit from an unknown file. Besides, if you learn later that the attachment was truly important, you can always ask the sender to send another copy.

- **Never install a patch or update you receive by e-mail.** If you receive an e-mail message that seems to be from Microsoft or another software maker with an attachment that purports to be a security patch, delete it immediately. This is a favorite tactic of virus writers. Reputable software makers post patches on their Web sites and send e-mail alerts that describe the patch and include a link to the download site. (The only exception to this rule is if you're troubleshooting a problem with a legitimate support person who sends you a file containing an unpublished hotfix or registry file to help you solve the problem.)

- **Never accept a file sent over an Internet messaging service unless you're certain the file is safe.** If you visit sites where online vandals share tools and techniques, you quickly learn that ICQ, AOL Instant Messenger, and Windows Messenger are favorite transmission vectors for Trojan horse programs disguised as MP3 files or graphics. Children are especially vulnerable to this sort of attack and need to be warned about the dangers of exchanging files with friends and strangers alike.

> **Tip** **Use test files to educate users**
>
> One powerful technique you can use to educate inexperienced users, especially children, is to send them an e-mail attachment that contains a fake virus file with the EICAR test (described in "Inside Out: Run your own virus tests," page 477.) Use this technique to demonstrate what they're likely to see when their antivirus software detects a real virus; it's much easier to discuss the proper response to virus alerts with a safe test virus than to wait until the user receives a real virus and possibly panics.

Blocking Dangerous Attachments

In a perfect world, your antivirus software will reject any miscreant that tries to sneak in as an e-mail attachment, either as it arrives or when you try to open or save the infected file. But that precaution can fail if your virus definitions are out of date or your antivirus software is temporarily disabled. If you're rightly concerned about that possibility, add a second layer of protection in the form of software that blocks all attachments that might contain hostile code.

You might already have access to an effective attachment-blocking system. Many ISPs and hosting companies that provide e-mail accounts routinely reject all messages that contain potentially dangerous attachments. In addition, you can block attachments using your e-mail client software. If your primary e-mail program is Outlook Express 6, Outlook 2000 with SP2, Outlook 2002, or Outlook 2003, this capability is built into the program you use to download and read e-mail messages. In Outlook 2002 and Outlook 2003, in fact, attachment blocking is hard-wired into the program and can be turned off only with the help of third-party utilities.

> For a complete description of the features and limitations of attachment blocking in Microsoft e-mail clients, see "Protecting Yourself from Hazardous Attachments," page 494.

If you prefer a non-Microsoft e-mail program, or if the attachment-blocking capabilities of Outlook or Outlook Express are unacceptable, you have at least these two alternatives:

- If you run your own mail server, you can block or quarantine potentially dangerous attachments at the gateway where e-mail enters your network. Many e-mail server programs include this capability as a configuration option, or you can install a separate module, such as GFI's MailEssentials for Exchange/SMTP (*http://www.gfi.com*). On all but the smallest networks, server-based attachment-blocking tools are vastly preferable to software that must be installed, configured, and kept running on each individual desktop.

- On a single computer, you can use ZoneLabs' ZoneAlarm Pro, whose MailSafe option mirrors the attachment-blocking capabilities of Outlook 2002, while still enabling you to decide which attachments are safe to save or open. ZoneAlarm Pro works with any POP3 or IMAP e-mail client to intercept and quarantine any attachment that might be harmful, based on a customizable list of 48 file name extensions. (Don't confuse this capability with the limited MailSafe feature in the free ZoneAlarm firewall product from the same company, which blocks only files with the .vbs extension.)

Table 14-1 lists the file name extensions that ZoneAlarm Pro considers potentially dangerous, breaking them down into categories by type of file. (This list is current as of February 2005 for users of ZoneAlarm Pro 5.5.) A comparison with Table 15-1 (page 497), where we list the equivalent settings for Outlook 2000 SP2 and later versions, shows that the two lists are similar but not identical. For instance, ZoneAlarm Pro blocks files whose names include the extensions .dbx and .nch, both of which are used for Outlook Express data files (each Outlook Express folder has its own data file and index), as well as Windows Media Player skins (.wms extension); Outlook, on the other hand, blocks Office profile settings (.ops) files, which ZoneAlarm Pro ignores. Otherwise, the two lists are remarkably similar.

Table 14-1. File Types Blocked by ZoneAlarm Pro

Type of File	File Name Extensions	Description
Compressed files	.zip, .mht	Many attachment-borne viruses today are carried in files compressed by using the popular .zip standard; quarantining this type of attachment gives you a chance to examine it more carefully. The .mht format is used to pack Web pages and accompanying images into a single file that can contain dangerous code.
Executable files and program installers	.com, .exe, .hta, .msi, .msp, .pif, .scr	Executable files are among the most dangerous of all file types because they can perform literally any task the user has permission to do. The .scr extension identifies a screen saver, which can be programmed to perform harmful actions. Files using the .hta extension are potentially dangerous HTML applications.
Batch files and shortcuts	.bat, .cmd, .lnk, .scf, .url	Batch files (including those with the .cmd extension aimed at Microsoft Windows NT/2000/XP) can call any executable program, as can shortcuts. The .url extension (Internet shortcuts) is banned because it can be used to disguise exploits that affect Web browsers, such as buffer overrun attacks.
System configuration files	.inf, .ins, .isp, .prf, .reg	These files can alter crucial portions of the Windows registry, including those related to Microsoft Office; .ins and .isp files can change Internet connection settings.

Table 14-1. **File Types Blocked by ZoneAlarm Pro**

Type of File	File Name Extensions	Description
Script and Visual Basic files	.bas, .js, .jse, .mst, .sct, .vb,.vbe, .vbs, .wsc,.wsf, .wsh	Script files that use the JScript or Visual Basic Scripting Edition language can perform a startling array of destructive actions. Internet Explorer security settings block most damage, but vulnerabilities exist and can be exploited on an unpatched system.
Shell scrap objects	.shb, .shs	Scrap objects, introduced in Windows 95, are rarely used today but are still supported by Windows 2000 and Windows XP. Because a scrap object can contain an embedded executable program, this file type is considered very dangerous, and in fact one wide-spread virus (VBS.Stages.A) used this technique successfully.
Media Player files	.asx, .wms	These file types can exploit vulnerabilities in Windows Media Player.
System files that can contain exploits	.chm, .cpl, .crt, hlp, .msc.	This group consists of Help files, console objects, security certificates, and other types of files that typically contain data but can be crafted to exploit vulnerabilities in Windows.
Outlook Express data files	.dbx, .nch	By tampering with the contents of mail folders, a virus writer could sneak hostile code onto a machine.
Microsoft Access data and program files	.ade, .adp, .mda, .mdb, .mde, .mdz	Because Access can be used to develop stand-alone applications, files in this category are considered dangerous and should be treated with suspicion.
Photo CD images	.pcd	Scripts that can be included in this file type are potential sources of attack.

As Table 14-1 makes clear, hostile code can be hidden in an astonishing number of file types, not only in executable files and scripts. The use of double file extensions (described in "How Malicious Software Attacks Your Computer," page 458) increases the risk that a careless or unsophisticated user might fail to distinguish between safe files and those that are potentially damaging.

If you turn on the MailSafe feature in ZoneAlarm Pro to block access to dangerous file attachments, the program intercepts all incoming file attachments; if the file name extension is on the MailSafe list, the program changes the extension to one that is registered to ZoneAlarm. A file attachment with the extension .exe, for instance, is renamed using the extension .zl9. When you attempt to open that file, ZoneAlarm Pro displays the dialog box shown in Figure 14-2 on the next page, warning you that the file might be unsafe. You can then choose whether to save the file for further examination, open it, or delete it.

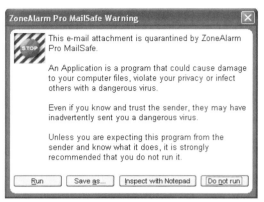

Figure 14-2. ZoneAlarm Pro intercepts potentially dangerous file attachments based on their file name extension; the program works with all POP3 and IMAP e-mail programs.

Tip   Look inside a script file

When you receive a script file as an attachment to an e-mail message, how do you know it's safe? If you have a basic knowledge of how scripts work, you can examine the file in a text editor before deciding whether to execute it. You can open a script file using Notepad or any text editor; you could also rename the script file using the .txt file name extension to ensure that it opens in Notepad rather than being inadvertently run when you double-click the file icon. Note that this precaution will not be effective with script files that have been encrypted.

Using Backups and System Restore

When a virus attacks your computer, one of the first actions it typically takes is to infect other files. If the virus remains undetected for days or weeks, you could find that some of the infected files have been copied as part of your regular backups. The System Restore feature in Windows XP, which takes regular snapshots of system files, can also keep copies of infected files. The risk? After you successfully clean up the infection, you restore your backed-up data files, only to discover that doing so inadvertently reinfects your computer.

To avoid this frustrating scenario, follow this advice:

- Always perform a complete virus scan before performing a full backup. If you schedule both tasks weekly, be sure to run the virus scan task *before* the backup task.

- After cleaning up a virus infection, install your antivirus software and the latest virus definitions before restoring any backed-up files. This precaution ensures that the antivirus program will detect any infected files in your backup set as they're restored.

Because of the design of Windows, it is not possible to repair or replace infected files saved in the System Volume Information folder during a System Restore operation. Antivirus programs can detect the presence of a virus in this location, but they can't clean it up. The solution is to completely purge all System Restore checkpoints and their accompanying saved files. To do so, follow these steps:

1 Open Control Panel and double-click the System icon (in the Performance and Maintenance category).

2 Click the System Restore tab and select the Turn Off System Restore On All Drives check box. (If your computer has only a single volume, this text will read simply Turn Off System Restore.)

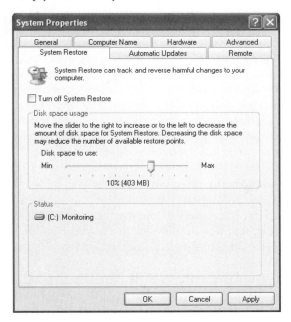

3 Click Apply, and then click OK to close the dialog box.

4 Restart your computer.

5 Update your antivirus software (the System Restore procedure might have removed recent updates to the scanning engine). Run a complete scan for viruses, using the most current virus definitions.

6 After verifying that the system is free of any infections, repeat steps 1 through 4, this time clearing the Turn Off System Restore check box.

Repairing an Infected System

What should you do if you suspect that your computer has been infiltrated by a virus? For starters, don't panic. If you indiscriminately begin deleting files or mucking with the registry, you could wind up making your ultimate cleanup job much more difficult. Follow the recovery instructions listed here to work your way through the cleanup process safely, without losing your sanity.

> **Tip** Should you start from scratch?
> Clean up or reformat? That's the difficult choice you face when your computer has been attacked by a virus or other hostile code. Given the choice, most people would prefer a simple cleanup in preference to the hassle and downtime involved in reformatting, reinstalling the operating system, reinstalling all programs, restoring backed-up data, and tweaking personal preferences. But don't let convenience overrule common sense. Can you be certain that the virus or worm is completely removed? If the malware contained a Trojan horse component, is it possible that it downloaded hostile software that you haven't detected? If you can't be 100 percent certain that the computer in question is completely clean, the prudent course of action is to start fresh, and take advantage of the opportunity to tighten the security gap that allowed the malware to sneak onto your computer. If the computer in question contains critical data and programs, especially if it runs any server software that is exposed to the Internet, you should bite the bullet and reformat.

- **Step 1: Positively identify the infection.**   The name of a file attachment or the text of the message that accompanied it might give you a clue as to the identity of the virus your computer contracted. Before you proceed further, confirm the exact diagnosis. Read the description of the virus in any of the online information sources listed in "Choosing an Antivirus Program," page 474, and verify all symptoms to be sure.

> **Tip** Don't rush to judgment
> Most major viruses mutate over time, with later versions of a specific attack often fixing bugs found in the original and adding new wrinkles. It's likely that the removal instructions for multiple strains of a single virus will vary in small but significant details. If you follow instructions that apply to a strain different from the one that infected your computer, you could leave bits of the infection behind, where they can reinfect your computer after you think you're up and running again. Take the time to make an accurate diagnosis. If you're uncertain, contact the support professionals at the company that makes your antivirus software.

- **Step 2: Isolate the infected computer.**   Because viruses can spread over networks and through internal e-mail servers, you should promptly pull the plug on your network and disconnect any modems to prevent further damage. Back up essential data files before you begin repairs, especially if the virus has destructive potential.

- **Step 3: Find explicit removal instructions.** From an uninfected computer, visit an authoritative source and find detailed removal instructions. Print out the instructions and keep them nearby as you work. Carefully read all instructions before beginning the cleanup.

- **Step 4: Gather your cleanup tools.** You might need to create a bootable floppy disk or CD or use your original Windows CD to boot into Safe Mode. The removal instructions should help you decide which tools are needed.

- **Step 5: Begin the cleanup process.** Depending on the virus, this task could take minutes, or it could require the better part of a day. The instructions you download in step 3 should help you prepare for this step.

  - Be prepared to delete all infected files and replace them with backup copies that are certain to be clean.

  - If you're lucky, one of the leading antivirus software companies has created an automated removal tool that can automate some or all of the cleanup process. Symantec offers an excellent collection at *http://www.sarc.com /avcenter/tools.list.html*. Download the removal tool and its instructions and save them, preferably to a CD or other removable media. This procedure is most effective when the virus that attacked you is relatively simple and its actions are thoroughly understood.

  - If no removal tool is available, follow the step-by-step removal instructions to the letter. Do not rush through this process, and don't skip any steps.

- **Step 6: Reinstall antivirus software.** After completing cleanup, this should be your first task. Use trusted media (the original CD), or a fresh download from an uninfected computer. Install the latest updates and rescan all local disks to verify that the virus is completely gone.

- **Step 7: Restore data and programs from backup copies.** Here, too, use only trusted media to reinstall programs. If you suspect that the original installation files might have been compromised by the virus, find fresh copies. Be especially vigilant for "data diddling" viruses, which can tamper with formulas in spreadsheets or alter text in documents. The notorious Melissa virus, for instance, randomly inserted a quote from Bart Simpson ("Twenty-two points, plus triple-word-score, plus fifty points for using all my letters. Game's over. I'm outta here.") into infected documents.

- **Step 8: Scan all other computers on your network.** Before you reconnect to your network, confirm that other computers are free of infection. This avoids the possibility that a blended threat will reinfect the newly cleaned-up computer. After you're certain that everything is back to normal, it's okay to reconnect.

Chapter 14

491

Securing E-Mail and Instant Messages

Electronic mail might be indispensable, but it can also be a major source of security concerns. E-mail attachments are the principal medium through which viruses, worms, and Trojan horses spread from one computer to another. Malicious scripts or insecure ActiveX controls in HTML-encoded messages can be harmful to your computer's health. Unencrypted message content can be subject to unwanted inspection, both while the message is in transit and after it has reached its destination. People who don't have your best interests at heart can impersonate you, sending messages to others that appear to have come from you. And messages can be altered by third parties while en route to recipients.

In some circles, instant messaging (IM) is a more popular communication medium than e-mail, spurring attackers to jump into the fray, hoping to exploit any software vulnerabilities and, in many cases, users' naïveté. IM scams can spread viruses, worms, and other malware. Other scams attract IM participants to phishing sites in an attempt to obtain personal information such as logon credentials and credit card data. IM users can also be targets of "spim" (the IM equivalent of spam); although spim doesn't threaten your security, it can be annoying.

Fortunately, you can take relatively simple measures to counter these various threats. For example, you can virtually eliminate the hazards associated with message attachments by applying a virus scanner to the attachments before opening them. (The current versions of Microsoft Outlook and Outlook Express provide additional protection against dangerous attachments, as you'll see in this chapter.) You can use security zones in Microsoft Internet Explorer to guard against rogue HTML in e-mail messages that you receive in Outlook or in Outlook Express. Public key encryption can ensure the privacy of your communications, and digital signatures can guarantee both the authenticity and the integrity of your e-mail messages.

In this chapter, we assume that you're reading, composing, and managing your e-mail using an up-to-date Microsoft client program—Outlook 2002 (part of Microsoft Office XP), Outlook 2003, or Outlook Express version 6 or later. If you use a different e-mail program, such as Thunderbird or Eudora, many of the basic principles still apply, but the step-by-step procedures for tasks, such as blocking dangerous attachments and installing digital certificates, are different.

Security Checklist: E-Mail and Instant Messages

- Be suspicious of any file attachment you receive through e-mail or instant messaging. Is it from someone you know? Did you expect to receive a file from that person?
- Configure your antivirus program to scan all attachments.
- Be sure you've updated your e-mail and instant messaging programs with the latest security updates.
- Be sure your e-mail program uses the Restricted Sites security zone for displaying HTML messages.
- If you use a public terminal to access a Web-based e-mail account, remember to log off and clear the cache when you're finished.
- Don't use a Web-based e-mail account as your registered address for sites with sensitive or financial information, such as your on-line banking access.
- Use encryption whenever you send an e-mail message that contains sensitive information.
- Use a digital signature to verify the identity of an e-mail message's sender and confirm that a message has not been altered.
- To prevent unwanted instant messages, block all users except those on your contact list.

Note A burgeoning problem that's often spread by e-mail is *phishing*, a scam in which someone tries to convince you to give them confidential information such as passwords, credit card numbers, personal identification numbers (PINs), and so on. For details about recognizing and avoiding phishing scams, see "Avoiding Losses from 'Phishing' Attacks," page 591.

Protecting Yourself from Hazardous Attachments

Every e-mail attachment is a potential threat to your computer's security. As we emphasize in Chapter 14, "Stopping Viruses, Worms, and Trojan Horses," you should be suspicious of any unexpected attachment from any source, even if it appears to be from a known and trusted contact. Regardless of its origin, never run or open any attachment from your e-mail program unless it has passed muster with an up-to-date virus checker. Even if your antivirus program does not scan inbound e-mail messages, it should intercept any infected attachment when you try to run or save it—that is, if you have your antivirus program set to scan all files as they're created or saved. If you're not certain that your antivirus software is protecting you automatically, save all attachments to your hard disk and scan them manually before you open them.

This advice applies to document files as well as executable programs. The macro languages that are incorporated into modern applications (for example, Microsoft Visual Basic for Applications, which is supported by Office and many other programs) allow full-fledged programs to be embedded in seemingly innocent document files. If you allow a macro to run unchecked, it can access essential resources on your system, including your disk drives and your address book. Hence, a Microsoft Excel workbook (.xls) or a Microsoft Word document (.doc) has the potential to do as much damage as an executable program (.exe). You should be most concerned with macro security if you're using an older version of Office, especially Office 97. Macro-based viruses are much less troublesome in Office 2003 and Office XP, and in Office 2000 when the appropriate security updates are installed; in each case, macro security levels are set to High by default, meaning that unsigned, untrusted macros simply won't run.

Attachment and Automation Security in Outlook

If you use Outlook as your e-mail client, you might already enjoy a considerable degree of protection against malicious attachments—perhaps even more protection than you need or want, thanks to the Outlook E-Mail Security Update. This sweeping set of restrictions was originally released as an add-in for Outlook 98 and Outlook 2000, and is incorporated into a default installation of Outlook 2002 or Outlook 2003; Outlook 2000 automatically adds the update when you install Microsoft Office 2000 Service Pack 2 (SP2) or later. The e-mail security update is designed to prevent viruses from using Outlook to propagate themselves. In particular, this security update does the following:

- Blocks access to attachments of a large number of file types
- Changes the default security zone for HTML-formatted e-mail from Internet to Restricted Sites
- Disables script stored directly in an Outlook item
- Implements protective measures that intervene and require the user's consent when any program attempts to send e-mail messages on behalf of an Outlook user, to access e-mail addresses from a user's message store or Contacts folder, or to save user messages as files

Note A detailed and balanced description of the Outlook E-Mail Security Update from a non-Microsoft perspective, as well as a wealth of other information about every aspect of Outlook, is available at *http://www.slipstick.com*.

Taken as a whole, the Outlook E-Mail Security Update provides remarkably effective protection against viruses and worms. To the best of our knowledge, in fact, this update alone would have protected you from every virus found in the wild since this update was introduced; as a result, attackers have taken to enclosing viruses in .zip archives that are sent as attachments. Some Outlook experts have called the security update "draconian" because its restrictions apply with equal force to experts and novices alike. But if you are willing to trade off some minor inconvenience for thorough virus protection, this is an essential update.

Determining Whether You Have the Security Update

Your version of Outlook includes the security update if any of the following is true:

- You're using Outlook 2002 or any subsequent version.
- You're using Outlook 2000 version 9.0.0.4201 or later.
- You're using Outlook 98 version 8.5.7806 or later.

To determine your version number, choose Help, About Microsoft Outlook. The version number appears near the top of the About dialog box.

How the Security Update Handles File Attachments

The most noticeable effect of the security update is that attachments of any file type included on Outlook's prohibited list become inaccessible in the Outlook e-mail client. You can neither open nor save such attachments. If you receive a message containing one or more proscribed attachments, Outlook identifies the blocked items in an informational header that appears above the message, as shown in Figure 15-1. The attachments remain attached; Outlook quarantines them, making them inaccessible to you, but it does not get rid of them until you delete the message containing the attachments.

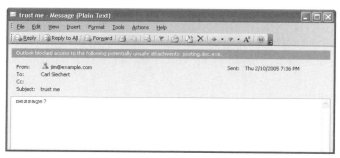

Figure 15-1.   Executable attachments are blocked in Outlook 2002/2003 and in versions of Outlook 2000 that include the security update.

Outlook also quarantines files attached to messages that were received before you installed the security update if their file type is on the proscribed list. Thus if you upgrade to Outlook 2002 or Outlook 2003 from an earlier version of Outlook, some of your existing e-mail attachments might become inaccessible.

Table 15-1 lists the file types blocked by the Outlook E-Mail Security Update. Note that in Outlook 2002 and Outlook 2003—but not in Outlook 2000—you can customize this list. (For information about altering the blocked attachment list, see "Customizing the Security Update in Outlook 2002 and Outlook 2003," page 502.)

Chapter 15

Table 15-1. FileTypes Blocked as Attachments by the Outlook E-Mail Security Update

Extension	File Type
.ade	Microsoft Access project extension
.adp	Microsoft Access project
.app	Executable application***
.asp	Active Server Page***
.bas	Microsoft Visual Basic class module
.bat	Batch program
.cer	Security certificate file***
.chm	Compiled HTML Help file
.cmd	Microsoft Windows command script
.com	MS-DOS program
.cpl	Control Panel extension
.crt	Security certificate
.csh	Script***
.exe	Program
.fxp	Microsoft FoxPro compiled source***
.hlp	Microsoft Windows Help file
.hta	HTML application
.inf	Setup information file
.ins	Internet settings file
.isp	Internet communication settings
.its	Internet document set***
.js	Microsoft JScript (JavaScript) file
.jse	Microsoft JScript encoded script file
.ksh	UNIX shell script***
.lnk	Shortcut
.mad	Microsoft Access module shortcut***
.maf	Microsoft Access file***
.mag	Microsoft Access diagram shortcut***
.mam	Microsoft Access macro shortcut***
.maq	Microsoft Access query shortcut***
.mar	Microsoft Access report shortcut***
.mas	Microsoft Access stored procedures***
.mat	Microsoft Access table shortcut***

Chapter 15

497

Table 15-1. **FileTypes Blocked as Attachments by the Outlook E-Mail Security Update**

Extension	File Type
.mau	Media attachment unit***
.mav	Microsoft Access view shortcut***
.maw	Microsoft Access data access page***
.mda	Microsoft Access add-in program*
.mdb	Microsoft Access program
.mde	Microsoft Access MDE database
.mdt	Microsoft Access workgroup information**
.mdw	Microsoft Access workgroup information**
.mdz	Microsoft Access wizard program
.msc	Microsoft Management Console document
.msi	Microsoft Windows Installer package
.msp	Microsoft Windows Installer patch
.mst	Visual Test source file
.ops	Microsoft Office XP settings**
.pcd	Photo CD image or Visual Test compiled script
.pif	Shortcut to MS-DOS program
.prf	Microsoft Outlook profile settings*
.prg	Program***
.pst	Microsoft Outlook personal folder file***
.reg	Registration entries (registry updates)
.scf	Microsoft Windows Explorer command*
.scr	Screen saver
.sct	Microsoft Windows script component
.shb	Shortcut into a document
.shs	Shell scrap object
.tmp	Temporary file***
.url	Internet shortcut
.vb	Microsoft VBScript file
.vbe	Microsoft VBScript encoded script file
.vbs	Microsoft VBScript script file
.vsmacros	Microsoft Visual Studio .NET macro project
.vss	Microsoft Visio stencil***
.vst	Microsoft Visio template***

Table 15-1. **FileTypes Blocked as Attachments by the Outlook E-Mail Security Update**

Extension	File Type
.vsw	Microsoft Visio workspace***
.ws	Microsoft Windows script file***
.wsc	Microsoft Windows script component
.wsf	Microsoft Windows script file
.wsh	Microsoft Windows Scripting Host settings file

*Blocked only in Outlook 2002 and later
**Blocked only in Outlook 2002 SP1 and later
***Blocked only in Outlook 2003

If you originate or forward a message containing proscribed attachments, Outlook warns you that your recipients might not be able to open those attachments but will send them if you choose to. Copying a message containing a blocked attachment into a new Outlook folder, importing that folder into Outlook Express, and opening the message after disabling the Attachment Security option in Outlook Express is one way to open a blocked attachment that you know is safe. For other workarounds, see "Workarounds for the Security Update," page 503.

How the Security Update Handles Microsoft Office Documents

You'll notice that the only core Office document types listed in Table 15-1 are those created by Access. Documents created in Excel, Word, Outlook, or Microsoft PowerPoint are exempt, even though Visual Basic for Applications (VBA), the macro language supported by all Office applications, has often been used to create viruses.

The security update does not block Excel, Word, Outlook, and PowerPoint documents because these applications include their own macro security mechanism. In Office XP and earlier versions, you can set macro security to one of three levels: High, Medium, or Low. Office 2003 adds a fourth level, Very High. The effects of these settings are as follows:

- **Very High (Office 2003 only).** VBA macros are allowed to run only if the Trust All Installed Add-ins And Templates option is enabled and the macros are stored in a specific trusted folder on the local hard disk. Macros contained in any other location, even digitally signed macros stored within documents, do not run.

- **High.** Only those macros that are digitally signed by sources you have explicitly added to a list of trusted sources are allowed to run. The Office application disables all other macros. (If you open a file containing a signed macro from a source that you have not explicitly trusted, the application gives you the opportunity to add the source to your trusted sources list.)

- **Medium.** The application prompts you whenever you open a file containing one or more macros from a source that you haven't explicitly trusted.

- **Low.** All macros are allowed to run.

In addition to these three settings, Office applications provide a check box that lets you accept all macros in currently installed add-ins and templates.

The Outlook E-Mail Security Update changes the macro security setting in Excel, Word, Outlook, and PowerPoint to High. If you regularly create your own macros or work with documents containing macros created by trusted associates, you'll probably find this default setting to be a nuisance. Changing the setting to Medium should give you an acceptable level of security. If you regularly write your own macros, you might want to switch to Low, provided you have an up-to-date virus checker that scans inbound e-mail messages. Be advised that Microsoft does not recommend this setting, and we agree that using this low level of protection is a bad idea. Serious macro developers have a much safer option: Add your own certificate and use it to sign any macros you create. If you share macros with other people, you can share the certificate as well. (For more details on installing certificates, see Chapter 20, "Installing and Using Digital Certificates.")

To change the macro security setting in Excel, Word, Outlook, or PowerPoint, choose Tools, Macro, Security. Set the level you want on the Security Level tab. To modify the trusted sources list, click the Trusted Sources tab. Note that although each application's security-level setting is independent of the other applications' settings, a source trusted in one application is trusted in all.

The Outlook Object Model and the Security Update

Outlook's object model—the collection of methods, properties, forms, and other internal elements that Outlook makes available for use by external programs—provides a convenient way for programmers to tap into Outlook and add e-mail features to their applications. However, the Outlook object model offers no easy way to distinguish between a legitimate program and a virus or other hostile intruder. As a result, in addition to blocking potentially dangerous attachments, the security update is designed to place a roadblock between Outlook and executable programs that attempt to access its object model. This layer of protection prevents rogue programs from propagating themselves by sending e-mail messages or accessing information from your messages or address books. Unfortunately, it has the side effect of interfering with legitimate applications and macros. It's particularly likely to hamper mail-merge operations and the exchange of information between Outlook and handheld devices running older versions of Windows CE or the Palm OS. (The latest versions of the operating system software for popular handheld devices do not suffer from these problems.)

If a process attempts to access your address book information, Outlook displays the warning shown here:

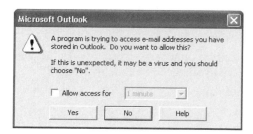

If you're sure that the attempted access is legitimate, you can allow the operation to proceed by selecting the check box and specifying a maximum duration. You can permit access for up to 10 minutes.

If a process attempts to send e-mail messages by using the Outlook object model, Outlook displays a similar prompt. In this case, however, the Yes button (which would allow the action to proceed) is disabled for five seconds. During this interval, you can click only No or Help. If a program uses Outlook's Send method repeatedly (as, for example, in an e-mail or fax mail-merge process), you must answer this prompt for each addressee—and wait five seconds each time.

In short, the Outlook E-Mail Security Update effectively precludes the use of Outlook for certain types of mail-merge operations. A program called Outlook Redemption, available at *http://www.dimastr.com/redemption/*, provides an effective workaround.

Adding the Security Update to Your System

As we noted earlier in this chapter, you can acquire the Outlook E-Mail Security Update either by upgrading to Outlook 2003 or Outlook 2002, or by installing Office 2000 SP2 or later. With an installation of Outlook 2000 or Outlook 98, you can also add the security update manually. Before you take any of these steps, be sure you have evaluated the tradeoffs that come with the extra security the update provides. (For an analysis of these tradeoffs, see *http://www.slipstick.com/outlook/esecup.htm*.) You can't remove the security update from Outlook 2002 (although you can customize the list of forbidden attachments). Removing the update from Outlook 2000 or Outlook 98 is not simple, but it is possible.

The update for Outlook 2000 is included in Office 2000 Service Pack 3; descriptions and download links are available in Knowledge Base article 326585. If you choose not to install Office 2000 SP3 for whatever reason, get the security update alone from *http://www.microsoft.com/technet/prodtechnol/office/office2000/support/o2ktool.mspx*. To add the security update to Outlook 2000, you must first have installed Office Service Release 1 (SR-1 or SR-1a). To determine whether you've already done this, choose Help, About Microsoft Outlook. The top line of the About dialog box will say SR-1 if you've installed either SR-1 or SR-1a. (SR-1a includes SR-1 and an additional patch for users who have upgraded from Microsoft Windows NT 4; if you're installing Office 2000 from scratch, you should download this version of the service release. For information about obtaining SR-1a, see Microsoft Knowledge Base article 245025).

To download the security update for Outlook 98, go to *http://office.microsoft.com/downloads/9798/Out98sec.aspx*.

If you install the security update for Outlook 2000 or Outlook 98 and then change your mind about using it, you can remove the update as follows:

- **Outlook 2000.** Open Add/Remove Programs in Control Panel and uninstall Office 2000. You then need to reinstall all of Office.
- **Outlook 98.** Open Add/Remove Programs in Control Panel and uninstall the update.

Chapter 15

Customizing the Security Update in Outlook 2002 and Outlook 2003

Administrators working with Outlook 2002 or Outlook 2003 in a Microsoft Exchange Server environment can tailor the security update to add or remove restrictions for particular users. To do this, you need the latest version of Admpack.exe, which is available on some versions of the Office CD and as a download from Microsoft. Microsoft Knowledge Base article 290499 provides an overview of this process. For details, see *http:// office.microsoft.com/en-us/assistance/HA011364471033.aspx* (for Outlook 2002) or *http://office.microsoft.com/en-us/assistance/HA011402911033.aspx* (for Outlook 2003). Using the Outlook Security Template, for example, an administrator for an Exchange Server–based mail system can use a graphical interface to control which types of files are restricted, among other things. For more information, see *http://office.microsoft.com /en-us/assistance/HA011402931033.aspx*.

Users of Outlook 2002 and Outlook 2003 (including those who are not using Exchange Server) can modify the registry to remove particular file types from the list of proscribed attachments. File types that you "unprotect" in this manner are demoted from Outlook's "Level 1" list (the list shown in Table 15-1) to a "Level 2" list that is initially empty. Attachments that you designate as Level 2 can be saved but not opened or run directly from Outlook. When you double-click such an attachment in an Outlook message, Outlook displays this warning:

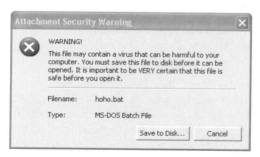

Click Save To Disk to proceed.

To move file types from Level 1 to Level 2, follow these steps:

1 Open Registry Editor.

2 Navigate to HKCU\Software\Microsoft\Office\11.0\Outlook\Security. (This is the correct key for Outlook 2003. If you use Outlook 2002, replace "11.0" with "10.0." Use "9.0" for Outlook 2000 SP3.)

3 Create the string value Level1Remove (if it doesn't already exist).

4 Double-click the Level1Remove value.

5 For the Level1Remove value data, enter a series of file name extensions, separated by semicolons.

For example, to add .bat, .com, and .pif files to the Level 2 list, you would enter this:

```
.bat;.com;.pif
```

6 Close Registry Editor.

7 If Outlook is running, close the application and restart it.

> **Caution** As always, we recommend that you exercise extreme caution before editing the registry manually. An incorrect modification can cause unintended side effects, up to and including an inability to restart your system. If you're not certain that you know how to use Registry Editor safely, we urge you to steer clear of this powerful but potentially dangerous tool.

Although the Outlook E-Mail Security Update blocks virtually all the potentially dangerous file types known at the time of its creation, miscreants are working overtime to figure out how to infect file types previously deemed safe. For example, vulnerabilities in .gif (graphic image) and .pdf (Acrobat document) files have been discovered, and these file types are not blocked. In addition, knowing that .zip archive files are not deemed dangerous, a number of virus writers now embed malicious code in a .zip archive attached to a message in the hope that recipients will open the .zip archive and then open the dangerous files it contains. If you want to add these potentially dangerous file types—or others that might be discovered later—to the list of blocked attachments, in the same registry key described in the preceding procedure, create a string value called Level1Add. Set its data in the same way as the Level1Remove value. For example, to add .zip and .gif files to the proscribed list, set the Level1Add value data as:

```
.zip;.gif
```

 Troubleshooting

Level1Add doesn't work in Outlook 2002

A bug in the initial release of Outlook 2002 causes it to ignore the Level1Add value, so you can't manually add attachment types to the prohibited list. Install the latest service pack for Office XP or Outlook 2002 to solve the problem. See KB article 312834 for more information.

A COM add-in called Attachment Options adds to the Options dialog box in Outlook a tab that lets you view and modify the lists of Level 1 and Level 2 attachment types. Attachment Options, written by Outlook MVP Ken Slovak, is available at *http://www.slovaktech.com/attachmentoptions.htm*.

Workarounds for the Security Update

The protection against rogue attachments offered by the Outlook E-Mail Security Update undoubtedly makes your use of e-mail in Outlook safer. If you're accustomed to receiving executable attachments from trusted parties, however, the security update also brings with it a nontrivial amount of inconvenience. In addition to moving Level 1 file types to the Level 2 list as described in the previous section, there are three other ways to ameliorate the inconvenience, listed at the top of the next page.

Chapter 15

503

● Ask trusted senders to compress all attachments, using the Compressed Folder feature in Microsoft Windows XP or a compression utility such as WinZip (*http://www.winzip.com*) before attaching and sending the files. Compressed files that use the .zip extension are not on the proscribed list by default.

● Instruct senders to upload files to an FTP server or a Web-based file storage service such as Xdrive (*http://www.xdrive.com*) or Box.net (*http://www.box.net*) and send you a link to the file via e-mail.

● Export messages with trusted attachments to Outlook Express.

Outlook Express 6 (the version that ships with Windows XP) *optionally* blocks executable attachments. If you choose to export one or more quarantined items from Outlook to Outlook Express 6, be sure that attachment blocking is turned off in Outlook Express. (For more details, see "Attachment Security in Outlook Express," page 504.)

Before you export messages to Outlook Express, create an Outlook folder to contain those messages (unless, of course, you intend to export your entire message store). Move or copy the messages containing the blocked attachments to the folder you just created. Then, in Outlook Express, follow these steps:

1 Choose File, Import, Messages.
2 On the Select Program page, select Microsoft Outlook and then click Next.
3 On the Select Folders page, click the Selected Folders option, and then select the name of the folder that holds the messages you want to import. Click Next.
4 Click Finish.

Attachment Security Without the E-Mail Security Update

If you're using a version of Outlook that does not incorporate the E-Mail Security Update (that is, Outlook 98 or an unpatched version of Outlook 2000), Outlook doesn't block potentially dangerous attachments. But it can warn you (and does so by default). To change Outlook's behavior in this regard, choose Tools, Options and click the Security tab, and then click Attachment Security. The following dialog box appears:

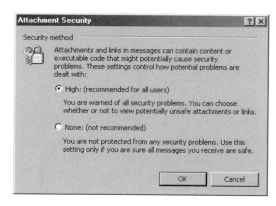

It's best to leave the warnings in place (the default setting in this dialog box). Of course, from a security standpoint, it's even better to retire that old e-mail client and upgrade to a more security-hardened version.

Attachment Security in Outlook Express

Beginning with version 6, Outlook Express provides a blanket attachment-blocking mechanism comparable to that in Outlook 2002/2003 or Outlook 2000 with the E-Mail Security Update. Previous versions of Outlook Express did not provide this capability. The specific workings of this feature vary depending on the operating system and service packs you have installed. The following is a summary of the different behaviors you're likely to see:

- With Windows XP Service Pack 2, Outlook Express 6 uses the new Attachment Execution Service interface. Attachment blocking is enabled by default but can be disabled by the user. Files that are known to be dangerous or whose behavior is unknown are blocked. Attachments that are safe may be opened or saved; for some file types that represent a low risk, you may have to deal with an additional prompt first.
- With Windows XP before SP2 and Windows 2000 with Internet Explorer Service Pack 1, attachment blocking uses a different mechanism. When blocking is enabled, file types known to be dangerous (typically executable files) are completely blocked; some other file types are blocked as well, although you can remove these file types from the blocked list by manually editing settings on the File Types tab of the Folder Options dialog box. Attachment blocking can be disabled completely.
- On a computer running Windows 2000 with any version of Internet Explorer and Outlook Express prior to version 6, no attachment blocking is available in Outlook Express. Any user can open, save, or execute any attachment, regardless of whether it's smart or safe to do so.

This security mechanism offers excellent protection against viruses and other hostile code. With Windows XP SP2, its operation is relatively unobtrusive, and it can be turned off any time if you need to open or save a blocked attachment that you know is safe. In Windows 2000 and in pre-SP2 versions of Windows XP, however, the default settings for the attachment-blocking feature are so restrictive that you're almost certain to be frustrated by its workings. If you're thinking of turning on attachment blocking in Outlook Express in either of these configurations, read this section carefully.

> **Tip** Upgrade to Internet Explorer 6
>
> Because Internet Explorer 6 is included with Windows XP, the Outlook Express features described in this section are available to all Windows XP users. With Service Pack 2, the user interface is unchanged, but the inner workings of the feature are much smoother. If you've chosen to stick with Windows 2000 and prefer to use Outlook Express as your e-mail client, we recommend that you upgrade to Internet Explorer 6 so that you have the option of enabling global protection against potentially harmful attachments. Installing Internet Explorer 6—a good idea in itself—automatically installs Outlook Express 6. To upgrade to Internet Explorer 6, go to *http://www.microsoft.com/windows/ie/default.mspx*.

In its original release, Outlook Express 6 does not implement attachment blocking unless you specifically enable this option. By default, all attachments arrive in your Inbox, where you can choose to open them directly or save them to disk. Beginning with Windows XP SP1 and Windows 2000 with Internet Explorer SP1, attachment blocking is enabled by default. To change the current setting for attachment blocking, choose Tools, Options and then click the Security tab. On the Security tab (shown in Figure 15-2), clear or select Do Not Allow Attachments To Be Saved Or Opened That Could Potentially Be A Virus.

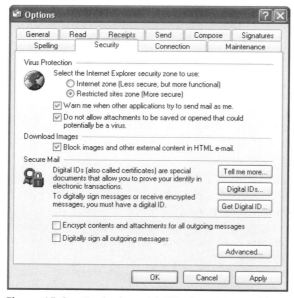

Figure 15-2.   Beginning with Windows XP SP1, blocking executable attachments in Outlook Express 6 is turned on by default.

With attachment blocking turned on, you can neither read nor save attachments that Outlook Express 6 regards as dangerous. What's on that list? In deciding which file types are potentially hazardous to your computer's health, Outlook Express uses the same list of file types that Internet Explorer checks when you download a file. This list consists of these two parts:

- A predefined, hard-coded list of file name extensions that are always considered dangerous. This list is composed of files that are traditionally considered "executable" (.exe, .bat, and so on). When attachment blocking is enabled, the user is always protected from these file types.

- A list of file types that may pose a risk. With Windows XP SP2, this list is managed by the Attachment Execution Service, and you see a security dialog box whenever you try to open, execute, or save a file that is on this list. In earlier versions, this second list is drawn from file types for which the Confirm Open After Download option has been selected. This very long list is far more extensive than the one employed by Outlook with the E-Mail Security Update. It includes some genuinely suspicious attachment types, such as JScript/JavaScript files (.js extension), Control Panel extensions (.cpl), and Windows Installer packages (.msi)—any of which could contain harmful code. It also includes Internet shortcuts (.url), compressed archives (.zip), Acrobat Portable Document Format files (.pdf), Office documents (.doc, .xls, and so on), and other benign file types.

Before SP2, Outlook Express blocked access to files on both lists. Figure 15-3 shows what happens to a typical message containing a variety of file attachments. Only a plain text file (.txt) and a graphics file (.gif) passed through the attachment filters.

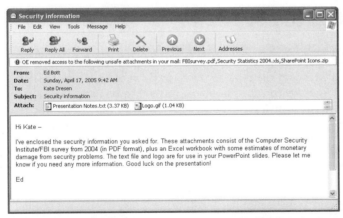

Figure 15-3. With attachment blocking turned on, Outlook Express 6 is overly cautious, rejecting even innocuous .zip files and Office documents.

If you intend to use this protective feature and you're not running Windows XP SP2, expect to fine-tune its behavior. For instance, you can specify that compressed files with the .zip extension are perfectly safe and should always be allowed to pass through the attachment-blocking filters. To modify the list, follow the procedure on the next page.

Chapter 15

1 Open Windows Explorer and choose Tools, Folder Options.

2 Click the File Types tab, and then scroll through the Registered File Types list until you find the extension for the file type you want to change. Select that entry in the list.

3 Click the Advanced button.

4 In the Edit File Type dialog box, clear the Confirm Open After Download check box.

5 Click OK to close the Edit File Type dialog box, and then click Close in the Folder Options dialog box.

Repeat this process for any other file types that you want to designate as safe. (Note that this option is not available for any file type on the hard-coded list of dangerous types.) Also be aware that changing this setting for any file type might affect the way it's handled in Internet Explorer.

With Outlook Express, unlike Outlook, you can easily disable this feature and grant access to attachments at any time. If you receive an e-mail message with an attachment that is blocked in Outlook Express, you can unlock access to it by disabling attachment blocking temporarily. From the main Outlook Express window, choose Tools, Options. Click the Security tab, and then clear the Do Not Allow Attachments To Be Saved Or Opened That Could Potentially Be A Virus check box. After you've saved or opened the attachment, you can turn the safety feature back on again.

Inside Out

Keep limited users out of trouble

Because the attachment-blocking setting is applied on a per-account basis, an administrator might want to turn it on for users with limited accounts while leaving the blocking feature disabled for your administrative account and those of other trusted users. Enabling blocking prevents inexperienced users from inadvertently executing a virus or a Trojan horse program. However, as an administrator, you cannot prevent a user who is poking around the Outlook Express Options dialog box from disabling this feature. If you're truly concerned that another user will deliberately bypass your controls and open a dangerous attachment, use the more powerful attachment-blocking feature included with Outlook.

Whether you choose to block executable attachments or allow them to be opened and saved, you should make sure that Outlook Express is set to warn you if an application (a virus, for example) attempts to send e-mail messages on your behalf. This option, controlled by the Warn Me When Other Applications Try To Send Mail As Me check box in the Options dialog box (see Figure 15-2), is enabled by default.

Protecting Yourself from Rogue HTML

Hypertext Markup Language (HTML) is the default display format for messages created in both Outlook Express and Outlook. In either program, you can override this default format for outbound messages. That is, you can set Outlook Express to compose messages in plain text instead of HTML; in Outlook you can choose to compose messages in plain text or Rich Text Format (RTF) if, for some reason, you don't want to use HTML.

By default, inbound messages formatted in HTML are displayed in HTML, which means that Outlook and Outlook Express are potentially exposed to the same HTML threats as a Web browser—malicious scripts or hostile ActiveX controls, for example. In their current versions, both programs include an option that causes incoming messages to be displayed in plain text; HTML coding and scripts are ignored. In Outlook 2003, choose Tools, Options. On the Preferences tab, click E-Mail Options and then select the Read All Standard Mail In Plain Text check box. (A related option lets you choose whether to use plain text for digitally signed messages. If you opt to use plain text, the digital signature can't be verified.) To force the use of plain text for incoming messages in Outlook Express 6 SP1 (or on Windows XP SP2), choose Tools, Options. On the Read tab, select Read All Messages In Plain Text. (In Windows XP—but not Windows 2000—Outlook Express also offers a command that immediately renders in full HTML a message that is displayed in plain text. In the message window, choose View, Message In HTML.)

Both Microsoft e-mail client programs deal with the potential hazards of HTML the same way Internet Explorer does—with security zones. (For information about Internet Explorer security zones, see "Using Security Zones," page 405.) The use of security zones in Outlook and Outlook Express differs from that in Internet Explorer, however, in the following ways:

- In Internet Explorer, you can choose from four security zones—Internet, Local Intranet, Trusted Sites, and Restricted Sites. In Outlook and Outlook Express, only the Internet and Restricted Sites zones are available.

- In Outlook and Outlook Express, ActiveX controls and scripts are always disabled, even if you have enabled them in the currently active security zone. (For information on how to run a script in Outlook 2002/2003, see "Activating Script in an Outlook 2002 or Outlook 2003 Message," below.)

- Outlook and Outlook Express always apply the specified security zone's settings to inbound messages, regardless of their source.

It's particularly important to understand the third point. In Internet Explorer, you can assign particular URLs to the Restricted Sites zone. For example, if you regard *www.edbott.com* as a purveyor of perilous prurience, you can add that site to the Restricted Sites zone and use the settings associated with Restricted Sites to keep Ed's wares from entering your system. If you set Outlook or Outlook Express to use the Internet zone, however, *all* e-mail—even messages originating at or passing through *edbott.com*—will be given the more relaxed settings typically associated with the Internet zone. In other words, the e-mail client doesn't care where the message comes from or who it has kept company with along the way; it uses the same security zone for all inbound messages.

Chapter 15

509

Changing the Security Zone

In Outlook 2002/2003 and Outlook Express 6, the default security zone is Restricted Sites. In all earlier versions of both programs, the default zone is Internet. For effective security in earlier versions of these e-mail clients, you should switch to Restricted Sites. The procedure for changing the zone is essentially the same in both programs:

1. Choose Tools, Options, and then click the Security tab.

2. In Outlook, select the zone you want from the Secure Content section of the dialog box. In Outlook Express, select a zone in the Security Zones section of the dialog box.

Activating Script in an Outlook 2002 or Outlook 2003 Message

Normally, you do *not* want script embedded in an HTML e-mail message to run within your message window. As a general rule, letting script run in this context is such a bad idea that Outlook and Outlook Express expressly forbid it, even if you have adjusted the security parameters associated with the Internet or Restricted Sites zone to allow script to run. But the message window in Outlook 2002 and Outlook 2003 does include a command that lets you temporarily override the scripting safeguards.

If an Outlook message includes script that you're certain is safe, you can run the script by choosing View, View In Internet Zone. This command, which appears only within the message window (not in the main Outlook window) and only when an HTML message is displayed, is a curiosity in several ways.

First, it does not implement the current security parameters of the Internet zone. If you turn scripting off in the Internet zone and then choose View, View In Internet Zone for a scripted message, the script will still run.

Moreover, when you choose View, View In Internet Zone, Outlook displays the warning shown here *whether or not* your message actually contains any script. (If your message really does contain script, Outlook indicates that fact in the information bar that appears directly above the message header, before you choose the View In Internet Zone command.)

Another HTML Concern: Linked Graphics

HTML-formatted messages often include photos, logos, and other graphic images that are not included as an attachment to the message. Rather, the HTML code contains a link to a graphic file that is stored on an external Web server. When you display the message, earlier versions of Outlook and Outlook Express automatically connected to the Internet and downloaded the image. While this isn't a security threat per se, it can be a privacy threat that can lead to the receipt of more spam. How? When the e-mail client retrieves a graphic file from a Web server, the server's logs record the message recipient's e-mail address, among other things. For spammers, this provides confirmation that the address is valid. Further, they might infer that you liked the message enough to at least open it and view its pictures. (Because of its value in this regard, some spammers and legitimate e-mail senders include a link to an invisible single-pixel image file—a so-called *web bug*—for the sole purpose of knowing whether you opened their message.) Linked images in e-mail messages also create an annoyance for users who do not have always-on Internet connections: When they open such a message, the e-mail client attempts to open a connection to the Internet.

In Outlook 2003 and in Outlook Express SP1 (the version included with Windows XP SP2), the issue of links to external servers has been addressed. By default, both programs display a placeholder instead of a picture that must be downloaded from an external server.

To view the picture in Outlook 2003, right-click any image placeholder and choose Download Pictures. Other options on the shortcut menu enable you to add the sender or the sender's domain to the safe senders list; pictures from designated safe senders download automatically. For additional options, choose Tools, Options. On the Security tab, click Change Automatic Download Settings to display the dialog box shown here:

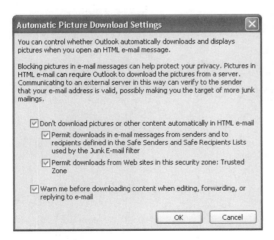

In Outlook Express, the feature is less complex. A message that includes links to external images shows "Some pictures have been blocked to help prevent the sender from identifying your computer. Click here to download pictures." You control this option with the Block Images And Other External Content In HTML E-Mail check box on the Security tab of the Options dialog box. (See Figure 15-2 on page 506.)

Chapter 15

Finally, although its effects on the current message are not the same as those you would get by setting Outlook to use the Internet zone globally, the command becomes unavailable if you set Outlook to use the Internet zone. Hence, if you want to let a script run in an Outlook message, you must first be sure that Outlook itself is set up to use the Restricted Sites zone and then choose View, View In Internet Zone.

Using Web-Based E-Mail Securely

Web-based e-mail systems such as MSN Hotmail, Gmail, or Yahoo! Mail offer you the convenience of being able to send and receive messages from any computer connected to the Internet, anywhere in the world. This ability is a genuine convenience when you're traveling without a computer of your own; you can sit down at any computer, including those in public libraries or Internet cafés, and catch up with your e-mail. If you use one of these services on a public or shared computer, however, you need to take a few precautions that you might not consider necessary at home:

- Be sure the system does not cache your logon credentials.
- Be sure to sign out explicitly when you've finished using an e-mail system.
- Be sure to clear the temporary Internet cache when you're finished browsing.

Many Web-based e-mail systems offer you the option of "remembering" your user name and password so that you can log on with one or two keystrokes instead of having to type everything out completely. (See Figure 15-4.) If you make the mistake of selecting the easy logon option at a computer that's available to the public, the public (or at least anyone who knows your user name) will have easy access to your password and your account.

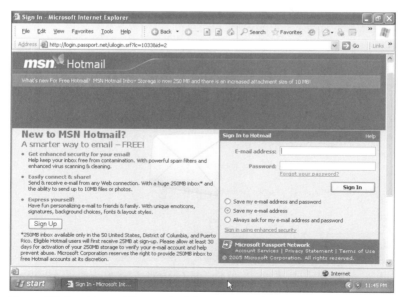

Figure 15-4. At a public terminal, be sure you do not select the option to save your username and password, and remember to sign out before walking away from the computer.

If your e-mail service doesn't offer to remember your logon credentials, your browser might. In Internet Explorer, an AutoComplete dialog box (or, in Mozilla-based browsers, Password Manager) might appear after you submit your name and password. You should, of course, decline its offer.

For more details on how to minimize the risks associated with the AutoComplete feature in Internet Explorer, see "Protecting Your Identity," page 587.

When you finish using e-mail at a public computer, don't simply pull up a different Web page or click off to some other application. You must sign out of the e-mail service, or you risk exposing your e-mail account to the next person who sits down at this computer. (In most cases, closing all browser windows is equivalent to signing out, but it's best to get in the habit of signing out explicitly.)

Some Web-based e-mail services, such as MSN Hotmail and Yahoo! Mail, offer the option of logging on over a secure (SSL—for Secure Sockets Layer) connection. (In Hotmail, click the Sign In Using Enhanced Security link.) Take advantage of this option if it's available. Doing so will keep your logon credentials encrypted as they're transmitted to the service provider, giving you an extra measure of protection against potential identity thieves.

If you log on securely, pages you view are encrypted and are typically not cached. If you don't have a secure logon option, you should clear the cache of temporary Internet files before you log off so that others can't revisit messages you viewed during a session. You can demonstrate this vulnerability at home: Browse the Internet, visit your e-mail site, and retrieve some messages. Log off and then, in Internet Explorer, choose File, Work Offline. Open the History pane, and then select By Order Visited Today from the View list. You should see several links to your e-mail site near the top of the History pane. Click a link in the History pane. If the browser gives you the option of reconnecting or staying offline, choose to stay offline. Your mail page should appear in plain view.

To clear the cache for Internet Explorer, choose Tools, Internet Options. On the General tab, click Delete Files. (On a public terminal, you might want to take a few seconds to erase other tracks as well: click Delete Cookies and Delete History.)

Troubleshooting

Your session expires immediately

Many Web-based e-mail systems use session cookies to track your identity while you're on line. If you log on to an e-mail service and then find yourself quickly booted out, it might be because, on the computer where you're working, the browser has inadvertently been set to disallow session cookies. You can use Internet Explorer 6 to reinstate session cookies, either globally or for particular URLs. For details, see "Protecting Your Identity," page 587.

> **Tip**   Don't use Web-based e-mail as your primary e-mail account
>
> If someone manages to learn your e-mail logon credentials (by observing or capturing your logon at a public terminal, for example), you might be putting at risk much more than your correspondence with Aunt Dora. First, of course, there is the matter of any sensitive messages that you have stored in your mailbox. Among those messages might be ones from secure sites advising you of your user name and password for those sites. Now whoever gains access to your e-mail also has access to those sites. It gets worse. Most sites that require you to log on have an "I forgot my password" link. On many sites, clicking this link causes the server to send your password to your registered e-mail address. So a thief with access to your e-mail account could attempt to log on to your bank account (for example), request that the password be sent to your e-mail address, retrieve the password, and then delete the message before you ever see it. There goes your savings.
>
> For this reason, we suggest not using your Web-based e-mail for receiving or storing any sensitive messages, nor for signing up for any other Web-based services. Instead, use it only for casual correspondence, and promptly delete any messages that contain sensitive information.

Handling Attachments and Script

Most Web-based e-mail services can scan inbound and outbound attachments for you, significantly reducing the chance that you'll infect your computer (or one in your local library or Internet café) by downloading a virus. This option also eliminates the possibility that you'll inadvertently transmit a virus by sending an e-mail message from an infected computer. MSN Hotmail, for example, automatically scans all attachments, without regard to file type, using software provided by Trend Micro.

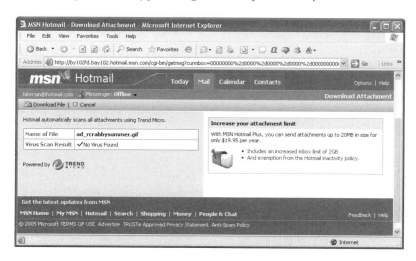

If your inbound attachments pass, MSN Hotmail lets you download them (but does not allow you to open them directly).

Before you commit to a Web-based e-mail service, you should familiarize yourself with its behavior toward attachments—particularly if you expect to be using the service at public computers that might not have adequate alternative forms of virus protection. If you plan to use the service as a secondary e-mail account (one to rely on while traveling, for example, or as an e-mail address to give out to online merchants in place of the address you normally use), try sending attachments of various file types from your primary account to the prospective secondary one to see what happens when they arrive.

If possible, you should perform the same experiment with a sample of benign script (VBScript or JavaScript or JScript). Most, but not all, Web-based e-mail services will refuse to run the script. You should avoid any service that allows the script to run. Some services (Yahoo!, for example) will display your script as text in the message body. If you know what you're looking at and can vouch for its safety, you can copy the script elsewhere and use it. Other services, such as MSN Hotmail, will do their best to hide the fact that a message has script. (To see the script in an MSN Hotmail message, click Options, and then click Mail Display Settings. In the Message Headers section of the Mail Display Settings page, choose Advanced, and click OK. Then return to your message, and in the expanded header, click View E-Mail Message Source.)

Protecting E-Mail from Prying Eyes

It's only a slight exaggeration to say that an unencrypted message sent by e-mail is about as private as a message written on a postcard. The problem is that packets of data moving from one e-mail server to another over the Internet travel through an unpredictable number of intermediaries; because these packets contain plain text, anyone who has access to any server along the way (your Internet service provider, for instance) can read the contents of messages in transit. The task might not be quite as simple as turning over a postcard, but it's not that much more difficult. For messages whose confidentiality is crucial, you can hide your communication from everyone but its intended recipients with the help of public key cryptography.

> For information about public key cryptography, see "What Are Digital Certificates?" page 672.

When you want to send someone a confidential message, you first obtain that person's public key. (You can do this through e-mail, or you might be able to download the key from a key server.) You encrypt your message with your recipient's public key before sending it, and the recipient decodes it with his or her private key once the message arrives. Anyone attempting to eavesdrop on your communication along the way is rewarded with an incomprehensible jumble of letters and numbers.

With public key cryptography, you also can add a *digital signature* to your messages. Digitally signing a message assures your recipient of two things: that the message is from you (not someone pretending to be you), and that it has not been altered en route. It does not encrypt your message or protect it in any way from being intercepted. For more information about digital signatures, see "Ensuring the Authenticity and Integrity of Your Messages," page 520.

How Private Is Your E-Mail?

The Electronic Communication Privacy Act (ECPA) of 1986 makes it illegal in the United States for third parties to intercept and read your e-mail. (Other countries might have laws that are more or less restrictive.) The amount of protection this law actually gives you is limited by enforcement difficulties and is subject to the following exceptions:

- E-mail sent to any kind of public forum (such as a newsgroup or bulletin board service) is not private.
- The privacy of a message is forfeited if you or any recipient of the message consents to making the message public.
- An employer can legally read any message sent or received through the employer's computer system.
- An Internet service provider (ISP) can legally read your e-mail, including unretrieved messages in your mailbox and messages you've recently sent or received.

You should also be aware that an ISP is entitled to make backup copies of your messages before they're deleted from the ISP's server. Law enforcement agencies can access these stored records with a legally obtained search warrant or subpoena.

Obtaining a Public Key/Private Key Pair

Many popular e-mail clients, including Outlook, Outlook Express, and Thunderbird, provide encryption and signing capabilities by supporting a standardized secure message format called Secure/Multipurpose Internet Mail Extensions (S/MIME). To encrypt messages using S/MIME, you must first obtain a *digital certificate*–sometimes called a *digital ID*. A digital certificate is to electronic communications what a driver's license or passport is to face-to-face transactions. It attests to your identity in a secure fashion.

For information about acquiring and managing digital certificates, see Chapter 20, "Installing and Using Digital Certificates."

> **Tip** **Password-protect your private key**
> When you apply to a certification authority (CA) for a certificate, you might be given the option to set a security level for your private key. (In the VeriSign forms, for example, this option appears under the heading "Additional Security for Your Private Key.") If you accept, Windows presents a dialog box giving you the choice of High, Medium, or Low security. If you select High, you are prompted for a password every time an application uses your private key (when you send a digitally signed message or decrypt an incoming message, for example). If you select Medium, you are prompted for permission when an application requests your key, but you do not need to supply a password. If you select Low, an application can use your private key without obtaining your explicit consent. Although it might be inconvenient to supply a password every time your key is used, selecting High is the best way to ensure that your private key remains under your exclusive control. If you select Medium or Low (or bypass this process altogether), your private key is secured only by your user account password, which means that it is accessible to administrators and to anyone with physical access to your computer if you step away without logging out.

Once you have obtained and installed your own certificate, you're in a position to add digital signatures to your messages. You can also receive encrypted messages from others. To send encrypted messages to someone else, you need to acquire that person's public key, as described in the following section.

Using S/MIME to Send Encrypted Messages

To send an encrypted message, you must have your recipient's public key, which is a component of the recipient's digital certificate. You can add that certificate to your certificate store by receiving a digitally signed e-mail message from your correspondent. When you receive the signed message, you need to install the attached certificate in your certificate store. To do this in either Outlook or Outlook Express, right-click the sender's name in the message window and then choose either Add To Contacts or Add To Address Book. If you already have a Contacts item or an Address Book record for the sender, a prompt will ask whether you want to update the existing record. Click Yes.

To confirm that you've successfully added your correspondent's certificate to your certificate store, open his or her Contacts item or Address Book record. On the Certificates tab (in Outlook) or the Digital IDs tab (in Outlook Express), you should find an entry for the person's certificate, as shown in Figure 15-5 on the next page. To inspect the certificate, select it and click Properties. If more than one certificate has been installed for this correspondent, the one marked Default will be used for outbound encrypted messages. If you need to change the default, select the certificate you want to use and click Set As Default.

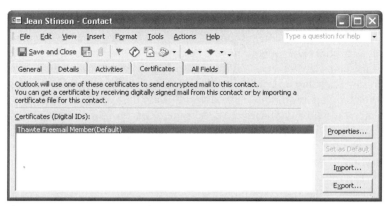

Figure 15-5.   You can confirm a successful installation of someone's certificate by opening his or her Contacts item or Address Book record.

If asking your correspondent to send you a digitally signed message is not convenient, and if you know which CA issued that person's certificate, you might be able to download and install the certificate from the CA's Web site. VeriSign and GlobalSign, for example, maintain directories at *https://digitalid.verisign.com/services/client/* and *http://secure.globalsign.net*, respectively.

After you have your recipient's public key, you can encrypt a message to that person. In Outlook 2000, do the following:

1   Begin creating a new message in the normal way. In the message window, click the Options button on the toolbar (not the Tools, Options command that is available if you use Word as your e-mail editor).

2   In the Message Options dialog box, select Encrypt Message Contents And Attachments.

If you are using Outlook 2002 or Outlook 2003, follow these steps:

1   Begin creating a new message in the normal way. In the message window, click the Options button on the toolbar (not the Tools, Options command that is available if you use Word as your e-mail editor).

2   In the Security section of the Message Options dialog box, click Security Settings.

3   In the Security Properties dialog box, select Encrypt Message Contents And Attachments.

In Outlook Express version 5 or 6, do the following:

1   Begin creating a message in the normal way.

2   In the message window, click Encrypt (on the toolbar) or choose Tools, Encrypt.

Encrypting All Outbound Messages

To encrypt every message you send in either Outlook or Outlook Express, choose Tools, Options. On the Security tab, select Encrypt Contents And Attachments For Outgoing Messages.

If you try to send an encrypted message to someone whose public key you do not have, Outlook warns you as follows:

If your message is addressed to multiple correspondents, clicking Continue will send the message in encrypted form to all recipients. Only those recipients for whom you have a certificate will be able to read the message; all others will be unable to read the message text.

> **Caution**   Encrypting all message content imposes a burden on anyone who receives a message from you. In some scenarios, in fact, the recipient might be unable to read messages you send. This can happen, for example, if the recipient uses Outlook on two computers—a desktop computer and a notebook, for instance—and keeps synchronized copies of the Outlook message store on each computer. If the recipient's certificate is saved only on the desktop computer, he or she will be temporarily unable to open the encrypted message on the notebook (and it's difficult to download a certificate when you're working on a notebook that isn't connected to the Internet). For the overwhelming majority of people, e-mail encryption is best performed on a message-by-message basis.

Reading Encrypted Messages

Outlook and Outlook Express identify encrypted messages by displaying an envelope icon with a blue padlock. For your protection, the message text does not appear in the preview pane in either program. When you open an encrypted message, your e-mail client retrieves your private key—after getting your permission or password, if you have protected your private key (see "Password-protect your private key," page 517)—and decodes the message. While you're reading, you can click the lock icon in the upper right corner of the message window to inspect the certificate that was used to encrypt the message.

An unauthorized person who tries to read an encrypted message will see an error message similar to the following (from Outlook Express):

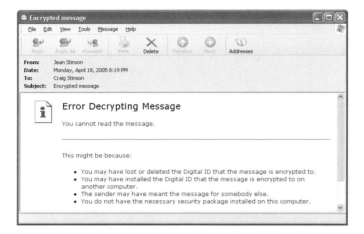

If you export an encrypted message, the message retains its encryption. If you forward an encrypted message, Outlook and Outlook Express assume that you want to encrypt the forwarded copy; you must, of course, have each new recipient's public key to accomplish this.

Ensuring the Authenticity and Integrity of Your Messages

As we mentioned at the start of this chapter, one of the hazards inherent in the use of e-mail is the possibility that someone might impersonate you—that is, send messages that appear to come from you. Making an e-mail message appear to come from someone other than its true sender is ridiculously easy. All you have to do is change the name and e-mail address that appear in the User Information section of the sending account's Properties dialog box. When your recipient opens your message, the information you entered is displayed in the From field.

That simple trick might fool a novice computer user, but anyone who knows how to view the full message header can usually spot a forged From address. (For details on interpreting a full message header, see "How to Decode an E-Mail Header," page 531.) Nevertheless, if someone chooses to embarrass you by sending a message that appears to originate under your name, you're powerless to prevent it, and some damage could well be done if a recipient does not recognize the hoax.

You can't eliminate this hazard. What you can do is use a *digital signature* to certify that what *you* send really does come from you. If you suspect that someone is abusing your good name, you can even adopt the practice of digitally signing all your messages.

A digital signature also ensures the recipient that your message has not been altered in any way. Consultants and software or hardware vendors often digitally sign their e-mail notifications of security vulnerabilities and updates; this precaution prevents a third party from counterfeiting a message and fooling a recipient into downloading a patch that contains a virus or a Trojan horse program.

When you add a digital signature to a message, your e-mail client program begins by applying a one-way *hash* function to your message. The hash function creates a *message digest*—a unique string of characters that is derived from the exact text of your message but that cannot be converted back into your text. (For that reason, hash functions are used only for authentication, not for encryption.) Usually, the message digest is much shorter than the message from which it is derived.

The message digest is then encrypted with your private key and attached (along with your certificate) to your message. If you, the sender, are not who you say you are, the signing process will fail at this point, and you will see something comparable to the following:

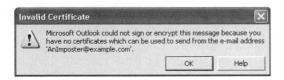

The recipient's e-mail program applies the same hash function to the received message text and then decrypts the message digest, using your public key (supplied as part of your certificate). If the message has been altered in any way, the recipient's hash function will not produce the same message digest as the sender's, and the recipient will see an error message similar to the one shown here:

Signing All Outbound Messages

To digitally sign every message you send in either Outlook Express or Outlook, choose Tools, Options. On the Security tab, select Digitally Sign All Outgoing Messages (in Outlook Express) or Add Digital Signature To Outgoing Messages (in Outlook).

Chapter 15

Using PGP for Signing and Encrypting

As an alternative to the S/MIME procedures described in the foregoing paragraphs, you can encrypt and sign messages using Pretty Good Privacy (PGP). PGP was the original standard for communications secured by public key cryptography—and some still regard it as the gold standard. Released in 1991 as freeware by its creator, Phil Zimmermann, PGP is now available from PGP Corporation (*http://www.pgp.com*) in a variety of editions. A free version is still available for personal, noncommercial use, but it's not promoted; if you're interested, search the site for PGP Freeware.

> **Tip** A great many Web sites and newsgroups can help you stay abreast of ongoing developments in the PGP world. We recommend, in particular, the Questions & Answers section of Tom McCune's PGP page (*http://www.mccune.cc/PGP.htm*) and the newsgroups *comp.security.pgp.discuss, alt.security.pgp,* and *comp.security.pgp.resources.*

PGP includes plug-ins for popular e-mail client programs, including Outlook and Outlook Express. If you use the PGP plug-in with Outlook, you should disable Word as your e-mail editor (choose Tools, Options; click the Mail Format tab; and then clear Use Microsoft Word To Edit E-Mail Messages) because the plug-in does not attach to Word.

With or without a plug-in, the PGPtray component of PGP adds a padlock icon to your computer's notification area. Clicking this icon opens a menu of PGP-related tasks:

You can use the Current Window submenu to encrypt, sign, decrypt, and verify (authenticate) the contents of an e-mail message window.

Because PGP is not based on the S/MIME protocol, it does not require the use of CAs. PGP digital signatures are appended to e-mail messages as blocks of plain text. You can create as many public key/private key pairs as you want, without using certificates. (You can distribute your public keys by copying them into an e-mail message, posting them on a personal or corporate Web site, attaching them as files to messages, or directing correspondents to a public key server, such as *http://pgp.mit.edu.*) Your recipient must also be a PGP user.

If you want encrypted or signed communications but you're not comfortable providing information about yourself to a CA, PGP might be the way to go.

Other Third-Party Encryption Tools

A growing number of vendors offer services and plug-ins that provide e-mail encryption, digital authentication and time-stamping, certified receipts, and other useful security features. Some services require both recipient and sender to subscribe; others do not. Some are free; others are inexpensive—at the personal level, at least. All relieve you of the need to acquire and manage certificates.

The following list is not exhaustive, but it will give you a sampling of what's available.

CertifiedMail.com

CertifiedMail.com (*http://www.certifiedmail.com*) uses SSL for encryption. The company stores your outbound messages on its server, notifying recipients by using ordinary e-mail. Recipients, who do not have to be subscribers, connect to the server through SSL and enter a password (if you've chosen to assign one) to pick up the mail. Senders receive time-stamped confirmation of delivery.

Plug-ins are available for Outlook, Outlook Express, and Lotus Notes. Subscribers with one of these plug-ins can send "certified" e-mail by clicking a toolbar button. Alternatively, any subscriber can use the service's Web site to compose and send.

Hushmail

Hushmail (*http://www.hushmail.com*) is a service that works like a Web-based e-mail account with encryption. You can log on to your Hushmail account from any Web browser and send encrypted or signed messages to any other Hushmail subscriber. The system is based on the OpenPGP standard.

Hushmail's principal disadvantage is that both sender and receiver must be Hushmail subscribers. (You can use Hushmail to send unencrypted mail to nonsubscribers, however.) It has two potential advantages over PGP: You can access your account from anywhere, and Hushmail manages your keys.

Sigaba Secure Email

Named for the American World War II encryption machine, the only such device that remained unbroken throughout the war, Sigaba (*http://www.sigaba.com*) provides encryption between corporate e-mail gateways, running the key management and authentication services. Sigaba Secure Email allows desktop-to-desktop encryption of messages and attachments using either a Web interface or standard e-mail client software. (Plug-ins are available for Outlook, Outlook Express, and other popular e-mail clients.) Sigaba Secure Email uses symmetric keys, rather than public and private keys, and assigns keys to messages, not to users. For desktop-to-desktop encryption, both sender and receiver must be registered with the service.

ZixMail

ZixMail (*http://www.zixcorp.com*) lets you exchange encrypted and signed mail with fellow subscribers and nonsubscribers alike. Subscribers receive ZixMail as attachments. Nonsubscribers receive notification that a secure message awaits them on ZixCorp's servers. Connection between the nonsubscriber and ZixCorp is secured by SSL, and recipients are required to create a password the first time they pick up their mail.

Senders can request a pickup receipt for any message; the receipt includes a digitally signed GMT time stamp. Messages remain on ZixCorp's servers for two weeks by default. (You can extend the period to three weeks.) If a message is not retrieved by its expiration date, the service notifies the sender.

ZixMail includes plug-ins for Outlook and Lotus Notes (but not for Outlook Express). In these programs, you can click a toolbar button to send e-mail through ZixMail or read incoming ZixMail messages. If you're using a program that doesn't have a ZixMail plug-in, you use ZixCorp's attractively designed mail client and address book instead.

Using Instant Messaging Safely

In the world of interconnected computers, the use of instant messaging programs such as AOL Instant Messenger, MSN Messenger, Windows Messenger, and Yahoo! Messenger is not without hazard. The biggest risks:

- Viruses, worms, and Trojan horses
- Unsolicited and unwanted incoming messages, or *spim*

Although some pundits and some companies that sell security software have hyped the risks of instant messaging, much of it is just that: hyperbole. Nonetheless, 2005 has seen a marked increase in the number of attacks carried out through IM software.

Instant messaging exploits rely primarily on unguarded users, rather than inherent vulnerabilities in instant messaging programs. IM-related problems don't require purchasing and using additional software or making arcane registry settings. Rather, the solution in most cases is awareness and education. The biggest threat is to IM users who are unaware of the risks of chatting with strangers, clicking unknown links, and downloading unknown files.

Avoiding Malicious Software

Like malicious e-mail messages and Web sites, instant messages can contain links to sites you shouldn't visit. In addition, IM clients allow the transfer of files—including executable program files—between computers. File transfers are particularly risky, because IM file transfers bypass the virus-scanning capability that's often configured for intercepting viruses at a gateway firewall or in incoming e-mail messages.

A typical attack, such as one by the widespread Bropia worm, comes in an instant message that *appears* to be from a known IM contact. The message encourages you to click an embedded link or to accept the download of file; doing so invariably attempts to launch malicious code. The code installs a program that causes your IM program to send a similar message to everyone on your IM contact list—without any indication to you of what's going on.

Other safeguards (such as up-to-date security patches and a real-time virus scanning capability with the latest virus signatures) might prevent the malicious code from running—but don't count on it. A better solution is to avoid suspicious links and file transfers.

Observe these guidelines when using IM software:

- **Think before you click.**   Do not click a Web link or accept a file download unless you know what it is.
- **Know who you're talking to.**   If a message appears to be from someone you know, be absolutely certain before you click a link or accept a file transfer. Ask them why they're sending it to you and what it's for. (So far, the worms haven't figured out a way to engage in conversation.)
- **Scan all downloaded files for viruses.**   Even a trusted friend who's sending you a legitimate file might not realize that the file is infected; after you've erected firewalls and taken other precautions, don't let IM be the entryway for viruses!

> **Tip**   If your antivirus program doesn't have provisions for automatically scanning files you download through instant messaging, your IM program might be able to invoke your antivirus program when needed. For example, with MSN Messenger 7, choose Tools, Options, and then click File Transfer. Select Scan Files For Viruses Using and then specify the path to your antivirus program.

- **Be sure your IM software is up-to-date.**   Use Automatic Updates or Microsoft Update to be sure that Windows Messenger has the latest security updates; for other IM clients, you might need to periodically visit the publisher's Web site to learn about updates.

> **Note**   IM programs have a significant security advantage over other virus vectors, such as Web browsers and e-mail programs: Because IM users must log on to a central server to use instant messaging, the publisher can *force* users to upgrade when a vulnerability is discovered and a security update is issued. For example, MSN Messenger can refuse a connection unless the latest patched software version is installed. (IM clients are generally free, as are their security updates.)

Preventing Spim

The scourge known as spim is the instant messaging equivalent of e-mail spam. At best, an unsolicited and unwanted advertising message that pops up on your screen is a momentary distraction. Because instant messaging accounts are reached by using an e-mail address, a spammer or spimmer who has managed to obtain legitimate e-mail addresses can quickly and automatically check to see if the target address is online and, if so, fire off a message.

Such intrusions can easily be blocked, regardless of which IM client you use. With Windows Messenger, when you block a user, if you're in that user's contact list your status is always shown as Not Online. If the blocked user tries to send a message (by entering your e-mail address), it's immediately returned to the sender. You never receive any indication that the blocked user is trying to contact you. To block all users except those you explicitly allow, choose Tools, Options, and click the Privacy tab, shown in Figure 15-6. The lists show everyone in your contact list as well as others you've contacted or blocked. To block unknown users, be sure that Other .NET Messenger Service Users is in the right-hand list (My Block List). If this entry is currently in the allow list, select it and click Block >>.

Figure 15-6. Blocking users prevents them from seeing whether you're online and sending you messages.

You might choose not to impose blanket blocking in this way, since it prevents "strangers" whom you want to converse with from reaching you. (For example, you wouldn't want indiscriminate blocking if you use instant messaging to hear from customers or prospective chat friends.) In this situation, you can block individual users—whether they're spimmers or annoying customers—in any of several ways:

- When you receive notification that the user has added you to his or her contact list, select the Block option.
- If the user is in your contact list, right-click the name and choose Block.
- If you are in a conversation with someone you want to block, click the Block button. (If you're conversing with more than one person, select the name of the person you want to block from the list that appears.) It will appear to the blocked user that you've gone offline. Conversation windows remain open on both computers.

Techniques similar to these are available in all instant messaging programs.

Chapter 16

Blocking Spam

Sooner or later, everyone who uses electronic mail begins receiving unsolicited commercial e-mail, often referred to as *UCE* or, simply, *spam*. Because e-mail is incredibly inexpensive, unscrupulous senders can blast out messages by the millions. As a result, junk e-mail can proliferate at a rate much faster than junk mail delivered by the postal service.

Make no mistake about it: Spam is a scourge, and it represents a threat to your computer's security. Unchecked, spam can literally overwhelm legitimate messages, making it impossible for you to find important mail from business associates, friends, and family. It consumes bandwidth when unwanted messages arrive at your mail server and again when you download those messages using your e-mail client software. Spam is a haven for scams, frauds, deceptive marketing practices, illegal chain letters, and extremely offensive, graphic pornography. A small but statistically significant number of spam messages include viruses, Trojan horses, and other hostile code, or use enticing and misleading language to trick you into clicking on Web site links that can be dangerous to your computer or your bank account. Porn sites in particular are notorious for their attempts to hijack your browser's home page or to fool you into downloading hostile ActiveX controls or installing "dialer" programs that silently rack up charges of several dollars a minute for their sleazy content. Scammers who practice the art of "phishing" create messages that appear to come from legitimate senders and entice recipients to give up passwords, bank account details, credit card numbers, and other valuable personal information. (We cover phishing scams in more detail in Chapter 18, "Protecting Your Privacy.")

By any objective measure, the problem with spam is getting worse. Although no one can produce a definitive count, companies that specialize in detecting spam and blocking it from corporate servers estimate that between 60 and 70 percent of all e-mail traffic is spam. Because each barrage might consist of hundreds or even thousands of individually addressed e-mail messages, the total number of spam messages sent yearly is almost certainly in the billions. Sometimes it feels like every one landed in your inbox, doesn't it?

Unfortunately, spammers are a case study in the survival of the fittest. For every countermeasure that spam-fighters develop, spammers figure out a workaround. That's why effectively battling spam requires constant vigilance and a willingness to outfox spammers. The good news? You already have most of the tools you need. In this chapter, we'll show you how to detect spam, how to block it at your mail server, how to filter out the messages that slip into your inbox, and how to fight back against spammers.

Security Checklist: Fighting Spam

Want to take charge of unwanted e-mail? Use this checklist to identify steps you can take. Some items might not be appropriate for your system configuration or e-mail client software; review the information in this chapter before you forge ahead.

- Check with your Internet service provider (ISP) or hosting company to see what spam-blocking options are available for your accounts.

- If you run a mail server, install spam-blocking software to reject unwanted messages before they reach users.

- If you use an external e-mail provider, experiment with settings to find the best way to block unwanted messages without inadvertently intercepting legitimate e-mail.

- Choose an e-mail program with robust filtering features.

- Set up message rules to sort and filter incoming e-mail.

- Set up at least one alternate e-mail address for use with untrusted recipients.

- Learn how to decode a message header.

What Is Spam?

The first challenge in devising your strategy for dealing with spam is defining it. Being able to distinguish different types of electronic mail is the crucial first step. Sorting incoming e-mail messages into categories forms the basis of virtually all filtering schemes. Done right, this winnowing process not only helps you identify unwanted bulk mail, it also helps you avoid false positives, in which a legitimate e-mail message is accidentally classified as spam and tossed or ignored.

In the broadest of terms, all e-mail messages you receive can be sorted into one of the following six categories:

- **Personal messages addressed directly to you.**   E-mail from friends, relatives, and business associates falls into this category. Ideally, every message in this category should be moved automatically into your inbox or a folder you designate with a mail-handling rule. Some spam-blocking software can mistakenly trap legitimate messages that contain words or phrases commonly found in spam messages.

- **Personal messages copied to you.**   This category consists of messages addressed to another person, with your address included on the Cc (courtesy copy) or Bcc (blind courtesy copy) line. Mechanical filtering systems often mistakenly identify blind copies as spam.

- **Messages sent to a mailing list of which you are a member.**   The software that runs most mailing list servers is designed to protect the privacy of individual recipients by hiding their names and e-mail addresses behind a single e-mail address called a *list alias* or *distribution list*. Subscribers to the list send a message to other users by addressing it to the alias, with the list server determining whether the message should be forwarded or rejected. Messages from mailing lists are frequently misidentified as spam, especially when they are not addressed directly to the recipient.

- **Commercial messages you requested or authorized.**   Many businesses and organizations use e-mail to maintain contact with their customers. Typically, you sign up for these messages by registering at the company's Web site, often when you set up an online account. The character of these commercial messages can vary widely. Software companies and developers often send important support bulletins or update notices to all registered users, for instance. An online business might send notices of special prices or new products to all their customers; the same company might also send individual e-mail messages to confirm purchases or shipping details. Sorting this type of mail is the most difficult challenge for any spam-fighting program.

- **Unsolicited commercial e-mail sent from an identified company or organization.**   Some businesses and marketing organizations insist on using e-mail as a blunt-edged marketing tool, blasting advertisements to prospective customers who haven't specifically requested such information. This category is the digital equivalent of the junk mail that clutters up your mailbox. Because it's unsolicited, it qualifies as spam, even if the sender is clearly identified. Many of these overaggressive senders claim that you signed up for their mailings and offer you the option of having your name removed from their mailing lists; those messages that don't include a usable removal option are relatively easy to filter out.

> **Caution**   If you see a "remove me from your list" link within a spam message, don't click it until you determine who really sent the message. Legitimate businesses and marketing companies provide clearly labeled options that allow recipients to "opt out" of future mailings either by clicking a link on a Web site or by sending a message to an e-mail address. But if the original message includes counterfeit headers and was sent through a hijacked mail server, the link in the message might be nothing more than window dressing intended to make the message look legitimate. If you're lucky, your request will go nowhere when you click such a link. But some shady companies that compile lists of e-mail addresses use these phony links to confirm that your e-mail address is valid. By responding to spam, you practically guarantee that you'll receive *more* spam.

- **Unsolicited bulk e-mail from an unknown or anonymous source.**   This category consists of messages sent using bulk-mail software designed to disguise the identity of the sender. This category includes the overwhelming majority of scams, chain letters, and come-ons for adult sites that make up the most vexing spam. Blocking this category of spam is an ongoing battle because developers of bulk-mail software regularly incorporate tricks designed to fool spam filters.

> **Tip** Don't count on CAN-SPAM
>
> In 2003, the United States Congress passed and the President signed the Controlling the Assault of Non-Solicited Pornography and Marketing Act (CAN-SPAM), which established a set of rules for those who send commercial e-mail, with penalties for those who refuse to abide by them. Under the terms of this statute, e-mail senders must include accurate header information and subject lines and must provide recipients with a way to "opt out" of any further e-mail. In addition, each commercial message must be labeled as an advertisement and must include a valid physical address. Anti-spam activists predicted that the new law would have no measurable effect on hardcore spammers, and the first year's results of the CAN-SPAM Act bore out those predictions. Experts estimate that the amount of spam sent in 2004 actually rose significantly over the previous year. For more details on how CAN-SPAM works, see *http://www.ftc.gov/bcp/conline/pubs/buspubs/canspam.htm*.

Sneaky Spammers' Secrets

When spammers unleash a flood of e-mail messages onto the Internet, they use a variety of tricks to hide their true identity. Their goal is to find suckers who will take the bait and call, click, or e-mail for the (often bogus) offering; disguising the source of the message makes it difficult for outraged recipients to complain. Here are the common tools of the spammer's trade:

- **Hijacked mail servers.** Virtually all bulk-mail programs do their dirty work by exploiting open e-mail relays—mail servers that are misconfigured to allow users from outside the local network to send e-mail without being authenticated. In recent years, many viruses have included software that turns the infected computer into a "zombie" e-mail server. A spammer who finds an open relay can pump thousands of messages through that server in a very short time, often without being detected, forging the message headers (information that documents a message's travels over the Internet) so that their true origin is virtually impossible to trace. Unfortunately, the supply of wide-open e-mail servers on the Internet is enormous and growing every day, and finding open relays is trivially easy. In the next section, we explain how you can decode a message header and spot a message that has been sent through a hijacked mail server.

- **Bogus addresses.** The From address of a spam message sent through an open relay is nearly always counterfeit. The To address is often faked as well. In fact, some bulk-mail software is clever enough to pick up the recipient's e-mail address and use it as the From address, resulting in a message that looks as if you sent it to yourself!

- **Misleading subject lines.** Many of the sleaziest spam attacks include innocuous or personalized subject lines. Porn peddlers in particular like to use innocent subject lines such as "Did you get my message?" or "Info you requested." The purpose, of course, is to slide past filtering software that looks for trigger words in the subject line.

- **"Word salads."**   You've no doubt received unwanted commercial e-mail filled with one or more paragraphs of nonsense words or a chunk of text from a newspaper or book. The idea is to fool spam filters by inserting some legitimate-looking content alongside the easy-to-spot offering for prescription drugs, cheap software, or a low-rate mortgage. In addition, spammers often misspell key words that would otherwise give away their content. Most modern filters have no trouble detecting these tricks.

- **Obfuscated URLs and scrambled sites.**   Spammers trying to sell worthless products often include a link to a "throwaway" Web page on a free service, which in turn redirects users to the real site. The throwaway page is usually taken down within hours or days, but not before at least a few suckers have been taken in. Determined spammers can make it extraordinarily difficult to determine the actual destination page by composing pages in JavaScript and using URLs that have been obfuscated using a variety of techniques.

Tip   **Decode sneaky spam messages**

If you're interested in learning more about the techniques spammers use to obfuscate URLs and disguise pages, read the news.admin.net-abuse.email FAQ at *http://www.spamfaq.net /spamfighting.shtml*. Section 1.3.1, "Spammer Tricks," is exceptionally well written and informative. An article by Keith Little entitled "How to Obscure Any URL" (*http://www.pc-help.org /obscure.htm*) goes into tremendous detail as well. For a suite of tools you can use to de-obfuscate misleading URLs, go to *http://www.gooby.ca/decrypt/* or *http://combat.uxn.com*.

How to Decode an E-Mail Header

Distinguishing legitimate e-mail messages from spam can be a daunting task. Opening or previewing a message doesn't give you enough information to make an intelligent judgment. The message shown in Figure 16-1 on the next page, for instance, displays many of the warning signs of spam, but it could also be legitimate. The trouble is, all visible indications shown in a message window can be counterfeited with ease.

Why does it matter whether a message is legitimate? When a sender honestly discloses the source of a message, you can contact that sender to demand that you be taken off the mailing list. If your request is ignored, you can filter out any further messages from that sender's address, and you can send a meaningful complaint to the company, to industry groups, and to consumer protection agencies. By contrast, when a spammer hides the origin of a message by forging addresses and relaying the mail through hijacked servers, filters using the From header are ineffectual and filing a complaint is much more difficult; in these cases, your goal is to set up a filter that detects similar messages by using criteria other than the sender's address. This way you can prevent those messages from appearing in your inbox again.

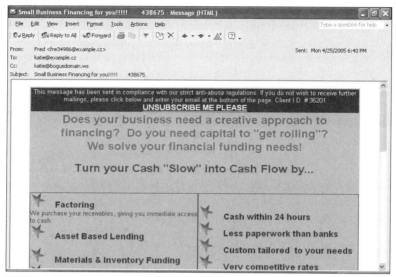

Figure 16-1. Is this message legitimate? You can't tell just by looking.

To determine whether a message came from a legitimate source, you need to check the message header. Although many parts of a message header can be forged, the crucial details that show which mail server a message passed through just before reaching your mailbox are usually accurate. Every e-mail client program uses a slightly different technique to reveal the full message headers.

Viewing Message Headers in Outlook Express

In Microsoft Outlook Express, follow these steps to view message headers:

1 Double-click the message to open it in its own window.

2 Choose File, Properties (or press Alt+Enter) to open the properties dialog box for the message.

3 Click the Details tab to see the full headers for the message. (You might need to scroll down or right to read details that are too wide to fit in the window.)

4   To copy the header text to the Clipboard, right-click any portion of the Details window and choose Select All; then right-click again and choose Copy. This enables you to paste the full header into an e-mail message (to complain to a spammer's Internet service provider, for instance) or another window, such as a browser-based tool for tracking down the true location of an IP address.

Viewing Message Headers in Outlook

If you use Microsoft Outlook 2000 or later, follow these steps:

1   Double-click the message to open it in its own window.
2   Choose View, Options to open the Message Options dialog box for the message.
3   Scroll through the Internet Headers box to see the full headers for the message.

Chapter 16

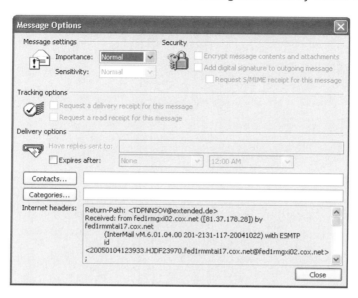

4. To copy the header text to the Clipboard, right-click any portion of the Internet Headers box and choose Select All; then right-click again and choose Copy. You can then paste the full header into an e-mail message or another window.

Viewing Headers in Other E-Mail Programs

If you use a different e-mail program, you'll need to search that program's documentation for instructions on how to read the full headers for a message. In Mozilla Thunderbird, for instance, you can choose View, Headers, All to see a complete display of message headers in the preview pane and in each message window. In Eudora for Windows, open the message and click the cleverly named Blah Blah Blah button. If you're using your Web browser to view messages sent to your MSN Hotmail account, choose Options from the main Hotmail screen, click the Mail tab on the left side of the window, click Mail Display Settings, and choose Full or Advanced instead of the default Basic setting for the Message Headers option.

Reading a Message Header

The most important pieces of information in an Internet message header appear near the top, in a block starting with the word *Received*. The entries in these headers are inserted by each Mail Transport Agent (MTA) that handles the message. Although the sender can attempt to forge a portion of this header, most mail servers add enough information for you to identify the chain of servers through which the message passed. The topmost entry shows the final transfer and should include the name of your mail server. One entry in the Received block should show the IP address of the sender, although a crafty spammer could try to disguise some of this information. Figure 16-2 shows a header from a spam message. (Although this example comes from a real message, the details have been changed to protect the guilty.)

```
❶ Return-Path: <324hal9000qwerty@hotmail.com>
❷ Received: from mail.im-not!a!spammer.com ([172.16.101.1]) by
     mail.example.com (Post.Office MTA v3.5.2 release 221 ID#
     0-71550U1400L100S0V35) with SMTP id com 1cF00-1855-1me for
     <katie@example.com>; Sat, 30 Apr 2005 03:33:57 -0700
❸ Received: from mail.bogus^server.com (dialup-10-100-185-123.my^isp.net
     [10.100.185.123]) by mail.im-not!a!spammer.com with ESMTP (SMTPD32-
     7.03) id A5AB1D9B0136; Fri, 29 Apr 2005 21:42:35 -0600
❹ Message-ID: <00000ba37ea4$00007353$00001799@mail.bogus^server.com>
❺ To: <Client List #1>
  From: "Contact List" <324hal9000qwerty@hotmail.com>
  Subject: Re: Information you requested
  Date: Fri, 29 Apr 2005 06:56:30 -0900
```

Figure 16-2. In this message header, only the block with "Received" details contains any useful information. Everything else is forged.

1 The Return-Path header is forged. Spammers often use bogus addresses from free e-mail services such as Hotmail or Yahoo. Anyone who tries to complain by hitting the Reply button will find that their message goes to a nonexistent address, or one that has been shut down by the e-mail provider, or worst of all, to an innocent bystander whose address was used (without permission) by the spammer.

2 This entry in the Received block shows the name and other identifying information for the recipient's mail server (in this case, mail.example.com) and the name of the server that last handled the message. That server's name might or might not be accurate, but the MTA has inserted the correct IP address for the server in brackets. Tracing that IP address can provide important clues that might help you determine whether the server name is accurate.

3 This entry in the Received block shows the origin of the message. Although the spammer has tried to disguise the name of the sending computer, the MTA has helpfully inserted the actual name and IP address of that computer in parentheses. Judging by the name, it's probably safe to assume that this sender was using a dialup account to connect to the mail server. By checking the message ID and the time stamps, the Internet service provider (ISP) might be able to identify the customer who sent this message.

Note that the server name at the end of this line is the same as the one at the beginning of the preceding line. Clever spammers can add fake Received lines to this list to cover their tracks, and some corporate firewalls or internal mail gateways might add additional gateways. The easiest means by which to spot a fake Received line is to match the receiving server at the end of one line with the sending server at the beginning of the line above it. If you can't see evidence of the message being handed from one server to another, you should be suspicious of that Received entry.

Chapter 16

> **Note** Some bulk mail programs include their own Simple Mail Transport Protocol (SMTP) servers, which run directly from the spammer's desktop. In this configuration, the Received header will typically point to the computer running that software. Spammers often use networks of "zombie" computers that have been commandeered by Trojan horse software. Because the spammer can operate these computers by remote control, they leave no traces of their real location. Another trick—less common today than in years past—is to hijack a Web site that contains a form intended for users to enter feedback or comments; if the form is powered by an older version of the popular FormMail CGI script, the spammer can take over the Web server and use it to pump out spam—usually a very short message containing a link to a Web site. If you see a message that begins by announcing that it's the result of your feedback form, this is the probable source.

  4 This header is a unique message ID tacked on by the original MTA. It could be useful if you ever need to trace the message through succeeding servers.

  5 Everything below this point can easily be forged.

Inside Out

Decipher message headers with ease

If the thought of manually decoding a message header gives you a headache, you can take your choice of several automated tools. SamSpade.org (*http://samspade.org*) has an amazingly complete set of online tools; you can also download the free Sam Spade for Windows network query tool from *http://samspade.org/ssw/*. If you've successfully decoded the header and now want to look up IP addresses, try the UXN Spam Combat page at *http://combat.uxn.com*, or the extremely thorough Elephants' Toolbox at Cotse.com (*http://www.cotse.com/iptools.html*).

Don't let message headers overwhelm you. Your goal in looking through the headers is to determine whether the sender is being honest about the source of the message. If you can match the domain of the return address with that of the server that sent the message, you can probably assume that the sender is using a legitimate address. If you're receiving multiple unwanted messages from that address and can't convince the sender to stop, use a filter to block it, as described later in this chapter.

Basic Spam-Blocking Techniques

When it comes to blocking spam, we have good news and bad news. The good news is that you can indeed devise a strategy to drastically reduce the amount of spam that appears in your inbox. The bad news is that devising an effective spam-blocking strategy requires a fair amount of up-front effort and ongoing maintenance; there is no simple solution that will block spam with a few easy clicks.

Following the six rules listed here should help you put together an effective anti-spam regimen:

Rule #1: Use server-based spam-blocking solutions when possible.   If you run your own mail server as part of a business, investigate anti-spam add-ins. If you get your mail through an ISP, find out whether they offer any spam-blocking options; some ISPs will provide this service, but only if you ask.

Tip   Use IMAP, if possible

Most ISPs store and forward mail using the Simple Mail Transport Protocol (SMTP) on the server, with clients using Post Office Protocol 3 (POP3) to retrieve messages. But a different industry standard, Internet Message Access Protocol (IMAP), gives users far more control over their mail. With an IMAP server, you can define rules that allow the server to process messages before they ever reach your client software. All versions of Microsoft Outlook since Outlook 2000 are fully capable of working with IMAP servers, as are Outlook Express and Mozilla Thunderbird. If this option is available to you, take advantage of it, and use server-side rules to block spam. To experiment with IMAP, set up a free account at FastMail (*http://www.fastmail.fm*); upgraded accounts are available for a fee.

Rule #2: Guard your e-mail address carefully.   Spammers compile mailing lists using a variety of sources. You can increase your odds of staying out of spam databases by not giving out your address to any untrusted person. Unfortunately, no matter how vigilant you are, every e-mail address begins to attract at least some spam eventually, especially if your user name is a common one (like Ed or Carl). That's because determined spammers use dictionary-based attacks to send mail to every likely address at every domain they can find; if they don't get a bounce message for a given address (like ed@example.com), they add it to their list. Also, well-meaning friends and relatives can inadvertently give your address away by entering it in online contests or "joke of the day" Web sites—many of which are designed specifically to harvest e-mail addresses for spam lists—or by including it on a Cc list that makes its way to an unscrupulous person.

Inside Out

Protect your identity

Don't overlook the need to guard your identity in public forums and on Web sites. If you include your e-mail address in messages you post to Usenet forums or Web-based bulletin boards, you can be certain that spammers will find it by using address-harvesting programs (called *spambots*). Use a secondary address, or practice what Usenet veterans call "address munging." Instead of entering your actual address, try spelling it out or add some obviously invalid characters and append the word *invalid* to the end of the address. For instance, katie@example.com could become katie.NOSPAM@REMOVE.THIS.example.com.INVALID or katie (at) example (dot) com. The munged address will trip up spambots, but a human being should have no trouble figuring out the real address. Also, never publish your personal e-mail address on a Web site. Businesses can add a secure form to enable customers and clients to contact them through the Web; many Web hosting companies include CGI scripts that can be used for this purpose. To fool simple address-harvesting robots, use a JavaScript tool that obfuscates the address using ISO character codes; you'll find one such tool at *http://www.albionresearch.com/misc/obfuscator.php*.

Rule #3: Use alternate addresses for transactions with untrusted parties.   Set up an e-mail account with a free service such as Hotmail and use it for Web sites and online services that require you to provide a valid e-mail address. If the address becomes flooded with spam, stop using it and open a new account.

Rule #4: Learn when and how to opt out of unwanted e-mail.   The best way to stop junk mail is before it ever reaches your inbox. Reputable businesses and online marketers provide a mechanism for you to remove your names from their mailing lists. Getting your name off those lists makes it easier to set up filtering rules.

Rule #5: Choose your e-mail client software carefully.   All e-mail programs are not created equal. Outlook Express, for instance, offers an extremely limited set of e-mail filtering features. If you plan to use filters extensively, you'll get better results from Outlook. If you use an older version of Outlook, consider an upgrade to Outlook 2003, which offers more sophisticated filtering capabilities than its predecessors.

Rule #6: Filter!   The secret of successful spam-blocking is to aggressively filter out unwanted messages. With virtually all Microsoft Windows–based e-mail programs, you can create rules that automatically sort messages into folders as they arrive in your inbox, based on their content or on information in the address block. More sophisticated filtering tools enable you to construct rules that examine the full message headers and can permanently delete messages instead of simply moving them to the trash. In this chapter, we discuss the built-in filtering options in Outlook Express and Outlook and list some third-party filtering products and services that work with any e-mail client software.

Tip   Master your own domain

If e-mail is a critical part of your business life, don't settle for the standard SMTP/POP3 account that your ISP throws in with your Internet service. Instead, consider setting up your own domain at a Web hosting firm that includes e-mail services as part of its package. For a relatively low cost, you can purchase a domain name that identifies you and your family or business, with the option to set up 5, 10, 25, or more individual accounts at that domain. You can create separate e-mail addresses within your domain that you can use to sort personal and business mail, even creating the illusion that a one-person company is bigger than it seems. Many of these accounts also include a feature that enables you to create forwarding rules for any message addressed to your domain, even if the address isn't one you previously set up. Use this option to create unique addresses for each of your favorite online merchants (for instance, ed-amazon@example.com), making it easy to filter incoming mail from each merchant based strictly on the address you provide. If one of your addresses lands on a spam list, you can filter it at your Web hosting company's server so that it never reaches your inbox.

Blocking Spam at the Source

We can't emphasize more strongly how important it is to turn away spam at your server, before it ever has a chance to reach your inbox. If you manage your own mail server, you can choose from a wide variety of spam-filtering solutions that work with the server package you've chosen. If you choose to let your ISP or a third-party hosting company manage the server, your options are limited to those that the server owner decides to make available.

Some ISPs offer crude spam-blocking software that has only an on-off switch. Think carefully before accepting this sort of solution. At a minimum, you'll need some assurance that the server won't intercept and delete e-mail from important contacts. Some ISPs and hosted mail providers offer multiple levels of filtering. At a minimum, you should be able to configure the server software to divert possible spam to a separate folder that you can check regularly. After a few weeks or months of monitoring, you can decide whether the software is accurate enough to allow you to simply trust its judgment and delete messages it identifies as spam.

The best ISPs and hosting companies offer highly configurable spam-blocking packages that let you maintain tight control over mail filtering without forcing you to write your own code. The most popular server-based program at hosting companies is SpamAssassin (*http://spamassassin.apache.org*). Each time a message arrives on a server running Spam-Assassin, the software runs a combination of tests that analyze its header information, body text, and character set. The source of the message is compared to several "real-time black-hole lists" (RBLs), which identify servers and ranges of IP addresses known to be sources of spam. Each of these tests is assigned a score, the value of which is based on how closely this characteristic is identified with spam. The results of an individual test are likely to be unreliable as a predictor of whether a message is spam, but the total score is surprisingly reliable.

SpamAssassin is highly configurable by users. You can adjust the numeric threshold that defines what is considered spam, dialing it up or down to change the sensitivity of the filters. You can change the weight assigned to individual tests to more accurately reflect the type of e-mail you receive. You can create blacklists and whitelists to supplement the logical test, and you can turn on Bayesian filtering (which uses a statistical model that becomes more accurate as you provide more samples of unwanted messages) and "train" the software to tell the difference between spam and ham (yes, that's how e-mail experts refer to legitimate e-mail).

If you own your own domain and your hosting company doesn't include a package with robust spam-filtering features, consider switching to a different hosting company. If that's not an option, consider subscribing to a third-party proxy service like SpamCop (*http://www.spamcop.net*). This commercial service retrieves e-mail from your server, analyzes it, and diverts probable spam to a separate folder. The service adds an extra layer of complexity and isn't for everyone, but if you have an e-mail address that is overwhelmed with junk mail and changing it is not an option, it's worth a try.

Using Filters

After you've turned away as much unwanted e-mail as possible at your server, message rules that work with your e-mail client software are your final line of defense. Although the procedures for creating rules vary from program to program, each rule typically consists of one or more conditions and an action that occurs when a message matches a condition. For instance, you might create a rule that examines each incoming message to see whether the sender has an address in your company's domain (the condition); if so, you want to move the message to your Company Mail folder (the action). Most people use filters ineffectively by trying to set up roadblocks for spam—by identifying suspicious words and phrases, for instance, or by blocking one sender at a time. (Both Outlook and Outlook Express, in fact, enable you to quickly add the sender of any message to a Blocked Senders list.) For most spam, which uses forged addresses and is sent through hijacked servers, that strategy is doomed to failure. In this section, we'll explain a filtering strategy that is much more effective at removing the clutter from your inbox.

> **Caution** Several years ago, a number of well-meaning would-be spambusters assembled lists of e-mail addresses designed to be downloaded and imported into your Blocked Senders list in Outlook Express or Outlook 2002 or later, or the Junk Mail filter of Outlook 2000. Each address was reportedly confirmed to have been used in the past by a spammer. One popular list we found contained more than 70,000 individual e-mail addresses. Most of those lists are gone now, and for good reason. While this strategy sounds tempting, it has two serious flaws. First, the overwhelming majority of addresses on these lists are throwaway accounts from free e-mail providers, created by a spammer for the specific purpose of sending one barrage of junk mail and then never used again—so the list isn't likely to turn up many matches and thus won't do much to cut down on spam. Second, and even worse, forcing your e-mail software to chug through a list of tens of thousands of bogus names every time you receive a new message could slow down your computer's performance substantially. We recommend that you avoid any anti-spam strategy that relies on the Blocked Senders list.

A smart filtering strategy starts with one golden rule: Use filters to identify the messages you *want* to read first! Leave those messages in your inbox, or move them to another folder reserved for messages that have been certified as legitimate. After you've sorted out the messages from friends, family, coworkers, and mailing lists to which you subscribe, you'll be left with confirmed junk mail and suspected spam, which can be diverted to other folders or deleted. This strategy is the best way to avoid false positives, in which a message from a trusted contact is mistakenly categorized as spam.

> **Tip** Keep rules in order
>
> Regardless of which e-mail client you use, the order in which you process rules is crucial. If you create a rule that categorizes anything with the phrases "$$$" or "XXX" as spam, make certain that rule goes into effect after you've sorted out messages from friends, families, and coworkers. If you put the $$$/XXX rule at the top of your list, you might inadvertently throw out a message from your mother asking what she should do with this chain letter someone just sent her. (And if she sends you the chain letter, you'll definitely want to educate her on why she shouldn't do it again!)

The first step in setting up an effective filtering program is to create a set of folders to hold each category of messages. Figure 16-3 shows an Outlook Express window with a basic set of folders defined. Although you can design a much more intricate filing system, this group of folders represents an excellent starting point. (And yes, the messages in the Probable Spam folder are real!)

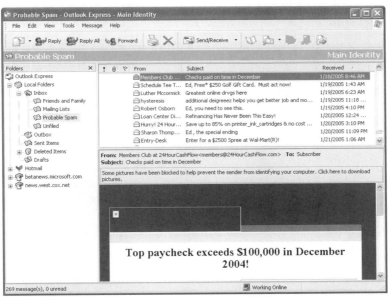

Figure 16-3. As the first step in your spam-filtering strategy, create a basic set of folders for sorting incoming messages.

Next, set up a basic set of message rules to successively filter out messages in each category and move them to the appropriate folder. If you're willing to put in the effort, you can build up a list of dozens or even hundreds of rules. However, five or six message rules (the conditions and actions for one such rule, for a user with the e-mail address *katie@example.com*, are shown in Figure 16-4 on the next page) are sufficient to filter out most spam without disturbing the messages you want to read. Table 16-1 on the next page describes how each rule works. In "Creating Custom Filters," page 544, we'll show you the steps you take to construct these rules.

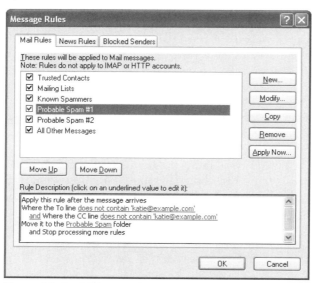

Figure 16-4. Make certain your message rules are processed in the correct order; this basic set of rules handles legitimate messages first, before dealing with suspicious e-mail.

Table 16-1. **Basic Message Rules**

Order	Message Rule	What It Does
1	Trusted Contacts	Create a list of trusted addresses (your mother's address at msn.com might be one) and domains (all messages sent from addresses at your company's domain, for instance). Choose "Stop processing additional rules" as the only action. This rule leaves all matching messages in the inbox and should remain at the top of the rules list.
2	Mailing Lists	Use individual e-mail addresses, domain names, or a fragment of unique text from the subject line or message body to identify each incoming message from mailing lists to which you subscribe. Move these messages to one or more separate folders and stop processing additional rules.
3	Known Spammers	This category includes all bulk mail from companies that identify themselves properly but refuse to remove your name from their mailing lists. In this rule, create conditions based on domain names, specific e-mail addresses, or message headers; for the rule actions, mark each matching message as read and then delete it. Be sure to choose "Stop processing additional rules" as the final action.

Table 16-1. **Basic Message Rules**

Order	Message Rule	What It Does
4	Probable Spam	In the example shown in Figure 16-4, we created two rules for this category. The first rule identifies all messages for which your specific address is not in the To or Cc fields. The second rule finds messages that contain words or phrases commonly found in spam. (If you use Outlook 2000 or 2002, the built-in Junk E-mail and Adult Content rules described in the section "Using Outlook's Junk E-Mail Filters," page 553, work well.) For the rule's action, mark messages as read and move them to the Probable Spam folder for further examination; most will eventually be deleted.
5	All Other Messages	If you've set up the preceding rules correctly, this group should include mostly spam that's addressed directly to you, plus a few messages from people who are not on your list of trusted contacts. Choose "For all messages" as the condition, and for the action move matching messages to an Unfiled folder for further examination.

Inside Out

Manage mailing lists

Setting up filters for mailing lists can be difficult. The format of the subject line might not be consistent, and the sender's address can change periodically as well. Your best strategy? Look at the boilerplate text at the beginning and end of a typical message. Thoughtful mailing list managers often include identifying prefixes (typically in brackets) that are designed to help you positively identify and filter messages from that list. Even without that tag, you might be able to pick out a unique phrase from the copyright line and use it to define the condition for a message rule.

Of course, you can customize these rules extensively. If you subscribe to a large number of high-traffic mailing lists, for instance, you might prefer to create a subfolder and a matching rule for each list. Likewise, you might create a series of rules designed to filter out spam and adult content—automatically, permanently deleting any message that contains a list of particularly vulgar words or phrases, for instance. Just make certain that each new rule goes in the same location within your list of rules as other rules in its category. If you create a new rule that sorts messages from the Lockergnome mailing list into their own folder, you need to move the rule into the group of rules that apply to other mailing list messages. After creating the rule and giving it a meaningful name, use the Move Up or Move Down button to put it in its proper place.

Microsoft Windows XP Networking and Security Inside Out

Caution Be extremely careful with two types of rules: those that permanently delete messages and those that respond automatically to incoming messages. Use the "permanently delete" option (available in Outlook but not in Outlook Express) only for message rules whose target is absolutely, positively certain. A loosely constructed rule that permanently deletes messages could end up erasing important mail without your knowledge. Rules that automatically respond to messages that meet certain conditions are even more dangerous because of the risk that the rule will create an "e-mail loop" in which your client software and an e-mail server automatically reply to each other's messages. If your auto-responder replies to a mailing list, you could end up being accused of spamming the list yourself! Outlook protects against the possibility of e-mail loops by firing off an auto-reply or auto-forwarded message in response to a rule only once per day or session, regardless of whether the rule is stored on the client or on the server; Outlook Express does not offer this protective feature and is thus more vulnerable to e-mail loops.

Creating Custom Filters

The procedures for creating message rules vary depending on the software you're using. In this section, we focus on techniques for Outlook Express and recent versions of Outlook. We also take a brief look at how to create and maintain a list of mail filters in other e-mail clients, including the Web-based offerings from MSN Hotmail.

Message Rules in Outlook Express

Creating a rule in Outlook Express involves filling in four options in a dialog box. The process is relatively straightforward, although it contains a few "gotchas."

Note In this section, we assume that you're using Outlook Express 6 (the default in all versions of Windows XP and included with Internet Explorer 6). If you're using an earlier version of Outlook Express with Windows 2000, we strongly recommend that you immediately upgrade to the latest version of Internet Explorer and Outlook Express to take advantage of security improvements in both programs.

To start creating a message rule, open the main Outlook Express window and choose Tools, Message Rules, Mail. If this is the first time you've created a rule, the New Mail Rule dialog box opens directly. If you have previously created any rules, the Message Rules dialog box opens and displays a list of all currently available rules. Click the New button to begin the four-part process. Figure 16-5 shows the New Mail Rule dialog box after all four steps have been completed.

Chapter 16

Figure 16-5. As you select options in steps 1 and 2, the Rule Description box (step 3) is filled in automatically. Click the underlined options to specify details for each message rule.

1. In the first box, Select The Conditions For Your Rule, click to select one or more options from the available list. Be aware of these general guidelines:

   ▪ You can filter based on information in the From, To, or Cc line, or based on text in the subject line or message body. You can also create rules that check the account from which the message was received, the size of the message, whether it contains an attachment, and other criteria.

   ▪ Although it's not immediately apparent, you can add "not" to any condition using an option in step 3. For instance, if you want to create a rule that selects messages in which your name is not in the To or Cc fields, select Where The To Or CC Line Contains People.

   ▪ When you select two or more options, Outlook Express automatically combines them using the "and" operator. You can change this operator to "or" in step 3.

   ▪ The last option in the list, For All Messages, is useful as the basis for the final rule in a list of rules, which might move all messages that weren't processed by previous rules to a specific folder. You could also use this condition in a rule that forwards a copy of all incoming messages to a separate e-mail account while you're away from the office and unable to connect with your regular mail server.

Chapter 16

2 In the next box, Select The Actions For Your Rule, click to select one or more options from the available list. Note the following suggestions:

- Although you can select any combination of actions, be sure that each combination makes sense. Moving a message to a folder and then deleting it is illogical, for instance.

- When you select two or more actions, Outlook Express performs all those actions on messages that match the rule's conditions. You cannot change the order of actions.

- Use the Flag It or Highlight It With Color actions to call attention to messages that remain in your Inbox folder. You might want all messages from your boss to appear in your Inbox folder in red, for instance.

- Don't select the Mark The Message As Watched Or Ignored option for a mail rule; this option is designed for working with newsgroups in Outlook Express.

- For any message that you plan to delete because you're certain it's unwanted, use the Mark It As Read and Delete It options.

> **Tip**   If you receive a large amount of spam and you use rules to mark it as read and delete it, you should disable the feature that automatically notifies you when new e-mail arrives. If you leave the notification option on, you're likely to be confused by the new message indicator, which is triggered by the arrival of any message in the Inbox folder and cannot be turned off by a message rule.

- Select the Stop Processing More Rules option if you want the action in the current rule to be the only one that applies to messages meeting that condition.

3 As you select each item in steps 1 and 2, Outlook Express fills in the Rule Description box. If a condition or action requires you to specify a value, that value is underlined and displayed in blue. Click the underlined text to fill in each value, as described here:

- For People, you can enter any valid e-mail address or select from the Address Book. Use the Add button (shown here) to enter each name. Enter a domain name without including a user name or the at sign (@) if you want the condition to apply to all messages from that domain.

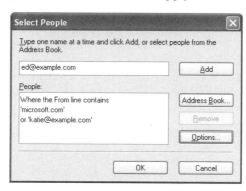

- For the Specific Words condition, you can enter one or more words or phrases.

- To customize a condition, click the Options button. As mentioned earlier (and shown here), the Rule Condition Options dialog box lets you add "not" to a condition. If the condition contains more than one item, use the second option to toggle between "and" and "or."

- If you select the option to move or copy a message to a specified folder, you can select that folder (or create a new one) from a dialog box.

- Before you can use the Reply With Message option in a rule, you must first create the message you want to use as your response. After creating the message, choose File, Save As in the new message window and save the message using the .eml extension. Select the saved message as the text of your automatic reply.

4 Replace the generic test in the Name Of The Rule box with a descriptive name for the newly created rule, and then click OK to save your changes.

After creating a new rule, you return to the Message Rules dialog box. Use the Move Up or Move Down button to place your new rule in the correct position. From this dialog box, you can edit any rule directly; to rename a rule or change the list of conditions or actions for a rule, click the Modify button.

Message Rules in Outlook

Although the basic principles behind message rules are the same in Outlook as in Outlook Express, the options available for creating a rule are considerably more extensive and, for the most part, more flexible. In Outlook, for example, you can create rules that act on messages you send as well as those you receive. You also have a much broader range of conditions and actions from which to choose.

Inside Out

Choose the right Outlook version

Which version of Outlook should you use? If you plan to use message rules, choose carefully. Outlook 97 isn't a viable option—the Rules Wizard was introduced as an add-on in Outlook 98. As we point out in Chapter 15, "Securing E-Mail and Instant Messages," both Outlook 97 and Outlook 98 have too many security problems for us to recommend them. Outlook 2000 is more robust, but you need to create a separate rule for each value you want to test, which can make the list of rules cumbersome and, if it gets large enough, virtually impossible to manage. Outlook 2002 (part of Office XP) adds several highly desirable tweaks to the Rules Wizard—most notable is the capability to specify multiple values as part of a single condition. Outlook 2003 uses a greatly improved rule-building interface and offers vastly improved Junk E-mail filtering. The combination can be extremely effective at blocking unwanted e-mail.

Creating a new rule in Outlook 2002 requires that you use a five-step wizard. To get started, open the Outlook Inbox folder and choose Tools, Rules Wizard. The Rules Wizard dialog box (Figure 16-6) displays a list of all currently available rules.

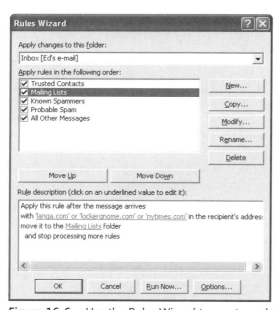

Figure 16-6. Use the Rules Wizard to create and manage e-mail filters in Outlook.

Click the New button to begin creating a rule, and then follow these steps:

1. Choose from a list of preconfigured templates or use a blank rule.
   - Templates, such as those shown in Figure 16-7, include preselected conditions and actions. If the template you choose meets all your needs, click the underlined links in the Rule Description box to fill in any required values and then click Finish.

Blocking Spam

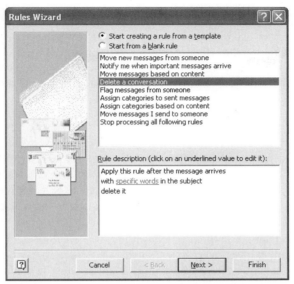

Figure 16-7. These templates cover the most common types of message rules. You can use a template to get started and then continue using the wizard to add more conditions or actions.

- If no template meets your needs, choose Start From A Blank Rule, choose Check Messages When They Arrive, and click Next.

2 Select the conditions for your message rule. If any of the selected conditions require that you specify values, click the underlined keyword in the Rule Description box and fill in the appropriate blanks. (When you add multiple values for a condition, the Rules Wizard separates them with "or," as shown here.)

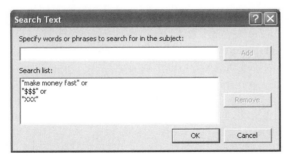

Click Next to continue. Use the following guidelines to get the most out of conditions:

- You can select multiple conditions, just as you can for rules in Outlook Express. In Outlook, however, multiple conditions are always joined with the "and" operator—that is, the rule will be applied if, for example, condition A is true *and* condition B is true. You cannot change this operator to "or."

> **Tip** Create an "or" rule
>
> If you need to test for two different conditions, either of which can be true, you need to do so in separate rules. (With Outlook Express, you can do this in a single rule.) Outlook doesn't let you create "exclusive or" rules, where the rule is triggered if A is true or B is true but A and B are not both true. However, you can easily achieve the same result using two consecutive rules. In the first rule, use the condition "A is true except when B is true." In the second rule, do the reverse: "B is true except when A is true."

- In addition to testing for words in the subject or body of the message and in the sender's or recipient's address, you can also select With Specific Words In The Message Header. With this option, you can create rules based on the name of a specific mail server, for instance, or to look for technical information found only in a message header, such as the name of the program that created the message or the name of a server through which it passed.

- Select Sender Is In Specified Address Book if you want the rule to be triggered for any address that appears in an Outlook address book you've set up. (If you use Internet standard SMTP mail servers, the default address book is the Contacts folder; if you connect to a Microsoft Exchange Server, you can choose from additional address books on the server.)

- Although you can do so in Outlook Express, you cannot add "not" to a condition in Outlook. Instead, create an exception using step 4.

3 Select an action for the rule. Here, too, you can select multiple actions, filling in any required values in the Rule Description box. Click Next to continue. Note the following suggestions:

- The Delete It option moves the message to the Deleted Items folder. The Permanently Delete It option eliminates all traces of the message. Be extremely careful with the latter option.

- If you delete or move a message because you are confident that it is spam, be sure to select the Mark It As Read action as well. This prevents you from being distracted by new messages that almost certainly aren't worth reading.

- Unless you're a skilled Microsoft Exchange developer, ignore the Perform A Custom Action option; this action requires that you create a dynamic-link library (DLL) for a custom rule for use with an Exchange server. Read more about this option in Microsoft Knowledge Base article 151690, "What Is the 'Custom' Rule Action For?"

4 Add any exceptions that the rule should take into account. The list of exceptions is essentially the same as the conditions list, enabling you to create more complex rules. For instance, if you've created a rule that tests for words and phrases commonly found in spam, you might add an exception for any message received from a person whose e-mail address is in your address book. Click Next to continue.

5 Give the rule a descriptive name and click Finish.

6 In the Rules Wizard dialog box, use the Move Up or Move Down button to place the new rule in the proper position.

> **Tip** **Troubleshoot message rules**
> If a message rule isn't behaving as you expected it would, the most likely reason is that another rule is performing an action on the message first. Two Knowledge Base articles, 291633, "How to Troubleshoot the Outlook Rules Wizard," and 197496, "Outlook Rules Wizard Troubleshooting," offer helpful suggestions.

To modify a rule after you've created and saved it, open the Rules Wizard dialog box and select the entry you want to modify from the list of available rules. If you simply want to add, change, or remove a value from the conditions or actions for the rule, you can do so directly in the Rule Description box at the bottom of the dialog box. Click the link for the value, add the new item, and save your changes. This is the correct technique to use if you have a Trusted Contacts or Known Spammers rule, for instance, and you want to add a new address or domain to either list. To make more substantial changes to a rule, such as adding or removing a condition or action, click the Modify button and run through the wizard for that rule.

In Outlook 2003, the general procedures for creating a rule are similar, although the user interface is different. To start, choose Tools, Rules And Alerts. On the E-mail Rules tab of the Rules And Alerts dialog box, click New Rule.

Follow the wizard's prompts to build the rule. To change a rule, select it in the Rules And Alerts window, choose Change Rule, and then click Edit Rule Settings.

Chapter 16

551

Filters in MSN Hotmail

Microsoft's Web-based e-mail service, MSN Hotmail, includes several built-in spam-filtering options. These options are the only way to filter mail received through this service. If you configure Outlook Express or Outlook to receive and send mail through an MSN Hotmail account, any message rules you create in your client software will be ignored when you connect to MSN Hotmail.

> **Note** With some Web-based mail services, including Google Gmail and Yahoo! Mail, you can configure an account for POP3 access. If you choose this option, your client software treats the incoming mail just as if it were coming from an Internet standard mail account. You can create rules to filter mail in this configuration.

To set up spam-filtering options in this service, go to the main MSN Hotmail page after logging on, choose Options, and configure any of the following options, all found by clicking the Mail heading in the left column and then clicking Junk E-Mail Protection:

- **Junk E-Mail Filter.** Choose Low, Enhanced, or Exclusive. The Exclusive option sends all mail to the built-in Junk Mail folder unless the sender is in your address book.
- **Delete Junk E-Mail.** Choose whether you want all junk mail deleted immediately or diverted to a Junk E-Mail folder. Choose the former option only if you're certain that your rules are set properly.
- **Mailing Lists.** Enter the To address for any mailing list to which you subscribe. This disables all junk-mail filtering for these list messages.
- **Block Senders.** Use this list to block specific addresses or entire domains. Any messages from these senders are removed on arrival and never appear in your Inbox, Junk E-Mail, or Deleted Items folders. Use the Block button on any message to automatically add the sender to this list. You can block up to 250 individual addresses and an apparently unlimited number of domains.
- **Safe List.** Specify the addresses that you do not want filtered as junk mail. When you open any message in the Junk Mail folder, you can click the This Is Not Junk Mail option to add its address to the Safe List automatically.
- **Junk E-Mail Reporting Confirmation.** Use this option to confirm whether you want to be notified each time an e-mail message is blocked.

One additional option on the Mail tab, Custom Filters, enables you to create and save a group of e-mail filters (according to the online Help files, you can create up to 10 filters with a standard MSN Hotmail account and up to 36 filters if you're subscribed to Hotmail Plus), which Hotmail uses to automatically move messages to other folders based on the subject or address block. These filters are not particularly useful for spam-blocking; they are most useful if you want to automatically divert mailing list messages to their own folder.

Any mail-handling rules you set using the Web-based MSN Hotmail interface will apply to all messages you receive through that account. This is true even if you have configured Outlook Express or Outlook to handle your MSN Hotmail account.

If you use the MSN Explorer client software to read your Hotmail or MSN messages, your spam-filtering options are far more limited. This software, which comes with Windows XP and is intended for users who are uncomfortable with too many technical options, includes an Inbox Protector feature that automatically shunts most unsolicited mail into a Bulk Mail folder. You can block senders and add addresses to a safe list. To set these options, start MSN Explorer, click the E-Mail button, and choose More Choices, Settings.

Using Outlook's Junk E-Mail Filters

Outlook 2003 includes extremely effective junk e-mail filtering capabilities. To use this technology, which is identical to the filtering features used in MSN Hotmail, choose Actions, Junk E-mail, Junk E-mail Options. The options available in this dialog box enable you to specify the level of filtering and whether filtered messages will be deleted or moved to the Junk E-mail folder.

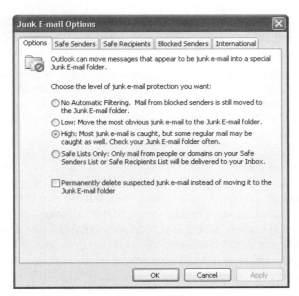

Chapter 16

> **Tip** Don't forget to update
> Since Outlook 2003 was released, Microsoft has issued regular updates to the program's junk filters. To download and install the latest updates, visit the Office Update Web site at *http://officeupdate.microsoft.com*.

The exact details of how the Junk E-mail filters work are undocumented, and the filter's configuration can't be fine-tuned. However, you can add individual senders or domains to a Safe Senders list (to allow them to bypass the filters) or to a Blocked Senders list. In addition, you can add specific addresses (mailing lists, for instance) to the Safe Recipients list so that they are not inadvertently filtered out.

The Outlook 2003 filters are highly automated and easy to use. Outlook 2000 and Outlook 2002, by contrast, include a pair of preconfigured message rules designed to automatically filter out junk mail and messages that contain adult content (that is, come-ons for pornographic Web sites). Used with their default settings, these rules are only marginally effective and can result in a fair number of false positives (legitimate messages incorrectly detected as junk mail) and outright misses, in which offending messages reach your inbox. However, with some judicious tweaking you can integrate these filters into your spam-fighting program and increase their effectiveness.

In their default configuration, the Outlook 2002 Junk Mail and Adult Content filters consist of three mechanisms:

- A list of words and phrases commonly found in spam messages. The settings file is documented in a readme file called Filters.txt; in Outlook 2002, this file is stored in the %ProgramFiles%\Microsoft Office\Office10*LocaleID* folder, where *LocaleID* is the locale identifier for your version of Office. (For U.S. English, this value is 1033.) Despite what you might read in some misinformed articles on the Web, these settings are not editable; the contents of Filters.txt consist of documentation only.

- A user-configurable list of Junk Senders and Adult Content Senders. These lists are maintained as text files in your user profile. You can edit this list manually (one address per line), although it's much easier to add senders to this list individually— select a message in the message list, right-click, and choose Junk E-Mail, Add To Junk Senders List (or Add To Adult Content Senders List). Note that Outlook does not create either list until you add at least one name to the list.

> **Tip** Spread your junk-mail net wider
>
> Using the options on the Junk E-Mail menu, you can specify that the sender of a particular message should be blocked or designated as "safe." When you use these menus to add an address to the Safe Senders, Blocked Senders, or Safe Recipients list in Outlook 2003, or to the Junk Senders list or the Adult Content Senders list in Outlook 2002, Outlook adds the entire address. If you edit the list of senders manually, however, you can add an entire domain to this list. Thus, if you want all e-mail you receive from a given domain to be treated as junk mail, add that domain name to the list.

- A user-configurable Exception list, which is also saved as a text file in the same location as the Junk Senders and Adult Content Senders lists. Any addresses found on this list are automatically exempted from the checks performed by the built-in junk mail rules.

The official method for turning on these filters is as follows:

1. From the Outlook 2002 Inbox folder, choose Tools, Organize.
2. Click the Junk E-Mail link in the Ways To Organize pane. This displays the options shown in Figure 16-8.

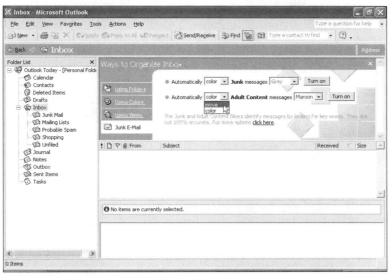

Figure 16-8. The default action for these filters merely changes the color of each message that is detected as junk mail or adult content. To move messages to a different folder, you must change these options.

3 By default, these rules are set to change the color of each matching message: junk e-mail to gray, adult content messages to maroon. Select Move instead of Color for each rule to move the messages to a different folder rather than simply changing their color.

4 Click the Turn On button to enable each rule. Doing so creates an Exception List rule at the top of the Rules Wizard. If you've chosen Move instead of Color as the action, Outlook creates a new rule in the Rules Wizard as well. (If you choose the Color option, this task is handled by the Automatic Formatting feature for the default view.)

So far, so good. Unfortunately, this seemingly simple set of steps has several drawbacks:

- The newly created rules are added to the top of the Rules Wizard. As a result, they're processed before any custom rules you've previously created. This practically guarantees that some legitimate messages will be handled improperly because they happen to contain a suspect phrase such as "special promotion" or "over 21" or "check or money order."

- If you choose the Move action, your messages are moved to a different folder, but they are not marked as unread.

- The filters' criteria haven't been updated in several years. Up-to-date spammers know about these filters and many avoid using the phrases contained in them. As a result, these filters trap only a fraction of the junk mail you're likely to receive.

- The rules created in the Organize pane cannot be customized.

Chapter 16

If you still want to use these built-in filters, ignore the Organize menu and create a custom rule instead. Follow these steps:

1 Use the Organize pane to turn on Junk E-Mail filtering. Choose the Move option and select a folder to which junk messages should be sent. This step creates the Exception List rule, which cannot be created manually.

2 From the Outlook Inbox folder, choose Tools, Rules Wizard.

3 Select the Junk E-mail rule and click Delete.

4 In the Rules Wizard dialog box, click New.

5 Select Start From Blank Rule, and then select Check Messages When They Arrive. Click Next, and follow the wizard's prompts to create a rule using the following conditions and actions:

■ Suspected To Be Junk E-Mail Or From Junk Senders

■ Move It To The Junk Mail Folder (or any folder you specify)

■ Mark It As Read

■ Stop Processing More Rules

■ Except If Sender Is In Contacts Address Book

6 Save this rule using a descriptive name, such as Junk Senders. When you finish, the result should look like the rule shown in Figure 16-9.

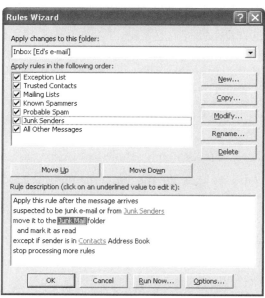

Figure 16-9. Use this improved custom version of the built-in junk mail filters.

7 Repeat steps 2 through 6 but use the condition Containing Adult Content Or Suspected To Be From Adult Content Senders.

8   Return to the Rules Wizard and move the newly created rules to the bottom of your list of message rules. Make sure the Exception List rule is above the Junk Senders and Adult Content Senders rules.

Tip   Handle exceptions

If you discover that the Junk Senders rule is regularly catching mail it shouldn't, you have two options. You can add the sender to your Outlook Contacts folder so that the sender's name isn't processed by your customized rule; or, if you'd prefer not to create a new address book record, add the name to the Exception list. Open the Rules Wizard and select the Exception List rule. In the description pane, click the Exception List link and type or paste the address you want to add. If this process seems too cumbersome, create a shortcut to %UserProfile%\Application Data\Microsoft\Outlook\Exception List.txt and add the shortcut to your Start menu or desktop. Use this shortcut to open the Exception List and edit it using Notepad.

By using this strategy, you ensure that the built-in junk filters are processed *after* any custom rules you've created to handle messages from trusted contacts, mailing lists, and other senders. These rules should also come after any spam-handling message rules you've created. In fact, these rules should be near the bottom of your list of message rules, above only the catch-all rule that handles messages that can't be handled by any existing rule.

Backing Up Message Rules

Creating a custom set of message rules and tweaking them so that they work exactly as you intend involves a significant amount of time and effort. Every so often, be sure to back up your filtering rules and save them to a safe place (*not* just on your computer, where the backup can vanish in the event of a disk crash).

In Outlook Express, message rules and the Blocked Senders list are stored in the registry, with a separate set of rules for each identity. To back up these settings manually, follow these steps:

1   Open Registry Editor (Regedit.exe).

2   Navigate to the following key, where *GUID* is the 32-character unique code for your identity: HKCU\Identities\{*GUID*}\Software\Microsoft\Outlook Express\5.0 \Rules.

3   Right-click the Rules key in the tree pane on the left and choose Export from the shortcut menu. (In Windows 2000, choose Export Registry File from the Registry menu.)

4   In the Export Registry File dialog box, enter a descriptive file name (My Message Rules, say) and a location for the saved settings. In the Export Range area at the bottom of the dialog box, keep the default setting, Selected Branch.

5   Click Save.

Chapter 16

6   If you've added any names to the Blocked Senders list, repeat steps 2 through 5 for the Block Senders key in the same branch of the registry.

To restore the backed-up rules, double-click the saved file and import the settings into the registry.

Tip   Make backing up easier

If exporting settings from the registry seems unnecessarily complex, try any of several third-party backup utilities to simplify the task. Express Assist completely backs up all messages, addresses, and settings, including message rules. OutBack Plus does the same task for all versions of Microsoft Outlook. Download a trial copy of either program from *http://www.ajsystems.com*. TweakIE (*http://www.tweakie.com*) performs the same functions and also manages Internet Explorer settings that handle cookies and the cache.

Outlook 2003 stores all message rules in the Personal Folders (.pst) file. To back up messages from Outlook 2000 or 2002, or to transfer message rules between Outlook 2003 and previous versions, use the export and import features. Exporting the rules saves a copy of all rules in a file; if you need to restore the rules later, on the same computer or a different one, use the import option and specify the same file. To export all rules, follow these steps:

1   From the Outlook Inbox folder, choose Tools, Rules Wizard. (In Outlook 2003, choose Tools, Rules And Alerts.)

2   Click Options.

3   In the Options dialog box, click the Export Rules button.

4   Browse to the folder you want to save the rules in, enter a descriptive file name and a location, and then click Save.

If you've customized the Junk Senders and Adult Content Senders lists, back them up as well. These text files (along with other Outlook settings) are stored in the %UserProfile%\Application Data\Microsoft\Outlook folder.

Third-Party Spam-Busting Solutions

If the message-filtering capabilities of your favorite e-mail software seem too cumbersome, consider using third-party software to do the dirty work. Literally dozens of spam-fighting utilities and services are available for Windows users to choose from. Look first at other security programs you might already own. Some antivirus developers have added spam-blocking features to their packages in recent years. Trend Micro, for instance, includes robust spam blocking with its full-featured PC-cillin product, and both Symantec and McAfee offer security suites that include spam-blockers.

If you prefer a stand-alone package, the following are among our favorites:

- **MailWasher Pro** gets consistently high marks for its constantly updated filters, which are built through a community-based spam-reporting system. The program works by querying your mail server before messages are downloaded to your e-mail client software; you can tag and delete unwanted messages before they reach your computer. Get more details at *http://www.mailwasher.net*.

- **SpamWeasel** from MailGate is available in a freeware version and a Pro version that you can evaluate for free for 30 days. We recommend the Pro version, which includes a huge database of preconfigured rules (the free version is outdated and difficult to configure). It operates with any Internet standard e-mail client, intercepting messages before they reach your inbox, examining the messages, and quarantining suspected spam. Get additional information at *http://www.mailgate.com/products/spamweas/swp_feat.asp*.

- **SpamKiller** is a commercial utility that also works with any e-mail program. Because it's driven by wizards, it's relatively easy to configure, and you can build new filters based on spam you receive. It works with POP3 accounts and MSN Hotmail, but not with AOL or Web-based services. Get more details at *http://www.spamkiller.com*.

- **SpamEater** from High Mountain Software comes in a free standard version and a paid version with some extra features. It's integrated with online databases of known spammer blacklists, and the full paid version supports online updates to the application and filter rules. It's also integrated with SpamCop, a service that enables you to automatically generate complaints about persistent spammers. For details, point your browser to *http://www.hms.com/spameater.asp*.

- **SpamhOle** is a free online service that creates temporary e-mail addresses you can use when you must provide an address to use a Web site that is not known to be trustworthy. The address you create is automatically forwarded to your real e-mail address and automatically expires after a period of time that you specify. Get details at *http://www.spamhole.com*.

Chapter 16

Fighting Back Against Spam

If you're inundated with unwanted e-mail, your natural inclination is to fight back. Surely there must be someone to whom you can complain, right?

Yes and no.

Given the free-for-all nature of the Internet, it should come as no surprise that no uniform laws govern unsolicited commercial e-mail. Depending on where you live, you might be able to file a lawsuit against the sender and even have a reasonable chance of succeeding—if you can identify the sender, that is. For an excellent overview of current anti-spam statutes in the United States, Europe, and around the world, visit David E. Sorkin's Spam Laws site at *http://www.spamlaws.com*.

If you live in the United States, or if the spam appears to have originated in the United States, you can send it to the U.S. Federal Trade Commission, by using the form at *http://www.ftc.gov/spam/* (click File A Complaint) or by forwarding the message to *spam@uce.gov*. You'll have the best chance of getting results if the spam in question is a come-on to a scam that has the potential to defraud investors or consumers. According to the FTC's Web site, the agency "uses the spam stored in this database to pursue law enforcement actions against people who send deceptive email…. The FTC's spam database has served as the basis for FTC cases involving pyramid schemes, money-making chain letters, credit card scams, credit repair scams, bogus weight-loss plans, fraudulent business opportunities, and other scams that were promoted via email."

The online SpamCop service (*http://www.spamcop.net*) specializes in helping Internet users track down the source of spam and then file complaints. You can use the reporting system for free or pay a small fee to remove banner ads and streamline the complaint process. The organization, founded by Julian Haight, also offers low-cost filtered e-mail accounts and comprehensive filtering options for corporate clients.

Whatever you do, don't try to fight back by spamming the spammers! The urge to flood an inconsiderate e-mail marketer with hundreds or thousands of reply messages can be overwhelming, but the consequences can be dire. You personally could be accused of spamming, and the IP address of your mail server could land in one of the Internet's "black hole" lists, which block suspected spammers from sending e-mail to subscribing servers.

Chapter 17

Securing Your Computer by Using a Firewall

Now that nearly every personal computer is connected to the Internet, either directly or indirectly, malicious hackers have plenty of tempting targets to attack. Widespread adoption of high-speed, always-on Internet connections presents new opportunities for vandals, thieves, and hostile code. Infections can spread quickly, and anyone who uses a computer is vulnerable to a wide range of troubling threats, including the following:

- Unauthorized users can access private data on a computer via the computer's Internet connection.

- Attackers can use an unprotected computer as a gateway to a corporate network by piggybacking onto the computer's virtual private network (VPN) connection to the network.

- An intruder can install software on an unprotected computer that allows that computer to be monitored or controlled from a remote location, capturing passwords and other sensitive information.

- A miscreant can use an unprotected computer as an unwitting accomplice. A so-called zombie computer can be used as a spam-relaying proxy or as a node in a distributed denial of service attack—an attack in which many computers are directed in concert to flood another computer with requests, effectively making it unusable.

Some of these vulnerabilities are mitigated by switching from older versions of Windows to a more secure operating system (especially Windows XP) and implementing password protection, NTFS permissions, antivirus software, and other techniques described in this book. But for effective protection from attacks by malicious intruders outside your local area network (LAN), you need a firewall.

In this chapter, we explore some of the threats presented by an unprotected Internet connection. We then explain how you can fine-tune the settings of your software firewall, with a special emphasis on Windows Firewall, included with Windows XP Service Pack 2 (SP2). With Windows Firewall and most of its third-party counterparts, you can keep a log of rejected connections. In this chapter, we explain how you can use this information to hunt down and stop some of the most persistent attackers.

Security Checklist: Fighting External Attacks

Here's a list of steps to take to prevent attacks from the outside:

- Keep your system up to date with security updates from Microsoft.
- Set up personal firewall software—Windows Firewall or a third-party alternative—on each computer that is part of your network.
- Install a perimeter firewall between your network and your Internet connection.
- Configure your firewall to block all ports except those you actually use.
- Be selective when you configure application-based rules; be certain that a program asking for Internet access legitimately needs it.
- If your router or firewall appliance can be accessed and managed from the Internet, disable this feature except when it's needed; in addition, change its default user name and assign a strong password.
- Monitor firewall logs for signs of attacks, such as probes of commonly exploited ports.

How Hack Attacks Work

Attackers—whether their intent is to steal information, commandeer computing resources, maliciously destroy information, or simply commit acts of electronic vandalism—employ a variety of methods to attack computers on the Internet.

Many attackers exploit software bugs in server applications, client applications, or operating systems. Like it or not, any but the most trivial application has bugs.

Most bug-related security holes are the result of buffer overrun vulnerabilities. A buffer overrun occurs when an input field in a program (including an operating system component or a Web-based application running in a browser window) receives more data than the program has allotted space for and the program is unable to process the input correctly. For example, a program might be set up to accept a URL that's no more than 256 characters long. If an attacker figures out how to send a 400-character string in the space where the URL normally goes, the program could crash. When this happens, the extra characters could go into an area of memory—a buffer—where the program interprets them as instructions to be executed. Hackers (good and bad) find these types of vulnerabilities by examining program code (the source code for many programs is widely available) or simply by trying to overflow any place a program accepts input.

If an overflow causes a program to crash, the system might be left in a state where it's vulnerable to executing instructions crafted by the attacker. The successful exploitation of this type of vulnerability could enable an attacker to run code on the local system, for example.

Other software bugs might cause a program to allow entry to an attacker who provides invalid input. Programs that handle valid input with aplomb sometimes don't fare as well with input outside the expected range. A determined attacker can exploit such bugs in a manner similar to buffer overrun vulnerabilities.

Attackers don't need to rely solely on bugs to gain entry to Internet-connected systems, however. Systems that are not securely configured are easy prey. Systems that act as file servers can expose shared folders; other types of servers can also provide access to a computer. (Many Trojan horse programs set up servers that attackers can contact and use to gain entry.) A common tool of attackers is a port scanner—an automated program that can cycle through thousands of IP address/port combinations in search of open ports. (An open port is one that is listening for connection requests.)

Would-be intruders also take advantage of systems on which security safeguards are disabled. While trying to troubleshoot a connection problem, for example, you might remove or relax some restrictions, such as NTFS permissions, firewall protection, and so on. If you forget to restore your secure settings after resolving the problem, you run the very real risk that an attacker will discover this lapse.

Tip Check for holes
Use Microsoft Baseline Security Analyzer (MBSA) or another security auditing program to search for insecure settings. For details about MBSA, see "Testing and Verifying Your Secure Status," page 229.

Security expert Robert Graham has cataloged a number of attacks using the vulnerabilities outlined in the preceding paragraphs. Although the information on his Web page titled "FAQ: Network Intrusion Detection Systems" is somewhat dated, it provides a useful introduction to the methods used by attackers. You can view an archived version of the page at *http://www.ticm.com/kb/faq/idsfaq.html*. The SANS Institute offers a similar, more up-to-date Intrusion Detection FAQ at *http://www.sans.org/resources/idfaq/*.

Chapter 17

DoS Isn't an Operating System

Another nasty trick is a denial of service (DoS) attack, in which the perpetrator attempts to crash a computer by overwhelming it with data. Doing so doesn't give the attacker access to the computer's information, but the attack effectively renders the computer unusable. The packets in a DoS attack are typically malformed in some way, which causes the computer to expend all its resources attempting to deal with the flood of erroneous data.

An attacker using a single computer can't do much to slow down a properly configured computer, but multiple computers working in concert to hammer a server with data requests can bring it to its knees quickly. This type of onslaught is called a distributed denial of service (DDoS) attack. In a DDoS, an attacker directs hundreds or even thousands of computers (usually computers that have been taken over by Trojan horse software and turned into "zombies") to launch coordinated DoS attacks against a particular computer or network. DDoS attacks have been used to knock several high-profile companies, including Yahoo!, Amazon.com, CNN, and eBay, off the Internet for hours or days at a time. More recent attacks have been aimed at smaller companies and individuals, especially researchers who specialize in security issues. But these companies and individuals weren't the only victims; many of the computers used to carry out the attacks belonged to unsuspecting individuals whose computers were also tied up to the point of paralysis.

Dave Dittrich, a security expert at the University of Washington, has assembled an exhaustive collection of links to information about DDoS and has also co-authored a book entitled *Internet Denial of Service: Attack and Defense Mechanisms* (Prentice Hall, 2005). If you want to know more about DDoS—how it works, prevention tools and techniques, news reports, and much more—visit his "Distributed Denial of Service (DDoS) Attacks/Tools" page at *http://staff.washington.edu/dittrich/misc/ddos/*.

Configuring a Host Firewall

The building blocks of a secure network include a perimeter firewall, such as a router, and a personal firewall on each workstation that prevents unsolicited network requests from reaching that computer. With this basic configuration in place, you're protected from most common outside attacks. Using a stateful-inspection firewall, the only packets of information allowed to reach your computer will be those that you specifically requested, or those originating from computers on your local network over approved ports.

> For a discussion of basic concepts behind network-based firewall devices and software firewalls, see "Blocking Attacks by Using a Firewall," page 10. For more details about setting up and using Windows Firewall, see "Using Windows Firewall in Windows XP," page 277.

But what if you want to allow other computers to initiate a connection to your computer? You probably want to share some folders with other users on your local network. You might run a personal Web server that is accessible to friends and family members over the Internet. Or perhaps you use an instant messaging program that requires inbound connections so others can contact you. In each of these cases, you set up an *exception* in your firewall software, which pokes a small hole in the firewall and allows a certain type of traffic to pass through.

In this section, we explain how to configure exceptions in Windows XP—a task you can typically perform at any time. If you use a third-party firewall program, the basic tasks are similar, although the steps you take will obviously vary.

Inside Out

When configuring your network to allow certain types of unsolicited traffic from the Internet, remember that you might have to make matching adjustments to both a software firewall and a hardware-based firewall device. If you want to allow traffic to reach a Web server running on your computer using nonstandard port 81, for instance, you'll first have to configure your router to send any incoming traffic on port 81 to the IP address assigned to your computer. Then you'll have to configure the software firewall to accept the incoming traffic. Until you complete both these steps, your Web server will be unreachable from the outside world.

Allowing Incoming Connections Through Windows Firewall

To allow specific types of incoming connections, you need to create a rule that defines the traffic you want to allow in. In Windows Firewall, you can do this in any of the following ways:

- You can click Unblock when Windows Firewall first detects that an external source is trying to connect with a program on your computer. By default, most programs are blocked; when you click Unblock, Windows adds the program to the global Exceptions list and allows it to receive data from outside sources over any port.

- You can manually add a program to the global Exceptions list. When you take this step, Windows Firewall allows that program to receive incoming traffic on any port whenever it is running.

- You can add a port to the global Exceptions list. This configuration allows incoming traffic on the specified port, regardless of which connection it uses, to pass through the firewall.

- You can open a port on a specific network connection. With this option, you can select from a list of predefined services on well-known ports (a Web server, for instance) or create a custom definition for a service that receives traffic only over the specified connection.

When creating or editing entries on the global Exceptions list, you can also define the scope of the exceptions—restricting allowed traffic to specific subnets or even IP addresses.

Chapter 17

Windows XP does some of this configuration automatically, without requiring any input from you. When you use the Network Setup Wizard to enable file and printer sharing, for instance, Windows creates an exception that allows unsolicited traffic from your local subnet (but not from the Internet) on TCP ports 139 and 445 and UDP ports 137 and 138. Likewise, when you configure Windows XP Professional to accept incoming Remote Desktop connections, Windows opens port 3389 for input from any computer, on your local network or outside. To see the list of currently enabled exceptions, open Control Panel, double-click the Windows Firewall icon (found in the Network and Internet Connections category), and then click the Exceptions tab. This dialog box displays a list of programs and services that are currently on the Exceptions list, as shown in Figure 17-1.

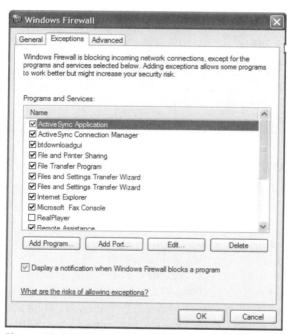

Figure 17-1. Most items on the Exceptions list are defined automatically the first time you use a program or service that connects to the Internet.

Each item in the Programs And Services list defines either a program or a port that is allowed to communicate with other computers; in addition, each entry specifies a *scope*, which defines the IP addresses or subnets (or both) that are allowed to make incoming connections. Selecting the check box to the left of any entry in the Exceptions list tells Windows Firewall to allow incoming connections that satisfy the conditions of that exception.

> **Note** Items in the Programs And Services list on the Exceptions tab define sets of conditions that apply to *incoming* requests only. These restrictions do not affect outgoing use of the services. By default, for instance, the Remote Desktop exception is not selected. This setting has no effect on outgoing connections, so you can freely connect to an external computer that is configured to accept Remote Desktop connections. But if you want to allow yourself to be able to access your computer by using a Remote Desktop connection from another location, you need to select the check box for this item—or better yet, let Windows enable this exception when you select Allow Users To Connect Remotely To This Computer on the Remote tab of the System Properties dialog box.

Creating a global exception increases your security risk to some degree, so you should clear the check box for all exceptions you don't need. If you're confident you won't ever need a particular exception, you can select it and then click Delete. (A handful of predefined exceptions don't allow deletion, but as long as their check boxes are not selected, there's no danger.)

Creating an Exception for a Program

Creating an exception for a program is the simplest way to allow a trusted program to communicate securely with the outside world. You don't need to know which port (or ports) the program uses. Windows Firewall opens ports dynamically while the program is running, whereas an exception created for a port you open allows any incoming traffic over that port, regardless of whether the affected program is actually running.

When a program attempts to open a listening port and you haven't allowed an exception for it, Windows Firewall displays a Windows Security Alert dialog box similar to this:

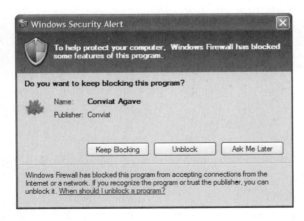

The exact effect of each of the three options in this dialog box is not obvious or intuitive:

- If you click Keep Blocking, Windows Firewall does not create an exception. This means that your program is unable to accept incoming connections, so it might not work properly.

Chapter 17

● If you click Unblock, Windows Firewall creates and then enables an exception for the program. The program's listening port is then open for incoming connections.

● If you click Ask Me Later, Windows Firewall creates an exception for the program— but it does not enable the exception. The program does not accept incoming connections unless you explicitly allow them.

If you choose Unblock or Ask Me Later, you can see the newly defined exception with a visit to the Exceptions tab in Windows Firewall. (See Figure 17-1.) You can learn more details about the exception by selecting its entry in the Programs And Services list and clicking Edit.

From the Exceptions tab, you can set up a program exception without waiting for the Windows Security Alert dialog box to appear. Follow these steps:

1 Click Add Program. The Add A Program dialog box appears.

2 In the Add A Program dialog box, select the program for which you want to allow incoming connections. Or click Browse and navigate to the program's executable file if it isn't shown in the Programs list.

3 Click Change Scope to display the dialog box shown in Figure 17-2.

4 Select the range of computers from which you want to allow incoming connections:

■ **Any Computer** means just that—any computer on your network or on the Internet. (Other defenses, such as NTFS permissions or some form of password authentication, might keep out unwanted users, but Windows Firewall will not.)

■ **My Network (Subnet) Only** allows inbound connections only from computers in the same subnet as yours. (For information about subnets, see "Setting IP Addresses," page 268.)

■ **Custom List** lets you specify one or more computers by their IP address. These can be computers on your LAN or computers with public IP addresses on the Internet.

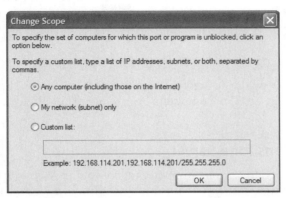

Figure 17-2. For any program or service, you can limit the set of computers that are allowed to make incoming connections.

Tip If you don't want to be bothered with the Windows Security Alert dialog box, clear the Display A Notification When Windows Firewall Blocks A Program check box on the Exceptions tab.

Opening a Port

Another way to create an exception for an incoming connection is to open a port. If the instructions for a program or service you want to use indicate that it needs to use a particular port (or ports), use the following procedure to open the specified port:

1 In Windows Firewall, click the Exceptions tab.

2 Click Add Port. The Add A Port dialog box appears.

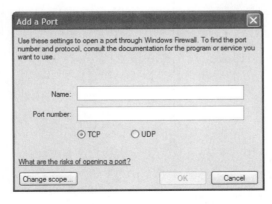

3 In the Add A Port dialog box, make the following entries:

- In the Name box, type a descriptive name for the program or service.

- In the Port Number box, type the port number needed by the program or service.

- Select either TCP or UDP to match the protocol needed by the program or service.

4 Click Change Scope.

5 In the Change Scope dialog box (see Figure 17-2 and step 4 in the previous section), select the range of computers from which you want to allow incoming connections.

Creating Exceptions for a Server

If you run a server program on your computer (a low-volume Web or FTP server, for example), you must create an exception that instructs Windows Firewall to allow outside users to make a connection to that server. (If the server runs on another computer on your network but the network connection through which outside computers will connect to the server is on your computer—for example, if your computer is configured as an Internet Connection Sharing (ICS) host—you will likewise need to create an exception on your computer.)

To enable a service, open the Windows Firewall application in Control Panel and click the Advanced tab. Select the connection from the list in the Network Connection Settings box, and click the Settings button to its right. This opens the Advanced Settings dialog box, which lists available services.

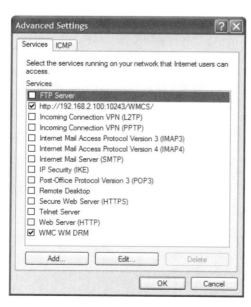

Select the check box for any service on your network that you want to be available to other users, regardless of their location. For example, to allow access to a Web server, select the Web Server (HTTP) check box. Doing so opens a dialog box in which you can specify the computer on your network that will receive the Web server requests. (See Figure 17-3.) In the case of a stand-alone system, you should use the local computer name, or you can use the name *localhost* instead. If the Web server is running on another computer on your network, enter its name; outside users direct their Web requests to your Internet gateway, and Windows Firewall redirects those requests to the computer you specify.

Figure 17-3. The only item you can change on the predefined services is the name of the computer that hosts the service.

If the service or port that you want to make available isn't listed on the Services tab, you can create a new entry. Click the Add button, and a Service Settings dialog box appears. Unlike in the dialog box for predefined services, in this dialog box you can edit all fields. Suppose you want to add support for an incoming connection to control the computer by using pcAnywhere, for example. pcAnywhere version 9 and later require the use of two different ports (TCP 5631 and UDP 5632); you must create a separate entry for each port. The details for the TCP port are shown in Figure 17-4.

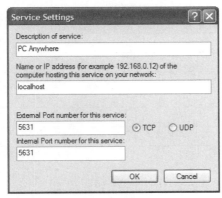

Figure 17-4. To add access to a service such as pcAnywhere, you must provide the port numbers. If the service requires multiple ports, create an entry for each port.

Chapter 17

You can enter any text you like in the Description Of Service box. In the two port number boxes, enter the port number associated with the service you're running. If you don't know the number, you'll need to refer to the documentation for the software that runs the service. (Ordinarily, you set the external and internal ports to the same number. The separate fields enable port redirection; if your ISP blocks incoming traffic on port 80, for example, you could allow outside users to specify port 81, the external port, and then have the request redirected to port 80 inside your network.) You must also select a protocol, which you can find wherever you find the appropriate port number. Most programs use TCP, but many multimedia programs use UDP.

Troubleshooting

A service doesn't work properly after you enable Windows Firewall

Windows Firewall is very effective—sometimes too effective. For example, after turning on Windows Firewall you might find that you can't access some services on your network that you were previously able to use. The most common reason is that Windows Firewall is blocking a port to which you need access. Windows Firewall logs can help you find the problem. By examining the logs, you can determine the port number and add it to the list that Windows Firewall will open. For details about Windows Firewall logs, see "Configuring Windows Firewall Logging," page 578.

Table 17-1 shows the details of the services predefined in Windows Firewall that are available on the Services tab, as well as details of ports you must open to use certain Windows Messenger features.

Table 17-1. Commonly Used Ports for Incoming Connections

Description	Port	Protocol
Services predefined in Windows Firewall		
FTP Publishing Service	21	TCP
Internet Mail Access Protocol Version 3 (IMAP3)	220	TCP
Internet Mail Access Protocol Version 4 (IMAP4)	143	TCP
Simple Mail Transfer Protocol (SMTP)	25	TCP
Post-Office Protocol Version 3 (POP3)	110	TCP
Remote Desktop (also used by Windows Terminal Services and by Remote Assistance in Windows XP)	3389	TCP
Secure Web Server (HTTPS)	443	TCP
Telnet Server	23	TCP
Web Server (HTTP)	80	TCP

Table 17-1. **Commonly Used Ports for Incoming Connections**

Description	Port	Protocol
Windows Messenger Services		
Windows Messenger file transfer (you need only a single port to receive a file; by opening all ports in this range, you can receive up to 10 files simultaneously)	6891–6900	TCP
Whiteboard and application sharing in Microsoft NetMeeting and Windows Messenger	1503	TCP

Note The only way to get full Windows Messenger capability (that is, instant messaging, audio, video, application sharing, whiteboard, file transfer, and remote assistance) across the Internet is to have Universal Plug and Play (UPnP)–compatible gateways at both ends of a connection. The most problematic features are audio and voice communication, which use dynamically assigned ports in the range of 5004 through 65535. Without UPnP, the two computers cannot negotiate a connection through firewalls or network address translation (NAT) devices. The good news is that Windows Firewall and ICS in Windows XP are UPnP compatible. For more information about UPnP, see "Why Your Router Should Be UPnP-Compatible," page 312.

Configuring ICMP Options

TCP and UDP are the most common protocols used to transmit data over the Internet. But some applications and command-line tools rely on Internet Control Message Protocol (ICMP) to communicate status, control, and error information between computers. In addition, widely used troubleshooting tools such as Ping and Tracert use ICMP to establish network connectivity. Because ICMP carries no data, it can't be used to break into your machine and steal information. But would-be attackers do use ICMP messages for scanning networks, redirecting traffic, and carrying out DoS attacks.

By default, Windows Firewall blocks most types of outgoing and incoming ICMP messages. From the Advanced tab of the Windows Firewall dialog box, click the Settings button in the ICMP area. By selectively enabling options in the ICMP Settings dialog box (see Figure 17-5 on the next page), you can allow certain types of ICMP packets over connections that are protected by Windows Firewall. Table 17-2 on the next page provides more information about these options. There's seldom a reason to enable any of these options except for troubleshooting purposes, and they can expose your computer to certain security risks.

Chapter 17

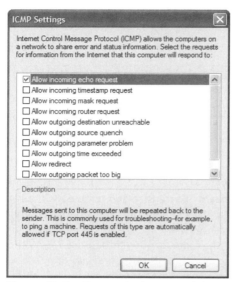

Figure 17-5.   Text at the bottom of this dialog box describes what the selected ICMP message is used for.

Table 17-2. **ICMP Options**

Option	Description
Allow incoming echo request	With this option enabled, your computer responds to Ping (echo) requests. This option is the one most likely to be useful for ordinary troubleshooting and is one of the few you should consider enabling. In fact, if you enable File and Printer Sharing over your local network, this option is selected and cannot be cleared.
Allow incoming timestamp request	When this option is enabled, your computer acknowledges certain requests with a confirmation message that indicates the time the request was received.
Allow incoming mask request	When this option is enabled, your computer listens for and responds to requests for information about the network to which it is attached.
Allow incoming router request	When this option is enabled, your computer responds to requests for information about its routing tables.
Allow outgoing destination unreachable	When this option is enabled, your computer responds to an unsuccessful attempt to reach it or another computer on your network with an explanatory acknowledgment of the failure.
Allow outgoing source quench	Enabling this option allows your computer to send source quench messages. A source quench message is a request to the sending computer to slow down its transmission rate because your computer can't handle packets as quickly as they arrive. In rare instances, this option can be useful for solving certain communications problems.

Table 17-2. **ICMP Options**

Option	Description
Allow outgoing parameter problem	When your computer receives data with an incorrect header, it discards the data; enabling this option allows your computer to report information back to the sending computer when this occurs. This option can be useful for solving certain communications problems.
Allow outgoing time exceeded	When a data transmission requires more time than allowed (based on the time to live value associated with each packet) and your computer is therefore unable to reassemble a fragmented datagram, it must discard the datagram. When enabled, this option allows your computer to report back to the sender with a "time exceeded" message. This option can be useful for solving certain communications problems.
Allow redirect	When enabled, this option allows your computer to respond to a request to redirect data to a different gateway. (The intent of this ICMP message is to allow gateway computers to direct traffic to a shorter path—but it's easy to imagine how this feature can be abused.)
Allow outgoing packet too big	This option is only applicable on a network connection using the IPv6 protocol. When it is enabled, the system sends an error message to a computer that sends data blocks that are too large to forward, instead of silently dropping the oversize blocks.

The procedure outlined above defines ICMP settings for all network connections. To specify ICMP settings for an individual connection, open the Windows Firewall dialog box, click the Advanced tab, and select the specific network connection. Click the Settings button in the Network Connection Settings area, and then click the ICMP tab in the Advanced Settings dialog box. The list of ICMP options here is identical to the global list, with one exception: If the connection you selected does not support IPv6—and most do not at this time—the list doesn't include Allow Outgoing Packet Too Big. Any per-connection settings you make here override the global settings you make in the dialog box shown in Figure 17-1.

Controlling Windows Firewall with Group Policy

On a computer running Windows XP Professional, Group Policy provides another way to control Windows Firewall. And like the Netsh command (described in the following section), it allows you to do some things you can't do by opening the application from Control Panel. To examine the available settings, at a command prompt, type **gpedit.msc** to open Group Policy. Navigate to Computer Configuration\Administrative Templates \Network\Network Connections\Windows Firewall, which contains two folders, Domain Profile and Standard Profile.

Why two profiles? You might want different settings depending on whether your computer is connected to a corporate network. For example, with a portable computer you might want the firewall to be locked up tight while you're traveling or working at home, but to have exceptions for certain programs when you're connected to the

Chapter 17

575

Microsoft Windows XP Networking and Security Inside Out

corporate network. Windows Firewall uses the settings specified in the Domain Profile folder whenever your computer is joined to a domain; it uses the settings in the Standard Profile folder at all other times. The available settings, which you can examine by clicking either folder, are the same in each folder. Select a policy to display information about how it works; double-click it to make settings.

For details about making Group Policy settings, see "Using the Group Policy Snap-In," page 754.

Using the Netsh Command to Manage Windows Firewall

If you need to adjust firewall settings repeatedly—on a single computer as conditions change or, perhaps, on a fleet of computers—you'll probably find working with the Windows Firewall application in Control Panel to be a bit cumbersome. Fortunately, Windows XP SP2 enables you to control the operation and configuration of Windows Firewall by using the Netsh Firewall command. Working with this command-line utility provides an alternative way to view or modify all manner of settings—more, in fact, than you can set by using the Control Panel application. For example, you can enable Windows Firewall with this command:

```
netsh firewall set opmode enable
```

This command enables logging of dropped packets in a file in the Shared Documents folder named Fw.log:

```
netsh firewall set logging c:\%allusersprofile%\documents\fw.log 4096 enable
```

With dozens of keywords and options, the Netsh Firewall command is quite complex. For a quick overview of command-line options, open the Help And Support Center, search for "netsh firewall," and read the topic page entitled "Configuring Windows Firewall from the command line." Help is also available from the command line, where you can start by entering **netsh firewall ?** at a command prompt. This returns a brief description of each keyword that you can put after **firewall**—Add, Delete, Dump, Help, Reset, and Set. Type **netsh firewall** *keyword* **?** (replacing *keyword* with a specific value), to learn about options for each keyword.

Note You can make settings for the Domain Profile or the Standard Profile by using Netsh Firewall, just as you can with Group Policy. In commands where it's relevant, you use the Profile parameter, which you can set to Domain, Standard, or All. (If you don't specify a profile, your settings apply to the current profile, which depends on whether your computer is joined to a domain.)

The ability to control the firewall with command lines (and with scripts) makes it possible to create little programs to perform oft-needed tasks easily. For a detailed discussion of options and a collection of sample scripts you can use when setting up Windows Firewall, see the Microsoft white paper "Deploying Windows Firewall Settings for Microsoft Windows XP with Service Pack 2," at *http://www.microsoft.com/technet/prodtechnol /winxppro/deploy/depfwset/wfsp2apb.mspx.*

Chapter 17

Blocking All Exceptions

In some circumstances, you might want to temporarily disable any exceptions you've created in Windows Firewall. On a portable computer, for instance, you might be comfortable allowing some types of traffic on a well-secured home network, but not when you're connected to a public wireless access point in an airport or coffee shop. To temporarily instruct Windows Firewall to ignore all exceptions, open the Windows Firewall dialog box and click Don't Allow Exceptions on the General tab, just below the On option. In this configuration, you can browse the Web and check e-mail, but that's about all.

To restore Windows Firewall to its default settings and remove any exceptions you've defined, either automatically or manually, click Restore Defaults on the Advanced tab.

Identifying Intruders

If you carefully monitor every unsolicited outside attempt to connect to your computer or network (some third-party personal firewalls pop up a message box at each attempt), you'll soon be overwhelmed at the sheer number of "attacks." Don't be alarmed. Most of the intrusion attempts are random port scans launched by software robots, and they're routinely rebuffed by your firewall. In fact, after you reassure yourself that a steady stream of unsuccessful intrusion attempts is perfectly normal, you'll probably want to disable those automatic alerts.

That doesn't mean you should completely ignore evidence of intrusion, however. Most personal firewall programs (including Windows Firewall) maintain a log of blocked connections and intrusion attempts. Inspecting this log occasionally can help you identify patterns and assure yourself that your computer and your network are properly shielded. Figure 17-6 on the next page shows the log page in ZoneAlarm Pro. Other programs provide similar information, which you can use to track down intruders.

Be on the lookout for repeat offenders. The reporting capabilities of personal firewalls vary widely, and some make this task much easier than others. In ZoneAlarm, for example, you can sort by any field in the log, including the Source IP or Count (number of times) columns. (These columns don't appear in Figure 17-6; you need to scroll to the right.)

Armed with the intruder's IP address, you can use any of several Whois utilities available on the Internet to try to figure out the intruder's identity. Some firewall programs make it even easier, by including a link to such information from within the firewall logs. If you use ZoneAlarm, several add-on programs are available that make it easier to analyze the information in the logs and follow up by notifying an intruder's ISP with a single click. Among the best are:

- ZoneLog Analyser, from Matt's Computer Solutions (*http://zonelog.co.uk*)
- ClearZone, from Brady & Associates, LLC (*http://www.y2kbrady.com /firewallreporting/clearzone/*)

Chapter 17

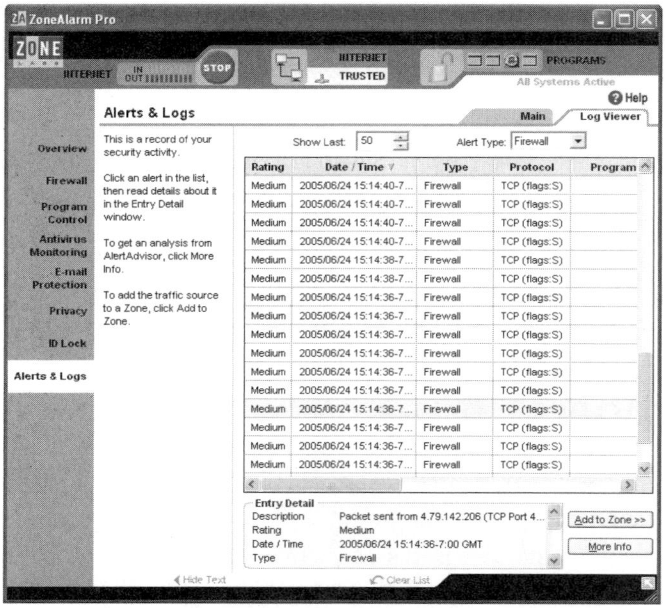

Figure 17-6. ZoneAlarm Pro provides details about each entry in a box at the bottom of the window.

Security expert Robert Graham (a cofounder of Network ICE, the company that produced BlackICE Defender) has published a document entitled "FAQ: Firewall Forensics," which explains the information in firewall logs. This lengthy document, which you can find archived at *http://security.uoregon.edu/firewalls/firewall-seen.html*, identifies a number of port probes and other suspicious activity.

Configuring Windows Firewall Logging

Like its predecessor, Windows Firewall blocks traffic silently; it doesn't display an on-screen alert as some personal firewalls do. However, you can configure Windows Firewall to store a record of its activity in a log file. When you turn on the logging option in Windows Firewall, it maintains a log of each connection that was blocked. It can also maintain a list of successful connections, but that tends to create very large log files, so it's not a good option for long-term use. The logs are useful for both security auditing and debugging. For purposes of security auditing, you can see which IP addresses on the Internet are probing your computer and take action against them if necessary.

To configure Windows Firewall logging, follow these steps:

1 From Control Panel, open Windows Firewall (in Network And Internet Connections, if you use Category view).

Note If the text in the Windows Firewall dialog box does not confirm that Windows Firewall is enabled, you'll need to configure the firewall settings first; for details, see "Enabling or Disabling Windows Firewall," page 278.

2 In the Windows Firewall dialog box, click the Advanced tab.

3 Click the Settings button in the Security Logging area.

4 Select Log Dropped Packets, as shown in Figure 17-7.

Figure 17-7. Always log dropped packets (packets that are blocked by the firewall) so that you can determine whether the access was an attempted attack or a legitimate connection that was denied.

5 Choose a location and filename. By default, the Windows Firewall log is named Pfirewall.log and is kept in the %SystemRoot% folder, but you can specify a different filename or location if you prefer.

6 Choose a maximum size for the firewall log. By default, this log file is limited to 4096 KB, which should be sufficient for most uses.

7 Click OK to save your changes.

Examining Windows Firewall Logs

For a quick look at the current contents of the Windows Firewall log file, open the %SystemRoot% folder in Windows Explorer and open Pfirewall.log with Notepad, as shown in Figure 17-8 on the next page. Each line in the file represents an event that Windows Firewall has logged. Fields on the line are separated by spaces, and the Fields entry near the top of the file defines the name of each field.

Chapter 17

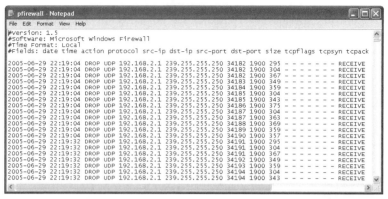

Figure 17-8. The Windows Firewall log can tell you what traffic is being blocked, providing useful information for security audits and debugging.

For more detailed analysis, you might want to import the Windows Firewall log into Microsoft Excel. To do so, follow these steps:

1 Start Excel, and choose File, Open.

2 In the Files Of Type box, select All Files; then browse to and select the firewall log file. If Windows Firewall is running, as it normally is, Excel warns you that the file is in use. Click Read Only to open the file. Excel starts the Text Import Wizard to convert the file to a spreadsheet.

3 Select the Delimited option. Start the import at row 4, which defines the field names, and then click Next.

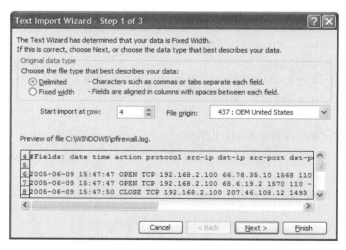

4 Change the delimiter to Space, and be sure the Treat Consecutive Delimiters As One check box is selected. The columns should look like this:

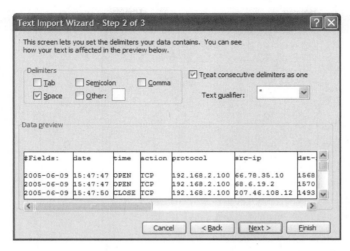

5 Click Next. You can fine-tune the import process in this step, but Excel does a good job using its default General type.

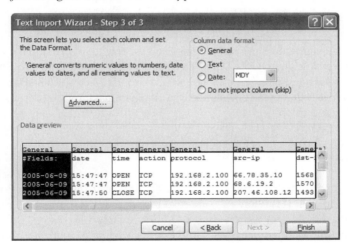

6 Click Finish. When the import is complete, right-click cell A1, which should contain the string "#Fields:", choose Delete, and then select Shift Cells Left. Click OK to put the column headings over the correct fields. Right-click cell A2, choose Delete, and then select Entire Row to eliminate the blank row between the headings and the data.

You can save the imported spreadsheet to a new file or use the sorting and filtering features of Excel to analyze the file. Figure 17-9 on the next page shows an imported log.

Chapter 17

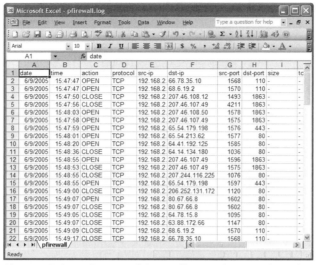

Figure 17-9. After you delete cell A1 and row 2, the column headings are correctly aligned, and the file is ready to be saved and analyzed.

> **Tip** The AutoFilter feature in Excel provides an easy way to analyze log data. To use it, select the entire table and choose Data, Filter, AutoFilter. Then click the arrow that appears by a column heading to filter the display. You can also use Microsoft PivotTables to create cross-tabulated lists that break down attacks by originating address, by destination port, by date and time, and so on.

Fighting Back

So what do you do if your computer is repeatedly attacked? You can track down and report the offenders to their ISP. A few ISPs are responsive to well-documented complaints and willing to pull the plug on system abusers. Unfortunately, most large ISPs are swamped with reports, understaffed because of competitive market conditions, and rarely willing to deal with any complaint that doesn't come from the FBI. But it's worth a try.

DShield (*http://www.dshield.org*), an organization sponsored by the highly regarded SANS Institute, tracks reports of intrusions. It compiles this information into interesting and useful reports that can alert you to trends in Internet attacks. But perhaps more important, DShield helps you to fight back by analyzing submitted log reports and, when the evidence is sufficient, contacting the ISP from which an attack originated. A message from DShield carries more credibility than a message from an unknown individual; as a result, many ISPs take prompt action to disconnect the offender and remove any viruses from their servers upon receipt of such a message.

You can also report an attack to law enforcement agencies. At this time, most law enforcement efforts are aimed at attacks on government and commercial computers;

individuals are a much lower priority. You can learn more about your options and current policies by visiting the US-CERT Web site (*http://www.us-cert.gov*), which is run by the United States Computer Emergency Readiness Team, the operational arm of the National Cyber Security Division (NCSD) of the United States Department of Homeland Security. At the site, you'll find educational material and links to other resources; if you believe you have discovered a new security incident or vulnerability, you can report it by using links on the Technical Users page at *http://www.us-cert.gov/nav/t01/*. In general, you should follow these guidelines when reporting an intrusion attempt:

- Respond quickly. Traces are often impossible if too much time is wasted before alerting law enforcement.

- If unsure of what actions to take, do not stop system processes or tamper with files. This might destroy traces of intrusion.

- Use the telephone or a computer on an uncompromised network to communicate. Be aware that an attacker might be capable of monitoring e-mail traffic.

- Make copies of files an intruder might have altered or left. If you have the technical expertise to copy files, this action will assist investigators as to when and how the intrusion might have occurred.

- DO NOT contact the suspected perpetrator.

Chapter 17

Protecting Your Privacy

The Internet is the greatest research tool ever invented. With it, you can learn almost anything—the symptoms of obscure diseases and their treatments, the names and birthdates of your distant ancestors, the favorite restaurants of your favorite restaurant critics—you name it. While you're out roaming and combing, however, keep in mind that parties on the other side of your screen are also busy conducting research. The object of their study is you. Unless you take certain precautions, putting the world at your fingertips can also mean having the world in your face.

Not all of the parties interested in you and your activities are located somewhere out in the ether. One or more could be down the hall or in the next cubicle. According to a 2001 study by the Privacy Foundation, more than a third of the people in the United States who use the Internet in their daily work are under some form of *continuous* (not just random or ad hoc) surveillance by their employers, and a 2004 study by the ePolicy Institute found that more than 60 percent of companies with 1000 or more employees have hired staff to read or analyze outgoing e-mail. Network packet sniffers, proxy servers, and other employee-monitoring tools are inexpensive, effective, and virtually impossible for the sniffee to detect.

In this chapter, we survey the major privacy hazards attendant on your computer use, at home and at work. We show you how to configure the privacy features in Microsoft Windows, Microsoft Internet Explorer, and the Firefox browser (also available in an open-source version as Mozilla Suite) and where to find alternatives that offer additional protection. We discuss the dangers of online con artists who use "phishing" e-mail messages to facilitate identity theft. Finally, we outline strategies for protecting what's yours to protect and for avoiding embarrassment in circumstances where your privacy is, to some extent, already compromised.

Security Checklist: Protecting Your Privacy

Here's a quick checklist of practices you might want to adopt to help keep the "researchers" at bay:

- Don't disclose personal or financial information to a third party unless you're certain the information is absolutely necessary. Once you hand over information, you have to trust that third party to keep it safe from theft and misuse.

- Make sure that any Internet site requesting a credit card number, your Social Security number, or your driver's license number is using a secure protocol such as Secure Sockets Layer (SSL) or Secure Electronic Transaction (SET).

- Be suspicious of anyone requesting personal identification numbers by e-mail. If you must send such information by e-mail, use Secure/Multipurpose Internet Mail Extensions (S/MIME) or Pretty Good Privacy (PGP) encryption. (For information about encrypting e-mail, see "Protecting E-Mail from Prying Eyes," page 515.)

- On any computer that's not under your exclusive control, do not use the AutoComplete feature of Internet Explorer for forms or passwords. Decline offers from all Web sites to remember your logon credentials.

- Teach your children how to surf the Web safely. In particular, be sure they understand that they should never reveal their real names or addresses on chat sites and never arrange face-to-face meetings with Internet contacts.

- Upgrade to the most recent version of Internet Explorer and configure its cookie management features to match your privacy requirements.

- Establish a cookie policy that gives you an acceptable balance of convenience and privacy. As one possibility, you might block all third-party cookies, accept all session cookies, and accept or block persistent first-party cookies on a case-by-case basis, adding the names of trusted sites to your browser's per-site list so that you don't continue to receive prompts for their cookies. (This approach is only one of many possibilities. Take the time to learn about the different types of cookies, as explained in "A Cookie Taxonomy," page 598, and about your browser's cookie-filtering options; then find the configuration that works for you.)

- Don't give away information that isn't requested. On Internet forms, fill out required fields only.

- Assume that your computer activities at work, both online and offline, are being monitored. Don't use your employer's computer for personal business without your employer's awareness and consent.

Protecting Your Identity

A thief who steals your identity can turn your life upside down. By appropriating information that uniquely identifies you—your mother's maiden name, the PIN for your online banking system, your driver's license number, or (for residents of the United States) your Social Security number—the crook can pretend to be you, with disastrous effects. Because many financial institutions and businesses accept a Social Security number as positive proof of identity, the criminal can apply for credit in your name, transfer money from existing credit cards and bank accounts, sign up for telephone service, and even initiate legal proceedings such as filing for bankruptcy. And thanks to the proliferation of online databases, cleaning the misinformation out of your credit report can take years.

According to the U.S. Federal Trade Commission (FTC), identity theft is on the rise. Fortunately, you can take a number of steps to minimize your chances of becoming a victim. (The FTC maintains an excellent Web site on identity theft at *http://www.consumer.gov /idtheft/*.) One way to keep a tight rein on your vital ID numbers is to make sure you never send them over a connection that isn't secure. In this context, *secure* nearly always means that the connection between you and the remote party is encrypted by Secure Sockets Layer (SSL). Using a secure connection offers two types of protection: First, it guarantees that the information is encrypted during transmission so that no one can intercept it as it travels from point to point on the Internet. Second, it provides a way to identify the recipient Web site by checking the details of its certificate.

To verify that your connection is using SSL, look for the following:

- The URL for the site begins with *https://*, not *http://*.
- A lock icon appears in the status bar of your browser window (both in Internet Explorer and in Mozilla-based browsers such as Firefox).

Note that many commerce sites begin their interaction with you over a standard HTTP connection and switch to SSL only when you need to send personally identifying data. This design is sensible and improves performance by using the more complex SSL process only for pages that require encryption. Also, a Web designer can construct a page in such a way that the secure portion of the page is embedded within a standard page. If you see a lock icon but the Address bar shows an *http:* prefix, right-click the portion of the page where you're being asked to enter data, choose Properties, and inspect the Address and Connection information to be sure the transmission is secure. (In Firefox or Mozilla, right-click the page, choose View Page Info, and then inspect the Security tab.)

SSL is a secure protocol originally developed by Netscape and supported by all major Web browsers. The protocol employs a combination of public key cryptography, one-way hashing, and symmetric cryptography to ensure that data sent and received is intelligible only to the appropriate parties. The public key and hash components of this process are used first to authenticate the server and then to create and encrypt a key that is used for the rest of the transaction. Once these steps are complete, the actual transmission of your personal data is encrypted symmetrically because symmetric encryption is considerably faster than public key encryption. Each connection uses a new key (created by your browser, not by the server), and the key itself is encrypted asymmetrically, so you can

Chapter 18

be confident that your transaction is secure. (For more details about how digital certificates work, see "What Are Digital Certificates?" page 672.)

In the initial "handshake" phase of the SSL connection, your browser uses the server's certificate to confirm the server's identity. You can inspect that certificate yourself if you have any doubts about the authenticity of the party involved in your transaction. To see the certificate in Internet Explorer, follow these steps:

1 Right-click anywhere on the page (except on a link or graphic), and choose Properties from the shortcut menu.

2 In the Properties dialog box, click the Certificates button.

In a Mozilla-based browser, such as Firefox or Netscape 6.2 or later, you can check a site's certificate this way:

1 Right-click anywhere on the page, and choose View Page Info from the shortcut menu.

2 In the Page Info dialog box, click the Security tab.

3 On the Security tab, click View.

As Figure 18-1 shows, the Firefox Security tab provides some useful information about the encryption used for the current connection. If your connection is not secure, this dialog box will tell you so in straightforward, nontechnical terms.

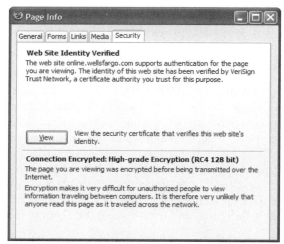

Figure 18-1. The Firefox Security tab describes the encryption used by your connection.

SSL confirms the server's identity but not yours. The remote server simply accepts that you are who you say you are. With credit card transactions, as long as your name, account number, expiration date, and billing address accord with the bank's records, the transaction is considered valid. For banking and trading activities, your identity is authenticated by your logon credentials (typically a user name and password).

Secure Electronic Transaction: An Alternative to SSL

Unlike SSL, the Secure Electronic Transaction protocol (SET) does authenticate both parties involved in a credit card transaction. SET was designed in the mid-1990s by major credit card firms to be a more secure alternative to SSL. To date, SET has not found widespread acceptance—in part because it entails expensive retooling by merchants and requires purchasers to acquire certificates. Nevertheless, you might find sites whose transactions are secured by SET, as an alternative or in addition to SSL. SET–enabled sites are more prevalent in Europe than in the United States.

You can feel doubly secure if you locate a Web-based merchant that uses SET, but don't go out of your way looking for such sites. Perhaps the biggest reason that SET has not become commonplace is that SSL is sufficiently secure for the overwhelming majority of online transactions. SSL has a long track record, and most vendors and banks have found it to be more than adequately secure.

In the United States, your liability for fraudulent credit card transactions is typically limited by law to $50, although there are important restrictions on the types of transactions that are protected. (The same protection doesn't apply to debit cards: A thief can use a debit card to drain your entire bank account, and you have no legal recourse.) Still, the hassle of dealing with stolen credit card credentials and canceling a compromised card is something that no one wants to undergo. As for banking and trading in stocks and online investment accounts, the fine print you agree to when you set up your accounts almost certainly makes you responsible for any action that occurs under a valid logon, which means that losing control of your credentials is a potential catastrophe.

In addition to using strong passwords, you can take the following steps to ensure control of your logon credentials:

- Restrict sensitive activities to computers over which you have complete physical control. (In other words, do your banking at home, not at work—if possible—and never, ever enter a password, PIN, or credit card number on a public terminal.)
- Disable your browser's password-memorizing feature.
- Never supply password or PIN information in an unencrypted e-mail message or Web-based form, in a newsgroup post, in an instant messaging session, or in a chat room.

Both Internet Explorer and Firefox/Mozilla can remember your logon IDs and passwords—and do so by default. This convenience is great if you're the only one using your computer, but it's a hazard if you're not. Unless you disable the feature, a user walking up to your computer might well be able to access vital accounts by guessing your user ID (or just pressing the Down Arrow key at a logon screen). If the guess is correct, the browser will dutifully supply the password.

Chapter 18

> **Tip**   **Manage passwords with user accounts**
> Your Internet passwords and other private information are stored in encrypted form and are available only while your user account is logged on. Therefore, for best security, each person who uses a computer should have his or her own user account. When leaving the computer unattended, you should either lock the workstation (the quickest way is to press the Windows logo key+L), log off, or shut down.

In Internet Explorer, the feature that remembers passwords is called AutoComplete. To turn it off, follow these steps:

1   Choose Tools, Internet Options.

2   Click the Content tab.

3   Click AutoComplete.

4   In the AutoComplete Settings dialog box (see Figure 18-2), clear the check boxes for Forms and User Names And Passwords On Forms.

Figure 18-2.   Do not use AutoComplete for forms or passwords if other people have access to your computer.

The corresponding feature in Firefox/Mozilla is called Password Manager. You can disable it in Firefox as follows:

1   Choose Tools, Options.

2   Click the Privacy icon on the left of the Options dialog box to display available privacy settings.

3   Click the plus sign to the left of Saved Passwords to display the options in this section.

4   Click Clear to delete all saved passwords from the current Firefox profile.

5   Clear the Remember Passwords check box to prevent any additional passwords from being saved.

6   If necessary, repeat steps 1 through 5 for any additional Firefox profiles.

> **Tip** **Zap a single saved password**
>
> If you occasionally share a computer with a trusted family member or coworker, you might decide that you can safely store some user names and passwords on your computer for the sake of convenience, but not for those sites that include sensitive personal or financial details, such as your bank or credit union. In this set of circumstances, you might opt to have Windows always require that you enter passwords for certain sites—an online bank, for instance. If you've saved a user name and password for a site and no longer want that combination to be available, you can remove that single entry. Navigate to the page that contains the logon form, and click in the box for your user name. Press the Down Arrow key to reveal the saved name (or a list of names, if you've saved more than one). Use the arrow keys to highlight the name, and then press the Delete key. Windows will prompt you to confirm that you want to delete both the user name and the saved password. To manage the complete collection of automatically saved information, download the *PC Magazine* utility AutoWhat? 2 from *http://www.pcmag.com/article2/0,1759,3116,00.asp* (subscription or purchase required).

Avoiding Losses from "Phishing" Attacks

Thieves and con artists have access to a full bag of online dirty tricks, including some that are decidedly low-tech in nature. The most successful method of attack in recent years has been the "phishing" e-mail, in which a con artist tries to fool a gullible or inattentive victim into giving up useful information. The scam works like this:

1. The criminal builds a counterfeit Web site designed to look like a legitimate site—typically a bank, brokerage, credit card issuer, or other site containing access to financial information. The site asks visitors to log on with their actual user name and password.

2. The scammer blasts out thousands (or even millions) of e-mail messages that appear to be from the same institution as the phony Web site. According to the message, the bank has observed fraudulent activity on the recipient's account or needs to update its billing records, and the recipient needs to click a link to supply the required information.

3. The victim visits the fake Web site and enters a valid user name and password, which are captured by the thief. If the scammer is clever, the page contains a script that passes the victim's logon credentials to the real site, so that nothing appears wrong. Meanwhile, the thief can log on at leisure and drain the bank account, make unauthorized charges, or steal personal information and apply for a new credit account.

Variations of this scam include e-mail messages that contain HTML–based forms requesting logon credentials, which then go out in a return e-mail or are sent to a Web site by script. In virtually all cases, the mail is sent through a hijacked server, using a throwaway mail account, and the phony site is usually hosted on a site that's been hacked into. The accounts and the fake page are typically shut down within hours, but by that time at least a little damage has been done.

Chapter 18

591

Phishing attacks work by exploiting the law of large numbers. The scammer sends out massive numbers of messages, knowing that most will go to people who don't have accounts with the institution he's targeted. But if he sends out 10 million messages and one in 1,000 reach people who have accounts at the targeted bank, that's a pool of 10,000 potential victims. Even if only a handful of those people are sucked in by the trick, the thief has come out ahead.

How can you avoid becoming a victim of a phishing attack? Follow these tips:

- Be suspicious of any e-mail reportedly from a bank or other financial institution, especially if it contains an urgent request or alarming details. Be especially wary if the message isn't personalized.

- Inspect the link in any suspicious e-mail carefully. The text used to identify the link might look legitimate, but hold the mouse pointer over the link and you'll see the URL to which it points. In the example shown here, the pointer to an IP address rather than a legitimate PayPal server is a dead giveaway.

- Don't follow links in an e-mail to visit an online bank or brokerage account. Type in the URL or use a saved shortcut. If you receive a notice warning you of irregularities with an account, call the institution and ask to speak with a customer service representative.

- Make sure you're using a secure (SSL) connection whenever you enter sensitive information.

- If you suspect that a message you receive is a phishing attempt, check the Recent Phishing Attacks list at the Anti-Phishing Working Group (*http://www.antiphishing.org*), to see if others have reported the same message.

- Forward suspicious messages, with all headers, to the Anti-Phishing Working Group (*reportphishing@antiphishing.com*), the U.S. Federal Trade Commission (*spam@uce.gov*), and the abuse alias at the institution being spoofed.

- Make sure anyone who uses a computer in your home or office is aware of the possibility that they'll be exposed to a phishing attempt.

- Consider installing software that can identify suspicious messages. The free Spoof-Stick utility (*http://www.spoofstick.com*), available for Internet Explorer and Firefox, displays the actual domain of any site you visit. The free EarthLink Toolbar (*http://www.earthlink.com/software/free/toolbar/*) includes a ScamBlocker button that maintains a list of known phishing sites and alerts you if you're about to visit one. Several popular security suites now include privacy modules that warn you when you're about to enter confidential information, such as a bank account number or your Social Security number, in an unsafe environment.

These social engineering attacks can also come over the phone. How can you keep from being duped? Treat the vital details of your personal and financial life with caution, and never hand them out unless you're absolutely, positively certain that the person asking for the information is legitimately entitled to it. Be especially suspicious of unsolicited offers that promise unrealistic returns. Above all, remember this: When in doubt, check it out.

Ensuring Your Children's Safety and Privacy

The Children's Online Privacy Protection Act of 1998 (COPPA) directed the FTC to develop various regulations governing the behavior of U.S. Web sites oriented toward children under the age of 13. You can read the text of the law and its resulting regulations, in the original legalese, at *http://www.cdt.org/legislation/105th/privacy/coppa.html* and at *http://www.cdt.org/legislation/105th/privacy/64fr59888.pdf*, respectively. A summary of the regulations, which went into effect in April 2000, is available at *http://www.ftc.gov/bcp/conline/edcams/coppa/index.html*. The key points of the act are as follows:

- Web sites oriented toward children are required to include a link to a statement describing their information practices. The statement must tell who is collecting information, how the information will be used, and whether it will be disclosed to third parties.

- Web sites must obtain "verifiable parental consent" for collecting information from children. This consent can take various forms, including postal mail or fax, a credit card number, or a digitally signed e-mail message.

- Parents must be given the option to consent to Web sites' data collection without allowing the sites to share that information with third parties.

- No parental consent is required for certain transactions, such as the disclosure of a child's e-mail address in connection with a one-time "homework help" request.

The upshot of these rules is to bring parents into the initial interaction between children and the Web sites that cater to them. That's a good thing, certainly; prior to COPPA, according to the FTC, only 24 percent of sites collecting personal data from children posted privacy policies, and only 1 percent required parental consent.

Nevertheless, COPPA doesn't begin to address all the hazards facing children online. In particular, the regulations do nothing to eliminate the possibility that a child will give out personal information to strangers over an instant-messaging connection, through e-mail, or in a chat room. Moreover, COPPA is concerned only with children under 13. Although teenagers might be more sensitive to privacy issues than younger children are, they are by no means immune to safety threats. Preserving the privacy and safety of all your children, teen and pre-teen alike, requires ongoing parental oversight.

All privacy decisions (and most parenting decisions, for that matter) involve tradeoffs. You could eliminate online risks completely by simply unplugging your computer from

Chapter 18

the Internet, but you'd be giving up far more in enrichment than you'd gain in protection. For a balanced perspective on the benefits and risks of children's Internet use, we recommend the site *http://www.safekids.com*, operated by the Online Safety Project. Here's a condensed summary of parental do's and don'ts that appear there:

- Don't let your children give out their names, school names, phone number, or address in a chat room or on a public newsgroup or bulletin board.
- Familiarize yourself with all the Web sites that your children use regularly.
- Never let your children arrange face-to-face meetings with strangers.
- Don't respond to obnoxious e-mail messages.
- Teach your children to be dismissive of all offers that are too good to be true.
- If possible, keep track of what your children download from Web sites.
- Consider using Content Advisor, a feature in Internet Explorer that helps control your children's access to objectionable sites. Third-party content filters are also available.

Privacy Options in Opera

In this book, we focus on the two leading Web browsers, Internet Explorer and Firefox. But Windows experts know that they have additional options, most notably the Opera browser (free with banner ads, or available in an ad-free commercial version; from *http://www.opera.com*). Opera has some worthwhile privacy features not available in Internet Explorer or Firefox/Mozilla. If you're interested in exploring all your options, you might want to download the free version of Opera and see whether its privacy features meet your needs better than your current browser.

For starters, Opera gives you the option of withholding referrer information when you log on to a new Web site. (The referrer information tells the new Web site the address of the site you're coming from.) Second, although Opera does not filter cookies on the basis of their Platform for Privacy Preferences (P3P) parameters, as Internet Explorer 6 does, it includes a simple option to downgrade all persistent cookies to session status. If you object to having any form of cookie stick to your hard disk, but you want the services that session cookies provide—such as the ability to store items in an online shopping cart—the Throw Away New Cookies On Exit option in Opera is an easy way to implement that policy.

Additionally, Opera includes some per-site cookie-filtering options not available elsewhere. For example, you can specify top-level domains, such as .gov or .org, in the per-site list so that cookies from all servers with URLs ending in the specified suffix are accepted or blocked.

Managing Cookies

In one of Charles Schulz's classic "Peanuts" cartoon strips, Charlie Brown and Snoopy are at the mailbox. A jury summons for Snoopy has arrived. Charlie Brown believes there has to be some mistake—dogs can't be required to perform jury duty. They talk it over, and in the last frame, Snoopy's thought bubble says he'll go ahead and do his civic duty—but only if the court hands out free cookies.

Snoopy would have loved the Internet, where he could have downloaded a bellyful every day. But over time, even he, like a growing number of human Internet users, might have come to regard Internet cookies with suspicion.

Cookies are snippets of text (not program code) that are saved on your computer and recalled when you return to the Web site that created the cookie and stored it on your computer. Used properly, cookies improve the quality of your interactions with Web sites in innumerable ways. They enable e-commerce sites to store your shopping-cart information as you browse their offerings. They allow news, weather, and sports services to tailor their offerings to your locality without pestering you for details about your location every time you visit. They make it possible for you to customize home pages at portals such as MSN so that those sites display only the information you actually care about, in a layout of your choosing.

> For a detailed description of cookie types and functions from Microsoft's perspective, see Knowledge Base article 260971, "Description of Cookies."

But because cookies also enable advertisers and market researchers to collect information about your shopping preferences and interests—information that you might prefer not to divulge—they are by no means an unmixed blessing. Some computer users simply don't care about cookies. At the opposite extreme, some users prefer to ban cookies completely, foregoing the convenience that cookies provide in order to close the blinds on intrusive clickstream trackers.

If you're willing to tolerate those cookies that play by a set of rules you define, you don't have to take such drastic measures. With its support for the Platform for Privacy Preferences (P3P) initiative, Internet Explorer 6 (and later versions) provides a way to keep the cookies that seem useful to you and reject those that do not. If you prefer to configure cookie options manually, you can do so as well.

> **Tip**   **Use Internet Explorer 6 or later**
> If you're using Internet Explorer 5 with Windows 2000, the superior cookie management offered by version 6 is just one of many good reasons to upgrade. In fact, we do not recommend the use of Internet Explorer 5, nor do we cover its features in this book. Internet Explorer 6 is included with every installation of Windows XP; you can get browser upgrades for earlier versions of Windows at *http://www.microsoft.com/downloads/*.

What Your Browser Gives Away

Cookies allow the owner of a Web site to store and recall information about how you use that site. But even without cookies, every time you log on to a Web site, your browser furnishes the following details to the Web server:

- The make and model of your browser
- Your IP address
- The site you were last visiting (the referrer site), if you reached the current page by clicking a link on that site (although some privacy utilities, such as *PC Magazine*'s CookieCop 2, *http://www.pcmag.com/article2/0,1759,6142,00.asp*, can prevent this information from being sent)
- Your Internet service provider
- Your operating system
- Your CPU type
- Your screen resolution and color depth (browsers other than Internet Explorer don't include this item)

The server needs at least some of this information (your IP address, for example) in order to furnish your browser with a properly formatted Web page. If you're not comfortable giving away this information, consider using an anonymous browser. (See "Browsing Anonymously," page 617, for links to these esoteric privacy tools.)

The Anatomy of a Cookie

A cookie is a short string of text characters. The mechanism for transmitting the contents of a cookie between a server and a browser is defined as part of the Hypertext Transfer Protocol (HTTP) specification. If your browser is Internet Explorer, each cookie is stored as a separate .txt file in the folder %UserProfile%\Cookies. As Figure 18-3 shows, your cookies' file names have the following format:

account_name@domain_name[subscript]

The naming convention and the profile-specific storage location ensure that multiple user accounts in use on a single computer can access common Web sites and maintain separate customizations for those sites.

> **Note** In Firefox/Mozilla, as in very early versions of Internet Explorer, all cookies are stored in a single file, called Cookies.txt. Internet Explorer has a way to move cookies between its format and that used by Mozilla-based browsers; for details, see "Backing Up, Restoring, and Deleting Cookies," page 613.

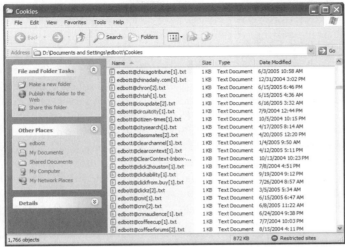

Figure 18-3. Internet Explorer stores cookies in %UserProfile%\Cookies and prefixes files with your account name.

How a Cookie Is Created

A Web site can create a cookie with an HTTP *set-cookie* header, which has the following format (the text shown here in italic—*name* and *value*, for instance—represents variables that are unique for each cookie):

```
Set-Cookie: name=value[; name=value] ... [; expires=date]
[; domain=domain_name] [; path=path_spec][; secure]
```

The significance of these elements is as follows:

name=value Name/value pairs are the main reason cookies exist. Each cookie can have an unlimited number of these (but must have at least one), and both the names and values can be whatever the site chooses to use. A site commonly uses this setting to assign a unique ID string to each visitor.

expires=date Cookies have a finite lifetime. This optional parameter specifies the cookie's expiration date and time (in Greenwich Mean Time). If this parameter is omitted, the cookie is a session cookie, which expires when you close your Internet connection. (Session cookies are stored in memory only.)

domain=domain_name and path=path_spec These parameters specify the domain and (optionally) the path on the Web server for which the cookie is valid. Cookie data is never sent to a domain other than the one that created the cookie.

secure If included, the Secure keyword ensures that the cookie's data will be transmitted only over an SSL (https) connection.

Chapter 18

597

Inside Out

Beware the secure cookie bug

The Secure keyword theoretically protects sensitive information (such as credit card numbers and passwords) from being sent "in the clear" over an unencrypted HTTP connection. In practice, a bug in versions 4 and 5 of the popular Microsoft Web server software Internet Information Services (IIS) causes this keyword to be ignored. If a secure Web site sets a cookie that includes sensitive information and then switches to a standard HTTP connection while using the same cookie, your data could be at risk. As a user, you have no way of knowing when a site is potentially exposing you to this bug. Fortunately, this feature is rarely used and does not represent a substantial risk. If you administer a Web site that uses either of these versions of IIS, make certain you apply the update that fixes this bug. You can read more details in Knowledge Base article 274149, "Cookies Are Not Marked as SSL-Secured in IIS."

A Cookie Taxonomy

Cookies can be classified by their origin and lifetime. A cookie served by a site that you explicitly visit (for example, by clicking a link, choosing a shortcut from your Favorites list, or typing a URL in the Address bar) is called a *first-party* cookie. Web pages aren't always put together using content from a single server, however. Banner ads, for instance, are usually placed at the top of Web pages by companies such as DoubleClick and 24/7 Real Media, which specialize in the complex process of selling advertising space to a variety of clients and placing those ads on a wide-ranging network of Web sites; these ads typically come from a central server managed by the advertising company and not from the Web server supplying the content for the main page. A cookie that the advertising company's server places on your computer is called a *third-party* cookie. (Older versions of the Netscape browser use the term *foreign* to describe cookies placed this way.) In either case, the cookie can be read only by the site that put it on your computer in the first place.

Cookies that expire when you close your Internet connection are called *session* cookies. Your browser stores these cookies in memory only. Cookies that are stored on your hard disk and have some expiration date in the future are known as *persistent* cookies. Session cookies are generally used for purposes such as recording the contents of shopping carts, and they constitute little or no privacy risk.

First-party cookies can enable a site to build a database of your preferences and interests and might or might not pose a privacy problem, depending on how the site uses this information and whether it shares it with other organizations. First-party cookies, particularly session cookies, are often essential to the functioning of a Web site; if you block a site's own cookies, you might find some of the site's features (or even the entire site) impaired or unavailable.

Third-party cookies are commonly used by advertising networks to develop profiles of Internet users' habits and predilections. An ad from a single network can be placed on many different "host" Web sites. Using the cookie associated with the ad network's server, the advertising company over time can build a comprehensive picture about what sites you visit, what ads you click, and so on. Of course, the cookie can't identify you in any meaningful way. However, if the advertiser can convince you at some point to supply your name, address, and other identifying details (by offering you an opportunity to enroll in a contest, for instance), the company can store this information in its database and use the unique ID in your saved cookie to associate your Web-browsing behavior with your stored data. Because the data accumulated in this fashion lets the advertiser serve up ads that are (at least in theory) targeted to your specific interests, advertising firms position this profiling as a service of sorts. You, on the other hand, might see this monitoring as a form of cyber-stalking.

Your browser has features that let you block particular kinds of cookies or that prompt you before accepting them. Understanding the difference between types of cookies is crucial to taking control of your privacy.

Reading Cookies

Because cookie files are plain text, you can open them in Notepad or another text editor. A typical cookie looks something like this:

Nonprinting characters make the data hard to read in Notepad. A number of independent software developers offer cookie-management utilities that make the data easier to read, if not necessarily easier to understand. (For a survey of such programs, see "Using a Cookie-Management Program," page 615.) If you don't have a cookie-management program, you can make the data more presentable by copying it into a spreadsheet program. When you paste cookie text into Microsoft Excel, for example, Excel parses fields into separate worksheet cells, making it easier to see what's there. The first three blocks in the cnn.com cookie shown in the preceding illustration look like this when pasted into Excel:

```
CNNid
Gaa5116-24478729-1088138319182-1
cnn.com/
1056
3919976448
30096012
1293793920
29645730
*
```

```
last5stocks
SBGI%2b
cnn.com/
1024
1866537600
30008150
2903970720
29668680
*
ecd
AZH05
cnn.com/
1024
1850283776
29744994
2499686992
29671848
*
```

As you can see, the cookie consists of several eight-line data blocks separated by asterisks. Each block includes a name/value pair, the cookie's domain, and five additional sets of numbers. In some cases, the field names and values are easy to figure out; in other cases, the cookie's contents are a mystery. In this example, it's easy to tell that the second cookie keeps track of the five most recent stock symbols entered in the search box. Without knowing the inner workings of cnn.com, however, it's hard to discern how the other two name/value pairs are used.

> **Tip** **View cookies in the Temporary Internet Files folder**
> In Internet Explorer, you can look at your cookie store by choosing Tools, Internet Options. On the General tab of the Internet Options dialog box, click Settings. In the Settings dialog box, click View Files. (If you prefer, you can open this location from the Run dialog box or an Address bar by entering **%userprofile%\local settings\temporary internet files**.) Switch the folder to Details view if necessary, and then click the Type heading to sort by file type. Your cookies will be listed as text documents. It takes longer to see your cookies this way than if you simply open the Cookies folder in Windows Explorer, but the Temporary Internet Files folder includes a heading that shows each cookie's expiration date.

Setting Cookie Preferences in Internet Explorer 6

Internet Explorer 6 is the first Microsoft browser to support the P3P initiative, an evolving standard developed by the World Wide Web Consortium (W3C). You can read a public overview of P3P at *http://www.w3.org/P3P/*; technical details about the specification for P3P version 1.0 (the version supported by Internet Explorer 6) are available at *http://www.w3.org/TR/P3P/*.

Among other things, P3P establishes a standard XML (Extensible Markup Language) syntax that Web sites can use to state their privacy policies, and a mechanism for transmitting those policies through HTTP. The XML vocabulary lets sites create two kinds of policy statements—a full description that a site can display or link to, and a tokenized compact description that can be embedded in an HTTP response header and read by your browser.

The compact privacy policy statement reports the following:

- The name of the organization that will collect user information
- The type of information that will be collected
- The purpose(s) for which the information will be used
- How the information will be retained
- Whether the information will be shared with third parties
- Whether users can access and change information
- Whether users can change the way information will be used
- How disputes can be resolved
- The location of the organization's complete privacy statement

Internet Explorer 6 (or another browser that supports P3P) can quickly read the tokenized policy statement, compare it with your stated privacy preferences, and then accept or reject the cookie as appropriate.

Using the Privacy Slider to Manage Cookies

In Internet Explorer 6, all cookie-management tasks are handled by using a group of controls on the Privacy tab of the Internet Options dialog box, shown in Figure 18-4 on the next page. (To display this dialog box, choose Tools, Internet Options and click the Privacy tab.) Adjusting the slider on the Privacy tab is one of several ways to manage cookies in Internet Explorer 6. (For others, see "Overriding P3P–Based Cookie Handling," page 607; and "Importing Custom Privacy Settings," page 609.)

Inside Out

The privacy slider affects only the Internet zone

In Internet Explorer 5, all settings that affect cookies were handled through the use of security zones; in Internet Explorer 6 and later versions, this architecture is fundamentally changed. The privacy slider—the default tool for managing cookies in Internet Explorer 6—affects only sites in the Internet zone. (By default, all cookies are accepted in the Trusted Sites and Local Intranet zones.) To apply P3P–based preferences to either of those zones, you must import a custom privacy settings file. (See "Importing Custom Privacy Settings," page 609.) Cookies from sites in the Restricted Sites zone are always rejected, and you can't override that default.

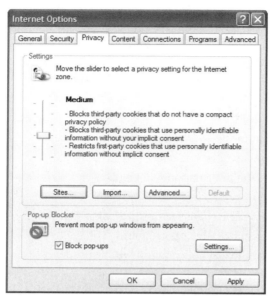

Figure 18-4.   The slider on the Privacy tab of Internet Explorer lets you choose from six built-in privacy settings.

Note   If you don't see a slider on your Privacy tab, you are currently using "advanced" or imported privacy settings. You can undo those settings and make the slider appear by clicking Default.

The privacy slider's default setting is Medium. Five other settings are available: Block All Cookies, High, Medium High, Low, and Accept All Cookies. Moving the slider from one setting to another is simple, but understanding the effects of each setting requires some careful attention to detail! In particular, be aware that, in all settings except Block All Cookies, cookies that already exist on your hard disk can be read by the Web site that placed the cookie there, even if you block new cookies from that site. To avoid uncertainty, it's best to back up and then delete all existing cookies before you set out for the Web with a new privacy setting in place. Also, note that the term *implicit consent*, used in the descriptive text next to the privacy slider, means that you have not taken an affirmative step to withhold consent; in other words, these settings assume that you have given your permission for a site to use personally identifiable information about you unless you have explicitly "opted out" of allowing the site to do so. Contrast this with the term *explicit consent*, which assumes that you do not grant this permission unless you "opt in"—that is, you must affirmatively grant permission before a site can use personally identifiable information about you in a cookie.

The effects of the six privacy slider settings are listed in Table 18-1 and (in an alternative view) Table 18-2 on the next page.

Table 18-1. **Privacy Slider Settings and Their Effects**

Setting	Effect
Block All Cookies	All new cookies are blocked. Existing cookies cannot be read. Per-site settings are ignored.
High	All cookies from sites without a compact privacy policy are blocked. Cookies that use personally identifiable information (for example, your telephone number or e-mail address) are blocked unless you have opted to permit them. Existing cookies are read, and per-site settings can override the High setting.
Medium High	Cookies from third-party sites without a compact privacy policy are blocked. Third-party cookies that use personally identifiable information are blocked, unless you have opted to permit them. First-party cookies that use personally identifiable information are blocked only if you have opted out. Existing cookies are read, and per-site settings can override the Medium High setting.
Medium (default)	Cookies from third-party sites without a compact privacy policy are blocked. Third-party cookies that use personally identifiable information are blocked only if you have opted out. Persistent first-party cookies for which you have opted out are accepted but are downgraded to session cookies. First-party cookies from sites without a compact privacy policy are accepted, but Internet Explorer prevents them from being read subsequently in a third-party context. Existing cookies are read, and per-site settings can override the Medium setting.
Low	Persistent cookies from third-party sites without a compact privacy policy are accepted, but Internet Explorer downgrades them to session cookies. Persistent first-party cookies for which you have opted out are accepted, but Internet Explorer prevents them from being read subsequently in a third-party context. Existing cookies are read, and per-site settings can override the Low setting.
Accept All Cookies	All new cookies are accepted. Existing cookies are read. Per-site settings are ignored.

Chapter 18

Table 18-2. **Privacy Slider Settings by Cookie Type**

Cookie Attributes	How Cookie Requests Are Handled					
	Block All Cookies	High	Medium High	Medium	Low	Accept All Cookies
Existing cookies	Cannot read	Unchanged	Unchanged	Unchanged	Unchanged	Can read
Third-party cookies, no compact privacy policy	Blocked	Blocked	Blocked	Leashed**	Down-graded*	Accepted
First-party cookies, no compact privacy policy	Blocked	Blocked	Leashed**	Leashed**	Leashed**	Accepted
Third-party cookies, personally identifiable information, no opt out	Blocked	Blocked	Blocked	Blocked	Leashed**	Accepted
First-party cookies, personally identifiable information, no opt out	Blocked	Blocked	Blocked	Down-graded*	Leashed**	Accepted
Third-party cookies, personally identifiable information, opt in	Blocked	Accepted	Accepted	Accepted	Accepted	Accepted
First-party cookies, personally identifiable information, opt in	Blocked	Accepted	Accepted	Accepted	Accepted	Accepted
Cookies from sites on per-site list	Blocked	Depends on per-site setting	Depends on per-site setting	Depends on per-site setting	Depends on per-site setting	Accepted

* Converted from persistent to session.
** Prevented from being read in a third-party context.

> **Note** Unless you import a custom privacy settings file that includes the XML element alwaysReplayLegacy, cookies that you had on your system before upgrading Internet Explorer 5 to version 6 are leashed in all privacy slider settings except Block All Cookies. That is, they are replayed in a first-party context only, or they are blocked altogether.

Limitations of P3P

P3P is by no means a solution for all privacy concerns. You should be aware of the following limitations as you work with any of the privacy settings in Internet Explorer 6:

- Not all sites are P3P–compliant (although a growing number are).

- P3P is intended to be a mechanism for industry self-regulation. It is not policed by any governmental agency.

- Some sites are certified by privacy agencies, such as TRUSTe (*http://www.truste.org*) or BBBOnLine (*http://www.bbbonline.com*). In theory, this means that a third party has declared that the site's behavior is consistent with its stated policies. In practice, independent privacy advocates recommend against relying solely on voluntary certifications when making important decisions about your personal privacy.

- Sites can change their privacy policies without notifying you.

Also be aware that P3P is still in the early stages of its development. Future revisions of the specification, as well as future versions of Internet Explorer and other browsers, might alter the range of privacy options available to you, for better or worse.

Fine-Tuning Your Privacy Settings with the Per-Site List

You can combine one of the privacy slider settings with the per-site list to fine-tune that setting. The per-site list lets you name specific domains from which you want to accept or reject all cookies. Figure 18-5 shows an example of the per-site list.

Figure 18-5. Combine per-site settings with privacy slider settings to fine-tune your cookie policy.

To add a domain to the per-site list, choose Tools, Internet Options; click the Privacy tab, and then click Sites. Type or paste the domain name in the Address Of Web Site box, and then click either Block or Allow. Note that you need only the domain name (including the top-level domain, such as .com or .org), not the site's entire URL. If you include an entire URL, Internet Explorer trims it to include only what it needs.

For example, suppose you've browsed to *http://www.truste.org/articles /preventing_spyware.php*, and you decide to add TRUSTe to your Always Allow list. You can select the Address bar, press Ctrl+C to copy the full URL to the Clipboard, go to the Per Site Privacy Actions dialog box (shown in Figure 18-5), press Ctrl+V to paste, and then click Allow. The TRUSTe site will take its place in your per-site list, trimmed from the full URL to truste.org.

> **Note** You can also populate the per-site list from the Privacy Policy dialog box; see the next section, "Reading the Privacy Report." Custom privacy settings files can create per-site lists as well; see "Importing Custom Privacy Settings," page 609.

Reading the Privacy Report

Whenever your privacy settings cause Internet Explorer to block one or more cookies, the following icon appears in your browser's status bar:

To learn more about what's been blocked, double-click the icon, or choose View, Privacy Report. A dialog box comparable to the one shown in Figure 18-6 appears.

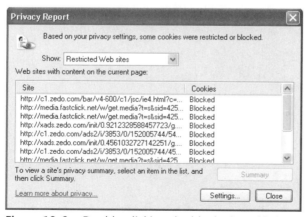

Figure 18-6. Double-clicking the blocked-cookie icon in the Internet Explorer status bar displays this Privacy Report dialog box.

You can set the Privacy Report dialog box to show only those sites from which cookies have been blocked or all sites that have contributed to the current page. When you open the dialog box by double-clicking the blocked-cookie icon, it initially displays the blocked sites only. To see everything, choose All Web Sites in the Show list.

> **Note** The Restricted Web Sites item in the Show list of the Privacy Report dialog box (see Figure 18-6) has nothing to do with your Restricted Sites security zone. It simply refers to those sites contributing to the current page that have had one or more cookies blocked by your privacy settings.

To find out more about a site that has had a cookie blocked, select it in the Privacy Report dialog box and click Summary. If the selected site has published a compact version of its privacy policy, the full P3P policy statement then appears in the Privacy Policy dialog box, shown in Figure 18-7. (If you see an error message instead of a privacy policy, visit the company's Web site to read the full policy.) After reading the privacy policy (and performing any additional due diligence), you might decide to add the site in question to your per-site list so that cookies from this site are henceforth always allowed or always blocked. Use the option buttons at the bottom of the dialog box for this purpose.

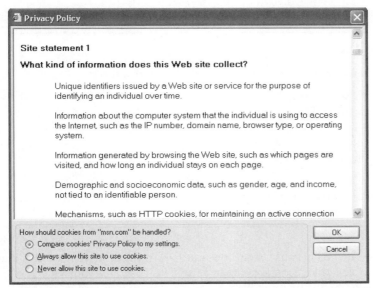

Figure 18-7. Selecting a site in the Privacy Report dialog box and clicking Summary displays the full P3P policy.

Overriding P3P–Based Cookie Handling

If you decide that none of the P3P–based privacy settings quite works for you, click the Advanced button on the Privacy tab of the Internet Options dialog box. In the Advanced Privacy Settings dialog box, select Override Automatic Cookie Handling, and then fill out the remainder of the dialog box to suit your preferences. Figure 18-8 shows the

Advanced Privacy Settings dialog box set to accept all session cookies without prompting, but to prompt for all persistent cookies.

Figure 18-8. In the Advanced Privacy Settings dialog box, you can override automatic (P3P–based) cookie handling and set your own policies instead.

Inside Out

Per-site settings and existing cookies trump advanced settings

If you decide to block first-party or third-party cookies (or both) through the Advanced Privacy Settings dialog box, be sure to remove any per-site settings that allow cookies. Otherwise, the sites on your Allow list will continue to drop cookies on your plate. To do this, click Sites on the Privacy tab of the Internet Options dialog box. Select specific sites and click Remove, or simply click Remove All.

Also be sure to back up and delete existing cookies for sites that you want to block (or to be prompted for). Otherwise, those sites will continue to read your current cookie data. For details, see "Backing Up, Restoring, and Deleting Cookies," page 613.

If cookies are blocked because of settings in the Advanced Privacy Settings dialog box, the same blocked-cookie icon appears in your status bar, and you can use it to display sites' policy statements. If your advanced settings result in a cookie prompt, you'll see something comparable to the Privacy Alert dialog box shown in Figure 18-9. (The Privacy Alert dialog box always appears initially in its collapsed form, but it's not very useful that way. You'll want to click More Info to open the full dialog box.)

The various fields in the Cookie Information section of this dialog box tell you which basic type of cookie (third-party or first-party, session or persistent) is being offered, who it's coming from, what name and value are being sent, when the cookie expires, and whether the cookie can be replayed only over a secure connection. In the Compact Policy field, you can even see the compact policy tokens (and, in some cases, the URL of the full policy statement). If you don't want to master the P3P specification (*http: //www.w3.org/TR/P3P/#compact_policy_vocabulary*) but do want to know what those tokens mean, go ahead and accept the cookie (without selecting Apply My Decision To All Cookies From This Web Site), and then choose View, Privacy Report. Select an item from the list of Web sites with content on the page (typically the second-level domain, such as microsoft.com or icann.org, is your best choice) and then click Summary to read the spelled-out version.

Figure 18-9. The expanded form of the Privacy Alert dialog box can help you decide whether to accept or reject a proffered cookie—or add its site to your per-site list.

Importing Custom Privacy Settings

The privacy options you can set with the privacy slider don't begin to cover all the available bases. They're applicable only to Web sites in the Internet security zone, and they deal with only some of the many possible combinations of tokens that can appear in a P3P compact privacy policy statement. In order to keep the user interface from becoming overwhelmingly complex, Microsoft implemented end-user settings for a half-dozen token permutations and gave advanced users an XML schema to deal with the rest. If you have some basic programming skills and an hour or two to master the schema (plus the P3P specification), you can create your own custom privacy settings files. These, unlike the built-in settings, can be applied to any security zone except Local Intranet and Restricted Sites.

To read an overview of how to create a custom privacy settings file, visit *http://msdn.microsoft.com /workshop/security/privacy/overview/privacyimportxml.asp*; for a detailed description of the XML elements that can be used, see *http://msdn.microsoft.com/workshop/security/privacy /customimportxml/customimportxml.asp*.

Chapter 18

> **Tip** **Take advantage of prefab custom privacy settings files**
> You can find prefabricated custom privacy settings files on the Internet. For example, Eric L. Howes has bundled more than 100 such files into a package called XML-Menu, which you can download free from *https://netfiles.uiuc.edu/ehowes/www/resource5.htm*. Even these settings will not cover every possibility (in particular, they include no per-site settings), but you can use these files (and the accompanying explanatory text) as an excellent starting point.

To import a custom privacy settings file, click Import on the Privacy tab of the Internet Options dialog box and specify the file name. Internet Explorer checks the XML syntax before accepting the file and confirms a successful import.

Note the following:

- Privacy settings that are not overridden by the custom settings file remain in effect. Thus, for example, you can use the privacy slider and per-site list to establish settings for the Internet zone and then use the custom settings file to configure only the Trusted Sites zones.

- If your custom settings file does configure a specific zone, and after importing it you adjust the privacy slider, your privacy slider setting overrides your custom Internet zone configuration.

- If your custom settings file uses the MSIESiteRules element to configure per-site settings in the Internet zone, the custom settings file takes precedence over existing per-site settings.

- If you import a new custom settings file, its configurations replace those of the previous one. That is, you cannot use custom settings files cumulatively.

Removing Custom Privacy Settings

To remove custom privacy settings and restore default cookie handling for the Internet, Local Intranet, and Trusted Sites security zones, follow these steps:

1 On the Privacy tab of the Internet Options dialog box, click Default.

   The Default button might be unavailable if the privacy slider was set to Medium (the default) before you imported the custom settings file. (This happens if the custom settings file includes only an alwaysReplaceLegacy element or if it does not include a p3pCookiePolicy element that specifies *zone = "internet"*.) If the button is unavailable, continue to step 2.

2 If your custom settings file configured per-site settings (with the MSIESiteRules element), click Sites on the Privacy tab to open the Per Site Privacy Actions dialog box and then remove any sites that were so configured.

3 If your custom settings file specified prompting for any Local Intranet sites, close the Internet Options dialog box and run Registry Editor. Remove the keys for any such sites that appear under HKCU\Software\Microsoft\Windows\CurrentVersion\Internet Settings\P3P\History.

These registry keys appear only if your custom settings file was set to prompt for them and you (or another user) subsequently used the Privacy Alert dialog box to change the per-site setting to Allow Cookie or Block Cookie. (For more about this issue, see Knowledge Base article 302831, "Unable to Remove Per Site Privacy Actions for Local Intranet Sites.")

4   If your custom settings file includes the alwaysReplaceLegacy element, use Registry Editor to remove the LeashLegacyCookies DWORD value (if it exists) from HKCU\Software\Microsoft\Windows\CurrentVersion\Internet Settings.

5   If your custom settings file includes a p3pCookiePolicy element that sets *zone* = *"intranet"*, use Registry Editor to remove the values {AEBA21FA-782A-4A90-978D-B72164C80120} and {A8A88C49-5EB2-4990-A1A2-0876022C854F} under the key HKCU\Software\Microsoft\Windows\CurrentVersion\Internet Settings \Zones\1.

6   If your custom settings file includes a p3pCookiePolicy element that sets *zone* = *"trustedSites"*, delete the same values listed in step 5, under the key HKCU \Software\Microsoft\Windows\CurrentVersion\Internet Settings\Zones\2.

For more information about these steps, see Knowledge Base article 301689, "How to Restore Default Settings After Importing Custom Privacy Preferences."

 ## Inside Out

A simple cookie strategy

If the complexities of devising per-zone cookie policies and importing custom XML files seem like more trouble than the results justify, we recommend this simple but effective strategy that uses the built-in cookie-management tools in Internet Explorer 6.

Start by deleting all cookies and clearing any sites on the Per Site Privacy Actions list. Then open the Internet Options dialog box and click the Advanced button on the Privacy tab. Then follow these steps:

1   Select the Override Automatic Cookie Handling option.

2   Under First-Party Cookies, choose Prompt.

    This option allows you to decide whether to accept or reject cookies each time you visit a new site.

3   Under Third-Party Cookies, choose Block.

    This prevents the most egregious instances of companies monitoring your movements on the Web.

4   Select the Always Allow Session Cookies check box. Session cookies are benign, in privacy terms.

5   Click OK to save your changes.

Chapter 18

Setting Cookie Preferences in Firefox/Mozilla

Firefox 1.0, like other browsers built on the Mozilla code base, is set by default to accept all cookies, no questions asked. The browser can distinguish first-party cookies from the third-party variety and makes it easy to block the latter. To do so, choose Tools, Options. Click the Privacy icon in the sidebar on the left side of the Options dialog box, and then click the plus sign to the left of the Cookies heading to view the settings shown in Figure 18-10.

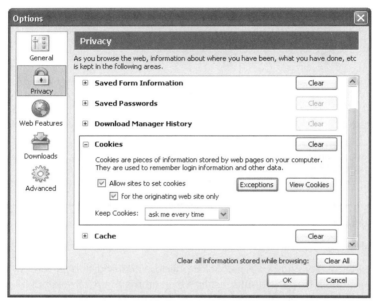

Figure 18-10. In Firefox, you can block third-party cookies (by enabling cookies for the originating Web site only) or request a warning before any cookie is stored.

If you ask to be warned before a cookie is stored, you'll find that the Firefox prompts are precise and informative:

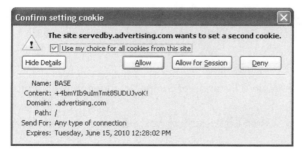

This message, for example, tells you that you have previously permitted one other cookie from the site in question. Assuming that you feel that first cookie has done you no harm, you might want to select Use My Choice For All Cookies From This Site before clicking Yes to accept the new cookie. Selecting the check box adds the serving site to the Exceptions list and sets its status to Allow, so that all subsequent cookies from the same site pass through without a prompt.

You can use a similar technique in Firefox and other Mozilla-based browsers to set the status for any site to Block. That is, if you select Use My Choice For All Cookies From This Site and click Deny, the site in question is barred from delivering cookies thereafter.

The cookie-handling options available in Firefox don't give you the same flexibility that you get with Internet Explorer 6. If you choose the option to disallow third-party cookies (by selecting Allow Sites To Set Cookies and For The Originating Web Site Only), you explicitly allow all first-party cookies. If you select Ask Me Every Time, you'll be prompted every time a first-party or third-party Web site lobs a cookie in your direction, without any regard for the option to set cookies only for originating sites.

The Ask Me Every Time option might not be *so* bad, however, if you use a limited number of sites most of the time. As you work with these "regulars," you can quickly segregate sites into Allow and Block categories. Once you've put a site into either group, you no longer need to deal with its prompts.

Suppose, for example, that you log on to a weather information site every evening to get the next day's forecast. The first time you visit the site, put its cookies on the Accept list by clicking Allow and selecting Use My Choice For All Cookies From This Site. The first time you're prompted for a cookie from a third-party site, click Deny with the same option to add its domain to the Exceptions list with the Block setting. In a short time, as you use your regular sites, you should see the prompt rate diminish.

Before you start compiling your Allow and Block lists, back up your current cookie store and then delete all your current cookies. (See the next section, "Backing Up, Restoring, and Deleting Cookies.") This will give you a clean start. If you find you can't manage without certain existing cookies, restore the lot and delete the ones you don't need. (A cookie-management utility can simplify this task. See "Using a Cookie Management Program," page 615, for some recommendations.)

> **Tip** Manage your Firefox cookie collection
> If you use Firefox, you might choose to review your cookie collection occasionally by clicking View Cookies in the Privacy section of the Options dialog box. If you see a site you'd prefer not to allow, select its entry in the Site list and click Remove Cookie. To automatically add sites to your Exception list and set their status to Block when you manually prune them in this fashion, click Don't Allow Sites That Set Removed Cookies To Set Future Cookies.

Backing Up, Restoring, and Deleting Cookies

As we noted in the previous section, backing up your cookies is a good idea if you're going to experiment with the privacy settings of Internet Explorer and you're concerned about losing functionality at particular Web sites if you block their cookies.

Chapter 18

613

All versions of Internet Explorer in Windows XP and Windows 2000 include an Import And Export command that you can use to back up and restore cookie files. (You can also use this command to back up and restore the contents of the Favorites folder.) The file created when you use Import And Export was originally intended as a means of transferring cookies and favorites between Internet Explorer and very early versions of Netscape browsers, but it also works just fine as a backup and restore tool.

To back up your cookies, choose File, Import And Export. When the wizard appears, click Next on the welcome screen, specify Export Cookies, and then click Next again.

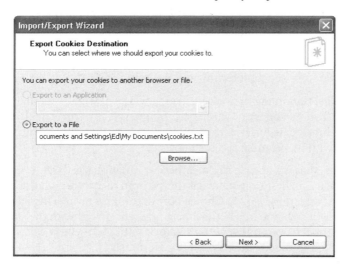

Choose Export To A File, specify a file name and location, click Next, and then click Finish. (If any Netscape browser is installed, the option to export to an application will also be available. This option is not available if your only Mozilla-based browser is Firefox.) To restore your cookies, follow the same procedure, but select Import Cookies instead of Export Cookies, and browse to the exported cookie file. It's that simple.

To delete all your cookies in one swoop, choose Tools, Internet Options. Then, on the General tab of the Internet Options dialog box, click Delete Cookies.

The quickest way to delete cookies selectively (if you're not using a cookie-management program) is to choose Start, Run and then type **%userprofile%\cookies** in the Run dialog box. In the ensuing Windows Explorer window, simply delete the cookies you want to get rid of.

Alternatively, you can delete cookies selectively from the Temporary Internet Files folder. To display this folder, choose Tools, Internet Options. On the General tab, click Settings;

and in the Settings dialog box, click View Files. When the Temporary Internet Files folder appears (it takes a moment or two, usually, because Temporary Internet Files is a virtual folder, and Internet Explorer has to "reconstitute" it from several hidden system folders), display the folder in Details view and sort it by Name. Your cookies will then appear together because their file names all begin with *Cookie*.

Using a Cookie-Management Program

A large number of free or inexpensive third-party cookie-management programs are available. Here are four that we like:

- **Karen's Cookie Viewer (free)**   *http://www.karenware.com/powertools /ptcookie.asp*
- **PurgeIE and PurgeFox (shareware)**   *http://www.purgeie.com* and *http: //www.purgefox.com*
- **CookieCop 2 (subscription or purchase required)**   *http://www.pcmag.com /article2/0,1759,6142,00.asp*

Karen's Cookie Viewer is a cleanly constructed utility that lets you look inside your existing cookies, determine what information they're sending and to whom, and delete those you don't need. The Microsoft Visual Basic source code is also available free at Karen Kenworthy's Web site.

PurgeIE and PurgeFox, from Assistance and Resources for Computing, Inc., is designed for covering your tracks—removing history files, temporary files, and anything else that would furnish clues to your recent activity on the Internet. Both programs also include tools for viewing and deleting cookies, and PurgeIE offers the incredibly useful ability to clean up "strays"—cookies or cached items in the Temporary Internet Files folder that are no longer indexed and cannot be removed by using Internet Explorer tools.

CookieCop 2, a *PC Magazine* utility, is also a privacy Swiss Army knife. In addition to filtering cookies, it can downgrade incoming cookies to session status, disable pop-up windows, and remove the referrer information that your browser normally sends (the address of the site you were most recently visiting).

> **Note**   If you're looking for a third-party cookie-filtering tool, be careful, especially when following links from advertisements or spam e-mails. Scammers and con artists are some of the most prolific advertisers of counterfeit and bogus security software. In the worst-case scenario, a program that promises to safeguard your security might actually install spyware, adware, or a surreptitious downloader. Caveat emptor!

Chapter 18

Inside Out

Windows Media Player and privacy

Windows Media Player incorporates its own Web browsing functionality, which uses the same components as Internet Explorer and thus creates the potential for privacy issues similar to those you experience when using a browser window. In older versions of Windows Media Player, privacy advocates complained, with good reason, about some design decisions implemented in the player. The good news is that Windows Media Player 9 Series and Windows Media Player 10 contain important changes in the player's architecture that give you control over personal information.

Three privacy issues are front and center with Windows Media Player:

- **Cookies.**   Because Windows Media Player uses the same underlying components as Internet Explorer, individual sites can, in theory, use cookies to track streaming content played on your computer. By using the cookie-management features described in this section, you can eliminate this possibility.

- **Unique identifier.**   When you connect to a streaming media server, the player sends a unique identifier called a Player ID. In earlier versions of this software, this ID could be used to personally identify your computer. In Windows Media Player 9 Series and later, the player sends a generic ID that changes each time you start a new session and cannot be used to track you. Note that some media providers might require a truly unique ID. This identifier (stored in the registry as the string value UniqueID, under the key HKCU\Software\Microsoft\Windows Media\WMSDK\General) can be used by Web sites for profiling purposes. If you encounter such a site and you agree to send this information, click Tools, Options, and select the Send Unique Player ID To Content Providers check box on the Privacy tab.

- **History.**   For each user account, Windows Media Player maintains a history that identifies media files, URLs, CDs, and DVDs you play. Anyone with physical access to your computer can inspect those lists and possibly draw conclusions based on their contents. Several settings on the Privacy tab of the Options dialog box enable you to control the compilation of these lists. Clear the Save File And URL History In The Player check box at the bottom, for instance, to disable the history list, and click the Clear History button to erase the file and URL history, and the Clear Caches button to erase the CD, DVD, and device information stored for the logged-on user.

To take advantage of these features, you might need to upgrade the Windows Media Player software on your computer (player updates are not included as Critical Updates with Windows Update, nor are they downloaded through the Automatic Updates feature in Windows XP). Download the latest version from *http://www.microsoft.com/windows /windowsmedia/*.

Watching for Web Bugs

A "Web bug" is a small object on a Web page whose purpose is to collect information. The term typically refers to a 1-pixel-by-1-pixel GIF image from a third party. Like any other object you download as part of a Web-page request, Web bug servers receive the basic data from your browser—your IP address, the page you linked from, your ISP, and so on. (See "What Your Browser Gives Away," page 596.) Like all other third-party objects, they can also transmit and replay cookies associated with the underlying site.

Web bugs disturb many computer users because of their stealthy nature. A 1-by-1 image is an unnoticeable speck on your screen, but its eyes and ears are as large as those of the tallest skyscraper ad. Knowing that Web bugs exist, people have the squirmy feeling they're being spied on (as indeed they undoubtedly are), that their "Web conversations" are bugged.

But are Web bugs a serious privacy threat? On Web pages, they're no different from any visible HTML object. The best way to deal with that sort of Web bug is to block third-party cookies. In addition, ad-blocking software such as AdSubtract Pro (*http://www.intermute.com/products/adsubtract.html*) or the AdBlock extension for Firefox can disable retrieval of Web page elements based on their originating domain, rendering any Web bugs harmless.

A more pernicious use of this technology is in HTML-formatted e-mail messages, where the URL for a graphic can be encoded with a unique ID that can then be associated with your e-mail address to personally identify you. Legitimate companies use this technique to track the effectiveness of e-mail marketing programs; unfortunately, spammers use the same tactic to identify active e-mail addresses, which can result in an increase in junk mail aimed at you. Most modern e-mail programs, including Microsoft Outlook 2003, Outlook Express, and Mozilla Thunderbird, block this tactic by disabling the display of images unless you specifically authorize the program to retrieve them.

You can read more about Web bugs at Bugnosis, *http://www.bugnosis.org* (a site sponsored by the Privacy Foundation). At this site, you can also download a free Web bug ferret called Bugnosis, an Internet Explorer add-in that looks for suspicious HTML objects and pops up a message to notify you when it finds them.

Browsing Anonymously

If you're concerned about the identifying information that your browser sends to Web sites as part of an HTTP request (see "What Your Browser Gives Away," page 596), you might want to consider an anonymous browsing service. Anonymous browsers interpose a proxy between you and the Web sites you visit. You give the proxy the URL of the site you want to see; the proxy fetches the page and sends it on to you, leaving the Web site in the dark about your own identity.

These companies are both good providers of anonymous browsing services:

- IDzap (*http://www.idzap.com*)
- Anonymizer (*http://www.anonymizer.com*)

Both providers offer paid (premium) subscription services. IDzap offers a limited free service as well, and Anonymizer allows you to visit Web sites anonymously by entering the URL in a box on the company's home page. If you plan to do a lot of anonymous Internet work, you'll probably want to sign up for one of the premium offerings. Both services also offer other inducements (the ability to block pop-up windows and banner ads, for example) to users who adopt their premium offerings.

A quick Web search using the term *anonymous proxy* turns up additional services, many of them from underground sites. The principal limitations of free services are these:

- The Web sites you interact with don't know who you are, but your ISP and—if you're using a company proxy server—your network administrator can track the pages you download (and their URLs). With a premium service from a reputable company, your connection to the anonymous host is itself secure, through SSL, so intermediaries on your side of the host can't see what you're doing.
- You have to trust the anonymous proxy to perform its promised functions and to preserve your confidentiality. If you can't verify that the anonymous connection point is trustworthy, you will need to be extremely careful about divulging any personal data—which defeats the purpose of the service.
- Free services typically support HTTP only. For secure connections (commercial transactions, for example), you'll need to connect in the traditional way, without the anonymous host. This might not be a serious problem, since you presumably trust the sites with which you transact secure business, but you might get tired of having to switch back and forth between two modes of connection.

Covering Your Tracks

In an effort to simplify recurrent tasks, Windows, Internet Explorer, and major applications all preserve evidence of your recent activities. They record these "tracks" in many different places—in %UserProfile%\Recent (which appears as My Recent Documents on the Windows XP Start menu), %UserProfile%\Local Settings\History, %UserProfile% \Local Settings\Temporary Internet Files, numerous separate registry keys, the Recycle Bin, the page file, and more.

Inside Out

Wiping the page file

If there's a possibility of your computer falling into the wrong hands, you should be sure that you don't leave any tracks in the page file. Because the page file acts as virtual memory, it contains snippets of everything you work on. By default, when you shut down your system, the page file remains intact. People who have access to your computer could conceivably pore through the unencrypted paging file to find out what you've been up to.

You can foil such snooping by enabling a security policy. In Control Panel, open Administrative Tools, Local Security Policy. In the Local Security Settings console, open Security Settings \Local Policies\Security Options. Double-click the Shutdown: Clear Virtual Memory Pagefile policy (in Windows 2000, the policy name doesn't include the word Shutdown), select Enabled, and click OK. After you do that, Windows fills the page file with zeros whenever you shut down. Because this could slow down your system, don't make this change unless your security needs demand it.

You can cover some of your tracks with simple menu commands. For more thorough or automated shredding, you can choose from a wide assortment of tools offered by independent software developers.

Eliminating Your Internet Explorer History

To erase the past in Internet Explorer, follow these steps:

1 Choose Tools, Internet Options.

2 On the General tab of the Internet Options dialog box, click Clear History.

   You can also use the spinner next to the Clear History button to control how many days of history Internet Explorer should record. Note, however, that if you set this value to 0, Internet Explorer's History bar continues to show where you've been on the current day. If you click Clear History, however, even today's travels are forgotten. Clearing your history also clears the Address bar's most-recently-used list.

3 Still on the General tab of the Internet Options dialog box, click Delete Files.

   This command cleans out the Temporary Internet Files folder, where Internet Explorer caches recently downloaded HTML pages and other objects to display pages more quickly on subsequent visits. When you do this, you'll see the confirmation prompt shown on the next page.

Chapter 18

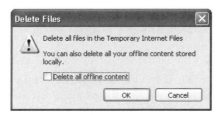

Internet Explorer preserves Web pages that you've marked for offline viewing in a cache separate from the Temporary Internet Files folder. Select the check box to eliminate these files as well.

Erasing Your Internet Explorer AutoComplete History

To thoroughly cover your tracks in Internet Explorer, you should erase not only the history that appears in the History bar but also the AutoComplete history that Internet Explorer uses to simplify your use of forms and logon screens. To take this additional step, follow this procedure:

1 Choose Tools, Internet Options and click the Content tab.
2 On the Content tab of the Internet Options dialog box, click AutoComplete.
3 In the AutoComplete Settings dialog box, click Clear Forms and Clear Passwords.
4 To turn off AutoComplete, clear all the check boxes in the AutoComplete Settings dialog box.

Turning Off Inline AutoComplete in Internet Explorer

Internet Explorer can remember URLs that you've typed before and assist you in retyping them. To prevent someone else from seeing the list of sites you've visited, you can turn off this feature. Follow these steps:

1 Choose Tools, Internet Options and click the Advanced tab.
2 On the Advanced tab of the Internet Options dialog box, clear the Use Inline AutoComplete check box (near the bottom of the Browsing section).

Clearing Your Recent Documents List

The Windows Start menu can be configured to display shortcuts to the 15 files you've used most recently. The items that appear there are derived from the folder %UserProfile%\Recent, which actually contains many more than 15 items. Anyone with physical access to your computer who wants to see at a glance what you've been up to lately can get a quick snapshot by viewing the contents of this folder.

One quick way to clear out your recent document history is to go to the folder by opening the Run dialog box and typing **recent**. Delete all the files you find in the folder. (If you open the %UserProfile% folder and can't see the Recent or My Recent Documents folder, be sure that Windows Explorer is set to display items with the Hidden attribute.)

> **Caution**   When you delete files from the Recent folder, they go into the Recycle Bin. To bypass the Recycle Bin, hold down the Shift key and press Delete. Or make certain to empty the Recycle Bin after you've finished deleting files.

You can also delete the cache of recent documents (including everything in the My Recent Documents folder, not just the 15 items shown on the Start menu) as follows:

In Windows XP:

1   Right-click the Start button or taskbar and choose Properties.
2   On the Start Menu tab of the Taskbar And Start Menu Properties dialog box, click Customize.
3   On the Advanced tab of the Customize Start Menu dialog box, click Clear List. (If you use the classic Start menu, click Clear in the Customize Classic Start Menu dialog box.)

In Windows 2000:

1   Right-click the taskbar and choose Properties.
2   On the Advanced tab of the Taskbar And Start Menu Properties dialog box, click Clear.

> **Note**   Clearing the list of recent documents also clears the most-recently-used list maintained by the Start menu's Run command.

Eliminating Recent Document History on Exit

With a Group Policy setting, you can eliminate the menu of recently used documents automatically every time you quit Windows. To do this, open Group Policy (at a command prompt, type **gpedit.msc**) and enable the setting Local Computer Policy \User Configuration\ Administrative Templates\Start Menu And Taskbar\Clear History Of Recently Opened Documents On Exit. To turn off this automatic cleansing, disable the same setting or set it to Not Configured (its default state).

> For information about using Group Policy, see Chapter 22, "Managing Security Through Group Policy and Security Templates."

Chapter 18

Inside Out

Wiping data from unused areas of a disk

Someone with the knowledge, desire, and proper tools can examine files on your disk even after you've deleted them. By default, files that you delete go to the Recycle Bin. The Recycle Bin is actually a hidden folder; deleting files merely moves them to that folder. A determined snoop with access to your computer can paw through your trash to dig up the dirt. If you're concerned about such access, configure the Recycle Bin so that deleted files don't go there. (Right-click Recycle Bin and choose Properties. On the Global tab, select Do Not Move Files To The Recycle Bin.) If you don't want to lose the benefit of Recycle Bin protection altogether, get in the habit of emptying the Recycle Bin before you log off.

However, your deleted files can still be dredged up, even if they're no longer in the Recycle Bin. That's because when you delete a file, Windows actually deletes only the file's directory entry; the file's data remains intact until another file uses its space. To prevent your files from being viewed by someone with file-recovery tools, you need a file-wiping utility. The version of Cipher.exe included with Windows XP Professional and Windows 2000 SP2 or later performs this task nicely: it overwrites all the unused areas of a drive with zeros, then fills all unused bits with ones, and finally overwrites all unused areas with random numbers. To wipe unused data, open a Command Prompt window and type **cipher /w:*directory***, where *directory* is the name of a folder—any folder—on the drive you want to wipe. The easiest way to wipe the current drive is to type **cipher /w:.** (a period is command-line shorthand for the current folder). To wipe a different drive, include the drive letter (for example, **cipher /w:e:**).

Eliminating Applications' Most-Recently-Used Lists and the Recent Documents Menu

A second Group Policy setting, considerably more powerful than the one just described, not only empties the Start menu's list of recent documents; it also works its magic on supporting applications (including those of Microsoft Office and other third-party applications certified for Windows 2000 or later versions) so that they no longer display your most recent selections on the File menu. The policy setting is Local Computer Policy \User Configuration\Administrative Templates\Start Menu And Taskbar\Do Not Keep History Of Recently Opened Documents.

When you enable this setting, Windows retains its knowledge of your recent documents but does not communicate it to the Start menu or supporting applications. If you subsequently disable the setting (or set it to Not Configured), the menu items that had been suppressed reappear.

> **Tip** **Beware the persistence of memory**
> Not all programs lose their most-recently-used lists when you enable Do Not Keep History
> Of Recently Opened Documents. Not even all Microsoft programs do this. (Microsoft Paint
> does not, for example.) Be sure that the program whose history you want to cover responds
> to this setting before you rely on it.

> **Note** Contrary to the descriptive text in Group Policy, enabling Do Not Keep History
> Of Recently Opened Documents does clear the most-recently-used list maintained by
> common Open and Save As dialog boxes.

Using Third-Party Cleaners

A variety of third-party products can help you rewrite history. To erase evidence of your Internet activities (and eliminate undesirable cookies as well), we recommend PurgeIE and its Firefox analog PurgeFox (from Assistance and Resources for Computing, Inc., *http://www.purgie.com* and *http://www.purgefox.com*). These programs can eliminate temporary Internet files, history folders, visited URLs, typed URLs, and more—on demand or every time you start Windows.

For more global cleaning operations, covering Windows in general as well as Internet Explorer and most Mozilla-based browsers, the most highly regarded program is Window Washer (from Webroot Software, Inc., *http://www.webroot.com/products/windowwasher/*). Window Washer erases your document history, the most-recently-used list maintained by the Windows Search command, the temporary files created by Scandisk, the various Microsoft Office most-recently-used lists, and more. You can even download custom plug-ins for eliminating most-recently-used lists held by a long list of third-party programs.

> **Note** Microsoft AntiSpyware includes amongst its Advanced Tools a "Tracks Eraser" that
> eliminates traces of your actions in your Web browser and dozens of other applications.
> Microsoft AntiSpyware was in beta testing at the time of this book's publication.

Whatever cleanup measures you take, if you really care about keeping your computing activities private, don't forget the obvious: Use strong passwords, lock your workstation when you step away, and put an old-fashioned lock on your office door.

Part 4

Extreme Security

Securing Ports and Protocols

Controlling network access is an important part of system security. On the Internet, where the flow of data is based on Transmission Control Protocol/Internet Protocol (TCP/IP), that means controlling access to ports. By monitoring and limiting the types of connections that applications and computers make to your system, you can greatly reduce the chances that the system will be compromised.

In this chapter, we first explain how ports and protocols work. We show you how to determine which ports are being used and, more important, which programs are using them. We then explain how you can restrict access to ports other than the ones legitimately used by programs you choose to allow.

The rest of the chapter covers the topic of services, which are specialized programs, routines, or processes that work closely with the operating system to perform functions that support other programs and services. Many services control, to one degree or another, the use of ports. For this reason—and because services typically run in the context of a privileged user account such as System or Local Service—understanding how to manage services is an important step in securing your computer and your network. The final sections of the chapter provide more details about a particular collection of services—Internet Information Services (IIS)—that enable other users to connect to your computer over the Internet. Naturally, you'll want to take extra care in configuring these services.

Security Checklist: Ports, Protocols, and Services

- Identify which ports are open for incoming connections.
- Determine which services and applications are using the open ports.
- Use TCP/IP filtering to block access to ports other than ones you explicitly need open.
- Disable unneeded services.
- If you use IIS as a server for Web, FTP, or SMTP access, disable the services you don't need.
- Unless you're using IIS for public Internet access, disable anonymous access.
- Run the IIS Lockdown tool.

How Ports and Protocols
Allow Access to Your Computer

For two computers to connect to each other through TCP/IP over the Internet, both have to agree on which ports and protocols they will use. A *port*, in this context, is not a physical connector, such as a serial port. Rather, it's a somewhat arbitrary number (from 1 to 65535) that is included in the header of a data packet and is used to identify a particular network communications channel. To establish a connection, the computer at the originating end specifies the IP address of the destination computer and the agreed-upon port number. The destination computer listens on the agreed-upon port number until a computer—any computer—sends it a message. The receiving computer can check the address of the originating computer and the information sent in the message to decide whether to accept the connection.

On the Internet, computers primarily use either of two communications protocols between ports: Transmission Control Protocol (TCP) and User Datagram Protocol (UDP). In TCP communication, the two computers set up a long-lasting connection to ensure that messages are received reliably. For example, if a computer sends a data packet on a TCP connection and the packet is lost or corrupted for any reason, the network software on both computers will cooperate to have the data retransmitted.

The second protocol, UDP, lets a computer send a simple one-packet message to another computer. If a UDP message is lost on its way to the destination, the sending computer has no way of knowing that it was lost. However, this lack of knowledge isn't always a disadvantage. Because UDP is a low-overhead protocol, little software is required to implement it. Applications can use UDP messages in situations in which data delivery isn't crucial and keeping communication overhead low is important. For example, applications that stream media such as video over the Internet typically use UDP messages. In such applications, a few lost bytes are less likely to be noticed than the delays that would be incurred by using an error-correcting protocol to retrieve lost packets.

Note More than a hundred Internet protocol types are defined, but only TCP and UDP are commonly used by applications. TCP/IP network software stacks use a third protocol, called Internet Control Message Protocol (ICMP), to communicate between themselves. ICMP messages do not use port numbers because the TCP/IP stack always processes them. One example of an ICMP message is the ECHO packet sent out by the Ping and Tracert command-line utilities.

How Ports Are Assigned

Ports and protocols are closely tied together because in most cases only one application listens on a port. To connect to an application, you must know what port it is listening on and what protocols it expects to use. Usually at least two protocols are involved. The low-level protocols (TCP and UDP) only transmit messages between the two computers; they don't concern themselves with the actual content or meaning of the messages.

Another application-layer protocol defines what the messages mean. For example, a Web browser communicates with a Web server by using the Hypertext Transfer Protocol (HTTP) application protocol on top of TCP. HTTP defines what it means for a Web browser to send "GET /default.htm" to a server; the TCP protocol simply makes sure that the message goes through.

The Internet community has agreed to certain standard application port number assignments so that when you want to contact the public Web server at *http://www.microsoft.com*, for example, you always use port 80, the designated port for HTTP. A group called the Internet Assigned Numbers Authority (IANA) is officially responsible for assigning port numbers in the range 0 through 1023 (well-known ports) and also coordinates the registration of port numbers in the range 1024 through 49151 (registered ports) as a service to Internet developers. Port numbers from 49152 through 65535 are not managed by the IANA at all and are generally used by each application in a unique way. The IANA has registered more than 6,000 ports; a complete list is available at *http://www.iana.org/assignments/port-numbers*. A text file containing a Windows-specific subset of this list is available in %SystemRoot%\System32\Drivers \Etc\Services.

Note The IANA list of ports indicates whether a particular application or service supports UDP, TCP, or both protocols. Two completely different applications or services on a computer can use the same port number but different protocols; the TCP/IP protocol stack always knows where to send the message based on the protocol type. Fortunately, the IANA doesn't allow this situation with well-known ports because it could cause human confusion.

Thanks to the standardization of port assignments, client and server applications that use common protocols such as HTTP, Simple Mail Transfer Protocol (SMTP), Post Office Protocol (POP3), and File Transfer Protocol (FTP) can use the standard port numbers and, virtually all of the time, their connection will be successful (providing, of course, that traffic on that port is not blocked by a firewall or a router at some point along the transmission path). Default port numbers are changed so seldom that most applications put that information in rarely visited setup dialog boxes.

Table 19-1 on the next page lists some common port numbers you're likely to encounter on a Microsoft Windows–based network. In some cases, the name of the service in this table won't match what you see on the IANA list. The table reflects real-life current names and usage, even if the use was never reflected in the official IANA document. The IANA lists port 3389, for example, as "MS WBT Server," indicating its early use by Windows-Based Terminal Server; but Microsoft's most recent name for this service is Remote Desktop Protocol. Contrary to the IANA assignments, port 22 was used by Symantec pcAnywhere until version 7.51 even though that port was originally intended only for the Unix-based Secure Shell Remote Login service. In later versions, pcAnywhere uses its own assigned ports (TCP 5631 and UDP 5632) by default, although it can be configured to use the old port numbers.

Table 19-1. **Commonly Used Ports and Protocols**

Port	Protocol	Description
21	FTP	File Transfer Protocol
22, 65301	PC Anywhere	pcAnywhere versions up to 7.51
23	Telnet	Character-oriented terminal connection
25	SMTP	Simple Mail Transfer Protocol
80	HTTP	Hypertext Transfer Protocol
110	POP3	Post Office Protocol version 3
119	NNTP	Network News Transfer Protocol
123	NTP	Network Time Protocol
135	epmap	Endpoint Mapper
137, 138, 139	NETBIOS	NetBIOS over TCP/IP
143	IMAP	Internet Message Access Protocol
161	SNMP	Simple Network Management Protocol
443	HTTPS	Secure HTTP
445	SMB	Server Message Block over TCP/IP
1723	PPTP	Point-to-Point Tunneling Protocol
1900, 5000	UPnP	Universal Plug and Play
3389	RDP	Remote Desktop Protocol (Terminal Services)
5190	AOL	America Online, AOL Instant Messenger
5631, 5632	PC Anywhere	pcAnywhere versions 7.52 and later
5900, 59xx	VNC	Virtual Network Computing

Unofficial Port Usage

Although some Internet conventions advise the use of specific ports for specific protocols, no rule absolutely decrees that you must use these ports. For example, you can set up your Web server to use port 21, even though the IANA has assigned that port to FTP. To connect to the server, remote computers would need to specify the nonstandard port number. Many applications that aren't full-blown Web servers need a way for users to manage them by using a Web browser; such applications can set up a simple HTTP-based Web interface on a port other than 80. Commonly used port numbers for Web-based services (other than the standard port 80) include 8080, 8081, 8181, 8282, and 8383. Web browsers such as Microsoft Internet Explorer make it easy to specify a nonstandard port number: Simply append a colon and a port number to the address. For example, to reach a Web server in the microsoft.com domain on port 8080, the URL would be *http://www.microsoft.com:8080/*. Other applications, such as an FTP client, usually provide a way to specify the port number as part of the connection setup.

Trojan horse programs are another type of software that can make use of obscure and nonstandard port numbers. The Trojan horse itself often enters a system through an e-mail message or a network share. Once it's on the system and activated, the program usually starts listening on a port for instructions. Hundreds of Trojan horse programs are floating around the Internet, and they use almost every port number you can imagine. The early versions of NetBus and Back Orifice used ports 12345 and 31337, respectively, but dozens of other ports are now in use. A Trojan horse might even intentionally use a standard port such as 80 or 21 in the hope that those ports won't be blocked at a firewall. In that approach, the risk for the attacker is that the Trojan horse might interfere with legitimate software and reveal itself.

> For more information about how Trojan horse programs work and how to stop them, see "Trojan Horse Programs," page 466.

How Connections to a Port Are Made

When an application on one computer (the "originator") wants to communicate with an application on another computer (the "destination"), it uses the operating system's application programming interface (API) to create a network connection. The originator creates a message that specifies the IP address for the destination and the port number to be used for communication. Generally, the originator knows the number of a specific service that it wants to reach, so it uses the service's well-known port number, such as 80 for HTTP. As part of the process of creating the connection, the API assigns the originator a dynamic port number (that is, a number from 1024 to 65535) that it can use for sending the message.

In the case of TCP messages, the originator opens a connection to the destination in order to send the message. It can then wait for a response from the destination, send additional messages, monitor the connection for errors, and at some point close the connection. UDP messages are much more primitive: The originator simply uses the API to send the message in the direction of the destination computer and hopes that it gets there. Meanwhile, the destination must be listening on the port that the originator specified in order to receive the message. If the destination computer is not listening on that port, its TCP/IP network stack will receive the message, determine that no application wants to receive it, and throw it away.

> **Note** This is a key point for TCP/IP port security. If an application is not listening on a particular port, the TCP/IP protocol stack on that computer simply drops any message that arrives for that port. Minimizing the number of ports that are being listened to thus reduces the chances of intrusions.

If the application on the destination computer is listening on the port, it can receive the originator's message. In a TCP connection, it can exchange multiple messages with the originator. For UDP, the connection is not persistent; the destination computer receives only the single message that was sent. Since the originator provides its source address and port number in the message it sends, the application on the destination computer already knows how to reach the originator when it replies. Thus, the originator's port number needn't be one of the well-known ports.

Determining Which Ports Are Active

To restrict the use of open ports, you need to know which ports are active on your system and which programs are using them. Although no single tool provides all the information you need, you can piece together the answers with a few tools and investigative skills. The instructions in this section show you how to combine the information provided by several tools to trace the program that is listening on a particular port.

When port sleuthing, it's often useful to have a list of programs that commonly use a particular port. Table 19-1 on page 630 presented a list of the most common ports; a complete listing of the official well-known port assignments is at *http://www.iana.org /assignments/port-numbers*. When tracking down Trojan horse programs, you might also want a list of the ports they commonly use. G-Lock Software maintains a list organized by port number at *http://www.glocksoft.com/trojan_port.htm*.

> **Note** Trojan horse programs often use port numbers that are also used by legitimate programs and system components. Do not assume that a system has been infected simply because you see a program listening on a port number that is known to be used by a particular Trojan horse. For example, the "Sockets de Trois" Trojan often uses port 5000, but so does the legitimate Simple Service Discovery Protocol (SSDP) Discovery Service. In addition, your computer assigns incoming ports by using arbitrary numbers beginning with 1024. One of these dynamic port numbers might match a number that's also used by a Trojan horse program; be sure to look at the port number on the destination computer before concluding that your computer has been compromised.

Task Manager, shown in Figure 19-1, is an important tool because it tells you what processes are running. To open Task Manager, press Ctrl+Shift+Esc. Click the Processes tab and be sure the Show Processes From All Users check box is selected. To sort by one of the columns, click the column heading; it's often convenient to sort by process identifier (PID) if you're looking up these numbers frequently. By default, Task Manager stays on top of all other windows, which can be annoying when you are working with multiple windows. You can turn off this option by choosing Options, Always On Top; a check mark next to the option indicates its status.

> **Tip** Make PIDs easier to identify
> In Windows XP, Task Manager doesn't display the PID on the Processes tab by default, but you can easily add it to the display. With the Processes tab showing, choose View, Select Columns. Then select PID (Process Identifier) and click OK.

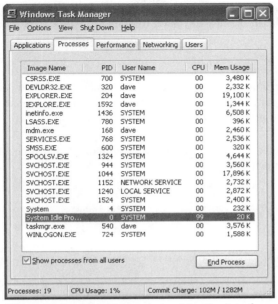

Figure 19-1. Task Manager provides the list of process identifier numbers you need to track down port usage.

Another valuable tool for the port tracker's kit is Tasklist (Windows XP) or Tlist (Windows 2000):

- The Tasklist command is part of the standard installation for Windows XP, so it's available from a command prompt. The most useful command option for matching up services with the ports on which they are listening is the command **tasklist /svc**, which displays the names of the services along with the PID and the image (.exe file) hosting that service.

- In Windows 2000, the Tlist command supplies comparable information. It is an optional component available on the Windows 2000 Professional CD. To install Tlist, navigate to the CD's \Support\Tools folder and run Setup. After Tlist is installed, you can run it from a command prompt. The command that helps identify ports is **tlist −s**, which shows the services running.

As a starting point for investigation, the Netstat command-line program can provide much of the detail you need about ports. To use it, open a Command Prompt window. If you type in the simplest form of the command, **netstat** with no command-line arguments, the command shows which ports are being actively used. To find out which program is using each connection, add the -o or -b argument to the command line. The -o argument, available in Windows 2000 and Windows XP Service Pack 1 (SP1) or earlier, displays the process identifier that has opened the connection. Using the PID displayed by Netstat, you can look up the name of the program in Task Manager. The -b argument, which was introduced in Windows XP Service Pack 2 (SP2), displays the same information and adds the name of the executable that created each connection or listening port. In most cases, using this switch will provide the details you need to determine how a connection was created.

> **Tip** Look up task command syntax
> The Netstat, Tasklist, and Tlist commands have many options besides the ones mentioned here. To see a full list of the options available for a command, type the command name followed by **-?** at the command prompt.

Here are the results of a Netstat -b command executed immediately after connecting to the *microsoft.com* site with Internet Explorer:

```
  Proto  Local Address     Foreign Address        State        PID
  TCP      tirebiter:3030    rad.msn.com:http      ESTABLISHED  2100
[iexplore.exe]
  TCP      tirebiter:3036    global.msads.net:http  ESTABLISHED  2100
[iexplore.exe]
  TCP      tirebiter:3038    www.microsoft.com.nsatc.net:http   ESTABLISHED
2100
[iexplore.exe]
  TCP      tirebiter:3039    www.microsoft.com.nsatc.net:http   ESTABLISHED
2100
[iexplore.exe]
```

In this case, the PID is the process identifier for Internet Explorer, as the final entry in each listing (iexplore.exe) confirms. By default, Netstat shows the names of the addresses and ports rather than the numbers when the names are available. The local system name is Tirebiter, and the four local ports listed are dynamically allocated and given to Internet Explorer as needed. Because Internet Explorer specified the "keep-alive" option for its connections with Microsoft's Web server, each connection stays active for about a minute after the last request is made. If you click to another page on the Microsoft site, Internet Explorer reuses the existing connection to make the access faster. (By the way, did you notice that each of the four connections resolves to a domain other than microsoft.com? That's a small sample of the difficulties you face when trying to track down the true source of a connection.)

If the system has no active connections on the network, the Netstat -b or -o command shows nothing. However, every network-connected system is listening on at least a few ports, waiting for connections. The -a option for Netstat shows all ports that have any kind of activity, including a program listening on them. Combining the -a and -b or -o options with the -n option tells Netstat to show the IP addresses and port numbers instead of names. If you enter **netstat -aon**, the output looks like this:

```
  Proto  Local Address     Foreign Address        State        PID
  TCP    0.0.0.0:135        0.0.0.0:0              LISTENING    944
  TCP    0.0.0.0:445        0.0.0.0:0              LISTENING    4
  TCP    0.0.0.0:1025       0.0.0.0:0              LISTENING    1044
```

TCP	0.0.0.0:1030	0.0.0.0:0	LISTENING	4
TCP	0.0.0.0:3389	0.0.0.0:0	LISTENING	1044
TCP	0.0.0.0:5000	0.0.0.0:0	LISTENING	1240
TCP	10.0.0.3:139	0.0.0.0:0	LISTENING	4
UDP	0.0.0.0:445	*:*		4
UDP	0.0.0.0:1031	*:*		1152
UDP	0.0.0.0:1049	*:*		1152
UDP	10.0.0.3:123	*:*		1044
UDP	10.0.0.3:137	*:*		4
UDP	10.0.0.3:138	*:*		4
UDP	10.0.0.3:1900	*:*		1240
UDP	127.0.0.1:123	*:*		1044
UDP	127.0.0.1:1900	*:*		1240

> **Note** If you enter the command **netstat –abn** instead of **netstat –aon**, the listing that results is identical except for the addition of one or more process names for each entry in the table.

Let's go through each item in this Netstat listing, which is typical for a system running Windows XP or Windows 2000. IP addresses, port numbers, and PIDs will vary on each system, of course.

The local IP addresses in the Netstat report all refer to the local system, although they're expressed in three ways: 0.0.0.0, 10.0.0.3, and 127.0.0.1. The third address alternative is the one assigned to the system by the network's Dynamic Host Configuration Protocol (DHCP) server. (Note that this is a private IP address, which indicates that the computer is connected to the Internet through a router that has its own public IP address.) The Foreign Address fields are all zeros in the case of the TCP connections, and *:* in the case of the UDP connections. Both values indicate that the ports are waiting to receive a message from any IP address and any port. No connections are currently established.

Now you can determine which programs are listening on these ports, starting from the top of the list. According to the IANA's list of well-known ports, port 135 is the Microsoft Locator Service, also known as the Endpoint Mapper. Remote computers can connect to this port on a destination computer to determine which ports are being used for a particular service. This lets services avoid the need to always use the same specific port number on a system. On this particular system, the port is opened by PID 944, which the Task Manager listing shows is an instance of Svchost.exe. Tasklist (or Netstat with the -b switch) tells you that this PID is the Remote Procedure Call subsystem (RPCSS).

> **Tip** Filter the Tasklist output
> When used with the /fi switch, Tasklist displays information only about the particular task in which you're interested. For example, to see which service is running as PID 944, you could type **tasklist /svc /fi "pid eq 944"** at a command prompt. This command filters the output to include only lines in which the PID is equal to 944. The online help for Tasklist explains other parameters you can use with the /fi switch.

The IANA lists port 445 (both TCP and UDP) as Microsoft's Server Message Block (SMB) over TCP protocol, which was first implemented with Windows 2000. This protocol was designed to replace the NetBIOS over TCP protocol used by older versions of Windows. (NetBIOS compatibility issues are discussed in "Inside Out: Securing the NetBIOS Ports," on the next page.)

Port 1025 (TCP) is a dynamically assigned port, so the port number alone does not help determine what this port does. Similarly, PID 1044, the process listening on this port, is for another process managed by Svchost.exe, which hosts no fewer than 24 services. Using Netstat with the –abn switch might narrow down the list to a few contenders, but given the tools available, determining which service actually has this port open isn't possible.

Port 1030, also a dynamically assigned port, is being used by PID 4, which is the System process.

Port 3389 (TCP) is for the Remote Desktop Protocol (RDP), also known as Terminal Services. Because both Remote Desktop and Fast User Switching are enabled on this system, this port must remain open to service those requests.

The IANA lists ports 5000 (TCP) and 1900 (UDP) as being used by the Universal Plug and Play (UPnP) protocol. If the SSDP Discovery Service is stopped, these ports no longer appear in the Netstat listing.

Ports 1031 and 1049 (UDP) are dynamically assigned ports, and they are being used by PID 1152, another Svchost.exe process. Task Manager shows that the process is owned by the Network Service user account. Looking at the list of services in the Services console, the only service currently running on this system that logs on as Network Service is the DNS Client service. The Tasklist display also shows PID 1152 hosting the Dnscache service, which is a good double-check. These outgoing ports are used to communicate with the Domain Name System (DNS) server so that the local computer can cache DNS name lookups to increase performance. If the DNS Client service is stopped, the ports no longer appear in the Netstat listing.

For information about various services and using the Services console, see "Shutting Down Unneeded Services," page 650.

Port 123 is assigned to the Network Time Protocol, so it is related to the Windows Time service. To confirm this, you can check its PID using Tasklist or Tlist. Alternatively, you can try an empirical test: Stop the Windows Time service. If the port disappears when you rerun Netstat, you've found the right program.

Ports 137, 138, and 139 provide support for NetBIOS. In most Windows-based networks, NetBIOS is used to provide Windows file and printer sharing as well as computer name resolution.

Inside Out

Securing the NetBIOS ports

The most common use for NetBIOS today is to carry NetBIOS messages over TCP/IP, referred to as NetBT. This eliminates the need to install a different protocol such as NetBEUI or IPX just to carry local NetBIOS traffic. The security downside of NetBT is that careless configuration can result in opening your network to intruders and even broadcasting your vulnerability to everyone on your local Internet segment.

Preventing Internet intrusions through NetBT is actually quite simple. Do not under any circumstances bind the File And Printer Sharing For Microsoft Networks item to any Internet-connected network segment. (That is, if you examine the properties dialog box for the network connection that connects your computer to the Internet, File And Printer Sharing For Microsoft Networks should *not* be selected. It's okay—necessary, in fact, if you're sharing your computer's files or printers with other network users—to select this item in the properties dialog box for your local area network connection. If your computer connects to the Internet through another computer on your network, only that computer's Internet connection needs to have File And Printer Sharing For Microsoft Networks disabled.) Using Windows Firewall or a third-party alternative can also protect you. Alternatively, if you are using a perimeter firewall such as a router, you are protected because the NetBIOS broadcasts are not passed through the firewall.

Starting with Windows 2000, Microsoft offers the SMB over TCP option. This protocol eliminates the need for NetBT in Windows file and printer sharing, which closes the NetBIOS ports and eliminates the broadcast messages that NetBT generates. However, there are several significant restrictions. Because SMB was introduced with Windows 2000 and is not backward-compatible, it cannot be used on networks that have Microsoft Windows NT, Windows 95/98, or Windows Me clients. Also, to eliminate NetBIOS as a name-resolution agent, you must provide a DNS server that can resolve computer names for local addresses. Most small networks do not have their own DNS server and instead depend on the DNS server of their Internet service provider.

Given the restrictions of the new SMB over TCP option, most small networks will need to stay with NetBT. Again, this is not a significant security problem as long as File And Printer Sharing is enabled only for the internal network and not for the Internet networking link.

Note Port Reporter is a free tool available from Microsoft that runs as a service and logs TCP and UDP port activity. On a computer running Windows 2000, Port Reporter maintains a log of the ports that are used. On Windows XP (and Windows Server 2003), Port Reporter also logs the processes that use the port, the modules that a process loads, and the user accounts that run a process. For details about Port Reporter and a link to download it, see Microsoft Knowledge Base article 837243.

Restricting Access to Ports

Internet architects originally envisioned assigning each new protocol or service its own port number so that it could be easily found and used on any computer. They succeeded, but their plan worked too well. Friendly computers in a local network can find the services easily, but so can any computer connected to the Internet, whether it's being used by friend or foe. Paring down the list of ports that can be accessed in your network is an essential security measure.

Windows includes three different mechanisms that can help secure a system by filtering traffic:

● Windows Firewall (available only in Windows XP) is an easy-to-configure tool that you can use to block all incoming traffic except for responses to communications initiated by your computer. This prevents would-be intruders from trying to access ports that might be running listeners.

● TCP/IP filters can be used to permit or deny traffic based on source address/port/protocol and destination address/port/protocol. This filter mechanism is typically used by a more sophisticated administrator who needs to allow incoming traffic to a listener.

● IP Security (IPSec) is similar to TCP/IP filters but it provides the ability to secure traffic through encryption and authentication. IPSec filters are typically used by very sophisticated administrators who want to permit incoming traffic while protecting against hackers and eavesdroppers.

The following sections discuss each of these mechanisms, as well as the use of a perimeter firewall.

Restricting Ports by Using Windows Firewall

The Windows Firewall feature of Windows XP lets you control which ports are open to the Internet. If you are also using the Internet Connection Sharing (ICS) feature, turning on Windows Firewall for the system that is running ICS protects the entire network. If your system has a direct connection to the Internet, you can protect that connection with Windows Firewall directly.

> For details about configuring Windows Firewall, see "Using Windows Firewall in Windows XP," page 277.

Restricting Ports by Using TCP/IP Filtering

In both Windows XP and Windows 2000, the TCP/IP protocol stack has an option that lets you apply a filter. This capability is limited because it filters only incoming packets and does not allow filtering by IP address. To configure TCP/IP filtering, follow these steps:

Securing Ports and Protocols

1 From Control Panel, open Network Connections. (In Windows 2000, the Control Panel item is named Network And Dial-Up Connections.)

2 Right-click the Local Area Connection icon and choose Properties.

3 On the General tab, select Internet Protocol (TCP/IP) and click Properties.

4 On the General tab of the Internet Protocol (TCP/IP) Properties dialog box, click Advanced.

5 In the Advanced TCP/IP Settings dialog box, click the Options tab.

6 In the Optional Settings box, select TCP/IP Filtering, and then click Properties.

7 In the TCP/IP Filtering dialog box, shown in Figure 19-2, select Enable TCP/IP Filtering (All Adapters) to enable filtering.

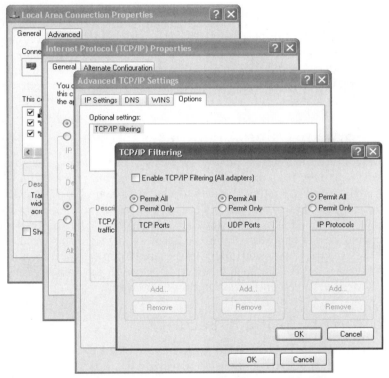

Figure 19-2. Options to restrict TCP/IP traffic are well hidden.

In this dialog box, you'll see the options to restrict traffic for TCP ports, UDP ports, and IP protocol numbers. For each option, you can permit all ports or protocols, or limit the allowed port or protocol numbers to a list that you provide. If you select Permit Only, you then add the port or protocol numbers on which you want to allow incoming connections; all others will be closed. Because the filtering you set here is for unsolicited incoming packets only, you need to open only the ports that you want other computers to access. For example, if you run a Web server, you need to open port 80 so that anyone wanting to reach your site can do so. You don't need to open port 80 to reach another Web site yourself because outgoing connections you establish are not blocked. Having the option to allow all ports except those you specify would often be useful, but that option is not available here.

The IP Protocol filter isn't very effective because nearly all Internet traffic you might want to block selectively comes through TCP, UDP, or ICMP (protocol numbers 6, 17, and 1, respectively). You can't filter out these protocols because they're essential to many services. One notable exception: Microsoft's Point-to-Point Tunneling Protocol (PPTP) uses the Generic Routing Encapsulation (GRE) protocol, number 47. The IANA maintains a complete list of protocol numbers at *http://www.iana.org/assignments/protocol-numbers.*

In most cases, the TCP/IP Filtering dialog box does not offer enough flexibility to serve as a useful security tool. The most critical limitation is that the filtering applies to all network adapters on the system. In a system acting as an Internet firewall, you typically want to apply more restrictive filters to the Internet connection than you would to the local network connection. If you're looking for a software filter on Windows XP systems, use Windows Firewall instead because it provides much better control over the types and methods of traffic filtering.

Restricting Ports by Using a Perimeter Firewall

Although software firewalls and filters offer some protection against intrusion, they have a major weakness: They're trying to protect the computer they're running on. A virus or a Trojan horse program that manages to run on a system can disable a software firewall, leaving it open to further attacks. A perimeter firewall reduces the risk from attacks by filtering Internet packets before they arrive at the computers on the local network. A perimeter firewall typically combines a hardware device with special-purpose software running only the most basic functions required to process and filter network packets. That makes it difficult for such common attackers as Trojan horses and virus-infected e-mail messages to compromise a perimeter firewall.

Restricting Ports by Using IP Security

IP Security (IPSec) is a broad security mechanism meant to overcome many of the security limitations of IP. Because all network activity in Windows XP and Windows 2000 uses IP by default, IPSec provides an important service for all network connections, incoming as well as outgoing. IPSec uses a filtering model to recognize specific IP traffic; recognized traffic can be blocked, permitted, or permitted after securing it with authentication, encryption, or both.

Because it supports authentication and encryption, IPSec is often associated with virtual private networks (VPNs) and wireless local area networks (WLANs)—situations in which eavesdropping is possible and must be foiled. But IPSec can be used to secure any network connection.

Securing Ports and Protocols

Unlike TCP/IP filtering, which merely determines which IP packets to allow into your computer, IPSec negotiates a security association between two computers (sometimes referred to as *end-to-end security*.) The security actions take place on each computer through the negotiated link. Although TCP/IP filtering is a part of IPSec, IPSec encompasses other security protocols, including packet filtering. The packet filtering that IPSec uses has more flexibility than the filtering discussed earlier in this chapter.

A combination of configuration settings for all the associated protocols in IPSec is called a *rule*, or a *filter rule*. An IPSec *policy* is a collection of one or more rules. You can enable only one IPSec policy at a time, but the policy might consist of several rules. Each rule is made up of five components:

- **Filter List.** Consists of one or more packet filtering definitions for filtering on protocol, source address/port/mask, and destination address/port/mask. Filter lists are named and stored for use in multiple rules. You can configure only one filter list per rule. A sample filter for closing port 139 is shown here. Although this example shows only one filter in the list, you can include as many filters as needed.

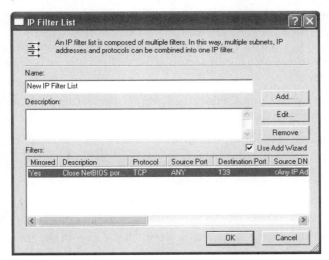

- **Filter Action.** Provides direction on what the filter does with connections matching the filter criteria: permit, block, or negotiate a secure connection.
- **Authentication Methods.** Offers a selection of user authentication methods: Kerberos, certificate, or code/key. Kerberos V5 protocol uses domain user accounts. Therefore, if the computers you are connecting are not in the same domain or in mutually trusted domains, you must use one of the other authentication methods. You can require that the computer attempting a connection have a server certificate from a selected certification authority (CA). You select the CA from your Trusted CA list. You can also use an alphanumeric key. If you use a preset key, both computers must have exactly the same key configured.

- **Tunnel Setting.**   Determines whether a connection can use a VPN. If you want the rule to allow a VPN connection, you configure the IP address of the requesting computer. Note that you can configure only one tunneling connection per rule. To allow multiple computers to request a VPN connection, you must create a rule for each computer and select each rule for the active policy.

- **Connection.**   Determines the connections to which this rule should be applied: all, dial-up, or network.

You might use a single filter or filter action in more than one rule. For example, if you want incoming SMTP and FTP communications to be encrypted, you need to set up a rule for SMTP and a rule for FTP that both use the same filter action. You can create reusable lists of filters and filter actions that facilitate setting up multiple rules with common elements.

Creating an IPSec Policy

IPSec policies are managed through the IP Security Policy Management extension of the Security Settings extension, which is itself an extension of the Group Policy snap-in for Microsoft Management Console (MMC). If you're using Windows XP Professional or Windows 2000, the easiest way to locate this extension is to open the Local Security Settings console: In Control Panel, open Administrative Tools (in the Performance And Maintenance category), Local Security Policy. Alternatively, type **secpol.msc** at a command prompt.

If you use Windows XP Home Edition, the Local Security Settings console is not available. To set up a console with the IPSec Security Policy Management snap-in, follow these steps:

1   At a command prompt, type **mmc** to open Microsoft Management Console.

2   Choose File, Add/Remove Snap-In (or press Ctrl+M).

3   In the Add/Remove Snap-In dialog box, click Add.

4   Select IP Security Policy Management and click Add.

5   In the Select Computer Or Domain dialog box, select Local Computer. Click Finish.

6   In the Add Standalone Snap-In dialog box, click Close. In the Add/Remove Snap-In dialog box, click OK.

Regardless of how you display the IP Security Policies extension in MMC, you need to select IP Security Policies On Local Computer in the tree pane in order to work with IPSec policies.

The user interface for creating IPSec policies can be a bit confusing. It provides property dialog boxes for the policy, each rule, each filter list, and each action. You must use at least one wizard but can use as many as four wizards. Use the IP Security Policy Wizard to create the shell for your new policy. From there, you can add rules to the policy and then add filter lists and filter actions to the rules—either by running wizards or by editing the properties dialog boxes for the rules, filter lists, and filter actions directly. The following sections explain each of these procedures.

Create the Policy Shell

1 Choose Action, Create IP Security Policy to start the IP Security Policy Wizard. Click Next.

2 Enter a name for the policy and, optionally, a description. Click Next.

3 The default response filter rule enforces Kerberos authentication and a custom security scheme and is used when no other filter rule applies. If you want to include this default rule in your policy, leave Activate The Default Response Rule selected. Otherwise, clear the check box. Click Next.

4 If you chose to use the default rule, the wizard asks you for an authentication method to use for that rule. Make a selection and click Next.

Add Filter Rules to the Policy

1 At this point, you have created the shell of your policy. You now need to fill out the filter rules.

2 Make sure that Edit Properties is selected, and then click Finish. The properties dialog box for your new policy appears. If you selected the default response rule, it is selected in the IP Security Rules list. Now you can add the primary rule(s) for this policy.

3 With the Use Add Wizard check box selected, click Add to start the Security Rule Wizard. (If you feel confident, clear the Use Add Wizard check box, and then click Add. The New Rule Properties dialog box appears. Fill out each tab according to the steps that follow.) Click Next.

4   If this rule is to allow a VPN connection, select The Tunnel Endpoint Is Specified
    By This IP Address, and enter the IP address of the computer that will be requesting
    the connection. Otherwise, leave This Rule Does Not Specify A Tunnel selected.
    (In the properties dialog box, these options are on the Tunnel Setting tab.) Click
    Next.

> **Note**   You need to create a rule for each computer that might be requesting a VPN
> connection.

5   Select the network connections to which you want to apply this policy (Connection
    Type tab). Remote Access refers to dial-up connections. Click Next.

6   Select the authentication method for this rule (Authentication Methods tab).
    Click Next.

Add Filter Lists to the Filter Rule

1   Now you need to select or define the filter list you want to use for this rule. If you're
    using the Security Rule Wizard, the list of predefined filters is displayed, as shown
    here. You'll find comparable settings on the IP Filter List tab of the properties
    dialog box.

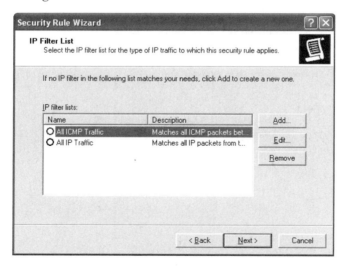

2   If the filter list you want to use is already defined, select it in the list and skip to
    the next section, "Finish Configuring the Rule." Otherwise, click Add to define a
    new filter list.

3   In the IP Filter List dialog box, which is a shell for new filter lists, enter a name
    and description for the new filter list.

4   With Use Add Wizard selected, click Add to add a filter to this list. (If you feel
    confident, clear Use Add Wizard. When you click Add, the Filter Properties dialog
    box appears. Fill out each tab according to the following steps.)

> **Note** Filter lists are saved by name and can be used in multiple rules.

5   On the first page of the IP Filter Wizard, click Next.

6   In the drop-down list, select the source address of the packets. (In the Filter Properties dialog box, the list is on the Addressing tab.) If you are creating a filter for a VPN connection, select A Specific IP Address for the source and My IP Address for the destination. Enter the IP address of the computer requesting the VPN connection as the source IP address. Click Next.

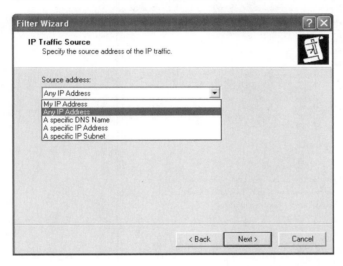

7   In the drop-down list, select the destination address of the packets. (In the Filter Properties dialog box, use the Addressing tab.) The options are the same as for the source. Click Next.

8   Select the protocol. (In the Filter Properties dialog box, use the Protocol tab.) Common selections are Any, TCP, UDP, and ICMP. Click Next. Depending on your selection, you might need to select the port numbers to filter.

9   Click Finish to return to the IP Filter List dialog box. If you want to add another filter, click Add and repeat the preceding process.

> **Note** Filters are not applied in the order in which they are listed; rather, they are generally applied from most specific to least specific. This ordering is not guaranteed during system startup, so some anomalous behavior can occur at that time.

10   When you finish adding filters to the filter list, click OK (or Close in Windows 2000) to return to the Security Rule Wizard. (If you've skipped the wizards, you return to the New Rule Properties dialog box.) Select the filter list you just created. Click Next.

Finish Configuring the Rule

1   Select an action to perform on packets matching the filter. (In the New Rule Properties dialog box, the list is on the Filter Action tab.) Pick one of the default actions or click Add to run the Filter Action Wizard and create a new action. (To see the properties dialog box for one of the default actions, select the action and then click Edit. The Require Security Properties dialog box is shown here.) Click Next and then click Finish.

On the wizard page, click Next and then click Finish.

> **Note**   Filter actions are saved by name and can be used in multiple rules.

2   Click OK. That rule is now defined. If you want to add another rule, click Add and repeat the process. As you add each rule, it appears in the IP Security Rules list in the properties dialog box for the policy. When you've added all the rules you want for your policy, click Close.

Enabling an IPSec Policy

In the Local Security Settings console, right-click the policy you want to enable and choose Assign (the IPSec term for *enable*). That policy is now enabled. If any other policy had been assigned previously, it becomes unassigned.

Modifying an IPSec Policy

As discussed earlier, IPSec policies have rules made up of filter lists, filter actions, authentication methods, tunnel settings, and connection types. Policies, filter lists, and filter actions are entities with names and associated configuration settings. Therefore, you can edit filter lists and filter actions on their own or through the policies that contain them.

In the IP Security Policies On Local Computer folder in the Local Security Settings console, choose Action, Manage IP Filter Lists And Filter Actions to open the dialog box shown in Figure 19-3. Select the filter list or filter action you want to modify, and click Edit. The corresponding properties dialog box opens, in which you can edit the configuration settings. These changes are reflected in each policy that uses the specific filter list or filter action.

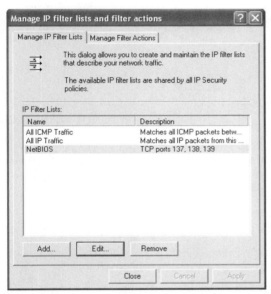

Figure 19-3. You can edit filter lists and filter actions directly.

To modify an IPSec policy, select the policy in the Local Security Settings console, and then choose Action, Properties. The policy's properties dialog box appears, similar to the one shown in Figure 19-4 on the next page. Select the rule you want to edit, and then click Edit to display the Edit Rule Properties dialog box. This is the same dialog box you see if you don't use the wizard to create new rules. Each tab in this dialog box contains the setting for one of the five elements of an IPSec rule.

Figure 19-4. You can modify an IPSec policy in its properties dialog box.

Monitoring IPSec

The IP Security Monitor tool displays information for each active security association. IP Security Monitor can also provide statistics about security associations, key usage, bytes sent and received, and other items.

In Windows XP, IP Security Monitor is implemented as an MMC snap-in, as shown in Figure 19-5. To create a console with IP Security Monitor, follow these steps:

1 At a command prompt, type **mmc** to open Microsoft Management Console.

2 Choose File, Add/Remove Snap-In (or press Ctrl+M).

3 In the Add/Remove Snap-In dialog box, click Add.

4 In the Add Standalone Snap-In dialog box, select IP Security Monitor, click Add, and then click Close.

5 In the Add/Remove Snap-In dialog box, click OK.

6 If you want to monitor other network computers running Windows XP, right-click IP Security Monitor in either pane, and choose Add Computer.

7 In the Add Computer dialog box, select or browse to the computer you want to add, and then click OK.

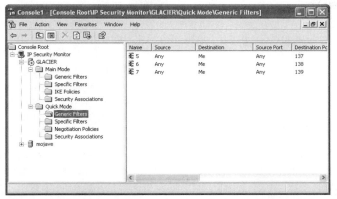

Figure 19-5. IP Security Monitor in Windows XP appears in MMC.

In Windows 2000, IP Security Monitor is a stand-alone program, as shown in Figure 19-6. To start IP Security Monitor, type **ipsecmon** at a command prompt.

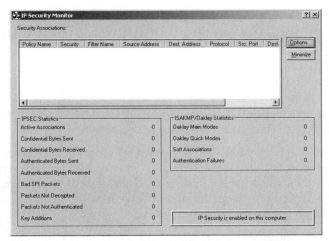

Figure 19-6. IP Security Monitor in Windows 2000 presents a plethora of statistics about IPSec.

Tip **Change IPSec from a command prompt**

If you find the graphical interface for setting IPSec policies cumbersome, you can use the command line alternative Ipseccmd instead. This utility, which is included with the Windows XP Service Pack 2 Support Tools, enables you to add, remove, view, and change IP Security policies in a directory or in a local or remote registry. For download details, see Microsoft Knowledge Base article 838079. The full syntax of the command is documented at *http: //www.microsoft.com/resources/documentation/windows/xp/all/proddocs/en-us /ipsecmd.mspx*.

Why Blocking Ports Isn't Enough

As firewall solutions became popular in the mid-1990s, some Internet application developers found that their software wouldn't work across firewall-guarded networks. Network administrators had done their job well and locked down all but a small handful of ports, such as HTTP port 80. Unfortunately, users behind a firewall now couldn't use services such as RealAudio or AOL Instant Messenger that used other ports. Users who wanted these services could ask their network administrators to open the ports, but users had to know enough to ask, and administrators weren't obligated to say yes.

To circumvent this problem of blocked ports, application developers started using commonly open ports like HTTP port 80 to provide their services. Newer standards such as Simple Object Access Protocol (SOAP) are based on the ability to send requests through HTTP using XML (Extensible Markup Language). With so many applications now sending their non-Web-page traffic over HTTP in some way or another, even a carefully firewalled network can be porous to a wide variety of services. Several Trojan horse programs that exploit HTTP have circulated as well. Because outgoing Web traffic is rarely blocked, these programs can effectively communicate on nearly any network.

Shutting Down Unneeded Services

One important countermeasure to combat malicious software is to minimize the amount of software that is run on your system. Windows XP and Windows 2000 offer a lot of services, many of which are enabled by default even when they're not needed. If a service or application isn't necessary, why allow it to run? Stopping or disabling unnecessary processes can improve performance and enhance security.

A service is a program that runs continuously in the background, processing requests from other programs or from the network. You don't interact directly with services, the way you might interact with an application such as Microsoft Word or Microsoft Excel. Instead, you usually configure the behavior of services through the Services console (shown in Figure 19-7) or, in some cases, through registry settings.

To start the Services console, open Control Panel, Administrative Tools (in the Performance And Maintenance category), Services. If you prefer to use a command prompt, simply type **services.msc**. The Services snap-in also appears as part of Computer Management, which you can start by right-clicking My Computer and choosing Manage or by typing **compmgmt.msc** at a command prompt.

In the Services console, services that are currently running are designated as Started in the Status field. All other services are not running. The Startup Type field indicates when and whether Windows starts the service: If the type is Automatic, the service starts when Windows does. A startup type of Manual means the service starts only if a program requests one of the features the service provides. A service whose startup type is Disabled never starts, even if another program needs it.

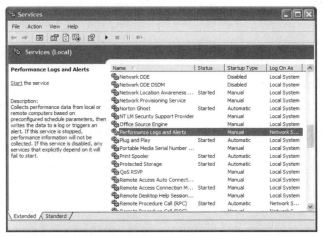

Figure 19-7. Windows provides a lot of services, but most systems don't need all of them running.

> **Caution** Disabling a service that's critical to system operation can render your computer unbootable. Stopping some services that appear to be unnecessary can cause subtle problems that are quite difficult to trace. In some cases, you need to take additional steps before stopping a service to make sure that Windows is properly informed that you don't want to use that service. Read the information for each service before deciding whether to change its startup type.

When turning off a service that you think your system isn't using, a safe first step is to stop the service without changing its startup type. Run your computer for a while—perhaps a few days—with the service stopped to be sure that it's really not needed. If you see any unusual system behavior, restart the service to see whether that solves the problem. If you return to the Services console and find a service running that you've previously stopped, you'll know that some part of the system restarted the service because it was needed and that setting the service to Disabled might cause trouble.

> **Tip** The Dependencies tab in the properties dialog box for a service provides additional clues about whether a service is expendable. It shows which other services depend on a particular service and which other services a particular service requires. Be sure to click the plus icons to fully expand the dependency trees.

If you run your computer for a few days without the service and all seems well, you can change the service's startup type to Manual. Usually, Windows starts a service that is set to Manual when it is needed. In contrast, you should use the Disabled startup type only sparingly. Disabling a service tells Windows never to run the service, even if it's needed for a critical operation. On a clean installation of Windows XP with SP2, a half-dozen services are disabled by default, including the Alerter and Messenger services, which were widely abused to send unwanted pop-up messages over the Internet. You might want to disable additional services that pose a significant security risk, such as Telnet or SMTP, but few others should receive this treatment.

Understanding Windows Services

In Windows XP (but not Windows 2000), the Services console displays a description for almost every service on the list—this information is rarely detailed or helpful, however. Nearly all descriptions include a variation on this refrain: "If this service is stopped, it won't work. If this service is disabled, services that depend on it won't work either." Table 19-2 provides some further detail about specific services, what they do, and whether it's safe to turn them off. Depending on your specific configuration, you might not have all the services listed here. You might also have other services not listed here if third-party software has installed services as well.

> **Caution** If you search the Internet, you might find sites that advocate stopping or disabling several services that we advise you to keep running. It is possible to run Windows with some of these additional services turned off, but you would be removing system functionality that Windows expects to be available. Windows and third-party applications might behave in unpredictable ways when these services are not running.

Determining the Name of a Service

As you view the properties dialog box for each service, you might notice that the service name (at the top of the General tab) often differs from the name that appears in the Services console (the display name) and that neither name matches the name of the service's executable file. (In fact, the executable for many services is Services.exe or Svchost.exe.) The General tab shows all three names.

When you use the Services console, you can find and work with a service by knowing only its display name. But if you use Tasklist or Tlist to determine which service is run by a particular PID shown in Task Manager (see "Determining Which Ports Are Active," page 632), you'll see only the service name. You'll also need to know the service name if you're forced to work with a service's registry entries, which are found in the HKLM\System\CurrentControlSet \Services*service* subkey, where *service* is the service's name. For these reasons, Table 19-2 includes the service name as well as the display name for default services included with Windows XP Professional, enabling you to correlate the two without poring through properties dialog boxes. Note that third-party programs frequently install their own services; as a result, your list might include entries not found in this table.

Like file names, the names of services are not case sensitive. In Table 19-2, we capitalize the service names as they appear in the registry. Although the programmers who developed Windows are obviously not very consistent in applying a capitalization style (or a naming convention), you're likely to see this same capitalization whenever a particular service name is mentioned in documentation.

Table 19-2. **Windows Services**

Display Name; Service Name	Description and Security Recommendation
Alerter; Alerter	Provides an administrative alert (a pop-up message box) function that can be accessed through the Net Send command. Because this feature can be abused and is rarely required in a small office work-group, it is disabled by Windows XP SP2. We recommend disabling this service in Windows 2000 as well.
Application Layer Gateway Service; ALG	Lets third-party software extend the functionality of ICS and Windows Firewall. Needs to run only on systems where ICS or Windows Firewall is being used. Keep this service set to Manual.
Application Management; AppMgmt	Intended for use in corporate installations where a network adminis-trator might, for example, want to make new applications available for users to install. Windows Installer appears to need this service for installing applications, so keep it set to Manual so that it will start when needed.
Automatic Updates; wuauserv	Checks the Windows Update site for updates and patches and optionally downloads and installs them automatically. We strongly recommend that this service remain set to Automatic. On systems that use an alternate means for managing updates, you can set the service to Disabled.
Background Intelligent Transfer Service; BITS	Lets programs download files over the Internet in a way that doesn't significantly interfere with the available bandwidth. The service doesn't provide a user interface to let you see which files are being transferred. With the service set to Manual, it should automatically start if a program needs it.
ClipBook; ClipSrv	Provides support for the obscure ClipBook Viewer application, which lets users share their Clipboard contents via cut and paste over the network. This service is rarely used and is disabled by Windows XP SP2.
COM+ Event System; EventSystem COM+ System Application; COMSysApp	Part of the Windows plumbing for Component Object Model (COM) components. Keep these services set to Manual for a faster startup in some cases, but do not set them to Disabled.

Table 19-2. **Windows Services**

Display Name; Service Name	Description and Security Recommendation
Computer Browser; Browser	Allows a system to act as a "browse master." In a Windows-based workgroup, one computer is always designated the browse master and keeps a list of computers that are present on the network. If the browse master becomes unavailable, the remaining network computers elect a new browse master. Leave this service set to Automatic for most situations. If you stop the Computer Browser service on a computer, that system will no longer be eligible to act as a browse master. If one computer on your network is always on and is very reliable, you can set Computer Browser to Automatic on that computer and set it to Disabled on the others.
Cryptographic Services; CryptSvc	Provides, among other things, digital signature verification for signed files such as device drivers and ActiveX controls. Leave it set to Automatic.
DCOM Server Process Launcher; DcomLaunch	Added in Windows XP SP2, this service provides additional security checks that prevent an unauthorized computer from using the Remote Procedure Call (RPC) protocol to launch a service on another computer. This service should be left at its default Automatic setting; disabling it will result in RPC errors.
DHCP Client; Dhcp	Retrieves network settings from a Dynamic Host Configuration Protocol (DHCP) server when the system starts. If you configure your network settings (IP address, subnet mask, DNS server, gateway) manually, you can disable this service. Most networks use DHCP, and in those cases the service should be left set to Automatic.
Distributed Link Tracking Client; TrkWks	Tracks the location of NTFS files and resources on the network and on a local computer. You can set this service to Manual on computers in a workgroup.
Distributed Transaction Coordinator; MSDTC	Supports Microsoft Transaction Server (MTS); primarily used in applications based on Microsoft SQL Server. Very few workstations on small networks need to have this service running, so you can keep it set to Manual.
DNS Client; Dnscache	Looks up and caches requests for Domain Name System (DNS) names, as a performance optimization. If the service is stopped, DNS requests are forwarded to the DNS server specified in your TCP/IP configuration settings. Leave this service set to Automatic if you want DNS caching, or set it to Manual if you do not.

Table 19-2. **Windows Services**

Display Name; Service Name	Description and Security Recommendation
Error Reporting Service; ERSvc	Supports the Windows Error Reporting feature that sends program and operating system crash dumps to Microsoft. If you want to turn off this feature, first open Control Panel, System, Advanced and click Error Reporting. After disabling Error Reporting in the dialog box shown in Figure 19-8, you can set this service to Disabled.

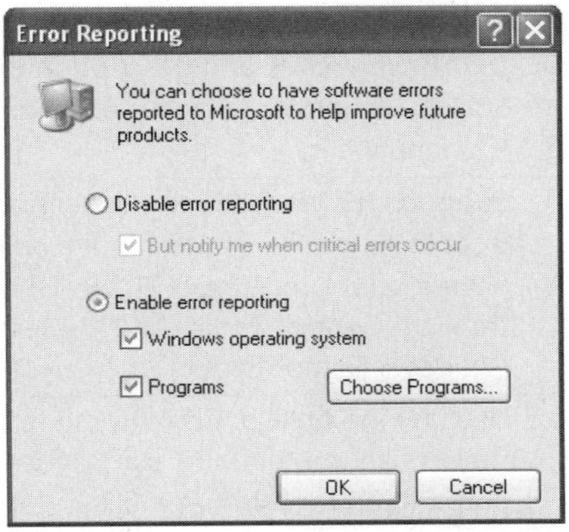

Figure 19-8. Error reporting helps Microsoft determine the cause of errors, but you might consider it a security risk.

Event Log; Eventlog	Maintains the system event log; this service should never be disabled. To see the event log, open Control Panel, Administrative Tools, Event Viewer.
Fast User Switching Compatibility; FastUserSwitchingCompatibility	Supports the multiple-logon feature of Windows XP. To disable Fast User Switching, open Control Panel, User Accounts and click Change The Way Users Log On Or Off. Fast User Switching is available only for stand-alone computers or computers in a workgroup.
Fax; Fax	Provides fax capabilities. This service is optional and is not installed by default. For information on installing and configuring this service, see Microsoft Knowledge Base article 306550.
FTP Publishing; MSFTPSVC	Part of IIS. For best security, disable the FTP Publishing service unless you know you have a specific need for it. Disabling this service in the Services console makes it impossible to start any FTP server in the Internet Information Services console; you'll get an error message about the service not being able to start.
Help and Support; helpsvc	Provides access to the Help and Support Center in Windows XP; some—but not all—such accesses cause this service to start. Set it to Manual so that it can start when needed.

Table 19-2. **Windows Services**

Display Name; Service Name	Description and Security Recommendation
HID Input Service; HidServ (Human Input Service Access in Windows XP SP1 and earlier)	Handles the special wheels and navigation buttons on human input devices, such as mice, keyboards, scanners, and remote controls. A standard keyboard and wheel mouse do not require this service, so you can set it to Manual if you don't have exotic input hardware.
HTTP SSL; HTTPFilter	This service, added in Windows XP SP2, enables applications to communicate in kernel mode using the Hypertext Transfer Protocol (HTTP); the name and description misleadingly refer to the Secure Socket Layer (SSL), which is not affected by this service. Leave it set to Manual.
IIS Admin; IISADMIN	Supports IIS; you will see this service if IIS has been installed. Leave it set to Automatic. If you require no IIS components (that is, you don't have a server for Web, FTP, NNTP, or SMTP access), uninstall IIS through Control Panel, Add Or Remove Programs, Add/Remove Windows Components.
IMAPI CD-Burning COM Service; ImapiService	Used by the built-in CD-burning feature in Windows XP. If you set the service to Manual, it starts when you send files to a CD drive in preparation for burning a CD.
Indexing Service; cisvc	Potentially generates an index of every file on all your drives, making this a very resource-intensive service. You can control which directories are indexed through Start, Administrative Tools, Computer Management, Indexing Service. If you find that this service has an unacceptable impact on performance, you might want to disable it. Before doing so, verify that no running programs, such as desktop search utilities, require it.
IPSEC Services; PolicyAgent	Supports the IP Security (IPSec) protocol, which is used to secure some VPNs, wireless networks, and other networks. If you are not using IPSec, you can set this service to Manual.
Logical Disk Manager; dmserver Logical Disk Manager Administrative Service; dmadmin	Supports the Disk Management console (Diskmgmt.msc). If you set these two services to Manual, they can be started as needed by Disk Management.
Messenger; Messenger	Used, along with the Alerter service, by the Net Send command-line utility to send administrative alerts. This service is not related to the Windows Messenger or MSN Messenger applications. This service is disabled by Windows XP SP2.
MS Software Shadow Copy Provider; SwPrv	Enables the Windows Backup volume shadow copy feature in Windows XP, which allows open files to be backed up. Keep this service set to Manual.
Net Logon; Netlogon	Used only for logon in domain-based networks. For workgroup configurations, you can keep this service set to Manual.

Table 19-2. **Windows Services**

Display Name; Service Name	Description and Security Recommendation
NetMeeting Remote Desktop Sharing; mnmsrvc	Supports the desktop sharing feature of Microsoft NetMeeting. If you don't use NetMeeting, or if you want to ensure that this feature is not used on your system, set the service to Disabled.
Network Connections; Netman	Manages network connectivity. Leave this service set to Manual; it starts automatically when it's needed.
Network DDE; NetDDE Network DDE DSDM; NetDDEdsdm	Supports Dynamic Data Exchange (DDE) over the network. The ClipBook service is one of very few programs that use Network DDE. Windows XP SP2 disables both of these services to ensure that they are not started remotely.
Network Location Awareness (NLA); Nla	Supports the ability to use two or more different network configurations; needed primarily for notebook computers (for example, using a home and office network). If the service is set to Manual, it is started automatically when needed. This service also starts if Windows Firewall or ICS is in use.
Network Provisioning Service; xmlprov	This service, available only in Windows XP SP2, sets up wireless networking and provides support for the Wi-Fi Protected Access (WPA) standard. Leave it set to Manual.
NT LM Security Support Provider; NtLmSsp	Provides authentication for some Remote Procedure Call (RPC) connections. Microsoft Exchange Server, which is rarely used in a workgroup environment, is one of the few applications that use this service. Keep it set to Manual.
Performance Logs and Alerts; SysmonLog	Provides options to run a program and send a message when specific conditions occur. If you are not using performance alerts (you specify alerts using the Performance console, which you can open with Control Panel, Administrative Tools, Performance or by entering **perfmon.msc** at a command prompt), set this service to Manual. (Note that the "Send a network message" action in a performance alert requires the Alerter service to be running.)
Plug and Play; PlugPlay	Detects and configures Plug and Play hardware devices. Keep this service set to Automatic, and never disable it.
Portable Media Serial Number; WmdmPmSp	Retrieves the serial number from portable music players connected to your computer. The serial number is required for transferring protected content to the player. If you don't have a portable music player, you can set this service to Manual or Disabled.
Print Spooler; Spooler	Helps to organize and send print jobs. Running this service is mandatory if you print to either a local or a remote printer. If this service isn't running, applications do not see any printers installed. You should leave this service set to Automatic in most cases.

Table 19-2. **Windows Services**

Display Name; Service Name	Description and Security Recommendation
Protected Storage; ProtectedStorage	Stores passwords, private keys, and form data in an encrypted state for security. Internet Explorer and Microsoft Outlook Express are two clients of this service. Keep the service set to Automatic.
QoS RSVP; RSVP	Provides a mechanism for an application to nicely share bandwidth with other applications. (The name stands for Quality of Service Resource Reservation Protocol.) An application must be QoS-aware for this service to be used; the only common QoS-aware application that ships with Windows is NetMeeting. Leave this service set to Manual.
Remote Access Auto Connection Manager; RasAuto	With a dial-up connection, automatically dials the connection when it detects that a message must be sent to the remote network. Most commonly, this service is used to connect to a dial-up Internet service provider. If you have no dial-up connections (for example, if you use a cable modem or DSL), you can set this service to Disabled.
Remote Access Connection Manager; RasMan	Creates network connections and manages the Network Connections folder. Windows Firewall and ICS also require this service. In most cases, it will be running. Leave this service set to Manual so that it will start if needed.
Remote Desktop Help Session Manager; RDSessMgr	Supports the Remote Assistance feature of Windows XP. By default, Remote Assistance is not enabled and must be turned on (Control Panel, System, Remote). Because this feature could be a security risk, the most secure setting is to keep Remote Assistance disabled. If you are not using Remote Assistance, keep this service set to Manual or Disabled.
Remote Procedure Call (RPC); RpcSs	Supports RPC functionality that is used by many components of Windows. Leave this service set to Automatic. If this service is turned off, the computer will not start.
Remote Procedure Call (RPC) Locator; RpcLocator	Helps other computers on the network find RPC-based programs on this computer. Because this is not a common situation for a workstation, you can usually set this service to Manual with no problem.
Remote Registry; RemoteRegistry	Lets a remote computer modify the Windows registry on your computer. For best security, you should disable this service. Leave this service set to Manual if you need it for remote management tasks through a corporate help desk, or if you use the Remote Desktop feature.

Table 19-2. **Windows Services**

Display Name; Service Name	Description and Security Recommendation
Removable Storage; NtmsSvc	Manages offline storage media such as magnetic tapes or CD-RWs. This service is not well documented and is totally unused on most systems. You can keep the service set to Manual so that it will start in the rare case in which it is needed. If you're curious, you can see the user interface in the Computer Management console; open Storage\Removable Storage.
Routing and Remote Access; RemoteAccess	Provides support for incoming dial-up and VPN connections. This service should be set to Manual or Disabled unless you want to provide remote access for the network through this computer.
Secondary Logon; seclogon (known as RunAs Service in Windows 2000)	Lets the system start a process under an alternative user account name. This service can be used by Scheduled Tasks or by administrators, and its setting should be left at Automatic.
Security Accounts Manager; SamSs	Manages user name and password information for some applications, along with Protected Storage. Leave this service set to Automatic.
Security Center; wscsvc	New in Windows XP SP2, this service manages the display of information in the Security Center. Leave this service set to Automatic unless you use an alternative security management program, in which case you can set it to Disabled.
Server; lanmanserver	Supports network file and printer sharing and RPC support. This service should usually be left set to Automatic. To prevent all incoming access to files on this system through file and printer sharing, remove the File And Printer Sharing For Microsoft Networks component from all network connections.
Shell Hardware Detection; ShellHWDetection	Sends information about newly detected hardware and media (digital cameras and CDs, for instance) to applications, and implements AutoPlay functionality. Keep it at the default setting of Automatic.
Simple Mail Transfer Protocol (SMTP); SMTPSVC	Provides e-mail message transport, as part of IIS. If you do not need this service (and most users do not), you should stop it in the Internet Information Services console and then set it to Manual or Disabled. (Besides being a security risk for your system, an incorrectly configured SMTP server can be hijacked by spammers. You might find your IP address, or even your entire IP address range, placed on several "known to send spam" lists, such as the Realtime Blackhole list at *http://mail-abuse.org/rbl/*. Many mail servers refuse to accept messages from any server on these lists, as they assume that the messages are spam.)
Smart Card; SCardSvr Smart Card Helper; SCardDrv	Supports smart card authentication hardware. If you don't have a smart card that you use to log in to your system, you can keep these two services set to Manual.

Chapter 19

659

Table 19-2. **Windows Services**

Display Name; Service Name	Description and Security Recommendation
SSDP Discovery Service; SSDPSRV	Provides a directory of UPnP devices that are available on the network. SSDP is part of UPnP support in Windows XP. UPnP is increasingly used for Internet gateway devices, media servers, network printers and scanners, and home automation systems, and the list is growing. In addition, the Windows Firewall depends on UPnP to provide incoming connections to systems behind the firewall. If SSDP is disabled, you can't use Remote Desktop and Remote Assistance to access systems across the Internet. Because of a UPnP vulnerability that was repaired in late 2001, some popular security sites recommend disabling this service completely; we believe that this advice is outdated and misguided and recommend instead that you set this service to Manual.
System Event Notification; SENS	Notifies system components and applications of events such as logon, screen saver start, or a switch to battery power. Keep this service set to Automatic.
System Restore Service; srservice	Maintains System Restore checkpoints. On most systems, you should keep this service set to Automatic. If you want to change System Restore behavior, open Control Panel, System and click the System Restore tab. If you turn off System Restore on all drives (which we don't recommend), you could set this service to Manual.
Task Scheduler; Schedule	Runs the programs in the Scheduled Tasks folder based on their schedules. Keep this service set to Automatic.
TCP/IP NetBIOS Helper; LmHosts	Provides NetBIOS name management services in Windows 2000. (See "Determining Which Ports Are Active," page 19xx.)
Telephony; TapiSrv	Supports modem connections. If you do not use a modem, you can keep this service set to Manual. However, when used on a system with Windows Firewall or ICS running, that service will start the Telephony service.
Telnet; TlntSvr	Provides remote command-line access to the system. This service is a security risk and should be set to Disabled.
Terminal Services; TermService	Supports all of Microsoft's multiple-login and remote access technologies: Windows Terminal Services, Remote Desktop, Fast User Switching, Remote Assistance, and Media Center Extenders (used with Windows XP Media Center Edition). If you do not plan on allowing any remote access, disable all the features that depend on it and set this service to Manual.

Chapter 19

Table 19-2. **Windows Services**

Display Name; Service Name	Description and Security Recommendation
Themes; Themes	Provides support for the new look and feel of Windows XP. This service should be left at Automatic with one possible exception. If you have reverted to the Windows Classic look (Control Panel, Display, Themes) and do not intend to use any of the new user interface features in the future, you can set this service to Manual. (When you do this, the Windows XP theme no longer appears as an option.)
Uninterruptible Power Supply; UPS	Supports the ability of an uninterruptible power supply (UPS) to notify the computer when power has gone out and the UPS battery is running low. This service is used only if you have a UPS, have connected the UPS to the computer via its USB or serial cable, and have configured the UPS Service via Control Panel, Power Options, UPS. In all situations, you can safely keep this service set to Manual.
Universal Plug and Play Device Host; upnphost	Lets the computer perform UPnP announcements on behalf of non-computer peripherals, such as a media player or home automation system. The peripheral must provide the drivers and software to support UPnP. It is safe to keep this service set to Manual.
Volume Shadow Copy; VSS	Manages the volume shadow, a feature of Windows XP that backup programs can use to take a snapshot and then back up volumes with open files. This service should be set to Manual.
WebClient; WebClient	Supports the Web-based Distributed Authoring and Versioning (WebDAV) extensions for HTTP. Microsoft Office and many Web-authoring tools use this feature. We recommend setting this service to Manual.
Windows Audio; AudioSrv	Supports playing sounds. You should leave this service set to Automatic. You cannot stop the service from the Services console, which is a strong hint that it should always be running.
Windows Firewall/Internet Connection Sharing (ICS); SharedAccess	Enables network address translation (NAT) for computers that share an Internet connection using ICS. Leave this service set to Automatic if you are using Windows Firewall or ICS. Otherwise, set it to Manual.
Windows Image Acquisition (WIA); stisvc	Provides support for scanners and cameras; not required unless you have one of these peripherals. You can keep the service set to Manual, and Windows will start it if necessary.
Windows Installer; MSIServer	Supports installation, repair, and removal of applications that use Windows Installer (.msi) files. The service can be set to Manual, and Windows will start it when needed.
Windows Management Instrumentation; winmgmt	Provides information about the system configuration to third-party applications and in some cases to Windows itself. This service, part of the plumbing of Windows, should remain set to Automatic.

Chapter 19

Table 19-2. **Windows Services**

Display Name; Service Name	Description and Security Recommendation
Windows Management Instrumentation Driver Extensions; Wmi	Supplies an interface to the driver, if you have installed a driver that provides Windows Management Instrumentation (WMI) functionality. By default, this service is set to Manual, and you can keep it that way.
Windows Media Connect (WMC); WmcCds Windows Media Connect (WMC) Helper; WmcCdsLs	These two services, available as updates to Windows XP, allow devices to share digital media files (music and video) over home networks. Leave both services set to Manual.
Windows Time; W32Time	Provides time synchronization services. Settings for this service are housed in Control Panel, Date And Time, Internet Time. If you plan to set the time on a system manually, you can set this service to Manual. Otherwise, keep it set to Automatic.
Wireless Zero Configuration; WZCSVC	Supports automatic configuration of most 802.11a/b/g wireless LAN cards. The documentation for your LAN card should indicate whether it uses Wireless Zero Configuration. Although you can set this service to Manual, there is no reason to change the default setting of Automatic.
WMI Performance Adapter; WmiApSrv	Implements performance counters as part of Windows Management Instrumentation. Keep this service set to Manual.
Workstation; lanmanworkstation	Makes network connections to other servers. Keep this service set to Automatic.
World Wide Web Publishing; w3svc	Provides Web server service, as part of IIS. If you have installed IIS, you should probably have this service set to Automatic so that it will run on startup. Otherwise, you should uninstall IIS.

Tightening Security on Internet Information Services

Although neither Windows XP Professional nor Windows 2000 Professional is intended for high-performance server applications, IIS can do quite well for a light-duty intranet or as a testing server on these systems. (IIS isn't supported on Windows XP Home Edition.) If you're not careful, however, installing IIS on a system can open security holes. Several powerful services are installed by IIS, and if they are not configured or maintained properly, they offer outsiders a way to gain access to and/or control files on the system.

To install IIS, go to Control Panel, Add Or Remove Programs, Add/Remove Windows Components. Select Internet Information Services (IIS) and then click Details to select the components you want to install, as shown in Figure 19-9. In Windows 2000, the FTP and SMTP services are selected for installation by default. Whether you use Windows 2000 or Windows XP, however, if you do not need these services, the best security move is to clear the check boxes so they won't be installed. If you're not sure whether you need the services, you can install them now and then disable them until you need them.

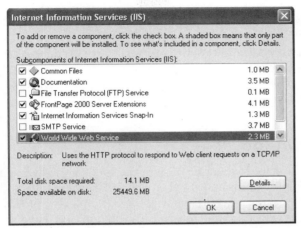

Figure 19-9. When installing IIS, choose only the components you need. Few people need the FTP or SMTP services.

Managing IIS Services

With IIS installed, you will see an Internet Information Services item in Administrative Tools. (In Windows 2000, the item is named Internet Services Administrator, but it's the same thing.) Figure 19-10 shows the Internet Information Services console, which also uses an MMC snap-in.

Figure 19-10. If you've installed the FTP and SMTP services but don't currently use them, stop them in the Internet Information Services console.

Unless you specify otherwise during the installation process, the default IIS configuration installs and enables the Web, FTP, and SMTP services. In most cases, you will be managing the server content through local files or file shares or through a site-management tool such as Microsoft FrontPage, so you should disable the FTP service unless you are absolutely sure you need it. Your current network usually has an existing SMTP mail server (or access to an external server through your ISP), so you should also disable the SMTP server.

> **Note** Security-conscious Web administrators might discover an IP Address And Domain Name Restrictions box. (Right-click Web Sites, choose Properties, and then click the Directory Security tab.) With IIS running on Microsoft Windows Server 2003 or Windows 2000 Server, this option lets you choose which remote systems can access the server. However, this option is unavailable through IIS running on Windows XP Professional or Windows 2000 Professional, and the corresponding Edit button is disabled.

Running the IIS Lockdown Tool

Given all the options that exist for configuring IIS, it can be confusing to determine which are required for your particular needs and which are optional and should be disabled. Fortunately, Microsoft has created a wizard that walks you through the process of determining which features you need, disabling the features you don't need and setting the security as tight as practically possible. You can read about the wizard (alternately called the Internet Information Services Lockdown Wizard and the IIS Lockdown tool) at *http://www.microsoft.com/technet/security/tools/locktool.mspx*, and you can download it from a link on the same page.

To use the Internet Information Services Lockdown Wizard, follow these steps:

1 Run the executable file, Iislockd.exe, from the folder where you downloaded it.

2 Click Next on the introduction and license agreement pages. The Select Server Template page appears.

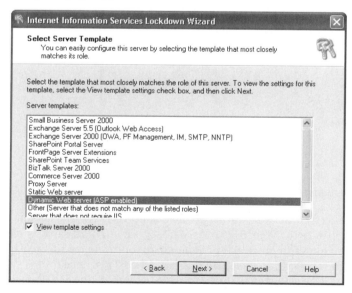

3 Select the template that most closely matches your use of IIS, and then click Next.

4 Select Install URLScan Filter On The Server and click Next. The URLScan feature protects the server from future URL-related exploits that might be uncovered. The Ready To Apply Settings page appears.

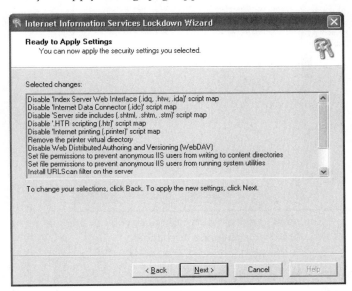

5 Click Next, and the wizard applies appropriate settings, disables unneeded services, and so on. Click Next and then click Finish to close the wizard.

A concise report of the actions taken by the wizard is saved as %SystemRoot% \System32\Inetsrv\Oblt-rep.log. A more detailed log file is saved in the same folder as Oblt-log.log.

Caution Do not delete the log files. The Internet Information Services Lockdown Wizard uses the Oblt-log.log file to undo its changes if that becomes necessary.

If you have problems accessing IIS after running the wizard, you can undo the changes it made. Just run the wizard again, and it offers to reverse all its modifications, as shown in Figure 19-11 on the next page, giving you the opportunity to lock down IIS with a different set of options. This behavior is useful because you can select or clear specific options and see whether they are the source of the problem you are experiencing.

Chapter 19

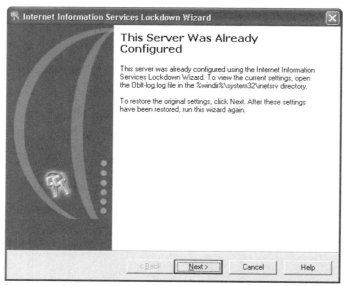

Figure 19-11. If something doesn't work right after you run the Internet Information Services Lockdown Wizard, you can undo its changes.

Blocking Anonymous Access to IIS

Most Web servers on the Internet are set up for anonymous access, but that usually isn't the first choice for a Web server running on your own system. If you're the only person planning to use the server, you should disable anonymous access. You don't incur the inconvenience of entering passwords, because when you go to your local Web site (using *http://localhost*) Internet Explorer automatically logs you in using your current user name and password.

> **Tip** **Configure Windows Firewall for Web access**
>
> If you set up a Web server on a computer running Windows XP Professional, network users (yourself included) will be denied access to the server's contents until you specifically allow incoming connections on port 80 (or an alternative port, if you change this setting in IIS). To configure access, open the Windows Firewall dialog box from Control Panel (open Security Center first if you use Control Panel in Category view), click the Advanced tab, select your local network connection from the list of available connections, and click Settings. In the Advanced Settings dialog box, select the Web Server (HTTP) check box, and click OK. If you've changed the port number, click Add and manually configure access on the appropriate port.

To disable anonymous access in IIS, open the Internet Information Services console. Right-click Default Web Site and choose Properties. On the Directory Security tab, click Edit in the Anonymous Access And Authentication Control box. In the Authentication Methods dialog box, shown in Figure 19-12, clear the Anonymous Access check box.

Figure 19-12. For the best security, disable anonymous access to your IIS server and do not enable Basic Authentication.

Integrated Windows Authentication was previously named NT Challenge Response, and the old name provides a clue to how it works. Instead of a client sending an actual password over the network, the server sends the client a "challenge phrase" consisting of some bytes of data. The server sends a different challenge phrase each time, but the actual content isn't important. The client takes the challenge phrase, modifies it using the password as a key, and sends the modified challenge phrase back to the server as the response. Meanwhile, the server has performed the same calculation on its end, using the password that it expects from the client. If the response sent by the client matches the server's calculated value, the two must have used the same password to perform the calculation, and permission is granted.

Basic Authentication takes the direct and nonsecure approach. The user name and password are sent across the network essentially in plain-text form. Anyone with network monitoring software can pick up this information and use it at any time to log in to the server. An attacker can obtain this information in several other ways, even without network monitoring. For example, a proxy server could cache this information and it could be retrieved if the security of the proxy was compromised.

Because Basic Authentication is so insecure, you should avoid turning it on for your server. However, you might encounter situations in which you can't avoid it. Some older non-Microsoft browsers don't support Integrated Windows Authentication; visitors who use an unsupported browser will see the error message "HTTP 401.2 - Unauthorized: Logon failed due to server configuration" when they go to your site. (This is confusing but technically correct; the server configuration issue is the lack of Basic Authentication.). Browsers in the Mozilla family, such as Firefox 1.0 and later, enable you to log on with your Windows credentials.

Regardless of which browser you use, you will be unable to log on to a Web site running IIS on Windows XP Professional if the following conditions are true:

- Anonymous access is disabled.
- Simple File Sharing is enabled on the IIS host machine.
- Integrated Windows authentication is the only option selected for access.
- You are attempting to connect from another computer across the network.

In this configuration, the Web browser displays a dialog box asking for a user name and password, but Windows XP ignores the user's credentials and tries to process the logon using the Guest account, which fails. The only way access across the network will succeed is if you disable Simple File Sharing and use the classic sharing model instead.

> For more details on Simple File Sharing versus classic sharing, see "Windows Sharing and Security Models," page 17.

> **Tip** Use Internet Explorer's automatic logon feature
>
> If you frequently access an IIS Web server on another system on your local network, you can avoid constantly typing your user name and password, even when you've disabled anonymous access in IIS. On the system running IIS, create a user with the same user name and password as the one you'll be using on the remote system. With its standard default settings, Internet Explorer will then automatically log on using your current user name and password, no prompting required. If you still receive prompts in Internet Explorer, select Tools, Internet Options, Security and select the Local Intranet zone. Click the Sites button and select the Include All Local (Intranet) Sites Not Listed In Other Zones check box. Click OK, and then click the Custom Level button and scroll to the bottom of the list. Under User Authentication, select Automatic Logon Only In Intranet Zone.

Using Server Logs

IIS maintains log files that you can use to ensure that no unauthorized access to the server is being made. Each access to the server for any type of file creates an entry in the log file. Failed accesses, such as pages that are not found or requests by users who are not authorized to access the server, are logged as well. One user loading a single Web page can create dozens of entries in the log if the page contains images that are also hosted on the server.

To enable logging, open the Internet Information Services console, right-click Default Web Site, and choose Properties. On the Web Site tab, select Enable Logging. To configure logging options, click Properties to display the dialog box shown in Figure 19-13.

For a lightly used Web server, you can simply review the file with Notepad to see whether any suspicious activity has occurred, as shown in Figure 19-14 on the next page. You can also import the file into Excel using the process described for Windows Firewall log files. (See "Examining Windows Firewall Logs," page 579.) Neither approach is practical for a busy Web server; even one that gets a few thousand accesses a day would be difficult to analyze this way. Instead, you might want to use a log analysis program. These programs read in the log files for a period of time (day, week, month, or longer) and summarize the accesses by user, page name, directory, or other groupings. To find a wide selection of commercial and free log analyzers, enter **web log analysis utilities** in your favorite Internet search engine.

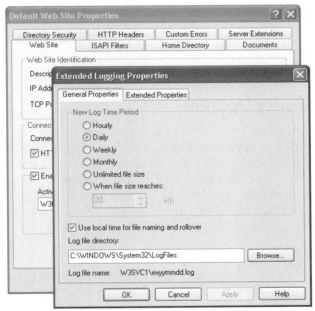

Figure 19-13. Enable IIS access logs so you can monitor whether unauthorized users are using the server.

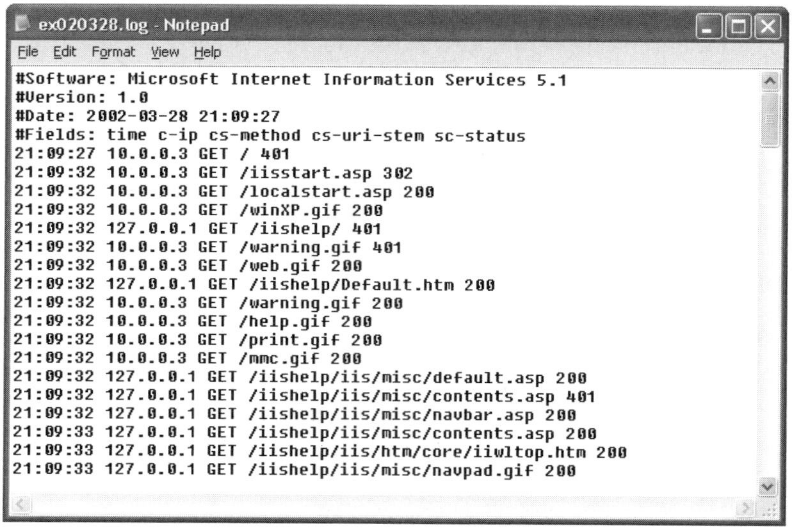

Figure 19-14. You can view the IIS log file with Notepad, import it into Excel for further analysis, or use a log file analysis program.

Keeping Up with IIS Security Updates

A poorly maintained Web server or FTP server is a disaster waiting to happen. New exploits are constantly being discovered and fixed, but your server is protected only if you apply the updates. After you've installed IIS, Windows Update should automatically notify you of new IIS updates and fixes if you have enabled Automatic Updates. Still, it is a good idea to occasionally run the Microsoft Baseline Security Analyzer (MBSA). For details about this program, see "Testing and Verifying Your Secure Status," page 229.

Chapter 20

Installing and Using Digital Certificates

Digital certificates (sometimes called *digital IDs*, *public key certificates*, or, more simply, *certificates*) are an important component of security in Microsoft Windows. Although they're widely used, they're seldom seen and little understood. In short, a *certificate* is a record that's used for authentication (that is, for proving one's identity), encryption (scrambling the content of sensitive documents to keep out prying eyes), or both.

Certificates are a basic component of the public key infrastructure (PKI). As such, a certificate securely links the value of a public key to the user, computer, or service that holds the corresponding private key. Certificates are issued by another integral PKI component, a certification authority (CA). The CA verifies the identity of each party in an electronic transaction before issuing a certificate.

In this chapter, we help make sense of these concepts, explain how to obtain certificates, and describe the tools available in Windows for managing your certificates. Elsewhere in this book, we explain how to use certificates for specific security-related purposes:

- Chapter 12, "Making Internet Explorer More Secure," explains how certificates are used to establish encrypted communications with secure Web sites and how to work with certificates for ActiveX controls.

- Chapter 15, "Securing E-Mail and Instant Messages," describes how to use certificates to digitally sign and encrypt your important messages.

- Chapter 19, "Securing Ports and Protocols," explains the use of Internet Protocol security (IPsec) for secure network communications.

- Chapter 21, "Encrypting Files and Folders," covers the way in which certificates are used by the Encrypting File System to protect data files from unauthorized access.

What Are Digital Certificates?

Digital certificates form the basis of two important security features: authentication and encryption.

Authentication is the means by which the identities of individuals, organizations, and devices are validated. For example, if you receive a digitally signed e-mail message or download a digitally signed program, the signature assures you that the identity claimed by the sender or the originating organization is genuine.

Encryption hides information from people who are not authorized to see it. Encryption uses keys to translate data from its base format to another, unintelligible format. The only way to make the data intelligible again is to translate it back—and of course it takes a key to translate the data back to its base format.

The most efficient and longest-used encryption method, called *symmetric encryption*, uses the same key for both encrypting and decrypting (that is, the same key at both ends of the process). Because both the sender and the recipient need the key, transmitting the key from the sender to the recipient can be a significant problem in itself.

Another method of encryption, called *asymmetric encryption*, uses different keys to encrypt and decrypt data. The asymmetric encryption method commonly used today is called *public key cryptography*. Public key cryptography uses a private key, known only to a single entity, and a public key, which is made available by the owner of the private key to anyone who needs it. Data encrypted with a public key can be decrypted only with its corresponding private key.

For example, say that you want to send a private message to Pat. If you use Pat's public key to encrypt the message, only Pat can decrypt it, because she is the only one with the corresponding private key. How do you get Pat's public key? She sends it to you, of course. But how do you know the key is really from Pat and not from someone pretending to be Pat? The answer to this question goes back to the other primary role of certificates: authentication. The message in which Pat sends her public key is signed with the private key of a third party—trusted by both you and Pat—that verified Pat's identity. Because the trusted third party is the only one who could sign a message with its own private key, you're assured that the message from Pat containing her public key actually came from Pat.

> **Caution** It's essential to keep your private keys secure. Any unauthorized access to them compromises your entire security scheme.

Digital certificates provide the storage and transport mechanism for public keys. The person, organization, computer, or service to whom a certificate is issued (the *subject*) can distribute the public key by sending a certificate. Certificates contain several pieces of information, including the following:

- The subject's public key
- The subject's identity, such as a name or an e-mail address

- The certificate's valid dates
- The identity of the CA that issued the certificate
- The digital signature of the CA

Certificate Purposes

We've mentioned the use of certificates for signing and encrypting e-mail messages, but you can employ public key cryptography in many more situations. The public key infrastructure, in fact, is used to create a complete system of security and authentication that can be tracked back to a trusted source.

Each certificate has one or more specified purposes, which are listed within the certificate. The certificate can be used only for these allowed purposes. A certificate can have more than one purpose. The General tab of the Certificate dialog box (see Figure 20-1 for an example) lists the certificate's purposes. Table 20-1 on the next page describes the most common certificate purposes. As Figure 20-2 on the next page shows, the Certificates snap-in for Microsoft Management Console (MMC) can organize certificates by purpose.

Figure 20-1. A certificate can have several purposes, but it can be used only for the purposes specified on the General tab.

Table 20-1. **Common Certificate Purposes**

Purpose	Description
Server Authentication	Used by servers (for example, secure Web servers using Secure Sockets Layer, or SSL) to authenticate themselves to clients
Client Authentication	Used by clients (such as Web users) to authenticate themselves to servers
Code Signing	Used by software producers to authenticate software (such as ActiveX controls or downloaded programs) to users
Secure E-mail	Used to sign and encrypt e-mail messages using Secure/Multipurpose Internet Mail Extensions (S/MIME)
Microsoft Trust List Signing	Used to create certificate trust lists
Encrypting File System	Used with the symmetric key for encrypting and decrypting files
File Recovery	Used with the symmetric key for recovering encrypted files

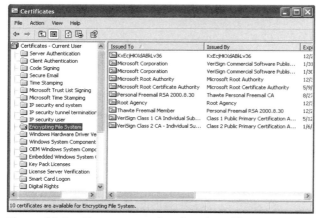

Figure 20-2. To see a complete list of certificate purposes, in the Certificates snap-in choose View, Options, and then select Certificate Purpose.

Certificate Stores

The storage location for the certificates on your computer is called, logically enough, a *certificate store*. Within the certificate store, certificates can be grouped according to the role they play within the PKI or in the specific application that uses them. Table 20-2 describes the logical stores that contain the most commonly used certificates. Some applications that use certificates create a logical group. Microsoft NetMeeting is an example.

Table 20-2. **Logical Certificate Stores**

Store	Description
Personal	Any certificates assigned to you and associated with your private keys.
Trusted Root Certification Authorities	Self-signed certificates of CAs that are implicitly trusted. This store includes certificates issued by third-party CAs, by Microsoft, and by your organization (if it has a domain-based certificate server).
Enterprise Trust	Any certificate trust lists you create. Certificate trust lists let you trust self-signed root certificates from other organizations.
Intermediate Certification Authorities	Certificates issued to other CAs.
Trusted Publishers	Certificates issued to publishers you've designated as always trustworthy or that are trusted by software restriction policies.
Untrusted Certificates	Certificates that you explicitly do not trust. Certificates are stored here if you select Do Not Trust This Certificate in a dialog box displayed by your e-mail program or Web browser.
Third-Party Root Certification Authorities	A subset of Trusted Root Certification Authorities that includes trusted root certificates from CAs other than Microsoft and your organization.

Certification Authorities

A certification authority is an integral part of the PKI. The essential role of a CA is to establish and vouch for the authenticity of public keys belonging to users or other certification authorities. To perform this role, a CA issues certificates signed with its own private key, manages certificate serial numbers, and, when necessary, revokes certificates.

For a certificate to be considered valid, both parties in an electronic transaction must trust the CA. Before granting a certificate to an individual or organization, the CA is responsible for verifying the identity of the entity that is applying for the certificate. After the requester's identity is verified, the CA assigns the requester both a public key and a private key and then supplies a digital certificate signed with the CA's private key. The validity of the certificate, then, is only as good as the credibility and level of trust maintained by the CA.

Certificate authentication works within a hierarchy of trust. At some point, you trust the CAs you trust because you choose to trust them. Unless you remove them, the certificates for all the CAs installed by default in your Trusted Root Certification Authorities store are trusted without question. Trusted root authority certificates are self-signed— that is, they authenticate themselves. By contrast, the certificates of an intermediate CA are signed not by that CA itself but by another CA. If the other CA is a trusted root authority, the first CA is trusted by inference. You might have a whole chain of CA authentication—called the *certification path*—ending with a trusted root authority. The Certificate dialog box contains a tab called Certification Path that displays this chain of authentication back to a trusted root authority, as shown in Figure 20-3.

For more information about certification paths and chain building, see "Troubleshooting Certificate Status and Revocation" on the Microsoft TechNet Web site at *http://www.microsoft.com/technet /security/topics/crypto/tshtcrl.mspx.*

Figure 20-3. The certification path of each certificate leads back to a trusted root authority.

Tip Windows XP includes a feature called Update Root Certificates. If this feature is enabled (the default setting), whenever you are presented with a certificate issued by an untrusted root authority, Windows contacts the Windows Update Web site to see whether Microsoft has added the CA to its list of trusted authorities. If the CA has been added to the Microsoft list of trusted authorities, Windows adds its certificate to your Trusted Root Certification Authorities store.

To enable or disable this feature, open Add Or Remove Programs in Control Panel, and then click Add/Remove Windows Components. In the Components list, select or clear the Update Root Certificates check box.

By contrast, Figure 20-4 shows a certificate that is not trusted because the chain of authentication cannot be traced back to a trusted root authority. You can choose to trust such certificates, but you should do so only if you're certain of the source's integrity. In the example shown, examining the details for the certificate purportedly held by the U.S. Navy shows that it was granted by an issuer claiming to be the U.S. Department of Defense. This certificate happens to be legitimate, but without the verification of a trusted certification authority, you can't really tell.

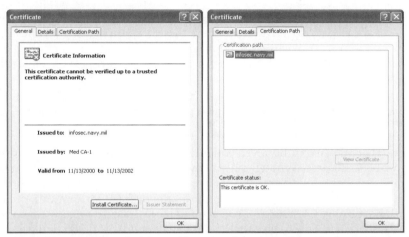

Figure 20-4. Although this certificate is otherwise valid, as indicated in the Certificate Status box, it is not trusted because it was not issued by a trusted certification authority.

When You Can't Trust a Certification Authority

Through a breakdown in its safeguards, even a trusted certification authority can issue a certificate to someone it shouldn't. In a well-publicized incident, VeriSign announced in March 2001 that it had issued two certificates to an individual who had fraudulently claimed to be a Microsoft employee. The certificates were promptly revoked (in fact, you can see them in the Untrusted Certificates store if you have Windows XP), and potential damage by someone sending out malicious code purportedly signed by Microsoft was avoided.

If you have Windows 2000 (or earlier versions of Windows) and you haven't applied the appropriate update to revoke these certificates, you might be at risk. For information about the erroneously issued certificates, see Microsoft Knowledge Base article 293817. This article explains how to identify the certificates and also includes links to Microsoft Security Bulletin MS01-017, which provides complete details, and to article 293811, which offers a tool that revokes the certificates' trusted status.

Obtaining a Personal Certificate

A quick journey to the Certificates snap-in or the Certificates dialog box reveals that you already have lots of certificates installed on your computer. (For details about these two tools, see "Managing Your Certificates," page 681.) Microsoft Internet Explorer comes with a whole passel of certificates, mostly for trusted CAs. Internet Explorer uses these certificates when you begin to download a program that has been digitally signed. Whenever you download a signed program, therefore, you're using certificates, whether you know it or not. Also, when you connect to a secure Web site (indicated by a lock icon on the Internet Explorer status bar), you're using a certificate to create the encrypted link.

> **For more information about downloading signed programs and using secure Web sites, see Chapter 12, "Making Internet Explorer More Secure."**

For several good reasons, however, you might want to go a little further and begin to actively use certificates. Although only a few people today digitally sign their e-mail messages, the number is increasing. If you have reason to be cautious about who reads your e-mail, you'll want to acquire public keys from the people to whom you intend to send clandestine messages. Likewise, if you want to receive secure e-mail from someone, you need to understand how to give the sender your public key. If you publish software on the Internet, you need a digital signing certificate, which involves much more than the simple personal certificates we discuss here.

> **Caution** The fact that you're reading this book indicates that you take computer security seriously. Therefore, you probably do have situations in which the authentication and encryption services provided by certificates are essential. But don't go overboard by signing and encrypting every document and message you handle. Along with the benefits of certificates come certain headaches; for example, a message with an expired certificate might not be accessible, and some mailing lists choke on digitally signed messages. Use these features only when they're needed.

> **Note** You don't need to obtain a certificate to begin using the Encrypting File System for encrypting files on your computer. Windows automatically creates a self-signed certificate when you begin using encryption. For more information, see Chapter 21, "Encrypting Files and Folders."

Certification authorities grant or deny a certificate when a requester applies for one. It is the CA's responsibility to confirm the identity of the requester, and the requester's responsibility to provide verifiable identification data to the CA. Each CA applies its own set of requirements to requests. The requirements might depend on the purpose of the certificate. It is relatively easy to get a certificate for signing e-mail messages and harder to get one for signing software.

Installing and Using Digital Certificates

You can request a certificate from one of the many certification authorities available on the Internet. Microsoft offers a short list of CAs that specialize in personal certificates at *http://office.microsoft.com/en-us/assistance/HA010547821033.aspx*. Most of these companies charge a fee for granting certificates, and each has its own method of verifying your identity. The fees and verification process might also vary based on the type of certificate you request. If you are granted a certificate from a CA whose certificates are included among the trusted root certificates by default, you can be fairly sure that your certificate will be accepted by any Internet Explorer user and most likely by anyone else.

Several third-party CAs are available to provide personal certificates to you for various purposes. You can find more information about their offerings at the following Web sites:

- GlobalSign (*http://www.globalsign.net/digital_certificate/*)
- Thawte (*http://www.thawte.com/buy/*)
- VeriSign, Inc. (*http://digitalid.verisign.com*)

To request a certificate from one of these CAs, go to its site and follow the instructions. When your certificate is approved, you download it and import it into your certificate store. Some sites perform the import as part of the download; other sites download a file that you must then manually import. (For details about importing, see "Importing Certificates," page 696.)

If your computer is part of an Active Directory domain, you can use your organization's internal certification authority to obtain a certificate. Microsoft Windows 2000 Server and Windows Server 2003 can offer certificate-granting services to computers in the domain or network. Microsoft Certificate Services is a CA with two means of access:

- Certificate Services can be run as an enterprise service. In this case, it is available to all domain computers and grants certificates based on the requester's permissions in Active Directory. The Certificate Request Wizard works only with enterprise-wide Certificate Services.

  You use the Certificates snap-in to request a new certificate from enterprise Certificate Services on your domain. If you have enterprise Certificate Services, select the Certificates – Current User\Personal folder and choose Action, All Tasks, Request New Certificate. Follow the wizard's instructions to request a certificate.

- Certificate Services can also be run in stand-alone mode. In this case, Certificate Services is available through an HTML interface, as shown in Figure 20-5. The stand-alone service does not automatically grant or deny requests. Requests are placed in a queue, and an administrator manually reviews them and decides whether to grant them. After you submit a request for a certificate from stand-alone Certificate Services on your network, you must return to the service to find whether your request has been granted. The address of the stand-alone service is *http://*servername/*certsrv*, where *servername* is the name of the computer running Certificate Services.

Just How Does a CA Know Who You Are?

The hierarchy of certificate authentication and trust rests on the certification authorities. It is their job to verify the identity of everyone who requests a certificate. But how do they do that? Policies among CAs differ, but we can look at one example. Thawte is a CA that provides, among other things, free personal certificates (*http://www.thawte.com/email/*). These certificates have two possible purposes: e-mail signing or encryption, and personal identification. The procedure Thawte uses to verify your identity depends on which purpose you specify in your request.

If you request a certificate for e-mail signing or encryption, the verification is quite simple. Thawte sends an e-mail message to the address listed in the request. The message contains the URL of a reply page on Thawte's Web site. To open the page, you must sign on with your Thawte user name and password. Thawte interprets your opening that page as verification of the e-mail address, and grants the certificate. This certificate contains your e-mail address but not your name. Then, whenever anyone receives an e-mail message signed with this certificate, he or she can be assured that you actually own the source e-mail account (even if the recipient has no assurance that you are who you say you are).

If you request a certificate for personal identification (that is, a certificate containing your name), the verification process is a bit more complicated. Thawte has created a "Web of Trust"—essentially a worldwide group of notaries who verify your identity face to face. You must personally visit at least two notaries and present some valid identification, such as a driver's license or passport. If the notary is satisfied with your documents, he or she can award you between 10 and 35 points. When you receive 50 points, your identity is validated. In this system, you must identify yourself to at least two and as many as five people before Thawte validates your identity. Then Thawte approves your request for a certificate containing your name.

If you receive an e-mail message signed with a certificate that itself is signed by Thawte, and the certificate contains the name of a person, you know that person had to go through the steps just described to get that certificate. If the certificate is signed by Thawte but does not include a person's name, you know that the person confirmed only his or her e-mail account with Thawte.

Note You might think that an unscrupulous system administrator could use Certificate Services to create falsified certificates. In fact, he or she could. But remember that other users won't necessarily trust this certification authority. (Because it's not included in your list of trusted CAs, Windows displays a warning message if such a certificate is sent to you.)

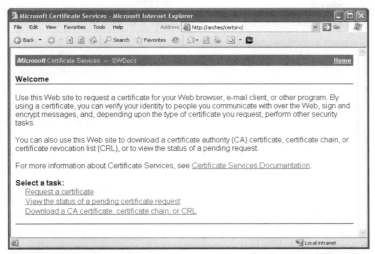

Figure 20-5. Certificate Services can issue certificates to domain users through an HTML interface.

A discussion of installing and configuring Certificate Services on a domain controller is beyond the scope of this book. For information about operating certification authority for your own organization, see *Microsoft Windows Server 2003 Administrator's Companion*, by Charlie Russel, Sharon Crawford, and Jason Gerend (Microsoft Press, 2003) and *Microsoft Windows Server 2003 PKI and Certificate Security* by Brian Komar with the Microsoft PKI Team (Microsoft Press, 2004). You can also find plenty of helpful information at *http://www.microsoft.com/windowsserver2003 /technologies/pki/default.mspx* and *http://www.microsoft.com/technet/prodtechnol/winxppro /plan/pkienh.mspx*.

Managing Your Certificates

For the most part, you can leave your certificates alone. Internet Explorer and Windows automatically take care of business and trouble you only when necessary. However, you might have occasion to examine and work with your certificates, particularly if you use personal certificates for e-mail, file encryption, and the like.

Note If you use a browser other than Internet Explorer, you will need to manage certificates for that browser using its tools. The popular Firefox browser, for instance, keeps its own store of trusted root certificates and adds certificates to the store when you visit secure Web sites. To view and manage the Firefox certificate store, open the Firefox browser window, open the Tools menu, and click Options. Select the Advanced icon in the sidebar at the left of the Options dialog box, and then expand the Certificates section. Click Manage Certificates to open a dialog box that displays all saved certificates.

You need to manage a number of components when you start using certificates, and keeping track of everything can be difficult. You might have personal certificates with private and public keys, client certificates, and—if you administer a server—server certificates. These are just for your own computer. You might also have public certificates for people to whom you send encrypted e-mail and for companies from whom you download software. If that's not enough, you might also have certificates from trusted third parties who authenticate your certificates and the certificates of those you do business with.

> **Note** Users—even users with administrative privileges—can manage only their own personal certificates.

You shouldn't be surprised that Windows offers more than one way to manage certificates. In fact, Windows gives you two distinct tools for certificate management:

- The Certificates dialog box
- The Certificates snap-in for Microsoft Management Console

Both tools allow you to perform essentially the same tasks. The Certificates dialog box is less complicated and easier to use. The Certificates snap-in has a few more options. We suggest you try the Certificates dialog box first. If you can't accomplish your goal with that, try the MMC snap-in. We discuss both in this chapter.

Where Do They All Come From?

When you first venture into the certificate-management tools, you might be surprised (and overwhelmed!) at the number of certificates that are already installed on your computer. How did they get there? The certificates in your computer's certificate stores generally arrive in one of these ways:

- As part of a default Windows installation.
- When you visit a secure Web site using SSL and trust is established. (Therefore, as you use the Internet and connect to servers that use certificates for authentication and other purposes, your certificate collection continues to grow.)
- When, while installing a signed program or downloading an ActiveX control in Windows XP, you select the option to always install software signed by that publisher.
- When using Windows XP with Service Pack 2 (SP2) installed, you specify in a Security Warning dialog box that you never want to install software signed by a particular publisher.
- When someone sends you a digitally signed or encrypted e-mail message or document.
- When you request a certificate from a CA, including personal certificates for signing and encryption, certificates needed for access to certain resources (such as a virtual private network), and so on.

Using the Certificates Dialog Box

You can open the Certificates dialog box by opening Internet Options from Control Panel or by choosing Tools, Internet Options in Internet Explorer. In Internet Options, click the Content tab, and then click Certificates.

Inside Out

Avoid annoying modal dialog boxes

If you open Internet Options (and then click Certificates on the Content tab) from Internet Explorer, you can't use that Internet Explorer window until you close those two dialog boxes. If you find so-called *modal* dialog boxes such as this annoying, be sure to open Internet Options from Control Panel or from an Internet Explorer window that you're not actively using.

Tip In Windows 2000, you can use an alternative method to open the Certificates dialog box: In Control Panel, open Users And Passwords. On the Advanced tab, click Certificates.

However you open it, the Certificates dialog box you see looks similar to the one shown in Figure 20-6.

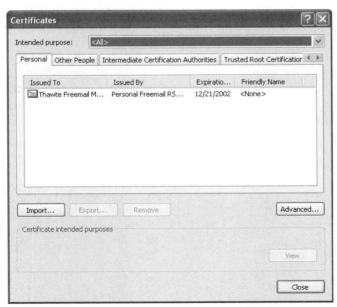

Figure 20-6. You can manage all your certificate components from one dialog box.

Chapter 20

The Certificates dialog box organizes your certificates on tabs that correspond roughly to the logical stores:

- **Personal.** This tab contains certificates with an associated private key (typically, your own personal certificates).
- **Other People.** This tab contains certificates for users with whom you've shared access to one or more encrypted files.
- **Intermediate Certification Authorities.** This tab contains certificates from CAs other than those with trusted root certificates.
- **Trusted Root Certification Authorities.** This tab contains self-signing certificates. You intrinsically trust content from people and publishers with certificates issued by these CAs.
- **Trusted Publishers.** This tab, which appears only in Windows XP, contains certificates that are added when you select the Always Trust Content From check box in a Security Warning dialog box. After you install SP2, the wording in this dialog box changes to read Always Install Software From.
- **Untrusted Publishers.** This tab, which appears only in Windows XP after installing SP2, contains certificates from software publishers for whom you have selected the Never Install Software From option in a Security Warning dialog box, as well as the two revoked certificates issued by VeriSign in January 2001 (see the sidebar "When You Can't Trust a Certification Authority," page 677).

You can filter the certificates listed on each tab according to their purposes. In the Intended Purpose box at the top of the Certificates dialog box, you can choose to see all certificates with any purpose (All), those with a particular purpose (the purposes listed are those that are not selected in the Advanced Options dialog box), or only those certificates with advanced purposes. To set up or change the Advanced Purposes list, click the Advanced button. The Advanced Options dialog box presents a list of certificate purposes, as shown in Figure 20-7. From this list, select the purposes that you want to include in the Advanced Purposes list.

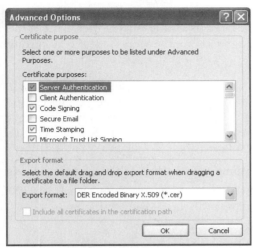

Figure 20-7. The certificate purposes selected here are included in the Advanced Purposes list.

Using the Certificates Snap-In

When you first open a console with the Certificates snap-in, each logical store is represented by a folder in the console tree. Certificates appear in the details pane, as shown in Figure 20-8.

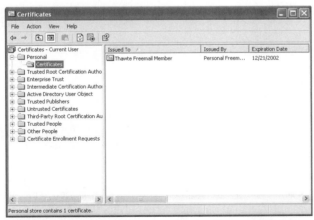

Figure 20-8. The Certificates snap-in allows you to manage all your certificates from an MMC console.

The easiest way to open the Certificates snap-in in Windows XP is to use Certmgr.msc, a predefined console that shows certificates for the current user. To start this console, open the Run dialog box (or a Command Prompt window) and type **certmgr.msc**.

Creating a Console

Users of Windows 2000 must first create a console that incorporates the Certificates snap-in. (Like Windows XP, Windows 2000 includes a predefined console named Certmgr.msc. It's configured, however, to look for a nonexistent file, so it displays only an error message and an empty certificate store.) To create a console, follow these steps:

1 At a command prompt type **mmc** to start Microsoft Management Console.

2 On the File menu (Windows XP) or the Console menu (Windows 2000), choose Add/Remove Snap-In (or simply press Ctrl+M).

3 In the Add/Remove Snap-In dialog box, click Add.

4 In the Add Standalone Snap-In dialog box, select Certificates and click Add.

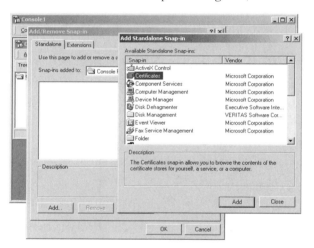

5 In the Certificates Snap-In dialog box, select the account for which you want to manage certificates: My User Account, Service Account, or Computer Account. For most purposes, you'll want to select My User Account.

> **Note** The Certificates Snap-In dialog box appears only if you're logged on as an administrator. Nonadministrative users can manage certificates only for their own user account, so that choice is made automatically for them.

6 In the Certificates Snap-In dialog box, click Finish if you selected My User Account, or click Next and then Finish if you selected Service Account or Computer Account.

7   If you're logged on as an administrator and you want to include the service or computer accounts (or both) in *your* console, repeat steps 4 through 6 to add the other accounts you want.

8   In the Add Standalone Snap-In dialog box, click Close. In the Add/Remove Snap-In dialog box, click OK.

9   Customize your console as you like, and then choose File, Save to save it as an .msc file that you can easily launch from Windows Explorer, from a shortcut, or from a command prompt.

Inside Out

View certificates for different accounts and computers

Note that the Certificates snap-in is capable of handling any of three accounts: current user, services, and computer. (You can direct the services and computer options at your own local computer or at another computer on your network for which your user account has administrative permissions.) Certificates can be associated with one or more of these accounts. To include all three accounts in one console, you must add the snap-in three times, selecting a different account each time.

The predefined Certificates console (Certmgr.msc) included with Windows XP displays certificates only for the current user account. If you want to view certificates for the services or computer accounts—on your own computer or on another network computer—you can follow the same procedure we outlined to create a console for Windows 2000 users.

Changing View Options

By default, the Certificates snap-in displays certificates organized by logical stores. But you can set up views that organize them differently. Select a top-level Certificates snap-in and then choose View, Options to display the dialog box shown in Figure 20-9.

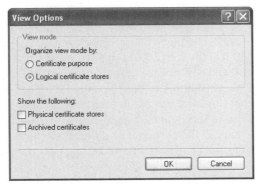

Figure 20-9.   The Certificates snap-in organizes its display of certificates by purpose or logical store.

Chapter 20

The View Options dialog box offers two view modes: Certificate Purpose and Logical Certificate Stores (the default). Selecting Certificate Purpose displays the certificates in folders organized according to purpose, as shown in Figure 20-2, page 674. If you select to view by Logical Certificate Stores, you can also select to show Physical Certificate Stores. If both logical and physical stores are displayed, the console tree is organized as shown in Figure 20-10. By default, the snap-in does not display archived certificates, but you can select Archived Certificates in the View Options dialog box to display them.

> **Note** *Archived certificates* are certificates that have expired. It's usually best to keep such certificates instead of deleting them upon expiration. You'll need them, for example, in order to confirm the digital signature on old messages or documents that were signed using the key on the archived certificate. More importantly, you'll want the archived certificate if it's needed to decrypt a document that was encrypted with the now-expired key.

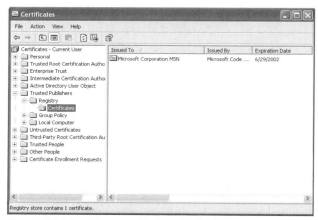

Figure 20-10. You can display physical locations within each logical store.

Viewing and Modifying Certificate Properties

You might want to view the contents of a certificate to note its expiration date, purpose, or certifying authority. Whether you use the Certificates dialog box or the Certificates snap-in, you can view certificate properties simply by double-clicking the certificate of interest. When you open a certificate, you see a Certificate dialog box. The General tab provides a clearly formatted summary of the certificate's purposes, subject, issuer, Certification Authority, and valid dates. (See Figure 20-1, page 673, for an example.) The Details tab, shown in Figure 20-11, lists all the parameters of the certificate and their values. The Certification Path tab shows the chain of authentication back to a root certification authority. (See Figure 20-3, page 20xx, for an example.)

Chapter 20

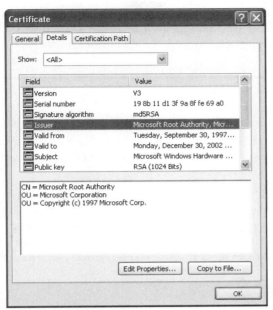

Figure 20-11. The Details tab provides a comprehensive summary of a certificate's contents.

Determining a Certificate's Validity

The icon near the top of the General tab offers some important information about a certificate's validity. If a yellow warning triangle appears in the corner of the icon, Windows does not have enough information to verify the certificate. If a red X appears in the corner, as shown in Figure 20-12, the certificate has a problem, which is explained in the text below the icon. A red *X* appears in these cases:

● The certificate was not issued by a trusted CA. This occurs with your own self-signed certificates, among others. If you *know* the issuer is valid, you can move the certificate to your Trusted Root Certification Authorities store.

● The certificate was issued without verification, which is often the case with free certificates obtained on a trial basis from third-party CAs.

● The certificate has expired or has been revoked, or is not yet valid.

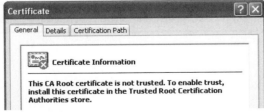

Figure 20-12. Seeing a red *X* on the General tab should raise your alert level.

Examine the Issued To and Issued By fields for additional clues about a certificate's validity, and click the Issuer Statement button if it is available. Do you know and trust the CA and the organization or person to whom the certificate was issued?

⚙ Inside Out

Find a particular certificate

You won't always know which store holds a certificate you're looking for. Because of the number of stores and the large number of certificates in some stores, browsing to find a particular certificate can be tedious, at best.

The Certificates snap-in (but not the Certificates dialog box) offers a search feature that makes it easy to find that proverbial needle in a haystack. The Find Certificates dialog box, shown here, also offers a quick way to perform common tasks with the certificates you find. Select a certificate from the search results list and then open the File menu, where you'll discover commands to renew, export, delete, open, or display the properties of a certificate.

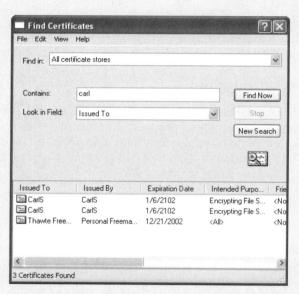

To use the Find Certificates feature, in the console tree select the Certificates folder or one of its first-level subfolders. Then open the Action menu and choose Find Certificates.

Changing a Certificate's Properties

You can modify certain properties of a certificate—although you'll seldom have reason to do so. If you find a certificate's Issued To name (the field by which certificates are normally listed and identified) to be inscrutable, you can assign (or change) the certificate's friendly name or description. (The Friendly Name column appears by default in the details pane of the Certificates snap-in, although it's so far to the right that it's usually hidden. If you end up relying on the Friendly Name column for any reason, you might want to move it to a more prominent position. Drag the column title to the new position, and drag its right border to adjust the width. You can also change the column order by opening the View menu and choosing Add/Remove Columns.)

The other change you can make to certificate properties is to enable or disable certain certificate purposes—although you can enable only purposes that are allowed by the certificate issuer.

To view or modify the friendly name, description, or enabled purposes, open a certificate, click its Details tab, and click Edit Properties. (Alternatively, if you're using the Certificates snap-in, right-click a certificate and choose Properties.) A dialog box such as the one shown in Figure 20-13 appears, in which you can read or modify the properties.

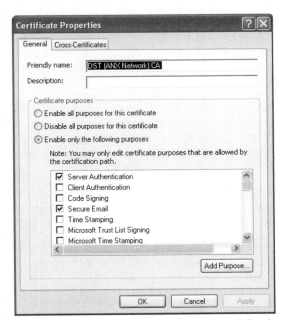

Figure 20-13. The Certificate Properties dialog box lets you create your own "friendly name" for a certificate.

Examining Certificates in Microsoft Office

Using Microsoft Office 2003 (or its predecessor, Office XP) you can attach a digital certificate to a document, spreadsheet, form, or presentation. As with e-mail messages, a certificate provides a digital signature that authenticates the document signer and ensures that the document has not been modified. In Office 2003, Microsoft introduced a new feature called Information Rights Management (IRM), which allows the creator of a document to assign permissions to that document, preventing its contents from being accessed, forwarded, edited, or copied by unauthorized individuals. These permissions are persistent and remain with the document even if it leaves the domain.

To add a digital signature to a document, spreadsheet, or presentation, open the Office application's Tools menu and choose Options. On the Security tab, click Digital Signatures and then click Add. (In Microsoft InfoPath 2003, open the Tools menu and choose Digital Signatures.) You can view the certificate attached to a document in the same dialog box. Select a certificate and choose View Certificate to see the same Certificate dialog box that you'd find if you located the certificate in the Certificates dialog box or the Certificates snap-in.

To use Information Rights Management in Microsoft Office Word 2003, the creator and anyone who wants to work with the protected document must install a small piece of client software. In addition, you need access to a Windows Server 2003 domain with Internet Information Services (IIS), Active Directory, and a computer running Windows Rights Management Services (RMS). To apply IRM restrictions to a document, open the document, click File, and then click Permissions. If the necessary client software is not installed, a wizard will walk you through the process of setting it up.

All versions of Office since Office 2000 also allow digital signing of macro projects. It's a good thing, too, because Word macros have been the source of numerous security problems. If your Office macro security setting (choose Tools, Macro, Security) is set to Medium or High, Office displays a warning when you open documents that are unsigned or signed with untrusted certificates.

To view the certificates for a signed macro project, choose Tools, Macro, Visual Basic Editor. In the Visual Basic Editor, select the macro project and choose Tools, Digital Signature. In the Digital Signature dialog box, click Detail.

For certificates attached to documents, a red *X* on the General tab can indicate that the document has been modified by someone other than the signer. A red *X* also appears if the certificate was not valid at the time it was used to sign the document.

For more details about RMS, see *http://www.microsoft.com/technet/technetmag/issues /2005/01/OfficeSpace/*.

Exporting Certificates for Safekeeping

You can export certificates from your certificate stores to ordinary files. You might want to do this in these situations:

- To create a backup copy for safekeeping
- To copy or move a certificate for use on another computer

To export a certificate from the Certificates dialog box, simply select the certificate and click Export. In the Certificates snap-in, select the certificate and choose Action, All Tasks, Export. Either action starts the Certificate Export Wizard. Like most wizards, the Certificate Export Wizard is pretty intuitive—except for the Export File Format page, shown in Figure 20-14. For more information about your choices here, see the sidebar "File Formats for Exported Certificates," page 694.

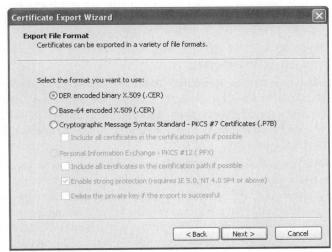

Figure 20-14. The Certificate Export Wizard supports four standard file formats.

When you export a personal certificate that contains a private key, you have the option of exporting the private key with the certificate. If you choose to export the private key, you must supply a password to protect it. You'll want to export the private key if you are exporting the certificate in order to import it to another computer of yours where you want to use the same keys.

File Formats for Exported Certificates

You can export and import certificates in any of several formats with rather cryptic names:

- **DER encoded binary X.509.**   Distinguished Encoding Rules (DER) X.509 defines a platform-independent method (that is, a method that can be used on computers running any operating system) for encoding certificates and other files for transmission between computers. Certificates you receive from CAs that do not use Windows 2000 might use this format, but there's no reason for you to use X.509 for exporting certificates that will be used only on Windows-based computers. This file type uses a .cer or .crt file name extension.

- **Base-64 encoded X.509.**   This X.509 variant uses an encoding method designed for use with S/MIME, a standard method for securely sending attachments over Internet e-mail. The entire file is encoded as ASCII characters, which ensures that it will survive a trip through various mail gateways unscathed. Unless you have problems sending a certificate file as an e-mail attachment, you don't need to use this format for exporting certificates that will be used only on Windows-based computers. This file type uses a .cer or .crt extension.

- **Cryptographic Message Syntax Standard – PKCS #7 Certificates.**   Unlike the X.509 formats, PKCS (Public Key Cryptography Standard) #7 certificates enable you to combine a certificate and all the certificates in its certification path in a single file, making it easy to move a trusted certificate from one computer to another. This file type uses a .p7b or .spc extension.

- **Personal Information Exchange – PKCS #12.**   Sometimes called Personal Interchange Exchange format (which, strangely enough, is abbreviated PFX), this format enables you to transfer your certificates along with their corresponding private keys. It's the only supported format that can include private keys. To permit the inclusion of the private key, the key must be marked as exportable; this is controlled by the CA that issues the original certificate. This file type uses a .pfx or .p12 extension.

- **Microsoft Serialized Certificate Store.**   This format is used only when you choose to export or import an entire certificate store. This file type uses an .sst extension.

Which format should you use? For encryption certificates or other certificates with a private key to be included in the exported file, use PKCS #12. (Include the private key only for your own backups or for installation on your own computers. Don't send a certificate with your private key to anyone else!) For all other certificates that you want to import to a computer running Windows, use PKCS #7. Computers running other operating systems might not support PKCS #7; to create a certificate for use on such a computer, use either of the X.509 formats. X.509 is the most widely accepted format for certificates.

Inside Out

Use drag and drop to export

From the Certificates dialog box (but not the MMC snap-in), you can drag a certificate to your desktop or to a folder in Windows Explorer. No wizard appears, and you don't have to answer any questions; an exported certificate file simply appears wherever you drop the certificate.

By default, the drag-and-drop export feature creates a DER encoded binary X.509 file. You can select another certificate file type by clicking the Advanced button in the Certificates dialog box. The Advanced Options dialog box (shown in Figure 20-7, page 685) offers a list of export formats. Note, however, that the Personal Information Exchange (PKCS #12) file type is not available. Including this option doesn't make sense because it's the only format that can include private keys (and because it's not available for most certificates).

You can export multiple certificates into a single file in any of three ways:

- In the Certificates dialog box or the Certificates snap-in, select multiple certificates before you begin the export. (You do that the same way you make multiple selections in Windows Explorer and other applications: drag a lasso around the entire group or hold down the Ctrl key as you click each item you want to select.) The Certificate Export Wizard combines the selected certificates into a single PKCS #7 file.

- To export a certificate and all the certificates in its certification path, in the Certificate Export Wizard, select PKCS #7 and Include All Certificates In The Certification Path If Possible.

- In the Certificates snap-in, you can export an entire store as a single file. To do so, you must first display physical certificate stores within logical certificate stores. (For details, see "Changing View Options," page 687.) Select a physical store (such as Registry, Local Computer, or Group Policy) that contains the certificates you want to export, and then choose Action, All Tasks, Export Store. The Certificate Export Wizard combines the files in the selected store into a single Microsoft Serialized Certificate Store file.

When you subsequently import a file that contains multiple certificates, the Certificate Import Wizard imports all the certificates contained in the file.

Importing Certificates

Once you have a certificate in a standard certificate file—one that you exported or one that was sent to you by someone else—you can import it into your certificate store. You'll want to import a certificate to accomplish the following tasks:

- To install a new certificate that you receive from another person or from a CA
- To restore a damaged or lost certificate from your backup copy
- To install your personal certificate on another computer

To import a certificate while using the Certificates dialog box, click Import. If you're using the snap-in, select any folder in the console tree, then open the Action menu and choose All Tasks, Import. The Import Certificate Wizard leads you through the simple process.

> **Tip** Import certificates directly from files
>
> You can import certificates without opening the Certificates dialog box or snap-in. Simply right-click the certificate file in Windows Explorer (or on your desktop) and choose Install Certificate. This command launches the Certificate Import Wizard, bypassing the step in which you must browse to find the certificate file.

Copying or Moving a Certificate

Using the Certificates snap-in (but not the Certificates dialog box), you can copy or move certificates from one store to another. You might do this to move a certificate that you know to be good—but that was not issued by a trusted CA—to the Trusted Root Certification Authorities or Trusted People store, for example.

To copy or move a certificate, you must use the snap-in's logical certificate stores view. (For details, see "Changing View Options," page 687.) Select the certificate and then choose Copy or Cut (to move it) from the Action menu or from the shortcut menu that appears when you right-click the certificate. Select the destination store and then choose Action, Paste.

You can also use the drag-and-drop feature just as you would in Windows Explorer: Drag a certificate (or multiple certificates) to another store to move it; hold down the Ctrl key as you drag to copy the certificate. (And if you can never remember which action copies and which one moves, drag using the right mouse button. When you drop the certificate, a shortcut menu opens to ask whether you want to move or copy.)

> **Note** You can't use these techniques to copy or move a certificate to a file folder; to do that, you must export the certificate. For details, see "Exporting Certificates for Safe-keeping," page 693.

Deleting a Certificate

If you're moving to a new computer and passing your old computer on to someone else (without formatting its drives), you should delete your personal certificates. Or you might want to delete a certificate if, for example, you no longer trust the person or organization to whom the certificate was issued. This is a rare situation, however, and you should consider moving the certificate to another store (for example, Untrusted Certificates) instead of deleting it.

Regardless of your reason for deleting a certificate, you should first export the certificate so that you have a backup copy available if you need it later.

> **Caution**   Maintaining an exported backup copy is especially important if the certificate was used for encrypting messages or other files. Without the certificate, you won't be able to decrypt the encrypted information.

To delete a certificate while working with the Certificates dialog box, select the certificate and click Remove. If you're using the Certificates snap-in, select the certificate and choose Action, Delete (or simply press the Delete key). You'll be given a final chance to reconsider when a confirmation dialog box appears.

> **Tip**   Don't worry about deleting Trusted Publishers
> You can safely delete certificates from the Trusted Publishers store. (These publishers are ones for which you selected the Always Trust Content From or Always Install Software From check box in the Security Warning dialog box that appears when you download active software.) If you've already installed software from the publisher whose certificate you're deleting, it will continue to run; the only effect of deleting a Trusted Publisher certificate is that the next time you attempt to install software from the publisher, you'll again be presented with the Security Warning dialog box.

Renewing a Certificate

When certificates issued by an enterprise Certificate Services server expire, they can be renewed. The Certificates snap-in gives you two options for renewing expired or about-to-expire certificates: You can renew them with the same keys or with new keys. If you are concerned that the keys might be compromised, you might want to renew the certificate with new keys. You renew a certificate by right-clicking its icon and choosing All Tasks, Renew Certificate With Same Key or All Tasks, Renew Certificate With New Key.

Chapter 21

Encrypting Files and Folders

Throughout this book, we explain various methods for keeping snoops away from your data: password-protected user accounts, restrictive NTFS permissions, prudent network sharing, firewalls, and so on. But what if, despite your best efforts, your files fall into the wrong hands? This is certainly a risk if you travel with a portable computer—a popular target for thieves. But even offices and homes in low-crime neighborhoods are sometimes burglarized, putting your desktop computers at risk. A stealthier thief—perhaps a coworker or someone who manages to penetrate your computer's defenses through the Internet—can also make off with your files.

Nearly every computer, whether it's in a business or a home, contains some sensitive data that must never be available outside your most trusted circle (or, in some cases, to anyone else at all). In addition to financial data—such as your accounting records or personal finance files—your computer might be the repository for marketing plans, trade secrets, medical history, diaries, address books, and similar information. If someone can obtain a file by downloading it from your computer or by borrowing (or stealing) your portable computer, they know your secrets.

In this chapter, we discuss the Encrypting File System (EFS), a feature of Microsoft Windows XP Professional and Windows 2000 that can prevent the loss of such confidential data. EFS encodes your files so that even if thieves are able to obtain a file, they can't read it. The files are readable only when you log on to the computer with your user account (which, presumably, you have protected with a strong password). In fact, even someone else logging on to your computer won't have access to your encrypted files, which provides protection on systems that are shared by more than one user.

> **Note** EFS is not available on computers running Windows XP Home Edition.

Security Checklist: Encrypting Data

Once you set up EFS, it works silently in the background, requiring no further attention. If you don't implement EFS correctly, however, you can undermine your security efforts. For example, your editing program can leave unencrypted temporary files on your drive. To adequately protect your data and, more important, to avoid permanently and irrevocably locking yourself out of your own folders, be sure to observe these guidelines:

- If you use Windows 2000, install the latest service pack to enable 128-bit encryption.
- Encrypt a file or folder to create a personal encryption certificate.
- Export the personal encryption certificate for each account.
- If you use Windows XP, be sure you have a Password Reset Disk. Also consider creating and designating a data recovery agent.
- Export and protect the private keys for recovery accounts, and then remove them from the computer. This prevents someone from accessing your files using the data recovery agent account.
- Encrypt the My Documents folder and any other local folder you use for storing documents.
- Always encrypt folders, not files. When a folder is encrypted, all files created in that folder are encrypted. (Many programs save a new copy of the document you are editing. This copy will be encrypted if you encrypt the folder, but it will be not be encrypted if you encrypt only the original file.)
- Don't destroy file recovery certificates and private keys when you change data recovery agent policies. Keep them until you are sure that all the files they protect have been updated.
- Configure a policy so that the page file is cleared when you shut down your computer. Otherwise, data from files that were decrypted during a working session might remain in the page file, which a thief could peruse. (For details, see "Exploring Security Options," page 736.)
- Disable hibernation (a power-saving option you configure in Control Panel, Power Options). If your system goes into hibernation while encrypted files are open (and therefore decrypted), the data is accessible to a thief who views the Hiberfil.sys file.

Note EFS in Windows XP Professional offers several features that are not available in Windows 2000. We note these additional features throughout this chapter, but here's a preview of the significant differences in Windows XP:

- You can share your encrypted files with other users you designate.
- You can store encrypted files in a shared Web folder on a remote computer.
- You can encrypt offline files.
- Names of encrypted files and folders are displayed in green in Windows Explorer.
- Stronger encryption algorithms are available.
- No default data recovery agent is required.
- Local administrators can't gain access to your encrypted files by changing your password.

Installing Strong Encryption in Windows 2000

Before you begin relying on EFS to protect your data, you should ensure that your copy of Windows 2000 uses strong encryption. (*Strong encryption* refers to cryptographic operations that use keys of 128 bits or more.)

All versions of Windows XP have built-in support for strong encryption. However, the original Windows 2000 Professional CD includes only 56-bit encryption—the maximum allowed for export from the United States at the time Windows 2000 was completed. In January 2000—only a few weeks before the retail release of Windows 2000—the U.S. government issued new export regulations allowing companies to ship strong encryption products to almost all countries.

If you haven't already done so, you should upgrade to 128-bit encryption, which provides strong encryption for encrypted files on NTFS volumes; for secure network connections, such as those using Internet Protocol Security (IPSec); and for all other encryption-based services. (To find out whether strong encryption is installed on your computer, search for a file named Rsaenh.dll; the file exists in %SystemRoot%\System32 only if strong encryption has been installed.) You can upgrade to strong encryption in any of these ways:

- Install the latest service pack for Windows 2000; strong encryption is included with Service Pack 2 and later. We recommend this method because the service pack also includes a large number of security updates, fixes, and enhancements.
- Install from the High Encryption Floppy Disk included in the Windows 2000 Professional retail package. Run Encpack.exe from the floppy disk.
- Download and then install the High Encryption Pack from *http://www.microsoft.com /windows2000/downloads/recommended/encryption/*.

Using the Encrypting File System

The Encrypting File System enables you to encrypt files on an NTFS volume so that only you can use them. This offers a level of protection beyond that provided by NTFS permissions, which you can use to restrict access to your files by others who log on to your computer. NTFS permissions are vulnerable for a couple of reasons. First, all users with administrative privileges can grant themselves (or others) permission to access your files. What's worse, anyone who gains physical access to your computer can boot from a CD or floppy disk (or from another operating system, if your computer is set up for dual booting) and use a utility such as NTFSDOS (available from Sysinternals, *http://www.sysinternals.com*) to read the files on your hard disk—without having to provide a user name or password. Portable computers, which are more easily stolen, are especially vulnerable to this type of information loss.

> **Tip** **Require a startup password on portable computers**
> On most computers, you can use BIOS settings to construct another obstacle for anyone who steals your computer. Set your BIOS so that a password is required to start the computer or to enter the BIOS setup program, and set the boot options so that the computer can't be booted from a floppy disk or CD. Unfortunately, this type of protection can also be circumvented. For example, removing the hard disk and installing it in another computer makes its files available to someone with the proper tools.
>
> A much more effective method is to remove the Syskey startup key from the computer. To start the computer, you'll then need to enter a password (or insert a floppy disk that contains the startup key, depending on how you set up Syskey protection) before you can log on. For details about configuring this protection, see "Adding Another Layer of Protection with Syskey," page 132.

EFS provides a secure way to store your sensitive data. Windows creates a randomly generated file encryption key (FEK) for each file to be encrypted and then transparently encrypts the data using this FEK as data is written to disk. Windows then encrypts the FEK using your public key. (Windows creates a personal encryption certificate for you with a public/private key pair the first time you use EFS.) The FEK is a symmetric key (that is, the same key is used for encrypting and decrypting data), which is orders of magnitude faster than public key encryption. The FEK, and therefore the data it protects, can be decrypted only with your certificate and its associated private key, which are available only when you log on with your user name and password. (Designated data recovery agents can also decrypt your data. For information about data recovery agents, see "Recovering Encrypted Data," page 715.) Other individuals who attempt to use your encrypted files receive an "access denied" message. Even administrators and others who have permission to take ownership of files are unable to open your encrypted files.

You can encrypt individual files or entire folders. We recommend that you encrypt folders instead of individual files. When you encrypt a folder, the existing files it contains are encrypted, and new files that you create in the folder are encrypted automatically, as are temporary files that your applications create in the folder. (For example, Microsoft Word creates a copy of a document in the folder where it's stored when you open the document for editing. If the document's folder isn't encrypted, the temporary copy isn't encrypted—giving prying eyes a potential opportunity to view your data.) For this reason, you should also consider encrypting your %Temp% and %Tmp% folders, which many applications use to store temporary copies of documents that are open for editing. (Note, however, that doing so might slow your system considerably, and it might prevent some installation programs from running properly.)

Inside Out

Avoid the risk of plaintext shreds

To prevent loss of data caused by a sudden system crash or hardware failure, EFS begins its encryption process by creating a plaintext backup of the original file. When the original has been successfully encrypted, EFS deletes the backup file. But like other files that are "deleted," the file remains on the hard disk; only the directory entry for the file is deleted. Using a file recovery tool, someone could retrieve these plaintext shreds and view the unencrypted backup copy of your file.

You can avoid this vulnerability by encrypting folders instead of individual files. When you do that, EFS never creates a plaintext backup file; your file exists on your hard disk only in encrypted form.

Before You Begin: Learn the Dangers of EFS

EFS provides secure encryption of your most important information. The encryption is so secure that if you lose the key that enables you to decrypt your data, the information is effectively lost. Windows provides no "back door" if your private key is lost (you're responsible for creating your own backup key and safely storing it), nor is there any practical way to hack these files. (If there were, it wouldn't be very good encryption.)

You can innocently lose your key in a number of ways. Suppose, for example, that you have stored your data in encrypted folders on a second volume (such as drive D). You notice that your computer is running sluggishly and its hard disk is overflowing with junk files—so you decide to reinstall Windows from scratch. Not worrying about your files on another partition, you format drive C and reinstall Windows. Although it's not apparent, reinstalling Windows creates new security identifiers (SIDs) for each user, even if you do everything exactly the same way as the last time you ran Setup. As a result, each user's encryption certificates are also different from the ones they replaced, and they can't be used to access the encrypted data stored on drive D. Even the Administrator account—which also has a new SID—can't decrypt the files from a different Windows installation.

Fortunately, with a little care, you can prevent these drastic scenarios. To learn about EFS and then begin safely using it for your important files, we recommend that you follow this approach:

1 Create an empty folder and encrypt it. (For details, see the next section, "Encrypting Your Data.")

2 Create a nonessential file in the encrypted folder (or copy a file to the folder)—and check to see that you can use it just as you would any ordinary file.

3 If your computer is not part of a domain, create a *data recovery agent*—a second user account that can be used to decrypt files should your personal encryption certificate become lost or corrupt. (For details, see "Creating a Data Recovery Agent," page 720.)

4 Back up your file recovery certificate and your personal encryption certificate along with their associated private keys. (For details, see "Backing Up Your Certificates," page 724.)

> **Note** You won't have a certificate to back up until you have encrypted at least one folder or file. A new Windows installation doesn't have encryption certificates; one is created the first time a user encrypts a folder or file.

Now you're ready to begin using EFS for your important confidential files.

> **Tip** If you encrypt files on a computer that is not joined to a domain, be sure to set up a data recovery agent. Back up both your personal certificate and the data recovery agent's file recovery certificate.

Encrypting Your Data

You'll want to encrypt any folders that contain confidential files. The most likely container for such files is your My Documents folder, although you might have documents stored in other folders, too.

To encrypt a folder, follow these steps:

1 Right-click the folder, choose Properties, click the General tab, and then click the Advanced button. (If the properties dialog box doesn't have an Advanced button, the folder is not on an NTFS-formatted volume and you can't use EFS.)

2 Select Encrypt Contents To Secure Data.

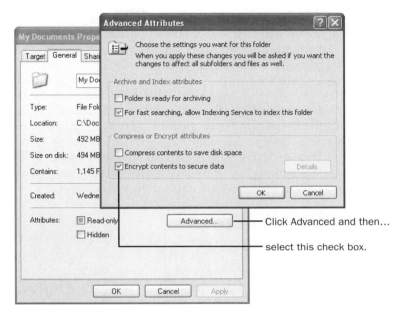

Click Advanced and then...

select this check box.

3 Click OK twice. If the folder contains any files or subfolders, Windows displays a confirmation message:

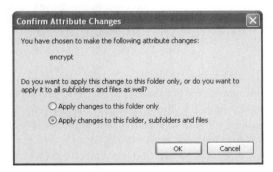

Note If you select Apply Changes To This Folder Only in the confirmation dialog box, Windows doesn't encrypt any of the files currently stored in the folder. But any new files that you create in the folder, including files that you copy or move to the folder, will be encrypted.

Chapter 21

To encrypt one or more files, follow the same procedure. You'll see a different confirmation message, shown in Figure 21-1, reminding you that the file's folder is not encrypted and giving you an opportunity to encrypt it. It's generally better not to encrypt individual files because the information you intend to protect can too easily become decrypted without your knowledge. For example, with some applications that create a copy of a document you have open for editing, the application saves the copy—which is not encrypted—and deletes the original, encrypted document. Furthermore, EFS itself creates a plaintext version of the file during the encryption process; although the copy is subsequently deleted, it remains on the hard drive, available to anyone with the proper snooping tools. You can safely encrypt static files that you use for reference only—but that you never edit—without encrypting the parent folder. Even in that situation, however, you'll probably find it simpler to encrypt the whole folder.

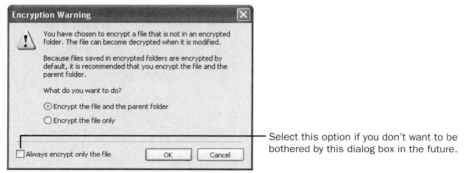

Select this option if you don't want to be bothered by this dialog box in the future.

Figure 21-1. When you encrypt individual files, Windows encourages you to encrypt the parent folder as well.

Note Some files can't be encrypted. For example, you can't encrypt any files that have the System attribute, including the page file. Those files are usually system files, and the system might be rendered unusable if some of its essential files were encrypted. For the same reason, you can't encrypt any files in the %SystemRoot% folder or any of its subfolders. Files in roaming user profiles also can't be encrypted. And files can't be both compressed and encrypted; if you encrypt a compressed file, Windows decompresses it. Your account must have Write permission for the file to encrypt or decrypt it.

Troubleshooting

Windows reports an "error applying attributes"

If you see a message box similar to the one shown here when you attempt to encrypt a file, EFS has been disabled on your computer. (The text of the message can vary, depending on whether encryption is disabled for a particular folder or for the computer.) Although the four buttons might lead you to believe that you have a choice in the matter, you don't. Regardless of which button you click, Windows refuses to encrypt your files—just as if you had clicked Cancel.

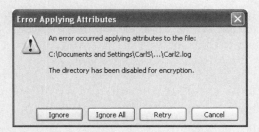

To solve this problem, you need to enable the Encrypting File System. For instructions, see "Disabling or Reenabling EFS," page 716.

Inside Out

Add encryption commands to shortcut menus

If you frequently encrypt and decrypt files and folders (for most users, it's a one-time "set it and forget it" operation), you'll find that it's tedious to right-click, choose Properties, click Advanced, select or clear a check box, and click OK twice every time you want to change encryption status. If you're comfortable using a command-line interface, you can use the Cipher command to perform these tasks. (For details, see "Using the Cipher Command," page 709.) But if you'd prefer to work with Windows Explorer, you can use an easier method: Add encryption commands to the shortcut menu that appears when you right-click a folder or file.

You can do that with Tweak UI for Windows XP (*http://www.microsoft.com/windowsxp /downloads/powertoys/xppowertoys.mspx*). In the left pane of Tweak UI, select Explorer; in the Settings box, select the Show "Encrypt" On Context Menu check box.

If you'd rather roll up your sleeves and make the change directly in the registry, follow these steps:

1 Use Registry Editor to open the HKLM\Software\Microsoft\Windows\CurrentVersion \Explorer\Advanced key.

2 Open the Edit menu, and choose New, DWORD Value.

3 Name the new value EncryptionContextMenu.

4 Double-click the EncryptionContextMenu value and set its data to 1.

This change takes effect the next time you start Windows Explorer. When you right-click a folder or file that's not encrypted, the shortcut menu includes an Encrypt command; a Decrypt command appears if the target is already encrypted.

Encrypting Offline Files

With the offline files feature, introduced with Windows 2000, you can cache a copy of files from a network share on your local computer. This capability is particularly useful for a mobile computer because it enables you to continue working with your files even when your computer is not connected to the network. (When you reconnect to the network, Windows synchronizes the local and network versions of each file.) As we have pointed out, however, mobile computers are the most vulnerable to theft, so it would be terrific to be able to encrypt the local versions of your offline files. With Windows XP (but not Windows 2000), you can.

To encrypt your offline files, do the following:

1 In Windows Explorer, choose Tools, Folder Options.

2 On the Offline Files tab, shown in Figure 21-2, select both Enable Offline Files and Encrypt Offline Files To Secure Data.

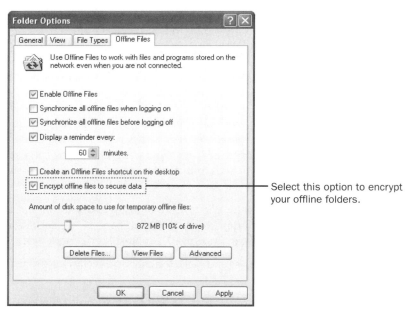

Select this option to encrypt your offline folders.

Figure 21-2. When you select this option, the local copy of your offline files is always encrypted, regardless of the files' setting in the network folder.

Chapter 21

> **Caution** The offline files feature runs under a system process, not in the context of the user currently logged on. For this reason, the offline files database (a single file that comprises all the offline files) is encrypted using the System startup key instead of the user's public key. Offline files—even when encrypted—are therefore available to all local administrators. That is, anyone who logs on with an administrator account (or any thief who makes off with your computer and figures out how to log on) has access to all offline files. You can effectively stymie thieves by removing the System startup key from the computer; you'll need to provide it each time you turn on the computer. For details, see "Adding Another Layer of Protection with Syskey," page 132.

Using the Cipher Command

Cipher.exe provides a command-line alternative for encrypting and decrypting folders and files. To encrypt or decrypt a folder or file, include the path and the appropriate switches. Use the /E switch to encrypt the folders or files you specify or the /D switch to decrypt them. For example, to encrypt the My Documents folder, including its files and subfolders, type **cipher /e /a /s:"%userprofile%\my documents"** at a command prompt.

In the file specification, you can use wildcards. You can also specify multiple folders and files in a single instance of the command; simply separate each name with a space. Table 21-1 shows Cipher's command-line switches for basic encryption and decryption operations. Cipher can also generate file encryption keys for users, create file recovery certificates, wipe unused data areas, and perform other tasks. For a complete list, type **cipher /?** at a command prompt.

> **Note** An updated version of Cipher.exe with additional capabilities was released in 2003. That version is included in Windows XP SP2, but Windows 2000 users must download it. See Microsoft Knowledge Base article 827014 for more information.

Table 21-1. **Common Command-Line Switches for Cipher.exe**

Switch	Description
/E	Encrypts the specified folders
/D	Decrypts the specified folders
/S:*folder*	Performs the operation on *folder* and its subfolders (but not on files)
/A	Performs the operation on specified files and files in specified folders

Using Encrypted Data

You'll notice no significant difference in working with encrypted folders or files if you're logged on with the same account you used when you encrypted them. In fact, you might forget that you're using encrypted files.

Inside Out

Identify encrypted files

Because EFS works transparently, knowing which folders and files are encrypted requires a close look. The process of right-clicking each file and then choosing Properties, General, Advanced (followed by Cancel, Cancel) is tedious. Fortunately, you can determine whether a folder or file is encrypted in any of these additional, and easier, ways:

- In Windows XP (but not Windows 2000), you can tell at a glance: By default, Windows Explorer displays the names of encrypted objects in green. (If they're not green, you need to set an option. In Windows Explorer, choose Tools, Folder Options. On the View tab, select Show Encrypted Or Compressed NTFS Files In Color.)

- In Windows Explorer, use Details view. Encrypted files show the letter *E* in the Attributes column. (If the Attributes column does not appear, open the View menu, click Choose Details, and then select the Attributes check box.)

- In a Command Prompt window, type **cipher** with no parameters to display the encryption state of the current folder and its files. Cipher precedes the name of each encrypted file with an *E*; a *U* (for unencrypted) identifies other files. To display only specific files (or files in another folder), append a file specification (including wildcards if you like) to the Cipher command line.

- To list all encrypted files on all local drives, type **cipher /u /n** in a Command Prompt window.

Encrypted files differ from unencrypted files in several subtle but important ways:

- **When you are logged on with an account different from the one you used when you encrypted a file...** If you try to open an encrypted file, you get an "access denied" message. Likewise, if you try to decrypt an encrypted file by clearing the encryption attribute, you get an "access denied" message. However, if you have Modify or Full Control permission, you can delete or rename an encrypted file.

- **When you copy or move an unencrypted file to an encrypted folder...** The copy you add to the encrypted folder becomes encrypted.

Tip You can override the default automatic encryption behavior by configuring a policy. In Group Policy (Gpedit.msc), open Computer Configuration\Administrative Templates \System. Double-click Do Not Automatically Encrypt Files Moved To Encrypted Folders and select Enabled.

- **When you copy an encrypted file...** If you copy an encrypted file to an NTFS volume on your computer or another computer running Windows XP or Windows 2000, it remains encrypted. (If EFS is disabled on the target computer, Windows refuses to copy the file, instead displaying a red-herring "access denied" message.) If you copy an encrypted file to a FAT volume (including floppy disks) or to an NTFS volume on a computer that is running Microsoft Windows NT, the file becomes decrypted.

- **When you move an encrypted file...**   If you move an encrypted file to another folder on the same volume, the file remains encrypted. Moving the file to another volume is essentially a "copy and then delete" process; moving your own encrypted files is handled the same way as the copy operation just described. If you move someone else's encrypted file to a FAT volume, you get an "access denied" message.

- **When you rename an encrypted file...**   The file is renamed and it remains encrypted.

- **When you delete an encrypted file...**   The restorable file (if you delete to the Recycle Bin) remains encrypted.

- **When you back up an encrypted file using Windows Backup...**   You've picked the best way to back up encrypted files or move them between systems! The files on the backup media remain encrypted, whether they're on disk or tape. (Because most removable media can't be formatted as NTFS, an ordinary copy becomes decrypted.)

- **When you use encrypted files on a different computer...**   Your personal encryption certificate and its private key must be available on the computer. You can copy the keys manually. For details, see "Backing Up Your Certificates," page 711. If you use roaming profiles, your encryption keys are automatically available on all computers you log on to with that user account. (Note, however, that if you roam between Windows 2000 and Windows XP computers, you can't access your files from Windows 2000 until you install a hotfix. See Knowledge Base article 891308 for details.)

Chapter 21

> **Caution**   Other users with permission to delete a file (that is, users with Modify or Full Control permission) can't use your encrypted files—but they can make them difficult for you to use. Any such user can rename your files, which can make them difficult to find, and also can delete your files. (Even if the user merely deletes them to the Recycle Bin and doesn't remove them altogether, the deleted files are unavailable to you because you don't have access to any other user's Recycle Bin.) Therefore, if you're concerned about protecting your files from other authorized users as well as from a thief who steals your computer, you should modify the NTFS permissions to prevent any type of modification by other users. For more information, see "Sharing Documents Securely on a Multiuser Computer," page 164.

Like the encryption process, decryption is done transparently. That is, you work with your encrypted files exactly the same way you work with unencrypted files. When Windows detects that a file you're accessing is encrypted, it finds your certificate and uses its private key to decrypt the data as it is read from the disk.

To permanently decrypt a folder or file, clear the Encrypt Contents To Secure Data check box in the Advanced Attributes dialog box. If you decrypt a folder, Windows asks whether you want to decrypt only the folder or the folder and its contents. If you choose the latter option, Windows prohibits you from decrypting any files for which you don't hold a valid encryption certificate. If you change the attribute for a file that you encrypted, Windows decrypts it without further ado. If you attempt to decrypt a file that someone else encrypted, you get an "access denied" message.

Sharing Your Encrypted Files with Other Users

A new feature in Windows XP enables you to share access to your encrypted files with one or more trusted users. The users you specify might share the computer with you or have access to the encrypted files over the network.

The only prerequisite for sharing access to an encrypted file is that each user with whom you want to share the file must have an encryption certificate on your computer. The easiest way for a user who shares your computer to create a certificate is for that user to log on and encrypt a file. Network users should export their own certificate (see "Exporting a Personal Encryption Certificate," page 726); you can then import the certificate to your computer.

> **Tip** **Checking for encryption certificates**
>
> To find out whether another user already has an encryption certificate on your computer, use the Certificates snap-in for Microsoft Management Console. (For details, see "Using the Certificates Snap-In," page 685.) Self-signed certificates, whether created on your computer or imported to your computer, appear in the Trusted People\Certificates store. Certificates issued by a certification authority (CA) appear in the Other People\Certificates store. (Note that EFS will not use certificates issued by an untrusted CA.) If Encrypting File System appears in the Intended Purposes column—you might need to enlarge the window or scroll to the right to see the column—you can share your encrypted files with this person.

To enable another user to use one of your encrypted files, follow these steps:

1 Right-click an encrypted file and choose Properties. On the General tab, click Advanced.

2 In the Advanced Attributes dialog box, click Details.

> **Note** The Details button is unavailable when you initially encrypt a file. To use this button, you must encrypt the file and then return to the Advanced Attributes dialog box. Note also that the Details button is available only when you display properties for a single file; if you select a folder or multiple files, the button is unavailable.

3 In the Encryption Details dialog box, click Add. The Select User dialog box appears, as shown in Figure 21-3.

Encrypting Files and Folders

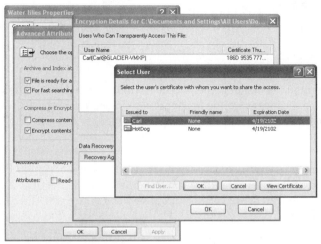

Figure 21-3. You can provide access to any account that has an Encrypting File System certificate on your computer.

4   Select the name of the user to whom you want to give access, and then click OK.

The users specified in the Encryption Details dialog box now have access to the encrypted file. Of course, they'll also need sufficient NTFS permissions to use the file and, if the file is in a shared network folder, permissions to access the network share.

Caution   Grant EFS access only to users you trust. Users who are granted access permissions also can share files with other users of their choosing. The only way you can prevent such sharing is to remove the user's Write permission for the file—but that might prevent the type of access you need. A more robust and flexible solution is available through Windows Rights Management Services (RMS), which requires Microsoft Office 2003 and Windows Server 2003 properly configured for RMS.

Accessing Encrypted Data on Remote Shares

You can use your encrypted files (or ones to which you've been granted access, as described in the previous section) when they're stored on another computer in your network. This, of course, makes it feasible for multiple users to access encrypted files, but it has other advantages as well; in particular, storing your network's important documents on a single server can simplify backup of these essential files. You can encrypt and decrypt files that are stored on a network share or, if you're using Windows XP, in a Web Distributed Authoring and Versioning (WebDAV) Web folder.

Using files stored on a network share requires a Windows 2000 Server or Windows Server 2003 domain environment, which places this topic beyond the scope of this book. Don't feel shortchanged, however; despite the otherwise superior security imposed by such domains, remote access to encrypted files on a network share is less secure than using Web folders. When files are stored on a network share, the encryption and decryption are performed on the computer where the files are stored, and the files are transmitted between computers in unencrypted form. When a file is stored in a Web folder, the file remains encrypted during transmission; all encryption and decryption take place at the user's computer.

> **Tip**   **Securely share your files over the Internet**
> Storing an encrypted file in a document folder at MSN Groups (*http://groups.msn.com*) provides the same security as storing in a local Web folder. You can share your documents with others (or retrieve them yourself from another location), and your encrypted documents remain encrypted when they're transferred across the Internet.

In addition, the use of Web folders for remotely accessing encrypted files is easier to set up and administer. And, if the Web folder is available over the Internet, you can securely access your encrypted files from anywhere in the world with an ordinary Internet connection.

You can set up a Web folder on a server that is running Internet Information Services (IIS) 5.0 or later. (Windows 2000 includes IIS 5.0; Windows XP Professional includes IIS 5.1.) To set up a Web folder, follow these steps:

1   Install IIS if you haven't already done so.

> **For information about installing and securing IIS, see "Tightening Security on Internet Information Services," page 662.**

2   Right-click the folder you want to share as a Web folder and choose Properties.

3   On the Web Sharing tab, select Share This Folder. The Edit Alias dialog box appears:

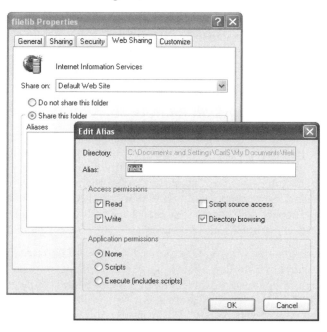

Chapter 21

4   Specify an alias (the name by which users will access the folder). Select the Read, Write, and Directory Browsing permissions. Select None in the Application Permissions box. Click OK in each dialog box.

Users can then access the Web folder in much the same way as they'd use a local folder. Its URL is *http://servername/alias*, where *servername* is the name of the server and *alias* is the alias you assigned in step 4 of the preceding procedure.

Recovering Encrypted Data

The security policy for a computer or a domain can include a data recovery policy. (In Windows 2000, a data recovery policy is required.) This policy designates one or more users as data recovery agents; these users can decrypt encrypted files even if the personal encryption certificate used to encrypt the file is no longer available. This capability makes it possible to recover encrypted files after an employee leaves a company, for example.

If your computer is running Windows 2000 and is not part of a Windows domain, the local Administrator account is the default data recovery agent. In Windows XP, stand-alone computers have no default data recovery agent; you should create one. (For details, see "Creating a Data Recovery Agent," page 720.) In a domain environment, the default data recovery agent is the Administrator account for the first domain controller in the domain.

If your computer is a member of a domain, the domain administrator can designate additional users as data recovery agents. Using the domain's Enterprise Certificate Authority, the domain administrator creates file recovery certificates for these users and adds them to Public Key Policies\Encrypted Data Recovery Agents in Local Security Settings or, more likely, in the domain security policy.

Whether your computer is a domain member or in a workgroup, running Windows XP or Windows 2000, best practices suggest not storing the private key associated with the data recovery agent's file recovery certificate on the computer. (If it's stored on the computer, the data recovery agent has access to all users' encrypted files, a situation that removes the privacy protection that EFS is designed to provide.) To restore the data recovery agent's file recovery certificate or private key when it's needed, take these steps:

1   Log on as an administrator.
2   Use the Certificates dialog box to import the file recovery certificate. The procedure is the same as that used to import a personal encryption certificate; for details, see "Importing a Personal Encryption Certificate," page 727.

If you need to recover encrypted files, it might be useful to know who encrypted the files in the first place. With Windows alone, you have no easy way to find out. However, you can use a tool named Efsinfo to show who encrypted each file and who has permission to decrypt it, including any data recovery agents. If you have a Windows XP Professional CD, you can install Efsinfo (along with a number of other useful tools) by running \Support\Tools\Setup on the CD. Efsinfo is also available as a free download from

Chapter 21

715

Microsoft; browse to *http://www.microsoft.com/windows2000/techinfo/reskit/tools/existing/efsinfo-o.asp*. (If you prefer to type a shorter URL and don't mind clicking a few links, go to *http://www.reskits.com* and look for the Windows 2000 Resource Kit Tools.)

> **For more information about Efsinfo, see the Microsoft Knowledge Base article 243026.**

A utility called EFSDump, from the good people at Sysinternals, is available at *http://www.sysinternals.com/ntw2k/source/misc.shtml*. Like Efsinfo, EFSDump shows who encrypted a file and who has access to it.

Disabling or Reenabling EFS

If you want to prevent users from encrypting files on a particular machine, you can disable EFS. If your computer is part of a domain, domain-level policies determine whether EFS can be used on a workstation. For stand-alone computers and computers that are part of a workgroup, the following sections explain how to control the availability of EFS.

Disabling or Reenabling EFS in Windows XP

To disable EFS on a computer running Windows XP Professional that is not part of a domain, follow these steps:

1 Open Registry Editor. (At a command prompt, type **regedit**.)
2 Open the HKLM\Software\Microsoft\Windows NT\CurrentVersion\EFS key.
3 Choose Edit, New, DWORD Value.
4 Type **EfsConfiguration** as the name for the new value.
5 Double-click the EfsConfiguration value and change its value data to **1**.
6 Restart the computer.

To reenable EFS, return to the same value and change it to **0**.

> **Note** Intrepid tweakers might come across a check box called Allow Users To Encrypt Files Using Encrypting File System (EFS) and assume that clearing it disables EFS. Unfortunately, this action has no effect in a workgroup environment. If you want to check it out for yourself, open Local Security Settings (Secpol.msc), select Public Key Policies, right-click Encrypting File System, and choose Properties.

Disabling or Reenabling EFS in Windows 2000

If you're using Windows 2000, follow these steps to disable EFS on a computer that is not part of a domain:

1 Open Local Security Settings. (In Control Panel, open Administrative Tools, Local Security Policy. Or, more simply, type **secpol.msc** at a command prompt.)
2 In Local Security Settings, go to Public Key Policies\Encrypted Data Recovery Agents.

3 Right-click the Administrator certificate and choose Delete.

> **Caution** Before you delete a certificate, be *sure* you have exported the file recovery certificate and its private key so that the key is available for data recovery. (For details, see "Backing Up the File Recovery Certificate," page 725.) Without it—or another valid data recovery agent certificate, such as one from a domain controller—you won't be able to reenable EFS unless you reinstall Windows 2000.

4 In response to the confirmation dialog box, click Yes.

This procedure creates an *empty recovery policy*. When the policy is empty—that is, all the data recovery agent certificates have been deleted—users who attempt to encrypt files will see the error message "There is no valid encryption recovery policy configured for this system."

To reenable EFS after you've set an empty recovery policy, you reinstall the data recovery agent certificate, as follows:

1 In Local Security Settings, go to Public Key Policies\Encrypted Data Recovery Agents.

2 Right-click Encrypted Data Recovery Agents, and choose Initialize Empty Policy. (If the command is not on the shortcut menu, you already have an empty policy; skip this step.)

3 Right-click Encrypted Data Recovery Agents, and choose Add to launch the Add Recovery Agent Wizard. Click Next.

4 On the Select Recovery Agents page, click Browse Folders and then navigate to the folder that contains the .cer file for the data recovery agent you want to add. (The Browse Directory button searches Active Directory, a feature of Windows 2000 Server–based domains.) Click Open.

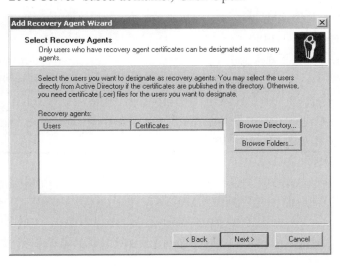

5   Here's where the wizard becomes confusing. The Select Recovery Agents page now shows the new agent as USER_UNKNOWN. This is normal. Simply click Next and then click Finish.

6   A message appears: "The certificate cannot be validated." Again, this is normal. Click OK.

The certificate for the data recovery agent (with the correct user name shown) now appears in the details pane, and you can begin encrypting files again.

Disabling EFS for Individual Folders or Files

You might want to prevent the encryption of files in a certain folder to ensure that they remain available to everyone who has access to the folder. To disable encryption within a folder, use Notepad (or another text editor) to create a file that contains the following lines:

```
[Encryption]
Disable=1
```

Save the file as Desktop.ini in the folder in which you want to prevent encryption. Any encrypted files already in the folder remain encrypted, but users who attempt to encrypt any other files will be stopped with this message: "The directory has been disabled for encryption."

Disabling encryption in this fashion doesn't disable encryption altogether, even within the folder you've set up. If you copy or move encrypted files into the folder, they remain encrypted. And if you create a subfolder within the folder, you can encrypt the subfolder and any files it contains.

Troubleshooting

Files still become encrypted after you've disabled EFS for a folder

You might discover that files added to a folder become encrypted even after you create the Desktop.ini file described here and store it in the folder. This can occur if encryption was already enabled for the folder when you added the Desktop.ini file. (With the file in place, you won't be able to set the encryption attribute for the folder.) To prevent new files from being encrypted, right-click the folder, choose Properties, click Advanced, and clear the Encrypt Contents To Secure Data check box.

It's possible, but generally not practical, to prevent certain files from being encrypted. You can do this in any of the following ways, each of which has a drawback:

- Store the file in %SystemRoot% or one of its subfolders—folders in which encryption is never allowed. (Drawbacks: Windows makes it difficult to browse to these folders, and storing the file here might not fit your system of organizing files.)

- Use the Attrib command to set the file's System attribute. (Drawback: By default, Windows Explorer does not display system files, so they're difficult to find.)

- Remove Write permission from the file for users you want to prevent from encrypting. (Drawback: Removing Write permission also prevents users from editing the file.)

Strengthening EFS Protection

EFS provides extremely strong protection against attackers. Multiple levels of encryption make it all but impossible to crack. Windows 2000 and the original release of Windows XP use expanded Data Encryption Standard (DESX), a variant of the DES developed by the United States government. By default, Windows XP SP1 and later (as well as Windows Server 2003) use Advanced Encryption Standard (AES) with a 256-bit key. In Windows XP (but not Windows 2000), you can strengthen security even more by using Triple Data Encryption Standard (3DES) to encrypt and decrypt files instead of the default algorithm. Although 3DES is more secure, it's slower because it processes each block of each file three times.

To enable 3DES protection in Windows XP, follow these steps:

1 Open Local Security Settings (Secpol.msc).

2 Select Security Settings\Local Policies\Security Options.

3 In the details pane, double-click System Cryptography: Use FIPS Compliant Algorithms For Encryption, Hashing, And Signing.

4 Select Enabled and click OK.

 Troubleshooting

Encrypted files appear corrupted

If you use a computer running Windows 2000 or Windows XP without any service pack applied, when you try to open a file encrypted on a computer running Windows Server 2003 or Windows XP SP1 or later, it appears garbled. That's because the DESX encryption used by the earlier operating systems is incompatible with the stronger AES used in the more recent operating systems. If you must maintain compatibility between systems, you can specify which of three encryption algorithms (DESX, AES, or 3DES) you want to use by editing the registry. Before you do that, however, use a system running Windows XP SP1 or later to decrypt the encrypted files; you can re-encrypt them after you change to a compatible encryption algorithm.

To specify an encryption algorithm on systems running Windows XP SP1 or later, follow these steps:

1   In Registry Editor, open the HKLM\Software\Microsoft\Windows NT\CurrentVersion \EFS key.

2   Open the Edit menu and choose New, DWORD Value.

3   Change the new value's name to AlgorithmID.

4   Double-click the AlgorithmID value and set its value data to one of the following hexadecimal values:

- ■ For DESX, type **6604**. This is compatible with all versions of Windows 2000 and Windows XP.

- ■ For AES, type **6610**. This is compatible with Windows XP SP1 and later.

- ■ For 3DES, type **6603**. This is compatible with Windows XP, regardless of service pack level.

For more details, see Knowledge Base article 329741.

Inside Out

Protect encrypted files from wily administrators

If you use EFS extensively and your computer is not a member of a domain, you might consider upgrading to Windows XP if you haven't already. That's because Windows XP adds another level of protection that directly affects the security of your encrypted files. In Windows 2000, an administrator can reset your password—a valuable trick if you forget the password. However, that means an unscrupulous administrator can reset your password, log in using your account, and peer into your encrypted files. The underhandedness won't go undetected (because your password has been changed, you'll need to contact the same administrator to reset it for you), but the damage will have been done. With Windows XP, in contrast, if anyone other than yourself changes your password, your certificates (which are needed for decrypting files, among other things) become inaccessible. Should a devious, but uninformed, administrator try to get your secrets by changing your password, you can restore access to your certificates by resetting your password to its previous value or by using your Password Reset Disk. For more information, see "Recovering a Lost Password," page 115.

Creating a Data Recovery Agent

Designating a data recovery agent—another user who can access your encrypted files— enables you to recover encrypted files if something happens to your private key.

In Windows 2000, the Administrator account is set up as the default data recovery agent. If your computer is a member of a domain, the domain administrator is the default data recovery agent. But if you're using Windows XP and your computer is not in a domain, there is no default data recovery agent.

> **Note** In Windows 2000, a data recovery agent is required. If no data recovery agent exists, you can't encrypt files. In Windows XP, however, a data recovery agent is optional (but usually desirable).

To create a data recovery agent, you must create a file recovery certificate and then designate a user to be the data recovery agent.

Generating a File Recovery Certificate

To generate a file recovery certificate, follow these steps:

1 Log on as an administrator.

2 At a command prompt, type **cipher /r:***filename*, where *filename* is the name you want to assign to the stored certificate files. Do not include a file name extension.

3 When prompted, type a password that will be used to protect the files you create.

These steps generate both a .pfx file and a .cer file with the file name you specify.

> **Caution** These files enable anyone to become a data recovery agent. Be sure to copy them to a disk and put it in a secure, safe place. Then erase these files from your hard disk.

 Inside Out

An alternative to data recovery agents

The reason Windows XP does not have a default data recovery agent for stand-alone computers is to provide enhanced security. In Windows 2000, a thief who's able to crack the Administrator account (the default data recovery agent) has access to all the encrypted files on a stolen computer. With Windows XP, the only way a thief can get your encrypted data is by knowing your user name and password.

This extra security comes with some risk: If you forget your password, you're locked out of your own files, and you have no practical way to get them back. For that reason, we suggest creating a data recovery agent as one solution. However, another solution that's easier and, perhaps, more secure is to create a Password Reset Disk. For details, see "Using a Password Reset Disk," page 116.

Designating Data Recovery Agents

You can designate any user as a data recovery agent. We recommend that you use the Administrator account.

> **Caution** Do not designate the account you use to create encrypted files as a data recovery agent. Doing so provides little or no protection. If the user profile is damaged or deleted, you will lose all the keys that allow decryption of the files.

Follow these steps to designate a data recovery agent:

1 Log on with the account that you want to designate as a data recovery agent.

2 Using the Certificates snap-in (in Windows XP, type **certmgr.msc** at a command prompt), go to Certificates – Current User\Personal.

3 Choose Action, All Tasks, Import to launch the Certificate Import Wizard. Click Next.

4 Enter the path and file name of the encryption certificate (a .pfx file) you exported (see Figure 21-4). If you click Browse, you must select Personal Information Exchange or All Files in the Files Of Type box to display .pfx files. Click Next.

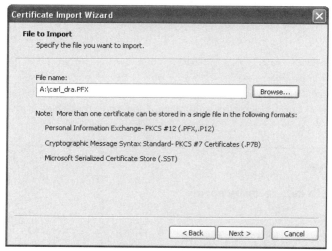

Figure 21-4. Be sure to specify the .pfx file—not the .cer file to which the Browse button leads you by default.

5 Enter the password for this certificate, and then select Mark This Key As Exportable. Click Next.

6 Select Automatically Select The Certificate Store Based On The Type Of Certificate, and then click Next. Click Finish.

7 In Local Security Settings (Secpol.msc), go to Security Settings\Public Key Policies \Encrypting File System.

8 Choose Action, Add Data Recovery Agent. Click Next.

9 On the Select Recovery Agents page, click Browse Folders and then navigate to the folder that contains the .cer file you created. (The Browse Directory button searches Active Directory.) Select the file and click Open.

10 The Select Recovery Agents page now shows the new agent as USER_UNKNOWN. Don't be alarmed by the USER_UNKNOWN text; simply click Next and then click Finish.

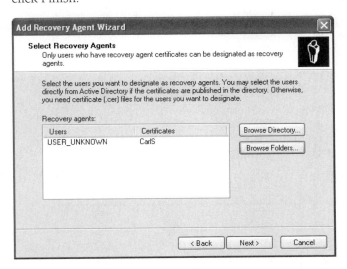

The current user is now the data recovery agent for all encrypted files on this system.

Removing the Private Key

To prevent someone from simply logging on as Administrator (or another designated data recovery agent) and viewing another user's encrypted files, you can export and remove the data recovery agent's private key. Keep the key in a secure location—without it, you can't use the file recovery certificate.

To remove the data recovery agent's private key, follow these steps:

1 Log on with the account you designated as a data recovery agent.

2 In Certificates (Certmgr.msc), go to Certificates – Current User\Personal \Certificates.

3 Right-click the File Recovery certificate (so identified in the Intended Purposes column), and then choose All Tasks, Export to launch the Certificate Export Wizard. Click Next.

4 Select Yes, Export The Private Key, and then click Next.

5 Select Enable Strong Protection and Delete The Private Key If The Export Is Successful. Click Next.

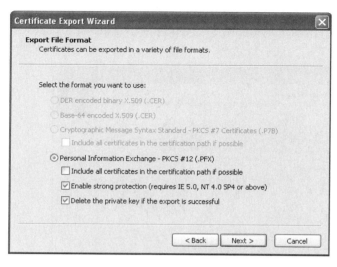

6   Enter a password twice, and then click Next.

7   Specify the path and file name for the exported file.

8   Click Next and then click Finish.

As with the file recovery certificates, you should copy the file to a removable disk, store it in a secure location, and then remove the file from your hard disk.

The data recovery agent's public key is now used to encrypt a copy of the FEK with each encrypted file, but because the private key is not available, the data recovery agent can't view the files. To reestablish the data recovery agent's access to encrypted files, import the private key you just exported, using the same procedure as for importing a personal certificate. For details, see "Importing a Personal Encryption Certificate," page 727.

Backing Up Your Certificates

When you use encryption for the first time (and you don't already have a certificate that's valid for EFS), Windows creates a self-signed certificate for EFS. (*Self-signed* means that the certificate has not been granted by a trusted certification authority that can confirm your identity. Such verification is unnecessary for this purpose; in this case, the signature merely confirms that the certificate was created while your account was logged on.) This certificate becomes your personal encryption certificate, and it contains the public/ private key pair used for encrypting and decrypting files while you're logged on.

Each user who encrypts files on a system has a personal encryption certificate. In addition, Windows can create a certificate for the designated data recovery agent. This certificate, whose purpose is shown as File Recovery, is not the same as that user's personal encryption certificate, whose purpose is shown as Encrypting File System.

All users should have a backup of their personal encryption certificate. More important, the system administrator should have a backup of the file recovery certificate and the data recovery agent's private key. Without one or the other of the certificates, encrypted files are unusable.

Backing Up the File Recovery Certificate

The file recovery certificate provides an administrative alternative for decrypting files if a user's personal encryption certificate is unavailable for any reason. Having a backup of this certificate is essential if you plan to use EFS.

To back up the file recovery certificate, follow these steps:

1 At a command prompt, type **certmgr.msc** to open the Certificate console.

2 In the console tree, open Certificates – Current User\Personal\Certificates.

3 Find the certificate that shows File Recovery in the Intended Purposes column. (You might need to scroll to the right to see the column.)

4 Right-click the file recovery certificate and choose All Tasks, Export.

5 In the Certificate Export Wizard, click Next on the welcome page.

6 Select Yes, Export The Private Key and click Next.

7 On the Export File Format page, select Personal Information Exchange – PKCS #12 (.PFX). Then select the Enable Strong Protection check box. Click Next.

Chapter 21

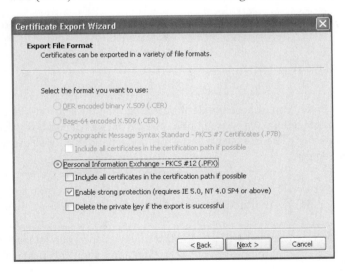

8 On the Password page, type a password to protect the exported certificate file, type it again, and then click Next.

9 On the File To Export page, specify a path and file name for the exported file, and then click Next. Confirm your settings and click Finish.

Exporting a Personal Encryption Certificate

To back up a personal encryption certificate, take these steps:

1 Log on as the user whose certificate you want to back up.

2 In Microsoft Internet Explorer, choose Tools, Internet Options. On the Content tab of the Internet Options dialog box, click Certificates to open the Certificates dialog box.

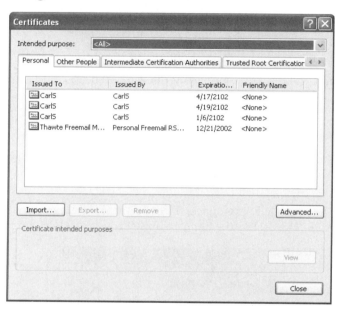

> **Note** If you prefer, you can use the Certificates snap-in for Microsoft Management Console for this procedure. We chose to open the Certificates dialog box through Internet Options because this route is available and easily understandable for all users; no special privileges are required.

3 On the Personal tab, select the certificate that shows Encrypting File System in the Certificate Intended Purposes box at the bottom of the dialog box.

> **Note** Windows creates this certificate the first time you encrypt a folder or file. Unless you have encrypted something—or you created an encryption certificate in some other way—the certificate won't exist.

4   Click Export to launch the Certificate Export Wizard, and then click Next.

5   Select Yes, Export The Private Key, and then click Next two times.

6   Specify a password for the .pfx file. It doesn't need to be the same as your logon password. Click Next.

7   Specify the path and file name for the exported file.

8   Click Next and then click Finish.

As you'll see in the next section, the import process makes it easy to install your certificate on another computer—and thereby provide access to your encrypted files. For that reason, be careful to observe these guidelines:

● When you export your certificate, be sure to protect it with a password that can't be guessed easily. Unlike the case of logon attempts, no policies exist to prevent further attempts after a certain number of incorrect guesses. (On the other hand, be sure to use a password that you can remember when the need arises!)

● Be sure to keep your certificate files—whether they're on a floppy disk, a hard disk, or some other medium—in a secure place.

Importing a Personal Encryption Certificate

You will need to import your personal certificate—one that you exported to disk using the procedure in the preceding section—in either of the following situations:

● You want to use your encrypted files on a different computer.

● Your original personal certificate is accidentally lost or becomes corrupt.

To import a personal encryption certificate, follow these steps:

1   In Internet Explorer, choose Tools, Internet Options. On the Content tab of the Internet Options dialog box, click Certificates to open the Certificates dialog box.

2   Click Import to launch the Certificate Import Wizard, and then click Next.

3   Enter the path and file name of the encryption certificate (a .pfx file) you exported, and then click Next. If you click Browse, you need to select Personal Information Exchange in the Files Of Type box to see .pfx files.

4   Enter the password, select other options if you want, and then click Next.

Chapter 21

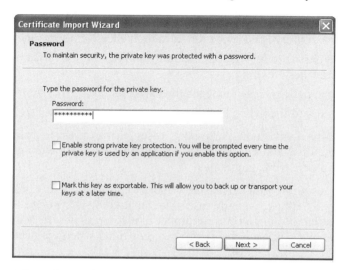

5   Select Place All Certificates In The Following Store, click Browse, and then select Personal. Click OK, Next, and then Finish.

> **Tip**   As a quick alternative to the first three steps of the preceding procedure, you can simply double-click the encryption certificate file in Windows Explorer. Doing so launches the Certificate Import Wizard.

Creating a New Personal Encryption Certificate

If you lose your personal encryption certificate, you can create a new one using Cipher.exe, the command-line encryption utility. At a command prompt, simply type **cipher /k** to create a new personal encryption certificate for the user running Cipher. (By using the RunAs command to launch Cipher, you can create certificates for other users.) Of course, you can't use the new certificate to decrypt files that were encrypted using the public key from your old certificate.

Chapter 21

Managing Security Through Group Policy and Security Templates

Group Policy is a feature of Microsoft Windows XP Professional and Windows 2000 that lets an administrator configure a computer and, optionally, prevent users from changing that configuration. Administrators can use Group Policy to set standard desktop configurations; restrict what settings users are allowed to change; specify scripts to run at startup, shutdown, logon, and logoff; redirect users' special folders (such as My Documents) to network drives; and more. In addition—and more pertinent to the topic of this book—administrators can use Group Policy to control a number of security settings.

> **Note** To manage Group Policy in Windows XP Professional or Windows 2000, you must be logged on as a member of the Administrators group. Group Policy is not available in Windows XP Home Edition.

The ideal environment for using Group Policy is a Microsoft Windows Server 2003 or Windows 2000 Server domain, in which administrators can centrally configure computers throughout sites, domains, or organizational units. In a domain environment, administrators can specify unique policies for different computers, users, or security groups. Managing Group Policy in an Active Directory domain environment is well documented in a number of books about administering Windows servers; two good examples are *Microsoft Windows Server 2003 Administrator's Companion* by Charlie Russel, Sharon Crawford, and Jason Gerend (Microsoft Press, 2003) and *Microsoft Windows 2000 Server Resource Kit* (Microsoft Press, 2000).

In this book, however, we focus on using Group Policy to make settings on a computer running Windows XP Professional or Windows 2000 in a workgroup environment. We further narrow our focus by concentrating on security-related policy settings. Our earlier book, *Microsoft Windows XP Inside Out, Second Edition* (Microsoft Press, 2005), provides more general information about using Group Policy in a workgroup environment. A comprehensive collection of Group Policy tools, white papers, reference materials, and deployment information is available online by visiting *http://www.microsoft.com/grouppolicy/*.

In this chapter, we first examine the security settings you can make through Group Policy and explain how to apply these settings using Microsoft Management Console (MMC) snap-ins. In a workgroup, you must make Group Policy settings on each computer where you want such restrictions imposed; you can't apply Group Policy settings to all computers, users, or groups on the network in a single operation, as you can in a domain. However, by using security templates—another subject covered in this chapter—you can store all your security-related settings in a file that you can then use to apply the settings on each computer. The final topic of this chapter is the Security Configuration And Analysis MMC snap-in that enables you to compare your current security settings with those of a security template and apply the template settings if you choose.

Security Checklist: Group Policy and Security Templates

Although the default configuration for Windows is reasonably secure for most situations, you should consider taking the following steps to tighten your computer's security:

- Learn about the available security-related policies.
- Use Group Policy to apply settings in the Administrative Templates folders.
- For a one-time configuration of a single computer, use Local Security Settings (or Group Policy) to apply security settings.
- Consider making different security settings for different groups of users. (Using a workaround described in this chapter, you can do that even on computers that are not part of an Active Directory domain.)
- Modify or create a security template to incorporate the security settings you want to apply to multiple computers (or multiple times to a single computer).
- Perform a security analysis to see how your current security settings compare with those in your security template.
- Apply the settings from your security template.

Exploring Security-Related Policies

Before you begin setting security policies, you need to understand what sorts of policies and settings are available. You can then configure the policies that most interest (and concern) you—either by making settings directly or by configuring and applying a security template. You can view most of the security-related policies in an MMC console named Local Security Settings, which is shown in Figure 22-1.

You can open Local Security Settings in either of two ways:

- In Control Panel, open Administrative Tools, Local Security Policy. (If you use Category view in Windows XP, you'll find Administrative Tools in the Performance And Maintenance category.)
- At a command prompt, type **secpol.msc**.

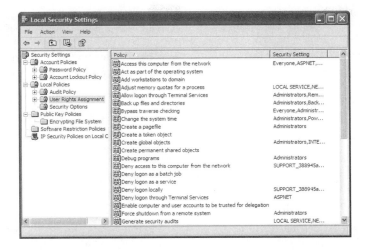

Figure 22-1. Local Security Settings controls a number of settings that affect all users on a single computer.

In tables in this chapter and throughout the book, we explain the various policies presented in Local Security Settings:

- **Security Settings\Account Policies\Password Policy:** See Table 4-3, "Password Policies," page 115.

- **Security Settings\Account Policies\Account Lockout Policy:** See Table 4-4, "Account Lockout Policies," page 132.

- **Security Settings\Local Policies\Audit Policy:** See Table 23-1, "Audit Policies for Security Events," page 775.

- **Security Settings\Local Policies\User Rights Assignment:** See Table 22-1, "User Rights Assignment Policies," page 733.

- **Security Settings\Local Policies\Security Options:** See Table 22-2, "Security Options Policies," page 737.

- **Security Settings\Public Key Policies:** See "Disabling or Reenabling EFS," page 716.

- **Security Settings\IP Security Policies On Local Computer:** See "Restricting Ports Using IP Security," page 640.

> **Note** The path to each policy folder shown in this list assumes that Security Settings is the console root, which is the case in Local Security Settings (Secpol.msc). To display these policy folders in the Group Policy console (Gpedit.msc), open Local Computer Policy \Computer Configuration\Windows Settings\Security Settings.

Chapter 22

> **Tip** An excellent resource for discovering the huge range of available group policies is a Microsoft Excel spreadsheet titled "Group Policy Settings Reference." For more detail, a document titled "Threats and Countermeasures" provides in-depth information. You can download both files from *http://www.microsoft.com/downloads*; search for each file by entering its title in the Keywords box.

Exploring User Rights

User rights are a collection of policies that determine what actions specified users and members of specified security groups can perform. Unlike permissions and access control lists (ACLs), which control access to a specific object (such as a file or a printer), user rights apply to operations that affect the entire computer.

User rights comprise two broad categories of rights: logon rights and privileges. *Logon rights* determine who is allowed to log on to the computer. *Privileges* determine who can perform other actions on the computer, such as backing up files or setting the system time. In Local Security Settings, logon rights and privileges are displayed in the Security Settings\Local Policies\User Rights Assignment folder.

You can specify which user accounts and security groups are granted each user right. To see all the users and groups who have a particular right, double-click the name of the right in the details pane. A dialog box similar to the one shown in Figure 22-2 appears.

Table 22-1 lists the user rights that you can control in Windows XP and Windows 2000 and shows the users and groups who are assigned the right in a default workstation configuration. For any right whose purpose isn't obvious from its name, a description appears in parentheses. The users assigned to each right by default are appropriate in most situations, and you'll seldom need to add a built-in user or group to the defaults. If you've created your own security groups, you might want to grant certain rights to members of those groups.

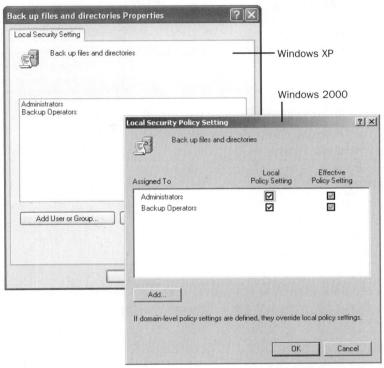

Figure 22-2. To modify the list of user accounts and security groups that have a particular right, double-click the right to display its properties dialog box.

Table 22-1. **User Rights Assignment Policies**

Policy (Description)	Default
Logon Rights	
Access this computer from the network	Administrators, Backup Operators, Everyone, Power Users, Users
Allow logon through Terminal Services* (Enables a user to log on through Remote Desktop.)	Administrators, Remote Desktop Users
Log on as a batch job (Enables a user to be logged on using a batch-queue facility. Scheduled Tasks and certain other services use this method for logging on users; Scheduled Tasks automatically grants this right as needed.)	Administrator, Support_*xxxxxxxx* (System has the right inherently)
Log on as a service (To run a service under a user account, this right must be granted to the account.)	Network Service (Local Service and System have the right inherently)

Table 22-1. **User Rights Assignment Policies**

Policy (Description)	Default
Log on locally (Enables a user to log on by working directly at the computer's keyboard.)	Administrators, Backup Operators, Guest, Power Users, Users
Deny access to this computer from the network (Takes precedence over the "Access this computer from the network" right.)	Support_*xxxxxxxx*
Deny logon as a batch job (Takes precedence over the "Log on as a batch job" right.)	No one
Deny logon as a service (Takes precedence over the "Log on as a service" right.)	No one
Deny logon locally (Takes precedence over the "Log on locally" right.)	Guest, Support_*xxxxxxxx*
Deny logon through Terminal Services* (Takes precedence over the "Allow logon through Terminal Services" right.)	No one
Privileges	
Act as part of the operating system (Enables a process to authenticate as any user and gain access to the same resources as that user.)	No one (System has the right inherently)
Add workstations to domain (Valid only on domain controllers.)	No one
Adjust memory quotas for a process** (Can be misused to instigate a denial-of-service attack—another reason not to use an administrator account as your everyday account.)	Administrators, Local Service, Network Service
Back up files and directories (Enables a user to back up files and folders, including those for which the user has not been granted any permissions in the object's ACL.)	Administrators, Backup Operators
Bypass traverse checking (Enables a user to traverse file folder trees, even through a folder for which the user has no other permissions. This privilege doesn't enables a user to list the contents of a folder; that ability is controlled by ACLs.)	Administrators, Backup Operators, Everyone, Power Users, Users
Change the system time	Administrators, Power Users
Create a pagefile (Enables a user to create and adjust the size of the virtual memory page file.)	Administrators
Create a token object (Enables a process authenticated as a user to create a token that can be used to access local resources.)	No one (System has the right inherently)
Create global objects*** (Enables a user to create global objects in a Terminal Services session.)	Administrator, Local Service

Table 22-1. **User Rights Assignment Policies**

Policy (Description)	Default
Create permanent shared objects (Enables a process to create a directory object. This task is ordinarily handled by kernel-mode components, which already have this right—so you shouldn't grant it to any users or groups.)	No one (System has the right inherently)
Debug programs (Most programming languages come with a debugger of some sort, and you don't need this right to use those debuggers. This right enables a user to attach a de-bugger to any process, including critical operating system components.)	Administrators
Enable computer and user accounts to be trusted for delegation (Valid only on domain controllers.)	No one
Force shutdown from a remote system (Enables a user to shut down a computer from another network location.)	Administrators
Generate security audits (Enables a process to generate entries in the Security log.)	Local Service, Network Service (System has the right inherently)
Impersonate a client after authentication***	Administrators, Local Service
Increase scheduling priority (Enables a user to change the scheduling priority of a task in Task Manager.)	Administrators
Load and unload device drivers (Enables a user to install and remove drivers for Plug and Play devices. Because device drivers run as highly privileged programs, attackers can use them to install malicious code that appears to be a device driver. You should grant this right only to users who are careful enough to install only drivers that have verified digital signatures or that are known to be valid.)	Administrators
Lock pages in memory (Enables a process to keep data in physical memory, preventing it from using virtual memory. This privilege is a relic from Microsoft Windows NT and no longer serves any purpose.)	No one (System has the right inherently.)
Manage auditing and security log (Enables a user to configure auditing for objects such as files, printers, and registry keys. Also allows a user to view and clear the Security log.)	Administrators
Modify firmware environment values	Administrators
Perform volume maintenance tasks* (Enables a user to run disk management programs, such as Disk Cleanup, Disk Defragmenter, and Disk Management.)	Administrators

Chapter 22

Table 22-1. **User Rights Assignment Policies**

Policy (Description)	Default
Profile single process (Enables a user to use Performance Monitor to monitor non-system processes.)	Administrators, Power Users
Profile system performance (Enables a user to use Performance Monitor to monitor system processes.)	Administrators
Remove computer from docking station (Enables a user to undock a portable computer by choosing the Eject PC command on the Start menu.)	Administrators, Power Users, Users
Replace a process level token (Enables a parent process to replace the access token that is associated with a child process.)	Local Service, Network Service (System has the right inherently.)
Restore files and directories (Enables a user to restore backed-up files and folders, including those for which the user has not been granted any permissions in the object's access control list.)	Administrators, Backup Operators
Shut down the system	Administrators, Backup Operators, Power Users, Users
Synchronize directory service data (Valid only on domain controllers.)	No one
Take ownership of files or other objects (Allows a user to take ownership of any securable object, such as files and folders on an NTFS volume, printers, and registry keys.)	Administrators

*Not available in Windows 2000.
**In Windows 2000, this right is called Increase Quotas.
***Added to Windows 2000 with SP4 and to Windows XP with SP2.

Exploring Security Options

The security options policies provide a number of interesting options for locking down your system. Table 22-2 explains the settings available in Security Settings\Local Policies\Security Options. You should carefully read the name of the policy and its description before you change any of the default settings, which provide a reasonable (but not extreme) level of security for most users in small businesses and homes. In particular, be sure you understand whether you need to enable or disable a setting to increase security; the effect of each setting is not always obvious.

Note Security options policies that are effective only on servers running Windows Server 2003, Windows 2000 Server, or another server operating system are not included in Table 22-2.

Tip   Change policies selectively

Table 22-2 describes dozens of policies, most of which have little or no effect on stand-alone computers or computers in a workgroup in most home and small business settings. So which policies should you consider changing? Those in the Accounts, Interactive Logon, and Shutdown categories are most likely to be of value to someone securing computers in such situations. The Devices and Network Security categories also have some policies of interest. The rest of the policies apply primarily to computers in large domains.

Table 22-2. **Security Options Policies**

Policy Name*	Security Setting
Accounts: Administrator account status**	Setting this policy to Disabled disables the Administrator user account. Even if you disable Administrator, the account remains available when you start your computer in Safe Mode. You can secure the Administrator account in less drastic ways; for details, see "Securing the Administrator Account," page 99.
Accounts: Guest account status**	Setting this policy to Disabled disables the Guest account. Traditional advice for securing Windows NT and Windows 2000 workstations recommends this action, but it can cause problems in Windows XP. If you use Simple File Sharing, and if you want to share folders or printers with other network users, the Guest account must be enabled. For details about this type of network setup, see "Windows Sharing and Security Models," page 17.
Accounts: Limit local account use of blank passwords to console logon only**	Enabling this policy (the default) prevents users from logging on remotely by using a user account that has no password. Accounts with blank passwords can't be used to log on over the network or for remote logons with Remote Desktop Connection, Terminal Services, Telnet, FTP, or other network services. For security, this policy should always be enabled.
Accounts: Rename administrator account	With this policy, you can assign a different user name to the security identifier (SID) associated with the Administrator account. This trick is useful for hiding the Administrator account from attackers; it forces them to obtain both a user name and a password (rather than a password only) to log on with this all-powerful account.
Accounts: Rename guest account	You can use this policy to change the user name for the SID associated with the Guest account. Such a smokescreen hides another potential entry point known to all attackers.
Audit: Audit the access of global system objects	This policy allows you to audit some additional system objects if you choose to audit object access. (For details about auditing, see "Auditing Security Events," page 773.) This policy is disabled by default, and few users have any reason to change this setting.

Chapter 22

Table 22-2. **Security Options Policies**

Policy Name*	Security Setting
Audit: Audit the use of Backup and Restore privilege	Ordinarily, nothing is recorded in the Security log when someone backs up or restores files, even if you choose to audit privilege use. Enabling this policy includes each use of the privilege, generating an audit event for every file that is backed up or restored. If you're concerned that a user in the Administrators or Backup Operators group is using Windows Backup to make off with your files, enable this policy and enable auditing of privilege use, as explained in "Enabling Security Auditing," page 774.
Audit: Shut down system immediately if unable to log security audits	Depending on how you configure event logging, the Security log might become full, allowing no additional entries. At this point, any actions that would ordinarily generate an event in the Security log go unrecorded. Enabling this policy prevents unrecorded events in a rather drastic fashion: by immediately halting the computer and displaying a blue screen error. To recover, an administrator must log on, clear the Security log (presumably after examining and exporting its contents), and then reset a registry value. For details, see "Ensuring That You Don't Miss Any Security Events," page 786.
DCOM: Machine Access Restrictions in Security Descriptor Definition Language (SDDL) syntax**	This policy, which is available only in Windows XP with Service Pack 2 (SP2) installed, sets access control entries that determine the level of access granted to users of Microsoft Distributed Component Object Model (DCOM) applications. (DCOM supports communication among objects on different computers. For more information, visit *http://go.microsoft.com/fwlink/?LinkId=20922*.) The default setting in SP2 prohibits remote access by anonymous users, which is a change from pre-SP2 behavior. Modifying these settings can cause DCOM applications to stop working or can expose security vulnerabilities, so they're generally best left unchanged.
DCOM: Machine Launch Restrictions in Security Descriptor Definition Language (SDDL) syntax**	This policy, which is available only in Windows XP with SP2 installed, sets access control entries that determine which users can launch DCOM applications. By default, members of the Administrators group can launch and activate applications locally and remotely; the Everyone group can launch and activate locally only.
Devices: Allow undock without having to log on**	When this policy is enabled, the command for removing a portable computer from its docking station is available from the Welcome screen or the Log On To Windows dialog box, which is available to anyone. Disabling this policy makes the undocking command available only after a user successfully logs on.

Chapter 22

Table 22-2. **Security Options Policies**

Policy Name*	Security Setting
Devices: Allowed to format and eject removable media (In Windows 2000: Allowed to eject removable NTFS media)	By default, only members of the Administrators group can format or eject certain types of removable media, such as Iomega Jaz drives or removable hard disks. (This policy does not restrict the use of floppy disks, CD-ROM discs, or USB flash drives (UFDs). For information about securing UFDs, see "Restricting Access to Removable Storage Devices," page 175.) To grant this ability to others, select an option other than Administrators. Note that Interactive Users is not the name of a security group; rather, it refers to any user who logs on locally.
Devices: Prevent users from installing printer drivers	When enabled, this policy allows only members of the Administrators or Power Users group to install a printer driver in order to add a network printer. If it's disabled (the default on workstations), any user can install a printer driver as part of adding a network printer. Regardless of this policy's setting, any user can add a network printer if the driver is already installed on the local machine. Also, this policy does not affect the installation of drivers for local (non-network) printers.
Devices: Restrict CD-ROM access to locally logged-on user only	Enabling this policy prevents remote users (including other network users) from accessing a computer's CD-ROM drives while anyone is logged on locally. If no one is logged on, other network users can access the drives. (This policy and the one that follows are intended more to prevent conflicts arising from two users accessing a resource simultaneously than as security measures to prevent use of your drives.)
Devices: Restrict floppy access to locally logged-on user only	Enabling this policy prevents remote users from accessing your computer's floppy drives while anyone is logged on to your computer. However, if no one is logged on locally, the floppy drive is accessible to network users, even when this policy is enabled.
Devices: Unsigned driver installation behavior	This policy determines what happens when a user attempts to install a device driver that hasn't been certified by the Windows Hardware Quality Lab (WHQL). You can set the policy to allow installation, prevent installation, or allow installation only after displaying a warning.
Domain member: Digitally encrypt or sign secure channel data (always)***	This policy affects only computers that are joined to a domain. Enabling it requires that all secure data channel communication with a domain controller be encrypted. If the domain controller isn't configured to sign or encrypt secure traffic, errors ensue.

Chapter 22

Table 22-2. **Security Options Policies**

Policy Name*	Security Setting
Domain member: Digitally encrypt secure channel data (when possible)***	This policy affects only computers that are joined to a domain. Enabling it ensures that all secure channel traffic is encrypted when the domain controller supports that capability.
Domain member: Digitally sign secure channel data (when possible)***	This policy affects only computers that are joined to a domain. Enabling it ensures that all secure channel traffic is digitally signed when the domain controller supports that capability.
Domain member: Disable machine account password changes**	When this policy is disabled (the default), a domain member computer periodically changes its computer account password. Computer account passwords (not to be confused with user account passwords) are used to establish secure channel communications between domain members and domain controllers.
Domain member: Maximum machine account password age**	This policy determines the maximum allowable age for a domain member computer's machine account password.
Domain member: Require strong (Windows 2000 or later) session key***	When enabled, this policy permits establishment of a secure channel only with a domain controller that supports 128-bit encryption; if disabled, this policy permits 64-bit session keys.
Interactive logon: Do not display last user name	When this policy is disabled (the default), the Log On To Windows dialog box displays the user name of the last person to log on. This setting is convenient for a workstation used primarily by one person, because that person can avoid typing his or her user name at each logon. Enabling the policy leaves blank the User Name box in the Log On To Windows dialog box, preventing someone from learning a valid user name simply by looking at the logon screen.
Interactive logon: Do not require CTRL+ALT+DEL (In Windows 2000: Disable CTRL+ALT+DEL requirement for logon)	When this policy is disabled, a user must press Ctrl+Alt+Delete before the Log On To Windows dialog box is displayed. (This policy has no effect if the computer is configured to use the Welcome screen in Windows XP.) Although the extra keystroke is inconvenient, it prevents attackers' use of programs that attempt to capture a user's password as it's entered.
Interactive logon: Message text for users attempting to log on	This policy sets the body text for a message that is displayed before each logon. For details, see "Displaying a Welcome Message—or a Warning," page 128.
Interactive logon: Message title for users attempting to log on	This policy sets the title bar text for a message that is displayed before each logon. For details, see "Displaying a Welcome Message—or a Warning," page 128.

Chapter 22

Table 22-2. **Security Options Policies**

Policy Name*	Security Setting
Interactive logon: Number of previous logons to cache (in case domain controller is not available)	This policy affects only computers that are joined to a domain. Ordinarily, when you log on using a domain account, Windows retrieves your account information from the domain controller (DC). If the DC is not available at logon time, a user can log on using account information cached on your local computer. This policy specifies the number of unique users whose account information is cached. Setting the policy to 0 disables it. Caching this information offers convenience when the DC is unavailable, but it does provide a slight opportunity for an attacker who disconnects the computer from the network.
Interactive logon: Prompt user to change password before expiration	This policy specifies the number of days in advance a user is warned of impending user account password expiration.
Interactive logon: Require Domain Controller authentication to unlock workstation**	This policy affects only computers that are joined to a domain. If this policy is disabled (the default), a workstation that has been locked by a domain user can be unlocked using locally cached account information. When the policy is enabled, a workstation can be unlocked only by authenticating with the domain controller.
Interactive logon: Require smart card**	This policy, when enabled, forces users to log on using a smart card. (A *smart card* is a credit card–sized device that stores certificates, passwords, and other personal information. On computers equipped with a smart card reader, users can log on by inserting the smart card and entering a personal identification number instead of entering a user name and password.)
Interactive logon: Smart card removal behavior	This policy specifies what happens if the smart card for the logged-on user is removed from the smart card reader. You can configure the policy to do nothing, lock the workstation, or log the user off.
Microsoft network client: Digitally sign communications (always)	Enabling this policy requires the use of signed packets with Server Message Block (SMB), an authentication protocol that can be used for communications between computers running Windows XP and Windows 2000. Both client and server computers must support SMB signing; and if this policy is enabled, it must be enabled or required on both ends. Although the use of SMB signing prevents certain types of attacks, it can slow down your computer slightly.
Microsoft network client: Digitally sign communications (if server agrees)	Enabling this policy causes the SMB client to digitally sign packets when communicating with an SMB server on which SMB signing is enabled or required.

Chapter 22

741

Table 22-2. **Security Options Policies**

Policy Name*	Security Setting
Microsoft network client: Send unencrypted pass-word to third-party SMB servers	Enabling this policy allows passwords to be sent in plain text to non-Microsoft SMB servers that do not support password authentication.
Network access: Allow anonymous SID/Name translation**	Enabling this policy allows a user who knows the security identi-fier (SID) of a user account to obtain the user name associated with the SID. This option would allow an attacker to discover the name of the built-in Administrator account even if you renamed it as a security precaution. Leave this policy disabled.
Network access: Do not allow anonymous enumer-ation of SAM accounts**	This policy prevents users with an anonymous connection to the computer from enumerating the user names of domain accounts. In certain network configurations with multiple domains, it's useful to disable this policy; all other users should leave it enabled.
Network access: Do not allow anonymous enumer-ation of SAM accounts and shares (In Windows 2000: Additional restrictions for anonymous connections)	Enabling this policy prevents users with an anonymous connec-tion from engaging in certain activities, including enumerating the names of domain accounts and network shares.
Network access: Do not allow storage of credentials or .NET Passports for network authentication**	When enabled, this policy prevents Stored User Names And Passwords from saving passwords and logon credentials. Stored User Names And Passwords provides a secure, convenient method of managing credentials for multiple Web sites, accounts, and domains.
Network access: Let Everyone permissions apply to anonymous users**	In Windows XP, when this policy is disabled, anonymous users are not considered members of the Everyone group, and there-fore permissions granted to the Everyone group do not apply to anonymous users. Anonymous users can access only resources for which the Anonymous group has been given explicit permis-sion. Enabling this policy includes anonymous users in the Everyone group, which is always the case in Windows 2000 and Windows NT.
Network access: Named Pipes that can be accessed anonymously**	This policy lists the named pipes that can be accessed by an anonymous connection. (A *named pipe* is an area of memory used for communication between two processes.) Programs and services that establish the pipes generally manage these settings; unless you really know what you're doing, it's best to leave this one alone.

Chapter 22

Table 22-2. **Security Options Policies**

Policy Name*	Security Setting
Network access: Remotely accessible registry paths**	In a domain-based environment, certain services require remote access to the registry. The list of registry keys in this policy controls which keys are available for this type of access. (By default, users with appropriate permissions have access to a much greater portion of the registry.) If your computer is not joined to a domain, you can safely delete these registry paths—although there's no compelling reason to do so. (To prevent remote access to your computer's registry, a better solution is to disable the Remote Registry service. For details, see "Shutting Down Unneeded Services," page 650.)
Network access: Shares that can be accessed anonymously**	This policy lists network shares that can be accessed by anonymous users. Except in rare situations, you'll want to include only the two administrative shares placed here by Windows itself: COMCFG and DFS$.
Network access: Sharing and security model for local accounts**	This policy is at the heart of the different sharing models available in Windows XP Professional for computers that are not joined to a domain. You can select between Classic and Guest Only; the latter setting is synonymous with Simple File Sharing. Setting this policy is merely an alternative to the Use Simple File Sharing option on the View tab of the Folder Options dialog box. For details about the two sharing and security models, see "Windows Sharing and Security Models," page 17.
Network security: Do not store LAN Manager hash value on next password change**	The *LAN Manager hash value* is a value derived from a user account password that is used for logging on to domains running Windows NT and other earlier operating systems. If all the computers on your network use Windows 2000, Windows XP, or Windows Server 2003, you don't need the LAN Manager hash. Because it presents a security risk (it's a useful piece of information for password crackers, and it's relatively easy for them to get), you should enable this policy if you don't need to log on to networks running earlier operating systems.
Network security: Force logoff when logon hours expire (In Windows 2000: Automatically log off users when logon time expires)	Although it might sound as though you can use this policy to forcibly log off users who are logged on when they shouldn't be, it works only with a domain controller and an SMB server. (Using the /Times switch with the Net User command, you can specify logon hours for particular users. They can't log on outside those hours, but if they're already logged on, they can continue working. For details, see Table 4-2, "Net User Parameters for Adding Accounts," page 90.)

Chapter 22

Table 22-2. **Security Options Policies**

Policy Name*	Security Setting
Network security: LAN Manager authentication level	This policy determines which challenge/response authentication protocol is used for network logons. The options for this policy appear in the list in increasing order of security. The less secure options (at the top of the list) are provided for compatibility with networks running Windows NT and other earlier operating systems. If all network computers that connect to your computer use Windows 2000, Windows XP, or Windows Server 2003, you should choose the most secure option, Send NTLMv2 Response Only\Refuse LM & NTLM. For more information about these choices and other operating systems, see "Controlling the Logon and Authentication Process," page 55.
Network security: LDAP client signing requirements**	This policy specifies whether your computer's communications with an LDAP server must be digitally signed.
Network security: Minimum session security for NTLM SSP based (including secure RPC) clients**	The four options in this policy determine the minimum client security requirements for communications between networked client/server applications. If all computers on your network use Windows 2000 (with 128-bit encryption), Windows XP, or Windows Server 2003, you can select all four options to provide additional security.
Network security: Minimum session security for NTLM SSP based (including secure RPC) servers**	This policy provides the same options as the preceding policy, but it affects the server side of the communication.
Recovery console: Allow automatic administrative logon	When this policy is disabled (the default), Recovery Console requires entry of the password for the Administrator account before granting access. Enabling this policy eliminates the password requirement, allowing anyone with physical access to your computer and a Windows CD to boot into Recovery Console with administrative privileges.

Table 22-2. **Security Options Policies**

Policy Name*	Security Setting
Recovery console: Allow floppy copy and access to all drives and all folders	When this policy is disabled (the default), Recovery Console allows access only to a few folders for the purpose of getting a corrupt system running. Specifically, Recovery Console allows full access to the root directory of any hard disk volume, to %SystemRoot% and its subfolders, and to \Cmdcons and its subfolders and allows read-only access to files and folders on removable disks. These limitations prevent thieves from copying files to removable media and from accessing non-system documents and programs. Enabling this policy eliminates these protections by enabling the Set command in Recovery Console. (In Recovery Console, type **set /?** for details about using Set to enable access to other folders; you can display Set's help without enabling this policy.)
Shutdown: Allow system to be shut down without having to log on	By default, the Log On To Windows dialog box includes a Shutdown button. (It appears only when you click Options to expand the dialog box.) Clicking the button shuts down the computer. If you disable this policy, the button appears dimmed, allowing only a user who successfully logs on to shut down the system. (Through another policy—the "Shut down the system" user right, described in Table 21-1—you can specify which logged-on users are allowed to shut down the computer.)
Shutdown: Clear virtual memory pagefile	Enabling this policy clears the content of the page file (\Pagefile.sys) each time you shut down. (Even when this policy is disabled, the page file is deleted at shutdown but, like files in the Recycle Bin, it can be recovered by someone with the know-how. Enabling this policy "wipes" the file by writing all zeros to the file area and deleting the file's directory entry.) The page file, also known as a swap file or virtual memory, contains information that is swapped out of memory during the course of normal operation. While Windows is running, the page file is accessible only by the System account and is secure from snoopers. But someone who boots your computer into another operating system might have access to the page file and might be able to find some sensitive information therein.

Chapter 22

Table 22-2. **Security Options Policies**

Policy Name*	Security Setting
System cryptography: Use FIPS compliant algorithms for encryption, hashing, and signing**	Enabling this policy causes the Encrypting File System (EFS) to use Triple Data Encryption Standard (3DES) to encrypt and decrypt files instead of the expanded Data Encryption Standard (DESX) algorithm. Because 3DES processes each block of each file three times, it's slower, but it's also more secure.
System objects: Default owner for objects created by members of the Administrators group**	This policy determines whether the initial owner of a new object (such as a file or a folder) created by a member of the Administrators group is the individual user who creates the object or the Administrators group. Because any member of the Administrators group can take ownership of an object, this distinction has little practical effect.
System objects: Require case insensitivity for non-Windows subsystems**	When this policy is enabled, names of files and other objects in non-Windows subsystems (such as POSIX) are case insensitive. With the policy disabled, subsystems can be case sensitive. Because few systems in homes and small businesses use any non-Windows subsystems, this policy generally has no effect.
System objects: Strengthen default permissions of internal system objects	This policy determines the default permissions for some objects; when the policy is enabled, stronger (that is, more restrictive) permissions are applied. Leave this policy enabled. (for example, Symbolic Links)

*Table entries provide the Windows XP name. In most cases, the name in Windows 2000 is the same, except that the category (the part of the name before the colon) is not included. By default, policies are listed in the Security Options folder in alphabetical order, so if you use Windows 2000, the order differs from the list shown here.

**Not available in Windows 2000.

***In Windows 2000, the name begins with "Secure channel" instead of "Domain member."

Exploring Other Group Policies

Literally hundreds of group policies are available in Windows XP Professional and Windows 2000. Most of these policies control elements of the user interface (for example, which icons appear on the desktop) and how certain programs operate (for example, allowing audio redirection in a Remote Desktop session). Others place limitations on what a user can do. Some of these limitations are intended to keep a user focused on his or her work, to eliminate options that might be distracting or confusing to inexperienced users, or to prevent users from making inadvertent changes. Although the limitations you can impose in some policies might provide a form of security, those policies are the subject for another book. Here we'll focus on a number of group policies that have clear security implications, as explained in Table 22-3.

For a complete list of available Group Policy settings, download the Group Policy Settings Reference spreadsheet, PolicySettings.xls, from *http://go.microsoft.com/fwlink/?linkid=22031*. The spreadsheet lists all Administrative Template policies, includes the help text for each one, and indicates which versions of Windows (including the service pack level) is required for each policy. The spreadsheet also provides similar information for all other settings in the Local Security Settings console.

If you use only Windows 2000 and you want a complete reference to its Group Policy settings without the distraction of newer Windows XP–only policies, visit *http://www.microsoft.com/resources /documentation/windows/2000/server/reskit/en-us/*. Look for Windows 2000 Group Policy Reference in the contents pane.

If you're a longtime user of Group Policy and you need information about the new policies added to Windows XP Professional with SP2, you might be interested in the white paper "Managing Windows XP Service Pack 2 Features Using Group Policy," which you can obtain at *http://go.microsoft.com/fwlink/?LinkId=31974*.

Caution　A determined attacker can bypass some of the protections these policies provide. For example, you can set a policy to hide the Security tab in the properties dialog box for a folder or a file. Although this setting removes the user interface to the ACLs, programs running in the context of a powerful user account can still make changes. Indeed, a user who knows about the Cacls command can perform many of the same tasks that are available through the Security tab. (However, you can mitigate that particular threat by enabling another policy, which prevents use of a Command Prompt window.) Nonetheless, these policies can provide protection against users inadvertently creating security vulnerabilities, as well as protection against less knowledgeable attackers.

Table 22-3. **Other Security-Related Group Policies**

Policy Name	Description
Computer Configuration\Administrative Templates\Windows Components\NetMeeting	
Disable remote Desktop Sharing	This policy disables only the remote desktop sharing feature of Microsoft NetMeeting. (This feature lets a remote user view and control your desktop.) If you use NetMeeting but want to prevent others from gaining access to your desktop, enable this policy.
Computer Configuration\Administrative Templates\Windows Components \Internet Explorer	
Security Zones: Use only machine settings	This policy applies the same Microsoft Internet Explorer security zone settings to all users of a single computer. If the policy is not enabled, each user can configure security zones independently. Enabling the policy ensures that the strong security zone settings you make apply to all users.
Security Zones: Do not allow users to change policies	This policy acts as an enforcement mechanism for the previous policy: Enabling this policy disables the Custom Level button and the security level slider on the Security tab in the Internet Options dialog box, preventing users from changing security zone settings.

Chapter 22

747

Table 22-3. **Other Security-Related Group Policies**

Policy Name	Description
Security Zones: Do not allow users to add/delete sites	When enabled, this policy disables the Sites button on the Security tab in the Internet Options dialog box, thereby preventing users from adding or removing sites from the Trusted Sites, Restricted Sites, and Local Intranet zones.
Disable Automatic Install of Internet Explorer components	When you visit a Web site that uses an installable component, a Security Warning dialog box asks whether you want to install the component. If you want to prevent users from downloading and installing potentially harmful components, you can take away the option to do so by enabling this policy.
Do not allow users to enable or disable add-ons	When enabled, this policy (available only in Windows XP SP2) prevents users from controlling add-ons through Add-On Manager in Internet Explorer.
Computer Configuration\Administrative Templates\Windows Components \Internet Explorer\Internet Control Panel\Security Page	
	This folder and its subfolders contain over 200 policies (!) that are new with Windows XP SP2. These policies provide detailed control of permissible actions in each security zone. Although there's generally no reason to make changes to these policies, their ability to lock down specific behaviors make it possible to prevent specific exploits as they're discovered. For information about security zones, see "Using Security Zones," page 405. For details on each of the settings in the Security Page folder, see *http://www.microsoft.com/technet/prodtechnol/winxppro /maintain/mangxpsp2/mngieps.mspx*.
Computer Configuration\Administrative Templates\Windows Components \Internet Explorer\Security Features	
	This collection of policies, which is available only on Windows XP Professional with SP2, provides granular control over a number of specific actions in Internet Explorer. For details on each of the settings in the Security Features folder, see *http://www.microsoft.com/technet/prodtechnol/winxppro /maintain/mangxpsp2/mngieps.mspx*.

Table 22-3. **Other Security-Related Group Policies**

Policy Name	Description
Computer Configuration\Administrative Templates\Windows Components\Security Center	
Turn on Security Center (Domain PCs only)	By default, Security Center, a feature of Windows XP SP2, is disabled on computers that are joined to a domain. Although you can open Security Center in this situation, it's nothing more than a collection of links; it doesn't monitor firewall, antivirus, and automatic update settings as it does on a computer that's not joined to a domain. Enabling this policy adds these Security Center capabilities to domain-based computers. For more information about Security Center, see "Monitoring Security in Windows XP," page 213.
Computer Configuration\Administrative Templates\Windows Components \Terminal Services\Encryption and Security	
Set client connection encryption level	If you use Remote Desktop on your Windows XP computer and the computers that connect to it are running Windows XP or Windows 2000 with the High Encryption Pack installed (in other words, they're using 128-bit encryption), you should enable this policy and set it to High Level. With any other setting, the client computer sets the encryption level.
Computer Configuration\Administrative Templates\System\Remote Assistance	
Solicited Remote Assistance	This policy restricts the use of Remote Assistance, a feature that can grant control to an outsider. (Although Remote Assistance has several safeguards built in, a disgruntled user inside your network could use it to allow entry by someone from the outside.) Disabling the policy prevents a user from sending an assistance request. If you enable the policy, you can configure it so that the person providing the assistance can view the computer but not control it.
Offer Remote Assistance	This policy restricts the ability of an outside expert to offer remote assistance without first receiving a remote assistance request. (When the expert offers assistance, the user must grant permission, so the expert can't take over unnoticed.) Disabling or not configuring this policy rejects all unsolicited assistance offers. If you enable the policy, you must specify a list of authorized experts, and you can limit how much control the remote expert will have.
Computer Configuration\Administrative Templates\Network\Offline Files	
Encrypt the Offline Files cache	Enabling this policy causes all local copies of Offline Files to be encrypted. This provides additional security (the files are already protected by NTFS permissions) in case an attacker gains access to your computer.

Chapter 22

749

Table 22-3. **Other Security-Related Group Policies**

Policy Name	Description
Computer Configuration\Administrative Templates\Network\Network Connections	
IEEE 802.1x Certificate Authority for Machine Authentication	This policy provides security for wireless networks by requiring authentication through a Certificate Authority. For more information about securing wireless networks, see Chapter 10, "Wireless Networking."
Computer Configuration\Administrative Templates\Network\Network Connections \Windows Firewall	
Windows Firewall: Allow authenticated IPSec bypass	This policy, which is available only on systems running Windows XP Professional with SP2 installed, allows IPSec-protected traffic to bypass Windows Firewall. To enable this policy, you enter a security descriptor for each remote computer; thereafter, your computer allows unsolicited incoming connections from specified computers that authenticate using IPSec. For information about IPSec, see "Restricting Ports by Using IP Security," page 640.
Domain Profile and Standard Profile folders	Each folder contains an identical set of policies, which enable you to make all settings to configure and control Windows Firewall on systems running Windows XP Professional with SP2. The Domain Profile settings are in effect when the computer is connected to an Active Directory network; the Standard Profile settings are effective when the computer is in a stand-alone configuration or connected to a non–Active Directory network.
User Configuration\Administrative Templates\Windows Components\NetMeeting	
Set Call Security options	This policy lets you require call security for all NetMeeting incoming and outgoing calls.
Prevent automatic acceptance of Calls	This policy prevents the use of NetMeeting's automatic answering feature, which could allow someone to connect to your computer when you're not there. (Even when the feature is enabled, however, it is effective only when NetMeeting is running.)
User Configuration\Administrative Templates\Windows Components\NetMeeting \Application Sharing	
Disable application Sharing	This policy disables NetMeeting application sharing altogether; when it is enabled, users can't share applications or use shared applications on another computer.
Prevent Sharing	This policy prevents users from sharing applications in NetMeeting themselves, but they can connect to others' shared applications.
Prevent Desktop Sharing	This policy prevents users from sharing the desktop in NetMeeting, although they can share individual applications.

Table 22-3. **Other Security-Related Group Policies**

Policy Name	Description
Prevent Sharing Command Prompts	This policy prevents users from sharing Command Prompt windows in NetMeeting. Such sharing can be dangerous because remote users can start other programs from a command prompt.
Prevent Sharing Explorer windows	This policy prevents users from sharing Windows Explorer windows in NetMeeting. Such sharing can be dangerous because remote users can start other programs from a Windows Explorer window.
Prevent Control	This policy prevents users from allowing remote users to control shared applications in NetMeeting.
User Configuration\Administrative Templates\Windows Components\NetMeeting \Options Page	
Hide the Security page preventing settings.	This policy hides the Security tab in NetMeeting and prevents users from changing call security and authentication
User Configuration\Administrative Templates\Windows Components\Internet Explorer	
Disable changing certificate settings	This policy disables the Certificates buttons on the Content tab of the Internet Options dialog box, thereby preventing users from adding or removing certificates for software publishers.
Do not allow AutoComplete to save passwords	If you enable this policy, Internet Explorer no longer saves passwords that you enter on Web pages, nor does it prompt to ask whether you want to save the password. Options in the AutoComplete Settings dialog box are disabled, preventing users from changing these settings. The risk of having Internet Explorer save passwords is that someone who gains access to your computer (and logs on to your account) has access to your password-protected Web sites.
User Configuration\Administrative Templates\Windows Components\Internet Explorer \ Internet Control Panel	
Disable the Security page	Enabling this policy hides the Security tab in the Internet Options dialog box, thereby preventing users from viewing or changing security zone settings.
User Configuration\Administrative Templates\Windows Components\Windows Explorer	
Hide these specified drives in My Computer	This policy allows a bit of subterfuge: By enabling it, you can prevent certain drives from appearing in My Computer, Windows Explorer, or common dialog boxes such as Open. The drive is still accessible by programs, at a command prompt, or by other non-obvious means—but it remains hidden from casual examination.

Chapter 22

Table 22-3. **Other Security-Related Group Policies**

Policy Name	Description
Prevent access to drives from My Computer	This policy prevents access to specified drives through Windows Explorer and most other means. (The drives still appear unless you hide them using the preceding policy, but they're unavailable.) Programs, however, can still access the drives.
Remove Security tab	Enabling this policy hides the Security tab in the properties dialog boxes for folders and files, preventing users from viewing or modifying access permissions. Knowledgeable users can use command-line tools such as Cacls or Xcacls to bypass this protection.

User Configuration\Administrative Templates\Windows Components\Windows Explorer \Common Open File Dialog

Hide the dropdown list of recent files	If this policy is disabled or not configured, the File Name box in the Open dialog box has a drop-down list of files you've recently opened. If you don't want others to know which files you've opened, enable this policy. (The files list is saved on a per-user basis, so only users who log in with the same account would see each other's file names.)

User Configuration\Administrative Templates\Windows Components \Microsoft Management Console

Restrict the user from entering author mode	This policy prevents users from creating or modifying MMC consoles, thereby allowing them to use only existing consoles for which they have sufficient permissions. This prevents access to potentially destructive snap-ins.
Restrict users to the explicitly permitted list of snap-ins	If you don't want to prevent users from creating or modifying consoles altogether, you can use this policy to limit them to certain snap-ins. If this policy is enabled, users have access only to the snap-ins and snap-in extensions that have been set to Enabled in the Restricted/Permitted Snap-Ins subfolder and its subfolders.

User Configuration\Administrative Templates\Start Menu and Taskbar

Do not keep history of recently opened documents	Ordinarily, Windows keeps track of documents you open by storing a shortcut to each one in the %UserProfile%\Recent folder. If you don't want others to know what documents you used recently, enable this policy. Doing so deletes the contents of the Recent folder and prevents new items from being added. It also prevents recent file names from appearing at the bottom of the File menu in many programs.

Table 22-3. **Other Security-Related Group Policies**

Policy Name	Description
Clear history of recently opened documents on exit	Unlike the preceding policy, this one does not prevent the accumulation of recent documents history. Within a logon session, you have convenient access (through the Recent Documents item on the Start menu) to documents you've already opened once. The information is purged when you log off. This policy does not affect the list of recent documents at the bottom of the File menu in some applications.
Turn off user tracking	Ordinarily, Windows tracks which programs and documents you use. The system uses this information to customize Windows to the way you work (for example, by displaying frequently used programs more prominently on the Start menu). When this policy is enabled, Windows does not track user actions.
User Configuration\Administrative Templates\Control Panel	
Prohibit access to the Control Panel	Enabling this policy prevents you from running Control Panel and removes it from the Start menu and from My Computer.
Hide specified Control Panel applets	This policy allows you to prevent certain items from appearing in Control Panel. A knowledgeable user can open these items from a command prompt, however.
Show only specified Control Panel applets	This policy provides the same protection as the preceding one: It causes certain items not to appear in Control Panel. (The difference is whether you want to specify only the items to hide or specify only the items to display.)
User Configuration\Administrative Templates\Control Panel\Display	
Password protect the screen saver	Enabling this policy causes all screen savers to be password-protected. That is, to restore the normal desktop when a screen saver is displayed, the user must enter his or her password. Therefore, someone who leaves the computer for a time doesn't leave its display open to anyone who walks by and jiggles the mouse. (However, no policy explicitly requires users to use a screen saver. If you want to do that, configure a screen saver and then enable the Hide Screen Saver Tab policy in this same folder, which prevents users from changing your screen saver configuration.)
User Configuration\Administrative Templates\System	
Prevent access to the command prompt	This policy prevents users from running Cmd.exe (Command Prompt), which can be used to launch all manner of programs, good and bad. It also prevents batch programs (those with a .cmd or .bat file name extension) from running.
Prevent access to registry editing tools	This policy disables Registry Editor (Regedit.exe and Regedt32.exe).

Chapter 22

Table 22-3. **Other Security-Related Group Policies**

Policy Name	Description
Run only allowed Windows applications	If you really want to lock down your computer (such as in a kiosk application), you can use this policy to specify a list of programs that a user is allowed to run from the Start menu or Windows Explorer.
Don't run specified Windows applications	With this policy, you can specify a list of programs that users are not allowed to run.
User Configuration\Administrative Templates\System\Ctrl+Alt+Del Options	
Remove Task Manager	Ordinarily, one of the buttons in the Windows Security dialog box, which appears when you press Ctrl+Alt+Delete, is one that opens Task Manager, a powerful application that lets you monitor and control running applications, among other things. Enabling this policy disables the Task Manager button in the Windows Security dialog box. It also prevents users from starting Task Manager by pressing Ctrl+Shift+Esc or running its executable file, Taskmgr.exe.
User Configuration\Administrative Templates\System\Power Management	
Prompt for password on resume from hibernate/ suspend	If you enable this setting, the computer is locked when it resumes after hibernating or a suspended low-power state. To gain access, the user who was logged on when the system shut down (or an administrator) must provide a password. If you use power management on a portable computer, you should enable this policy. Otherwise, someone who steals your computer might be able to pick up where you left off—logged in to your account.

> **Note** Group Policy settings take precedence over user settings (that is, settings that you make through Control Panel and other methods available to ordinary users). Group Policy settings are saved in different registry keys than settings made through other means. In cases of conflict, the value under the Policies key overrules the other.
>
> You might also notice that some policies appear in both User Configuration and Computer Configuration. If the settings conflict, the Computer Configuration setting always takes precedence.

Using the Group Policy Snap-In

The policies described in Tables 22-1, 22-2, and 22-3 can all be viewed and modified using the Group Policy snap-in for MMC. A console containing this snap-in is included with Windows XP and Windows 2000; the easiest way to open it is to type **gpedit.msc** at a command prompt. Figure 22-3 shows the Group Policy console.

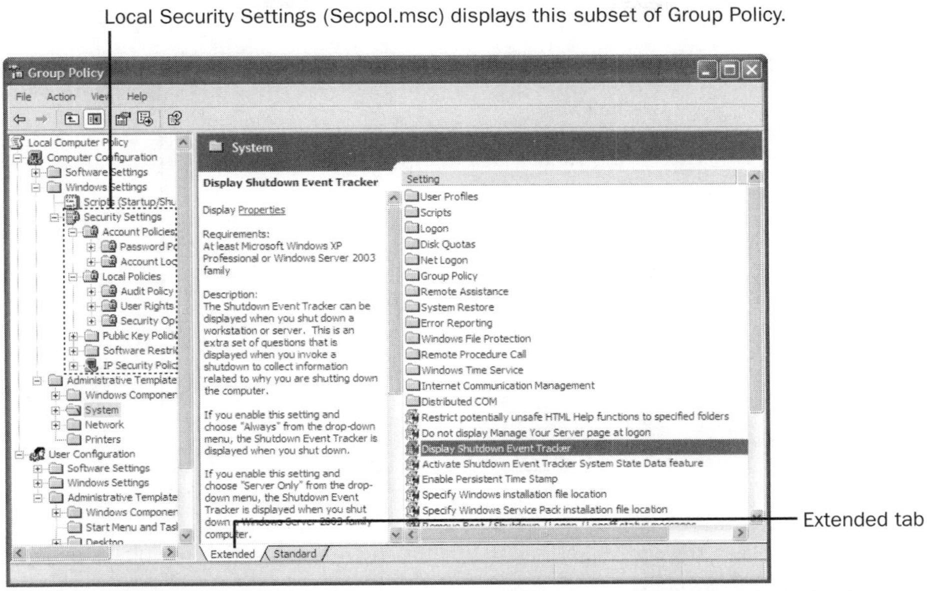

Local Security Settings (Secpol.msc) displays this subset of Group Policy.

Figure 22-3. Group Policy in Windows XP includes an Extended tab, which displays a description of any policy you select in the Administrative Templates folders.

Tip If your network includes at least one system running Windows Server 2003 or Windows 2000 Server, you can use Group Policy Management Console (GPMC), an MMC console that eases all aspects of Group Policy management by combining several functions into a unified console. GPMC provides tools for backing up, restoring, exporting, and importing GPOs. You can download GPMC from *http://go.microsoft.com/fwlink/?linkid=21813*.

Each policy in the Administrative Templates folders of Group Policy has one of three settings: Not Configured, Enabled, or Disabled. By default, all policies in the local Group Policy object are initially set to Not Configured.

To change a setting, simply double-click the name of the policy to open its properties dialog box. The properties dialog box for each policy under Administrative Templates looks much like the one shown in Figure 22-4 on the next page. The Setting tab (called Policy in Windows 2000) includes the Not Configured, Enabled, and Disabled options and an area where you can make policy-specific settings. (Many simple policies leave this area blank because the policy needs no further setting.) Controls in the center area appear dimmed unless you select the Enabled option. The Explain tab provides detailed information about the policy. Both tabs include Previous Setting and Next Setting buttons (called Previous Policy and Next Policy in Windows 2000), which make it convenient to go through an entire folder without opening and closing the properties dialog box for each policy individually.

Chapter 22

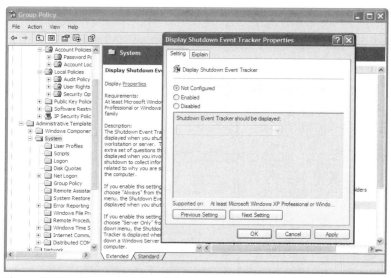

Figure 22-4. The properties dialog box for any Administrative Templates policy is similar to the one shown here.

> **Note** Pay close attention to the name of each policy because the settings can be counter-intuitive, particularly in Windows 2000. A number of policies begin with the word *disable* (for example, Disable Autoplay, a policy that's included in Computer Configuration \Administrative Templates\System). For those policies, if you want to *allow* the specified option (Autoplay in this example), you must select the Disable setting. (In other words, you must disable the disabling policy.) Conversely, if you want to prohibit the option, you must select Enable.
>
> The potential for confusion is reduced in Windows XP because its designers have renamed many of the policies. For example, Disable Autoplay is now called Turn Off Autoplay.

Using the Security Settings Extension

You can use Group Policy to work with user rights, security options, and other settings within the Security Settings folder. You can avoid much of the clutter, however, by opening Local Security Settings (shown in Figure 22-1, page 731), a console that includes only the Security Settings extension for the Group Policy snap-in.

You examine and set policies within the Security Settings extension in much the same way as you do for policies in the Administrative Templates folders. As shown in Figure 22-5, however, you'll discover that convenient touches such as the setting description and the Previous and Next buttons are missing.

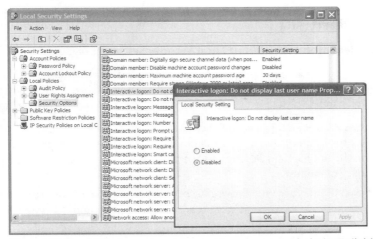

Figure 22-5. Aside from descriptive policy names, no help is available within the console.

How Policies Are Applied

When you configure a policy in the Account Policies or Local Policies subfolder of Security Settings, Windows immediately saves the information to the appropriate registry key. (Although the information is written to the registry immediately, some policy changes don't take effect until you log off and then log back on.)

Policy configuration changes in the Administrative Templates folders are applied indirectly. When you configure one of these policies (that is, you select either Enabled or Disabled and, optionally, set a value), Group Policy stores the information as a custom registry setting in one of the two Registry.pol files. As you'd expect, Group Policy uses the copy of Registry.pol in %SystemRoot%\System32\GroupPolicy\Machine for settings you make in the Computer Configuration\Administrative Templates folder in Group Policy and uses the copy in User for settings you make in User Configuration \Administrative Templates.

Computer-related Group Policy settings—those stored in Machine\Registry.pol—are copied to the appropriate registry keys in the HKLM hive when the operating system initializes and during a periodic refresh that occurs at intervals you define as a Group Policy setting. User-related settings (in User\Registry.pol) are copied to the appropriate keys in HKCU when a user logs on and during the periodic refresh.

Chapter 22

Troubleshooting

You need detailed information about Local Security Settings policies

If you need to find out more about the policies in the Security Settings extension, in addition to the information this book provides, online resources are available. (They're just not easy to find.) You can find a detailed description of each policy in the following places:

- In Windows XP, from either Group Policy or Local Security Settings, choose Action, Help. Click the Contents tab and then, in the Contents pane, open Security Settings \Concepts\Security Setting Descriptions\Local Policies. From here, you can drill down to the policy of interest.

- In Windows XP, use your Web browser to open *http://www.microsoft.com/resources /documentation/windows/xp/all/proddocs/en-us/localpoliciestopnode.mspx*. Click links in the right pane to see the description of a particular policy.

- In Windows 2000, use your Web browser to open *http://www.microsoft.com/resources /documentation/windows/2000/server/reskit/en-us/*. In the left pane, open Windows 2000 Group Policy Reference\Computer Configuration\Windows Settings \Security Settings\Local Policies. Continue expanding the table of contents until you reach the policy you want.

Inside Out

Apply different settings for different users

Centrally managed Group Policy settings—that is, those stored in Active Directory in Windows Server 2003 or Windows 2000 Server—can be applied to individual users, computers, or groups of either. You can have multiple sets of Active Directory–based Group Policy objects, enabling you to create an entirely different collection of settings for different users or computers.

Such is not the case with local Group Policy. Despite the (misleading) separate Computer Configuration and User Configuration folders, local Group Policy settings apply to all users who log on to the computer. You can't have multiple sets of local Group Policy objects.

Although you can't customize settings for each of several different groups, you can effectively have two groups of users: those who are affected by local Group Policy settings and those who are not. This duality affects only the User Configuration settings; Computer Config-uration settings are applied before anyone logs on.

You can do this because local Group Policy depends on users having read access to the local Group Policy object, which is stored in the %SystemRoot%\System32\GroupPolicy folder. Policies are not applied to users who do not have read access; therefore, by denying read access to administrators or others whom you don't want to restrict, you free those users from restrictions in local group policies. To use this method, follow these steps:

1 Make the Group Policy setting changes.

2 In Windows Explorer, choose Tools, Folder Options. On the View tab, select Show Hidden Files And Folders. If you're using Windows XP Professional, clear the Use Simple File Sharing (Recommended) check box. Click OK.

3 Right-click the %SystemRoot%\System32\GroupPolicy folder and choose Properties.

4 On the Security tab of the GroupPolicy Properties dialog box, select the Administrators group, and select the Deny check box for the Read permission. (If you want to exclude any other users or groups from Group Policy control, add them to the list of names and then deny their Read permission.)

5 Restore the Folder Options settings (the ones you set in step 2) to their previous states.

At your next logon using one of the user accounts for which you denied read access, you'll find that you're no longer encumbered by Group Policy settings. Without Read permission, however, you're also unable to run Group Policy—so you can't view or modify Group Policy settings. To regain that power, you need to revisit the GroupPolicy Properties dialog box and grant yourself Full Control permission.

If using group membership as the basis for customizing the effects of Group Policy settings is important to you, you should install Windows Server 2003 or Windows 2000 Server and set up Active Directory. The methods described here can provide an easy compromise in the meantime.

Starting Group Policy for a Remote Computer

When you start Group Policy as described earlier in this chapter, it displays the local Group Policy object (GPO) for your computer. You can, however, start Group Policy with its gaze turned toward another computer. To do that, you must have administrative privileges on both your own computer and the other computer. You can use either of two methods to start Group Policy for a remote computer: a command-line parameter or a custom MMC console.

Note Running Group Policy remotely provides full access to the policies in the Administrative Templates folders, enabling you to administer all the computers on your network from a single console. However, you can't manage the policies in the Security Settings folder remotely. To work with those policies, you must work directly at each workstation (unless you have Windows 2000 Server or Windows Server 2003 and domain-based policies).

The simplest method is to append the /Gpcomputer parameter to the command for running Group Policy, as in this example:

```
gpedit.msc /gpcomputer:"redwood"
```

The computer name that follows /Gpcomputer can be either a NetBIOS-style name (as shown here) or a DNS-style name (for example, redwood.contoso.com), which is the primary naming format used by Windows 2000 Server and Windows Server 2003 domains. In either case, you must enclose the computer name in quotation marks.

Chapter 22

759

An alternative is to create a custom console that opens the local Group Policy object on another computer. The advantage of this approach is that you can create a single console that can open Group Policy on each computer you want to manage. To create a custom console, do the following:

1 At a command prompt, type **mmc**.
2 Open the File menu (the Console menu in Windows 2000), and then choose Add/Remove Snap-In.
3 On the Standalone tab, click Add.
4 Select Group Policy and click Add.
5 In the Select Group Policy Object dialog box, click Browse.
6 On the Computers tab, select Another Computer, and then type the name of the computer or click Browse to select it from a list.
7 Click OK and then click Finish.
8 Repeat steps 4 through 7 to add other computers to the console.
9 Click Close, and then click OK.

Local Group Policy vs. Active Directory–Based Group Policy

Group Policy is primarily a feature for domain-based networks that use Active Directory in Windows 2000 Server or Windows Server 2003. In an Active Directory–based domain, Group Policy objects are stored at the domain level and affect users and computers on the basis of their membership in sites, domains, and organizational units. (A *Group Policy object*, or GPO, is simply a collection of Group Policy settings.) Each computer running Windows XP Professional or Windows 2000 (any version) has a single *local Group Policy object*, which is the one we focus on in this book. If your computer is part of an Active Directory network, it might be affected by Group Policy settings other than those you set in the local Group Policy object. Group Policy settings are applied in this order:

1 Settings from the local Group Policy object
2 Settings from site Group Policy objects, in administratively specified order
3 Settings from domain Group Policy objects, in administratively specified order
4 Settings from organizational unit Group Policy objects, from largest to smallest organizational unit (parent to child organizational unit), and in administratively specified order at the level of each organizational unit

Policies applied later overwrite previously applied policies, which means that if settings conflict, the highest-level Active Directory–based policy settings take precedence. The policy settings are cumulative, so all settings contribute to the effective policy.

Using Security Templates

If you decide to change some of the default settings for the policies shown in Tables 22-1 and 22-2, you can make the changes in Group Policy or in Local Security Settings, as described in the preceding sections. If you want to apply the same changes to a number of computers in your network, however, making the settings can be tedious. In this common situation, you're better off using *security templates*, files that contain preconfigured security settings for various purposes. You can also use security templates to restore your security settings to a known condition if experimentation with various settings has compromised your secure system. A security template can contain the following types of settings:

- Account Policies, including Password Policy and Account Lockout Policy settings. (For details about these settings, see Table 4-3, "Password Policies," page 115; and Table 4-4, "Account Lockout Policies," page 132.)

- Local Policies, including Audit Policy, User Rights Assignment, and Security Options settings. (See Table 23-1, "Audit Policies for Security Events," page 775; Table 22-1, "User Rights Assignment Policies," page 733; and Table 22-2, "Security Options Policies," page 737.)

- Event Log. (See "Viewing the Log of Security Events," page 781.)

- Restricted Groups. (See "Controlling Security Group Membership," page 767.)

- System Services, which determines the startup type for each service. (For information about services, see Table 19-2, "Windows Services," page 653.)

- Registry, which sets permissions on registry keys. (See "Configuring Permissions on Folders, Files, and the Registry," page 768.)

- File System, which sets permissions on folders and files. (See "Configuring Permissions on Folders, Files, and the Registry," page 768.)

Inside Out

Distribute local Group Policy settings

Security templates do not include settings for policies in Group Policy's Administrative Templates folders, including the settings shown in Table 22-3, page 747. Therefore, you can't use security templates to apply those settings to other computers. (The ability to centrally manage and apply Group Policy settings is one of the strengths of domain-based networks that use Windows 2000 Server or Windows Server 2003.)

However, you can promulgate your policy settings to other computers relatively easily: After you make the necessary changes on one computer, simply copy the Registry.pol files to each computer on which you want to apply the policies. For the settings in Computer Configuration\Administrative Templates, copy %SystemRoot%\System32 \GroupPolicy\Machine\Registry.pol to the same folder on the target machine. For the User Configuration\Administrative Templates settings, copy the Registry.pol file stored in %SystemRoot%\System32\GroupPolicy\User.

Chapter 22

Security templates are saved as ordinary text files with an .inf file name extension. By default, they're stored in %SystemRoot%\Security\Templates. Although you could edit these plain-text (but rather cryptic) files in Notepad or another text editor, you don't need to. The Security Templates snap-in for MMC provides a much better and easier means to view, modify, create, and delete security templates.

Each security template that comes with Windows is configured for specific purposes. You can use one of these templates as is, modify it, or create a new one from scratch. Table 22-4 describes the templates included with Windows XP Professional and Windows 2000 Professional.

Table 22-4. Security Templates Included with Windows

Template Name	Windows XP	Windows 2000	Description
Basicdc, Basicsv, and Basicwk		Yes	These templates configure a moderate level of security—slightly higher than an out-of-the-box installation—by setting a number of security options, configuring startup services, and applying permissions to registry keys and folders. They're intended for use on domain controllers (Basicdc), stand-alone servers (Basicsv), and workstations (Basicwk).
Compatws	Yes	Yes	This template removes all users from the Power Users group and relaxes the default permissions for members of the Users group. This setting allows members of the Users group to run certain applications that aren't properly designed for Windows security, without granting them the additional administrative privileges (such as the ability to create user accounts) granted to Power Users. Note that, unlike the other provided templates, which contain settings that are equal to or more restrictive than the default settings in Windows, Compatws.inf actually *reduces security.* Use it only if absolutely necessary.

Table 22-4. **Security Templates Included with Windows**

Template Name	Windows XP	Windows 2000	Description
Hisecdc and Hisecws	Yes	Yes	These templates are intended for configuring a highly secure domain. They include all the settings in the Securedc and Securews templates, plus additional settings that require more secure authentication, restrict security group membership, and require data signing and encryption in most network communications. Hisecdc is intended for domain controllers; Hisecws is for workstations.
Ocfiless and Ocfilesw		Yes	These templates apply default file permissions to all folders and files included with Windows 2000 Server and Windows 2000 Professional, respectively.
Rootsec	Yes		This template applies permissions to the root folder of the system drive, using the permissions introduced with Windows XP. If you inadvertently change those permissions, this template provides a quick and easy way to restore the default permissions. The permissions propagate to all child objects that inherit permissions from the parent, but they aren't applied to child objects for which explicit permissions have been set.
Securedc and Securews	Yes	Yes	These templates configure strong password, lockout, and audit settings; require the use of strong authentication protocols; restrict anonymous users; and configure Server Message Block (SMB) packet signing. They're intended for creating secure domains. Use Securedc on domain controllers and Securews on workstations.

Chapter 22

Table 22-4. **Security Templates Included with Windows**

Template Name	Windows XP	Windows 2000	Description
Setup Security	Yes	Yes	This template contains the default security settings that were applied when Windows was set up on your computer. As such, it makes a good disaster-recovery template, enabling you to easily go back to the original Windows configuration.

Note Except for Setup Security.inf, none of the furnished templates includes a complete set of security settings. Instead, they're designed to modify only a specific subset while leaving other settings unchanged.

Tip "Windows XP Security Guide v2," a document available from Microsoft, includes additional administrative templates. Go to *http://www.microsoft.com/downloads* and search for the document by title.

Inside Out

Restore default NTFS permissions with a hidden template

Windows includes another template, Defltwk.inf, that includes all the default security settings (including NTFS permissions, user rights assignments, policies, registry permissions, and so on) as originally configured by Microsoft for a clean installation of Windows on a new machine. (For a number of reasons, some of these settings might be different from the settings in Setup Security.inf.) Unlike the other predefined templates, Defltwk.inf is stored in %SystemRoot%\Inf, a hidden folder. Because of its storage location, it doesn't appear by default in the Security Templates snap-in—where it's more likely to get changed inadvertently. Instead, Defltwk.inf (and its companion for servers, Defltsv.inf) is intended to be used only with Security Configuration And Analysis or Secedit.exe, the tools for analyzing current settings and applying settings. Read more about Defltwk.inf in Knowledge Base article 266118. (The article refers only to Windows 2000, but Defltwk.inf is also included with Windows XP.)

Using the Security Templates Snap-In

Security Templates is an MMC snap-in that enables you to view and edit security templates. No console furnished with Windows includes the Security Templates snap-in; you'll have to create your own, as follows:

1 At a command prompt, type **mmc**.

2 Open the File menu (the Console menu in Windows 2000), and then choose Add/Remove Snap-In.

3 On the Standalone tab, click Add.

4 Select Security Templates, and then click Add.

5 Click Close, and then click OK in the Add/Remove Snap-In dialog box.

By default, the Security Templates snap-in displays the templates stored in %SystemRoot%\Security\Templates, as shown in Figure 22-6. To view templates stored in another folder, including those stored on a network drive, right-click Security Templates in the console tree and choose New Template Search Path.

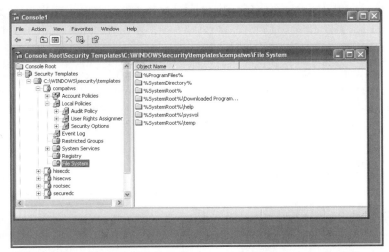

Figure 22-6. The Security Templates snap-in lets you set permissions on folders and files and make other security settings.

To create a new template, in the console tree, right-click the folder where you want to store the template and choose New Template. Enter a name and, optionally, a description of the template. You can view the description for a template in two ways:

● In the console tree, select the folder that contains the templates. The description of each template appears next to its name in the details pane.

● Right-click a template name (in the console tree or the details pane) and choose Set Description.

If you want to modify the settings in an existing template and also want to keep the original template unchanged, right-click the template name and choose Save As. After you specify a name for your copy of the template, it appears in the console tree. Note that none of the changes you make to a template are saved to disk unless you select the template and choose Action, Save or right-click a template name and choose Save. (The Save command on the File menu saves the console layout and settings—not the template settings.) If you have unsaved templates when you close the MMC console, Windows asks which of these templates you want to save. Select the ones you want to save and click Yes.

> **Note** The Security Templates snap-in is a tool for viewing and modifying templates only. Changes you make in the snap-in are saved in template files, but this snap-in does not apply template security settings to a computer. To apply the settings in a template, use the procedures described in "Applying Template Settings," page 769.

Reviewing Account Policies, Local Policies, Event Log, and System Services Settings

In the Security Templates snap-in, expand the folders in the console tree until the policy in which you are interested is displayed in the details pane. Then double-click the policy name to open the properties dialog box; Figure 22-7 shows an example. If you want the policy to be controlled by the security template, select Define This Policy Setting In The Template and then specify the setting you want. Your choices for policy setting depend on the specific policy. (For example, some policies require you to select among two or more option buttons, whereas others provide a text box or spin box with which you can specify a numeric value.)

Figure 22-7. The properties dialog box for each policy has options comparable to those in the Local Security Settings console.

Controlling Security Group Membership

With restricted groups policies, you can control membership in security groups. When you apply a security template with restricted groups policies, any user accounts that are currently members of a group whose membership is restricted are removed from that group. For example, if you create a restricted group policy for Administrators that includes only Ed and Carl in that group, applying the template adds Ed and Carl to the group (if they're not already members) and removes all other accounts. Restricting group membership in this way is a one-shot deal; administrators can subsequently add or remove members from the group.

To add a group to the list of restricted groups, right-click Restricted Groups and choose Add Group. In the Add Group dialog box, type the name of the security group you want to add, or click Browse to display a list of all security groups. (In Windows XP, click Advanced and then click Find Now to display the list.)

To control the membership of a restricted group, double-click the group name to display the properties dialog box for the group, as shown in Figure 22-8. Next to the Members Of This Group box, click Add. In the Add Member dialog box, type the user name you want, or click Browse to display a list of user names. You can separate multiple names with semicolons, or you can simply repeat the process to add other names.

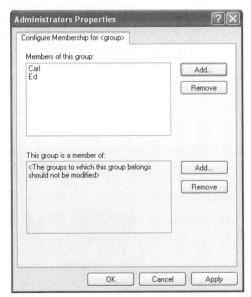

Figure 22-8. After applying the template, only user accounts listed in the top box remain in the group; if no names appear, the group is empty.

Chapter 22

Configuring Permissions on Folders, Files, and the Registry

The File System and Registry sections of a security template let you apply permissions to folders, files, and registry keys, overriding any permissions currently protecting the items you specify. Just as you can within Windows Explorer and Registry Editor, you can specify a discretionary access control list (DACL), which grants (or denies) access permissions to users and groups. You can also specify a system access control list (SACL), which specifies the security events to be recorded in the Security log.

> For information about permissions on folders and files, see "Using NTFS Permissions for Access Control," page 136. For information about applying permissions within Registry Editor and the effect of registry permissions, see "Restricting Access to the Registry," page 170.

If the folder or file on which you want to configure ACLs does not appear in the details pane when you select File System, right-click File System (or right-click an empty area of the details pane) and choose Add File. The Add File command opens the Add A File Or Folder dialog box, which lets you browse all folders and files in My Computer. The steps for adding a registry key are similar: Right-click Registry and choose Add Key. In the Select Registry Key dialog box, you can expand the registry hierarchy and select the key you want to configure.

When the folder, file, or registry key of interest appears in the details pane, simply double-click it to configure it. A dialog box similar to the one shown in Figure 22-9 appears. To set ACLs, select the first option button and then specify how you want to set permissions on child objects (subfolders and files within the specified folder, or subkeys within the specified registry key). The options to propagate inheritable permissions and replace existing permissions correspond to the similarly worded options in the Advanced Security Settings dialog box (Access Control Settings in Windows 2000), which opens when you click the Advanced button on the Security tab in Windows Explorer or Registry Editor.

Select Do Not Allow Permissions On This File Or Folder To Be Replaced if you want to ensure that permissions on this folder, file, or key are *not* changed when a security template is applied. Why not just omit this object name from the Registry or File System folder in the template? This option prevents changes that might be inflicted through inheritance by settings on a parent object.

Finally, of course, you need to specify the permissions for the object. Click Edit Security, and you'll see a dialog box that includes a Security tab just like the one in Windows Explorer or Registry Editor. This dialog box shows the object's current security settings.

Figure 22-9. The dialog box for setting registry key permissions is nearly identical to this one. Minor wording variations refer to keys instead of files and folders.

Applying Template Settings

After you've configured a template to include the settings you want, you can apply the settings to your local computer. You do this with Security Configuration And Analysis, an MMC snap-in that manages a database of security settings from one or more templates. You can also use this snap-in to compare your current settings to those in the database.

> **Tip** Before you apply your template settings, you might want to analyze your configuration to see what differences exist between your current settings and the settings in your security template. For details, see "Analyzing System Security," page 771.

To use Security Configuration And Analysis, you must add it to an MMC console. Use the same procedure as described for Security Templates; for details, see "Using the Security Templates Snap-In," page 765.

> **Tip** To house all your security-management tools in one place, create a console that includes the Group Policy, Security Templates, and Security Configuration And Analysis snap-ins. Save the console in your Administrative Tools folder.

Initially, the Security Configuration And Analysis snap-in looks like no other, displaying only an empty console tree and, in the details pane, sparse instructions for tasks whose purpose isn't clear. Go ahead and follow these instructions:

1 Right-click Security Configuration And Analysis and choose Open Database.

2 In the Open Database dialog box, type a name for a new database and then click Open. (If you want to use a database that you've created previously, select it instead.)

Chapter 22

769

3 In the Import Template dialog box, select a security template, and then click Open.

4 If you want to import another security template into the database, right-click Security Configuration And Analysis and choose Import Template.

Now you're ready to actually apply your settings. Right-click Security Configuration And Analysis and choose Configure Computer Now. In the Configure System dialog box, type the path and name for a log file if you don't want to accept the default file. Click OK. (Why it's called an *error* log file is another mystery of Security Configuration And Analysis; it's a log of all configuration actions, not only errors.) Windows applies your settings, and you're once again left at the same cryptic console display. To see what has occurred, right-click Security Configuration And Analysis and choose View Log File; the log file appears in the details pane.

Inside Out

Apply template settings with Secedit.exe

You might find it convenient to apply template settings with Secedit.exe, a command-line utility. This utility can make applying settings on multiple computers easier. You could, for example, store the security database (.sdb) file on a shared network drive, along with a one-line batch program that applies the settings. A command-line utility also makes it easy to set up security configuration as a scheduled task.

Before you use Secedit, you must create a security database file with Security Configuration And Analysis, as described in the numbered steps in the preceding section. Then, to apply your settings, use the command **secedit /configure /db *databasefile***, where *databasefile* is the path and name (including extension) of the database file. You can omit the path if the database is in the current directory. For example, if you leave the security database file in the default location, you'd enter the following:

```
secedit /configure /db "%userprofile%\my
        documents\security\database\mysettings.sdb"
```

With additional command-line parameters, you can instruct Secedit to apply only certain types of settings specified in the database, control the location and display of the log file, and set other options. In addition, you can use Secedit to compare your computer settings with security database settings, extract a security template file from a security database, and more. For details, type **secedit /?** at a command prompt.

Analyzing System Security

The Security Configuration And Analysis snap-in has that name for a reason: In addition to applying template settings (configuration), it compares a computer's current security settings with those in a security database file (analysis). This comparison provides an easy way to comprehensively review security settings. You can see which settings have been changed, how your computer compares with one of the highly secure template configurations, and so on.

To perform an analysis, open Security Configuration And Analysis in MMC and then create or open a security database. (See the preceding section, "Applying Template Settings," for details.) Right-click Security Configuration And Analysis and choose Analyze Computer Now. In the Perform Analysis dialog box, modify the log file name if you want and then click OK. After the analysis is complete, the console tree sprouts new branches, identical to those in a template in the Security Templates snap-in.

For each policy in the Account Policies, Local Policies, and Event Log folders, the details pane shows the database setting and the current computer setting. A symbol in a policy's icon indicates at a glance the results of the analysis of that policy:

	A circled green check mark indicates that the two settings match.
	An *X* in a red circle identifies policies in which the database setting differs from the computer setting.
	A circled exclamation point or question mark indicates that the computer setting was not analyzed; this typically occurs on policies that are relevant only on a domain controller.

Double-click a policy to see its properties dialog box, as shown in Figure 22-10 on the next page. The dialog box displays the current settings for the computer and in the database. If you want to change the setting in the database, select Define This Policy In The Database, make your setting, and click OK.

Differences between the database settings and computer settings in the Restricted Groups, System Services, Registry, and File System folders are indicated with icons similar to those just shown. Instead of displaying the settings in the details pane, however, Security Configuration And Analysis displays the word *Investigate* alongside items with differences. Double-click any such items in the Restricted Groups or System Services folder to display a properties dialog box, similar to the dialog box shown in Figure 22-10, that shows both settings and enables you to modify the database setting.

Security Configuration And Analysis has another quirk as well. Double-clicking an item in the Registry or File System folder doesn't open the properties dialog box unless the item is at the bottom of the hierarchy. To view the properties dialog box for a folder or a key that has child objects, right-click it and choose Properties.

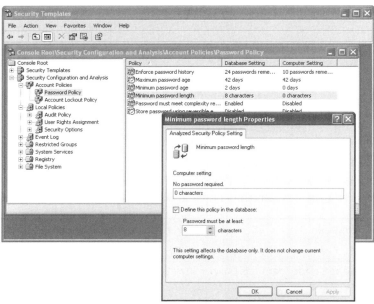

Figure 22-10. The properties dialog box for a policy initially shows the value in the security database. You can change the database value if you want.

Chapter 23

Monitoring Security Events

You can't keep an eye on your computer—let alone all the other computers on your network—all the time. Although you might have put in place all the proper safeguards to protect your data from unauthorized access (such as strong passwords, appropriate permissions, and a firewall), you can't be sure that those safeguards are always working properly. By taking advantage of improper settings inadvertently made by a user, or simply by making a determined effort, an attacker might still gain access to resources that should be off limits.

Fortunately, Microsoft Windows XP Professional and Windows 2000 provide the ability to audit your security setup, by recording attempts to access objects on the system, and by recording security-sensitive changes to the system's configuration. When properly configured, Windows monitors usage of a computer, enabling you to record unauthorized events or other security lapses in a log file that is accepted by the legal system as evidence. Using this information, you can plug any security holes to prevent a recurrence.

Windows records security events in the Security log, one of three logs that you can peruse in Event Viewer. (The others are the Application log and the System log. Computers running Windows 2000 Server or Windows Server 2003 might have additional logs, including Directory Service, DNS Server, and File Replication Service.) In this chapter, we explain how to configure your system to audit security events, offer some suggestions on which events to audit, and show you how to work with the Security log in Event Viewer.

Auditing Security Events

Auditing tracks the activities of users and security-sensitive changes to the system by recording in the Security log the events that you specify. For example, you can choose to audit failed logon attempts, which might indicate that someone is trying to log on with an invalid password (perhaps using a program to automate the attack). Or you might want to monitor the use of a particularly sensitive file. You can also choose to monitor changes to user accounts and passwords, changes to security policies, and use of privileges that might reveal that someone is trying to "administer" your computer— perhaps not with your best interests in mind.

Enabling Security Auditing

Unlike the other logs that appear in Event Viewer, the Security log is disabled by default in Windows XP Professional and Windows 2000. No events are written to the Security log until you enable auditing, which you do through Local Security Settings. (In Windows XP Home Edition, security auditing is enabled for certain events. Because Home Edition doesn't include Local Security Settings, you cannot change which events are audited unless you use a tool like Auditpol.exe, which is included in the Windows 2000 Resource Kit.) Even if you set up auditing for files, folders, or printers, as explained later in this chapter, the events you specify aren't recorded unless you also enable auditing by setting a high-level audit policy in Local Security Settings.

> **Note** To enable auditing, you must be logged on with an account that has the Manage Auditing And Security Log privilege. By default, only members of the Administrators group have this privilege. For information about privileges, see "Exploring User Rights," page 732.

To enable auditing, follow these steps:

1 In Control Panel, open Administrative Tools, Local Security Policy. (If you use Category view in Windows XP, you'll find Administrative Tools under Performance And Maintenance.) Alternatively, you can type **secpol.msc** at a command prompt.

2 In the console tree, select Security Settings\Local Policies\Audit Policy.

3 Double-click each policy for which you want to enable auditing, and then select Success, Failure, or both. Figure 23-1 shows the properties dialog box for an audit policy.

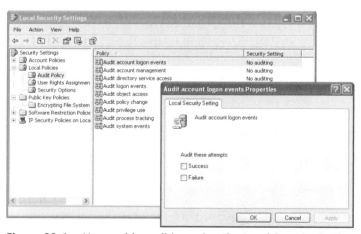

Figure 23-1. You enable auditing using the Local Security Settings console.

Figure 23-1 also shows the types of activities you can audit. Some, such as account management and policy change, provide an audit trail for administrative changes. Others, such as logon events and object access, help you monitor who is attempting to use your system. Still others, including system events and process tracking, can assist you in locating problems with your system. Table 23-1 provides more details.

Table 23-1. Audit Policies for Security Events

Policy	Description
Audit account logon events	Account logon events occur when a user attempts to log on or log off across the network, authenticating to a local user account.
Audit account management	Account management events occur when a user account or security group is created, changed, or deleted; when a user account is renamed, enabled, or disabled; or when a password is set or changed.
Audit directory service access	Directory service access events occur when a user attempts to access an Active Directory object. (If your computer is not part of a Microsoft Windows Server domain, these events won't occur.)
Audit logon events	Logon events occur when a user attempts to log on or log off a workstation interactively.
Audit object access	Object access events occur when a user attempts to access or take ownership of a file, folder, printer, registry key, or other object that is set for auditing.
Audit policy change	Policy change events occur when a change is made to user rights assignment policies, audit policies, trust policies, or password policies.
Audit privilege use	Privilege use events occur when a user exercises a user right (other than logon, logoff, and network access rights, which trigger other types of events).
Audit process tracking	Process tracking includes events such as program activation, handle duplication, indirect object access, and process exit. Although this policy generates a large number of events to wade through, it can provide useful information, such as which program a user used to access an object.
Audit system events	System events occur when a user restarts or shuts down the computer or when an event affects the system security or the Security log.

Note In Windows XP Home Edition, account logon, account management, logon, policy change, and system events are audited for both successful incidents and failed attempts. You cannot enable auditing for directory service access, object access, privilege use, or process tracking events, or disable the categories that are already enabled, without additional tools.

Chapter 23

Local Security Settings has some additional policies that affect auditing, but they're not in the Audit Policy folder. Instead, look to the Security Settings\Local Policies\Security Options folder for these policies:

- **Audit: Audit the use of Backup and Restore privilege.**   Enable this policy if you want to know when someone uses a backup program to back up or restore files. To make this policy effective, you must also enable Audit Privilege Use in the Audit Policy folder.

- **Audit: Shut down system immediately if unable to log security audits.**   For details about this extreme security policy, see the sidebar "Ensuring That You Don't Miss Any Security Events," page 786.

- **Audit: Audit the access of global system objects.**   This policy affects auditing of obscure objects (mutexes and semaphores, for example) that aren't used in most home and small business networks; you can safely ignore it.

> **Note**   In Windows 2000, the word "Audit:" does not precede the policy names.

Configuring Auditing of Access to Files, Printers, and Registry Keys

If you want to audit use or attempted use of certain files, folders, printers, registry keys, or other objects, you must select Success, Failure, or both options in the Audit Object Access policy, as described in the preceding section. Then you must set auditing options for the particular objects you want to monitor, as described in the following paragraphs. (In general, it's best to select both Success and Failure in the Audit Object Access policy, and then be more selective when you configure auditing options for each object.)

> **Note**   Because you can't make Audit Object Access policy settings in Windows XP Home Edition, you won't be able to audit access to files, printers, and other objects. Even if you know the trick to bypass Simple File Sharing (boot into Safe Mode), which would enable you to make audit settings for an object, those settings have no effect without the high-level policy in place.

Windows can audit a variety of events and can audit different events for different users. You must be logged on as a member of the Administrators group (or the Manage Auditing And Security Log right must have been granted to your logon account) to set up auditing of objects.

> **Note**   If you want to audit access to files or folders, those objects must be stored on an NTFS volume; FAT volumes do not support auditing.

Use the Security tab in the properties dialog box for a file, folder, printer, or registry key to display the audit settings for that object. You can specify the users and groups whose access to the selected object you want to audit; and for each user and group, you can specify which types of access should generate entries in the Security log. You should audit the minimum number of accesses necessary to accomplish your logging goal. For instance, if you want to audit changes to permissions, the only access you need to audit is Write Permissions.

To set up auditing for object access, follow these steps:

1 If you haven't done so already, visit Local Security Settings to enable auditing. Be sure to set the Audit Object Access policy to track both success and failure. (See the preceding section, "Enabling Security Auditing.")

2 If you use Windows XP Professional and your computer is not a member of a domain, choose Tools, Folder Options in Windows Explorer. Click the View tab and then clear the Use Simple File Sharing (Recommended) check box. Click OK. Disabling Simple File Sharing allows the Security tab to appear when you look at the properties dialog box for a file, folder, or printer. (You can skip this step if you're configuring auditing for a registry key.)

Note   After you make the appropriate audit settings for various objects (as described in the following steps), you can restore Simple File Sharing by returning to Folder Options and selecting the same check box. Although the Security tab will no longer be visible in the properties dialog box for files, folders, and printers, the audit settings you have made remain in effect.

3 Display the Security tab for the object, as follows:

- For a file or folder, right-click the object in Windows Explorer and choose Properties. In the properties dialog box, click the Security tab.

- For a printer, right-click the printer in the Printers folder (in Control Panel) and choose Properties. In the properties dialog box, click the Security tab.

- For a registry key in Windows XP, right-click the key in Registry Editor (that is, a folder icon in the console tree—not a registry value in the details pane) and choose Permissions.

- For a registry key in Windows 2000, open Regedt32.exe (not Regedit.exe), select the key, and choose Security, Permissions.

4 Click the Advanced button to open the Advanced Security Settings dialog box (in Windows 2000, the Access Control Settings dialog box).

5 Click the Auditing tab. For each object, you can specify different audit settings for different users.

Chapter 23

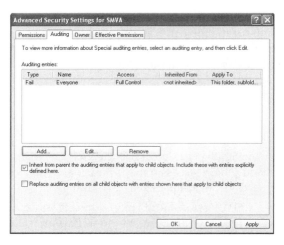

6   Click Add to add a new user or group, or select an existing user or group and then click Edit to change its audit settings.

If you click Add, the Select User Or Group dialog box appears. You enter the names of user accounts or security groups the same way you do on the Security tab. (For details, see "Setting NTFS Permissions Through Windows Explorer," page 136.) Click OK.

7   In the Auditing Entry dialog box, select the types of access you want to audit for the selected user or group.

The types of access you can audit for success or failure are the same types of access for which you can set permissions; specifically, the list of auditing permissions matches the object's list of special permissions. Figure 23-2 shows the options for different object types.

> **Note**   For information about special permissions for files and folders, see "Basic and Advanced Permissions," page 141.

If you select the Successful check box for a specific type of access, Windows generates a Security log record containing (among other information) the date and time of each successful use of the specified file or folder by the specified user or group. Similarly, if you select the Failed check box, Windows generates a Security log record each time the specified user or group unsuccessfully attempts to access the specified file or folder.

File or Folder

Printer

Registry Key

Figure 23-2. The types of access you can audit are the same as those for which you can set permissions. For each type of access, you can audit successful accesses, failed attempts, or both.

8 If you're making audit settings for an object other than a file, select the scope of the objects you want to audit from the Apply Onto list. Click OK.

9 On the Auditing tab of the Advanced Security Settings dialog box, you can select inheritance options. These options work exactly like (but independent of) the comparable options on the Permissions tab. For more information, see "Applying Permissions to Subfolders Through Inheritance," page 151.

Chapter 23

> **Tip**   Change audit settings for multiple objects in one fell swoop
> You can change audit settings for multiple files or folders (but not printers or registry keys) simultaneously. If you select more than one file or folder in Windows Explorer before you click the Security tab in the properties dialog box, the changes you make affect all the selected files or folders. If the existing security settings are not the same for all the items in your selection, a message appears, asking whether you want to reset the audit settings for the entire selection.

Deciding What to Audit

Avoid auditing if you don't need it. Security audits, like tax audits, can be time-consuming and can waste a lot of resources. When you enable auditing, the system must write an event record to the Security log for each audit check the system performs. This activity can degrade your computer's performance, so you'll want to be selective about which events you choose to monitor. In addition, indiscriminate auditing adds to the log events that might be of little value to you, thereby making the real security issues more difficult to find. And because the Security log has a fixed size, filling it with unimportant events could displace other, more significant events.

Here are some suggestions for what you should consider auditing:

- Audit failed logon attempts, which might indicate that someone is trying to log on with various invalid passwords.
- If you're concerned about someone using a stolen password to log on, audit successful logon events.
- To detect use of sensitive files (such as a payroll data file, for example) by unauthorized users, audit successful read and write access as well as failed attempts to use the file by suspected users or groups.
- If you use your computer as a Web server, you'll want to know whether an attacker has defaced your Web pages. By auditing write access to the files that make up the Web pages, you'll know whether your site has been vandalized.
- Logging printer failures quickly identifies people who attempt to access a printer for which they don't have permission. You might also want to log successes (at least for users or groups suspected of abusing the privilege) to determine, for example, who's using all the expensive color ink cartridges.
- To detect virus activity, audit successful write access to program files (files with .exe, .com, and .dll file name extensions).
- If you're concerned that someone is misusing administrative privileges, audit successful incidents of privilege use, account management, policy changes, and system events.

Viewing the Log of Security Events

Windows records the security events that you've chosen to audit in the Security log. To view the Security log, you use Event Viewer, a Microsoft Management Console snap-in. The Event Viewer snap-in is in Computer Management, under System Tools. Windows also offers an uncluttered view in a predefined console that contains only the Event Viewer snap-in. To open this console, go to Control Panel, Administrative Tools, Event Viewer, or simply type **eventvwr.msc** at a command prompt. You can use Event Viewer to examine any of the three logs: Application (Appevent.evt), Security (Secevent.evt), or System (Sysevent.evt). (Servers and computers with certain additional components installed might have additional logs available.) If you select the Security log, you'll see a window similar to the one shown in Figure 23-3.

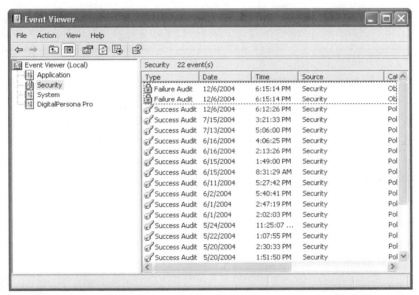

Figure 23-3. The Security log can show at a glance that an unauthorized user has attempted to access an object.

Events in the Security log are displayed with one of two icons:

	Indicates a successful performance of an audited event
	Indicates a failed attempt to perform an audited event

Chapter 23

Event Logs and Permissions

By default, the Application log and the System log can be viewed by Everyone, a built-in security principal that includes all users who access the computer, including members of the Guests group. (In Windows XP, Everyone does not include Anonymous logons, however.) In addition, Everyone has write access to these two logs; in effect, that means any application can make entries in the logs, regardless of the user context in which it's running. Only members of the Administrators group can clear these logs, however. You can prevent guests from viewing the Application and System logs by creating a DWORD entry named RestrictGuestAccess in HKLM\System\CurrentControlSet\Services\EventLog\Application and HKLM\System\CurrentControlSet\Services\EventLog\System. Set each value to 1.

The Security log can be viewed or cleared only by members of the Administrators group. In addition, only the LocalSystem account (a built-in security principal that represents the operating system) can write to the log, preventing rogue applications from filling the log.

Working with Logged Events

If you want more information about an event in the Security log, double-click the event to open the Event Properties dialog box, shown in Figure 23-4. By carefully examining all unsuccessful events, you might notice a pattern in attempts to gain access to a system or to particular objects.

Figure 23-4. The details shown in this Event Properties dialog box indicate that CarlS has attempted to access a file named Advanced Appearance.doc without permission.

You can search for particular events in the current log by using the Find command on Event Viewer's View menu. This command displays the dialog box shown in Figure 23-5. By clearing all check boxes except Failure Audit and not entering anything in the other fields, you can quickly step through each failed attempt to use your system. Naturally, if you're looking for a specific event, you can fill in other details about the event to speed your search.

Figure 23-5. Use the View, Find command to locate a particular event.

To examine several similar event entries, you can filter the list of events. You might want to restrict the display to include only events of a certain type or only those that occurred within a particular range of dates and times, for example. To filter a log, right-click the log's name and choose Properties. Then fill out the Filter tab of the log's properties dialog box, shown in Figure 23-6 on the next page. To restore the unfiltered list, return to this dialog box and click Restore Defaults.

> **Tip** Switch between views
> You can quickly switch between filtered and unfiltered views of a log—or between one filtered view and a different filtered view. Right-click the log's name, and choose New Log View. Event Viewer adds the new view to the console tree. Select the new view and filter as needed. (You might also want to give the new view a meaningful name; right-click it and choose Rename.) Now you can move between views by clicking different logs in the console tree. If you no longer need a view you create, right-click it and choose Delete.

Chapter 23

Figure 23-6. The Filter tab lets you restrict the list to events of particular interest.

Working with Log Files

The log files require little maintenance, and the default settings are appropriate in most cases. But you might want to limit the size of the logs, archive their content, or clear them—tasks that are explained in the following sections.

Setting Log File Size and Longevity

By default, each log file has a maximum size of 512 KB. You can adjust that downward or upward in 64-KB increments. If you want to maintain a long history of events, you can increase the log file size significantly; for the best performance, however, the combined size of all log files shouldn't exceed 512 MB.

Also by default, events in each log file have a minimum longevity of seven days. That means that if a file reaches its maximum size, new events overwrite the oldest ones—but only if the oldest ones are at least seven days old. This too is an adjustable parameter.

To change either a log file's maximum size or the minimum longevity of the events it contains, right-click the log and choose Properties. Figure 23-7 shows a log file's properties dialog box. (You must have administrative privileges to use this dialog box; otherwise, all the controls appear dimmed.)

If the Event Log service is unable to add new events to a log, either because you have told it never to overwrite log entries or because a log file has reached its capacity before the oldest events have reached their minimum age, you'll receive a warning message. You can remedy the situation, either by simply clearing the log or by archiving and then clearing it.

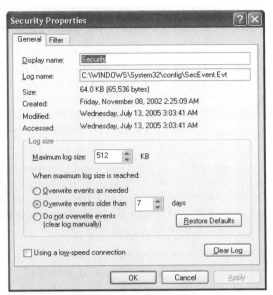

Figure 23-7. The properties dialog box enables you to control the size of your event logs and the lifespan of the events they contain.

Archiving and Exporting Log File Information

To archive a log, right-click it and choose Save Log File As. In the resulting dialog box, choose the default file type, Event Log (*.evt). Saving a log in its native (.evt) format creates a complete replica of the log, but you can view that replica only in Event Viewer (or a third-party application capable of reading native event logs).

Event Viewer can also export log data to tab-delimited and comma-delimited text files, however, and you can easily import these into database, spreadsheet, or even word processing programs. When you save a log in one of these formats, you get everything in the log except the binary data associated with certain events. To save an entire log file in a text format, select either Text (Tab Delimited) or CSV (Comma Delimited) from the Save As Type list.

The Save Log File As command always saves all events in the selected log, regardless of how the log might be filtered for display purposes. If you want to generate a text report showing only particular kinds of events, first filter the log to display those events, and then use the Action menu's Export List command. Like the Save Log File As command, Export List provides options for saving a tab-delimited or comma-delimited text file. Don't select the Save Only Selected Rows check box in the Export List dialog box unless you want a report that includes only column headers and a single event.

Ensuring That You Don't Miss Any Security Events

By default, when the Security log fills up, Windows erases the oldest entries when it needs to make a new entry—just as it does with the System log and the Application log. If security is critical to your operation, however, you can make a policy setting that ensures that events are never deleted automatically. With or without this setting, only administrators—and others with the Manage Auditing And Security Log right—can view the Security log or clear its contents. To prevent people from covering their tracks, no one can delete individual entries; authorized individuals must delete all or none.

Choosing this policy setting is a rather drastic solution, and you should implement it only when it's essential to preserve every security event. With this setting, the system halts with a blue screen when the Security log becomes full, preventing all further use—and possibly causing logged-on users to lose data if document files happen to be open at the time. If you want to enable this level of security, follow these steps:

1 In Event Viewer, right-click Security and choose Properties.

2 On the General tab, select Do Not Overwrite Events (Clear Log Manually).

3 In Local Security Settings (Secpol.msc), open Security Settings\Local Policies \Security Options.

4 Double-click Audit: Shut Down System Immediately If Unable To Log Security Audits. Select Enabled and click OK.

5 Restart the computer.

After you've followed these steps, the computer will halt when the Security log becomes full while a nonadministrative user is logged on. (Note that if you're logged on as an administrator, you can continue to work undisturbed—and growth of the Security log stops without any notice. Therefore, even this security safeguard has a serious flaw.) At that point, you need to restart the computer and log on as a member of the Administrators group; no other accounts are allowed to log on.

Your first action after logging on should be to review, export if desired, and clear the Security log. You then need to reset the shutdown policy by disabling it, reenabling it, and then restarting the computer. (The operating system automatically sets the registry value the policy controls to an invalid value; this is the mechanism that prevents others from logging on.) To restore the computer to normal operation (that is, it continues to run even if the Security log is full), revisit Local Security Settings and disable the policy.

Naturally, if you employ this trick, you should take steps to avoid having the Security log fill up, since it can lock the computer at inopportune moments. Review and then clear the log periodically. (Export the log contents first if you want to preserve them.) You might also want to increase the size of the log.

Inside Out

Use security templates to configure auditing

With security templates, you can save all your settings as a template, which you can then apply to other computers (templates provide an easy way to apply uniform settings on multiple computers) or on the same computer (a template can be useful for restoring security settings to a known state). The configuration of audit policies and Event Viewer can be part of a security template.

> For information about configuring policies with security templates and applying template settings, see "Using Security Templates," page 761.

To configure audit policies (those described in "Enabling Security Auditing," page 774), visit a template's Local Policies\Audit Policy folder.

To configure auditing for object access (as described in "Configuring Auditing of Access to Files, Printers, and Registry Keys," page 776), use the template's File System and Registry folders. (You can't configure printer auditing using security templates.) In those folders, right-click the object of interest, choose Properties, and then click Edit Security.

You can also configure certain Event Viewer options using security templates. You'll find the relevant policies in each template's Event Log folder. (In Windows 2000, the policies are in a subfolder named Settings For Event Logs.) The following template settings affect the Security log:

- **Maximum security log size.** This corresponds to the like-named setting in the Security Properties dialog box, shown in Figure 23-7, page 785.

- **Prevent local guests group from accessing security log (in Windows 2000, Restrict guest access to security log).** This setting controls the RestrictGuestAccess value in the registry's HKLM\System\CurrentControlSet\Services\Eventlog\Security key.

- **Retain security log.** This sets the value of the Overwrite Events Older Than __ Days box in the Security Properties dialog box.

- **Retention method for security log.** This setting corresponds to the When Maximum Log Size Is Reached option in the Security Properties dialog box.

The same folder contains analogous policies for the Application and System logs. Security templates in Windows 2000 also include a Shut Down The Computer When The Security Audit Log Is Full policy, which is merely another avenue to the like-named policy in Local Policies\Security Options.

Chapter 23

Displaying an Archived Log File

After you have saved a log file in the .evt format, you can redisplay its contents at any time by using the Open Log File command on the Action menu.

A reopened archive appears as a new entry in the console tree. You can view it, filter it, and search it, just as you would any other log file. You can also delete it—something you can't do to the default Application, Security, and System logs.

Clearing Log Files

To clear a log, either click the Clear Log button in the log's properties dialog box (shown in Figure 22-7, page 766) or right-click the log and choose Clear All Events. You must have administrative privileges to clear any log.

 This book's companion CD includes two example security templates that configure auditing. One template (named Forensic) is for forensic purposes, and it enables success auditing for most events. The other (Intrusiondetection) is for intrusion detection purposes, and it enables both success and failure auditing. Both templates create many access settings for the %SystemRoot% folder and the files and folders it contains to track modifications to system files. To see which events and audit policy settings the templates create, open the .inf file for the template. The companion CD also includes a pair of batch programs (Applyforensic.cmd and Applyid.cmd) that use Secedit.exe to apply the templates.

> For information about applying security templates and using Secedit, see "Applying Template Settings," page 769.

Viewing Other Security-Related Logs

Some applications and services generate their own logs of security-related events. The security log format, location, and options are likely to be different for each application or service, so you'll need to do some sleuthing. We mention the possibility here so that you can start your own investigation. Here are a few clues to get you started:

- If you use Windows Firewall, you can configure it to keep track of blocked (or successful) connections. It stores the log in %SystemRoot%\Pfirewall.log by default. Although it's a standard text file, it's difficult to read in its raw form.

> For information about configuring the Windows Firewall log and instructions for displaying it in a more useful form, see "Configuring Windows Firewall Logging," page 578.

- If you use another type of firewall (software or hardware), it undoubtedly has some logging capabilities that record connection attempts.
- Many antivirus programs have built-in viewers for their activity logs. Such logs will show events such as scanning your system for viruses, updating virus definitions, quarantining viruses, and so on.

Note Only the operating system itself can write to the Security log. Otherwise, malevolent applications could fill the Security log with meaningless events, thereby clearing out the noteworthy events you want to record. Therefore, applications and services are limited to making entries in the Application log or the System log—or in a separate log managed by the specific application or service. (Of course, if the application or service performs actions that generate security events you've chosen to audit, the events appear in the Security log.)

Chapter 23

Part 5

Appendix

The Ten Immutable Laws of Security

> **Note** This article, reprinted with permission of the Microsoft Security Response Center, is widely regarded as one of the most important statements on computer security and is on our must-read list. You'll find this article and many more essential resources, including security bulletins and white papers, on the Microsoft Security Web site at *http://www.microsoft.com /security/*.

Here at the Microsoft Security Response Center, we investigate thousands of security reports every year. In some cases, we find that a report describes a bona fide security vulnerability resulting from a flaw in one of our products; when this happens, we develop a patch as quickly as possible to correct the error. In other cases, the reported problems simply result from a mistake someone made in using the product. But many fall in between. They discuss real security problems, but the problems don't result from product flaws. Over the years, we've developed a list of issues like these, that we call The Ten Immutable Laws of Security.

Don't hold your breath waiting for a patch that will protect you from the issues we'll discuss below. It isn't possible for Microsoft—or any software vendor—to "fix" them, because they result from the way computers work. But don't abandon all hope yet—sound judgment is the key to protecting yourself against these issues, and if you keep them in mind, you can significantly improve the security of your systems.

Law #1:   If a bad guy can persuade you to run his program on your computer, it's not your computer anymore.

It's an unfortunate fact of computer science: When a computer program runs, it will do what it's programmed to do, even if it's programmed to be harmful. When you choose to run a program, you are making a decision to turn over control of your computer to it. Once a program is running, it can do anything, up to the limits of what you yourself can do on the computer. It could monitor your keystrokes and send them to a Web site. It could open every document on the computer, and change the word "will" to "won't" in all of them. It could send rude e-mails to all your friends. It could install a virus. It could create a "back door" that lets someone remotely control your computer. It could dial up an ISP in Katmandu. Or it could just reformat your hard drive.

That's why it's important to never run, or even download, a program from an untrusted source—and by "source," I mean the person who wrote it, not the person who gave it to you. There's a nice analogy between running a program and eating a sandwich. If a stranger walked up to you and handed you a sandwich, would you eat it? Probably not. How about if your best friend gave you a sandwich? Maybe you would, maybe you wouldn't—it depends on whether she made it or found it lying in the street. Apply the same critical thought to a program that you would to a sandwich, and you'll usually be safe.

Law #2:   If a bad guy can alter the operating system on your computer, it's not your computer anymore.

In the end, an operating system is just a series of ones and zeroes that, when interpreted by the processor, cause the computer to do certain things. Change the ones and zeroes, and it will do something different. Where are the ones and zeroes stored? Why, on the computer, right along with everything else! They're just files, and if other people who use the computer are permitted to change those files, it's "game over."

To understand why, consider that operating system files are among the most trusted ones on the computer, and they generally run with system-level privileges. That is, they can do absolutely anything. Among other things, they're trusted to manage user accounts, handle password changes, and enforce the rules governing who can do what on the computer. If a bad guy can change them, the now-untrustworthy files will do his bidding, and there's no limit to what he can do. He can steal passwords, make himself an administrator on the computer, or add entirely new functions to the operating system. To prevent this type of attack, make sure that the system files (and the registry, for that matter) are well protected. (The security checklists on the Microsoft Security Web site will help you do this).

> **For more information,** refer to "Security Checklists and Resource Guides" at
> *http://www.microsoft.com/technet/security/chklist/default.mspx.*

Law #3:   If a bad guy has unrestricted physical access to your computer, it's not your computer anymore.

Oh, the things a bad guy can do if he can lay his hands on your computer! Here's a sampling, going from Stone Age to Space Age:

- He could mount the ultimate low-tech denial-of-service attack, and smash your computer with a sledgehammer.
- He could unplug the computer, haul it out of your building, and hold it for ransom.

- He could boot the computer from a floppy disk, and reformat your hard drive. But wait, you say, I've configured the BIOS on my computer to prompt for a password when I turn the power on. No problem—if he can open the case and get his hands on the system hardware, he could just replace the BIOS chips. (Actually, there are even easier ways.)

- He could remove the hard drive from your computer, install it into his computer, and read it.

- He could make a duplicate of your hard drive and take it back to his lair. Once there, he'd have all the time in the world to conduct brute-force attacks, such as trying every possible logon password. Programs are available to automate this and, given enough time, it's almost certain that he would succeed. Once that happens, Laws #1 and #2 above apply.

- He could replace your keyboard with one that contains a radio transmitter. He could then monitor everything you type, including your password.

Always make sure that a computer is physically protected in a way that's consistent with its value—and remember that the value of a computer includes not only the value of the hardware itself, but the value of the data on it, and the value of the access to your network that a bad guy could gain. At a minimum, business-critical computers such as domain controllers, database servers, and print/file servers should always be in a locked room that only people charged with administration and maintenance can access. But you may want to consider protecting other computers as well, and potentially using additional protective measures.

If you travel with a laptop, it's absolutely critical that you protect it. The same features that make laptops great to travel with—small size, light weight, and so forth—also make them easy to steal. There are a variety of locks and alarms available for laptops, and some models let you remove the hard drive and carry it with you. You also can use features such as the Encrypting File System in Windows 2000 to mitigate the damage if someone succeeded in stealing the computer. But the only way you can know with 100 percent certainty that your data is safe and the hardware hasn't been tampered with is to keep the laptop on your person at all times while traveling.

Law #4: If you allow a bad guy to upload programs to your Web site, it's not your Web site anymore.

This is basically Law #1 in reverse. In that scenario, the bad guy tricks his victim into downloading a harmful program onto his computer and running it. In this one, the bad guy uploads a harmful program to a computer and runs it himself. Although this scenario is a danger anytime you allow strangers to connect to your computer, Web sites are involved in the overwhelming majority of these cases. Many people who operate Web sites are too hospitable for their own good, and allow visitors to upload programs to the site and run them. As we've seen above, unpleasant things can happen if a bad guy's program can run on your computer.

Appendix

If you run a Web site, you need to limit what visitors can do. You should allow a program on your site only if you wrote it yourself, or if you trust the developer who wrote it. But that may not be enough. If your Web site is one of several hosted on a shared server, you need to be extra careful. If a bad guy can compromise one of the other sites on the server, it's possible he could extend his control to the server itself, in which case he could control all of the sites on it—including yours. If you're on a shared server, it's important to find out what the server administrator's policies are. (By the way, before opening your site to the public, make sure you've followed the security checklists for IIS 4.0 and IIS 5.0.)

Law #5:   Weak passwords trump strong security.

The purpose of having a logon process is to establish who you are. Once the operating system knows who you are, it can grant or deny requests for system resources appropriately. If a bad guy learns your password, he can log on as you. In fact, as far as the operating system is concerned, he is you. Whatever you can do on the system, he can do as well, because he's you. Maybe he wants to read sensitive information you've stored on your computer, such as your e-mail. Maybe you have more privileges on the network than he does, and being you will let him do things he normally couldn't. Or maybe he just wants to do something malicious and blame it on you. In any case, it's worth protecting your credentials.

Always use a password—it's amazing how many accounts have blank passwords. And choose a complex one. Don't use your dog's name, your anniversary date, or the name of the local football team. And don't use the word "password"! Pick a password that has a mix of upper- and lower-case letters, numbers, punctuation marks, and so forth. Make it as long as possible. And change it often. Once you've picked a strong password, handle it appropriately. Don't write it down. If you absolutely must write it down, at the very least keep it in a safe or a locked drawer—the first thing a bad guy who's hunting for passwords will do is check for a yellow sticky note on the side of your screen, or in the top desk drawer. Don't tell anyone what your password is. Remember what Ben Franklin said: Two people can keep a secret, but only if one of them is dead.

Finally, consider using something stronger than passwords to identify yourself to the system. Windows 2000, for instance, supports the use of smart cards, which significantly strengthens the identity checking the system can perform. You may also want to consider biometric products such as fingerprint and retina scanners.

Law #6:   A computer is only as secure as the administrator is trustworthy.

Every computer must have an administrator: someone who can install software, configure the operating system, add and manage user accounts, establish security policies, and handle all the other management tasks associated with keeping a computer up and running. By definition, these tasks require that he have control over the computer. This puts the administrator in a position of unequalled power. An untrustworthy administrator can negate every other security measure you've taken. He can change the permissions on the computer, modify the system security policies, install malicious software, add bogus users, or do any of a million other things. He can subvert virtually any protective measure in the operating system, because he controls it. Worst of all, he can cover his tracks. If you have an untrustworthy administrator, you have absolutely no security.

When hiring a system administrator, recognize the position of trust that administrators occupy, and hire only a person who warrants that trust. Call his references, and ask them about his previous work record, especially with regard to any security incidents at previous employers. If appropriate for your organization, you may also consider taking a step that banks and other security-conscious companies do, and require that your administrators pass a complete background check at hiring time, and at periodic intervals afterward. Whatever criteria you select, apply them across the board. Don't give anyone administrative privileges on your network unless they've been vetted—and this includes temporary employees and contractors, too.

Next, take steps to help keep honest people honest. Use sign-in/sign-out sheets to track who's been in the server room. (You do have a server room with a locked door, right? If not, re-read Law #3.) Implement a "two person" rule when installing or upgrading software. Diversify management tasks as much as possible, as a way of minimizing how much power any one administrator has. Also, don't use the Administrator account— instead, give each administrator a separate account with administrative privileges, so you can tell who's doing what. Finally, consider taking steps to make it more difficult for a rogue administrator to cover his tracks. For instance, store audit data on write-only media, or house System A's audit data on System B, and make sure that the two systems have different administrators. The more accountable your administrators are, the less likely you are to have problems.

Law #7: Encrypted data is only as secure as the decryption key.

Suppose you installed the biggest, strongest, most secure lock in the world on your front door, but you put the key under the front door mat. It wouldn't really matter how strong the lock is, would it? The critical factor would be the poor way the key was protected, because if a burglar could find it, he'd have everything he needed to open the lock. Encrypted data works the same way—no matter how strong the crypto algorithm is, the data is only as safe as the key that can decrypt it.

Many operating systems and cryptographic software products give you an option to store cryptographic keys on the computer. The advantage is convenience—you don't have to handle the key—but it comes at the cost of security. The keys are usually obfuscated (that is, hidden), and some of the obfuscation methods are quite good. But in the end, no matter how well-hidden the key is, if it's on the computer it can be found. It has to be—after all, the software can find it, so a sufficiently-motivated bad guy could find it, too. Whenever possible, use offline storage for keys. If the key is a word or phrase, memorize it. If not, export it to a floppy disk, make a backup copy, and store the copies in separate, secure locations. (All of you administrators out there who are using Syskey in "local storage" mode—you're going to reconfigure your server right this minute, right?)

Law #8:   An out-of-date virus scanner is only marginally better than no virus scanner at all.

Virus scanners work by comparing the data on your computer against a collection of virus "signatures." Each signature is characteristic of a particular virus, and when the scanner finds data in a file, e-mail, or elsewhere that matches the signature, it concludes that it's found a virus. However, a virus scanner can scan only for the viruses it knows about. It's vital that you keep your virus scanner's signature file up to date, as new viruses are created every day.

The problem actually goes a bit deeper than this, though. Typically, a new virus will do the greatest amount of damage during the early stages of its life, precisely because few people will be able to detect it. Once word gets around that a new virus is on the loose and people update their virus signatures, the spread of the virus falls off drastically. The key is to get ahead of the curve, and have updated signature files on your computer before the virus hits.

Virtually every maker of anti-virus software provides a way to get free updated signature files from their Web site. In fact, many have "push" services, in which they'll send notification every time a new signature file is released. Use these services. Also, keep the virus scanner itself—that is, the scanning software—updated as well. Virus writers periodically develop new techniques that require that the scanners change how they do their work.

Law #9:   Absolute anonymity isn't practical, in real life or on the Web.

All human interaction involves exchanging data of some kind. If someone weaves enough of that data together, they can identify you. Think about all the information that a person can glean in just a short conversation with you. In one glance, they can gauge your height, weight, and approximate age. Your accent will probably tell them what country you're from, and may even tell them what region of the country. If you talk about anything other than the weather, you'll probably tell them something about your family, your interests, where you live, and what you do for a living. It doesn't take long for someone to collect enough information to figure out who you are. If you crave absolute anonymity, your best bet is to live in a cave and shun all human contact.

The same thing is true of the Internet. If you visit a Web site, the owner can, if he's sufficiently motivated, find out who you are. After all, the ones and zeroes that make up the Web session have been able to find their way to the right place, and that place is your computer. There are a lot of measures you can take to disguise the bits, and the more of them you use, the more thoroughly the bits will be disguised. For instance, you could use network address translation to mask your actual IP address, subscribe to an anonymizing service that launders the bits by relaying them from one end of the ether to the other, use a different ISP account for different purposes, surf certain sites only from public kiosks, and so on. All of these make it more difficult to determine who you are, but none of them make it impossible. Do you know for certain who operates the anonymizing

Appendix

service? Maybe it's the same person who owns the Web site you just visited! Or what about that innocuous Web site you visited yesterday, that offered to mail you a free $10 off coupon? Maybe the owner is willing to share information with other Web site owners. If so, the second Web site owner may be able to correlate the information from the two sites and determine who you are.

Does this mean that privacy on the Web is a lost cause? Not at all. What it means is that the best way to protect your privacy on the Internet is the same as the way you protect your privacy in normal life—through your behavior. Read the privacy statements on the Web sites you visit, and do business only with ones whose practices you agree with. If you're worried about cookies, disable them. Most importantly, avoid indiscriminate Web surfing—recognize that just as most cities have a bad side of town that's best avoided, the Internet does, too. But if it's complete and total anonymity you want, better start looking for that cave.

Law #10:   Technology is not a panacea.

Technology can do some amazing things. Recent years have seen the development of ever-cheaper and more powerful hardware, software that harnesses the hardware to open new vistas for computer users, as well as advancements in cryptography and other sciences. It's tempting to believe that technology can deliver a risk-free world, if we just work hard enough. However, this is simply not realistic.

Perfect security requires a level of perfection that simply doesn't exist, and in fact isn't likely to ever exist. This is true for software as well as virtually all fields of human interest. Software development is an imperfect science, and all software has bugs. Some of them can be exploited to cause security breaches. That's just a fact of life. But even if software could be made perfect, it wouldn't solve the problem entirely. Most attacks involve, to one degree or another, some manipulation of human nature—this is usually referred to as social engineering. Raise the cost and difficulty of attacking security technology, and bad guys will respond by shifting their focus away from the technology and toward the human being at the console. It's vital that you understand your role in maintaining solid security, or you could become the chink in your own systems' armor.

The solution is to recognize two essential points. First, security consists of both technology and policy—that is, it's the combination of the technology and how it's used that ultimately determines how secure your systems are. Second, security is a journey, not a destination—it isn't a problem that can be "solved" once and for all; it's a constant series of moves and countermoves between the good guys and the bad guys. The key is to ensure that you have good security awareness and exercise sound judgment. There are resources available to help you do this. The Microsoft Security Web site, for instance, has hundreds of white papers, best practices guides, checklists and tools, and we're developing more all the time. Combine great technology with sound judgment, and you'll have rock-solid security.

Index to Troubleshooting Topics

Index to Troubleshooting Topics

Index

Numerics

A

E

About the Authors

Ed Bott is an award-winning computer journalist and the author or coauthor of more than 20 books on Microsoft Windows, Microsoft Office, and personal computers, including two editions of *Microsoft Windows XP Inside Out*. In nearly 20 years in the computer industry, he has written countless magazine articles and served as a top editor of *PC Computing* and *PC World* magazines. After spending three years in Microsoft's backyard in Redmond, Washington, Ed and his wife Judy moved to the sunny Southwest, where they live with their two cats, Katy and Bianca, and have never been happier. You can learn more about Ed and his current projects by visiting *http://www.edbott.com/weblog/*.

Carl Siechert began his writing career at age 8 as editor of a neighborhood newsletter that reached a peak worldwide circulation of 43 during its eight-year run. Following several years in the printing industry, Carl returned to writing with the formation of Siechert & Wood Professional Documentation, a Pasadena, California, firm that specializes in product documentation for the personal computer industry. Carl is a coauthor of more than a dozen books published by Microsoft Press, including *Microsoft Windows XP Inside Out* and *Microsoft Windows 2000 Professional Expert Companion*. Carl hiked the Pacific Crest Trail from Mexico to Canada in 1977 and would rather be hiking right now. He and his wife Jan live in southern California.

For *Windows Server 2003* administrators

Microsoft® Windows® Server 2003 Administrator's Companion
ISBN 0-7356-1367-2

The comprehensive, daily operations guide to planning, deployment, and maintenance.
Here's the ideal one-volume guide for anyone who administers Windows Server 2003. It offers up-to-date information on core system-administration topics for Windows, including Active Directory® services, security, disaster planning and recovery, interoperability with NetWare and UNIX, plus all-new sections about Microsoft Internet Security and Acceleration (ISA) Server and scripting. Featuring easy-to-use procedures and handy workarounds, it provides ready answers for on-the-job results.

Microsoft Windows Server 2003 Administrator's Pocket Consultant
ISBN 0-7356-1354-0

The practical, portable guide to Windows Server 2003. Here's the practical, pocket-sized reference for IT professionals who support Windows Server 2003. Designed for quick referencing, it covers all the essentials for performing everyday system-administration tasks. Topics covered include managing workstations and servers, using Active Directory services, creating and administering user and group accounts, managing files and directories, data security and auditing, data back-up and recovery, administration with TCP/IP, WINS, and DNS, and more.

Microsoft IIS 6.0 Administrator's Pocket Consultant
ISBN 0-7356-1560-8

The practical, portable guide to IIS 6.0. Here's the eminently practical, pocket-sized reference for IT and Web professionals who work with Internet Information Services (IIS) 6.0. Designed for quick referencing and compulsively readable, this portable guide covers all the basics needed for everyday tasks. Topics include Web administration fundamentals, Web server administration, essential services administration, and performance, optimization, and maintenance. It's the fast-answers guide that helps users consistently save time and energy as they administer IIS 6.0.

To learn more about the full line of Microsoft Press® products for IT professionals, please visit:

microsoft.com/mspress/IT

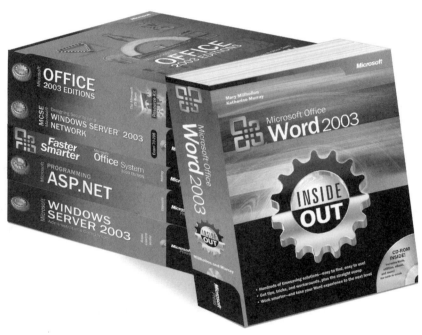